Handbook of Augmented Reality

Borko Furht
Editor

Handbook of Augmented Reality

 Springer

Editor
Borko Furht
Department of Computer and Electrical Engineering
  and Computer Science
Florida Atlantic University
Glades Road 777
33431 Boca Raton, Florida
USA
bfurht@fau.edu

ISBN 978-1-4939-0127-2   ISBN 978-1-4614-0064-6 (eBook)
DOI 10.1007/978-1-4614-0064-6
Springer New York Dordrecht Heidelberg London

Printed on acid-free paper

Springer is part of Springer Science+Business Media (www.springer.com)

To my granddaughter Sophia Rolleri. Her contribution to augmented reality.

Preface

Augmented Reality (AR) refers to a live view of physical real world environment whose elements are merged with augmented computer-generated images creating a mixed reality. The augmentation is typically done in real time and in semantic context with environmental elements. By using the latest AR techniques and technologies, the information about the surrounding real world becomes interactive and digitally usable.

The objective of this Handbook is to provide comprehensive guidelines on the current and future trends in augmented reality technologies and applications. This Handbook is carefully edited book – contributors are worldwide experts in the field of augmented reality and its applications. The Handbook Advisory Board, comprised of 11 researchers and practitioners from academia and industry, helped in reshaping the Handbook and selecting the right topics and creative and knowledgeable contributors.

The Handbook comprises of two parts, which consist of 33 chapters. The first part on *Technologies* includes articles dealing with fundamentals of augmented reality, augmented reality technologies, visualization techniques, head-mounted projection displays, evaluation of AR systems, mobile AR systems, and other innovative AR concepts.

The second part on *Applications* includes various articles on AR applications including applications in psychology, medical education, edutainment, reality games, rehabilitation engineering, automotive safety, product development and manufacturing, military applications, exhibition and entertainment, geographic information systems, and others.

With the dramatic growth of augmented reality and its applications, this Handbook can be the definitive resource for persons working in this field as researchers, scientists, programmers, engineers, and users. The book is intended for a wide variety of people including academicians, designers, developers, educators, engineers, practitioners, researchers, and graduate students. This book can also be beneficial for business managers, entrepreneurs, and investors. The book can have a great potential to be adopted as a textbook in current and new courses on Augmented Reality.

The main features of this Handbook can be summarized as:

1. The Handbook describes and evaluates the current state-of-the-art in the field of augmented reality.
2. The book presents current trends and concepts of augmented reality, technologies and techniques, AR devices, interfaces, tools, and systems applied in AR, as well as current and future applications.
3. Contributors to the Handbook are the leading researchers from academia and practitioners from industry.
   We would like to thank the authors for their contributions. Without their expertise and effort this Handbook would never come to fruition. Springer editors and staff also deserve our sincere recognition for their support throughout the project.

Boca Raton, Florida   Borko Furht
2011   Editor-in-Chief

Editor-in-Chief

 Borko Furht is a professor and chairman of the Department of Computer and Electrical Engineering and Computer Science at Florida Atlantic University (FAU) in Boca Raton, Florida. He is also Director of the NSF-sponsored Industry/University Cooperative Research Center on Advanced Knowledge Enablement. Before joining FAU, he was a vice president of research and a senior director of development at Modcomp (Ft. Lauderdale), a computer company of Daimler Benz, Germany, a professor at University of Miami in Coral Gables, Florida, and a senior researcher in the Institute Boris Kidric-Vinca, Yugoslavia. Professor Furht received Ph.D. degree in electrical and computer engineering from the University of Belgrade. His current research is in multimedia systems, video coding and compression, 3D video and image systems, wireless multimedia, and Internet, cloud computing, and social networks. He is presently Principal Investigator and Co-PI of several multiyear, multimillion dollar projects including NSF PIRE project and NSF High-Performance Computing Center. He is the author of numerous books and articles in the areas of multimedia, computer architecture, real-time computing, and operating systems. He is a founder and editor-in-chief of *the Journal of Multimedia Tools and Applications* (Springer). He has received several technical and publishing awards, and has consulted for many high-tech companies including IBM, Hewlett-Packard, Xerox, General Electric, JPL, NASA, Honeywell, and RCA. He has also served as a consultant to various colleges and universities. He has given many invited talks, keynote lectures, seminars, and tutorials. He serves as Chairman and Director on the Board of Directors of several high-tech companies.

Contents

Handbook Editorial Board

Contributors

Zhuming Ai Naval Research Laboratory, Washington, DC, USA

Frank Angermann Metaio, Munich, Germany, Frank.Angermann@metaio.com

Shu'nsuke Asai Shimane University, Shimane, Japan

Yohan Baillot Naval Research Laboratory, Washington, DC, USA

Francesca Beatrice Instituto Universitario de Automática e Informática Industrial, Universidad Politécnica de Valencia, Valencia, Spain

Selim Benhimane Research, metaio GmbH, Munich, Germany

Benjamin Berg SimTiki Simulation Center, University of Hawaii, Honolulu HI, USA, bwberg@hawaii.edu

Mark Billinghurst The Human Interface Technology Laboratory, New Zealand (HIT Lab NZ), The University of Canterbury, Christchurch, New Zealand, mark.billinghurst@canterbury.ac.nz

Lisa Blum Collaborative Virtual and Augmented Environments, Fraunhofer FIT, Schloss Birlinghoven, 53754 Sankt Augustin, Germany, lisa.blum@fit.fraunhofer.de

Fernando Boavida Centre for Informatics and Systems, University of Coimbra, Portugal

Markus M. Broecker University of South Australia, Wearable Computer Laboratory, Mawson Lakes, Australia, markus.broecker@unisa.edu.au

Wolfgang Broll Collaborative Virtual and Augmented Environments, Fraunhofer FIT, Schloss Birlinghoven, 53754 Sankt Augustin, Germany, wolfgang.broll@fit.fraunhofer.de

Department of Virtual Worlds and Digital Games, Ilmenau University of Technology, Ilmenau, Germany, wolfgang.broll@tu-ilmenau.de

Leonard D. Brown Department of Computer Science, The University of Arizona, Tucson, Arizona, USA

Dennis G. Brown Naval Research Laboratory, Washington, DC, USA

Julie Carmigniani Department of Computer and Electrical Engineering and Computer Sciences, Florida Atlantic University, Boca Raton, Florida, USA, jcarmign@fau.edu

Jeff Chastine Department of Computing and Software Engineering, Southern Polytechnic State University, Marietta, Georgia, USA, jchastin@spsu.edu

Mike Y. Chen Yuan Ze University, Taiwan, 7533967@gmail.com

Jean-Marc Cieutat ESTIA Recherche, Bidart, France, j.cieutat@estia.fr

Benjamin Close University of South Australia, Wearable Computer Laboratory, Mawson Lakes, Australia, benjamin.close@clearchain.com

Mathis Csisinko Institute of Software Technology and Interactive Systems, Vienna University of Technology, Vienna, Austria

Henry B.L. Duh Department of Electrical and Computer Engineering/Interactive and Digital Media Institute, National University of Singapore, Singapore, duhbl@acm.org

Andreas Dünser The Human Interface Technology Laboratory, New Zealand (HIT Lab NZ), The University of Canterbury, Christchurch, New Zealand, andreas.duenser@canterbury.ac.nz

J. Edward Swan II Naval Research Laboratory, Washington, DC, USA

Pedro Ferreira Centre for Informatics and Systems, University of Coimbra, Portugal, pmferr@dei.uc.pt

Jonas Fredriksson Chalmers University of Technology, Department of Signals and Systems, Gothenburg, Sweden, jonas.fredriksson@chalmers.se

Philippe Fuchs Virtual Reality and Augmented Reality Team, École des Mines ParisTech, Paris, France, philippe.fuchs@ensmp.fr

Borko Furht Department of Computer and Electrical Engineering and Computer Science, Florida Atlantic University, Boca Raton, Florida, USA, bfurht@fau.edu

Marina Gavrilova University of Calgary, Canada, mgavrilo@ucalgary.ca

Raphael Grasset HIT Lab NZ, University of Canterbury, New Zealand, raphael.grasset@canterbury.ac.nz

Institute for Computer Graphics and Vision, Graz University of Technology, Graz, Austria.

Jian Gu KEIO-NUS CUTE Center, National University of Singapore, Singapore, eledbl@nus.edu.sg

Pascal Guitton LaBRI (IPARLA), Université Bordeaux I & INRIA, Bordeaux, France, guitton@labri.fr

Jan Herling Department of Virtual Worlds and Digital Games, Ilmenau University of Technology, Ilmenau, Germany, jan.herling@tu-ilmenau.de

Masahito Hirakawa Shimane University, Shimane, Japan, hirakawa@cis.shimane-u.ac.jp

Hong Hua College of Optical Sciences, The University of Arizona, Tucson, Arizona, USA, hhua@optics.arizona.edu

Yetao Huang Beihang University, Beijing, China, 6666@bit.edu.cn

Olivier Hugues ESTIA Recherche, MaxSea, LaBRI, Bidart, France, o.hugues@net.estia.fr

Tia Jackson Metaio, Munich, Germany, tia.jackson@metaio.com

Zhiguo Jiang Beihang University, Beijing, China

M. Carmen Juan Instituto Universitario de Automática e Informática Industrial, Universitat Politècnica de València, C/Camino de Vera, s/n, 46022-Valencia, Spain, mcarmen@dsic.upv.es

Simon J. Julier Naval Research Laboratory, Washington, DC, USA

Denis Kalkofen Institute for Computer Graphics and Vision, Graz University of Technology, Graz, Austria, kalkofen@icg.tugraz.at

Tai-Wei Kan Graduate Institute of Networking and Multimedia, National Taiwan University, Taiwan, 7533967@gmail.com; d99944001@ntu.edu.tw

Shuhei Kanagu Roots Co. Ltd, Shimane, Japan, kanagu@roots.selfip.com

Hannes Kaufmann Institute of Software Technology and Interactive Systems, Vienna University of Technology, Vienna, Austria, kaufmann@ims.tuwien.ac.at

Kazuhiro Koyama Roots Co. Ltd, Shimane, Japan, koyama@roots.selfip.com

Antonio Krüger German Research Center for Artificial Intelligence DFKI, University of Saarland, Saarbrücken, Germany

Georg Kuschk Research, metaio GmbH, Munich, Germany

King Lai Department of Electrical and Computer Engineering, Michigan State University, East Lansing, MI, USA

Marion Langer Research, metaio GmbH, Munich, Germany

Hongen Liao The University of Tokyo, Tokyo, Japan, liao@bmpe.t.u-tokyo.ac.jp

Sebastian Lieberknecht Research, metaio GmbH, Munich, Germany, Sebastian.Lieberknecht@metaio.com

Gunnar Liestøl Department of Media & Communication, University of Oslo, Norway, gunnar.liestol@media.uio.no

Yue Liu Beijing Institute of Technology, Beijing, China

Mark A. Livingston Naval Research Laboratory, Washington, DC, USA, mark.livingston@nrl.navy.mil

Markus Löchtefeld German Research Center for Artificial Intelligence DFKI, University of Saarland, Saarbrücken, Germany, markus.loechtefeld@dfki.de

Paul Maassel Naval Research Laboratory, Washington, DC, USA

Michael R. Marner University of South Australia, Wearable Computer Laboratory, Mawson Lakes, Australia, michael.marner@unisa.edu.au

Peter Meier Metaio, Munich, Germany

Alessandro Mulloni Institute for Computer Graphics and Vision, Graz University of Technology, Graz, Austria, mulloni@icg.tugraz.at

Olivier Nannipieri Université du Sud, Toulon, and Université de la Méditerranée, Marseille, France, fk.olivier@mac.com

A.Y.C. Nee Department of Mechanical Engineering, National University of Singapore, Singapore, mpeneeyc@nus.edu.sg

Jonas Nilsson Vehicle Dynamics and Active Safety Centre, Volvo Car Corporation, Gothenburg, Sweden

Department of Signals and Systems, Chalmers University of Technology, Gothenburg, Sweden, jnilss94@volvocars.com

Anders C.E. Ödblom Volvo Car Corporation, Gothenburg, Sweden, aodblom1@volvocars.com

S.K. Ong Department of Mechanical Engineering, National University of Singapore, Singapore, mpeongsk@nus.edu.sg

Leif Oppermann Collaborative Virtual and Augmented Environments, Fraunhofer FIT, Schloss Birlinghoven, 53754 Sankt Augustin, Germany, leif.oppermann@fit.fraunhofer.de

David Pérez Instituto de Investigación en Bioingeniería y Tecnología Orientada al Ser Humano, Universitat Politècnica de València, Valencia, Spain

Shane R. Porter University of South Australia, Wearable Computer Laboratory, Mawson Lakes, Australia, shane.porter@unisa.edu.au

Michael Rohs Department of Applied Informatics and Media Informatics, Ludwig-Maximilians-University (LMU) Munich, Munich, Germany

Lawrence J. Rosenblum Naval Research Laboratory, Washington, DC, USA

Kengo Sakata Shimane University, Shimane, Japan

Christian Sandor Magic Vision Lab, University of South Australia, Adelaide, South Australia 5001, Australia, christian.sandor@unisa.edu.au

Dieter Schmalstieg Institute for Computer Graphics and Vision, Graz University of Technology, Graz, Austria, schmalstieg@icg.tugraz.at

Gregory S. Schmidt Naval Research Laboratory, Washington, DC, USA

Jie Shen School of Computer Science and Engineering, University of Electronic Science and Technology of China, Chengdu, China, zeropoint17@hotmail.com

Y. Shen Mechanical Engineering Department, National University of Singapore, Singapore

Andrei Sherstyuk Avatar Reality Inc., Honolulu HI, USA, andrei@avatar-reality.com

Ross T. Smith University of South Australia, Wearable Computer Laboratory, Mawson Lakes, Australia, ross@r-smith.net

Bo Song Department of Electrical and Computer Engineering, Michigan State University, East Lansing, MI, USA

Yasuhiro Sota Roots Co. Ltd, Shimane, Japan, sota@roots.selfip.com

Quintus Stierstorfer Research, metaio GmbH, Munich, Germany

Takehiro Tawara Riken, 2-1 Hirosawa Wako-Shi, 351-0198 Saitama, Japan, takehirotwr@riken.jp

Chin-Hung Teng Department of Information and Communication, Yuan Ze University, Taiwan, 7533967@gmail.com

Bruce H. Thomas University of South Australia, Wearable Computer Laboratory, Mawson Lakes, Australia, bruce.thomas@unisa.edu.au

Anton Treskunov Samsung Information Systems America Inc (SISA), San Jose, CA, USA, anton.t@sisa.samsung.com

Daniel Ulbricht Research, metaio GmbH, Munich, Germany

Dale Vincent Internal Medicine Program, Tripler Army Medical Center (TAMC), Honolulu HI, USA, dale.vincent@amedd.army.mil

Yongtian Wang Beijing Institute of Technology, Beijing, China, 6666@bit.edu.cn

Richard Wetzel Collaborative Virtual and Augmented Environments, Fraunhofer FIT, Schloss Birlinghoven, 53754 Sankt Augustin, Germany, richard.wetzel@fit.fraunhofer.de

Sean White Nokia Research Center, Santa Monica, CA, USA, sean.white@nokia.com

Ning Xi Department of Electrical and Computer Engineering, Michigan State University, East Lansing, MI, USA, xin@egr.msu.edu

Ruiguo Yang Department of Electrical and Computer Engineering, Michigan State University, East Lansing, MI, USA

Adeel Zafar Volvo Car Corporation, Gothenburg, Sweden, azafar3@volvocars.com

J. Zhang Department of Mechanical Engineering, National University of Singapore, Singapore

Rui Zhang College of Optical Sciences, The University of Arizona, Tucson, Arizona, USA, hhua@optics.arizona.edu

Part I
Technologies

Chapter 1
Augmented Reality: An Overview

Julie Carmigniani and Borko Furht

1 Introduction

We define Augmented Reality (AR) as a real-time direct or indirect view of a physical real-world environment that has been enhanced/*augmented* by adding virtual computer-generated information to it [1]. AR is both interactive and registered in 3D as well as combines real and virtual objects. Milgram's Reality-Virtuality Continuum is defined by Paul Milgram and Fumio Kishino as a continuum that spans between the real environment and the virtual environment comprise Augmented Reality and Augmented Virtuality (AV) in between, where AR is closer to the real world and AV is closer to a pure virtual environment, as seen in Fig. 1.1 [2].

Augmented Reality aims at simplifying the user's life by bringing virtual information not only to his immediate surroundings, but also to any indirect view of the real-world environment, such as live-video stream. AR enhances the user's perception of and interaction with the real world. While Virtual Reality (VR) technology or Virtual Environment as called by Milgram, completely immerses users in a synthetic world without seeing the real world, AR technology *augments* the sense of reality by superimposing virtual objects and cues upon the real world in real time. Note that, as Azuma et al. [3], we do not consider AR to be restricted to a particular type of display technologies such as head-mounted display (HMD), nor do we consider it to be limited to the sense of sight. AR can potentially apply to all senses, augmenting smell, touch and hearing as well. AR can also be used to augment or substitute users' missing senses by sensory substitution, such as augmenting the sight of blind users or users with poor vision by the use of audio cues, or augmenting hearing for deaf users by the use of visual cues.

J. Carmigniani (✉)
Department of Computer and Electrical Engineering and Computer Sciences,
Florida Atlantic University, Boca Raton, Florida, USA
e-mail: jcarmign@fau.edu

B. Furht (ed.), *Handbook of Augmented Reality*, DOI 10.1007/978-1-4614-0064-6_1,
© Springer Science+Business Media, LLC 2011

Fig. 1.1 Milgram's
reality-virtuality
continuum [1]

Azuma et al. [3] also considered AR applications that require removing real objects from the environment, which are more commonly called *mediated* or *diminished reality*, in addition to adding virtual objects. Indeed, removing objects from the real world corresponds to covering the object with virtual information that matches the background in order to give the user the impression that the object is not there. Virtual objects added to the real environment show information to the user that the user cannot directly detect with his senses. The information passed on by the virtual object can help the user in performing daily-tasks work, such as guiding workers through electrical wires in an aircraft by displaying digital information through a headset. The information can also simply have an entertainment purpose, such as Wikitude or other mobile augmented reality. There are many other classes of AR applications, such as medical visualization, entertainment, advertising, maintenance and repair, annotation, robot path planning, etc.

2 History

The first appearance of Augmented Reality (AR) dates back to the 1950s when Morton Heilig, a cinematographer, thought of cinema is an activity that would have the ability to draw the viewer into the onscreen activity by taking in all the senses in an effective manner. In 1962, Heilig built a prototype of his vision, which he described in 1955 in "The Cinema of the Future," named Sensorama, which predated digital computing [4]. Next, Ivan Sutherland invented the head mounted display in 1966 (Fig. 1.2). In 1968, Sutherland was the first one to create an augmented reality system using an optical see-through head-mounted display [5]. In 1975, Myron Krueger creates the Videoplace, a room that allows users to interact with virtual objects for the first time. Later, Tom Caudell and David Mizell from Boeing coin the phrase Augmented Reality while helping workers assemble wires and cable for an aircraft [1]. They also started discussing the advantages of Augmented Reality versus Virtual Reality (VR), such as requiring less power since fewer pixels are needed [5]. In the same year, L.B Rosenberg developed one of the first functioning AR systems, called Virtual Fixtures and demonstrated its benefit on human performance while Steven Feiner, Blair MacIntyre and Doree Seligmann presented the first major paper on an AR system prototype named KARMA [1]. The reality virtuality continuum seen in Fig. 1.1 is not defined until 1994 by Paul Milgram and Fumio Kishino as a continuum that spans from the real environment to the virtual environment. AR and AV are located somewhere

Fig. 1.2 Ivan Sutherland's
HMD [5]

in between with AR being closer to the real world environment and AV being closer
to the virtual environment. In 1997, Ronald Azuma writes the first survey in AR
providing a widely acknowledged definition of AR by identifying it as combining
real and virtual environment while being both registered in 3D and interactive in
real time [5]. The first outdoor mobile AR game, ARQuake, is developed by Bruce
Thomas in 2000 and demonstrated during the International Symposium on Wearable
Computers. In 2005, the Horizon Report [6] predicts that AR technologies will
emerge more fully within the next 4–5 years; and, as to confirm that prediction,
camera systems that can analyze physical environments in real time and relate
positions between objects and environment are developed the same year. This type
of camera system has become the basis to integrate virtual objects with reality in
AR systems. In the following years, more and more AR applications are developed
especially with mobile applications, such as Wikitude AR Travel Guide launched
in 2008, but also with the development of medical applications in 2007. Nowadays,
with the new advances in technology, an increasing amount of AR systems and
applications are produced, notably with MIT 6th sense prototype and the release of
the iPad 2 and its successors and competitors, notably the Eee Pad, and the iPhone 4,
which promises to revolutionize mobile AR.

3   Augmented Reality Technologies

3.1   Computer Vision Methods in AR

Computer vision renders 3D virtual objects from the same viewpoint from which the images of the real scene are being taken by tracking cameras. Augmented reality image registration uses different method of computer vision mostly related to video tracking. These methods usually consist of two stages: tracking and reconstructing/recognizing. First, fiducial markers, optical images, or interest points are detected in the camera images. Tracking can make use of feature detection, edge detection, or other image processing methods to interpret the camera images. In computer vision, most of the available tracking techniques can be separated in two classes: feature-based and model-based [7]. Feature-based methods consist of discovering the connection between 2D image features and their 3D world frame coordinates [8]. Model-based methods make use of model of the tracked objects' features such as CAD models or 2D templates of the item based on distinguishable features [7]. Once a connection is made between the 2D image and 3D world frame, it is possible to find the camera pose by projecting the 3D coordinates of the feature into the observed 2D image coordinates and by minimizing the distance to their corresponding 2D features. The constraints for camera pose estimation are most often determined using point features. The reconstructing/recognizing stage uses the data obtained from the first stage to reconstruct a real world coordinate system.

Assuming a calibrated camera and a perspective projection model, if a point has coordinates $(x, y, z)^T$ in the coordinate frame of the camera, its projection onto the image plane is $(x/z, y/z, 1)^T$.

In point constraints, we have two principal coordinate systems, as illustrated in Fig. 1.3, the world coordinate system W and the 2D image coordinate system. Let $p_i(x_i, y_i, z_i)^T$, where $i = 1, \ldots, n$, with $n \geq 3$, be a set of 3D non-collinear reference points in the world frame coordinate and $q_i(x_i', y_i', z_i')^T$ be the corresponding camera-space coordinates, p_i and q_i are related by the following transformation:

$$q_i = Rp_i + T \tag{1.1}$$

where

$$R = \begin{pmatrix} r_1^T \\ r_2^T \\ r_3^T \end{pmatrix} \text{ and } T = \begin{pmatrix} t_x \\ t_y \\ t_z \end{pmatrix} \tag{1.2}$$

are a rotation matrix and a translation vector, respectively.

Let the image point $\mathbf{h_i}$ $(u_i, v_i, 1)^T$ be the projection of $\mathbf{p_i}$ on the normalized image plane. The *collinearity equation* establishing the relationship between h_i and p_i using the camera pinhole is given by:

$$h_i = \frac{1}{r_3^T p_i + t_z}(Rp_i + T) \tag{1.3}$$

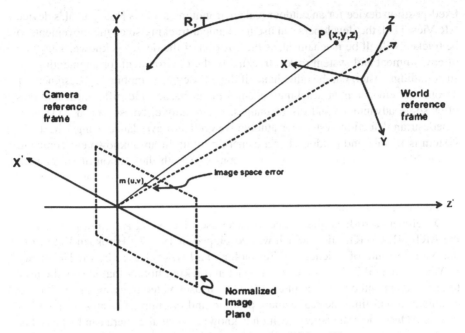

Fig. 1.3 Point constraints for the camera pose problem adapted from [9]

The image space error gives a relationship between 3D reference points, their corresponding 2D extracted image points, and the camera pose parameters, and corresponds to the point constraints [9]. The image space error is given as follow:

$$E_i^p = \sqrt{\left(\hat{u}_i - \frac{r_1^T p_i + t_x}{r_3^T p_i + t_z}\right)^2 + \left(\hat{v}_i - \frac{r_2^T p_i + t_y}{r_3^T p_i + t_z}\right)^2} \qquad (1.4)$$

where $\hat{m}_i \left(\hat{u}_i, \hat{v}_i, 1\right)^T$ are the observed image points.

Some methods assume the presence of fiducial markers in the environment or object with known 3D geometry, and make use of those data. Others have the scene 3D structure pre-calculated beforehand, such as Huang et al.'s device AR-View [10]; however, the device will have to be stationary and its position known. If the entire scene is not known beforehand, Simultaneous Localization And Mapping (SLAM) technique is used for mapping fiducial markers or 3D models relative positions. In the case when no assumptions about the 3D geometry of the scene can be made, Structure from Motion (SfM) method is used. SfM method can be divided into two parts: feature point tracking and camera parameter estimation.

Tracking methods in AR depend mostly on the type of environment the AR device will be introduced to as well as the type of AR system. The environment might be indoor, outdoor or a combination of both. In the same way, the system might be mobile or static (have a fixed-position). For example, if the AR device is a fixed-position device for an outdoor real environment, such as Huang et al.'s device AR-View [10], the developers can use mechanical tracking since the movements to be tracked will all be mechanical, as the position of the device is known. This type of environment and system makes tracking of the environment for augmenting the surroundings easier. On the other hand, if the AR device is mobile and designed for an outdoor environment, tracking becomes much harder and different techniques offer some advantages and disadvantages. For example, Nilsson et al. [11] built a pedestrian detection system for automotive collision avoidance using AR. Their system is mobile and outdoor. For a camera moving in an unknown environment, the problem for computer vision is to reconstruct both the motion of the camera and the structure of the scene using the image and additional sensor data sequences. In this case, since no assumption about the 3D geometry of the scene can be made, SfM method is used for reconstructing the scene.

Developers also have the choice to make use of existing AR libraries, such as the ARToolKit. ARToolKit, which was developed in 1999 by Hirokazu Kato from the Nara Institute of Science and Technology and was released by the University of Washington HIT Lab, is a computer vision tracking library that allows the user to create augmented reality applications [12]. It uses video tracking capabilities to calculate in real time the real camera position and orientation relative to physical markers. Once the real camera position is known, a virtual camera can be placed at the same exact position and 3D computer graphics model can be drawn to overlay the markers. The extended version of ARToolKit is ARToolKitPlus, which added many features over the ARToolKit, notably class-based APIs; however, it is no longer being developed and already has a successor: Studierstube Tracker.

Studierstube Tracker's concepts are very similar to ARToolKitPlus; however, its code base is completely different and it is not an open source, thus not available for download. It supports mobile phone, with Studierstube ES, as well as PCs, making its memory requirements very low (100KB or 5–10% of ARToolKitPlus) and processing very fast (about twice as fast as ARToolKitPlus on mobile phones and about 1 ms per frame on a PC) [13]. Studierstube Tracker is highly modular; developers can extend it in anyway by creating new features for it. When first presenting Studierstube in [13], the designers had in mind a user interface that "uses collaborative augmented reality to bridge multiple user interface dimensions: Multiple users, contexts, and locales as well as applications, 3D-windows, hosts, display platforms, and operating systems." More information about Studierstube can be found at [13–15].

Although visual tracking now has the ability to recognize and track a lot of things, it mostly relies on other techniques such as GPS and accelerometers. For example, for a computer to detect and recognize a car it is very hard. The surface of most cars is both shiny and smooth and most of the feature points come from reflections and thus are not relevant for pose estimation and even sometimes recognition [16]. The few stable features that one can hope to recognize, such as the windows corners or wheels, are extremely difficult to match due to reflection and transparent parts. While this example is a bit extreme, it shows the difficulties and challenges faced by computer vision with most objects that have irregular shape, such as food, flowers, and most objects of art.

Fig. 1.4 HMD from [17]

A recent new approach for advances in visual tracking has been to study how the human brain recognizes objects, also called the Human Vision System (HVS), as it is possible for humans to recognize an infinite number of objects and persons in fractions of seconds. If the way of recognizing things by the human brain can be modeled, computer vision will be able to handle the challenges it is currently facing and keep moving forward.

3.2 AR Devices

The main devices for augmented reality are displays, input devices, tracking, and computers.

3.2.1 Displays

There are three major types of displays used in Augmented Reality: head mounted displays (HMD), handheld displays and spatial displays.

HMD is a display device worn on the head or as part of a helmet and that places both images of the real and virtual environment over the user's view of the world (Fig. 1.4). HMD can either be video-see-through or optical see-through and can have a monocular or binocular display optic. Video-see-through systems are more demanding than optical-see-through systems as they require the user to wear two cameras on his head and require the processing of both cameras to provide

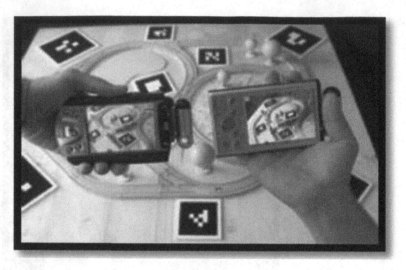

Fig. 1.5 Handheld displays from [18]

both the "real part" of the augmented scene and the virtual objects with unmatched resolution, while the optical-see-through employs a half-silver mirror technology to allow views of physical world to pass through the lens and graphically overlay information to be reflected in the user's eyes. The scene as well as the real world is perceived more naturally than at the resolution of the display. On the other hand, in video-see-through systems, augmented view is already composed by the computer and allows much more control over the result. Thus, control over the timing of the real scene can be achieved by synchronizing the virtual image with the scene before displaying it while in an optical-see-through application, the view of the real world cannot be delayed, so the time lag introduced in the system by the graphics and image processing is perceived by the user. This results in image that may not appear "attached" with the real objects they are supposed to correspond to, they appear to be unstable, jittering, or swimming around.

Handheld displays employ small computing devices with a display that the user can hold in their hands (Fig. 1.5). They use video-see-through techniques to overlay graphics onto the real environment and employ sensors, such as digital compasses and GPS units for their six degree of freedom tracking sensors, fiducial marker systems, such as ARToolKit, and/or computer vision methods, such as SLAM. There are currently three distinct classes of commercially available handheld displays that are being used for augmented reality system: smart-phones, PDAs and Tablet PCs [18]. Smart-phones are extremely portable and widespread, and with the recent advances present a combination of powerful CPU, camera, accelerometer, GPS, and solid state compass, making them a very promising platform for AR. However, their small display size is less than ideal for 3D user interfaces. PDAs present much of the same advantages and disadvantages of the smart-phones, but they are becoming a lot less widespread than smart-phones since the most recent advances, with Android-based phones and iPhones. Tablet PCs are a lot more powerful than

Fig. 1.6 SAR from [21]

smart-phones, but they are considerably more expensive and too heavy for single handed, and even prolonged two-handed, use. However, with the recent release of iPad, we believe that Tablet PCs could become a promising platform for handheld AR displays.

Spatial Augmented Reality (SAR) make use of video-projectors, optical elements, holograms, radio frequency tags, and other tracking technologies to display graphical information directly onto physical objects without requiring the user to wear or carry the display (Fig. 1.6) [19]. Spatial displays separate most of the technology from the user and integrate it into the environment. This permits SAR to naturally scale up to groups of users, thus allowing collaboration between users, increasing the interest for such augmented reality systems in universities, labs, museums, and in the art community. There exist three different approaches to SAR which mainly differ in the way they augment the environment: video-see-through, optical-see-through and direct augmentation. In SAR, video-see-through displays are screen based; they are a common technique used if the system does not have to be mobile as they are cost efficient since only off-the-shelf hardware components and standard PC equipment is required. Spatial optical-see-through displays generate images that are aligned within the physical environment. Spatial optical combiners, such as planar or curved mirror beam splitters, transparent screens, or optical holograms are essential components of such displays [19]. However, much like screen-based video see-through, spatial optical-see-through does not support mobile applications due to spatially aligned optics and display technology. Finally, projector-based spatial displays apply front-projection to seamlessly project images directly onto physical objects' surfaces, such as in [20]. More details about SAR can be read in [19]. Table1.1 shows a comparison of different types of displays' techniques for augmented reality.

3.2.2 Input Devices

There are many types of input devices for AR systems. Some systems, such as Reitmayr et al.'s mobile augmented system [17] utilizes gloves. Others, such as ReachMedia [22] use a wireless wristband. In the case of smart-phones, the phone itself can be used as a pointing device; for example, Google Sky Map on Android phone requires the user to point his/her phone in the direction of the stars or planets s/he wishes to know the name of. The input devices chosen depend greatly upon the type of application the system is being developed for and/or the display chosen. For instance, if an application requires the user to be hands free, the input device chosen will be one that enables the user to use his/her hands for the application without requiring extra unnatural gestures or to be held by the user, examples of such input devices include gaze interaction in [23] or the wireless wristband used in [22]. Similarly, if a system makes use of a handheld display, the developers can utilize a touch screen input device.

3.2.3 Tracking

Tracking devices consists of digital cameras and/or other optical sensors, GPS, accelerometers, solid state compasses, wireless sensors, etc. Each of these technologies has different level of accuracy and depends greatly on the type of system being developed. In [24], the authors identified the general tracking technology for augmented reality to be: mechanical, magnetic sensing, GPS, ultrasonic, inertia, and optics. In [25], the authors use a comparison from DiVerdi [26] based on range, setup, resolution, time, and environment. We further adopted their comparison method to this survey in Table 1.2.

3.2.4 Computers

AR systems require powerful CPU and considerable amount of RAM to process camera images. So far, mobile computing systems employ a laptop in a backpack configuration, but with the rise of smart-phones technology and iPad, we can hope to see this backpack configuration replaced by a lighter and more sophisticated looking system. Stationary systems can use a traditional workstation with a powerful graphics card.

Table 1.1 Comparison of different techniques for different types of display

Types of displays / Techniques	HMD		Handheld			Spatial		
	Video-see-through	Optical-see-through	Video-see-through — HMD	Video-see-through — Handheld	Handheld	Video-see-through	Optical-see-through	Direct augmentation
Advantages	complete visualization control, possible synchronization of the virtual and real environment	employs a half-silver mirror technology, more natural perception of the real environment	portable, powerful CPU, camera, accelerometer, GPS, and solid state compass	portable, widespread, powerful CPU, camera, accelerometer, GPS, and solid state compass	more powerful	cost efficient, can be adapted using off-the-shelf hardware components and standard PC equipment	more natural perception of the real environment	displays directly onto physical objects' surfaces
Disadvantages	requires user to wear cameras on his/her head, require processing of cameras video stream, unnatural perception of the real environment	time lag, jittering of the virtual image	small display	becoming less widespread, small display	more expensive and heavy	does not support mobile system	does not support mobile system	not user dependent: everybody sees the same thing (in some cases this disadvantage can also be considered to be an advantage)

Table 1.2 Comparison of common tracking technologies (adapted from Papagiannakis et al. [25] and DiVerdi et al. [26]). Range: size of the region that can be tracked within. Setup: amount of time for instrumentation and calibration. Precision: granularity of a single output position. Time: duration for which useful tracking data is returned (before it drifts too much). Environment: where the tracker can be used, indoors or outdoors

Technology	Range (m)	Setup time (hr)	Precision (mm)	Time (s)	Environment
Optical: marker-based	10	0	10	∞	in/out
Optical: markerless	50	0–1	10	∞	in/out
Optical: outside-in	10	10	10	∞	in
Optical: inside-out	50	0–1	10	∞	in/out
GPS	∞	0	5,000	∞	out
WiFi	100	10	1,000	∞	in/out
Accelerometer	1,000	0	100	1000	in/out
Magnetic	1	1	1	∞	in/out
Ultrasound	10	1	10	∞	in
Inertial	1	0	1	10	in/out
Hybrid	30	10	1	∞	in/out
UWB	10–300	10	500	∞	in
RFID: active	20–100	when needed	500	∞	in/out
RFID: passive	0.05–5	when needed	500	∞	in/out

3.3   AR Interfaces

One of the most important aspects of augmented reality is to create appropriate techniques for intuitive interaction between the user and the virtual content of AR applications. There are four main ways of interaction in AR applications: tangible AR interfaces, collaborative AR interfaces, hybrid AR interfaces, and the emerging multimodal interfaces.

3.3.1   Tangible AR Interfaces

Tangible interfaces support direct interaction with the real world by exploiting the use of real, physical objects and tools. A classical example of the power of tangible user interfaces is the VOMAR application developed by Kato et al. [27], which enables a person to select and rearrange the furniture in an AR living room design application by using a real, physical paddle. Paddle motions are mapped to intuitive gesture based commands, such as "scooping up" an object to select it for movement or hitting an item to make it disappear in order to provide the user with an intuitive experience.

A more recent example of a tangible AR user interface is TaPuMa [28]. TaPuMa is a table-top tangible interface that uses physical objects to interact with digital projected maps using real-life objects the user carries with him as queries to find locations or information on the map. The advantage of such an application is that using objects as keywords eliminates the language barrier of conventional graphical interfaces (although most of them do have multiple languages, they are often mistranslated). On the other hand, keywords using objects can also be ambiguous, as there can be more than one mapping to actions or information possible, and different people from different places, age-group, and culture have different meanings for different objects. So although this system might seem rather simple to use, it opens the door to a main problem in user interfaces: showing the user how to utilize the real objects for interacting with the system. White et al.'s [29] solution was to provide virtual visual hints on the real object showing how it should be moved.

Another example of tangible AR interactions includes the use of gloves or wristband such as in [22] and [30].

3.3.2 Collaborative AR Interfaces

Collaborative AR interfaces include the use of multiple displays to support remote and co-located activities. Co-located sharing uses 3D interfaces to improve physical collaborative workspace. In remote sharing, AR is able to effortlessly integrate multiple devices with multiple locations to enhance teleconferences.

An example of co-located collaboration can be seen with Studierstube [13–15]. When first presenting Studierstube in [13], the designers had in mind a user interface that "uses collaborative augmented reality to bridge multiple user interface dimensions: Multiple users, contexts, and locales as well as applications, 3D-windows, hosts, display platforms, and operating systems."

Remote sharing can be used for enhancing teleconferences such as in [31]. Such interfaces can be integrated with medical applications for performing diagnostics, surgery, or even maintenance routine.

3.3.3 Hybrid AR Interfaces

Hybrid interfaces combine an assortment of different, but complementary interfaces as well as the possibility to interact through a wide range of interaction devices [7]. They provide a flexible platform for unplanned, everyday interaction where it is not known in advance which type of interaction display or devices will be used. In [32], Sandor et al. developed a hybrid user interface using head-tracked, see-through, head-worn display to overlay augmented reality and provide both visual and auditory feedbacks. Their AR system is then implemented to support end users in assigning physical interaction devices to operations as well as virtual objects on which to perform those procedures, and in reconfiguring the mappings between devices, objects and operations as the user interacts with the system.

3.3.4 Multimodal AR Interfaces

Multimodal interfaces combine real objects input with naturally occurring forms of language and behaviors such as speech, touch, natural hand gestures, or gaze. These types of interfaces are more recently emerging. Examples include MIT's sixth sense [20] wearable gestural interface, called WUW. WUW brings the user with information projected onto surfaces, walls, and physical objects through natural hand gestures, arms movement, and/or interaction with the object itself. Another example of multimodal interaction is the work from Lee et al. [23], which makes use of gaze and blink to interact with objects. This type of interaction is now being largely developed and is sure to be one of the preferred type of interaction for future augmented reality application as they offer a relatively robust, efficient, expressive, and highly mobile form of human-computer interaction that represent the users' preferred interaction style. They have the capability to support users' ability to flexibly combine modalities or to switch from one input mode to another depending on the task or setting. In addition, multimodal interfaces offer the freedom to choose which mode of interaction the user prefers to use depending on the context; i.e. public place, museum, library, etc. This freedom to choose the mode of interaction is crucial to wider acceptance of pervasive systems in public places [75].

3.4 AR Systems

Augmented reality systems can be divided into five categories: fixed indoor systems, fixed outdoor systems, mobile indoor systems, mobile outdoor systems, and mobile indoor and outdoor systems. We define a mobile system as a system that allows the user for movement that are not constrained to one room and thus allow the user to move through the use of a wireless system. Fixed system cannot be moved around and the user must use these systems wherever they are set up without having the flexibility to move unless they are relocating the whole system setup. The choice of the type of system to be built is the first choice the developers must make as it will help the developers in deciding which type of tracking system, display choice and possibly interface they should use. For instance, fixed systems will not make use of GPS tracking, while outdoor mobile system will. In [25], the authors conducted a study of different AR systems. We conducted a similar study using 25 papers that were classified according to their type of system, and determined what the tracking techniques, display type and interfaces were for each. Tables 1.3 and 1.4 show the results of the study and Table 1.5 the meaning of the abbreviation used in Tables 1.3 and 1.4.

The papers used for the study were all published between 2002 and 2010 with a majority of papers (17 papers out of 25) published between 2005 and 2010.

Note that in the mobile indoor and outdoor systems, one of the system studied (Costanza's eye-q [49]) does not use any tracking techniques, while others use multiple type of tracking techniques. This is due to the fact that this system was

Table 1.3 AR system comparison

System type	Method	Application domain					Tracking and registration					Display	Interface
		Adv.	Ent. and ed.	Nav. and info.	Med.	Gen.	Optical	GPS	Mechanical	Sensors	Wireless		
Fixed indoor	Bichlmeier et al. [34]				X		IO, OI, MB					HMD	tangible
	Luo et al. [35]				X		IO					HMD	tangible
	Mistry et al. [28]			X			OI			RFID		spatial	tangible
	Magic Mirror	X					OI, MB					spatial	tangible
	Botella et al. [36]				X		IO, MB					HMD	tangible
	Cooper et al. [30]		X				OI, MB					spatial	shared
	Takahashi et al. [37]			X			MB					spatial	tangible
	Akinbiyi et al. [38]				X					force		HMD	tangible
	Sandor et al. [32]					X	IO					HMD	hybrid
Fixed outdoor	Huang et al. [10]		X						X			spatial	tangible
Mobile indoor	Miyashita et al. [39]		X				ML			rotation,		handheld	tangible
	Bruns et al. [40]		X				ML			RFID	Bluetooth	handheld	tangible

(continued)

Table 1.3 (continued)

System type	Method	Application domain					Tracking and registration					Display	Interface
		Adv.	Ent. and ed.	Nav. and info.	Med.	Gen.	Optical	GPS	Mechanical	Sensors	Wireless		
	Caruso et al. [41]					X	MB			IR LEDs		HMD	tangible
	Lee et al. [23]					X	IO					HMD	multimodal
	Arvanitis et al. [42]		X				IO					HMD	tangible
	Reitmayr et al. [17]			X			MB			inertial		HMD	tangible
	Stutzman et al. [43]	X					X			inertial		handheld	shared
Mobile outdoor	Brown et al. [44]			X			X	X		inertial		HMD	shared
	Dahne et al. [45]		X				ML	X		EC		HMD	tangible
	Chen et al. [46]			X			ML	X		inertial		spatial	tangible
	Schneider et al. [47]		X				X	X		rotation		HMD	tangible
	Wang et al. [48]			X			X	X		inertial		handheld	tangible
Mobile indoor and outdoor	Mistry et al. [20]					X	X					spatial	multimodal
	Feldman et al. [22]					X				RFID, inertial	X	handheld	multimodal
	Costanza et al. [49]					X				inertial		HMD	tangible

Table 1.4 Systems preferred type of tracking, display and interfaces

		Fixed indoor systems		Fixed outdoor systems		Mobile indoor systems		Mobile outdoor systems		Mobile indoor and outdoor systems	
		Number	Percentage	Number	Percentage	Number	Percentage	Number	Percentage	Number	Percentage
Application domain	Adv.	1	11%	0	0%	1	14%	0	0%	0	0%
	Ent. and ed.	1	11%	1	100%	3	43%	2	40%	0	0%
	Nav. and info.	2	22%	0	0%	1	14%	3	60%	0	0%
	Med.	4	44%	0	0%	0	0%	0	0%	0	0%
	Gen.	1	11%	0	0%	2	29%	0	0%	3	100%
Tracking	Optical	7	78%	0	0%	2	29%	0	0%	1	33%
	GPS	0	0%	0	0%	0	0%	0	0%	0	0%
	Sensor based	1	11%	0	0%	0	0%	0	0%	0	0%
	Wireless	0	0%	0	0%	0	0%	0	0%	0	0%
	Mechanical	0	0%	1	100%	0	0%	0	0%	0	0%
	Hybrid	1	11%	0	0%	5	71%	5	100%	1	33%
Display type	HMD	5	56%	0	0%	4	57%	3	60%	1	33%
	Handheld	0	0%	0	0%	3	43%	1	20%	1	33%
	Spatial display	4	44%	1	100%	0	0%	1	20%	1	33%
Interface	Tangible	7	78%	1	100%	5	71%	5	100%	1	33%
	Shared	1	11%	0	0%	1	14%	0	0%	0	0%
	Hybrid	1	11%	0	0%	0	0%	0	0%	0	0%
	Multimodal	0	0%	0	0%	1	14%	0	0%	2	67%
Total number of papers:		9	36%	1	4%	7	28%	5	20%	3	12%

Table 1.5 Abbreviations

Abbreviation	Meaning	Abbreviation	Meaning
Adv	Advertising	IO	inside out
Ent. and ed.	Entertainment and education	OI	outside in
Med.	Medical	MB	marker-based
Nav. and info.	Navigational and informational	ML	markerless
Gen.	General	EC	electronic compass

developed as a personal, subtle notification display. Also notice that there was only one paper studied that discussed fixed outdoor systems because this type of system is not popular due to its inflexibility. The results from this study thus can also be used to show the most popular type of system developed so far. However, we need to take into account the fact that mobile system are now on the rise and while mobile indoor and outdoor systems represented only 12% of the papers studied, developers are looking more and more into this type of system as they have the most chance for making it into the market.

Although these results cannot be used as a general rule when building an AR system, they can serve as a pointer of what type of tracking techniques, display, or interface is more popular for each system type. Developers should also keep in mind that these choices depend also on the type of applications, although as can be seen, the application does not necessarily guide the type of system.

From this study, we see that optical tracking is mostly preferred in fixed systems, while a hybrid approach is most often preferred for mobile systems. HMDs are often the preferred type of display choice; however, we predict that they will need to become more fashionably acceptable for systems using them to reach the market. When it comes to interfaces, the most popular choice is tangible interfaces, but we predict that multimodal interfaces will become more famous with developers within the next years as we believe that they also have a better chance to reach the public industry.

4 Augmented Reality Mobile Systems

Augmented reality mobile systems include mobile phones applications as well as wireless systems such as MIT's sixth sense [20] and eye-q [49]. AR mobile systems involve the use of wearable mobile interfaces for the user to interact with digital information overlapped on physical objects or surfaces in a natural and socially acceptable way. Mobile phones for augmented reality present both advantages and drawbacks. Indeed, most mobile devices nowadays are equipped with cameras making mobile phones one of the most convenient platforms on which to implement augmented reality. In addition, most cell phones provide accelerometers, magnetometers and GPS from which AR can benefit. However, in spite of rapid advances in mobile phones, their computing platform for real-time imaging applications is still rather limited if done using the cell phone's platform. As a result, many applications send data to a remote computer that does the computation and sends the result back to the mobile device, but this approach is not well adapted to AR due to limited bandwidth. Nevertheless, considering the rapid development in mobile devices computing power, it can be considered feasible to develop real-time AR application locally processed in the near future.

We define a successful AR mobile system as an application that enables the user to focus on the application or system rather than on the computing devices, interacts with the device in a natural and socially acceptable way, and provides the user with private information that can be shared if necessary. This suggests the need for lightweight, wearable or mobile devices that are fashionably acceptable, private and possess robust tracking technology.

4.1   Socially Acceptable Technology

Many research groups have raised the problem of socially acceptable technology. Mobile systems in particular are constantly faced with social acceptance issues to go from the laboratories to the industry. For systems to be successful in the market, developers need to take into account that the device needs to be socially acceptable, natural to interact with, and fashionably acceptable.

4.1.1   Social Acceptance

Mobile phones and PDAs reminders, messages, calls, etc. have been judged to be distractions and are mostly considered not to be socially acceptable as they not only disrupt the person whose phone or PDA is receiving a message or reminding its owner of more or less important information, but also the other persons present in the same room, whether they are having a conversation with the disruptor (as this is how the person whose phone is disrupting the room will be seen) or the disruptor is in a public place, such as a bus. As a result, research groups such as [22, 49], [others], have decided that interaction with Augmented Reality systems implemented in mobile applications need to be subtle, discrete and unobtrusive, so to not disrupt the user if s/he is under a high load of work and the disruption is not of priority level. A system that is subtle, discrete and unobtrusive becomes socially acceptable. Indeed, the main problem with social acceptance comes from the level of disruption portable devices create in public places and during conversations. In [49], the authors study the peripheral vision and adapt their mobile device, eye-q, so that it does not occlude the foveal field of view, which is the main focus in the human field of view. The cues become less and less visible depending on the level of concentration and work-load of the user, making it naturally adaptive to users' cognitive workload and stress. And since the cues are only visible to the user, they can be considered socially acceptable as they will only disrupt the user depending on his level of concentration and he can choose not to answer to the cues. In addition, Sorce et al. [33] have come up to the conclusion that multimodal interfaces are crucial to wider acceptance of pervasive systems in public places as they offer the user the freedom to choose from a range of interaction modes. As a result, users are presented with the freedom to choose the most appropriate and socially acceptable mean of communication with their devices.

4.1.2 Natural Interaction

Another important factor to socially acceptable devices is that the user has to be able to interact with them in a natural way. If the interaction between the user and the device is unnatural, it will appear awkward of use in public places. In [22], the authors have created an augmented reality system that uses a wireless wristband that includes an RIFD reader, 3-axis accelerometer and RF communication facilities, a cell phone and a wireless earpiece to allow the user to interact with services related to objects using RFID tags through implicit touch-based gestures. Once an object is detected in the user's hand, the user can interact with information about this object using natural slight wrist gestures while previous commercial interfaces that supported hands-free and eyes-free operations required speech recognition, which not only suffers from poor performance and noisy conditions, but is also not socially acceptable.

4.1.3 Fashion Acceptance

Mobile AR systems that wish to step from the laboratories to the industry will also be facing fashion issues as the users will not want to wear a HMD or other visible devices. As a result, developers of mobile systems should take into account fashion trends as this might be a big obstacle to overcome. Groups such as MIT Media Lab, constantly try to reduce the amount of undesirable visible devices or arrange them in different design choice. WUW's first development stage integrated the camera and projector into a hat and the second development integrated it into a pendant. The group is also researching a way to replace the need to wear colored markers on fingers' tips [20]. Although these might not yet look very fashionable, they are a good step in the direction of fashionably acceptable AR mobile systems. Another example is ReachMedia [22] which integrates a wristband with a smartphone in order to interact with everyday objects using natural hand and wrist slight gestures. Here the authors avoid the use of unstylish head mounted display for using acceptable wristband and phones. However, the audio interaction with the phone might require the use of headphones in order to remain discrete and subtle.

4.2 Personal and Private Systems

Augmented reality mobile systems need to be personal, meaning that the displayed information should only be viewed by others if the user allows it. MIT's SixthSense technology [20] although very advanced, does not offer such privacy to its user due to the use of direct augmentation technique without using any viewing device for protecting the information. Anyone can see the same thing as the user at any time. This poses a dilemma as not needing to wear or carry any extra viewing device for the WUW is an advantage for fashionable acceptable devices; however, it is a problem when it comes to privacy. Systems such as Costanza et al. eye-q [49] or Babak Parviz's contact lens [50] offer such privacy to the user with information that can only be viewed by the user. These systems can also be considered socially acceptable as they are discrete and subtle as well as fashionably correct. However, these systems do not offer the ability of sharing information if the user desires to. A successful AR mobile system should provide the user with private information that can be shared when the user wishes to.

In addition, AR mobile systems need to be careful not to violate other users' and non-users' privacy in new ways. Indeed, information that are available and not considered private on social networks, for instance, can be considered private in everyday life. As a result, technologies such as WUW [20] that make use of online available information about other persons to display them for the user might face privacy issues due to the way the information are being disclosed.

4.3 Tracking Technology for Mobile AR Systems

It is well known that for AR to be able to trick the human senses into believing that computer-generated information coexist with the real environment, very accurate position and orientation tracking is required.

As was seen in the AR systems section, the most common type of tracking systems for mobile systems is by combining a few complimentary tracking techniques to comprise the advantages of both and support the disadvantages of the other, which creates hybrid tracking. Outdoors systems make mostly use of GPS and inertial tracking technique with the use of accelerometers, gyroscopes, electronic compasses and/or other rotation sensors, along with some computer vision tracking techniques. GPS system, although lacking in precision, provide an easy tracking system for outdoor systems that allows for better estimating the position of the user and its orientation once coupled with some inertial sensors. In this way, the user's interest point is narrowed down and allows for easier visual tracking with fewer options. Indoors systems were GPS cannot be used unite visual tracking with inertial techniques only. Visual tracking achieve the best results with low frequency motion, but are highly likely to fail with rapid camera movement, such as the ones that will occur with HMDs. On the other hand, inertial tracking sensors perform best with high frequency motion while slow movements do not provide good results due to noise and bias drift. The complementary nature of these systems leads to combining them together in most hybrid systems.

Other systems, such as [23] and [42], rely on computer vision for tracking, but most are indoor systems with which the environment can be somewhat controlled. When it comes to visual outdoor tracking, a couple of factors, such as lightning, make tracking extremely difficult. Moreover, some objects present tracking difficulties. One of the most advanced visual tracking mobile systems is Google Goggles [51]; however, this application can only track objects of regular form such as barcodes and books, or places thanks to its GPS and accelerometer that help the application recognize where the user is standing and the user's orientation to narrow down the options. Google Goggles cannot recognize things of irregular shapes such as leaves, flowers or food.

5 Applications

While there are many possibilities for using augmented reality in an innovative way, we have cornered four types of applications that are most often being used for AR research: advertising and commercial, entertainment and education, medical, and mobile application for iPhones. Below, we study why AR could bring a better solution to some areas, a cheaper solution to others, or simply create a new service. We also discuss the challenges augmented reality is facing to go from the laboratories to the industry.

Note that it was decided here to replace the navigational and informational domain application that was encountered in the AR systems section by a study of the augmented reality mobile applications as these applications most often have navigational and informational use.

5.1 Advertising and Commercial

Augmented reality is mostly used by marketers to promote new products online. Most techniques use markers that the users present in front of their webcam either on special software or simply on the advertising company's website. For example, in December 2008, MINI [52], the famous car company, ran an augmented reality advertisement in several German automotive magazines [53]. The reader simply had to go to the MINI's website [52], show the ad in front of their webcam, and a 3-D MINI appeared on their screen, as seen in Fig. 1.7. Beyond Reality [54] released a marker less advertisement magazine of 12 pages that could be recognized and animated by a software the user could download on the publisher's website as a starting point to their Augmented Reality Games. They see that with such a system, they could add a "paid" option on the software that would allow the user to access

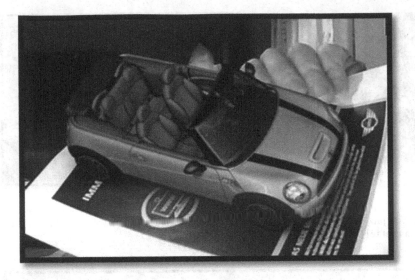

Fig. 1.7 MINI advertisement [53]

additional content, such as seeing a trailer and then being able to click on a link to view the full movie, turning the magazine into a movie ticket [54].

AR also offers a solution to the expensive problem of building prototypes. Indeed, industrial companies are faced with the costly need to manufacture a product before commercialization to figure out if any changes should be made and see if the product meets the expectations. If it is decided that changes should be made, and this is more often than not the case, a new prototype has to be manufactured and additional time and money are wasted. A group of the Institute of Industrial Technologies and Automation (ITIA) of the National Council of Research (CNR) of Italy [21] in Milan works on AR and VR systems as a tool for supporting virtual prototyping. The ITIA-CNR is involved in the research for industrial contexts and application using VR, AR, realtime 3D, etc. as a support for product testing, development and evaluation. Some examples of applied research projects where the above technologies have been applied include motorcycle prototyping (Fig. 1.8), virtual layout of a factory and an office (Figs. 1.9 and 1.10), virtual light simulation (Fig. 1.11), and virtual trial of shoes with the Magic Mirror interface, which will be discussed next.

Shoes are the accessories that follow fashion trends the most and are renewed annually, especially for those who live in fashion capitals, such as Milan, New York and Paris. For these people, it is more important to wear trendy shoes at the sacrifice of comfort. With the Magic Mirror, the ITIA of CNR in Milan [21] has created a system which, combined with high-tech footwear technology for measurement, enables the user to virtually try on shoes prior to buying/ordering them. The user is able to see his/her reflection in the Magic Mirror with a virtual model of the pair of shoes s/he would like to try on. The advantage of such a system over going to the

Fig. 1.8 Right picture: Picture of a virtual motorcycle prototype (on the *right*) next to a physical motorcycle prototype (on the *left*) in the real environment; left picture: virtual prototype in a virtual environment [21]

Fig. 1.9 Virtual factory prototype [21]

store is that once the user selects shoes for trial, s/he has the ability to change a few details, such as the color, the heel, and/or even the stitching. To do so, the user puts on some special "socks" with spherical, infrared reflective painted-on markers that serve as a tracking system for the Magic Mirror, which is in fact an LCD screen that actually processes the information from the electronic catalog and inputs data from the client to see if the model chosen is approved, to detect and mirror the movements of the customer.

To build such a system, the ITIA-CNR in Milan created their library, called GIOVE library. The GIOVE library has been developed (and is continuously under development) not only to approach this specific project, but for the ITIA-CNR to use as a software library when needed for any application since any type of functionality can be added to the GIOVE library as it has been made from scratch by the ITIA-CNR. The system first has to be calibrated using a bigger version of ARToolKit markers onto which one of the small tracking sphere (similar to the ones place on

Fig. 1.10 Virtual office prototype [21]

Fig. 1.11 Virtual testing of a lighting system [21]

the "socks") is placed in the middle. The marker is then laid on the orange pad that is used to help the system recognize the position where virtual elements have to be inserted. A couple of infrared lights camera track the IR lights reflected from the markers and since the system knows in advance the geometric placement of the

Fig. 1.12 User trying on
virtual shoes in front of the
Magic Mirror [21]

markers, the virtual position can be reconstructed accurately. The "socks" are of the some orange color, which is the color specified to the system for tracking. This color was chosen by the group because it is an unusual color for pants; however, the system could track any color it is indicated. Another challenge the ITIA group had to face with such a system was due to the camera lens distorting the real image while the virtual image to be added to the environment would remain perfect. This detail is not always perceived in every system, but with the Magic Mirror application, it was too noticeable. The solution to such a problem is to either compensate the real image so that the distortion is not so perceptible anymore or to distort the virtual image so that it is not so perfect anymore. The ITIA group chose to compensate their real image using some of the MatLab's software formulas to figure out the degrees of distortion to compensate are (Fig. 1.12).

Similar examples to Magic Mirror use of AR for advertising and commercial applications lies in fully replacing the need to try on anything in stores, thus saving considerable amount of time for clients, which would most likely be used for trying on more clothing (shirts, dresses, watches, pants, etc.) and thus increasing the stores chances for selling (Fig. 1.13).

Augmented reality has not fully reached the industrial market in advertisement application mostly because a few improvements need to be made to systems similar to the Magic Mirror or Cisco's retail fitting room. Indeed, for the product to be viable in the market it needs to provide the user with a flawless representation of the

Fig. 1.13 Cisco's AR commercial where a client is trying on clothes in front of a "magic" screen

prototype; the user should have the impression that they are looking at a physical prototype. In the case of the Magic Mirror system, this would mean flawless tracking so that when the user looks at the magic mirror s/he feels like s/he is actually wearing the shoes and can really see what the shoes would look like.

5.2 Entertainment and Education

Entertainment and education applications include cultural apps with sightseeing and museum guidance, gaming apps with traditional games using AR interfaces, and some smart-phone apps that make use of AR for an entertainment and/or educational purpose.

In cultural application, there exists a few systems that uses AR for virtually reconstructing ancient ruins, such as in [10] (Fig. 1.14), or for virtually instructing user about site's history such as in [47].

There are also a few systems that exploit AR for museum guidance such as [40] and [39]. In [40] and [39], both systems are mobile, but [40] also uses a mobile phone as an interface while [39] simply uses a magic lens configuration. In [40], the authors identified the benefits of using augmented reality as an interface for their cultural applications as: efficient communication with the user through multimedia presentations, natural and intuitive technique and low maintenance and acquisition costs for the museum operators' presentation technology in the case of smart-phone being used as an interface. And indeed, using a smart-phone or even

Fig. 1.14 Augmented view of Dashuifa from [10]

another hand-held display is a more intuitive and natural technique than looking up
a number randomly assigned to the object in a small written guide, especially when
the user can simply make use of his/her own phone in a world where everybody
already possesses one. Similarly, users can relate easier to multimedia presentations
brought to them and will more willingly listen, watch and/or read about information
that they can acquire by simply pointing at an object using their phone rather than
have to look it up in a guide (Figs. 1.15 and 1.16).

AR can also be used for a learning purpose in the educational field. In fact,
AR recently emerged in the field of education to support many educational
applications in various domains, such as history, mathematics, etc. For instance,
Mark Billinghurst et al. [55] developed the Magic Book, a book whose pages
incorporated simple AR technology to make the reading more captivating. Malaka
et al. [56,57] built a mobile outdoor augmented reality system application using their
previously developed GEIST project for assisting users in learning history through
a story-telling game where the user can release ghost from the past.

AR gaming applications present many advantages other physical board with, for
example, the ability to introduce animations and other multimedia presentations.
The ability to introduce animations can not only add excitement to a game, but
it can also serve a learning purpose with, for example, indication to help players
learn the game or know when they are making an invalid move. In [30], the authors
create an augmented reality Chinese checkers game, called ARCC that uses three
fiducial markers and cameras fixed on the roof to track the markers. Two of their
fiducial markers are used for positioning the checkerboard and the third is used for
manipulating the game pieces. Having only one tool for manipulating the pieces

Fig. 1.15 Mobile
phone-enabled guidance
in a museum from [40]

Fig. 1.16 Visitor with guidance system from [39]

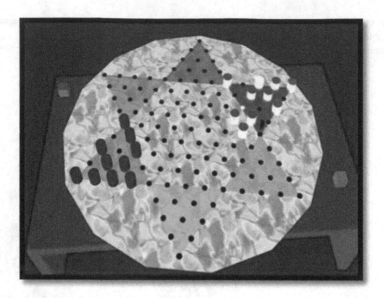

Fig. 1.17 ARCC from [30]

allows the authors the adapt their setup to different types of games as all they have
to change is the GUI (Graphic User Interface) that is the board game and the game's
logic (Fig. 1.17).

Beyond Reality [54], which was the first to introduce a marker less magazine,
presents two board games, PIT Strategy and Augmented Reality Memory. In PIT
Strategy, the player is the "pit boss" in a NASCAR race and must act according
to given weather condition, forecast and road condition. In Augmented Reality
Memory, the player turns a card and sees a 3D object, turns a second card and sees
another 3D object. If they match, a celebration animation will appear; otherwise, the
player can keep looking for matches. These two games are still under development
and further information can be found on [54].

Here again, augmented reality has not fully reached its potential to enter the
industrial market. Once again, this is mostly due to technological advances such
as tracking system. For example, we saw that the few museum guidance systems
developed were only applicable to the museum or exhibition they were developed
for and could not be utilized for other museums. This is due to the fact that both these
systems relied on the organization of the museum or the exhibition to recognize the
artifacts as opposed to detecting the artifacts solely using computer vision. So why
hasn't computer vision been used to recognize the objects instead of relying on
knowing the user's position in the museum? As was seen in the Computer Vision
Methods in AR section, some objects have irregular forms and although it might
seem easy for us to recognize them, it is very hard for a computer to detect what
these objects are, and this is the case of most artifacts. Paintings do not present such

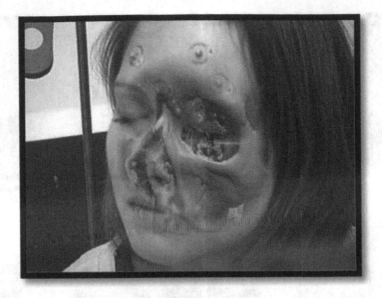

Fig. 1.18 Bichlmeier et al. system for viewing through the skin [34]

a big trouble for system such as Google Goggles [51] due to their regular shape, but objects, such as objects of modern art have very irregular shape that makes it hard to track a defined feature.

5.3 Medical Applications

Most of the medical applications deal with image guided and robot-assisted surgery. As a result, significant research has been made to incorporate AR with medical imaging and instruments incorporating the physician's intuitive abilities. Significant breakthrough has been provided by the use of diverse types of medical imaging and instruments, such as video images recorded by an endoscopic camera device presented on a monitor viewing the operating site inside the patient. However, these breakthroughs also limit the surgeon's natural, intuitive and direct 3D view of the human body as the surgeons now have to deal with visual cues from an additional environment provided on the monitor [34]. AR can be applied so that the surgical team can see the imaging data in real time while the procedure is progressing. Bichlmeier et al. [34] introduced an AR system for viewing through the "real" skin onto virtual anatomy using polygonal surface models to allow for real time visualization. The authors also integrated the use of navigated surgical tools to augment the physician's view inside the human body during surgery (Fig. 1.18).

Teleoperated robot-assisted surgery provide the surgeons with additional advantages over minimally invasive surgery with improved precision, dexterity,

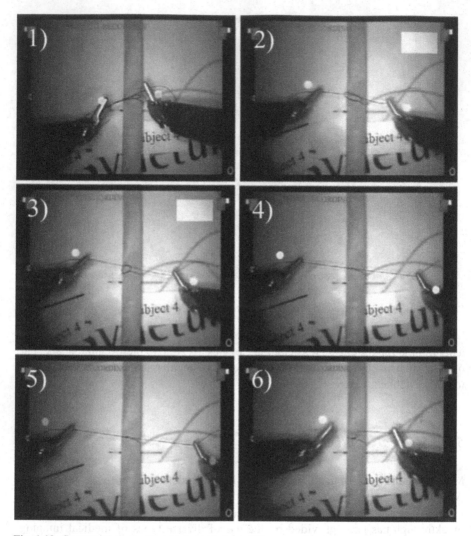

Fig. 1.19 Sequential shots of knot tying task from [38]

and visualization [58, 59]; however, implementing direct haptic feedback has been limited by sensing and control technology and thus is restricting the surgeon's natural skills. The lack of haptic feedback has been proved to affect the performance of several surgical operations [60]. In [38], the authors propose a method of sensory substitution that provides an intuitive form of haptic feedback to the user. The force applied by the surgeon is graphically represented and overlaid on a streaming video using a system of circles that discretely change colors across three pre-determined ranges (Low Force Zone (green), Ideal Force Zone (yellow) and Excessive Force Zone (red)) according to the amount of bending forces detected by strain gages (Fig. 1.19).

The need to reduce surgical operations is not the only one to depend upon seeing medical imaging data on the patient in real time; the necessity to improve medical diagnosis also relies on it. In this research field, the ICAR-CNR group of Naples [62,77] is working on an AR interactive system for checking patient's hand and wrist for arthritis by overlaying in real time 3D MR imaging data directly on top of the patient's hand. Since arthritis disabilities are strongly associated with pain intensity and so require a direct manipulation of the hand and wrist region to be diagnosed, the system may support physicians by allowing them to perform morphological and functional analyses at the same time [62]. AR could also be used to manage clients' medical history. Imagine if all a doctor had to do to check a patient's medical history was to put on a head mounted display and look over the patient to see virtual labels showing the patient's past injuries and illnesses.

The use of AR in the medical field to provide better solutions to current problems than already existing solutions is infinite. In [35], the authors use AR to provide a low cost and smaller in size solution to the post-stroke hand rehabilitation problem, which has the potential to being use in clinics and even at home. In [36], the authors use AR to help patients fight against the phobia of cockroaches and thus show that AR can be used to treat psychological disorders as well.

Additionally, AR can be used to assist the impaired, such as for instance supporting the visually impaired through augmented navigation. In [63], Hara et al. developed a multimodal feedback strategies for augmented navigation of the visually impaired. The feedback device consisted of a Wiimote which provided audio and haptic feedback to operate as a guiding tool and warn the user when they were getting close to walls and other obstacles.

Unfortunately, on top of facing a few technological advances issues such as displays and tracking issues, medical applications also face privacy concerns. Displays challenges mostly arise from the fact that the preferred type of display to use for medical applications is a HMD as it allows the physician not only to use both hands, but it is also easier to track where the doctor is looking to augment the right surfaces; however, it is challenging to implement HMD to medical applications. There are challenges that arise because of the HMD itself, such as accurately placing and applying depth perception to 3D models, and challenges that are due to the medical field itself, such as for a surgeon to still be able to see his tools through the projected images. Another possible type of display that could be used would be spatial display to allow the whole surgical team to see the same thing at the same time; however, it is then very hard to track where the surgeon is looking and what the desired place for augmenting is.

Privacy concerns always arise in the medical field, especially when discussing the treatment of the very confidential medical history of patients.

Another type of issues that medical application in augmented reality will most likely have to face is the problems that arise with retraining the medical staff for using new tools. Most AR applications aim at simplifying the use of AR tools such that they correspond to what the physician is used to; for instance in [38], the feedback system developed by the authors did not require the surgeons to truly learn how to use it as the application was easily integrated onto the da Vinci Surgical

System that most surgeons know how to use. Even with this system, the surgeons still have to get use to this type of haptic feedback system, although the training is rather short and inexpensive. However, there are some systems that will require a complete retraining of the staff to interact with the application. For example, applications that will require the user to interact with a 3D input device as opposed to 2D input devices such as a mouse, will present some training problems as they might be too costly for the medical field to judge them viable.

5.4 Mobile (iPhone) Applications

Many AR mobile applications for iPhone already exist; however, no development has been done for the iPad due to the lack of camera in the first generation of iPad. Moreover, most iPhone applications either have an entertainment and/or educational purpose or a navigational and/or informative purpose, such as orienting the user.

Examples of such applications include WikitudeDrive [64], which is a GPS-like application that allows the user to keep his/her eyes on the road while glancing at the GPS; Firefighter 360, which has an entertainment purpose that permits the user to fight a virtual fire like a real firefighter; and Le Bar Guide that has a navigational function to guide the user to the nearest bar that serves Stella Artois beer. Websites such as Mashable, the Social Media Guide [65] and iPhoneNess [66] have all come up with the best augmented reality applications for iPhone and we encourage interested readers to have a look at them.

Due to the relatively new side of adding AR to mobile applications, there currently are not many libraries, kits or codes available for iPhone program developers to add some augmented reality to their application. Studierstube Tracker and Studierstube ES support iPhone platforms; however, they are not open sources [14]. We found two sources to help iPhone developers in using AR for the mobile application. SlideShare, Present Yourself [61] is a slideshow presentation that shows the viewer how to develop augmented reality applications on iPhone with codes for retrieving GPS position, using the compass and accelerometer, and getting the image from the camera. iPhone ARKit [67] is a small set of class that can offer developers augmented reality on any iPhone application by overlaying information, usually geographic, over the camera view. The iPhone ARKit's APIs were modeled after Map Kit's [68], which is a framework for providing an interface to embed maps directly into the windows and views and to support annotating the map, adding overlays, and performing reverse-geocoding lookups to determine place mark information for a given map coordinate (Figs. 1.20–1.22).

Augmented reality mobile applications are one of the only augmented reality applications that we can find in the general public. However, even these applications are facing a few challenges issues. There are, for instance, problems due to GPS systems not being accurate enough for other applications that require very precise placement of virtual tags. There are issues with working with limited hardware capability when we require image processing power. In the iPhone category, there

Fig. 1.20 WikitudeDrive [64]

Fig. 1.21 Firefighter 360 [65]

were challenges due to accessing the video APIs as Apple would not open its APIs enough for the developers to be able to get in there and work with the video. However, with the release of the iPhone 4/iOS4, augmented reality sees more doors opening for AR applications on mobile phones: the developers now have the ability to access the camera images APIs, enhanced image tracking, gyroscopic motion sensing, and faster processor and high resolution display [69].

Similar to mobile systems, mobile applications also face social acceptance issues, as the applications also need to be subtle and discrete. Mobile applications should not be able to make random noises at inopportune times for the user. No matter

Fig. 1.22 Le Bar Guide [65]

how accustomed to mobile phones our society has become, it is still considered to be rude and obnoxious when someone is on the phone in a public place; when a person's phone is ringing in public, the first reflex for this person is to search for their phone to turn off the sound and then check who is calling or what the reminder is. Of course, social acceptance has the advantage of changing through the generations much like fashion.

6   Future of Augmented Reality Applications

AR is still in infancy stage, and as such, future possible applications are infinite. Advanced research in AR includes use of head-mounted displays and virtual retinal displays for visualization purposes, and construction of controlled environments containing any number of sensors and actuators [1]. MIT Media Lab project "Sixth Sense" (Fig. 1.23) [20] is the best example of AR research. It suggests a world where people can interact with information directly without requiring the use of any intermediate device. Other current research also include Babak Parviz AR contact lens (Fig. 1.24) [50] as well as DARPA's contact lens project (Fig. 1.23) [70], MIT Media Lab multiple research applications such as My-Shopping Guide [71] and TaPuMa [28]. Parviz's contact lens opens the door to an environment where

Fig. 1.23 From top to bottom and left to right: Examples of futuristic augmented reality [74, 76] and Babak Parviz's contact lens [50]

information can only be viewed by the user. Of course, this can also be done by using glasses as opposed to contact lens, but the advantage in both cases over using a cell phone, for instance, is that no one else but the user can see the information projected, making it very personal. Cisco has imagined a world where AR could be used for replacing the traditional fitting rooms by trying on virtual clothes, thus saving time and providing the ability to try on more clothes, increasing the chance for stores to sell.

Augmented reality also brings the possibility of enhancing missing senses for some users. For example, AR could be used as a sensory substitution device. Hearing-impaired users could receive visual cues informing them of missed audio signals and sightless users could receive audio cues notifying them of unknown visual events.

We believe that new mobile devices, such as iPhone, Android-based devices, and iPad are not well used in AR. Indeed, most of the current applications include gaming, entertainment and education, and while most already believe that these are "amazing apps" [65].

Fig. 1.24 From top to bottom and left to right: DARPA's contact lens project [70], MIT's Sixth Sense [20], Contactum's AR Solutions [72]

Even the future is not far from challenges for augmented reality. We see social acceptance issues, privacy concerns, and ethical concern arising with the future of augmented reality applications in the industry.

Social acceptance mostly arise from mobile devices with the need for the devices to be subtle, discrete and unobtrusive as well as fashionably acceptable as was discussed in the Augmented Reality Mobile Systems section, but also with systems that will require retraining of the personnel and staff in order to be utilized. We have seen that this might be the case with some medical applications and that the health system might decide against the use of augmented reality if they decide that the retraining is too costly. A system for easy integration of such system will have to be developed to avoid such issues.

Privacy concerns arise not only with medical applications, but also with technologies that have the ability to detect and recognize people. For instance, MIT's WUW technology video presentation [73] has an application that is capable of recognizing people and displaying information about these persons for the user to see. Although those information could be found online by anyone on websites such as social networks, it will raise problems as a lot of people will not appreciate being spotted that way, even if they do not mind having these information available online for anyone to see. A solution for applications like ones similar to WUW recognizable feature would be to create a social network within the users of this technology for them to decide whether or not they want to be recognized or what information about them they allow to be displayed. Non users of this technology should not be recognized by the system unless they allow it by joining the social network.

When it comes to ethical concerns, the apprehension mostly comes from the fact that people tend to get carried away by technologies with things they see in Hollywood movies. We do not know where to put down limits for the use of technology and keep researching as we see the potential grow. However, with augmented reality, it will be very important for the developers to remember that AR aims at simplifying the user's life by enhancing, *augmenting* the user's senses, not interfering with them. For instance, when reading the comments following Babak Parviz's contact lens article (Fig. 1.23) [50], there were suggestions from readers including "tapping the optic nerve" or "plugging in to the optic nerves and touch and smell receptors" and suggested that these would eventually be "more marketable approach" and a "much more elegant solution." Although the commentators do realize that as of today research simply does not know enough about the human nervous system do such things, the fact that thoughts and ideas have started to emerge in this direction raises questions about ethical concerns: is having technology coming in direct interaction with our human senses something we want? As was mentioned earlier, AR is about augmenting the real environment with virtual information; it is about augmenting people's skills and senses not replacing them.

7   iPhone Projects: AR

7.1   Ideas

After conducting research on iPhone's current AR application, it was found that many of the most useful iPhone's applications for the user are GPS-like applications that are used to guide and provide information to the user about where the user might find the closest bars (Le Bar Guide), Wi-Fi spots (WorkSnug), or anything the user might be interested in. We believe that incorporating a "tag" application to such already existing application would present a great success among the customers. The "tag" application would enable the user to tag any place by writing a note about it. The location might be one of the spots the user was looking for, such as a coffee shop, and the user would like to make a note (tag) about it, or it could be another location that might bear meaning to the user, such as the user's home or a nice spot during an excursion the user found. The tags could carry any sort of information; for example, it could be a comment about a site or strictly informative, such as Home, and guide the user back to these spots. The tags could be private or they could be shared with all other users of this application. As a next development of this application, it would be nice to expand into a social network where the user can have friends and comment about public tags can be made, etc.

Another type of application we believe would have a great success is a cultural application. It was seen in the Entertainment and Education Applications section that some of the most useful use of AR for cultural applications was done through museum guidance as it is intuitive, natural and efficient of communication. One of the applications visited even made use of a mobile phone as its interface. However, in both cases, the system was limited to the museum for which it was build. Therefore, we propose an AR mobile phone system for providing information to the user about artifacts in a museum which is not limited to one museum. For object detection, the user will take a picture of the artifact s/he wishes to learn more information about and the system will identify the object by comparing it through a database that we may have to create. Once the object is identified, the application will display multimedia information, such as text, audio, video, and/or pictures about the work for the user.

Augmented reality could also be used on iPhone as a device to help impaired people. It could, for instance, be used as a hearing device for those who can't hear very well or at all through the use of visual information or as an eye for those who cannot see, i.e. blind people or those who have very poor vision and require special help, through the use of audio of information. For example, augmented reality could in this way augment some people's view in an unconventional manner for AR not by imposing virtual tags in the real environment, but by the use of audio tags. The application that could be developed for this use could be an application to help blind or poorly sighted people know whether cars in the street are in movement or at a stop. This type of application would of course have to be very careful to accurately inform the users that the cars the device is pointing at are in movement or at a stop and not that it is necessarily advised to cross the street as this is what street signs are for. The problem arises from the fact that, unlike in Florida and most of the US where street signs informing pedestrians to cross the road also emits audio cues in addition to visual cues, street signs in most of Europe only make use of visual cues which are impossible to interpret for someone that cannot see them. Moreover, blind people normally had to refer to their hearing sense to determine whether cars were in movement; however, with the increasing advances, cars are becoming quieter and it is a difficult task.

Acknowledgements This material is based upon work supported by the National Science Foundation under Grant No. OISE-0730065.

References

1. Wikipedia, the free encyclopedia, http://en.wikipedia.org/wiki/Augmented_reality, AugmentedReality, 2010.
2. P. Milgram and A.F. Kishino, "Taxonomy of Mixed Reality Visual Displays" (http://vered.rose. utoronto.ca/people/paul_dir/IEICE94/ieice.html) *IEICE Transactions on Information Systems,* E77-D(12), pp. 1321–1329, 1994.
3. Ronald Azuma, Yohan Baillot, Reinhold Behringer, Steven Feiner, Simon Julier, Blair MacIntyre, "Recent Advances in Augmented Reality", *IEEE,* November/December 2001.
4. Wikipedia, the free encyclopedia, http://en.wikipedia.org/wiki/Sensorama, Sensorama, 2009.
5. https://www.icg.tugraz.at/~daniel/HistoryOfMobileAR/, History of Mobile Augmented Reality, 2009.
6. 2005 Horizon Report Johnson, Laurence F. and Smith, Rachel S. *2005 Horizon Report.* Austin, TX: The New Media Consortium, 2005.
7. Feng Zhou, Henry Been-Lirn Duh, Mark Billinghurst, "Trends in Augmented Reality Tracking, Interaction and Display: A Review of Ten Years of ISMAR", 2008.
8. Byungsung Lee, Junchul Chun, "Interactive Manipulation of Augmented Objects in Marker-Less AR Using Vision-Based Hand Interaction," itng, pp.398–403, *2010 Seventh International Conference on Information Technology,* 2010
9. Ababsa, F.; Mallem, M.;, "Robust camera pose estimation combining 2D/3D points and lines tracking," *Industrial Electronics, 2008. ISIE 2008. IEEE International Symposium on,* vol., no., pp.774–779, June 30 2008-July 2 2008 doi: 10.1109/ISIE.2008.4676964 URL:http:// ieeexplore.ieee.org/stamp/stamp.jsp?tp=&arnumber=4676964&isnumber=4676877
10. Yetao Huang, Yue Liu, Yongtian Wang, "AR-View: and Augmented Reality Device for Digital Reconstruction of Yuangmingyuan", *IEEE International Symposium on Mixed and Augmented Reality,* 2009.
11. Jonas Nilsson, Anders C.E. Odblom, Jonas fredriksson, Adeel Zafar, Fahim Ahmed, "Performance Evaluation Method for Mobile Computer Vision Systems using Augmented Reality", *IEEE Virtual Reality,* 2010.
12. Wikipedia, the free encyclopedia, http://en.wikipedia.org/wiki/ARToolKit
13. Dieter Schmalstieg, Anton Fuhrmann, Gerd Hesina, "Bridging Multiple User Interface Dimensions with Augmented Reality", *IEEE,* 2000.
14. Handheld Augmented Reality, http://studierstube.icg.tu-graz.ac.at/handheld_ar/stbtracker.php, Studierstube Tracker, 2010.
15. Dieter Schmalstieg, Anton Fuhrmann, Gerd Hesina, Zsolt Zsalavari, L. Miguel Encarnacao, Michael Gervautz, Werner Purgathofer, "The Studierstube Augmented Reality Project", *Presence,* Vol. 11, No. 1, February 2002, 33–54, Massachusetts Institute of Technology, 2002.
16. Lepetit, V., "On Computer Vision for Augmented Reality," *Ubiquitous Virtual Reality, 2008. ISUVR 2008. International Symposium on,* vol., no., pp.13–16, 10–13 July 2008
17. Gerhard Reitmayr, Dieter Schmalstieg, "Location based Applications for Mobile Augmented Reality", *AUIC2003,* 2003.
18. Daniel Wagner and Dieter Schmalstieg, "Handheld Augmented Reality Displays", Graz University of Technology, Austria.
19. Oliver Bimber, Ramesh Raskar, Masahiko Inami, "Spatial Augmented Reality", *SIGGRAPH 2007 Course 17 Notes,* 2007.
20. Pranav Mistry, Pattie Maes, Liyan Chang, "WUW – Wear Ur World – A Wearable Gestural Interface", *ACM, CHI 2009,* Boston, April 4–9, 2009.
21. Marco Sacco, Stefano Mottura, Luca Greci, Giampaolo Vigan, *Insitute of Industrial Technologies and Automation,* National Research Council, Italy.
22. Assaf Feldman, Emmanuel Munguia Tapia, Sajid Sadi, Pattie Maes, Chris Schmandt, "ReachMedia: On-the-move interaction with everyday objects", iswc, pp.52–59, *Ninth IEEE International Symposium on Wearable Computers (ISWC'05),* 2005.

23. Jae-Young Lee; Seok-Han Lee; Hyung-Min Park; Sang-Keun Lee; Jong-Soo Choi; Jun-Sik Kwon; "Design and implementation of a wearable AR annotation system using gaze interaction," *Consumer Electronics (ICCE), 2010 Digest of Technical Papers International Conference on*, vol., no., pp.185–186, 9–13 Jan. 2010

24. Li Yi-bo; Kang Shao-peng; Qiao Zhi-hua; Zhu Qiong; "Development Actuality and Application of Registration Technology in Augmented Reality", *Computational Intelligence and Design, 2008. ISCID '08. International Symposium on*, Vol.2, No., pp.69–74, 17–18 Oct. 2008

25. George Papagiannakis, Gurminder Singh, Nadia Magnenat-Thalmann, "A survey of mobile and wireless technologies for augmented reality systems", *Computer Animation and Virtual Worlds*, v.19 n.1, p.3–22, February 2008

26. DiVerdi, S.; Hollerer, T., "GroundCam: A Tracking Modality for Mobile Mixed Reality," *Virtual Reality Conference, 2007. VR '07. IEEE*, vol., no., pp.75–82, 10–14 March 2007

27. H. Kato, M. Billinghurst, I. Poupyrev, K. Imamoto, K. Tachibana, "Virtual Object Manipulation on a Table-Top AR Environment", *ISAR'00*, 111–119, 2000.

28. Pranav Mistry, Tsuyoshi Kuroki, and Chaochi Chuang, "TaPuMa: Tangible Public Map for Information Acquirement through the Things We Carry", MIT Media Lab, *Ambi-sys'08*, February 2008.

29. S. White, L. Lister, and S. Feiner, "Visual Hints for Tangible Gestures in Augmented Reality", *In ISMAR '07*, 47–50, 2007

30. Nicholas Cooper, Aaron Keatley, Maria Dahlquist, Simon Mann, Hannah Slay, Joanne Zucco, Ross Smith, Bruce H. Thomas, "Augmented Reality Chinese Checkers", *The Australasian Computing Education Conference; Vol. 74, Proceedings of the 2004 ACM SIGCHI International Conference on Advances in computer entertainment technology*, Singapore, pp 117–126, 2004

31. Istvan Barakonyi, Tamer Fahmy, Dieter Schmalstieg, "Remote collaboration using Augmented Reality Videoconferencing", *Proceedings of Graphics Interface 2004*, p.89–96, May 17–19, 2004, London, Ontario, Canada

32. C. Sandor, A. Olwal, B. Bell and S. Feiner, "Immersive mixed-reality configuration of hybrid user interfaces", In *ISMAR '05*, pp. 110–113, 2005

33. Salvatore Sorce, Agnese Augello, Antonella Santangelo, Antonio Gentile, Alessandro Genco, Salvatore Gaglio, Giovanni Pilato, "Interacting with Augmented Environments," *IEEE Pervasive Computing*, vol. 9, no. 2, pp. 56–58, Apr.-June 2010, doi:10.1109/MPRV.2010.34

34. Christop Bichlmeier, Felix Wimmer, Sandro Michael Heining, Nassir Navab, "Contextual Anatomic Mimesis: Hybrid In-Situ Visualization Method for Improving Multi-Sensory Depth Perception in Medical Augmented Reality", *IEEE*, 2007

35. Xun Luo; T. Kline; H.C. Fischer; K.A. Stubblefield; R.V. Kenyon; D.G. Kamper; "Integration of Augmented Reality and Assistive Devices for Post-Stroke Hand Opening Rehabilitation," *Engineering in Medicine and Biology Society, 2005. IEEE-EMBS 2005. 27th Annual International Conference of the*, vol., no., pp.6855–6858, 2005

36. Juan, M.C.; Botella, C.; Alcaniz, M.; Banos, R.; Carrion, C.; Melero, M.; Lozano, J.A.; "An augmented reality system for treating psychological disorders: application to phobia to cockroaches," *Mixed and Augmented Reality, 2004. ISMAR 2004. Third IEEE and ACM International Symposium on*, vol., no., pp. 256–257, 2–5 Nov. 2004

37. Takahashi, H., Shimazaki, S., Kawashima, T.: "Augmented reality system for development of handy information device with tangible interface", In: Shumaker (ed.) *Virtual Reality, HCII2007. LNCS*, vol. 4563, pp. 564–573. Springer, Berlin (2007)

38. Akinbiyi, T.; Reiley, C.E.; Saha, S.; Burschka, D.; Hasser, C.J.; Yuh, D.D.; Okamura, A.M.; "Dynamic Augmented Reality for Sensory Substitution in Robot-Assisted Surgical Systems," *Engineering in Medicine and Biology Society, 2006. EMBS '06. 28th Annual International Conference of the IEEE*, vol., no., pp.567–570, Aug. 30 2006-Sept. 3 2006

39. Miyashita, T.; Meier, P.; Tachikawa, T.; Orlic, S.; Eble, T.; Scholz, V.; Gapel, A.; Gerl, O.; Arnaudov, S.; Lieberknecht, S., "An Augmented Reality museum guide", *Mixed and Augmented Reality, 2008. ISMAR 2008. 7th IEEE/ACM International Symposium on*, vol., no., pp.103–106, 15–18 Sept. 2008

40. Bruns, E.; Brombach, B.; Zeidler, T.; Bimber, O., "Enabling Mobile Phones To Support Large-Scale Museum Guidance", *Multimedia, IEEE*, vol.14, no.2, pp.16–25, April-June 2007
41. Caruso, G.; Re, G.M.; "AR-Mote: A wireless device for Augmented Reality environment," *3D User Interfaces (3DUI), 2010 IEEE Symposium on*, vol., no., pp.99–102, 20–21 March 2010
42. Theodoros N. Arvanitis, Argeroula Petrou, James F. Knight, Stavros Savas, Sofoklis Sotiriou, Michael Gargalakos, Elpida Gialouri, "Human factors and qualitative pedagogical evaluation of a mobile augmented reality system for science education used by learners with physical disabilities", *Personal and Ubiquitous Computing*, v.13 n.3, p.243–250, March 2009
43. Stutzman, B.; Nilsen, D.; Broderick, T.; Neubert, J., "MARTI: Mobile Augmented Reality Tool for Industry," *Computer Science and Information Engineering, 2009 WRI World Congress on*, vol.5, no., pp.425–429, March 31 2009-April 2 2009
44. Brown, D.; Julier, S.; Baillot, Y.; Livingston, M.A., "An event-based data distribution mechanism for collaborative mobile augmented reality and virtual environments," *Virtual Reality, 2003. Proceedings IEEE, vol., no., pp. 23–29*, 22–26 March 2003
45. Dahne, P.; Karigiannis, J.N.; "Archeoguide: system architecture of a mobile outdoor augmented reality system," *Mixed and Augmented Reality, 2002. ISMAR 2002. Proceedings. International Symposium on*, vol., no., pp. 263–264, 2002
46. Ian Yen-Hung Chen, Bruce MacDonald, Burkhard Wünsche, "Markerless augmented reality for robotic helicoptor applications", *Lecture Notes In Computer Science, Proceedings of the 2nd international conference on Robot vision*, pp 125–138, 2008
47. Rainer Malaka, Kerstin Schneider, Ursula Kretschmer, "Stage-Based Augmented Edutainment", *Smart Graphics 2004*, pp.54–65
48. Patricia P. Wang, Tao Wang, Dayong Ding, Yimin Zhang, Wenyuan Bi, Yingze Bao, "Mirror world navigation for mobile users based on augmented reality", *International Multimedia Conference, Proceedings of the seventeen ACM international conference on Multimedia*, pp 1025–1026, 2009.
49. Enrico Costanza, Samuel A. Inverso, Elan Pavlov, Rebecca Allen, Patties Maes, "eye-q: Eyeglass Peripheral Display for Subtle Intimate Notifications", *Mobile HCI 2006*, September 13–15, 2006.
50. Babak A. Parviz, "Augmented Reality in a Contact Lens" (http://spectrum.ieee.org/biomedical/bionics/augmented-reality-in-a-contact-lens/0) *IEEE Spectrum*, September 2009.
51. Google, http://www.google.com/mobile/goggles/#text, Google Goggles, 2010
52. MINI, www.mini.com
53. Geekology, http://www.geekologie.com/2008/12/14-week, Cool: Augmented Reality Advertisements, Dec. 19 2008
54. Beyond Reality, http://www.augmented-reality-games.com
55. Mark Billinghurst, "The MagicBook: A Transitional AR Interface", Ivan Poupyrev, 2001.
56. Ursula Kretschmer, Volker Coors, Ulrike Spierling, Dieter Grasbon, Kerstin Schneider, Isabel Rojas, Rainer Malaka, Meeting the spirit of history, *Proceedings of the 2001 conference on Virtual reality, archeology, and cultural heritage*, November 28–30, 2001, Glyfada, Greece [doi>10.1145/584993.585016]
57. Malaka, R., Schneider, K., and Kretschmer, U. Stage-Based Augmented Edutainment. In LCNS 3031 (2004), 54–65
58. Wikipedia, the free encyclopedia, http://en.wikipedia.org/wiki/Robotic_surgery, Robotic surgery, 2010
59. Wikipedia, the free encyclopedia, http://en.wikipedia.org/wiki/Invasiveness_of_surgical_procedures, Invasiveness of surgical procedures, 2010
60. Brian T. Bethea, Allison M. Okamura, Masaya Kitagawa, Torin P. Fitton, Stephen M. Cattaneo, Vincent L. Gott, William A. Baumgartner, David D. Yuh, "Application of Haptic Feedback To Robotic Surgery", *Journal of Laparo Endoscopic and Advanced Surgical Techniques*, 14(3):191–195, 2004.
61. SlideShare, Present Yourself, http://www.slideshare.net/OmarCaf/augmented-reality-on-iphone-applications, Augmented Reality on iPhone Applications, Paolo Quadrani, Omar Caffini, 2010.

62. L. Gallo, A. Minutolo, and G. De Pietro, "A user interface for VR-ready 3D medical imaging by off-the-shelf input devices", *Computers in Biology and Medicine*, vol. 40, no. 3, pp. 350–358, 2010.doi:10.1016/j.compbiomed.2010.01.006

63. Hara, Masayuki; Shokur, Solaiman; Yamamoto, Akio; Higuchi, Toshiro; Gassert, Roger; Bleuler, Hannes, Virtual Environment to Evaluate Multimodal Feedback Strategies for Augmented Navigation of the Visually Impaired, *32nd Annual International Conference of the IEEE Engineering in Medicine and Biology Society (EMBC'10)*, Buenos Aires, Argentina, September 1–4, 2010.

64. Wikitude, http://www.wikitude.org/dewikitude-drive-eyes-road-againenwikitude-drive-eyes-road, WikitudeDrive: Never take your eyes off the road again, 2009.

65. Mashable, The Social Media Guide, http://mashable.com/2009/12/05/augmented-reality-iphone/, 10 amazing Augmented Reality iPhone Apps, 2009.

66. iPhoneNess, http://www.iphoneness.com/iphone-apps/best-augmented-reality-iphone-applications/, 26 Best Augmented Reality iPhone Applications.

67. Github, Social Coding, http://github.com/zac/iphonearkit/, iPhone ARKit, 2009.

68. iPhone OS Reference Library, http://developer.apple.com/iphone/library/documentation/MapKit/Reference/MapKit_Framework_Reference/index.html, Map Kit Framework Reference, 2010.

69. Read Write Web, http://www.readwriteweb.com/archives/how_iphone_4_could_change_augmented_reality.php, How iPhone 4 Could Change Augmented Reality, Chris Cameron, June 10, 2010

70. Wired, http://www.wired.com/dangerroom/2008/03/darpa-wants-con/, Pentagon: 'Augment' Reality with 'Videogame' Contact Lenses (Updated), Noah Shachtman, March 20th, 2008.

71. David Merrill and Patties Maes, "Augmenting Looking, Pointing and Reaching Gestures to Enhance the Searching and Browsing of Physical Objects", *MIT Media Lab*.

72. Contactum, Augmented Reality Solutions, http://www.augmented-reality.com/, Where reality meets the virtual world, 2006.

73. Sixth Sense – a wearable gestural interface (MIT Media Lab), http://www.pranavmistry.com/projects/sixthsense/, Sixth Sense – integrating information with the real world, Pranav Mistry, Fluid Interface Group, MIT Media Lab, 2010

74. Compute Scotland, http://www.computescotland.com/optical-ingenuity-from-fraunhofer-ipms-2321.php, Optical ingenuity from Fraunhofer IPMS, May 8th, 2009.

75. Encyclopidia, http://encyclopedia.jrank.org/articles/pages/6843/Multimodal-Interfaces.html, Multimodal Interfaces.

76. Nineteen fortyone, http://www.nineteenfortyone.com/2009/08/reality-is-so-boring/, Reality is SO boring, 2009.

77. Dr. Giuseppe De Pietro and Dr. Luigi Gallo of ICAR-CNR group, National Research Council, Italy.

Chapter 2
New Augmented Reality Taxonomy: Technologies and Features of Augmented Environment

Olivier Hugues, Philippe Fuchs, and Olivier Nannipieri

Abstract This article has a dual aim: firstly to define augmented reality (AR) environments and secondly, based on our definition, a new taxonomy enabling these environments to be classified. After briefly reviewing existing classifications, we define AR by its purpose, ie. to enable someone to create sensory-motor and cognitive activities in a new space combining the real environment and a virtual environment. Below we present our functional taxonomy of AR environments. We divide these environments into two distinct groups. The first concerns the different functionalities enabling us to discover and understand our environment, an augmented perception of reality. The second corresponds to applications whose aim is to create an artificial environment. Finally, more than a functional difference, we demonstrate that it is possible to consider that both types of AR have a pragmatic purpose. The difference therefore seems to lie in the ability of both types of AR to free themselves or not of location in time and space.

1 Introduction

It is indisputable that augmented reality (AR) is the result of a series of technological innovations. However, does reducing AR to a set of technical characteristics in behavioural interfacing not lead us to underestimate the wealth of AR and its functionalities? We are therefore entitled to naively ask the following question: what is augmented in augmented reality? If reality is by definition everything that exists, then strictly speaking reality cannot be augmented since it is already everything. So what is augmented? Initially the answer seems obvious: it is not reality, but the perception of reality which is augmented. From this perspective, the question

O. Hugues (✉)
ESTIA Recherche, MaxSea, LaBRI, Bidart, France
e-mail: o.hugues@net.estia.fr

B. Furht (ed.), *Handbook of Augmented Reality*, DOI 10.1007/978-1-4614-0064-6_2,
© Springer Science+Business Media, LLC 2011

of what is real, existence and properties is not examined here. The issue concerns perception, ie. the phenomenon – reality as it is perceived, not the noumen – reality in itself, to use Kant's words [1].

2 Augmented Perception?

We can find in literature two main movements which define perception. On the one hand (a passive conception), the sensory system passively receives stimulations and processes this information so as to refer to internal representations. On the other (an active conception), it is the extraction of regularity between actions and stimulations which enable perception. It seems that the current movement is rather to consider perception using the sensory-motor approach (the second case), in opposition to the linear and sequential approach of the perception process, the first case [2]. Furthermore, this is confirmed by Gibson [3] who considers the senses as full perceptory systems ("perception is to extract, thanks to movements, this information by detecting its invariants"). It is important to emphasise that like Auvray and Fuchs [2] who used the theoretical framework proposed by Bergson in "Matrer and Memory" [4], that any perception and any knowledge have only one final aim – whether conscious or not: action. We do not perceive and do not attempt to familiarise ourselves in order to know but rather to act. Inherited from the pragmatic conception of William James [5], the Bergsonian theory insists on the nature itself of our perception and any search for information in the real world: perception is never disinterested, knowledge is only ever a means to acting better in the real world [4] – and surviving for wild animals or being happier for humans. Although any increase in the quantity of information – and consequently, any increase in our understanding of reality – admitted by AR aims for greater mastery of what is real, it is clear that, from a technological point of view, AR can offer interfaces which propose either, more explicitly, information, or, more explicitly, a better mastery of our actions with regard to real events. But how do technical devices modify our perception? According to [2], "using a new technical device modifies our sensory-motor relationship with the environment; and subsequently it modifies our perception". Technical tools modify our "perceptory space". The step is decisive. However, we cannot "only" endeavour to perceive better since perception is not a final aim in itself, but rather a means of achieving a target action [4]. In the manner of virtual reality (VR), augmenting reality may satisfy two objectives for the user: encourage understanding and mastery of the real world and therefore, an *augmented perception of reality* on the one hand and, on the other hand, propose a *new environment* whose aim does not appear to be obey either requirements in terms of knowledge or practical requirements.

3 Final Aim and Birth of a Taxonomy

Globally, the aim of AR is to enable a person to carry out sensory-motor and cognitive activities in a new space by associating the real environment and a virtual environment. Yet, like VR [6], AR can propose either a modelisation of the real world based on an environment which imitates or symbolises the real world, or the creation of an artificial environment which does not correspond to anything which exists. It is on the basis of this distinction that it is possible to propose a functional taxonomy of AR and draw a certain number of relative implications, namely, with regard to variations in space and time references allowed by AR.

4 Taxonomy of Interactives Mixed Systems

There have been many attempts to classify augmented reality environments since this technology is in fact a sub-set of environments or mixed systems.

Whether technical, functional or conceptual, these taxonomies often aim to describe, compare and generate [7]. We present an overview of some of the taxonomies present in literature. Readers will find a more complete review of classifications in [8].

4.1 Conceptual Taxonomies

In [9], the authors proposed a framework for analysis with which they explore different mixed environments so as to identify the common use of human abilities linked with the physical world, the body and the social environment. However, since the advantage of mixed environments is their ability not to faithfully reproduce reality [10], the authors proposed six factors like the power of expression, efficiency, ergonomics and accessibility enabling the use of the physical world to be weighted. This classification enables a large number of possibilities for interaction generated by mixed systems to be highlighted. In [11], Mackay proposes a classification of mixed interfaces whose common denominator is the target of augmentations. Different targets are users, objects of interaction and the environment. Dubois [12] extends this classification by introducing a methodology rating known as ASUR, extended in 2003 [13] and whose discretisation includes the user, the adaptor,[1] the system and real entities. Later, Renevier [14] defined methods of interaction as passive (determined by the system) or active (determined by the user). Creating,

---

[1] Adaptors transfer data from one world to the other and may be the system's input or output.

accessing, modifying and destroying links depends on the methods of interaction. A link is defined as being short-lived or persistent and can be located with regard to users. Different types of locating are possible. The authors also define three types of interaction: the users interact with objects via links and inversely, and links are used for communication between users.

4.2 Technical Taxonomies

In [15,16], the authors propose a technological classification now well known under the name of "virtuality-reality continuum". They endeavour to discretise and classify the environment according to four categories. This continuum highlights the fact that there is a progressive transition from real to virtual and inversely. The authors of [17] chose to analyse the user's movements in order to extract its framework based on expected movements, captured movements and desired movements. By using Norman's theory of action [18], the authors proposes dissociating the systems which augment performance from systems which augment evaluation.

4.3 Functional Taxonomies

With the aim of clarifying concepts which underlie the combination of the real world and virtual world, Dubois et al. [19] propose a classification broken down into two distinct parts: the first characteristic is the purpose of the task and the second is the type of augmentation. Whilst the purpose of the task enables the authors to augment and specify the Milgram continuum [15] by adding to it two continua so as to distinguish augmented reality from virtual reality, the second characteristic enables the existence of two different functional types of augmentations to be underlined. The first consists of an "augmented performance" whilst the second is an "augmented perception". According to the authors, the first type of augmentation enables users to carry out tasks in the real world in a new way like for example with the "Active Badge" [20] whilst the second, much more common concerning AR systems, enables relevant information to be provided for the task in hand.

5 Proposal for a Functional Taxonomy for AR

We propose distinguishing several AR functionalities whose organisation is presented in Fig. 2.1.

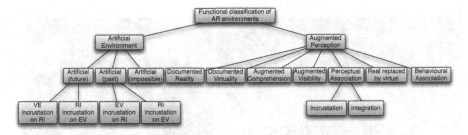

Fig. 2.1 Functional classification of AR. (RI : image with "real" content, VE : virtual entity)

5.1   Functionality 1: Augmented Perception of Reality

This first functionality consists of highlighting the fact that AR constitutes a tool for assisting decision-making. It can provide information which will enable a better understanding of reality and which will ultimately optimise our action on reality.

Fuchs [21] proposes a taxonomy which considers the means by which AR enables this objective to be achieved. Five types of environments can be distinguished. To these five type of environment, we can add another type to which Fuchs [21] attributes the functionality 0. This is the case where real images (RI) and virtual entities (VE) are displayed on the same screen, but without any relationship between the two. In this case, the user has a single screen with two independent displays. We then talk about functionality 0 because there is no relation between the content of VE and RI. With the exception of this case of a limited AR environment, which is possible but not relevant, other environments are possible and more relevant. Specifically, the *augmented perception of reality functionality* can be divided into five sub-functionalities.

5.1.1   Sub-functionality 1: Documented Reality and Documented Virtuality

This is the minimum functionality of augmented reality: RI and VE are in two different display boxes, but their information is related. Augmentation thus consists of informing users, like for example, without the mediation of a technical device, an assembly manual for kit furniture. The aim of the second display box (mostly text) is to help users understand and guide their action. This is documented reality.

Inversely, in some specific cases, for example, the synoptic of an industrial process (VE) with the "real time" incorporation of one or several windows displaying real parts of the process (RI) , the "document" no longer consists of a virtual environment, but of images of the real object. In this particular case, we can talk about documented virtuality. In both these cases it involves improving the understanding of the real or virtual scene by adding passive semantic information provided on another display support.

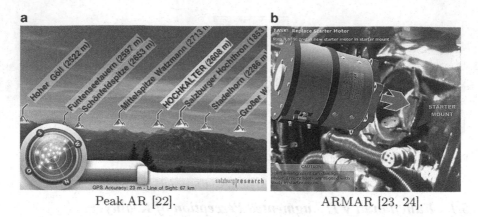

Peak.AR [22].   ARMAR [23, 24].

Fig. 2.2 Example of applying the augmented understanding of reality

5.1.2 Sub-functionality 2: Reality with Augmented Perception or Understanding

In this functionality, RI ad VE are in the same display box. Two levels can be distinguished according to the contribution of augmentation.

First Level: Reality with Augmented Understanding

This involves augmenting the understanding of images from the real scene by incrusting passive semantic information (Fig. 2.2). VE (titles, keys, symbols, etc.), more or less visually close to real objects, providing complementary information on the latter (eg. functions, references). Inverting RI and VE in this functionality cannot be envisaged.

Second Level: Reality with Augmented Visibility

This is the augmented visibility of images from real scenes (if we limit ourselves to visual perception). VE (eg. "iron wire" model of real objects) geometrically match the contours of real objects (Fig. 2.3). They enable objects to be highlighted so as to see them better. This involves, amongst other things, calibrating cameras. It is then possible either to improve the clarity of images by highlighting the apparent contours of objects so as to perceive them more easily or to improve the understanding of objects by virtually representing their visible and invisible contours.

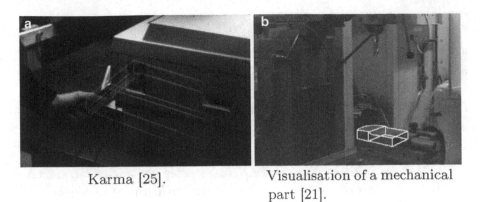

Karma [25].   Visualisation of a mechanical
                           part [21].

Fig. 2.3 Reality with augmented visibility with objects' visible and invisible contours represented

5.1.3 Sub-functionality 3: Perceptual Association of the Real and Virtual

In this functionality new virtual objects are added to the real scene. We can distinguish between both cases according to the level of integration of virtual objects in the real scene.

First Level: Incrustation of Virtual Objects on Real Images

Virtual objects are incrusted (overlay) on top of real objects. Therefore virtual objects are not concealed by real objects. We can refer to this as association by superposition (Fig. 2.4a).

Second Level: Integration of Virtual Objects on Real Images

Virtual objects are integrated with real objects. The latter conceal virtual objects which are positioned behind them. This is a 3D association. However integration with real time occlusion remains a major technological hurdle (Fig. 2.4b).

5.1.4 Sub-functionality 4: Behavioural Association of the Real and Virtual

In addition to the conditions of the previous functionality, we semantically modellise virtual objects by taking into account their physical properties according to the laws of gravity, contact, elasticity, fluidity, etc. so as to enrich the scene. Prior knowledge is used in the real scene and its objects. This functionality defines geometrical and physical interactions between real and virtual objects. For example, we can mention the behaviour and attraction functions of virtual objects with real objects.

Incrustation of objects.   Integration of objects.

Fig. 2.4 Examples of perceptual associations between the real and virtual (Extract from [26])

Fig. 2.5 The teleoperated robot is displayed simultaneously in real 3D images and using 3D artificial images

5.1.5   Sub-functionality 5: Substituting the Real by the Virtual or Virtualised Reality

If we know the geometrical modelisation of the real scene observed, we can replace the video image display for the real scene by the synthetic image of the model, determined from the same point of view. By going from the video image to the synthetic image, and vice versa, the understanding for the environment is augmented. In this case we can talk about virtualised reality. We can then also change the point of view for the synthetic image, without moving the camera filming the real scene, which enables a better understanding of the scene. For example, we can mention teleoperation work carried out at the DER by EDF (Fig. 2.5). In their visualisation device, the video image display for the real scene is not replaced by the model's synthetic image, but they are displayed on two neighbouring screens. The robot, which the operator is handling, is simultaneously displayed in real 3D images and synthetic 3D images. Whatever the point of view of real cameras, the operator can always observe on a screen in virtualised reality the mechanical configuration of the robot with "real time" animated synthetic images.

5.2 Functionality 2: Create an Artificial Environment

In the first functionality, AR enables objects, beings or relations which exist in reality but which cannot be perceived by users to be visualised, eg. underground stations [27] exist in reality, but are not always easily identifiable. An iPhone® application shows (or highlights) what exists in reality but cannot be seen. It is clear that with regard to the Bergsonian theory of perception, all our activities, even the most speculative (eg. thinking, modellising) concern actions [4]. However, humans have an ability which seems to partly escape this law: imagination. We can reasonably acknowledge that the production of mental images may not satisfy a practical objective, although what we imagine may or not have voluntary effects on our perception and actions in the real world. The production of unconscious mental images (ie. dreams) and conscious mental images (ie. fantasies, defined as the production of mental images during the awakening phase, eg. when we imagine that we are in other places) does not seem to serve any practical function. When we form mental images of an imaginary environment it is not in order to act in the real world, but perhaps, on the contrary, an attempt to escape reality. However, AR is able to produce such environments which are no longer subject to practical requirements. In such cases, AR offers environments which present not reality as they are perceived – by augmenting the amount of information which we are unable to perceive, but which, however, is present in reality – but reality, as it could be in the future or even an impossible reality.

5.2.1 Sub-functionality 1: Imagine Reality as it Could be in the Future by Associating the Real and the Virtual

Overall this is not about being informed, understanding or even acting with regard to what really exists, but digitally creating a possible world which combines either a real environment with virtual images (level 1) or a virtual environment with real images (level 2). Each level can be broken down into two sub-levels according to the type of association. This type of functionality can use two types associations: with occlusion versus without occlusion.

Fig. 2.6 Example of a possible future environment by incrusting virtual elements [28]

First Level: Imagine a Possible Future Environment by Incrusting Virtual Objects on/in Real Images

First Sub-level: No Occlusion

In this functionality, new virtual objects are added to the real scene by superposition and are not concealed, not to better understand and/or act in reality, but with a disinterested aim, for example, strictly aesthetic.

Second Sub-level: With Occlusion

This involves adding virtual objects which conceal part of the real environment. Obviously, this is more efficient at the sub-level than the real/virtual association because it enables users to visualise what the possible future environment looks like if these virtual objects incrusted in the real environment really existed. Thus, an interface enabling one of the rooms of a real apartment to be visualised (eg. the user's) by adding virtual furniture [28] would not enable them to know or master reality any better, but to imagine what the future reality would be like (Fig. 2.6).

Second Level: Imagine a Possible Future Environment by Incrusting Real Objects in/on a Virtual Environment

First Sub-level: Without Occlusion

In this functionality, we added by superposition, without occlusion, new real objects to the virtual environment. Here again, for example, to satisfy an aesthetic objective, it would involve seeing in what type of room (virtual), the real object would be best suited, by revealing all its aesthetic qualities. We could, for example, virtually move the real image of a sculpture in virtual rooms of a future exhibition venue so as to estimate the optimal location (according to constraints such as light, access for visitors, etc.).

Second Sub-level: With Occlusion

Here again, the this second sub-level takes on its full meaning with the integration of real images in a virtual environment: the designer of the future exhibition venue may visualise what visitors really see if they visited this venue with such a configuration.

5.2.2   Sub-functionality 2: Imagine Reality as it was by Associating the Real and Virtual

Likewise, it is possible, either to associate virtual objects which no longer exist with a real environment (level 1) or associate objects which still exist but which were present in an environment which no longer exists and which is, consequently, digitally created (level 2). And in each of these cases, this association can be done without (sub-level 1) or with occlusion (sub-level 2).

First Level: Imagine a Past Environment by Incrusting Virtual Objects on/in Real Images

First Sub-level: With Occlusion

With this objective in mind, the objective is to visualise what current scenes looked like in the past without incrusting virtual objects belonging to the past and concealing the current environment.

Second Sub-level: With Occlusion

Partial occlusion of the real present environment by virtual objects enables the past to be imagined as faithfully as possible. AR therefore plays the role of a "virtual memory". For example, the mixed environment which proposes adding, with occlusion, to the current Cluny Abbey building architectural items which have since disappeared enables the abbey to exist as it did then [29]. We can thus see Cluny Abbey as it was when it was built in the tenth century (Fig. 2.7).

Second Level: Imagine a Past Environment by Incrusting Real Objects in/on a Virtual Environment

First Sub-level: Without Occlusion

This functionality is clearly very limited: it is certainly possible to put in its past context the real image, for example, of a column in the city of Ephesus in tact in a

Present environment.   Both past and present environment.

Fig. 2.7 Present Cluny Abbey augmented with items belonging to its past [29]

virtual environment by digitally creating the city of Ephesus (today in ruins) without occlusion. Yet, the advantage of such as association is almost non-existent.

Second Sub-level: With Occlusion

On the other hand, incrusting with occlusion the real image of the column of Ephesus in a virtual environment representing the city of Ephesus before it was subject to the ravages of time enables us to much more easily imagine the place and function of this column at the time when it was built on the site of Ephesus.

5.2.3 Sub-functionality 3: Imagine an Impossible Reality

This functionality makes better use of the potential of AR with regard to its possible distance from reality by taking advantage of the imaginary dimension of mixed environments. Here the objective is not to inform, or encourage understanding or optimise users' actions. This functionality emphasises the potentially disinterested nature of mixed environments: it is possible to create an environment which cannot really exist, eg. artistic creations or systems whose final aim is purely aesthetic. Designers therefore have greater relative freedom and are not limited to the types of environments which they can use: they can go beyond the possibilities that this environment really offers and the means used may be very varied. Concretely, it is possible to use all types of environments in the *augmented reality perception functionality*. Without systematically and exhaustively listing all the types of artificial mixed environments, it is possible to give a few examples. The principle for all possible sub-functionalities consists of diverting the primary function of AR, ie. *augmented perception of reality*. Creating an *artificial AR environment* can for example be envisaged thanks to a semantic gap produced by the incoherence of the overall meaning of the mixed environment. Diverting sub-functionality n°1 (*documented reality* and *documented virtuality*) of the first functionality (*augmented perception of reality*) involves associating, for example, with a real environment

Chocapic and Nestlé [30].

"Virtual windows" [31].

Fig. 2.8 Examples of artificial AR environments

a virtual "document" providing information out of step with this environment with the aim of provoking in users a modification of the meaning of reality as it is perceived by users due to the difference between the real image and virtual information. We could for example associate with a real environment a virtual "document" erroneously describing this environment. Synthesising these mutually incompatible meanings would provoke in users the representation of an impossible mixed artificial environment. We could create an environment where a real image is augmented with erroneous meanings (ie. "documents"), ie. incoherent with the real image, but this would be a minimum functionality. The potential of AR is best exploited in environments which for example propose diverting the primary function of integrating virtual objects in a real scene (second level of sub-functionality 3: *perceptual association of the real and the virtual*). This is the case of the AR game developed by Dassault Systems for Nestlé [30] (Fig. 2.8a), where a virtual character moves, partially concealing the real image, on a cereal box. Although this environment obeys objectives defined by a marketing strategy (eg. increasing traffic to Chocapic®'s website and creating a strong emotional link between the brand and its target, in this case young children), these objectives are merely an indirect consequence of the experience of young users. Basically, this environment creates an impossible artificial universe where a Minimoys® character runs across a cereal box. The aim is neither about better understanding reality nor more effectively mastering it. Although the final objective is interested (ie. making young consumers loyal), the system in itself could well have not obeyed any practical objective. It suffices to see how adults (who are not the target of this PR operation) adapt this game. In other words, what this type of environment attempts to create is a feeling of presence in an artificial world. And what at the end of the day this world contributes to strengthening the links between players and the brand of cereals is not fundamental, even though the game was created with this objective in mind. It is possible to distance oneself even further from the practical constraints when for example proposing an impossible mixed artificial environment such as the view of a US city "through the windows" of an apartment located in France [31] (Fig. 2.8b). An application which enables users to enjoy the view of a suspension bridge in the US from the window of their Parisian apartment has no practical, only an aesthetic use. With Wiimote® placed on the window ledge between two windows and an infrared sensor on the user's head, when moving around the room, the corner view of windows changes so as to give the illusion that the apartment is located in the US.

6 Discussion

The distinction between AR environments whose function is to *augment the perception of reality* and those whose function is to immerse users in an *artificial environment* has a double implication. The first concerns the fact that the taxonomy cannot be designed as a classification with a merely descriptive vocation. Taxonomy has a generative dimension [7]. Concretely, more than just a simple classification tool of what already exists, it enables environments which it is possible to design to emerge. In this respect, taxonomy is a tool for assisting the creation of virtual and augmented reality environments. This reflection leads to the second major implication of analysing what has been done here. The difference between the two types of AR goes further than a simple distinction in terms of functionality: if the first type of AR (ie. functionality 1: *augmented perception of reality*) is a prisoner of the present, the second type (ie. functionality 2: *imagine*) goes far beyond it. In short, AR enables us, admittedly, to see, understand and master the present better, and it also enables us to propose an environment with which the designer and, consequently, users can play with location in time. When I see, thanks to an AR interface today the ruins of Cluny Abbey augmented with parts of this abbey which have disappeared [29], I see an environment which is neither pure present nor pure past, but a mixture of both the past and present. Likewise, when I see my currently empty living-room augmented with its future furniture [28], I am neither in the present nor the future, but in a reality where both present and future are mixed. And when "hrough" the windows of my Parisian apartment I see a US city [31], I perceive a world which is simply not possible. This is why AR enables us, not only, to free ourselves from reality's time categories (ie. past vs present vs future), but also from the spatial unity which characterises reality, which, for example, means I cannot see a US city by looking through the window of my apartment. When, for example, I am looking for the closest underground station thanks to an application available on my mobile [27], this enables me to go there here and now: the first functionality of AR (ie. AR with an informative and practical aim) does not modify the space perceived, it only aims to unveil parts of that space – in this case underground stations – which are not perceived, but which may rightly be perceived since they do exist. On the other hand, whether it is Cluny Abbey [29] or a furnished room [28], the items added modify the structure of current real spatial relations. In short, from the spatial point of view, the first type of AR does not modify anything, it only reveals what already exists: it updates the spatial structure of reality, whether this structure can be directly perceived by the senses (eg. Paris underground stations) whether it is the expression of causal relations scientifically shown based on calculations (eg. an environment which shows the existing electrical voltage between two items on an electric meter) or whether it can only be apprehended via an artificial technique (eg. an AR environment which would make something visible thanks to a thermal camera for light waves whose frequency escapes human sight). On the contrary, the second type of AR modifies the spatial structure by adding objects, beings or relations which do not belong to it: it modifies the spatial configuration of reality.

7 Conclusion

To summarise, strictly speaking, there are two major differences between the two types of AR: it is functional in so far as both AR do not satisfy the same objectives – one is practical, the other imaginary. However, this distinction is not fundamental because it can be argued that, just like the interface enables me to locate underground stations on my mobile [27], the aim of Cluny Abbey in mixed reality [29] is to at least provide knowledge (ie. knowing what this abbey looked like when it was built) and even my virtually furnished has a practical function (ie. enabling me to buy furniture or not according to the layout of the room). The basic distinction between the two AR therefore seems to correspond to the ability of both to be go beyond location in space and time or not. Whilst the first type of AR presents us reality (what I can see, what I can do), the second type, on the contrary, presents us what is imaginary: what I cannot really see – since it is not actually real – but which I can, paradoxically, see thanks to an AR interface. In short, the second type of AR enables us to go from what is put into action (ie. current) to what is not: the imaginary. And this imaginary may be possible or not. Finally, AR makes the impossible possible.

References

1. E. Kant, *Kritik der reinen vernunft, J.F Hartknoch. Critique de la raison pure.* éd. Riga (trad. fr. Delamarre, A. et Marty F.). Gallimard, Paris, 1980, 1781-1787.
2. M. Auvray and P. Fuchs, "Perception, immersion et interaction sensorimotrices en environnement virtuel," *In A. Grumbach & E. Klinger (Eds.), Réalité Virtuelle et Cognition. Numéro spécial de Intellectica,* vol. 45, no. 1, pp. 23–35, 2007.
3. J. Gibson, *The senses considered as perceptual systems.* Boston: Houghton Mifflin, 1966.
4. H. Bergson, *Matière et mémoire. Essai sur la relation du corps à l'esprit.* Première édition : 1939. Paris : Les Presses universitaires de France, 1965, 72e édition. Collection : Bibliothèque de philosophie contemporaine, 1939.
5. W. James, *Pragmatism: A new name for some old ways of thinking.* New York : Longman Green and Co, 1907.
6. P. Fuchs and G. Moreau, "Le Traité de la Réalité Virtuelle," *Presse de l'Ecole des Mines de Paris,* Troisième Edition. Mars 2006.
7. M. Beaudouin-Lafon, "Instrumental interaction: an interaction model for designing post-wimp user interfaces," in *CHI '00: Proceedings of the SIGCHI conference on Human factors in computing systems,* (New York, NY, USA), pp. 446–453, ACM, 2000.
8. L. Nigay and J. Coutaz, "Espaces conceptuels pour l'interaction multimédia et multimodale," *TSI spécial multimédia et collecticiel, AFCET et Hermes Publ.,* vol. 15, no. 9, pp. 1195–1225, 1996.
9. R. J. Jacob, A. Girouard, L. M. Hirshfield, and M. S. Horn, "Reality-Based Interaction: A Framework for Post-WIMP Interfaces," pp. 201–210, ACM Press, Florence, Italy, April 5-10 2008.
10. P. Dourish, *Where the Action is : The Foundations of Embodied Interaction.* MIT Press, Décembre 2001.
11. W. E. Mackay, "Augmenting reality: A new paradigm for interacting with computers," *World Proceedings of ECSCW'93, the European Conference on Computer Supported Cooperative Work,* vol. 7, 1996.
12. E. Dubois, Laurence Nigay, J. Troccaz, O. Chavanon, and L. Carrat, "Classification space for augmented surgery, an augmented reality case study," *In A. Sasse and C. Johnson (eds.), Proceedings of Interact'99, IOS Press. Edinburgh (UK),* pp. 353–359, 1999.
13. E. Dubois, P. Gray, and L. Nigay, "ASUR++: supporting the design of mobile mixed systems," *Interacting with Computer,* pp. 497–520, 2003.
14. P. Renevier, *Système Mixtes Collaboratifs sur Supports Mobiles : Conception et Réalisation.* Spécialité informatique, Université Joseph Fournier - Grenoble 1, Grenoble, Juin 2004.
15. P. Milgram and F. Kishino, "A taxonomy of mixed reality visual displays," in *IEICE Transactions on Informations Systems* [16], pp. 1–15.
16. P. Milgram, H. Takemura, A. Utsumi, and F. Kishino, "Augmented reality: A class of displays on the reality-virtuality continuum," *Telemanipulator and Telepresence Technologie,* vol. 2351, pp. 282–292, 1994.
17. S. Benford, H. Schnädelbach, B. Koleva, R. Anastasi, C. Greenhalgh, T. Rodden, J. Green, A. Ghali, T. Pridmore, B. Gaver, A. Boucher, B. Walker, S. Pennington, A. Schmidt, H. Gellersen, and A. Steed, "Expected, sensed, and desired: A framework for designing sensing-based interaction," *ACM Trans. Comput.-Hum. Interact.,* vol. 12, no. 1, pp. 3–30, 2005.
18. D. A. Norman, "Cognitive engineering," *Book chapter of User Centered System Design, New Perspectives on Human-Computer Interaction,* pp. 31–61, 1986.
19. E. Dubois, L. Nigay, and J. Troccaz, "Combinons le monde virtuel et le monde réel : Classification et principe de conception," *Actes des Rencontres Jeunes Chercheurs en Interaction Homme-Machine,* pp. 31–34, Mai 2000.
20. R. Want, A. Hopper, V. Falc ao, and J. Gibbons, "The active badge location system," *ACM Trans. Inf. Syst.,* vol. 10, no. 1, pp. 91–102, 1992.

21. P. Fuchs, G. Moreau, and J. Papin, "Le Traité de la Réalité Virtuelle," *Presse de l'Ecole des Mines de Paris. Première Edition*, Mars 2001.
22. S. Research, "Peak.ar : http://peakar.salzburgresearch.at/."
23. S. Henderson and S. Feiner, "Augmented reality for maintenance and repair (armar)," *Technical Report AFRL-RH-WP-TR-2007-0112, United States Air Force Research Lab*, Jul 2007.
24. S. J. Henderson and S. Feiner, "Evaluating the benefits of augmented reality for task localization in maintenance of an armored personnel carrier turret," *Mixed and Augmented Reality, IEEE / ACM International Symposium on*, pp. 135–144, 2009.
25. S. Feiner, B. Macintyre, and D. Seligmann, "Knowledge-based augmented reality," *Commun. ACM*, vol. 36, no. 7, pp. 53–62, 1993.
26. S. Gibson, A. Chalmers, G. Simon, J.-F. Vigueras Gomez, M.-O. Berger, D. Stricker, and W. Kresse, "Photorealistic Augmented Reality," in *Second IEEE and ACM International Symposium on Mixed and Augmented Reality - ISMAR'03*, (Tokyo, Japon), p. 3 p, IEEE, ACM, none, 10 2003.
27. Presselite, "Metro paris : http://www.presselite.com/iphone/metroparis/."
28. Meine Wohnung, "Click & Design : http://www.meinewohnung.cc/."
29. ENSAM - On-Situ, "Dispositif de réalité augmentée pour l'abbaye de cluny . Rayon. http:// www.on-situ.com/."
30. D. Nestlé, "Minimoys : http://minimoys.3ds.com/press/3DVIA-Nestle.html."
31. Rationalcraft, "Winscape : http://www.rationalcraft.com/Winscape.html."

Chapter 3
Visualization Techniques for Augmented Reality

Denis Kalkofen, Christian Sandor, Sean White, and Dieter Schmalstieg

Abstract Visualizations in real world environments benefit from the visual interaction between real and virtual imagery. However, compared to traditional visualizations, a number of problems have to be solved in order to achieve effective visualizations within Augmented Reality (AR). This chapter provides an overview of techniques to handle the main obstacles in AR visualizations. It discusses spatial integration of virtual objects within real world environments, techniques to rearrange objects within mixed environments, and visualizations which adapt to its environmental context.

1 Introduction

Augmented Reality (AR) applications enrich the real world environment with a certain amount of synthetic information, ideally just enough to overcome the limitations of the real world for a specific application. Azuma et al. [3] define three requirements of an Augmented Reality application. They claim that in addition to a mixture of real and virtual imagery, AR applications have to run in real time and virtual objects have to be aligned (registered) with real world structures. Figure 3.1 shows an example of a common AR system and the data which is acquired, computed, and presented. In order to register the virtual monster, the AR system derives tracking information from the video input. After rendering the registered 3D structure, its overlay allows to generate the impression of a virtual figure standing on a real world paper card.

This kind of visualization is a powerful tool for exploring real world structures along with additional contextual information. For example, by augmenting textual annotations, AR displays are able to provide semantics to real world objects or places. AR visualizations may also use the real world environment to provide

D. Kalkofen (✉)
Institute for Computer Graphics and Vision, Graz University of Technology, Graz, Austria
e-mail: kalkofen@icg.tugraz.at

B. Furht (ed.), *Handbook of Augmented Reality*, DOI 10.1007/978-1-4614-0064-6_3,
© Springer Science+Business Media, LLC 2011

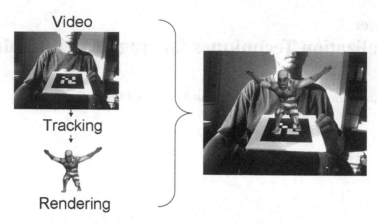

Fig. 3.1 Data flow in a common AR system. Real world imagery is delivered by the system's video feed and processed by vision based tracking algorithms. To align virtual and real data, the derived tracking data has been applied to transform the virtual content. Finally, the rendering is overlaid on top of the video feed

contextual information to computer generated graphics. For example, visualizations in AR are able to automatically select information relative to the current real world environment by using the user's location and orientation.

Since virtual information does not necessarily have to follow real world physical rules, AR displays are furthermore able to present a variety of nonnatural effects in a real world environment. This ranges from fictional characters living in a real world game environment [12] to a presentation of structures hidden in reality. By augmenting the virtual counterpart of a real world object, AR displays are able to uncover hidden objects, yielding the impression of seeing through formerly obscuring objects.

Azuma's definition of an AR application guarantees that the dynamics of real world environments remain unchanged after virtual renderings have been added. However, in order to comprehensibly fuse real and virtual information, both images have to be carefully combined rather than simply pasted together. If the computer graphics are generated independently from the information visible in the real environment, a successful visual interaction between both types of data may not be achieved. For example, without considering the information which is about to be removed by an augmentation, the resulting visualization may cause problems in depth perception. Our cognitive system interprets a set of depth cues (see Sect. 2.1) in order to pick up the spatial arrangements of the 3D objects in the environment. However, when carelessly adding computer graphics to the real-world imagery, the AR system may override some of those depth cues. This problem is illustrated in the simulated surgery depicted in Fig. 3.2. It demonstrates that spatial relationships between virtual and real data are lost after carelessly uncovering the hidden object. This effect happens due to the lack of occlusion cues. If no partial occlusion exists, judgment concerning the order of objects becomes difficult. Other existing depth cues (such as object size or object detail) are not strong enough to communicate the order of objects in such a visualization [48].

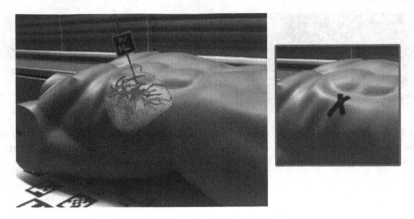

Fig. 3.2 Improper augmentation. In this example, careless augmentations of hidden structures cause two key problems: they override useful information (such as landmarks) and they lack depth cues. (*Right*) Original scene before augmentation, the *black cross* indicates the insertion point for the rfa-needle. (*Left*) Augmentation of the liver with its portal & hepatic vessel trees and a tumor

Furthermore, careless replacement of parts of the real world imagery may also hide important structures present in the real environment. Figure 3.2 shows how the computer-generated rendering of some of the inner anatomy obstructs the view of highly relevant landmarks which are present in the real-world imagery. In this example, the objective is to insert a needle into a patient's abdomen using a pre-defined entry point (black markings). By overlaying virtual organs on top of the real world imagery, the user is left unable to see the entry points which are marked on the skin of the patient.

In addition to the problems caused by overriding (and thus removing) real world imagery, careless generation of visualization in AR environments may lead to misleading interactions of colors and shades representing the real and the virtual objects. If the rendering of virtual objects does not take the prospective real world surroundings into account, the composition of both may fail to transport the intention of the visualization. Comprehensible visualizations in AR environments require that the appearance of the added 3D computer graphics fits into the real-world environment. Consequently, successful visualizations have to consist of easily distinguishable elements. For example, Fig. 3.3a shows an x-ray visualization with similar appearance of both hidden and occluding structures. Even though depth cues are preserved, it is difficult to make out the elements of the visualization. As a result the spatial relationships are difficult to perceive.

Quite a number of visual deficiencies may be caused by a naïve combination of virtual and real world imagery. To avoid this, the limitations of the AR systems itself have to be considered in order to generate comprehensible visualizations. For example, AR visualization have often to be generated from imperfect data. Incomplete descriptions of the environment as well as erroneous or unsynchronized tracking information may affect the impact of the resulting visualization [26].

Fig. 3.3 Visual interaction between real and virtual renderings. The visualizations in (**a**) and (**b**) use the same parameters. However, while the visualization in (**a**) clearly presents all important objects, the augmented elements are hardly visible in (**b**)

Moreover, AR visualizations often have to deal with hardware restrictions such as small display sizes, limited field of view or restrictions caused by the egocentric nature of AR visualizations itself.

In the remainder of this chapter, we will first discuss techniques to enable a comprehensible integration of virtual objects into real world environments (Sect. 2). Then, we present techniques to manipulate mixed environments enabling to overcome limitations such as narrow fields of view (Sect. 3). Finally, we present context driven visualization techniques which allow to automatically adapt AR visualizations to their real world surrounding as well as to the uncertainty of the data involved in generating the rendering (Sect. 4).

2   Data Integration

A simple overlay of hidden structure on top of the system's video feed can cause a number of cognitive problems, caused by the processes involved in creating the impression of depth. Understanding these causes allows to develop rendering techniques which successfully add and preserve such information in AR visualizations.

2.1   Depth Perception

Our cognitive system takes approximately 15–20 different psychological stimuli into account in order to perceive spatial relationships between 3D objects [21]. These so called depth cues can be divided into monocular and binocular. While binocular depth cues require the use of two eyes, monocular cues appear even when one eye is closed.

Monocular depth cues can be further divided into pictorial cues, dynamic depth cues and oculomotor cues. Dynamic depth cues are caused by the fact that objects further away seem to move slower than objects close by when moving our viewpoint. Our cognitive system translates the difference in speed into an approximation of distances between the objects. Consequently, those depth cues appear if either the objects in the 3D environment or the observer move.

Oculomotor cues are caused by the feeling which occurs when the eyes converge and change shape in order to focus nearby objects. The feeling caused by the contraction of the muscles of the eye and the alteration of the shape of its lens is interpreted as distance from the object. While focusing on objects, which are very close, stresses the eyes more (causing more of the noted feeling), focusing on further away structures relaxes muscles and the lenses; this causes less of this particular feeling.

Pictorial depth cues are those that can be found in a single image including:

- Occlusion: if the 2D projections of two objects in the environment overlap, objects which are closer to the observer occlude objects which are further away.
- Relative size: more distant objects appear to be smaller than closer objects.
- Relative height: objects with bases higher in the image appear to be further away (compare the stakes of the bridge).
- Detail: objects which are closer offer more detail.
- Atmospheric perspective: due to dust in the atmosphere, objects which are further away appear more blurry than those which are nearby.
- Shadows: depending on the position of the light source, shadows can be cast from one object onto another.
- Linear perspective: parallel lines converge with increasing distance. Notice how the sidewalks seem to converge at some infinite place although in reality they appear to be approximately parallel.

Even though monocular depth cues enable one to make depth judgments, our typical impression of a 3D object is caused by binocular depth cues. This type of cue exploits the difference between the 2D projections of a point in 3D space on the retinas of the left and the right eye. Corresponding retinal points move further away the closer a 3D point gets. Nevertheless, in order to provide the user of an AR application with binocular depth cues, special stereoscopic display devices have to be used to provide the user with both renderings at the same time. Therefore, in the remainder of this chapter we will concentrate on monocular depth cues, in particular on those which can be found in a single static visualization.

2.2 Augmenting Pictorial Depth Cues

By rendering the virtual structure using a camera which uses parameters reflecting the characteristics of the real camera, the fusion of virtual and real world imagery will automatically provide pictorial depth cues which match to those present in the real world environment.

Figure 3.4 shows an example of an augmentation of a virtual Lego figure which stands (a) behind and (b) to the left of two real Lego figures. Among others factors, linear perspective, relative height (the virtual figure bases higher in the image) and relative size (the virtual figure is smaller) indicate the spatial relation of the virtual figure relative to the real ones. Since the parameters of the virtual camera have been

Fig. 3.4 Synchronizing the parameter of the virtual and the real camera allows to align real and virtual pictorial depth cues. The virtual Lego figure in (**a**) is correctly perceived next to the real figures, whereas the virtual one in (**b**) is correctly perceived behind both. This effect is achieved by aligning depth cues such as perspective distortion and relative size

aligned with those of the real one, the depth cues from both presentations line up. Even though a number of depth cues are missing (for example no shadows are cast and the virtual and the real world lighting do not match), the virtual Lego figures in (a) and (b) are perceived in its correct position in 3D space.

Synchronization of other parameters can further increase the perception of AR visualization. For example, Fischer et al. [17] as well as Okumura et al. [35] demonstrated the alignment of image noise and blur caused by defocusing and motion. Later Klein et al. [31] showed a more extensive set of synchronized parameters including color and lens distortion.

If the AR rendering framework is able to synchronize camera parameters, depth cues of 3D objects will line up with those present in the environment. Using this fact, additional virtual objects are able to enrich the perception of the real environment. The fact that renderings of registered 3D objects add a number of depth cues to the environment was used by Wither and Höllerer [47] as a means to increase the accuracy of depth judgments in real world environments. They additionally render carefully designed virtual objects, such as a chess board pattern, to encode additional depth cues.

2.3   Occlusion Handling

While renderings from synchronized real and virtual cameras are already able to align depth cues, as soon as occlusions between real and virtual objects appear, those depth cues are no longer sufficient to produce believable augmentations (Fig. 3.5a). Even though all other depth cues would have been added to the AR display, the virtual object will be perceived as floating in front of the video image. A believable integration of virtual structure into the real world environment becomes only possible if occlusions between real and virtual objects have been resolved (Fig. 3.5b).

Fig. 3.5 Importance of occlusion cues (**a**) Even though a number of different depth cues exist, depth order is ambiguous and perception is wrong if occlusions have been ignored (**b**) The same rendering as in (**a**) with occlusion correctly resolved. This visualization is able to communicate the spatial relationship between its real and virtual content

---

Algorithm 1 Occlusion handling using phantom objects

---
1. Draw Video
2. Disable writing to color buffer
3. Render virtual representations of real objects (Phantoms)
4. Enable writing to color buffer
5. Draw virtual objects

2.3.1 Phantom Objects

To identify occlusions between virtual and real world structures, we have to compare the depth values of both types of objects per pixel in the screen space of the AR display. A common method to assign virtual and real world fragments has been presented by Breen et al. [7] and is called *Phantom Rendering* (outlined in Algorithm 3.1). Registered virtual counterparts of real world objects are included in the representation of the virtual environment, which subsequently enables to compare depth values in a common space. Phantom objects (which represent the virtual counterparts of real world objects) are rendered invisible (only to the z-buffer), before purely virtual objects are being rendered. Assuming that phantom objects are properly registered with their real world counterparts, the AR display becomes able to reject hidden virtual fragments using ordinary OpenGL depth testing. This strategy reveals occlusion by allowing only visible fragments of virtual structure to pass (Fig. 3.6).

Note that rendering of phantom objects does not only allow for occlusion handling but also enables for efficiently casting shadow from virtual to real world objects which can be used to provide further depth cues [23].

Fig. 3.6 Phantom Rendering in AR. The invisible phantom object prevents occluded virtual fragments from passing the render pipeline. The augmentation consists of only nonoccluded virtual fragments

Fig. 3.7 Uniform Transparency Modulation. Complex color arrangements will result in ambiguous presentations if uniform transparency modulations are applied

2.3.2 Advanced Occlusion Handling Using Video-Textured Phantom Objects

One strength of AR is the ability to uncover hidden structure and thus altering the original order of occluding and occluded elements. This *x-ray visualization* is a powerful tool in exploring hidden structures along with related real world information. However, as outlined before, without considering the information which is to be removed, the augmentation may lead to perceptual problems.

The easiest approach to present both hidden and occluding structure is to make the occluding one transparent so that hidden structure is visible. However, a simple uniform modification of the transparency values of occluding structures will most often result in ambiguous presentations. Figure 3.7 demonstrates the presence of clutter after blending the occluding structure uniformly with hidden objects. Even though very uniformly colored occluders covering high contrastive structures may allow one to perceive both types of data. The study of Buchmann et al. [8] showed that spatial relationships are lost if transparency is uniformly altered. The users in their experiment perceived hidden text on top of an occluding hand.

Rather than uniformly modulating transparency, comprehensible x-ray visualizations vary transparency values non-uniformly over the object. This results in

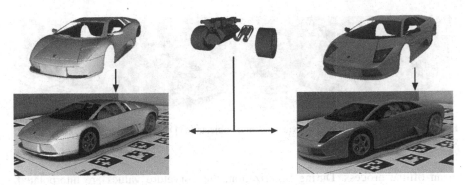

Fig. 3.8 Video Phantoms. Since ordinary phantom objects resolve occlusions by rejecting occluding virtual fragments occluding structure are not directly identified. Video phantoms (image on the *right hand side*) make use of current real world video information instead of virtual shades

a so called *ghost presentation* of occluding elements. In order to automatically generate ghost illustrations, a number of different approaches have been applied to control the means of modulation. Very early work from Crow proposes a function of the cosine [14] of the angle between a surface normal and the current viewing vector. To simulate different transparent media, Crow additionally uses the cosine to a modifiable power which can vary the drop-off function of his transparency modulation. Even though he didn't explicitly point it out, this allows for modulating transparency depending on the silhouette of the occluding structure. Notice that the silhouette of a 3D object is defined at those points where the viewing vector hits a surface point within an angle of 90 degree to its normal vector [22].

In order to render such effects in AR, we have to extend the idea of phantom rendering. Basic phantom rendering was only intended to resolve occlusions using a cheap process that can be executed on fixed function graphics hardware. The algorithm does not specifically identify real world pixels, which are suitable to be turned transparent. Instead of real world occluding fragments, only visible virtual fragments will be identified by this algorithm. Consequently, a system to generate ghost renderings has to use a slightly modified version of the original idea of Phantom Rendering. Instead of rendering the phantom invisible, the new approach renders a virtual and fully opaque presentation of real world structure (Fig. 3.8). Since this will obscure the real world object, the phantom object uses color information from the video feed. The implementation passes the current video frame to a fragment shader, which renders the phantom visible, resulting in a video textured phantom. Instead of using shades of virtual material (Fig. 3.8 left side), a texture lookup at the fragment's position after its projection to image space provides the output values (Fig. 3.8 right side).

By using a Video Phantom Object, we are able to apply any model based stylization technique to generate a ghost representation of occluding structure in AR. Figure 3.9 shows an example of two ghost renderings, which were generated from a video phantom. Their stylization uses principal curvature information [32] of the registered 3D mesh. The curvature values are defined per vertex and computed

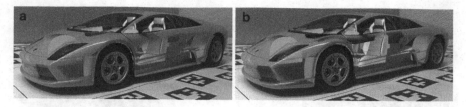

Fig. 3.9 Ghost presentations using video phantom objects (**a**) Dense ghost presentation (**b**) Sparse ghost presentation

in an offline process. During rasterization, the curvature values are interpolated between vertices, so that for each fragment (and thus for each pixel covered by the video phantom object) a curvature value is carried out. Finally, curvature values are linearly mapped to transparency values using (3.1). To control the object's transparency the parameters k and $tShift$ have to be modified. While $tShift$ linearly changes the mapping from curvature to opacity values, k changes the shape of the mapping function. High curvature values map to high opacity values while low curvature values map to low opacity values.

$$O_i = \frac{C_i}{k} + tShift; \; k \neq 0.0 \tag{3.1}$$

i:Current fragment; O: Opacity; C: Maximal curvature; k: Curvature weight; tShift: Transparency shift

2.4 Image Based X-Ray Visualization

Perfectly registered virtual models of real world objects enable to resolve occlusions between real and virtual objects. However, AR scenes commonly suffer from incomplete virtual representations. Often only the video in combination with the object of interest is available to the AR system. In such situations, the AR system requires knowledge about the organization of the scene in order to correctly sort their elements. While this information is often difficult to acquire for a general visualization, in case of applications using x-ray visualization to "see through" real world structure, the virtual data can often be assumed as being completely covered by real world objects. In this case, the depth order is known, and the AR system can analyze the video stream only in order to preserve important depth cues. In the following, we will review the extraction and preservation of image features which have been used to aid depth perception in x-ray visualizations in AR.

2.4.1 Edge Features

Several researcher have demonstrated the value of preserving or enhancing the result of an edge detector on the AR system's video feed [2, 28]. For example, Figs. 3.10 and 3.11 show edge preservations by applying an image based edge detector to the

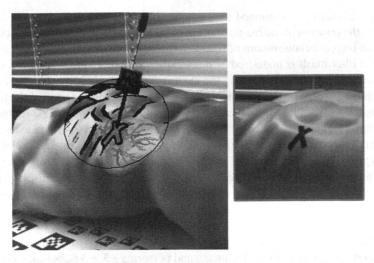

Fig. 3.10 Image based Ghosting using Edge Preservation. Preserving edges on the entire image clutters the presentation. An interactive Flat Magic Lens allows to control cluttering video ghosting. Edges have been preserved by operators in 2D image space only. Each video frame is processed and discrete edges are detected using and ordinary edge detector (such as the Canny operator [9])

Fig. 3.11 The Augmented Reality system uses a priorly acquired textured reconstruction of a remote scene (*center*) based on captured images and derived models. The textured reconstruction is overlaid on the user's view of the environment (*left*). In combination with highlighting the edges of occluding structure, only where hidden elements can be revealed, a comprehensible x-ray visualization is achieved while at the same time edge clutter is avoided (*right*)

current video feed. Note, by using only the video data as a source for preservation, other features than those which belong to the occluding object have been detected. In Fig. 3.10 the edges on the puppet, but also the edges of the ARToolkit marker and the needle (which is inserted into a tumor in this simulated surgery) have been detected and emphasized in black.

Even more confusing than edges from unwanted objects, is that edges extracted from video may clutter the whole view. As a remedy, a hybrid approach using features from video and tracked objects as stencil masks is able to reduce the image clutter. Figure 3.10 has been enhanced with edges from the video stream which were stenciled by the region covered by a Flat Magic Lens [43]. The Magic Lens has been interactively positioned to augment only relevant edges from the video. However, the position of the magic lens has to be adjusted in each frame which may require an inappropriate amount of interaction. Therefore, if the manipulation of an additional filter mask is undesired or practically impossible, the visualization may filter depth cues automatically using the 2D footprint of the hidden elements (which describes the 2D area on the screen which is covered by the rendering of the hidden elements). Note that this area can easily be controlled by scaling the 2D footprint.

The implementation of such an information filter was demonstrated using GPU fragment shader in combination a multi-pass render-to-texture strategy [27] as well as by exploiting the capabilities of stencil buffering [2]. The video image captured from a user worn camera is rendered as a 2D background on the display before any other rendering occurs. Then, the occluded objects are rendered to the display and either to the stencil buffer or to a texture map. After this, the video image is re- rendered to the display while stencil tests (or fragment based texture lookups) ensure that edges are only drawn over the occluded objects. A fragment shader operates on each pixel of the video image and performs a 3×3 Sobel edge operator on surrounding pixels, and outputs opaque pixel colors for edges while preventing their rendering otherwise. Rendering of soft edges can be achieved by altering the alpha values near the edges. This can be achieved by applying a blur filter to the alpha channel of the edge texture.

2.4.2 Salient Features

Preserving edges from occluding elements helps to maintain context and improves spatial perception. However, visually important information about the occluding elements may still get lost. For example, contrasts in the visual features of the image, including color, luminosity, orientation and motion, determine *salient regions* and thus should be preserved as well. Salient regions can be understood as the regions in an image, which are most likely to attract the viewer's gaze [41]. In the following we discuss three salient features: hue, luminosity, and motion. The goal of this approach is to provide users with richer information about the occluding structure.

The presented saliency model is based on Walther's approach [44] (for a more thorough presentation, please refer to [38]). The sensory properties of the human eye are recognized to form a hierarchy of receptive cells that respond to contrast between different levels to identify regions that stand out from their surroundings. This hierarchy is modeled by subsampling an input image I into a dyadic pyramid of $\sigma = [0 \ldots 8]$, such that the resolution of level σ is $1/2^\sigma$ the resolution of the original image. From this image pyramid, P_σ, we extract the visual features of luminosity l, color hue opponency c, and motion t.

While motion is defined as observed changes in the luminosity channel over time, luminosity is the brightness of the color component, and is defined as:

$$M_l = \frac{r+g+b}{3}$$

Color hue opponency mimics the visual system's ability to distinguish opposing color hues. Illumination independent Red-Green and Blue-Yellow opponency maps are defined as following before the maps M_{rg} and M_{by} are combined into a single map M_c.

$$M_{rg} = \frac{r - g}{max(r,g,b)} \qquad M_{by} = \frac{b - min(r,g)}{max(r,g,b)}$$

Contrasts are modeled in the dyadic feature pyramids as across scale subtraction $\ominus$ between fine and coarse scaled levels of the pyramid. For each of the features, a set of feature maps are generated as:

$$F_{f,p,s} = P_p \ominus P_s$$

where f represents the visual feature $f \in \{l,c,m\}$. p and s refer to pyramid levels and are applied as $p \in \{2,3,4\}$, $s = p + S$, and $S \in \{3,4\}$. Features maps are combined using across-scale addition $\oplus$ to yield conspicuity maps C. Finally, all conspicuity maps are combined to form the saliency map S.

$$C = \bigoplus_{p=2}^{4} \bigoplus_{s=p+3}^{p+4} F_{p,s} \qquad S = \frac{1}{3} \sum_{k \in \{l,c,t\}} C_k$$

In the next stage, occluded and occluder regions have to be composed using their saliency information to create the final x-ray visualization. Figure 3.12 illustrates the composition of the different maps into the final x-ray visualization. Saliency maps S_o and S_d are generated for both the occluder I_o and occluded I_d images respectively. Further to this, we highlight edges in the occluder to emphasize structure. An edge map E is generated from the occluder region and weighted with the occluder saliency map.

$$E = \gamma(I_o) \times S_o \times \varepsilon$$

Where γ is a Sobel edge function and ε is a weighting constant. This edge map is combined with the occluder saliency map as an addition, $S_{o'} = S_o + E$. We combine $S_{o'}$ and S_d to create the final saliency map indicating the transparency of the occluder. We assume that salient regions of the occluder should take precedence over salient regions of the occluded. Additionally, a mask M and inverse mask M' is generated to reveal only the portion of the occluded region we are concerned with. Given this, the final image is composed as:

$$I_c = S_{o'} \times M + P_o \times M + P_d \times M'$$

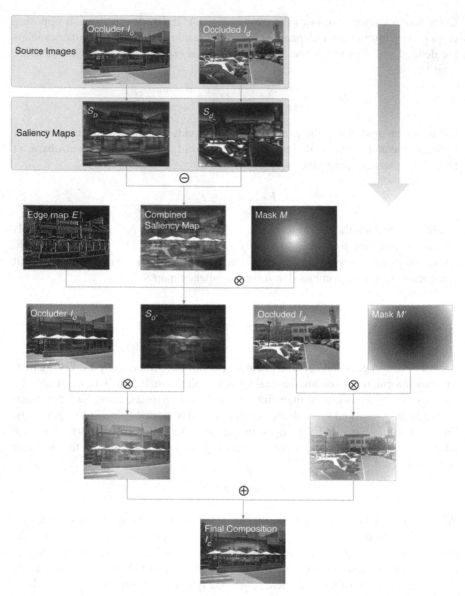

Fig. 3.12 Composition: source images are processed through a series of filters and combinations to produce the final output image. $\oplus$, $\ominus$, and $\otimes$ denote addition, subtraction, and multiplication of pixel values

Fig. 3.13 Image based X-Ray Visualization using Feature Evaluation per Area. By using feature analyzes per area the AR system is able to assign the same stylization of video elements within an entire region of the image. Notice how the white crossings in (**a**) appear similar ghosted in (**b**), and how most of the pixels belonging to the concrete have been assigned to the same transparency modulation

2.4.3 Area Based Feature Preservation

While the algorithms discussed so far compute a transparency value for each pixel, Zollmann et al. [49] demonstrated occlusion handling per area. In addition to per pixel evaluations of image features, she computes saliency values on a superpixel representation of the image [36]. Such a hybrid approach enables for two advantages compared to an exclusive pixel based one. Firstly, it allows to evaluate further features such as the amount of texture in a region. If occluding elements do not provide a sufficient amount of detectable features, the resulting x-ray visualization will suffer from a lack of occlusion cues. However by inserting synthetic features (such as hatch marks or stipplings [22]) depth perception can be rectified in such cases. In order to decide when and where to augment additional depth cues, Zollmann computes the amount of texture as a local variation of illumination per superpixel.

An area based approach furthermore provides the data to apply similar transparency modulations on similar regions in the image. Since an image naturally consists of homogeneous areas, transparency modulations per area will introduces less noise than frequently changing values. For example, most of the street markings in Fig. 3.13 have been assigned to similar transparency values. The pixel in the red as well as those belonging to the white markings have been automatically grouped to form two classes of occluding structure. Finally, all pixel in a group have been assigned to the same transparency modulation.

3 Scene Manipulation

Whereas naïve combination of virtual and real world imagery may easily cause visual deficiencies, the limitations of the AR system itself has to be considered as well in order to generate comprehensible visualizations. In addition, hardware restrictions such as small display sizes, narrow fields of view or the limitations caused by the egocentric nature of AR influence the comprehension of their visualization.

As a remedy, spatial rearrangements of the objects within the mixed environment have been demonstrated to be effective. For example, non linear distortions allow to increase the current field of view and rearrangements of real and virtual objects enable to increase their visibility.

This section provides techniques that deliberately modify real world imagery in order to increase the information content. First, we present techniques to relocate real-world objects (Sect. 3.1). Then, we present two space-distorting techniques (Sect. 3.2), that apply non-linear transformations to real-world objects.

3.1 Rearranging Real World Objects

Rearranged AR scenarios consist of real, virtual and relocated real information. To correctly compose an image out of all three types of information, the rendering algorithm has to fulfill three requirements. Firstly, it must be able to convincingly relocate real-world structures. Therefore, visual information has to be transferred from its original to the target location after the explosion was applied. Secondly, new imagery has to be generated to fill the original locations. Thirdly, the rendering algorithm has to correctly resolve occlusions between all used data.

To relocate real world information, we exploit the idea of video-textured phantom objects (see Sect. 2.3.2). To texture a phantom object with video information, we calculate the (u,v) coordinates for each fragment, as if the video background was applied using projective texture mapping from the camera's point of view. This is implemented by multiplying each vertex of a phantom with the model-view-projection (MVP) matrix before other transformations will be applied.

By using a vertex shader, relocation of video information can be achieved in two ways. One can either render the phantom geometry in their real location, look up the color from the video feed before the transformation to relocate the elements will be applied, or one can compute the MVP matrix for each phantom beforehand and use it in the shader which renders the phantom object in its new location. Since the second approach fits better into a scene graph framework, leveraging its ability to cascade transformations, we choose it in our implementation. We pass the matrix to transform a vertex from object to world space before the explosion's transformation is applied. The necessary interpolation of the calculated (u,v) coordinates is performed by passing the calculated values from the vertex shader to the pixel shader. Note that interpolation of (u,v) coordinates rather than color values is necessary to avoid artifacts.

Since all objects are rendered only once and no shading is used, the computation of pixel colors only consists of a calculation of texture coordinates and a lookup of the current video feed per fragment. Therefore, rendering of video-textured phantoms has negligible overhead compared to simple phantom rendering and also works if no relocation is applied.

3.1.1 Dual Phantom Rendering

With video-textured phantoms, we can relocate real world objects to another location in the image, thereby revealing the virtual objects behind the relocated objects. This assumes that the complete area of the relocated object is covered with virtual objects, which overrides the part of the image originally covered by the relocated object. However, frequently only a part of the uncovered area is occupied by a virtual object. Without special measures, the remaining area will still show the original video image (Fig. 3.14c). We must therefore extend the algorithm to invalidate any relocated real world information in its original location, to be able to either create a cut-out or to supplement incomplete hidden information (Fig. 3.14d).

To identify invalid pixels, we add a second render pass in which we project all fragments of a phantom onto their original real world location. This generates a 2D mask, consisting of only those pixels which will occur twice in a simple video-textured phantom rendering. This mask can then be used to remove redundant real world information, resulting in, e.g., a black background where no information is available. This algorithm is called *dual phantom rendering* [29], and can be described as follows:

1. *Enable and initialize framebuffer-object*

   (a) *Enable rendering to target 1 (T1)*
   (b) *Clear depth buffer and render target (T1 is cleared with 100% transparent pixels)*

2. *Render all video-textured phantoms (as described in Sect. 3.1) to T1*
3. *Render all virtual objects to T1*
4. *Switch rendering to target 2 (T2)*
5. *Render all phantoms in its original location to T2*
6. *Disable render-to-framebuffer-object and switch back to on-screen rendering*
7. *Fill the color-buffer with the current video feed*
8. *Cut out invalid real world information using T2*
9. *Superimpose T1*

Note that in step 5 of our algorithm, we are only interested in a binary 2D mask. This allows us to disable shading, thereby accelerating the rendering process. Furthermore, in cases where only a simple cut-out (and no restoration) of invalid real world information is desired, steps 7 and 8 can be combined by filling the color buffer depending on the 2D mask of the invalid video pixel (T2).

The algorithm as outlined only marks those fragments as invalid that will be visible in the final composition. This is controlled by the values in the depth buffer after virtual objects- and video-textured phantoms are rendered (after step 3). Not touching the depth buffer before rendering the phantom objects (step 5) allows us to reject all fragments which are hidden by either virtual or relocated real world information. This is an appropriate approach for those cases where a simple cut out of invalid information is desired. However, if the restoration of hidden information is requested, a 2D mask representing the entire phantom object produces better

Fig. 3.14 Distributing real world information. (**a**) Exploded virtual phantom object (**b**) Transferred real world information to the phantom object (**c**) Incomplete virtual scene and phantom rendering (**d**) Dual phantom rendering is used to remove void information (**e**) Phantoms with overlapping 2D footprints using the same video information (**f**) Synchronized dual phantom rendering to control the usage of video information

results, because it presents the 2D footprint of the entire object and not only its visible portion. Such a 2D mask can be computed by clearing the depth buffer before phantom rendering is initiated (before step 5).

Even though dual phantom rendering can be accelerated in many cases, it still incurs a considerable performance overhead because of the required second rendering pass. Therefore, this approach is only recommended if required by the AR application.

3.1.2 Synchronized Dual Phantom Rendering

Labeling transferred video information in those places where a part of an explosion has been originally located enables us to remove redundant information. However, in those cases where phantoms overlap in screen-space, we will still transfer the same real world information to more than one object (Fig. 3.14e). To completely avoid duplicate usage of real world information, we have to further restrict the transfer of information to only those fragments of the phantom that are actually visible in its original location (Fig. 3.14f).

Therefore, instead of directly texturing a relocated phantom, we will first render the phantom object at its original location. However, instead of simply marking the information as invalid, it is labeled with the phantom's object ID. By using regular OpenGL depth tests we obtain an ID buffer of only visible fragments. This ID buffer allows us to restrict the transfer of video information to only those fragments which have been identified as visible in their original location. The algorithm to synchronize the transfer of real world information can be outlined as following:

1. *Enable and initialize FBO*

   (a) *Enable rendering to target 1 (T1 = ID-Buffer)*
   (b) *Clear depth buffer and render target*

2. *Render IDs of all phantoms in its original location to ID-Buffer (T1)*
3. *Disable FBO / Switch back to on-screen rendering / Clear depth buffer*
4. *Fill color-buffer with the current video feed*
5. *Cut out invalid real world information using the ID-Buffer as 2D mask (phantom ids >0)*
6. *Render all video-textured phantoms. Use ID-Buffer (T1) to control the usage of video information*
7. *Render all virtual objects*

While Synchronized Dual Phantom Rendering [29] requires both a second render pass and an ID buffer, we favor this approach over an unsynchronized Dual Phantom Rendering only in scenarios where the phantoms may overlap in screen space. Most of the real world scenarios consist of a set of objects which overlap in 2D, but some applications may only focus on a subset, allowing the use of the simpler unsynchronized dual phantom rendering.

3.1.3 Restoration

Since the video feed of an AR system delivers only information about visible real world objects, their rearrangement may introduce spots without any available information. Virtual objects are used to fill out these empty places, but often the virtual model fails to completely cover this area (Fig. 3.15).

We therefore utilize a restoration technique to fill in empty areas resulting from relocating real world objects. In our current implementation we identify the background information on the border of a mask, resulting from a relocation of parts

Fig. 3.15 Bad example of an explosion diagram in AR. No further shading of the transferred real world information is used. Notice the clutter of real and virtual information

of an object. The empty area is filled using the mean value of the all identified real world background information. This technique was chosen because it is simple and fast, and leads to acceptable results for a number of different applications. However, more advances techniques such as inpainting [6] exist and should be considered if this simple method fails.

The chosen strategy to visually unify the occurring material depends on the ratio of visible virtual to real world information. The visible pixels are counted with an occlusion query before pixel shading is applied. If the amount of available video pixel is too small (empirically set to less than 50%), we will only use the virtual color of an object (Fig. 3.16). However, if enough video information is present and only some virtually shaded fragments may disturb the perception of an object, we will re-shade the virtual information to visually fit to the used real world imagery. We have implemented this re-shade operator similar to the restoration of video background, by computing the mean value of real world color information on the border to the virtual fragments. This is implemented by computing the sum of all rgb values of all pixels at the border, which is divided by the amount of pixel at the border.

3.2 Space-Distorting Visualizations

Being able to perceive points of interest in detail within the user's current context is desirable, however, it is challenging to display off-screen or occluded points of interest. Sandor et al. [39] present a system which allows for space-distorting visualizations to address these situations (see Fig. 3.18). While this class of visualizations has been extensively studied in information visualization (for example [10]), this system presents the first instance of applying it to AR.

Fig. 3.16 Two animations (labeled 1 and 2 on the starting frame in the middle of the upper row) demonstrating reorganization of real world objects within an AR display

The system uses the approach of video-textured phantom objects (see Sect. 2.3.2), implemented by projecting the current video feed onto a 3D reconstruction of the environment. When the reconstructed model is distorted, the video image is distorted accordingly, minimizing the dissonance between the real-world and reconstructed model, and therefore reducing the cognitive load required to understand the distorted space.

To further reduce cognitive load, the system uses a *Ray* cue which acts as an overview and unifying signpost for the visualizations – a "cognitive anchor" for space distortion. Rays are rendered as wedges, emanating from the user towards the point of interest. Rays that pass through objects such as buildings become semi-transparent as an added depth cue. When distortions such as the Radial Distort occur, the Rays bend towards the distortion, indicating both their original direction in the near half of the ray and the distorted location in the far half. The amount of distortion is reinforced in the ray color, akin to stress visualization, where a ray under no distortion is green and a heavily distorted ray is rendered red. These ray cues were added from informal user feedback and are invaluable in providing a grounding for users who have no experience with space distortions.

This visualization technique builds upon the aforementioned cues to distort the space while keeping semblance with the real-world. To bring POIs outside the user's FOV into view, the system radially distorts the world around the user, compressing regions of the FOV that don't contain a POI. To reveal occluded POIs, it melts the occluding geometry. To reveal a POI that is both outside the FOV and occluded, it first radially distort the POI into view and then melts the occluding objects.

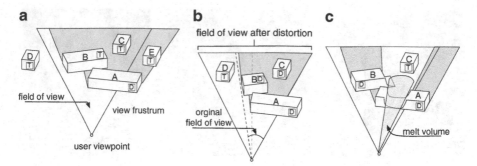

Fig. 3.17 The adaption of the Elmqvist and Tsigas occlusion model and how they apply to Melt and Radial Distort. (**a**) Elmqvist and Tsigas occlusion model to include targets outside the FOV. Target objects are flagged with "T" and distractors are flagged with "D". (**b**) Shows a schematic of the Radial Distort after distortion. (**c**) The melt volume with distractor objects flattened

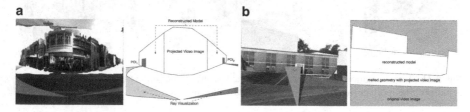

Fig. 3.18 The space distortion visualizations enable users to rapidly grasp the location of points of interest (POIs) that are either outside their field of view or otherwise occluded. (**a**) illustrates Radial Distort, revealing POIs that are outside the field of view of the user. (**b**) illustrates Melting, for discovering occluded POIs

3.2.1 Melt

The purpose of Melt is to reveal occluded targets. Occluded targets are revealed by virtually melting the distractor objects (Fig. 3.19d–f). A circle sector volume originating from the user in the direction of the POI defines the melt volume (Fig. 3.17c). The POI may be zoomed to gain more screen space and therefore present more information about its immediate context (Fig. 3.19g–h). Melt fits into the Elmqvist and Tsigas occlusion taxonomy [16] as a volumetric probe design pattern; however, it is passive/offline. The user selects the target from a list and the system animates the melting of distractors within the melt volume.

The melting metaphor replicates a common metaphor which we reinforce through animation. Like Virtual X-Ray, which is inspired by the 'superman'-like ability to see through buildings, Melt is inspired by the superman-like ability to melt buildings. Compared to Virtual X-Ray, Melt is suited to situations where there is more than one occluding object, such as POIs that are two or more streets over from the user. In this case, Virtual X-Ray loses most depth information besides the most

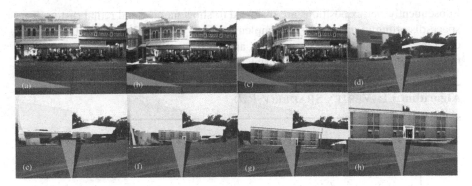

Fig. 3.19 The visualization applied in a city location. It enables users to rapidly grasp the location of points of interest that are outside their FOV by using our Radial Distort visualization. (**a–c**) show three frames of the animated Radial Distort visualization. (**d–f**) Show that occluded locations can be observed by our Melt visualization: the occluding geometry is flattened while projecting the video onto it. (**e–h**) POIs are zoomed closer to the user for visibility

immediate distractor. Virtual X-Ray also introduces high visual complexity when rendering transparency, decreasing depth perception and increasing cognitive load.

3.2.2 Radial Distort

The purpose of Radial Distort is to bring targets outside the FOV within the FOV, as illustrated in the Fig. 3.17b. Figure 3.19a–c show a video sequence of the visualization where one POI is outside the FOV. This POI is rotated inwards, so that it lies at the border of the FOV. The center of the FOV is compressed accordingly. The video image is projected in realtime onto the deforming geometry.

The benefit of such a technique is the ability to bring a POI to the attention of the user without forcing them to change their viewing direction, thereby keeping current context. Users can then turn their view towards the POI, with the distortion interactively unravelling as they do. In our experience, this interaction is more natural than using arrows to point to offscreen content.

Like Vallance [42], Radial Distort presents both immediate detail and continuous global context. Exact spatial relationship is degraded in favor of representing relative location to the user's current point of view. This follows the projection distorter design pattern. The user's current point of view is merged into n points of view for each point of interest, benefitting POI discovery at the cost of POI invariance.

3.2.3 Implementation

The video information is applied to the 3D reconstruction by using a video-textured phantom object (Sect. 2.3.2). A vertex shader projects texture coordinates for the current video image onto the front-most vertices of the undistorted scene.

Subsequently, vertex positions are distorted to show melting and radial distort. The space-distorting visualizations are implemented as GLSL 1.2 shaders. The pseudo code in 3.1 describes all POIs $p \in P$ as angles p_{angle_min} and p_{angle_max}, relative to the user's viewing direction, and a distance p_z, relative to the user's current position.

Algorithm 3.1: VERTEX SHADER(V, P, d)

---

for each $v \in V$

    // calculate γ, the angle of v relative to the user's current
    // viewing direction d
    $\gamma \leftarrow$ ANGLE(v, d)

do

    // radial distortion
    $\gamma \leftarrow \gamma *$ RADIALDISTORT(γ)

    // melt any occluding objects
    for each $p \in P$
        do $\begin{cases} \textbf{if } p_{angle\_min} \geq \gamma \leq p_{angle\_max} \textbf{ and } v_z \leq poi_z \\ \quad \textbf{then } v_z \leftarrow 0 \end{cases}$

Where V is the set of all vertices and RADIALDISTORT returns an angular coefficient that radially distorts the vertex into view. Our RADIALDISTORT implementation linearly compresses the FOV until all POIs are visible, and is defined by the following equation:

$$r = \begin{cases} \dfrac{1/2\,FOV}{\arg\min(p_{angle\_min}|p \in P)} & \text{for } \gamma \leq 0, \\[3ex] \dfrac{1/2\,FOV}{\arg\max(p_{angle\_max}|p \in P)} & \text{for } \gamma \geq 0. \end{cases}$$

Where r is the angular coefficient returned by RADIALDISTORT, such that it is the ratio of half the FOV to the greatest angle of a POI outside the FOV. At this stage, all visualizations have been calculated and are rendered by the fragment shader.

4 Context Driven Visualization

In previous sections, we have discussed techniques for integrating virtual structures into real world scenes through depth cues and occlusion handling (Sect. 2) and rendering techniques for manipulation of physical objects and scenes (Sect. 3). In this section, we focus on visualizations that alter appearance based on context by considering visualizations that are relevant to the physical context in which they are displayed (Sect. 4.1).

Virtual data presents additional contextual information to real world objects (Sect. 4.2), can represent invisible aspects of a scene (Sect. 4.3), or it gains from showing the object of interest within a specific real world context (Sect. 4.4). In addition, information about the quality of the data of the AR system provides the context of the application from a system's point of view. In order to improve the comprehensibility of AR displays their visualizations have to furthermore be able to adapt to those information (Sect. 4.5).

4.1 Situated Visualization

AR visualizations differ from more traditional computer visualization in that the virtual information is displayed in a physical context. Visualization typically appears on a computer screen, mobile device, or virtual world where the background is under the complete control of the visualization designer. However, the visualization itself often has no relevance to the surrounding environment. For example, a visualization of molecular structures in a virtual world might be presented with 3D data floating in front of a black background. AR visualization inherently has some form of background from the physical world but the background may have no relevance to the displayed data. For example, Fuhrmann et al. present an AR visualization of dynastic cycles of ancient China [18]. In this case, the background for the visualization is a white room. Moving to a different room would not change the meaning of the visualization. White et al. [46] use the term *situated visualization* to describe visualizations that are displayed in the context in which they are relevant. For example, carbon monoxide data presented on the street where the sensors collect the data.

The goal of a situated visualization is often to make meaning from the combination of the physical world and the virtual representation. In this case the visual data needs to clearly be associated with the physical location or object and take into account the user, task, and physical context. In the case of information visualization, this can change the representation or spatial layout of the visualization.

Here we focus on the challenges of information visualization situated in the physical world. Several challenges arise in data visualization in AR: the individual data points must be clearly associated with their proper physical world relationships, visualizations must take into account the background and user to assure legibility of the data, appropriate mapping from data to representation and meaningful representations must be chosen, and spatial layout of the visualization must reflect any existing spatial constraints in the data.

Some of these issues have been addressed in previous sections of this chapter. Here we focus on changes driven by context. Sources of context include objects in the scene, the scene itself, type of data being displayed, changes in live sensor data, user, type of display, and even the task. Changes to the visualization include the mapping and representation, spatial layout and coordinate system,

Fig. 3.20 The physical leaf species is identified using computer vision techniques. The visualization changes based on semantic context, in this case based on the specific species identified

4.2 Object as Context

Some of the most meaningful visualizations use an object in the scene as the focus. If the object is already known, a static visualization can be crafted to convey the appropriate information. However, if the focus of the visualization is unknown, the representation and layout made need to change based on the object. The approach taken by White et al. [46] uses computer vision to identify the object of focus and changes the visualization based on object classification. In the Tangible Electronic Field Guide (Fig. 3.20), a leaf is placed at the center of a clipboard to begin the task. Moving a handheld fiducial marker under the leaf triggers the matching algorithm and a best match for species is found using the inner distance shape context developed by collaborators Ling and Jacobs [34]. As the list of matching species is completed, the visualization forms proximal to the physical leaf. The spatial layout of the visualization can be flexible here because proximity is the primary constraint. Thus, the visualization can be arranged linearly or oriented in a circle around the leaf, depending on the size of the leaf. Each leaf node can be picked up and examined by the user and compared with the physical leaf. The images are dependent on the physical leaf itself and the task of the user. If the user changes modes by flipping the handheld marker, the leaf images change to full tree image or bark images to aid in the identification process.

4.2.1   Implementation

The architecture of the EFG incorporates aspects from context-aware computing, image identification, and visualization. In particular, our architecture borrows from Chi's Information Visualization Data State Reference Model (or Data State Model) [11] and Abowd et al.'s Cyberguide [1].

In the Data State Model, Chi describes four states of data for visualization (value, analytical abstraction, visualization abstraction, and view) and the transformations between states (data transformation, visualization transformation, and visual mapping transformation). The data transformation converts data values to an analytical abstraction. For example, data transformation could involve taking a set of ranked matching species data and transforming them into an ordered list. The visualization transformation converts the analytical abstraction into a visualization abstraction. For example, it could transform an ordered list into a set of images displayed in row-major order. The visual mapping transformation then provides a view onto the visual abstraction. For instance, it might render an overview of the entire set of images or a zoomed view of a single image. Heer and Agrawala suggest a design pattern based on this model that they refer to as the Reference Model pattern [25].

The advantage of this model is that we can separate out both analytical models and views with view transformations from the original data set. We find this useful in that we can take the original data from both the entire dataset or matching results, convert to hierarchies or lists, and then provide appropriate views such as quantum tree maps [4] or row-major layouts.

The Cyberguide tour guide is a mobile system that provides information based on the relevant context of the user (e.g. the physical location of the user). It has four service components: map, librarian, navigator, and messenger. The map component provides a set of maps for the system. The librarian maintains information about a tourist site. The navigator maintains the position of the user in the system. The messenger handles communication between the user and other users or systems (see Fig. 3.21). In our case, we are interested in context services that represent location, time, explicit meta-information from the user, and object matching. By using this context service, we can change the underlying values based on object context or visualization abstraction.

4.3   Sensor Data as Context

Visualizing sensor data can also provide a challenge because the specific data coming from the sensor will change and the location of that data may change. In the Sitelens system, White et al. [45] use situated visualization to visualize carbon monoxide (CO) data in the Manhattanville area of New York City. CO levels are measured using a CO sensor together with a combined DRM+GPS system. Each measurement is represented as a sphere. For the red spheres, location of the measurement is mapped to sphere location and CO level for each sample location

Fig. 3.21 Sitelens. Colored spheres represent geocoded sensor data that is invisible to the eye

is mapped to the altitude of each sphere. For the green spheres, the measurements come from a static sensor source provided by the Environmental Protection Agency, which is meant to represent CO levels in this area. The location is mapped to the same location as the local CO measurements to provide a comparison of two sensors meant to represent a given location.

Note that care must be taken in mapping sensor data to visual representations in situated visualizations. In a pilot study, White et al. [45] found that mapping data to size provided visual cues that were confused with depth cues. In a typical 2D visualization, size can be used and even in an AR visualization that is not 3D, size can be used. There is no control over the background in the situated visualization case so visual mapping that might be mistaken for depth cues are avoided and redundant encoding of data using multiple channels (e.g. color and shape) can be helpful.

4.3.1 Implementation

The SiteLens architecture borrows from our Electronic Field Guide architecture in the previous sections, extending it in several areas. First, we now need to know the orientation and location of the display relative to the physical world. A new tracking component, which gathers orientation, GPS, and fiducial marker orientation and position, manages this information to represent spatial context. Second, we use the same concepts for visualization management but maintain a collection of visualizations that are currently active, either display-referenced or world-referenced. Third, we incorporate a component for importing and loading georeferenced data. Fourth, we incorporate a component within the context service for gathering live sensor data via Bluetooth.

The visualization manager is similar to the EFG visualization manager. However, here each visualization is initialized with specific abstract representations for each data element in a data set and these representations can be changed to represent different colors, shapes, and mappings. Each visual representation is a subclass of a data node in our architecture, so we can easily create new visual representations and data mappings.

4.4 Scene as Context

The background scene provides both semantic and optical context for the visualization. This becomes important in avoiding placing information over relevant aspects of the scene (as discussed in the previous section on saliency), reflecting relevant parts of the physical scene through outlining, highlighting, or lowlighting, and insuring that the visualization itself is legible.

In terms of legibility, Gabbard et al. [19,20] conducted a set of studies to compare the readability of different text styles on different textured backgrounds, such as brick or pavement, under different illuminance conditions. Their studies focused on optical see-through displays and found that billboarding and fully-saturated green text provided best results while fully-saturated red text styles were problematic. They also suggest that the right active text style will result in better performance than static text drawing styles although they were unable to show this conclusively.

Placement of virtual information must also take into account the background scene. Leykin and Tuceryan used a machine learning approach to address this problem [33]. In their experiment, they use text overlaid on a variety of textured backgrounds. Each example was ranked by a human for readability and this was then used as training data for an SVM. The feature extracted from the training data was the response from a Gabor Filter across the 90×90 pixel sample and was meant to represent texture. Their approach then subdivides the scene into 90×90 blocks which are fed to the SVM. The block with the highest readability rank is then used for displaying text.

Tanaka et al. [40] also address this problem by focusing on color space characteristics. Their approach subdivided the image based on a grid and analyzes averages in RGB and HSV color spaces and variances in RGB, YCbCr, and HSV color spaces. Each grid subdivision is then ranked and information is placed in the location with the maximum viewability.

These techniques are related to view management developed by Bell et al. [5] in that we look for the best location to place information. However, Bell takes advantage of knowledge of the spatial layout of a model of the scene and does not take into account the actual image of the scene.

Fig. 3.22 Erroneous Phantom Rendering. (**a**) The phantom object does not perfectly reflect its real world counterpart. (**b**) The error causes wrong depth sorting at some pixels. Notice the error close to the shoulder of the *red* Lego figure

4.5 Uncertainty as Context

To allow visual interaction between virtual and real world data, the virtual information has to be integrated into the real environment instead of simply being layered on top of real imagery. To be able to resolve occlusions, both types of data have to be analyzed and compared in a common space, using e.g. a phantom or a video phantom object. The corresponding algorithms transfer real world information into the coordinate system of the virtual camera, followed by an analysis of all depth values using ordinary 3D computer graphics hardware.

However, to perfectly map a virtual object to its real world counterpart, the virtual model has to exactly reflect the real object's shape, and its 3D registration has to transform the virtual model perfectly to fit to its real location. While both steps are prone to errors, both also influence the quality of the resulting visualization in AR. Figure 3.22 shows the effect of a virtual counterpart which does not perfectly reflect the real world object. The classification falsely identifies parts of the background as being in front of the virtual figure. To avoid ambiguous AR visualizations we have to consider the existence of erroneous data and thus have to support error-friendly visualizations which are robust enough to either overcome or lower the problems resulting from errors.

A pragmatic approach to handle imperfect data is to either refine the data using fusions of multi data sources or to refine the augmentation itself. For example, while Klein et al. [30] use additional sensors to adjust an object's registration, Diverdi and Höllerer [15] refine the prospective overlay in image space, so that it fits to its real world counterpart. Both algorithm search for edges in the augmentation which correspond to edges detected from the video feed. However, while Klein adjusts the pose of the virtual camera, Diverdi alters the resulting rendering in favor of a more precise augmentation.

An approach to deal with registration error is to incorporate the error estimate as a parameter of the visualization technique. As demonstrated by Coelho and his colleagues [13], information about the current uncertainty of the data can be used

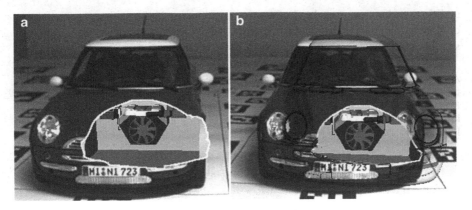

Fig. 3.23 Error Communication (**a**) The error is not communicated (**b**) An additional presentation of contextual structure is able to communicate the error. The additional augmentation is augmented as a ghost stylization of the structure in the context of the object of interest

as contextual information to the application in order to change the way textual annotations will be arranged. Coelho shows how a switching from an internal to an external placement strategy (see [24] for an overview of annotation strategies) can be used to resolve disambiguations in case of registration errors.

As outlined by Robertson et al. [37]), by additionally presenting easily perceivable augmentations of virtual counterparts of real scene elements helps in understanding the current error. This technique is able to visually communicates the current error to the user and thus enables them to ameliorate scene understanding in AR. For example, compared to Fig. 3.23a, the AR visualization in Fig. 3.23b has been enriched with a sparse representation of elements in the surrounding of the object of interest. By providing such an additional augmentation, the user of the AR system becomes able to mentally correct the error.

5 Closing Remarks

Augmented reality displays extend the viewer's perception via the addition of computer generated information. The visual interaction between virtual and real world imagery is the main advantage of AR visualizations compared to traditional visualizations. AR visualizations have a high potential, however, their success is dependent on their comprehensibility. If heedlessly implemented AR visualizations easily fail to visually communicate their information.

The complex character of AR environments requires complex visualization techniques to neither isolate certain structures nor to generate ambiguous presentations. In this chapter we have provided an overview of the fundamental techniques to comprehensibly fuse virtual and real world imagery. We have provided techniques to spatially integrate virtual objects within real world environments. In addition, we have presented techniques to use contextual information to increase the comprehension of AR visualizations and we have explained techniques to enable spatial manipulations of objects within AR environments.

Acknowledgments For valuable discussions on the topics presented in this chapter we would like thank Markus Tatzgern, Stefanie Zollmann, Steve Feiner, Peter Belhumeur, David Jacobs, John Kress, Sarah Williams, Petia Morozov, Andrew Cunningham and Arindam Dey. This research was in part funded by Nokia Research Center, a grant from the Boston Society of Architects, NSF Grant IIS-03-25867, and a gift from Microsoft.

References

1. Gregory D. Abowd, Christopher G. Atkeson, Jason Hong, Sue Long, Rob Kooper, and Mike Pinkerton. Cyberguide: a mobile context-aware tour guide. *Wireless Networks*, 3:421–433, 1997.
2. Ben Avery, Christian Sandor, and Bruce H. Thomas. Improving spatial perception for augmented reality x-ray vision. In *Proceedings of the IEEE Conference on Virtual Reality*, pages 79–82, 2009.
3. Ronald Azuma. A survey of augmented reality. *Presence: Teleoperators and Virtual Environments*, 6(4):355–385, 1997.
4. Benjamin B. Bederson, Ben Shneiderman, and Martin Wattenberg. Ordered and quantum treemaps: Making effective use of 2d space to display hierarchies. *ACM Transactions on Graphics*, 21:833–854, 2002.
5. Blaine Bell, Steven Feiner, and Tobias Höllerer. View management for virtual and augmented reality. In *Proceedings of the ACM symposium on User interface software and technology*, pages 101–110, 2001.
6. Marcelo Bertalmio, Guillermo Sapiro, Vincent Caselles, and Coloma Ballester. Image inpainting. In *Proceedings of ACM SIGGRAPH*, pages 417–424, 2000.
7. David E. Breen, Ross T. Whitaker, Eric Rose, and Mihran Tuceryan. Interactive occlusion and automatic object placement for augmented reality. *Computer Graphics Forum*, 15(3):11–22, 1996.
8. Volkert Buchmann, Trond Nilsen, and Mark Billinghurst. Interaction with partially transparent hands and objects. In *Proceedings of the Australian User Interface Conference*, pages 17–2, 2005.
9. John F. Canny. A Computational Approach to Edge Detection. *IEEE Transactions on Pattern Analysis and Machine Intelligence*, 8(6):679–698, 1986.
10. M. Sheelagh T. Carpendale, David J. Cowperthwaite, and F. David Fracchia. Extending distortion viewing from 2D to 3D. *IEEE Computer Graphics and Applications*, 17(4):42–51, 1997.
11. Ed H. Chi. A taxonomy of visualization techniques using the data state reference model. In *Proceedings of the IEEE Symposium on Information Vizualization*, pages 69–75, 2000.
12. Ben Close, John Donoghue, John Squires, Phillip De Bondi, Michael Morris, Wayne Piekarski, Bruce Thomas, Bruce Thomas, and Unisa Edu Au. ARQuake: An outdoor/indoor Augmented Reality first person application. In *Proceedings of the IEEE International Symposium on Wearable Computers*, pages 139–146, 2000.
13. Enylton Machado Coelho, Blair MacIntyre, and Simon J. Julier. Osgar: A scene graph with uncertain transformations. In *Proceedings of the IEEE and ACM International Symposium on Mixed and Augmented Reality*, pages 6–15, 2004.
14. Franklin C. Crow. Shaded computer graphics in the entertainment industry. *Computer*, 11(3):11–22, 1978.

15. Stephen DiVerdi and Tobias Hollerer. Image-space correction of ar registration errors using graphics hardware. In *Proceedings of the IEEE conference on Virtual Reality*, pages 241–244, 2006.
16. Niklas Elmqvist and Philippas Tsigas. A taxonomy of 3d occlusion management for visualization. *IEEE Transactions on Visualization and Computer Graphics*, 14:1095–1109, 2008.
17. Jan Fischer, Dirk Bartz, and W. Straßer. Enhanced Visual Realism by Incorporating Camera Image Effects. In *Proceedings of the IEEE and ACM International Symposium on Mixed and Augmented Reality*, pages 205–208, 2006.
18. Anton Fuhrmann, Helwig Löffelmann, Dieter Schmalstieg, and Michael Gervautz. Collaborative visualization in augmented reality. *IEEE Computer Graphics and Applications*, 18:54–59, 1998.
19. Joseph Gabbard, Edward Swan, II, and Deborah Hix. The effects of text drawing styles, background textures, and natural lighting on text legibility in outdoor augmented reality. *Presence*, 15:16–32, 2006.
20. Joseph L. Gabbard, J. Edward Swan, II, Deborah Hix, Robert S. Schulman, John Lucas, and Divya Gupta. An empirical user-based study of text drawing styles and outdoor background textures for augmented reality. In *Proceedings of the IEEE Conference on Virtual Reality*, pages 11–18, 2005.
21. Eugen Bruce Goldstein. *Sensation and Perception*. Brooks/Cole, Pacific Grove, CA, 2001.
22. Amy A. Gooch and Bruce Gooch. *Non-Photorealistic Rendering*. AK Peters, Ltd., 2001.
23. Michael Haller, Stephan Drab, and Werner Hartmann. A real-time shadow approach for an augmented reality application using shadow volumes. In *Proceedings of the ACM Symposium on Virtual Reality Software and Technology*, pages 56–65, 2003.
24. Knut Hartmann, Timo Götzelmann, Kamran Ali, and Thomas Strothotte. Metrics for functional and aesthetic label layouts. In *Proceedings of International Symposium on Smart Graphics*, pages 115–126, 2005.
25. Jeffrey Heer and Maneesh Agrawala. Software design patterns for information visualization. *IEEE Transactions on Visualization and Computer Graphics*, 12:853–860, 2006.
26. Richard L. Holloway. Registration error analysis for augmented reality. *Presence*, 6(4):413–432, 1997.
27. Denis Kalkofen, Erick Mendez, and Dieter Schmalstieg. Interactive focus and context visualization for augmented reality. In *Proceedings of the IEEE and ACM International Symposium on Mixed and Augmented Reality*, pages 191–200, 2007.
28. Denis Kalkofen, Erick Mendez, and Dieter Schmalstieg. Comprehensible visualization for augmented reality. *IEEE Transactions on Visualization and Computer Graphics*, 15(2):193–204, 2009.
29. Denis Kalkofen, Markus Tatzgern, and Dieter Schmalstieg. Explosion diagrams in augmented reality. In *Proceedings of the IEEE Conference on Virtual Reality*, pages 71–78, 2009.
30. Georg Klein and Tom Drummond. Sensor fusion and occlusion refinement for tablet-based AR. In *Proceedings of the IEEE and ACM International Symposium on Mixed and Augmented Reality*, pages 38–47, 2004.
31. Georg Klein and David W. Murray. Simulating low-cost cameras for augmented reality compositing. *IEEE Transactions on Visualization and Computer Graphics*, 16:369–380, 2010.
32. Shoshichi Kobayashi and Katsumi Nomizu. *Foundations of Differential Geometry*. Wiley-Interscience, 1996.
33. Alex Leykin and Mihran Tuceryan. Determining text readability over textured backgrounds in augmented reality systems. In *Proceedings of the ACM SIGGRAPH international conference on Virtual Reality continuum and its applications in industry*, pages 436–439, 2004.
34. Haibin Ling and David W. Jacobs. Shape classification using the inner-distance. *IEEE Transactions on Pattern Analysis and Machine Intelligence*, 29:286–299, 2007.
35. Bunyo Okumura, Masayuki Kanbara, and Naokazu Yokoya. Augmented reality based on estimation of defocusing and motion blurring from captured images. In *Proceedings of the IEEE and ACM International Symposium on Mixed and Augmented Reality*, pages 219–225, 2006.

36. Xiaofeng Ren and Jitendra Malik. Learning a Classification Model for Segmentation. In *Proceedings of the IEEE International Conference on Computer Vision*, pages 10–17, 2003.
37. Cindy M. Robertson, Blair MacIntyre, and Bruce N. Walker. An evaluation of graphical context as a means for ameliorating the effects of registration error. *IEEE Transactions on Visualization and Computer Graphics*, 15(2):179–192, 2009.
38. Christian Sandor, Andrew Cunningham, Arindam Dey, and Ville-Veikko Mattila. An augmented reality x-ray system based on visual saliency. In *Proceedings of the IEEE and ACM International Symposium on Mixed and Augmented Reality*, pages 27–36, 2010.
39. Christian Sandor, Andrew Cunningham, Ulrich Eck, Donald Urquhart, Graeme Jarvis, Arindam Dey, Sebastien Barbier, Michael Marner, and Sang Rhee. Egocentric space-distorting visualizations for rapid environment exploration in mobile mixed reality. In *Proceedings of the IEEE Conference on Virtual Reality*, pages 47–50, 2010.
40. Kohei Tanaka, Y. Kishino, M. Miyamae, T. Terada, and S. Nishio. An information layout method for an optical see-through head mounted display focusing on the viewability. In *Proceedings of the IEEE and ACM International Symposium on Mixed and Augmented Reality*, pages 139–142, 2008.
41. Anne M. Treisman and Garry Gelade. A feature-integration theory of attention. *Cognitive psychology*, 12(1):97–136, 1980.
42. Scott Vallance and P. Paul Calder. Context in 3D planar navigation. *Australian Computer Science Communications*, 23(5):93–99, 2001.
43. John Viega, M. Conway, G. Williams, and R. Pausch. 3d magic lenses. In *Proceedings of the ACM symposium on User interface software and technology*, pages 51–58, 1996.
44. Dirk Walther. *Interactions of visual attention and object recognition : computational modeling, algorithms, and psychophysics*. PhD thesis, California Institute of Technology, 2006.
45. Sean White and Steven Feiner. Sitelens: situated visualization techniques for urban site visits. In *Proceedings of the international conference on human factors in computing systems*, pages 1117–1120, 2009.
46. Sean White, Steven Feiner, and Jason Kopylec. Virtual vouchers: Prototyping a mobile augmented reality user interface for botanical species identification. In *Proceedings of the 3D User Interfaces*, pages 119–126, 2006.
47. Jason Wither and Tobias Höllerer. Pictorial depth cues for outdoor augmented reality. In *Proceedings of the IEEE International Symposium on Wearable Computers*, pages 92–99, 2005.
48. Shumin Zhai, William Buxton, and Paul Milgram. The partial-occlusion effect: utilizing semi-transparency in 3d human-computer interaction. *ACM Transactions on Computer-Human Interaction*, 3:254–284, 1996.
49. Stefanie Zollmann, Denis Kalkofen, Erick Mendez, and Gerhard Reitmayr. Image-based ghostings for single layer occlusions in augmented reality. In *Proceedings of the IEEE and ACM International Symposium on Mixed and Augmented Reality*, pages 19–26, 2010.

Chapter 4
Mobile Augmented Reality Game Engine

Jian Gu and Henry B.L. Duh

1 Introduction

The recent fusion of Augmented Reality (AR) and mobile technologies has enabled the creation of novel mobile AR applications. As the image processing algorithms and processing capabilities of mobile hardware continue to improve, mobile AR will become more commonplace. In addition, the mobile game industry itself has grown significantly in recent years. This is partly because of the development of 3D game engines which are being widely used not only in game applications, but also in the areas of virtual reality, virtual architecture, and education.

However, despite the respective growth in both 3D game engines and mobile AR applications, there is little focus on the integration of the two. Our aim is to study existing AR libraries and mobile game engines, and then to develop a 3D mobile AR game engine ideally suited for developing mobile AR applications. The key development tasks include: (1) To extend game functions for AR Libraries (i.e. supplementary math functions, network library, etc). (2) To improve or optimize 3D performance in current mobile AR applications. (3) To enable our libraries to operate across a wide range of mobile phone handsets without significant porting efforts.

We explored the feasibility of building a mobile AR game engine that can be used to develop stationary maker-driven image based AR games [1]. In the following sections, we will discuss related work on both current mobile AR and game engine applications, provide an overview of our game engine, and finally showcase several mobile AR applications using our mobile AR game engine.

H.B.L. Duh (✉)
Department of Electrical and Computer Engineering/Interactive and Digital Media Institute,
National University of Singapore, Singapore
e-mail: duhbl@acm.org

B. Furht (ed.), *Handbook of Augmented Reality*, DOI 10.1007/978-1-4614-0064-6_4,
© Springer Science+Business Media, LLC 2011

2 Related Works

In this section, we reviewed three types of related work; (1) AR libraries, (2) mobile game engines and (3) mobile AR games. The AR library and games we describe here are suitable for all mobile platforms.

2.1 Existing Mobile AR Libraries

One of the most popular AR libraries is ARToolKit[1] [2]. It calculates 3D camera poses from a single square-tracking marker. In 2003 the ARToolKit library was ported to the PocketPC platform and was used in the first fully self-contained PDA AR application [3]. A year later, Möhring [4] created the first mobile phone based AR application that showed a simple 3D virtual car model with 500 polygons that was rendered at 4–5 frames per second (FPS). In 2005, Anders Henrysson [5] ported ARToolKit to the Symbian platform, it become a new platform fo the mobile ar games.

NyARToolKit[2] is a complete port of ARToolkit to Java. This makes it slower in execution efficiency, but is completely architecture independent. NyARToolKit is a library of functions that integrates virtual objects into the physical environment, invoking real-time camera vision functionality and 3D renderings of virtual objects as an integrated output stream. Despite being Java-native, the toolkit also works with C# (Apple iPhone) and Google's Android operating system.

A higher level programming library for mobile AR applications is the Studier-stube ES [6] (StbES) library. This is a C++ based application framework for developing AR applications for mobile devices. It is cross-platform and operates on Windows, Windows Mobile, Apple iPhone and Symbian operating systems. Studierstube ES provides support for 2D and 3D graphics, video capture, tracking, multimedia output, persistent storage, and application authoring. Constituents of this library include Studierstube Core, Math, IO, Muddleware, Scenegraph and Studierstube Tracker (STBtracker).

STBtracker[3] [6] is the core tracking library in Studierstube ES. STBtracker is able to detect different types of markers including Template Markers, Frame Markers, DataMatrix Markers, Split Markers, Grid Markers and ID Markers. The tracking concept is very similar to that of ARToolKit's, but its code base is completely unique. STBtracker has been written from scratch with high performances for both personal computers as well as mobile phones. STBtracker's memory requirements are very low ($\sim$100 KB or 5–10% of the ARToolKit's memory footprint) and its

---

[1] http://www.artoolworks.com/Home.html.
[2] http://nyatla.jp/nyartoolkit/wiki/index.php?FrontPage.en.
[3] http://handheldar.net/stbtracker.php.

processing capability is about twice as fast as ARToolKit's on mobile phones. This tracking library serves as a standard benchmark for the comparisons of other mobile phone AR applications to be conducted. However, it is not open source and thus the detailed information on the library is very limited.

In 2008, Gu, Mukandan and Billinghust [7] developed a computer vision library for Java 2 Micro Edition (J2ME)-based mobile applications. It is able to support image processing and determine 3D camera poses. Based on this library, Gu et al. [7] presented several sample AR applications on J2ME-enabled mobile phones, however these applications performed significantly slower than comparable Symbian C++ based applications. Despite this, for portability support, J2ME would be preferred as Java is natively platform independent.

In the commercial market, Metaio[4] has released the Metaio Unifeye Mobile AR SDK. This allows iPhone, Android, Symbian and Windows Mobile developers to more easily create augmented reality applications on smartphone devices. However this SDK does not support many game features and functions.

QualComm[5] released an augmented reality SDK for Android smart phones very recently. Qualcomm's SDK will enable a new breed of applications that delivers interactive 3D experiences on everyday objects, such as 3D gaming experiences on tabletops and interactive media experiences on product packaging and promotional items. With compare to other SDKs in performance factor, QualComm supports to build high performance augmented reality applications for mobile devices (low processing power devices). It uses various rendering techniques and new algorithms for image/video rendering to archive this high performance. Some of the features of the SDK include the ability to track 2D planar surfaces, such as standard markers or more sophisticated image markers. QualComm is a free SDK and anyone can use QualComm SDK for building next generation mobile AR applications. Unfortunately it is not an open source SDK. Developers cannot see what happen inside the SDK. This feature will limit the innovative products built on QualComm SDK.

2.2   Existing Mobile Game Engines

We considered three factors for studying existing game engines: 3D performance, extendibility and platform independence.

* 3D performance: For static image-based AR applications, the real-time 3D rendering capability is more vital than other functions.

---

[4]http://www.metaio.com/.
[5]http://developer.qualcomm.com/ar.

• Extendibility: The game engine should be extendable in order for additional functions to be implemented. The availability of an open source framework is a feature we considered.
• Platform independence: The engine can operate across a wide range of mobile phone operating systems without significant porting efforts. C/C++ is the lower-level language of choice because such implementation is more efficient than Java and that majority of the AR libraries are written in C/C++.

There are currently nine popular engines for the mobile platform. They include: Unreal 3[6], Unity3D[7], Torque 3D[8], Bork 3D[9], SIO2[10], Oolong[11], EDGELIB[12], Irrlicht[13] and Shiva (Stonetrip) 3D[14]. However, many game engines are not available as open source and hence did not form part of this study.

The SIO2 game engine is a 3D engine that is written in C and uses Blender in its production pipeline for scene and model creation. It incorporates nearly all the most advanced technologies currently available on portable devices which have been modified and optimized to get the most out of the Apple[15] iPhone and iPod Touch devices. However, this engine is limited by its use of uncommon proprietary model file formats.

Irrlicht is an excellent open source engine that has the support for a wide variety of file formats, and is completely cross-platform, using D3D, OpenGL and its own software renderer. There are also numerous third-party tools that have been created for this engine. However, resources are very limited for developers to set up the Irrlicht game engine on the iPhone platform.

The Oolong game engine is a 3D engine that is written in C++ with good performance and a wide range of supported features. Game titles developed with the engine include Block2, iPunt and Kids vs. Zombies. It is ideal for our high-level game engine structure. More detail is described in Sect. 3.2.

Although there are already several open source mobile 3D game engine options available, our aim is to build a custom game engine that is able to run AR applications well. The game engines mentioned are designed for the general mobile game development context and often do not factor in the restrictive limitations of image based AR (See Table 4.1). For example, if we load a static 3D object that has 30,000 polygons into a common game engine, a frame rate of 40–45 FPS is likely

---

[6]http://www.unrealtechnology.com/.

[7]http://unity3d.com/.

[8]http://www.torquepowered.com/products/torque-3d.

[9]http://bork3d.com/engine.

[10]http://sio2interactive.com/.

[11]http://code.google.com/p/oolongengine/.

[12]http://www.edgelib.com/.

[13]http://irrlicht.sourceforge.net/.

[14]http://www.stonetrip.com/.

[15]http://www.apple.com/iphone/.

Table 4.1 Development requirements for different platforms

	iPhone OS	Android	Symbian
Requirement	iOS 4.1	Android OS 1.6/2.1	Symbian OS V9.x
			S60 third Edition
SDK	Xcode 3.2.3	Android SDK 2.1	S60 third Edition SDK
	iPhone SDK 3.2		
NDK	–	Android NDK r4	–
Test phones	iPhone 3G	Nexus one	Nokia N95, N96
	iPhone 3GS	HTC Magic	
	iPhone 4		
Programming language	Objective C C++	Java, C++	C++

to be attainable but if the same object is loaded into an AR application, the achieved frame rate can only be 6–8 FPS at best. In addition the 3D camera's position in the 3D world is usually fixed or has its paths predefined (constrained mode) in a typical mobile game, but in an AR context the camera is in free movement all the time.

2.3   Existing Mobile AR Games

Mobile phone based augmented reality is become a popular concept in recent years. Based on the mobile augmented reality software development kits which we discussed previously, thousands of Mobile AR applications have been built.

In 2002 the first prominent mobile AR game, ARQuake [8], was developed. ARQuake was an AR version of the famous first-person PC shooter game – Quake [8]. Players would each wear an AR system consisting of a laptop (in a backpack) that had several sensors embedded for position tracking including differential GPS (for orientation) and a camera for marker-based computer vision tracking. In 2004, AR Soccer [9] was the first handheld-based AR game to be released. AR Soccer was a computer vision-based smartphone game. The player was able to kick a virtual ball with his/her real foot into the virtual goalpost. The foot was tracked with the integrated camera on the PDA.

In 2005, Henrysson ported ARToolKit to the Symbian platform and created a collaborative AR Tennis game [5]. With AR Tennis, players would see a virtual tennis court that is superimposed over a piece of paper with the tracking squares on it.

Another AR game that was developed at the same time was the Invisible Train [10]. The goal of this multiplayer game (PDAs connected via Wi-Fi) was to steer a virtual train over a real wooden railroad track. The player was able to interact using the touch screen to adjust the train speed and toggle track switches.

In 2009, Duy [11] discussed the potential uses and limitations of mobile AR games, and presented the Art of Defense (AoD), a cooperative mobile AR game. The AoD AR Board Game combines camera phones with physical game pieces to create a combined physical/virtual game on the tabletop.

Int13[16] released a Mobile AR game called Kweekies, an AR pet game that allows gamers to interact with their virtual pets by using the embedded cameras of their smartphones. In 2010, Japanese advertising agency, Dentsu[17], started an experimental coupon download platform called iButterfly. The free iPhone application allows users to collect coupons, using AR and the device's inbuilt GPS functions. Other mobile AR games include PIT Strategy[18], ARhrrrr Zombies[19], Spacecraft Racing[20], Marbles[21], and Pacman[22].

3   Mobile AR Game Engine

Although different mobile game engines have been used for the development of many mobile games/applications, no AR-based open source option is currently available. To overcome this limitation, we developed MARGE based on several existing AR libraries and game engine components.

3.1   MARGE on Multi Platforms

In order to make our game engine compatible across the widest range of platforms, we developed it to support the three Apple iPhone, Google Android and Symbian operating systems.

There are few vision-based AR applications on the Google Android platform because it is a newer platform, and due to hardware delay issues such as camera calls that are raised through Java's interface. The Native Development Kit (NDK) for Android enables us to improve the performance of Android-based AR applications. NDK contains tools that can tap into the native libraries that have been built using $C/C++$ sources. This provides the reusability of existing $C/C++$ codes and offers improved performance for specific applications. Using a combined J2ME library and ARToolkit to build our Android AR toolkit, a frame rate of 8 FPS on the HTC Magic (Android OS 1.5) can be achieved. However, since there is no hardware acceleration support in HTC Magic for rendering 3D graphics, its 3D performance (using OpenGL ES 1.0) is very much inferior to the Apple iPhone 3GS/4.

---

[16]http://www.int13.net/en/.

[17]http://www.dentsu.com/.

[18]http://arnewsroom.com/arnews/.

[19]http://www.augmentedenvironments.org.

[20]http://www.genckolik.org/.

[21]http://www.augmentedrealityarena.com/archives/481.

[22]http://www.gizmag.com/go/3512/.

The Apple iPhone Operating System (OS) is one of the most popular mobile OS available. We used the iPhone 4 (iOS 4.1) as the development platform and built its higher level structure by incorporating several selected functions from oOlong. The lower level layer is formed using the ARToolkit tracking library (ARToolkit v4.4.2) that has been ported over to the iPhone , but it relies on functional parts from the higher level game engine counterpart and the OpenGL ES graphics (1.1 and 2.0) library in order to complete its mobile AR application workflow.

MARGE was originally designed to run on the Symbian S60 platforms. The lower-level AR library we used for this particular implementation is the STB-Tracker. However, the STBTracker library became inaccessible to us so our next step would be to enable our code to be executable on the Maemo[23] operating system by using ARToolkit. Table 4.1 shows the requirements of the development tools for the various platforms.

3.2   System Structure of MARGE

As mentioned, MARGE includes two levels of structure. At the lower level, AR-Toolkit performs image processing and tracking functions, and conveys information to the higher level game engine. The higher level game engine combines AR technology together with game functionalities and features. MARGE's AR library support is not limited to ARToolkit only, as different AR libraries can be loaded as well. However, only ARToolkit is currently free for use to us.

At the higher level, MARGE offers two different traits, functionalities and features, both in the game context. In Fig. 4.1, all of the components in MARGE are listed. We will describe each component in more detail in the next three sub-sections.

3.3   AR Library and Bridge Functions of MARGE

The ARToolkit Library[24]: We used v4.4.2 of the ARToolkit for our development which was first released by ARToolworks in 2009. This is the first fully-featured AR framework that supports native operations on various platforms. ARToolKit's basic tracking works as follows:

- The camera captures a live video feed of the real world and sends it to the phone.
- Algorithms on the phone searches through each video frame for any square shapes.

---

[23]http://maemo.org/.
[24]http://www.artoolworks.com/Home.html.

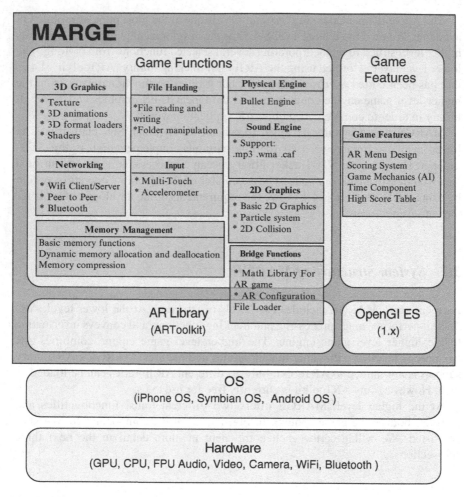

Fig. 4.1 System structure of MARGE

- If a square is found, ARToolKit calculates the position of the camera relative to the black square.
- Once the position of the camera is known, a 3D model is drawn from that same position.
- This model is drawn on top of the video of the real world and so appears stuck on the square marker.

The final output is shown back in the phone's screen, so the user sees virtual graphics overlaid on the real world.

The most difficult portion for AR libraries operating across the different phones is the low level API calls to obtain raw video data from the camera, as different firmware makes use of different ways to call the camera functions. For example, the iPhone OS 3.x uses PLCameraController to obtain the video frame, which is different for calling camera in its OS 2.x. The AR library adds the PLCameraController's previewView function to the preview window in order to solve a camera call problem on the iPhone.

In the Android OS, raw video data from the camera is obtained by registering a PreviewCallBackListener on the camera activity. The raw video data (in YUV420sp format) becomes accessible to the programmer in the call back function whenever it is available. In order for ARToolkit to work with the video frame, a YUV2RGB converter should be in place to decode the real time video frame to RGB888 format for image processing.

Supplementary Math Library: Although ARToolkit has many math functions for AR applications, they are insufficient as full game features. So we built several supplementary math functions that can be used to enhance the interaction possibilities between users and virtual objects. For example: we rewrote the "gluUnProject" transformation function to convert the mobile phone screen coordinates to OpenGL coordinates. This means that users are able to use the multi-touch screen to translate the tracked positions of a user's finger input in a corresponding 3D coordinate (x, y, z) in the OpenGL environment. The other function that was included in our game engine is the provision of distance information between the camera and marker. We read several relevant parameters of the marker's pose from the matrix belonging to the lower level AR library, and then insert the parameter to our math function to calculate the distance:

```
#define LENGTH(v) (sqrt(v[0]*v[0] + v[1]*v[1] + v[2]*v[2]))
ARdouble position[3], distance;
position[0] = pose[0][3];
position[1] = pose[1][3];
position[2] = pose[2][3];
distance = LENGTH(position);
```

AR Configuration File Loader: In order to allow the user to be able to change the AR tracking patterns and 3D objects without changing the original code, we also included external file support to enable the loading of the custom patterns and 3D objects. Users simply need to copy the respective pattern and 3D object files to the required folder and update the relevant file names in the predefined configuration file, loadConfig.txt, by using any text editor. This function enables users to create and load their custom 3D characters into the AR application.

3.4 Game Functions of MARGE

Here we describe the MARGE functions that we created to produce better AR game performance than other platforms. MARGE typically provides a sustained frame rate of 15–20 FPS on the iPhone platform.

3.4.1 3D Graphic Performance Optimization

In this section we will discuss the 3D graphics optimizations on the Apple iPhone 3GS that significantly improves performance. The most important task for us when developing MARGE was to look for functions that could be optimized. They should be ideal for operating on less powerful processors without a significant tradeoff on efficiency. The performance of processing 3D scenes and objects in a game environment is a vital factor that affects the efficiency of a game engine. Mobile AR processing is more demanding than that of a typical mobile game engine. Low-level AR libraries consume much of the available mobile processor power for calculations, which makes it a challenge when selecting an appropriate algorithm to draw the higher-level aspects.

The loading and handling of resources is a complex part of a 3D engine. Numerous decisions have to be made about which file formats to support, how the files should be created and manipulated, the organization of data in these files and memory management issues pertaining to data that is loaded into the application's memory. In a mobile game, objects are generally divided into two types, dynamic and static objects. Static objects are those that do not undergo any form of geometry shape or positional changes, while dynamic ones refer to those that may change their relative positions and/or geometry shapes. Different techniques are applied to render the two object types.

POD format loader: Firstly, we created a dynamic object loader for use with the OpenGL ES 3D graphics library. On the Apple iPhone, OpenGL ES runs on the embedded PowerVR hardware. Imagination Technologies[25] released a supplementary API to allow developers to take advantage of the PowerVR hardware. The model format for PowerVR is the POD format which supports node animations and bone animations. Animations are exported from 3DS MAX to POD files and the animation data for positioning, rotating and scaling is stored in each node that is animated within the scene file. The POD scene file's loading performance in an AR environment is able to achieve a frame rate of 18–22 FPS while drawing an animated object consisting of 3,800 polygons on the Apple iPhone 4.

To support the loading of more complicated static 3D models, we developed two additional functions. One loads the 3DS format and the other loads the OBJ format. These two formats are very widely used in standard commercial 3D packages such as Autodesk's 3DS MAX and Maya. These loaders can only load static models.

3DS Format loader: MARGE uses Lib3ds as the 3DS loader library and a wrapper class is written in order to use this library in the game engine. Lib3ds is a free library for handling 3DS files. It supports modules for vector, quaternion, and matrix mathematics, all of which have simple data structures that allow the easy manipulation of 3D object data. This makes it ideal for the AR game engine.

---

[25] http://www.imgtec.com/.

OBJ format loader (Kagamine Rin)   POD format loader (Rohan)
        (116844 polygons 8 FPS)   (3842 polygons 18 FPS)

Fig. 4.2 Static and dynamic format loader in MARGE

OBJ Format loader: We wrote a class that can load Wavefront OBJ 3D files and render the contents on the iPhone using OpenGL ES. We chose this file format because it is a simple text-based format that is supported by many 3D packages. However we found that the biggest issue for the OBJ loader is its prolonged loading times and the application is prone to crashing if an overly complex object is loaded. This is due to the fact that there is too much auxiliary information in the OBJ file format that may be too intensive for loading on the phone. We are still looking ways to improve this loader. Its performance can attain a frame rate of 8 FPS with 116844 polygons (Fig. 4.2).

Shader: OpenGL ES 2.0 supports high level programmable shaders in the form of vertex and fragment shaders. oOlong features supports the creation of a custom vertex shader that can generate or modify any vertex attributes such as position, color or texture coordinates, and fragment shaders that operate on individual fragments. We included this feature in our engine as an adopted function from the oOlong engine.

3.4.2   Network Features of MARGE

Networking support is an essential feature for a complete Mobile AR gaming experience. This is also included in our game engine and is demonstrated it through a remote AR table fighting game prototype. Wireless networking is necessary for communication between other users and systems while on the move, as defined in [12].

We designed two main structures for our network functions, a client-server architecture and a peer-to-peer architecture. In the client-server architecture, a computer server hosts the game and is assumed to have known addresses so that the clients may conveniently connect to the server with a pre-configured IP address. Players' interactions and messages are sent from mobile clients to the server as they are generated. The server processes game state messages to facilitate decision-making processes. It then sends the connected clients (two clients in this case) the update to their current game state. With a peer-to-peer model, each user would also have to simulate the position of the other user's virtual character, since it is no longer able to rely on a central server. We will explain the peer-to-peer model in details.

Socket Class Hierarchy: Given a peer-to-peer architecture, each peer should be capable of initiating and hosting a game for some other peer to join, or joining an existing game. Each peer would be able to function as a client (where it joins an existing game) or as a host (where it creates a game waits for another player).

Initialisation of the network communication of a peer differs slightly depending on if the peer is a host or a client. For instance, a peer hosting a game has to listen for an incoming connection whereas a peer joining a game need not listen for anything. Therefore, each peer has two types of sockets available to it: the server socket and the client socket.

The server socket and the client socket shares a common interface known as the SuperSocket. The SuperSocket consists of methods that are common to both the sockets. It also consists of a series of methods whose implementation is provided by the subclasses. For instance, the send, recv, and isOffline methods need to be implemented by the subclass as it is dependent on how the socket is structured.

Mutual discovery: Without the presence of a central server with a known address, the discovering of a peer's IP address becomes an issue. We solve this by allowing a mobile client to act as a game host and by revealing its IP address in the GUI. The second player can then connect to this game by entering the IP address of the host peer.

The disadvantage of our current approach is that both players need to have a communication channel outside of the game to communicate this IP address. It is not possible for two players to join each other just within the game without having to exchange IP addresses verbally or other such means. However, this is not a pressing problem as it is possible to create some kind of directory service where players advertise their IP address. The game can then retrieve the available games by querying this directory.

Performance: The network connection between the two players can be interrupted at any time. Once the connection is lost, we replace the lost player with AI so that game is able to continue. To achieve robustness, we maintain a flag to indicate the connection status. During each simulation step, we check the state of the socket and set the flag immediately when a disconnection is detected. We rely on the state of the TCP socket to know whether a disconnection has occurred and do not use any explicit heartbeat messages.

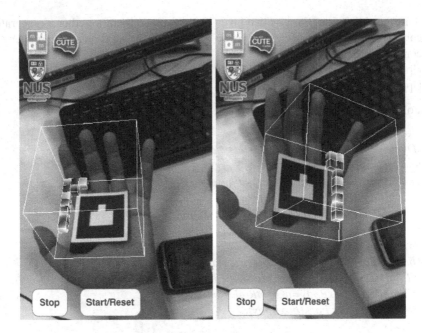

Fig. 4.3 "Falling cubes" with the physics engine support

3.4.3 Physics Engine

MARGE uses Bullet Physics[26] for 3D physics simulation. Bullet Physics is a library that supports 3D collision detection, soft body and rigid body dynamics and is available as open source. We created a simple application using this physics library (see Fig. 4.3) by combining physics and collision in an AR environment. A white wire mesh box serves as the bounding volume of the contained smaller color boxes. Ten colored boxes are set up to fall from a top-down orientation. Then, when the user tilts the marker, the color boxes are cascaded and the moving direction of the boxes is simulated by the gravity of the physical engine. The boxes can collide with each other as well. We calculate the angle between camera and the marker by using supplementary math library (mention in Sect. 3.3) to simulate the effect of tilting marker. The application's achieved frame rate is between 15 FPS and 18 FPS in iPhone 4. The logic for this application is as follows:

- Set up a dynamic physic world
- Create six planes for walls.
- Create 10 boxes and add Rigid Body for the boxes
- Calculate the distance between marker and camera
- Calculate the angle between marker and camera

---

[26]http://bulletphysics.org/wordpress.

- Start the simulation. For any two given boxes, collide them together to generate contact points. Returns 0 if there is no contact, otherwise return the number of contacts generated
- Update the angles
- Update the gravity of color boxes.

Part of code is showing below:

```
sDynamicsWorld = new btDiscreteDynamicsWorld
for (int i=0;i<6;i++)
{worldBoxShape->getPlaneEquation(planeEq,i);
btCollisionShape* groundShape =
new btStaticPlaneShape(-planeEq,planeEq[3]);
}
for (int i=0;i<10;i++)
{btRigidBody::btRigidBodyConstructionInfo
rbInfo(mass,myMotionState,boxShape,localInertia);
btRigidBody* boxBody=new btRigidBody(rbInfo);
sBoxBodies.push_back(boxBody);
}
sDynamicsWorld->
setGravity(btVector3(AccelerometerVector[0]*scaling,
AccelerometerVector[1]*scaling,AccelerometerVector[2]*scaling));
sDynamicsWorld->stepSimulation(frameRate, 2);
```

3.4.4 Input

MARGE provides Sensor Reading and Multi-touch functionalities for interaction in AR games:

Sensor Reading: The accelerometer is used in our game engine to enhance game interactivity. The iPhone's in-built accelerometer is a three–axis device that it is capable of detecting either movement or the gravitational forces in three-dimensional space. In the AR game, Pan Master (Sect. 5), the accelerometer is used to detect shakes in order to enhance the interaction experience between player and the game's 3D virtual pan.

Multi-touch: The term "touch" refers to a finger being placed on the iPhone's screen. The iPhone supports multi-touch interactions in that multiple simultaneous input is possible (i.e. several fingers on the screen at the same time). We also use the multi-touch feature in our game of Pan Master to allow the player to interactively "stir" the ingredients in the virtual pan on the screen as with the stirring action in a real cooking process.

3.4.5 Other Functions

In this section, we listed several other important incorporated features of the Mobile AR Game Engine:

Sound engine: There are generally two purposes for playing a sound in a game application, to serve as background music, and to serve as sound effects. Sound effect files tend to be short, ranging from 1 to 10 s long and do not take up much memory, partly because their sound quality can be lower than that of background music tracks. For our application, we included sound effects to correspond to gaming tasks in our Pan Master game and AR Fighter game. However, as music files tend to be relatively longer in duration and larger in file sizes, they are usually compressed to reduce their file sizes. Unfortunately, that will also mean that such files will need to be uncompressed whenever playback is required and this step would require additional CPU usage. Since it is unlikely that multiple files will be played at any one time, this constraint is still manageable. MARGE supports the .mp3 .caf and .wav file formats.

2D Graphics: We will skip many of the basic 2D functions in the game engine such as 2D image display, drawing text, drawing primitives and image rotation and scaling etc, because the emphasis is on the presentation of 3D objects. Only two functions which are used in our AR game are marked as important 2D Graphics features; 2D bounding boxes and particle systems.

MARGE supports 2D bounding box collision detection. It compares two rectangles for any intersection by attempting to detect whether two rectangular volumes are in any way touching or overlapping with each other. The rectangles to be tested for overlapping are the vertical and horizontal extents of the two images that the collision detection is to be performed on. This feature is used in our AR game "Pan Master" (see Sect. 5) to detect whether two scallops are colliding with each other in a 2D mode. This feature can be a game enhancement feature.

Integrated as part of the 2D graphic module of MARGE, the particle system is simply a group or groups of sprites that float about in virtual space. However, for each particle instance, not only the geometry, position, and orientation are tracked, but also the velocity, life span and animation speed as well. The original code originates from the Oolong engine and is ported into AR. In our particle system demo, a 600-point sprite setup achieved a frame rate of approximately 19 FPS. (See Fig. 4.4).

In order to extend more functionality in our mobile AR game engine. We build a mobile AR video player by using FFmpeg library and 2D graphic module. FFmpeg library is a cross-platform solution to record, convert and stream audio and video. We developed a video player API which can play videos in the AR environment. It can support wma, mov, mp4, mov, 3gpp, etc. Streaming video is also supported in the MARGE. The performance can be reach 14 FPS with a video resolution of 320*240. (See Fig. 4.5).

Fig. 4.4 Particle system (*left*) and mobile AR video player (*right*)

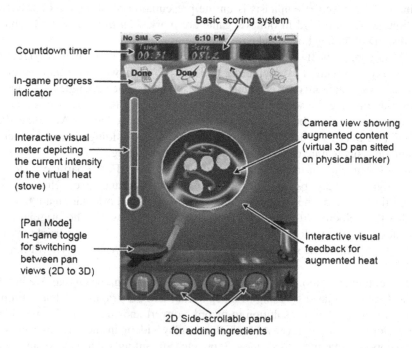

Fig. 4.5 Main user interface of mobile AR cooking game with hybrid 2D/3D elements

File Handling and Memory Management: File handling and Memory Management are adopted functions from the oOlong engine. The file module provides a way to access the file systems across different devices. Files can be opened, closed, created, read and written. The contents of a file folder (directory) can be read by opening them using the file module. This is used in the function of the AR configuration loader. Folders can also be created, renamed and deleted. Memory can be allocated and released dynamically through the memory module. It is allocated dynamically when attempting to store large amounts of game data.

4 Evaluation

There is no general standard to evaluate a game engine. As mentioned in Sect. 1, the purpose of MARGE is to create a game engine can combines AR technology with existing mobile game development contexts. We built our functions to fulfill the requirements of AR and optimize the overall performance. Since MARGE is intentionally designed for mobile platforms, three important features are considered across its design inception: extendibility, portability and 3D performance issues. Extendibility indicates that the game engine can add and/or remove functions easily. Comparing with Torque and EDGELIB, MARGE is open source that will allow developers to easily include their own functions. MARGE is written in C++ and uses many standard functions of the language that can be easily ported to support other platforms, with better portability than SIO2 for the iPhone platform. Currently MARGE supports three main mobile platforms (iPhone, Android, Symbian). While SIO2 is limited to using the Blender format in its 3D content creation workflow, MARGE supports the popular 3D packages, 3ds Max and Maya. MARGE is not limited to using the ARToolkit tracking – it can be extended to any other AR libraries by loading the respective APIs. MARGE has network capability which is an added advantage over Irrlicht.

Few AR applications currently have networking support. However, it is included in our engine to demonstrate its potential for collaborative mobile AR games. From (Table 4.2), it is clear that MARGE has an identifiable advantage by the exclusive incorporation of an AR library. It is a big challenge for developers to create AR applications on mobile phones with satisfactory 3D performance. We have also undertaken several approaches to improve the 3D performance of MARGE including the optimization of codes/3D model loaders and using simpler algorithms. In the next subsection, an experiment to test our 3D model loaders for the 3D performance optimization of MARGE is described. We compared MARGE with other game engines in Table 4.2.

5 Applications

In this section, we will describe two applications based on our mobile AR game engine.

Table 4.2 Comparison MARGE with other game engines

Mobile game engine	MARGE	EDGELIB	SIO2	Irrlicht	Torque
Multi-platform					
Apple iPhone	Yes	Yes	Yes	Yes	Yes
Windows Mobile 6	No	Yes	No	Yes	Yes
Google Android (2.0)	Yes	Yes	No	No	No
Symbian	Yes	Yes	No	Yes	No
Open source	Yes	No	Yes	Yes	No
Language	C++	C++	C	C++	C++
3D graphics					
3D animations	Yes	Yes	Yes	Yes	Yes
Texture support	.pvr .bmp, .png, .jpg, .tga, .gif, .jpe, .jfi, .tpic.	.bmp .png .jpg .tga .gif	.SIO2	.bmp .png .psd .jpg .tga .pcx	.jpg, .tga
3D format loaders	.pod .obj .3ds	.3ds .ms3d	blender	.obj .3ds .dae .b3d .ms3d .bsp .md2 .X	.dts .dif
Networking					
Client/server	Yes	Yes	No	No	Yes
P2P	Yes	No	No	No	Yes
Bluetooth	No	Yes	No	No	No
AR features					
AR library support	Yes	No	No	No	No
Supplemental math library	Yes	No	No	No	No
AR configuration file loader	Yes	No	No	No	No

5.1 *"Pan Master"*

"Pan Master" (see Fig. 4.6) is a game that allows players to enjoy the process of cooking, using a pan as the main mode of cooking. One of the key features of the AR technology is that the system is able to detect the distance between objects (e.g. fiducial markers) and the device (camera), and then provide a spatial/real sense of physical space to the users.

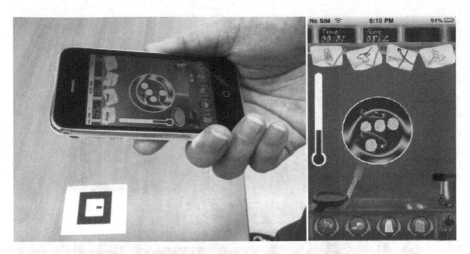

Fig. 4.6 Virtual 3D pan on a physical AR marker

The basic game mechanism of the game is such that the player needs to follow the sequential indications to finish several cooking steps within the stipulated time limit in order to induce game progress to advance to the next stage (see Fig. 4.5).

The heating control of the pan, and the cooking time are two essential factors which will affect the cooking process. Players can control the heating through adjusting the physical distance of the mobile device (camera) to the marker. It means that, the distance and time can be integrated to provide a more real cooking experience to player. The player enjoyment and engagement will be enhanced through integrating these two factors – physical distance and the timing.

Despite the migration of AR interfaces to mobile phones, there has been little research on proper interface guidelines and effective visualization techniques for mobile phone AR and almost no formal usability studies have been conducted [13, 14]. The main problems are the development of appropriate visual presentation designs and the implementations of suitable interaction mechanisms as these tend to differ quite significantly from desktop Graphic User Interface design [15].

"Pan Master" was conceived and developed in parallel during the initial development of the MARGE. In designing the user interface for "Pan Master", several important design considerations were factored and subsequently established as standard user interface features that enabled MARGE to be able to comprehensively provide and support. One of the key considerations was to address the four input options for mobile interaction techniques that [16] identified as "keypad input, tangible input, phone tilting detected through computer vision and gesture input from a camera in front of the phone".

In "Pan Master", user actions performed in the form of gaming tasks in 2D space (i.e. via on-screen interface elements) and accompanying tangible input (i.e. mobile phone's inbuilt accelerometer that detects tilts and shakes) are interlinked to

Fig. 4.7 Characters are fighting

associated game elements that completely reside in 3D space (i.e. virtual 3D pan with supporting visual elements that are registered onto a physical AR marker) and corresponding visual feedback is then delivered accordingly on the mobile phone screen. This integrated feedback is bi-directional ("2D to 3D" as well as "3D to 2D") and interface elements are domain-transferable (i.e. toggling a virtual pan between 2D and 3D modes of presentation with accompanying interaction and interface sets that appear in respective correspondence), thereby creating a continuous and unbroken interaction flow. This follows the concept of "Continuous Natural User Interface" in [17] in a task-focused domain approach (fulfilling the requirement of an AR user interface's specification of showing only information that is needed to solve the current task) in [18].

Future work will feature the incorporation of networking support to create a collaborative virtual cooking interaction for a better gaming experience.

5.2 "AR Fighter"

"AR Fighter" is a remote AR fighting table/card game (see Fig. 4.7) we developed for the Apple iPhone platform. The concept is derived from existing game titles

"Street Fighters"[27]. and "Eye of Judgment"[28]. The idea is combines mobile AR game with a common game. In the AR part, two users use different markers to virtually "fight" each other. The mobile networking feature is added to this game to allow connected users to fight each other through the use of a common virtual object. A particle system is used to enhance the visual effects and a physics engine plays the essential role of detecting the collision of two virtual objects. User can download new model via our Mac server.

The basic structure of our mobile AR game consists of two mobile phones that use a WiFi connection to link to each other for the AR game to be played. One phone acts as the server and the other acts as the client. We also established a server application in a Macintosh computer that acts as the server to manipulate and update the in- game models and to maintain high score tracking for the phone devices. When the iPhone application is started, it will check for the availability of updated models that a user may use and also list the high scores table.

The network connection between the two players can be interrupted at any time. Once the connection is lost, we replace the lost player with AI so that game is able to continue. To achieve robustness, we maintain a flag to indicate the connection status. During each simulation step, we check the state of the socket and set the flag immediately when a disconnected is detected. We rely on the state of the TCP socket to know whether a disconnection has occurred and do not use any explicit heartbeat messages. The performance of Mobile AR Fighter game with the network support can reach 14–17 FPS.

At the starting page, users need to determine if the mobile device will play as the host or as the client. They can then choose the character/avatar and arena as well as to see an overview of the opponent's avatar (see Fig. 4.8). Users can rotate the 3D avatar in the character viewport the choosing page by a finger swipe gesture across the screen of the mobile device.

In the AR interface, the accelerometer is used in our game to enhance game interactivity. The iPhones in-built accelerometer is a three axis device that it is capable of detecting either movement or the gravitational forces in three-dimensional space. User can tilt the phone to make the avatar move in the respective corresponding direction. We also used the multi-touch feature of the mobile phone in our game to allow players to control the virtual avatar. For example, a double tap makes the avatar move towards the corresponding point of the tap while a single tap is to initiate an attack move. The vibration function is used whenever a virtual avatar is hit.

---

[27] http://www.streetfighter.com/.
[28] http://www.eyeofjudgment.com/.

Fig. 4.8 Choosing the character

6 Conclusion

This chapter describes the development of an AR game engine for mobile phones. We introduced the structure and component constituents of MARGE. An evaluation is carried out by comparing MARGE with other game engines and establishing the efficiency of the different 3D model loaders in MARGE. We emphasized performance, portability and extendibility and compared them to some of the most current game engines -. Finally we also described several mobile AR games based on MARGE.

Future work will cover improvements in three areas:

- Wider range of supported platforms. The game will be playable across extended mobile platforms as a cross platform game.
- Improved performance of Android-based applications. We will attempt to enhance the real-time 3D performance on Google Android phones.
- Add Addition of more features for the AR Fighter and Pan Master applications. For "AR Fighter", the game is currently designed only for two players. We aim to extend our networking feature to include additional player support within the network. Physics engine also can be added the to the "AR fighter".
- Lighting sensitivity/condition is a common issue for AR applications. The relatively new Apple iPhone 4 features an embedded LED flash/bulb near its

camera lens. We plan to use the camera API to control this strong flashlight to reduce the effects of external lighting conditions (resulting in possible over or under exposures in image captures) so as to preserve a consistent user experience by preventing disruptions in interaction flows.

- Combining natural feature tracking with a faster AR library and then extending it as a cross platform Mobile AR SDK.

Acknowledgements The initiative is supported by the Singapore National Research Foundation (NRF-2008-IDM-001-MOE-016) and the National University of Singapore (R-263-000-488-112). We specially thank Dr. Mark Billinghurst to help us acquiring ARToolKit commercial version for our work. Also thanks to Raymond Koon Chuan Koh to give us comments in the early draft and Yuanxun Gus help for implementing networking features.

References

1. A. Phillips, Games in AR: Types and technologies, In proceedings of the IEEE International Symposium on Mixed and Augmented Reality 2009 (ISMAR 2009), 2009
2. H. Kato, and M. Billinghurst, Marker Tracking and HMD Calibration for a Video-Based Augmented Reality Conferencing System. In proceedings of the 2nd IEEE and ACM International Workshop on Augmented Reality, IEEE Computer Society, 1999
3. D. Wagner, D. Schmalstieg, ARToolKit on the PocketPC platform Augmented Reality Toolkit Workshop IEEE International 2003.
4. M. Moehring, C. Lessig, and O. Bimber, Video See-Through AR on Consumer Cell Phones, In proceedings of the third IEEE and ACM International Symposium on Mixed and Augmented Reality (ISMAR 2004), pp. 252–253, 2004
5. A. Henrysson, M. Billinghurst, M. Ollila, Face to Face Collaborative AR on Mobile Phones, In proceedings of the fourth IEEE and ACM International Symposium on Mixed and Augmented Reality (ISMAR 2005), 2005.
6. D. Wagner, Handheld Augmented Reality, PHD thesis, Graz University of Technology, 2007.
7. J. Gu, R. Mukundan, M. Billinghurst, 2008. Developing mobile phone AR applications using J2ME. In proceedings of IEEE Image and Vision Computing New Zealand, (IVCNZ 2008), 2008
8. W. Piekarski and B. Thomas, ARQuake: The Outdoor Augmented Reality Gaming System, In Communications of the ACM (Commun. ACM), vol. 45, no. 1, pp. 36–38. 2002.
9. C. Reimann, V. Paelke, and D. Stichling, "Foot-Based Mobile Interaction with Games," Proc. ACM SIGCHI Int'l Conf. Advances Computer Entertainment Technology (ACE 04), vol. 74, ACM Press, pp. 321–324. 2004.
10. D. Wagner, T. Pintaric, D. Schmalstieg, The invisible train: a collaborative handheld augmented reality demonstrator In proceeding of International Conference on Computer Graphics and Interactive Techniques archive ACM SIGGRAPH 2004 Emerging technologies, 2004.
11. N. Duy, K. Raveendran, Y. Xu, etc Art of defense: a collaborative handheld augmented reality board game Mixed and Augmented Reality, In proceedings of 8th IEEE International Symposium (ISMAR 2009), pages: 135–142. 2009
12. C. Huang, A. Harwood, S. Karunasekera, Directions for Peer-to-Peer based mobile pervasive augmented reality gaming Parallel and Distributed Systems, International Conference on, vol. 2, pp. 1-8, in proceedings of 13th International Conference on Parallel and Distributed Systems – Volume 2 (ICPADS 2007), 2007.
13. M. Bell, M. Chalmers and L. Barkhuus etc, Interweaving Mobile Games with Everyday Life, In proceedings of SIGCHI Conf. Human Factors in Computing Systems (CHI 06), ACM Press pp. 417–426. 2006

14. A. Henrysson, J. Marshall, and M. Billinghurst, Experiments in 3D interaction for mobile phone AR. In proceedings of the 5th international Conference on Computer Graphics and Interactive Techniques in Australia and Southeast Asia. (GRAPHITE 2007). ACM, New York, NY, 187–194. 2007
15. F. Zhou, H.B.L. Duh and M. Billinghurst, 2008. Trends in augmented reality tracking, interaction and display: A review of ten years of ISMAR. In proceedings of the 7th IEEE/ACM International Symposium on Mixed and Augmented Reality (ISMAR 2008), pp. 193–202. 2008
16. V. Paelke, J. Stocklein, C. Reimann, W. Rosenbach, Supporting user interface evaluation of AR presentation and interaction techniques with ARToolkit. Augmented Reality Toolkit Workshop IEEE International. vol., no., pp. 35–41. 2003
17. N. Petersen, D. Stricker, Continuous natural user interface: Reducing the gap between real and digital world. In proceedings of the 8th IEEE International Symposium on Mixed and Augmented Reality (ISMAR 2009). on, vol., no., pp.23–26. 2009.
18. A. Vitzthum, SSIML/AR: A Visual Language for the Abstract Specification of Augmented Reality User Interfaces. In proceedings 3D User Interfaces,. (3DUI 2006). IEEE Symposium on, vol., no., pp. 135–142, 25–29. 2006

Chapter 5
Head-Mounted Projection Display Technology and Applications

Hong Hua, Leonard D. Brown, and Rui Zhang

Abstract Recent advances in microelectronics and the rapid growth of digital information have led to exciting new display technologies which are suitable to a wide variety of application domains. Head-mounted projection display (HMPD) has been actively developed in the recent decade as an alternative to conventional eyepiece-type head-mounted displays. HMPD replaces the eyepiece-type optics with a projection lens and employs a retroreflective screen instead of the diffusing screens typical to standalone projection-based systems. This unique combination of projection and retroreflection gives HMPD technology several remarkable advantages that make it suitable for collaborative visualization and augmented reality applications. In this chapter, we will review the fundamentals of HMPD technology and outline design considerations relating to the human visual system. We will summarize recent technological advancements, including efforts to improve the field of view and enhance image brightness. We will examine the significance of the retroreflective materials and their effects on imaging resolution and user perception. Finally, we will discuss a variety of application directions and user interface capabilities that have been enabled through HMPD technology.

1 Introduction

The increased bandwidth of wireless networks, rapid expansion of digital information, and expansion of electronics and sensing technologies have stimulated the development of display solutions suitable for a wide variety of application domains. Among a wide range of display technologies developed in the past decades, head-mounted display (HMD) technology, also known as head-worn display, refers to a device that is typically attached in close proximity to the eyes

H. Hua (✉)
College of Optical Sciences, The University of Arizona, Tucson, Arizona, USA
e-mail: hhua@optics.arizona.edu

B. Furht (ed.), *Handbook of Augmented Reality*, DOI 10.1007/978-1-4614-0064-6_5,   123
© Springer Science+Business Media, LLC 2011

and requires an optical system to couple a miniature image source with the human visual system. Within military applications the acronym HMD has also been used to refer to helmet-mounted displays where the display is attached to a military helmet. HMD technology has become critical for many applications, spanning the fields of flight simulation, scientific visualization, medicine, engineering design and prototyping, education and training, tele-manipulation and tele-presence, wearable computing, and entertainment systems. For instance, in the domain of augmented reality [1], see-through HMDs are one of the enabling technologies for merging virtual views with physical scenes, which may enable a physician to see the 3D rendering of the anatomical structures or CT images of a patient superimposed onto the patient's abdomen [6].

In the fields of virtual reality and augmented reality, HMDs may be categorized into immersive and see-through displays. An immersive display immerses a user in a solely computer-generated virtual environment, while a see-through display blends real and computer-generated scenes either through a video-mixing approach or an optical combiner approach. A video see-through display blocks the direct view of the physical world and electronically fuses the view of a computer-generated virtual environment with the view of the real-world captured via one or two miniature video cameras mounted on the headgear. The core display optics of video see-through displays is similar to that of immersive displays. The resolution of the real-world view is limited by the resolution of video cameras. An optical see-through display, on the other hand, maintains the direct view of the real world and uses an optical combiner to superimpose a computer-generated virtual scene onto the real scene. The optical see-through approach allows a user to see the real world with full resolution and is less intrusive into the user's view of the real scene than the video see-through approach [50]. Therefore, it is a preferred method for tasks where hand-eye coordination or an unblocked view of the real world is critical. Both types of see-through displays have been applied in various augmented applications, from medical training to entertainment [1].

Since the pioneering work by Ivan Sutherland who demonstrated the first graphically-driven optical see-through HMD in the 1960s [57], researchers have made great advances in HMD designs with the advancement of optical technology, improvements on microdisplays, and miniaturization of electronics. The optical systems for near-eye displays fall into three broad design forms: eyepiece/magnifier type, objective-eyepiece compound magnifier type, and projection type. Although these design forms are well understood by optical designers, designing wide field-of-view (FOV), lightweight, compact, and high-performance optical see-through HMD systems continues to be a major challenge and pursuit for HMD developers. Over the past decades, different approaches have been applied to the optical design of HMD systems to improve one or several aspects of the HMD system performance. These methods include applying a catadioptric technique [11], introducing tilt and decenters to rotationally symmetric systems [49], and capitalizing on emerging optical technologies that are becoming more readily available such as aspheric surfaces, diffractive, optical element, holographic optical elements (HOE), and freeform technologies [8, 25, 32]. Comprehensive reviews on the advancements of HMD optics can be found in Rolland and Hua [53] and Cakmakci and Rolland [7].

Besides advancements in optical design methods, new display concepts have been explored. Head-mounted projection display technology (HMPD) is a new HMD concept which has been actively developed in the recent decade as an alternative optical design form to conventional eyepiece-based designs. HMPD technology has been explored for a wide range of augmented reality applications. This chapter will review the fundamentals of HMPD technology in Sect. 2, continue with a summary of technological developments in Sect. 3, discuss issues and studies related to image resolution and user perception in Sect. 4, and describe application examples in Sect. 5.

2 Fundamentals of Head-Mounted Projection Displays

Similar to a conventional HMD system, a head-mounted projection display (HMPD) integrates a pair of optical systems and microdisplays along with their drive electronics into a head-worn system. The positioning of the system with respect to the head of a user and the interface of the display optics with the eyes impose tight requirements on the overall system design. This Section will review the HMPD concept and the characteristics of the technology with respect to other related technologies, summarize the state-of-the-art in microdisplay technology, and discuss the interface requirements between the human visual system and HMPD optics.

2.1 Concept

Head mounted projection display technology, pioneered by Kijima and Hirose [35], Fisher [14], and Fergason [13], deviates from the conventional approaches to HMD designs. Unlike a conventional optical see-through HMD, an HMPD replaces eyepiece-type or objective-eyepiece compound type optics with a projection lens. Unlike a conventional projection system which employs a diffusing screen to reflect projected light toward a user's eyes, an HMPD utilizes a retroreflective screen instead.

As illustrated in Fig. 5.1, a monocular configuration of an HMPD consists of an image source (typically a miniature display), a projection lens, a beamsplitter combiner, and a retroreflective screen. The components and distances are not drawn to scale in the figure to allow for illustration of the entire system. The projected image is at least 250 mm away from the eyes to allow the user to accommodate properly. An image on the miniature display, which is located beyond the focal point of the projection lens, rather than between the lens and the focal point as in a conventional HMD, is projected through the lens and thus forms a magnified real image. The beamsplitter, placed after the projection lens and oriented at a 45°

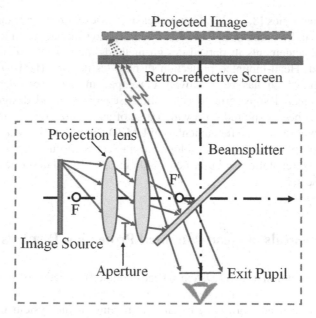

Fig. 5.1 Schematic design of an HMPD in a monocular configuration [25]

angle with respect to the optical axis, reflects the light from the projection lens toward the retroreflective screen which substitutes for a typical diffusing screen in a conventional projection system. The retroreflective screen will then redirect the light back toward the beamsplitter along the opposite direction of the incident rays. The retroreflected light forms the exit pupil of the system through which the eye views the projected image. The exit pupil of the system is located at the conjugate position of the aperture of the projection lens. Typically, the components inside the dotted-line box in Fig. 5.1 are integrated into a head-worn device, while the retro-reflective screen is positioned remotely, away from the user. To facilitate mobility, recent work by Martins et al. [43] demonstrated a design that integrates a screen within a head-worn device.

In a binocular HMPD configuration, the unique combination of projection and retroreflection eliminates the crosstalk between the projected images for the left and right eyes and thus enables stereoscopic and multi-viewing capabilities [18]. Considering its head-worn nature and projection principle, the HMPD technology, therefore, is considered as a technology lying on the boundary between conventional HMDs and CAVE-like projection displays [9].

Compared with conventional eyepiece or objective-eyepiece based HMDs, an HMPD technology can potentially have several advantages [18, 25]. First of all, a projection lens system has a relatively more symmetric lens structure with respect to the system stop position than an eyepiece. As a result, the size, weight and distortion of a projection lens do not scale with the FOV as rapidly as an eyepiece, whereas it is very challenging to design wide FOV, compact and low distortion eyepiece

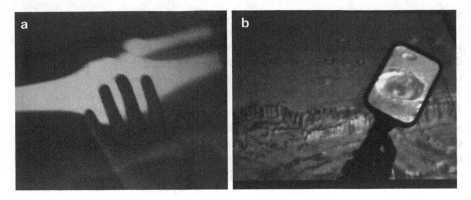

Fig. 5.2 Occlusion cue rendering through an HMPD: (**a**) natural occlusion of a computer-generated object (bone) by a real object (hand) [21]; (**b**) physical hand-held device blocks part of virtual scene (Mars terrain) and is augmented by high-detail view (magnified crater)

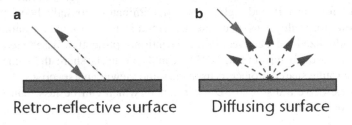

Fig. 5.3 (**a**) Retroreflective screen vs. (**b**) diffusing screen

optics. Second, an optical see-through HMD typically requires a large eye relief, which is the distance from the eye pupil to the center of the last surface of the HMD optics closest to the eye, to allow fitting all types of eyeglasses. In an HMPD system a large eye relief can be achieved by simply adjusting the distance between the projection lens and the beamsplitter without compromising the performance of the projection system. In an eyepiece-based HMD system, however, increasing the eye relief typically results in larger and heavier optics and higher distortion for the same FOV requirement and eventually leads to a compromise on FOV and optical performance. Third, an optical see-through HMPD system is capable of providing intrinsically correct occlusion of computer generated virtual objects by real objects, as demonstrated in Fig. 5.2, while in a conventional OST-HMD the virtual image always floats on the real object, except in the sophisticated occlusion-capable designs [40].

Compared with conventional projection-based stereoscopic systems such as CAVE [9] and 3D cinema projection, an HMPD system has several remarkable advantages due to the nature of retroreflection. Figure 5.3 illustrates the difference between a diffusing screen and a retroreflective screen. A retroreflective surface reflects an incident ray back in the opposite direction, while a diffusing surface spreads an incident ray in all directions. As a result, a retroreflective screen for an HMPD system can be applied to surfaces that do not necessarily coincide with the projected image plane, and can be tailored to non-planar shapes without introducing additional distortion in the virtual images. It is worth noting that, in practice, imperfect retroreflection leads to degradation in the imaging quality when a retroreflective screen is far from the nominal focal distance of the projection optics or results in vignetting-like effects when the screen is significantly curved [63]. A diffusing screen in a conventional projection system, however, needs to be placed at the focal distance of the projection optics, to remain orthogonal with the projection axis, and to be the same shape as that of the projected image plane. Off-axis projection and non-planar projection surfaces can result in warping and blurring effects in the image. Furthermore, a retroreflective screen is much more efficient in reflecting light toward specific view directions than a diffusing screen. As a result, an HMPD system can deliver much brighter images than conventional projection systems with the same luminous input, which makes it possible to miniaturize the projection unit for a wearable binocular system. Finally, a retroreflective screen naturally separates the images for the left and right eyes and eliminates crosstalk between users, which allows for multiple users to interact with a shared virtual environment from their individualized perspectives. In a conventional projection-based stereoscopic system using a diffusing screen, however, multiple users share the same images projected through shared projectors from the same viewing perspectives. As a result, users may perceive a distorted 3D environment which can be less than ideal for collaborative activities.

2.2 Microdisplay

Microdisplays are one of the core elements in HMD systems, including HMPDs, which integrate one or more image sources inside the device. As such, advancements in microdisplay technologies have great impact on HMD development. Historically, miniature cathode ray tubes (CRT) were the sole choice three decades ago, whereas limited resolution active-matrix liquid crystal displays (AM-LCDs) became the predominant technology for HMDs in the 1990s. More recently, a variety of new microdisplay technologies have evolved to become mainstream choices, including high-resolution AMLCDs, liquid-crystal-on-silicon (LCoS) panels, ferroelectric liquid-crystal-on-silicon (FLCoS) displays, and self-emissive organic light-emitting diode (OLED). These microdisplay technologies readily offer pixel resolutions from VGA and SVGA to SXGA and even full high-definition (HD) resolutions. Additionally, laser diodes-based image sources have been employed in scanning displays, which have demonstrated advantages in applications requiring high image brightness. Table 5.1 summarizes the major properties of several microdisplay technologies from major manufacturers.

AMLCD offers a potentially more compact system because its transmissive nature only needs a backlit panel rather than a bulky illumination unit. However,

Table 5.1 A survey of microdisplay technologies

	AM-LCD (backlit)	OLED	LCOS (color filter)	LCOS (color sequential)	FLCoS	Micron®	DLP
Manufacturer	Kopin®	Emagin®	HimaxDisplay	Holoeye®	Forth dimension®	Micron®	Texas instrument®
website	www.kopin.com	www.emagin.com	www.himaxdisplay.com	www.holoeye.com	http://www.forthd.com	www.micron.com	www.dlp.com
Size(diagonal) (inch)	0.97	0.78	0.62	0.55	0.88	0.463	0.95
Resolution (pixel)	1,280 × 1024	1,280 × 1,024	800 × 600	1,280 × 768	1280 × 1024	800 × 600	1920 × 1080
Contrast ratio	300:1	>10,000:1	200:1*	1,000:1	200:1	300:1	>1,000:1 depending on illumination
Pixel size (μm)	15 × 15	12 × 12	15 × 15	9.6 × 9.6	13.4 × 13.4	11.75 × 11.75	10.8
Color method	RGB sub-pixels	RGB sub-pixels	RGB sub-pixels	Color sequential	Color sequential	Color sequential	Color sequential
Color depth (bit)	24	24	N/A	24	24	24	23,148 patterns/s
Frequency (Hz)	60	60 or 85	60	60	60 or 85	60	
Fill factor	N/A	69%	N/A	89%	92%	91.7%	90%
Type of illumination	Backlight	Self-emissive	Front illumination optics				
Optical efficiency	<10% (estimated)*	<10% (estimated)*	<10% (estimated)*	66%	60–70%	62%	60%
Power consumption	200 mW	<180 mW	~200 mW*	N/A	N/A	90 mW	N/A

due to low transmission efficiency, it has a relatively low contrast ratio and yields a low luminance range and relatively narrow view angle. Furthermore, it requires three subpixel cells to form a color display, which leads to large pixel dimensions compared with other available microdisplay technologies.

The self-emission nature of OLED and its compact packaging offer potentially the most compact system design among these technologies, and it provides a good range of luminance. However, the resolution and contrast ratio of existing OLEDs are relatively low compared with FLCoS and LCoS microdisplays, and its life span is shortened when the display luminance is high (e.g. more than 100cd/m^2). Existing OLED microdisplays have relatively small panel size. For HMD designs, smaller panels have the advantage of enabling a more compact system, but often at the cost of a narrower FOV than is possible with a larger panel, because more optical magnification is required to achieve an equivalent FOV with a smaller panel. When the display panel is too small, it requires a shorter focal length and larger magnification to achieve a reasonable FOV, which leads to a challenging design of a low F/# system.

LCoS and FLCoS based microdisplays have an advantage in image brightness and life time over OLEDs. Currently LCoS and FLCoS microdisplays offer high pixel resolution (as high as 1080p), luminance output, optical efficiency, and image contrast. On the other hand, due to their reflective nature, they require a carefully designed illumination unit to illuminate the microdisplay, which makes the overall display system less compact than a system using AMLCD or OLED microdisplays. The LCoS and FLCoS microdisplays work most efficiently when the illumination rays are normally incident upon the display surface. In normal incidence, all the rays experience the same optical path through the liquid crystal material, while skewed incidence leads to a reduction in image contrast. To ensure the high contrast of the output image, it is recommended to limit the incident angle to the range of $\pm 16°$, which imposes a critical requirement on the design of both a light engine and imaging lens. Furthermore, the refresh rate of the liquid crystal used in some LCoS microdisplays may be inadequate to provide a full color display using a single panel with a color sequential method. In this case, either the color depth must be compromised, or multiple display panels must be employed with a bulky illumination system to achieve full color. Alternatively, the fast response speed of ferroelectric liquid crystal makes it possible to achieve a full-color display using a single-panel with a color sequential scheme.

2.3 HMPD Optics and Human Visual System

The human visual system (HVS) is the final core element in an HMPD system. Understanding some of the visual and anatomical properties of the HVS is not only critical for prescribing adequate design requirements for system development, but also for evaluating the performance and usability of a system. This section will briefly summarize these properties and discuss how they are related to the HMPD-HVS interface.

The instantaneous field of view (FOV) of a human eye is approximately 150° horizontally and 120° vertically and the binocular overlap region, within which a target is visible to both eyes, measures about 114° when the eyes converge symmetrically. The visual acuity of a normal eye is 1 arc minute or better in a fovea region of about 5° and degrades rapidly beyond 10–15° from the fovea (e.g. about 20–25% of the peak VA at 10° from the fovea) [56]. Although wide FOV and high resolution are both desirable characteristics of high-performance displays, in practice a tradeoff is often made to balance factors such as FOV, resolution, as well as weight and volume to address the needs imposed by specific tasks. With a fixed number of available pixels in microdisplays, the angular resolution of the display, defined as the angular subtense of each pixel in any direction, is inversely proportional to the FOV along that direction.

In the case of designing an HMPD system, the size of a projection lens does not scale as much as eyepiece type optics with the increase of FOV, thus it is relatively easier to design wide FOV, optical see-through HMPD systems than conventional HMDs. However, several factors impose limits on the FOV of HMPD systems. Firstly, the use of a planar beamsplitter (BS) oriented at 45° with the optical axis (Fig. 5.1) sets the FOV upper limit to 90°. Such a limit may be overcome by adopting a curved BS instead [39]. Secondly, a wide FOV requires a large-sized BS, which consequently challenges the compactness and weight of the display system. The limit of allowable BS dimensions is set by the interpupilary distance (IPD), which is in the range of 55–75 mm for over 95% of the population. Thirdly, previous investigations on retroreflective materials show that the retroreflectance of currently available materials drops off significantly for light incident at angles beyond ±35° [23]. A FOV beyond 70° will inevitably cause vignetting-like effects and compromise image uniformity.

The pupil is the optical aperture of the human eye which changes its size through dilation and contraction to respond to different lighting conditions. The diameter of the pupil varies from 2 mm under sunlight to about 8 mm in the dark [56]. An HMPD is a pupil-forming system where a physical stop surface is placed inside the projection lens to confine the light rays through the system. Therefore, the stop of the projection system needs to remain optically conjugate to the entrance pupil of the eye to view non-vignetted images, and in a binocular system the separation between the left- and right-arm optics needs to match with a user's IPD. The exit pupil of the projection system thus needs to be considerably larger than the diameter of the eye pupil for comfortable viewing. It is suggested that the exit pupil diameter of an HMPD should typically be at least 10–12 mm [25, 62]. This range of pupil size allows an eye swivel of about ±21° up to ±26.5° within the eye socket without causing vignetting or loss of image for a typical 3-mm eye pupil in the lighting conditions provided by HMPDs. Furthermore, it allows a ±5 mm to ±6 mm IPD tolerance for different users without the need to mechanically adjust the IPD of the binocular optics. Given that a short focal length is typically required for the projection optics to achieve a considerably large FOV, the requirement for a large pupil often leads to projection optics with a low F/#, which becomes an optical design challenge.

The entrance pupil of the eye, which is the image of the pupil through the corneal surfaces, is located inside the eyeball and is about 3 mm from the vertex of the anterior cornea [56]. The location of the exit pupil of the HMPD optics needs to match that of the eye entrance pupil and is best characterized by eye clearance, the point of closest approach of the eye to the HMD. An adequate eye clearance is required for viewing comfort with HMDs. The recommended smallest value of eye clearance is 17 mm, to allow the wearing of standard 2 mm-thick eyeglasses, and 23 mm of eye clearance is desired to accommodate most eyeglasses. Another commonly used figure of merit is the eye relief, which indicates the distance from the center of the last surface of the optical system to the expected location of the eye. Large values of eye relief do not necessarily provide sufficient clearance. Although it is generally less challenging to achieve large eye clearance in HMPD designs than in conventional eyepiece-type HMDs, the requirement for large eye clearance can be problematic in systems with wide FOV as the dimensions of the BS in Fig. 5.1 increase with eye clearance distances.

3 Technology Advancements

The 1990s saw pioneering efforts that led to the establishment of the HMPD concept. Among these efforts, Fisher first described the combination of projection optics and a retroreflective screen for a biocular HMD construction [14]; Fergason extended the biocular concept to binocular displays [13]; and Kijima et al. demonstrated the first head-mounted prototypes implemented from off-the-shelf components [35, 36]. Since these pioneering efforts, HMPD technology was explored extensively in the last decade as an alternative to the conventional designs of optical-see-through HMDs for various applications, and the technology has evolved significantly. This section reviews most of the recent technology developments, while Sect. 5 will focus on various application endeavors.

Advancements of optical design methods and fabrication technologies have played critical roles in HMPD development. Hua and Rolland investigated the engineering challenges in developing a fully custom-designed system [18, 19]. They designed the first wide FOV, low-distortion, and lightweight optics for HMPD systems using a diffractive optical element, aspheric surfaces, and plastic materials [20, 25]. Figure 5.4a, b show the lens layout and assembly of the projection lens, respectively. The lens has a FOV of 52°, a weight of 8 g, and a dimension of 15 mm in diameter by 20 mm in length. The lens design further led to the success of the first custom-designed compact prototypes. Based on a pair of 1.3" backlit LCD microdisplays as the image source, the 1st generation custom-designed HMPD prototype, shown in Fig. 5.4c, weighed about 750 g [19]. Using the same projection optics and microdisplays, Hua further developed a 2nd-generation prototype that was lighter and more compact, by employing an optical folding mechanism. The 2nd generation prototype is shown in Fig. 5.4d and weighed about 500 g.

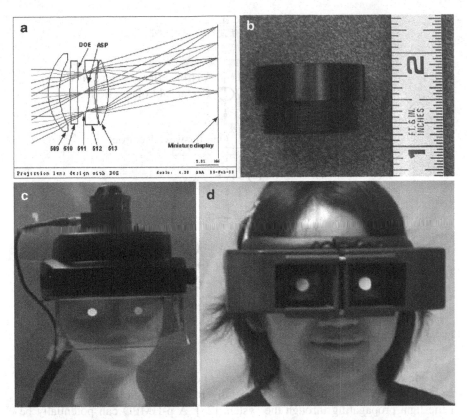

Fig. 5.4 Example of HMPD optics and prototype: (**a**), (**b**) Layout and assembly of a compact projection lens for HMPD systems [25]; (**c**), (**d**) Prototypes based on the lens in (**a**), (**b**) [21,53]

There have been several attempts thereafter to explore more compact and brighter HMPD designs. For instance, the Optical Diagnostic and Applications Laboratory (ODA Lab) led by Rolland has designed a 70° wide FOV projection lens [16], and has also developed an OLED-based 42° prototype, collaborating with NVIS Inc. [53].

In general, the prototypes above were based on the schematics illustrated in Fig. 5.1 and yielded low image brightness and contrast due to the inherently low-efficiency of an HMPD system. As illustrated in Fig. 5.1, the projected light is split twice through a beamsplitter and results in a loss of at least 75% of the light from a displayed image. Further accounting for the additional light loss by typical retroreflective screens, the overall luminous efficiency of an HMPD is around 5%. For instance, with a miniature backlit AMLCD as the image source, the luminance of the observed image of an HMPD is estimated to be $4\,\mathrm{cd/m^2}$, while the average luminance of a well-lit indoor environment is over $100\,\mathrm{cd/m^2}$. As a result, the image of an HMPD typically appears washed out in such well-lit environments.

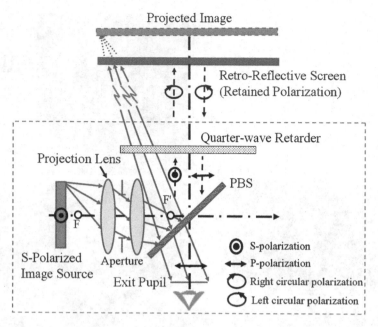

Fig. 5.5 Schematic design of a polarized HMPD [28]

To address the problem of high light loss, a polarized head mounted projection display (p-HMPD) was proposed to carefully manipulate the polarization states of the light propagating through the system [28]. A p-HMPD can potentially be three times brighter than a traditional non-polarized HMPD design using the same microdisplay technologies. A schematic design of a monocular p-HMPD configuration is illustrated in Fig. 5.5. The image on a microdisplay is projected through the projection lens, forming an intermediate image. The light from the microdisplay is manipulated to be S-polarized so that its polarization direction matches the high reflection axis of the polarized beamsplitter (PBS). After the projected light is reflected by the PBS, it is retroreflected back to the same PBS by a retroreflective screen. The depolarization effect by the retroreflective screen is less than 15% within ±20° and is less than 23% up to ±30° [61]. As a result, the retroreflected light remains predominantly the same polarization as its incidence light. In order to achieve high transmission through the PBS after the light is retroreflected, a quarter-wave retarder is placed between the PBS and the retroreflective screen. By passing through the quarter wave retarder twice, the incident S-polarized light is converted to P-polarization and transmits through the PBS with high efficiency. The overall light efficiency of a p-HMPD is at least 2.5 times that of an HMPD system [61] Hua and Gao first developed a p-HMPD prototype using a pair of transmissive AMLCDs and achieved much brighter images than HMPD systems [30]. However, since a transmissive AMLCD microdisplay has a low transmission efficiency of around 5%, the overall performance of the first p-HMPD prototype was

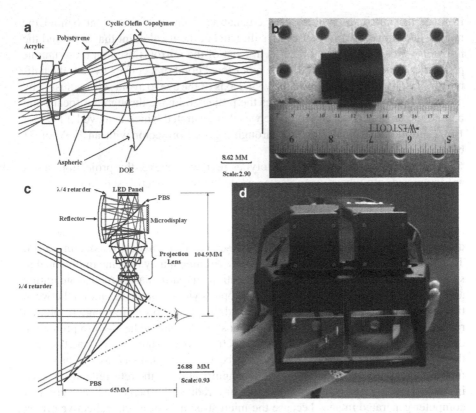

Fig. 5.6 Example of p-HMPD optics and prototype: (**a**), (**b**) Layout and assembly of a compact projection lens for a p-HMPD system; (**c**) Overall optical layout of the prototype system shown in (**d**) [62]

still unsatisfactory in a well-lit environment. To achieve higher image brightness and higher image quality, a 2nd generation of p-HMPD prototype using a pair of FLCoS microdisplays (1280 × 1024 pixels) was designed [62]. As opposed to the transmissive backlit LCD, the FLCoS microdisplay operates in a reflective mode and has much higher luminous efficiency, typically around 60%. Figures 5.6a, b show an optical layout and prototype of the projection lens, whereas Figs. 5.6c, d show the overall optical layout of the system and a protoype implementation. The system achieves a diagonal FOV of 55°, an angular resolution of 2.16 arc minutes per pixel, and a pupil of 10 mm. As shown in Fig. 5.6a, the projection lens consists of five plastic elements with aspheric surfaces and a diffractive optical element (DOE) introduced to help balance the optical aberrations. Each lens system weighs less than 9 g with an overall length of 34 mm.

In the effort of developing a very wide FOV HMPD system, Kiyokawa [39] employed a convex hyperbolic half-silvered mirror as the optical combiner rather than a planar beamsplitter which has been used in prior work. A convex hyperbolic mirror has two focal points. It reflects rays emanating from the focal point in front of the mirror as if they were emanating from the focal point behind the mirror, and conversely, it focuses rays directed at the focal point that is behind the mirror towards the focal point that is in front of the mirror. Based on these unique properties, a projector is placed at the outer focal point of a convex hyperbolic half-mirror, which is tilted away from the visual axis of the eye to avoid self-occlusion by the projector, while a viewer observes the projected image through the focal point behind the mirror. A bench prototype was demonstrated which achieved a FOV of 146.2° in the horizontal direction through a portal projector with an FOV of 31 by 22.2°.

In all of the existing HMPD prototypes reviewed above, the projection optics are integrated into a head-worn device while the retroreflective screen is placed at a remote location away from the user. Typically the projected image needs to be at least 250 mm away from the eyes to allow comfortable viewing, and the screen needs to be near to the projected image plane to avoid severe image quality degradation, due to the imaging artifacts of retroreflective screens that will be discussed in Sect. 4. The requirement for a remote screen in the environment may become impractical in some application scenarios, outdoor applications in particular. Directly integrating a retro-reflective screen with the projection optics yields a large separation between the screen and the projected image plane and thus leads to severe image resolution reduction. Martins et al. [43] recently demonstrated a mobile head-worn projection display (M-HMPD) by imaging a retroreflective screen which is integrated within the headset, so that the screen appears to be the same distance as the projected image plane of the projection optics. The magnification of the retroreflective screen in an M-HMPD configuration, however, may reduce the perceived resolution of computer-generated images because the microstructures of a retroreflective screen may become visible to the user. For instance, the corner cube microstructures of commercially available retroreflective materials are approximately 150 μm in size and, after considerable magnification by an imaging lens, the magnified structures are typically larger than the displayed pixels. Custom-designed retroreflective screens with substantially smaller corner cubes may address this resolution problem.

4 Imaging Properties of a Retroreflective Screen

As discussed in Sect. 2, employing a retroreflective screen in HMPDs enables several unique display capabilities compared with conventional HMD technologies. For instance, an ideal retroreflective screen may be applied to surfaces that are located at an arbitrary distance from the projected image and can be tailored to arbitrary shapes without introducing additional distortion in the virtual images. In practice, however, an imperfect retroreflective screen with artifacts can significantly degrade image quality.

Several pioneering efforts have been made to study the imaging properties of retroreflective materials and their effects on the image quality of an HMPD. Hua et al. [18] quantitatively described the effects of imperfect retroreflection on the perceived image and the exit pupil by assuming a nonzero deviation angle and a nonzero cone angle of the retroreflected light for an ideal incident ray. Subsequently, Hua et al. [23] measured the retroreflectivity of various retroreflective screens as a function of incident angles and examined the divergence profile of the retroreflected beam at a 4° incident angle. Zhang and Hua [61] evaluated the depolarization effects of a retro-reflective screen as a function of ray incident angles and wavelength and analyzed how the depolarization effects impact various aspects of display performances such as luminous efficiency, image uniformity, contrast, and colorimetric characteristics [61]. Recently, Fidopiastis et al. [15] reported a study to evaluate the resolution performance of an in-house built HMPD, which has a theoretical angular resolution of 4.2 arc minutes, under different lighting levels and different contrast levels. The results showed that the lighting levels did not have significant effects on the visual acuity, but type of the retroreflective screen affected performance at a low contrast level.

Recently, Zhang and Hua [63, 64] carried out a comprehensive study to examine the imaging properties of common, commercially available retroreflective screens made of micro corner-cube-reflector (CCR) arrays. In their study, they analyzed the effects of CCR arrays on the image resolution of an HMPD system, as well as the limits to the distance between an HMPD user and a retrorefelctive screen, as a function of the focal distance of the projection optics. They further analyzed how the imaging artifacts of a screen affected the tolerance range of a user's distance to the screen under various application scenarios. Through a visual acuity testing experiment, they objectively quantified the perceived image resolution of a p-HMPD system in relation to the screen placements and HMPD focus settings. Through a second depth-judgment experiment, they further objectively evaluated the effects of a retro-reflective screen on a user's depth perception [64, 65]. A summary of major findings is discussed below.

4.1 Effective Aperture and Retroreflectivity

Figure 5.7a illustrates a single CCR, which is an assembly of three reflective surfaces that are mutually orthogonal to each other, while Fig. 5.7b demonstrates the microscopic structure of a CCR – based retroreflective screen. Only a fraction of the rays incident upon a CCR aperture experience three consecutive reflections within a CCR and can be effectively retroreflected, which defines the effective aperture of a corner cube. The shape and size of the effective aperture of a CCR depend not only on the size of the CCR, but also on the angle of the incident rays. For a CCR with equilateral triangular aperture, normal incident rays yield the maximum effective aperture, which correspondingly is a hexagonal shape with an effective area of 66.7% of the entire CCR aperture [12, 38]. As the incident angle increases, the shape of the effective aperture deviates from a hexagonal shape and the size decreases. As a result, the retroreflectivity of a CCR-based retroreflective screen decreases as the angle of the incident rays increases [12, 38]. Furthermore, other factors such as

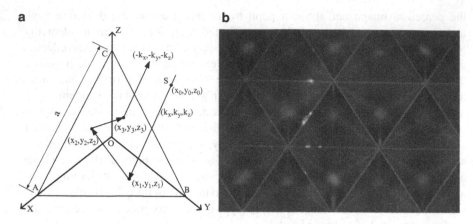

Fig. 5.7 (a) Schematics of a single corner cube reflector; (b) microscopic structure of a CCR array based retroreflective screen [63]

the quality of the CCRs and optical coating may also reduce the retroreflectivity of a screen and worsen the angle-dependence effects. For instance, Hua et al. [23] tested the retroreflectivity of four different samples. The peak retroreflectivity of these samples varied between ~40% and 15%, and their half angle width, which is defined as the angular width when the reflectivity of a sample drops down to half of its peak reflectivity, varied from about 25° (the sample with the highest peak reflectivity) to 50° (the sample with lowest peak reflectivity).

Such an angle-dependence property can have two different effects on an HMPD system. First of all, it sets a practical upper limit on the FOV of an HMPD system. Assuming the use of a flat screen, it is expected that the retroreflective efficiency for the peripheral visual fields is lower than that of the center fields due to the increasing incident angles upon the screen. Therefore, as the FOV of the projection optics increases, the peripheral fields may be perceived as being significantly vigetted and appear to be much darker than the center fields. A concave shape of a screen can help to reduce the vignetting effect and expand the FOV limit. For instance, in the SCAPE system design by Hua et al. [24, 26, 27], curved corners with a radius of curvature of 4 ft were chosen to create a 12 ft by 12 ft immersive wall display.

Secondly, as briefly discussed in Sect. 2, a truly retro-reflective screen may be tailored into arbitrary shapes without causing image blurring, introducing distortion in virtual images, or degrading image quality, whereas a diffusing screen does. Practically, to maintain dominant retro-reflection, the angle-dependence property sets up a constraint on the screen shape. A retro-reflective screen can be tailored into significantly curved shapes, but in approaching the marginal visual fields, the drop of reflectivity results in gradual vignetting effects on image brightness. A concave shape will improve marginal fields, while a convex shape will worsen them. Therefore, the shape of the screens and their orientation with respect to the observer are critical factors in constructing practical retroreflective display surfaces.

4.2 Effective Image Resolution and Screen Placement

From a geometrical imaging point of view, the image formed by a single CCR is point-symmetrical to the object with respect to the CCR vertex, meaning the image is rotated by 180° from the orientation of the object. The retroreflected ray bundle is virtually emitted from an image point that is symmetrical to the object point over CCR vertex [63]. In the case of a retroreflective screen, the incident ray bundle from a source point may impinge on multiple CCRs, each of which forms a virtual image point located at the symmetrical position of the object point with respect to the vertex of the corresponding CCR [63]. The retroreflected ray bundles from each of the CCRs, which are virtually emitted from different virtual image points, will converge toward the object point, and a minimally blurred image spot centered on the object point will be formed on the object plane. Thus, the image of the object point through a retroreflective screen coincides with the object plane and centers on the object point, but with a finite spot size approximately twice that of the corner cube [63].

Since the aperture size of a CCR in a retroreflective screen is small (i.e. in the magnitude of $100\,\mu m$), diffraction effects can have significant impact on the image resolution observed in the retroreflective path. Zhang detailed a theoretical model that combines of the effects of geometrical imaging and diffraction to quantify the effective image resolution of a retroreflective screen in various HMPD settings [63, 64]. In the model, the effective image resolution of a retroreflective screen in an HMPD is characterized by the subtended angle of the minimal blur spot in the unit of arc minutes. It is affected by multiple factors, such as the displacement of a retroreflective screen, d, from the projected image plane, the focusing distance, z_i, of the projection optics, the diameter of the ray bundle (RBD) projected by a projection lens, and the size, a, of the corner cubes [65]. Consider an example. A projection lens projects a ray bundle whose focusing distance (i.e. z_i) may vary between $1\,m$ and $4\,m$ from the viewer. The diameter of the projected ray bundle varies between $4\,mm$ and $10\,mm$, corresponding to the exit pupil diameter of the lens. The projected ray bundle approximates normal incidence upon a retroreflective screen which is made of corner cubes of $a = 200\,\mu m$. For a focusing distance of $z_i = 1\,m$, $2\,m$, and $3\,m$, respectively, Fig. 5.8a–c plot the effective angular resolution of the screen as a function of its displacement d from the focusing plane and the ray bundle size. The results indicate that the angular resolution of the screen degrades with the increase of its displacement from the focusing plane of the projection lens. In other words, when other parameters remain constant, the best image resolution is achieved when the screen coincides with the image plane of the projection lens. Furthermore, as the ray bundle diameter from the projection lens increases, the effective image resolution degrades. For instance, in an arm-length application (i.e. $z_i = 1\,m$), when the screen is placed in front of the projected image plane by $700\,mm$ (i.e. $d = -700\,mm$), the angular resolution of a retroreflective screen with a CCR size of $200\,\mu m$ can be as large as around 8.6 arc minutes for $RBD = 4\,mm$. Under the same distance d, the angular resolution increases to 11.6 arc minutes for $RBD = 10\,mm$. The results further suggest that increasing the focusing distance, z_i, of the projection lens helps

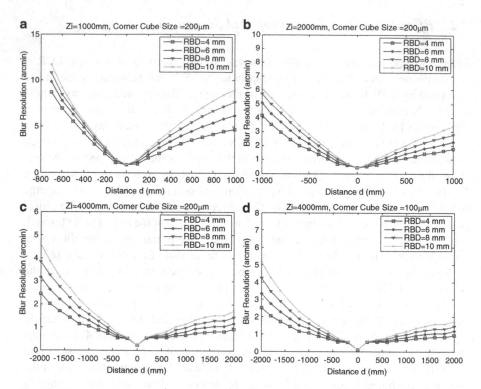

Fig. 5.8 The angular resolution of a retroreflective screen as a function of its displacement from the focusing plane and the size of projected ray bundle (RBD): (**a–c**) corner cube size $a = 200\,\mu m$ and focusing distance $z_i = 1\,m$, $2\,m$, and $4\,m$, respectively; and (**d**) corner cube size $a = 100\,\mu m$ and focusing distance $z_i = 4\,m$ [64]

to reduce the degradation effects on image resolution when the other parameters are fixed. As the focusing distance z_i increases, the effective resolution degrades less with the same screen displacement distance d. Finally, to demonstrate the effect of corner cube size, Fig. 5.8d plots the angular resolution of the screen for a corner cube of $a = 100\,\mu m$, while keeping other parameters the same as those for Fig. 5.8c. The effective image resolution of the screen noticeably degrades with the decrease in cube size, due to the diffraction effect.

These screen effects on the image resolution of an HMPD system were validated through a visual acuity testing experiment [65]. As the displacement of a retroreflective screen from the focusing plane of the projection system increases, the perceived image resolution through an HMPD degrades. Therefore, in practice, the placement of retroreflective screens and the focusing distance of the projection optics need to be tailored for the specific requirements of different applications. More specifically, the focusing distance z_i of the projection optics is typically set to match the viewing distance of an application, and the retroreflective screens should be at an approximately similar distance. For example, for scenarios where the 3D scene is at about an arm-length distance from the viewer (e.g. workbench-type applications and surgical visualization), the focus of the projection system and the screen should be configured at such range; for far-field applications where the 3D scene is considerably far from the viewer (e.g. flight simulation or battlefield visualization), the focus of the projection system and the screens should be configured at far distance.

Moreover, the resolution effects described above may limit a user's mobility in an HMPD-based augmented environment. In an interactive 3D environment, a user may walk around to explore the 3D environment. Assuming a fixed focusing setting for the projection optics, the displacement of the screen from the projection image plane varies depending on the user's location in the environment, except in a mobile HMPD system where the screen is fully integrated with the helmet [43]. Consequently, the image resolution observed by a user depends on his or her physical distance to the screen [64]. Establishing the tolerance range of a user's movement in a 3D environment is critical. Within this range, the degradation of effective image resolution caused by a retroreflective screen is visually acceptable. For instance, a user may be limited to move within a range such that the angular resolution of a retroreflective screen is smaller than a single pixel of the projection system without screen effects. In this case, users will not perceive any screen effects. Such a strict tolerance criterion, however, may impose too strong a limit on users' mobility in a 3D environment, leading to impractical application conditions. For instance, based on a p-HMPD prototype which has an angular resolution of 2.1 arc minutes per pixel and a retroreflective screen with a corner cube size of 200 μm, it was established that a user may move between −17.8 cm and 22.2 cm from the screen when the projection system is focused at a 1 m distance, or between −147.3 cm and 200 cm when focusing at a 4 m distance [64]. Realistically, imposing such a limitation on users' mobility without compromising on image resolution is barely acceptable for an interactive 3D environment. Therefore, the imaging artifacts of a retroreflective screen are the key limiting factors for the existing HMPD technology to be adopted for high-resolution 3D display systems.

5 Applications

Despite its drawbacks and relative youth, HMPD technology has been shown to offer a level of versatility that makes it suitable for many cutting-edge application directions. For example, the technology allows for new directions in Tangible User Interface [33] design by reducing the cognitive barriers between the real and virtual worlds. It promotes enhanced telepresence capabilities, giving remote users a fuller sense of "being there." Finally, HMPD allows for the creation of diverse and cohesive computer-supported workspaces, called Augmented Virtual Environments, which would otherwise be difficult to realize with many other display technologies. In this Section, we will address each of these application directions in further detail, providing domain-specific examples to illustrate their utility.

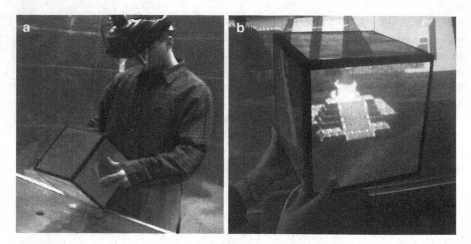

Fig. 5.9 The object-oriented display technique: (**a**) Manipulation of a retro-reflective cube serving as tangible container; (**b**) View through HMPD of augmented cube with 3D virtual object inside it [4]

5.1 Tangible User Interfaces

Tangible user interfaces (TUI) seek to reduce the cognitive seams between the real and virtual worlds by promoting interaction techniques that give physical form to computer-generated information [33]. As discussed in Sect. 2.1, HMPD technology allows the creation of augmented environments where computer-generated virtual information can be optically combined with the real world. Further, HMPD supports correct occlusion of virtual objects by real objects. Combined with appropriate haptic feedback, the augmentation capabilities of HMPD provide a powerful platform for making TUIs that enhance a user's sense of physically interacting with virtual data. For example, consider the Visuo-haptic interface proposed by [31]. In this system, a Phantom force feedback pen was used to draw onto virtual objects, which were overlaid directly onto the device using retroreflective material. Rather than having separate spaces for interaction and visualization, the Visuo-haptic interface "optically camouflaged" the force feedback device to closely couple the haptic responses with the virtual world being acted upon.

Force feedback devices are not the only means for creating useful TUIs. Augmenting physical props can be equally powerful, if those props have meaningful shapes and provide useful occlusion cues. To illustrate, consider how an HMPD-enabled system can be used to create an Object-Oriented Display [34]. In a typical immersive virtual environment, the user resides inside of the display system, and the virtual environment surrounds him/her. With an Object-Oriented Display, such as the one shown in Fig. 5.9 [4], a physical display container surrounds the virtual object and users can then manipulate the container with proper occlusion cues to gain a tangible understanding of the virtual object's size and structure. The display

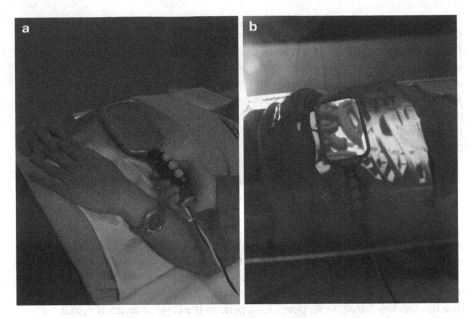

Fig. 5.10 A tangible interface for medical visualization: (**a**) Real view showing hand-held magic lens and patient covered in retro-reflective cloth; (**b**) View through HMPD of augmented patient [6]

container is simply a retroreflective prop that is tracked by motion sensors to allow proper registration of the virtual object with the physical prop. If the virtual object is well registered, the container itself dictates the extents of the object and gives a tangible form to the virtual data. As discussed in Sect. 4, a retroreflective screen can assume a variety of shapes without introducing distortion into the perceived image. This allows the display container to assume any number of shapes, such as cubes, spheres, or cylinders, as suited for the application needs.

The Object-Oriented Display demonstration underscores the possibilities for using HMPD to give tangible physical form to virtual data. Indeed, retroreflective displays can take on complex, specialized shapes as needed for a given task. For example, Brown et al. [6] have suggested a TUI using HMPD for teaching human physiology to medical and nursing students. In a simple demonstration shown in Fig. 5.10, a live patient was overlaid with a pliable, retroreflective cloth that served as a virtual window into his body. On the cloth, trainees could see a set of 3D anatomical models which simulated the patient's internal physiology, including various tissues, organs, and bones. By using a soft cloth, the setup offered convincing haptic feedback about the virtual anatomy superimposed onto the patient. For instance, the tactile sensations of touching the patient's ribs corresponded with the visual presentation of the virtual ribs in the patient's body. Similarly, a medical training platform has been created using HMPD that allows students to look inside the body of an artificial patient, while performing mock surgical procedures such as endotracheal intubation [51]. The intubation procedure involves inserting a breathing tube through an incision in the neck and down into the lungs. The system augments an existing training platform called the Human Patient Simulator (HPS), which is an anatomically-correct mannequin with fleshy internal structure simulating the upper torso. By employing a marker-based tracking system, the setup allowed dynamic and precise registration (<3mm RMS) of 3D virtual anatomy to be visualized through the HMPD. Users could then practice the intubation technique with actual surgical instruments, using the augmented mannequin to learn the proper location and course of the tube while doing the procedure.

Beyond simply grounding virtual data in physical objects, HMPD-enabled TUIs can couple virtual information to the real world in arbitrary but meaningful ways. For example, Kjima et al. [37] used HMPD technology to render virtual "see through" windows on real world objects. By holding a tracked sheet of retroreflective material up to an object, the user could virtually see through it, observing objects on the other side. Thus the real world object was augmented with pertinent virtual information in its correct real world context. The system worked by computing the pose of each hand-held, retroreflective window, using vision techniques and head-mounted cameras, and then rendering proper 3D information into the window based on its pose. As a perk to the HMPD-enabled visualization, retroreflective materials present a unique opportunity to simplify image segmentation – under coaxial infrared illumination, the retroreflective material appears bright while occluding real objects appear dark [22]. Additionally, the retroreflective windows provided a volume "slicing" capability, in which users could flip through a stack of MRI images by physically moving the window prop back and forth through space.

The Kijima demo demonstrates a simple example of an HMPD-enabled "Magic Lens" device. Originally proposed by Bier et al. [3], Magic Lens is a powerful complexity management technique that correlates alternate views of a dataset to provide details on demand. The Magic Lens technique has gained increasing use in virtual environments applications, where 3D information can have significant structural complexity and many overlapping layers [42, 60]. HMPD enables the creation of augmented, tangible Magic Lenses which provide users with intuitive metaphors for managing information complexity and tuning the level of detail to the needs of the application [6]. Tangible Magic Lenses can take many diverse forms, which differ in the way information is presented, the way a user's viewpoint is manipulated, and the way details are visually correlated with the overall structure of the dataset. To illustrate, two diverse applications of the technique are mentioned here. Considering again the anatomy simulator shown in Fig. 5.10, a hand-held, augmented Magic Lens was introduced to provide a detailed view in context, synonymous with how a user might employ a "magnifying glass" in the real world [6]. In this Magic Lens configuration, the augmented patient provided a contextual reference, while the hand-held display window provided a "focus" showing high-detail information only at the point of interest. In addition, the Magic Lens device allowed users to interactively tune the level of detail, by adding or subtracting tissues and organs, as well as a tangible "slicer" capability similar to [37]. In a

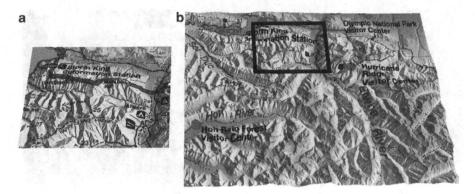

Fig. 5.11 A magic lens for map reading: (**a**) Detail view showing higher level-of-detail and greater magnification; (**b**) Overview map showing picture frame icon that indicates point of interest [48]

separate application, Oh and Hua [48] investigated embedded Magic Lenses as an aid for map reading tasks on a workbench. In their application, a user could select an area from a virtual overview map for closer inspection, by placing a "picture frame" icon on the map at their point of interest. The frame icon itself could be a tangible object, for instance tracked by vision techniques. Higher-magnification views of the selected area were rendered into a secondary detail window which was also embedded on the workbench. The Oh and Hua application illustrates an "overview+detail" Magic Lens configuration as shown in Fig. 5.11. Indeed, HMPD-enabled Magic Lenses offer intuitive, tangible viewing controls that can be tailored to the task and application; for a more thorough investigation of these techniques, refer to [6, 47, 48].

5.2 Remote Telepresence

In collaborative activities involving complex 3D datasets, a significant challenge rests providing an effective medium for remote users to illustrate complex ideas and intentions. Common devices, such as speakerphones and whiteboards, have limited expressive power and are not well-suited to tasks that involve complex 3D datasets. This can leave remote users at a disadvantage, in terms of understanding the thoughts of collaborators and reciprocating ideas. HMPD-enabled frameworks have been shown to be effective tools for promoting communication in remote collaboration, by both promoting better visualization capabilities with a more intuitive user interface, and by enhancing interpersonal communication among remote users through face-to-face interaction.

Hua et al. [22] have suggested an HMPD-based framework for remote collaboration that gave all users direct, symmetric control over a dataset through tangible interaction methods, such as those discussed in Sect. 5.1. This framework was

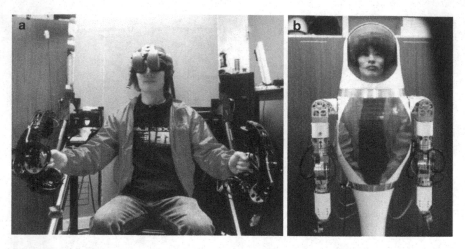

Fig. 5.12 The TELESAR system: (**a**) Cockpit with servo arms used in operating a remote surrogate; (**b**) View through HMPD of robotic surrogate augmented with user's upper body [45]

illustrated with a simple game of "GO" played between remote opponents. In the demo, each user played real stones onto an augmented "GO" board. By means of a COMPUTER vision system, the location of each real stone was tracked and relayed to the remote site, where a virtual stone was drawn in its place. The interface thus afforded symmetric and equally expressive controls over the dataset for both parties, as real stones indicated the player's moves and virtual stones indicated his/her opponent's moves.

In addition to an enhanced collaborative interface, HMPD-enabled frameworks have been used to promote interpersonal communication by giving the remote user a sense of virtual presence within the remote world. For instance, the Teleportal Face-to-Face System [2] augmented the workspace with a video avatar of the remote user's face, thus permitting non-verbal communication through eye contact and facial expressions. The Teleportal system consisted of a pair of side-mounted lipstick cameras and micro-mirrors, which were integrated into a compact HMPD prototype [54]. A homographic mapping technique was used to reconstruct a virtual front view of each user's face from the two side views, which could then be mapped onto selected physical objects in the workspace. For instance, a user's face could be rendered onto a retroreflective avatar which sat at a shared conference table, or it could be rendered into a window that was "teleported" around the workspace with the group's attention [52, 54].

The TELESAR project (TELExistence Surrogate Anthropomorphic Robot) [58, 59] furthered the visual telepresence idea by promoting a degree of "tele-existence" through robotic surrogates. The TELESAR system is illustrated in Fig. 5.12. Each robotic surrogate consisted of an upper torso with humanoid hands and arms. The surrogate was controlled remotely, through a special cockpit that afforded its operator with force feedback as the surrogate's hands contacted physical surfaces in the remote environment. Additionally, the TELESAR system leveraged HMPD's versatile imaging capabilities to provide two-way visual feedback in supplement of the surrogate's actionable characteristics. Extending the Teleportal idea, the surrogate itself was augmented with the human form of its controller. The user's head and upper torso were captured via a stereo imaging system and mapped onto the surrogate, which was coated in a retroreflective material, as shown in Fig. 5.12b. Likewise, acquisition cameras were mounted onto the surrogate itself, so that the operator could view the remote environment in stereoscopic virtual reality, using retroreflective screens enveloping the cockpit [45]. Indeed, new developments in robotics and imaging techniques may one day push this technology toward fully augmented, bi-pedal robots that offer us the ultimate in "mutual tele-existence" capabilities [58].

5.3 Augmented Virtual Environments

HMPD has been applied to meet a variety of visualization needs, ranging from hand-held, object-oriented displays to immersive cockpits used in tele-existence. In many real world scenarios, the needs of the application are often in flux and depend upon the particular task and objectives at hand. To illustrate, we draw motivation from the Reality-Virtuality (R-V) Continuum of Milgram [44], which orders all visualization experiences into a continuum ranging from the purely physical world of "Reality" to the wholly computer-generated world of "Virtuality." Display systems can be ordered in this continuum based upon the level of augmentation they offer. For example, the CAVE system [9] represents a "Virtual Reality" condition since it almost completely immerses the user in computer-generated information, whereas a see-through HMD supports a level of "Augmented Reality" by overlaying select digital information onto the real world. The augmentation capabilities of the display system are typically fixed for the duration of an application and are difficult to change; nonetheless, the needs of the application itself may change through time, as each subtask has differing or even competing requirements. Similar issues may arise in regards to a dataset's scale or level of detail, and in the way users collaborate as they alternate back and forth between group and independent work. Augmented Virtual Environments (AVEs) are a recent development in collaborative workspaces which leverage the capabilities of HMPD to address these changing needs, by providing users with more options and greater flexibility to interact with and visualize datasets.

In an early demonstration, Kijima et al. [35, 36] created a flexible compound environment that coupled a computer workstation within a semi-immersive virtual environment using an HMPD-type display. By tracking gaze position, users could operate on data in two modes: by looking at the computer screen, they could interact with high-resolution CAD images, or by looking away from the screen, they could visualize a 3D representation of the CAD model to gain a better understanding of its structure. By its optical see-through nature, HMPD allows the integration of other display technologies, in this case a high-resolution workstation monitor, to allow high-resolution CAD modeling, while augmenting those 2D models as needed with additional 3D spatial information. More recently, the ARC system (*i.e.* the Artificial Reality Center) [17] was proposed as a means to allow multi-user, co-located interaction in an HMPD-enabled workspace with variable level of immersion. The ARC consisted of a hemi-cylindrical display wall coupled with motion sensors for tracking users' head poses. The level of immersion could be controlled by simply changing the user's location with respect to the display wall or by adding additional segments to the display wall [52, 54]. In addition, HMPD allowed each user to have a unique view of the data, as discussed in Sect. 2.1, and so promoted co-located collaboration by allowing the group to communicate with natural hand gestures, such as pointing to common objects, while viewing from different, correct perspectives. The ARC system has been demonstrated in medical applications, such as visualizing the effects of radiation dosimetry on lung tumors and surrounding tissues [55].

In contrast to other display technologies, an HMPD-enabled workspace can potentially support multi-user interaction across a wide range of visualization and interaction modes. For example, such a workspace could offer augmentation capabilities that range from "Augmented Reality" to fully immersive "Virtual Reality." Each paradigm has particular strengths and weaknesses. For example, an augmented environment typically gives users a more tangible sense of grounding of the virtual dataset by registering it with the real-world, which imposes practical physical constraints on the dataset. Conversely, virtual environments provide users with a greater degree of freedom for exploring a datasets, irrespective of size and scale, as users can literally dive into the dataset in ways they never could in the real world. To bring together the strengths of both paradigms, an HMPD-enabled workspace called SCAPE (Stereoscopic Collaboration in Augmented Projective Environments) [24–27] was proposed to embed collaborative, Augmented Reality inside of immersive Virtual Reality, as shown in Fig. 5.13. The SCAPE system consisted of a retroreflective workbench which was suitable for augmented interaction, and a semi-cylindrical room display offering 360° field of regard, which supported immersive virtual reality. The system prototype is illustrated in Fig. 5.14. By embedding the AR workbench inside of the VR room display, users could collaborate face-to-face while visualizing an augmented environment on the common tabletop, and naturally transition their attention to the VR room display to explore immersive datasets as needed.

To illustrate the utility of an AVE, Hua [24, 26] demonstrated an archaeology teaching application that involved complex, 3D models of a World Heritage site (the Aztec city of Tenochtitlan) shown in Fig. 5.15. Using HMPDs, a group of students could view an augmented, 3D map of the site grounded on the workbench, and a life-sized, immersive view of the site on the room display. In their application, the tabletop provided an "exocentric" view of the virtual world, giving users an understanding of its overall structure and their location in it. Correspondingly, the room display provided an "egocentric" view of the dataset, giving users an understanding of its immense scale and fine details. Furthermore, the application

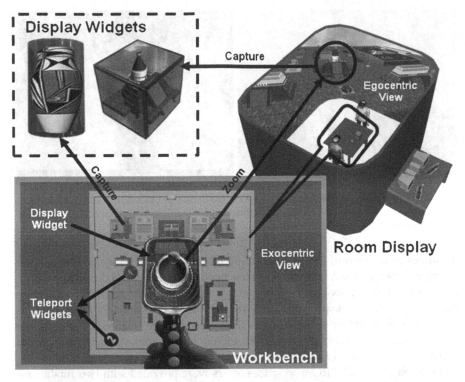

Fig. 5.13 A conceptual model of the SCAPE augmented virtual environment showing various modes of interaction and visualization [29]

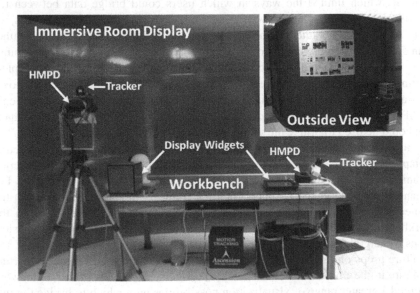

Fig. 5.14 A prototype implementation of the SCAPE augmented virtual environment [29]

Fig. 5.15 Exploring an archaeology site in an AVE: (**a**) Egocentric, immersive virtual environment viewed using room display; (**b**) Exocentric, augmented environment viewed using workbench and auxiliary display [26]

illustrates some interesting issues regarding the semantics of co-located interaction during collaborative tasks. Since users have personalized views of the virtual world, the views may not necessarily be consistent. For instance, although the users occupy the same physical workspace, they may feasibly explore completely different areas of the virtual world or interact with information on the augmented workbench in differing ways. A more detailed discussion of the consistency challenges to collaborative activities in AVEs may be found in [27] and [41].

In the SCAPE and ARC workspaces, users were provided with two fundamentally different and yet complementary paradigms for manipulating the same dataset. Although useful, there was a pronounced distinction between the worlds of AR and VR, which limited the ways in which users could bridge data between the paradigms, in terms of scale, viewpoint, and mode of interaction. In other words, the early AVEs separated interaction into two distinct and disconnected modes, rather than considering a more continuous range of interaction and visualization possibilities. An HMPD-enabled workspace could feasibly allow for a far more complete continuum of visualization experiences, simply by affording better controls over how and where data are visualized in the workspace [10, 29]. Toward this end, SCAPE was upgraded with a toolset of auxiliary displays and interaction widgets that could be used to bridge the worlds contained by the AR and VR views [4, 27]. The toolset, illustrated conceptually in Fig. 5.13, extended the tangible interaction metaphors discussed in Sect. 5.1 to provide a set of generic props and interaction techniques which could be introduced as needed during the application [6]. For instance, Object-Oriented Displays could be used to "miniaturize" data from the immersive virtual world, while hand-held Magic Lenses magnified data on the workbench. In addition, vision techniques allowed the use of arbitrary physical props as tangible controllers to the virtual dataset; in a simple demonstration, toy furniture props on the workbench were used to move equivalent pieces of virtual furniture in the immersive environment [5]. Together, the tools of this framework afforded a greater range of visualization possibilities with which to bridge the two display spaces.

By providing a continuum of visualization and interaction experiences, HMPD-enabled AVEs can greatly enhance the user's ability to respond to the changing needs of an application. To illustrate, we discuss how the workspace can meet the changing needs of augmentation in a manufacturing application that is motivated by [52]. In this hypothetical application, a design meeting considers the evolution of a complex mechanical part. The meeting starts out with users discussing a 1:1 physical mock-up of the mechanical part, which was rapidly prototyped from a previous meeting. The real model sits in the center of a shared conference table and represents a pure "Reality" viewing condition for the group. At some point, the users decide to make alterations to the part. A virtual 3D model is generated from the physical part and placed onto an immersive room display where it is greatly scaled. The users dive into the part, making structural changes to its geometry as needed. This view condition corresponds to an almost entirely "Virtual Reality" experience. Afterward, the group reduces the model's scale so that they can observe the new alterations in the context of its overall structure. The model is captured into a smaller, auxiliary display widget, which is placed back onto the conference table, where it can be viewed exocentrically from all sides. This view condition represents an intermediate level of "Augmented Virtuality." Finally, the group wishes to compare their alterations with the original mechanical part. The virtual model is overlaid onto the original mechanical part, back in 1:1 scale, where the structural differences between old and new parts are made obvious. This view condition represents a level of "Augmented Reality." Over the course of one design meeting, the group has already traversed many points just on the continuum of Reality-Virtuality [44] in meeting the needs of their design application. In the same respect, other important aspects of the visualization have also changed significantly – including scale, view perspective, level of detail, and mode of collaboration – and all of which are made possible by an HMPD-enabled Augmented Virtual Environment.

6 Conclusions and Future Research Directions

Driven by the need for lightweight, wide FOV, and compact optical see-through HMDs, in the past decade several groups have carried out research and development efforts on a relatively new display concept, head mounted projection displays. These efforts led to significant advancements and understanding of this ever-maturing technology and spurred great interest in applying it to a wide range of augmented reality applications. In this Chapter, we presented a review of the technology advancements, the imaging properties of a retroreflective screen and their effects on HMPD systems, and a broad range of application examples.

Head mounted projection displays hold great potential to enable many applications, but more research and development are needed to push the envelope of the technology and alleviate its limitations. It is clear that one of the key limits of HMPDs lies in the imaging artifacts caused by the imperfect retroreflective screens commercially available, which have typically been developed for non-imaging applications. Efforts should be made to optimize the screen design to be more suitable for imaging applications, to overcome its limitations on image resolution and user mobility discussed in Sect. 4. Furthermore, although a preliminary study was carried out by Zhang and Hua, additional studies are needed to examine and understand the effects of a retroreflective screen on a user's depth perception. Finally, mobility and portability of the technology must be improved. HMPDs typically require a screen that is located remotely, which limits its use for outdoor applications. A mobile HMPD configuration has the potential to address this limitation, if a customized retroreflective screen can be fabricated with a much smaller corner cube size. More compact projection optics and microdisplay technology can also help to further reduce the weight and size of the helmet and improve its portability.

References

1. R. Azuma, Y. Baillot, R. Behringer, S. Feiner, S. Julier, and B. Macintyre, "Recent advances in augmented reality," *IEEE Computer Graphics and Applications*, 21(6), 34–47, 2001.
2. F. Biocca and J.P. Rolland, "Teleportal Face-to-Face System," U.S. Patent 6,774,869, August 10, 2004.
3. E. Bier, M. Stone, K. Pier, W. Buxton, and T. DeRose, "Toolglass and Magic Lenses: The See-through Interface," *Proc. of ACM Conference on Computer Graphics and Interactive Techniques (SIGGRAPH)*, p. 73–80, 1993.
4. L.D. Brown, H. Hua, "A Widget Framework for Augmented Interaction in SCAPE," *CHI Letters/Proc. of ACM International Symposium on User Interface Software and Technology (UIST)*, 5(2), 1–10, 2003.
5. L.D. Brown and H. Hua, "Toward a Tangible Interface for Multi-Modal Interior Design Using SCAPE," *Proc. of IEEE Virtual Reality (IEEE VR) Workshop on 3D User Interfaces: Beyond Wand & Glove-Based Interaction (3DUI)*, Chicago, IL, p. 79–83, 2004.
6. L.D. Brown and H. Hua, "Magic Lenses for Augmented Virtual Environments," *IEEE Computer Graphics & Applications,* 26(4), 64–73, 2006.
7. O. Cakmakci and J. Rolland, "Head-work displays: a review," *J. of Display Technology*, 2(3),199–216, 2006.
8. A. Cameron, "The application of holographic optical waveguide technology to Q − Sight™ family of helmet mounted display," *Proc. of SPIE*, V. 7326, 73260H-1, 2009.
9. C. Cruz-Neira, D. J. Sandin, T.A. DeFanti, R.V. Kenyon, and J. C. Cart, "The CAVE: Audio visual experience automatic virtual environments". *Communications of the ACM*, 35(6), 65–72, 1992.
10. L. Davis, J.P. Rolland, F. Hamza-Lup, Y. Ha, J. Norfleet, B. Pettitt, and C. Imielinska, "Enabling a Continuum of Virtual Environment Experiences" *IEEE Computer Graphics and Applications,* 23(2), 10–12, 2003.
11. J. G. Droessler, D. J. Rotier, "Tilted cat helmet-mounted display," *Opt. Eng.*, V. **29**, 849, 1990.
12. H. Eckhardt, "Simple model of corner reflector phenomena," *Applied Optics* v. 10, 1559–1566, 1971.
13. J. Fergason, "Optical system for head mounted display using a retro-reflector and method of displaying an image," U.S. patent 5,621,572, 1997.
14. R. Fisher, "Head-mounted projection display system featuring beam splitter and method of making same," U.S. Patent 5,572,229, 1996.

15. C. Fidopiastis, C. Fuhrman, C. Meyer, and J. P. Rolland, "Methodology for iterative evaluation of prototype head-mounted displays in virtual environments: visual acuity metrics," *Presence: Teleoperators and Virtual Environments*, v. 14(5), 2005.
16. Y. Ha, H. Hua, R. Martins, and J.P. Rolland, "Design of a wearable wide-angle projection color display," *Proc. of International Optical Design Conference 2002* (IODC), 2002.
17. F. Hamza-Lup, L. Davis, and J.P. Rolland, "The ARC Display: An Augmented Reality Visualization Center," *Proc. of IEEE International Augmented reality Toolkit Workshop*, Darmstadt, Germany, September, 2002.
18. H. Hua, A. Girardot, C. Gao, and J.P. Rolland, "Engineering of head-mounted projective displays," *Applied Optics*, 39 (22), 3814–3824, 2000.
19. H. Hua, C. Gao, F. Biocca, and J.P. Rolland, "An ultra-light and compact design and implementation of Head-Mounted Projective Displays", *Proc. IEEE Virtual Reality Annual International Symposium 2001*, p.175–182, 2001.
20. H. Hua and J.P. Rolland, "Compact lens assembly for the teleportal augmented reality system," US Patent 6,731,734 B1, May 2004.
21. H. Hua, C. Gao, L.D. Brown, N Ahuja, and J. P. Rolland "Using a Head-Mounted Projective Display in Interactive Augmented Environments," *Proc. of IEEE International Symposium on Augmented Reality*, 217–223, 2001.
22. H. Hua, C. Gao, and L.D. Brown, "A Testbed for Precise Registration, Natural Occlusion, and Interaction in an Augmented Environment Using Head-Mounted Projective Display," *Proc. of IEEE Virtual Reality*, p. 81–89, 2002.
23. H. Hua, C. Gao, and J.P. Rolland, "Study of the imaging properties of retro-reflective materials used in head-mounted projective displays (HMPDs)," in *SPIE Aerosense 2002*, Orlando, FL, April 1–5, 2002.
24. H. Hua, L.D. Brown and C. Gao, "A New Collaborative Infrastructure: SCAPE," *Proc. of IEEE Virtual Reality (IEEE VR)*, p. 171–179, 2003.
25. H. Hua, Y. Ha, and J. P. Rolland, "Design of an ultralight and compact projection lens," *Applied Optics, 42*, 97–107, 2003.
26. H. Hua, L.D. Brown, and C. Gao, "SCAPE: Supporting Stereoscopic Collaboration in Augmented and Projective Environments," *IEEE Computer Graphics and Applications*, 24(1), p. 66–75, 2004.
27. H. Hua, L.D. Brown, and C. Gao, "System and Interface Framework for SCAPE as a Collaborative Infrastructure," *Presence: Teleoperators and Virtual Environments*, 13(2), p. 234–250, 2004.
28. H. Hua and C. Gao, "A polarized head-mounted projective display," *Proceedings of 2005 IEEE and ACM International Symposium on Mixed and Augmented Reality*, pp. 32–35, Oct. 2005.
29. H. Hua, "Merging the Worlds of Atoms and Bits: Augmented Virtual Environments," Optics and Photonics News, 17(10), 26–33, 2006.
30. H. Hua and C. Gao, "Design of a bright polarized headmounted projection display" Appl. Opt. **46**, 2600–2610, 2007.
31. M. Inami, N. Kawakami, D. Sekiguchi, Y. Yanagida, T. Maeda, and S. Tachi, "Visuo-Haptic Display Using Head-Mounted Projector," *Proc. of IEEE Virtual Reality*, p. 233–240, 2000.
32. K. Inoguchi, H. Morishima, N. Nanaba, S. Takeshita, and Y. Yamazaki, "Fabrication and evaluation of HMD optical system consisting of aspherical mirrors without rotation symmetry," *Japan Optics'95, Extended Abstracts*, 20pB06, pp. 19–20, 1995.
33. H. Ishii and B. Ullmer, "Tangible Bits: Towards Seamless Interfaces Between People, Bits, and Atoms," *Proc. of ACM Conference on Human Factors in Computing (CHI)*, p. 234–241, 1997.
34. N. Kawakami, M. Inami, D. Sekiguchi, Y. Yanagida, T. Maeda and S. Tachi, "Object-Oriented Displays: A New Type of Display Systems, from Immersive Display to Object-Oriented Displays," *Proc. of IEEE Systems, Man, and Cybernetics, (IEEE SMC)*, v.5, p. 1066–1069, 1999.
35. R. Kijima and M. Hirose, "A Compound Virtual Environment Using the Projective Head-Mounted Display," *Proc. of ACM International Conference on Artificial Reality and Tele-Existence/ ACM Conference on Virtual Reality Software and Technology (ICAT/VRST)*, p. 111–121, 1995.

36. R. Kijima and T. Ojika, "Transition between Virtual Environment and Workstation Environment with Projective Head-Mounted Display," *Proc. of IEEE Virtual Reality Annual International Symposium (VRAIS)*, p.130–137, 1997.
37. R. Kijima, K. Haza, Y. Tada, and T. Ojika, "Distributed Display Approach Using PHMD with Infrared Camera," *Proc. of IEEE Virtual Reality (IEEE VR)*, p. 33–40, 2002.
38. H. Kim and B. Lee, "Optimal design of retroreflection corner-cube sheets by geometric optics analysis," Opt. Eng. (Bellingham) **46**, 094002 (2007).
39. K. Kiyokawa, "A wide field-of-view head mounted projective display using hyperbolic half-silvered mirrors," *Proc. of IEEE International Symposium on Mixed & Augmented Reality (ISMAR)*, 2007.
40. K. Kiyokawa, M. Billinghurst, B. Campbell, E. Woods, "An occlusion-capable optical see-through head mount display for supporting colocated collaboration," *Proc. of IEEE International Symposium on Mixed & Augmented Reality (ISMAR)*, 133–141, 2003.
41. S.Y. Lee and H. Hua, "Effects of Viewing Conditions and Rotation Methods in a Collaborative Tabletop AR Environment," *Proc. of IEEE Virtual Reality (IEEE VR)*, p. 163–170, 2010.
42. J. Looser and M. Billinghurst, "Through the Looking Glass: Use of Lenses as an Interface Tool for AR Interfaces," *Proc. of ACM Conference on Computer Graphics and Interactive Techniques in Australia and South East Asia (GRAPHITE)*, p. 204–211, 2004.
43. R. Martins, V. Shaoulov, Y. Ha, and J.P. Rolland, "A mobile head-worn projection display," *Optics Express,* 15(22), 14530–38, 2007.
44. P. Milgram and F. Kishino, "Augmented Reality: A Class of Displays on the Reality-Virtuality Continuum," *SPIE Telemanipulator and Telepresence Technologies*, v. 2351(34), p. 42–48, 1994.
45. K. Minamizawa, M. Shinmeimae, H. Kajimoto, N. Kawakami and S. Tachi, "Study of Telexistence (XXXXVI): Optical System for Mutual Telexistence Using Retro-reflective Projection Technology," *Journal of Asia Society of Art Science*, v.2 (1), p. 31–36, 2006.
46. M. D. Missig, and G. M. Morris, "Diffractive optics applied to eyepiece design," Appl. Opt. **34**, 2452–2461, 1995.
47. J.Y. Oh and H. Hua, "User Evaluations on Form Factors of Tangible Magic Lenses," *Proc. of IEEE International Symposium on Mixed and Augmented Reality (ISMAR)*, p. 23–32, 2006.
48. J.Y. Oh and H. Hua, "Usability of Multi-Scale Interfaces for 3D Workbench Displays," *Presence: Teleoperators and Virtual Environments*, v. 17 (5), MIT Press, p. 415–440, 2008.
49. J. P. Rolland, "Wide-angle, off-axis, see-through head-mounted display," *Opt. Eng.*, Vol. **39**, 1760, 2000.
50. J.P. Rolland and H. Fuchs, "Optical versus video see-through head-mounted displays in medical visualization," *Presence: Teleoperators and Virtual Environments (MIT Press),* 9(3), 287–309, 2000.
51. J.P. Rolland, L. Davis, F. Hamza-Lup, J. Daly, Y. Ha, G. Martin, J. Norfleet, R. Thumann, and C. Imielinska, "Development of a Training Tool for Endotracheal Intubation: Distributed Augmented Reality," *Proc. of Medicine Meets Virtual Reality 2003 (MMVR)*, *Studies in Health Technology and Informatics*, v. 98, p. 288–294, 2003.
52. J.P. Rolland, F. Biocca, H. Hua, Y. Ha, C. Gao, and O. Harrisson, "Teleportal Augmented Reality System: Integrating Virtual Objects, Remote Collaborators, and Physical Reality for Distributed Networked Manufacturing," *Virtual and Augmented Reality Applications in Manufacturing* (Ch. 11), Eds. S.K. Ong and A.Y.C. Nee, Springer-Verlag: London, p. 183–202, 2004.
53. J.P. Rolland, and H. Hua, "Head-mounted displays," Encyclopedia of Optical Engineering, R. Barry Johnson and Ronald G. Driggers, Eds, 2005.
54. J.P. Rolland, F. Biocca, F. Hamza-Lup, Y. Ha, and R. Martins, "Development of Head-Mounted Projection Displays for Distributed, Collaborative Augmented Reality Applications," *Presence: Teleoperators and Virtual Environments*, v. 14(5), p. 528–549, 2005.
55. A.P. Santhanam, T.R. Willoughby, I. Kaya, A.P. Shah, S.L. Meeks, J.P. Rolland, and P. Kupelian, "A Display Framework for Visualizing Real-time 3D Lung Tumor Radiotherapy," *Journal of Display Technology* (Special Issue on Medical Displays), 4(4), 473–482, 2008.

56. J. Schwiegerling, *Field Guide to Visual and Ophthalmic Optics*, SPIE Press, 2004.
57. I.E. Sutherland, "A head-mounted three-dimensional display," *Proc. of Fall Joint Comput. Conf. AFIPS*, 33, 757–764, 1968.
58. S. Tachi, N. Kawakami, M. Inami and Y. Zaitsu, "Mutual Telexistence System Using Retro-reflective Projection Technology," *International Journal of Humanoid Robotics*, 1 (1), p. 45–64, 2004.
59. S. Tachi, N. Kawakami, H. Nii, K. Watanabe and K. Minamizawa, "TELEsarPHONE: Mutual Telexistence Master Slave Communication System Based on Retroreflective Projection Technology," *SICE Journal of Control, Measurement, and System Integration*, 1(5), p. 335–344, 2008.
60. J. Viega, M.J. Conway, G Williams, and R. Pausch, "3D Magic Lenses," *Proc. of ACM International Symposium on User Interface Software and Technology (UIST)*, p. 51–58, 1996.
61. R. Zhang and H. Hua, "Characterizing polarization management in a p-HMPD system," *Applied Optics*, 47(4):512–522, Jan. 2008.
62. R. Zhang, and H. Hua, "Design of a polarized head-mounted projection display using ferroelectric liquid-crystal-on-silicon microdisplays," *Applied Optics*, 47(15): 2888–96, 2008.
63. R. Zhang and H. Hua, "Imaging quality of a retroreflective screen in head-mounted projection displays," *Journal of Optical Society of America: A*, 26(5): 1240–1249, May 2009.
64. R. Zhang, *Development and Assessment of Polarized Head Mounted Projection Displays*, Ph.D. Dissertation, University of Arizona, 2010.
65. R. Zhang and H. Hua, "Effects of a Retroreflective Screen on Depth Perception in a Head-mounted Projection Display," *Proc. of 2010 IEEE and ACM International Symposium on Mixed and Augmented Reality (ISMAR'2010)*, 2010.

Chapter 6
Wireless Displays in Educational Augmented Reality Applications

Hannes Kaufmann and Mathis Csisinko

1 Introduction

Augmented Reality (AR) as defined by Azuma [1] does not pose restrictions on output devices to be used for AR. Starting with light-weight notebooks and ultra mobile PCs, recently smartphones became favorite AR output devices. They represent a class of self contained computing units, providing (usually limited) computing power as well as input and output peripherals – all in one device.

In contrast to that are output devices without a general computing processing unit which rely on external source to create and transfer image data. The latter are of interest in this work.

In this chapter we present wireless technologies that can be used to transmit uncompressed stereoscopic video signals to wireless displays in real time. We introduce two output devices, a stereoscopic head mounted display (HMD) and a TFT display module. Both of them have been adapted to act as wireless receivers in order to display wirelessly streamed AR content. Next we focus on advantages of wireless displays for educational AR applications. By way of example two educational AR applications are presented which were used to demonstrate and test wireless displays. A number of teaching scenarios are described where teachers and students greatly benefit from the use of wireless displays. We briefly summarize the results of our observations while developing and evaluating these displays.

H. Kaufmann (✉)
Institute of Software Technology and Interactive Systems, Vienna University of Technology,
Vienna, Austria
e-mail: kaufmann@ims.tuwien.ac.at

B. Furht (ed.), *Handbook of Augmented Reality*, DOI 10.1007/978-1-4614-0064-6_6,   157
© Springer Science+Business Media, LLC 2011

1.1 Motivation

If many users collaborate in a virtual environment, personal displays (e.g. head mounted displays) can be used to deliver user specific views or context sensitive information to each user privately. The reason why we started working on wireless displays is that in [2] we presented a low cost hardware setup that allowed attaching 12 and more HMDs to a single PC. For evaluation purposes a collaborative, educational, augmented reality application was used by six students simultaneously who were wearing HMDs. These devices were attached to a single PC which rendered six views of the application at interactive frame rates. The final evaluation revealed usability problems. A major hindrance for practical usage of such a setup was the number of HMD cables. Given a wireless tracking solution (e.g. optical tracking), the number of cables is at least equivalent to the number of displays. Cables lie on the floor and tend to get tangled as soon as participants start to move. Users have to be very careful not to stumble over cables. As a further consequence movement and interaction is restricted and the number of displays/users has to be limited. Therefore we started to look into wireless solutions to deliver personalized content to users.

1.2 Trend Towards Wireless Clients

In recent years there has been a trend towards smart mobile computing units. Popular examples of such mobile devices are nowadays smart phones, e-book readers and tablets. Technical advances in performance have lead to increasingly powerful devices while minimizing size and weight.

However, computing power of mobile devices is still inferior to desktop computer systems. Provisions to mobility requirements (size, weight, battery lifetime) are limiting factors for computing performance. In particular, there is a tradeoff between mobile device computing power vs. mass, form factor and power consumption. Handheld devices like smart phones have superior mobility features than netbooks and ultra mobile PCs (UMPCs). However, comparing the same devices in terms of computing performance, netbooks and UMPCs are ranked higher than smart phones.

Consequently, mobile computing units are not usable under the precondition that computing (and graphics) performance must be similar to desktop systems. This is exactly the case in real-time Virtual Reality (VR) application scenarios. For instance if we consider medical VR/AR applications with volume visualizations of large datasets, physics simulations or other high end application areas, the performance of mobile computing units will not be sufficient compared to desktop systems for many years to come.

In order to circumvent limitations of current autonomous mobile devices we follow a different approach: High fidelity computing is performed on ordinary state-of-the-art desktop systems and its output is transferred wirelessly to mobile display devices. By this means computing power does not affect size and weight of output devices. This approach is closely related to thin clients in the area of terminal computing.

In the area of terminal computing, a thin client is a computer terminal with the main purpose of providing a graphical user interface to the end user. Computing power and functionality are provided by a server. Lately, the trend towards lowering computer infrastructure costs has lead to the introduction of so called zero clients. While thin clients still require some local processing power and locally installed software, zero clients eliminate the need for locally installed software and connect directly to servers which are located elsewhere. Zero client hardware typically consists of a small box that connects to a keyboard, mouse and monitor. A zero client is able to connect with the server over a wired or wireless IP network.

In PC gaming a live streaming service (OnLive) became available recently. Latest computer games run on servers in the OnLive data center and the image output produced by these games is streamed in real time to PCs of home users at interactive frame rates. Internet connectivity with high network bandwidth is a prerequisite.

These examples illustrate that clients which simply display (wirelessly) streamed content are becoming more frequently used. Maintenance costs are lower because only servers need to be maintained; software synchronization between multiple clients to keep software versions current is not necessary. Output devices without computing power can be produced at much lower costs, have reduced power requirements and can be very light weight. These are important criteria in AR environments as well.

With the technologies presented in Sect. 3, existing standalone output devices can be converted into wireless displays. This encompasses head mounted displays, LCD/TFT/OLED display modules, video projectors and more.

2 Technological Background

2.1 Requirements

There are a number of requirements for wireless transmission of display signals. Virtual environments are real-time applications where users typically walk around, adapt their viewport and manipulate the surrounding environment. It is expected that the effects of these actions are perceivable immediately because the user depends on feedback. Hence, timing is very crucial, especially for visual feedback, the most dominant form of feedback. Therefore, low transmission latency is mandatory. High latency can cause a number of side effects; the degree of immersion and the feeling of presence decreases. The same can be observed if there are (temporary) failures in visual feedback. Thus, wireless transmission must make use of reliable communication channels.

Furthermore, it is desired to achieve the highest quality of display signal transmission possible. Unfortunately high quality graphics transmission at interactive frame rates requires quite high bandwidth. For example, a stereoscopic HMD running at a resolution of 800×600 at 24 bits color depth with 85 Hz frame rate (42.5 Hz per eye) requires nearly 1 Gbps. This is approximately 2 decades higher than digital TV program broadcasting, where the data rate is around tenths of Mbps.

Contrary to digital TV program broadcasting we cannot use sophisticated compression algorithms in order to cope with limited bandwidth. There are two main reasons:

First of all, transmission delays in TV program broadcasting are not as crucial as in AR application scenarios where low latency has to be enforced. Unfortunately, compression and decompression takes some time and therefore latency would increase.

Second, lossy compression algorithms cause visual artifacts on the receiver's side. This behavior is undesired especially in stereoscopic display signal transmissions which are being used for HMDs. Reconstruction artifacts in video frames may disturb the user. If no further provisions are taken into account, reconstruction errors between display frames for the left and the right eye will differ in general. Consequently, this will affect the aligning process in the human vision system in a negative way.

In summary we require a wireless solution with high bandwidth and low latency. In December 2009 Sensics conducted a worldwide survey (details in [3]) in order to evaluate user requirements for wireless HMD signal transmission. According to the results, both low latency and a refresh rate of 60 frames per second (or higher) were considered as top priority. The capability for true stereoscopic viewing and the ability to use multiple HMDs simultaneously had also high ranking.

2.2 Wireless Technology Overview

Our solution is based on the WHDI standard from AMIMON [4]. This technology is primarily targeted on consumer electronics, in particular HDTV, and establishes wireless HDMI signal transmission. HDTV resolutions require bandwidths in the range of about 1 Gbps up to 3 Gbps and WHDI is able to provide these data rates. Stereoscopic video signals (HMDs) with the demand for increased frame rates have bandwidth requirements close to these figures (approximately 1 Gbps, as mentioned before). The WHDI solution uses multi-input-multi-output (MIMO) technology and establishes wireless communication over the unlicensed 5 GHz frequency band.

In general the bit rate of a wireless connection is not constant over time. The WHDI implementation includes technology to adapt to the current conditions utilizing prioritization of more important components of the video signal. This differentiation between more and less important components include more vs. least significant bits (MSB vs. LSB) of video pixels, lower vs. higher spatial frequencies and luminance vs. chrominance information. More important parts are encoded and modulated in a way that correct reconstruction on the receiver's side is more likely than for less important components. This guarantees that even in the case of decreasing wireless channel capacity communication does not break down immediately and the video signal can be reconstructed, although in lower quality since less important components might have been lost. We did not observe such cases since we were not operating on the upper bandwidth limit.

There exists a competitive standard, called WirelessHD operating on the 60 GHz band with 7 GHz channel bandwidth. It features data rates up to 4 Gbps with a theoretical limit at 25 Gbps.

Furthermore there is a commercially available wireless solution for HMDs. Sensics offers a wireless link option for its HMD products. It is based on Wi-Fi wireless N technology and MPEG4 H.264 video compression. According to the specification a system latency of below 32 ms is maintained. However, Sensics is specialized in HMDs with wide field of view and high display resolutions (e.g. $1,280 \times 1,024$ pixels, $1,920 \times 1,200$ pixels). Thus its products are more targeted on a high price market and probably not affordable for every customer.

Finally for all these different wireless solutions there is no official statement in the specifications about display resolutions with frame rates above 60 Hz. Higher frame rates are required especially for HMDs operating in page-flipped (frame sequential) mode. Due to the fact that video frames are split between left and right eye, each eye perceives images at a frame rate which is only half as big as the display signal refresh rate.

Hence we had to test higher frame rate capabilities in our hardware setup in order to check whether we get acceptable results for frame sequential HMD signals.

3 Hardware Setup

The first-generation WHDI devices (ZWD-2500, see Fig. 6.1 left) that we used in our setup were produced by Zinwell. The slim dimensions ($180 \times 140 \times 39\,\text{mm}^3$) of

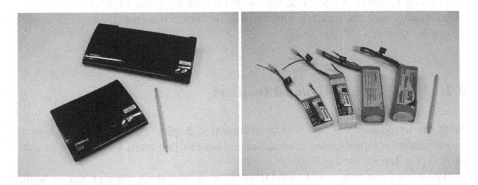

Fig. 6.1 WHDI devices (*left*), LiPo accumulators (*right*)

the receiving device and its mass of about 220 g were acceptable for our prototype solution. Contrary to the mobile receiving device, the transmitting device is not carried around by the user. Thus, mass, size and power consumption characteristics are not as critical as for the receiving device.

The transmitter (ZWD-2500T) contains four input ports (two HDMI and two sets of RCA video component ports). It selectively provides a wireless link of one of its input signals to the receiver (ZWD-2500R). On the receiver's side the transmitted signal is output by an HDMI port. Additionally, wireless transmission covers audio and remote control signals as well. However, these features were not used in our setup. These first-generation devices seem to have a bandwidth limitation of approximately 1.5 Gbps. Officially 1080p resolution is supported up to a frame rate of 30 Hz, whereas the second-generation WHDI devices support 60 Hz frame rate as well (approximately 3 Gbps data rate).

For our device setup latency is specified as being less than 1 ms, which is excellent for AR applications. Furthermore, it is possible to operate multiple pairs of WHDI receiving/transmitting devices simultaneously. During initialization the devices automatically negotiate radio channels but there is also the option to override them manually. In the latter case the devices offer selecting one out of ten different radio channels. In our tests we used automatic negotiation and successfully operated three pairs of WHDI devices.

Transmission range is specified as up to 20 m in a line of sight condition, which is reduced to a maximum of 10 m in cases beyond line of sight. This is sufficient and compatible for our indoor tracking scenarios.

True wireless display devices require mobile power support as well. Fortunately, light-weight accumulators are available nowadays. We have chosen Lithium-ion polymer (LiPo) accumulators, which evolved from Lithium-ion batteries. Compared to other kinds of mobile power sources they feature very high power capacity, low weight and small form factor at the same time. Hence, they can be found in various mobile electronic devices (e.g. music players) and are popular power supplies for radio-controlled scale aircraft models as well.

The WHDI receiver must be supplied with a voltage of approximately 5 V. We use LiPo accumulators (see Fig. 6.1 right) with a voltage of 7.4 V. This voltage is reduced to about 4.8 V by a regulator module in order to ensure electrical compatibility with the receiver. The masses for the LiPo accumulators used in our setups are between 100 and 400 g.

3.1 Wireless Head Mounted Displays

With the introduction of low cost head mounted displays, prices of HMD-based mixed reality setups dropped considerably. Two HMD models were tested in our prototype solution (see Fig. 6.2).

The Sony Glasstron model LDI-D100BE is an optical see-through device with an LCD display resolution of 800 × 600 pixels (each eye) at a maximum frame

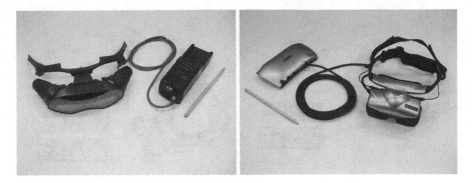

Fig. 6.2 HMD models: Sony Glasstron (*left*), eMagin Z800 (*right*)

rate of 85 Hz (42.5 Hz per eye). This HMD supports page-flipped (frame sequential) stereoscopic viewing. The head-worn display unit is connected to and controlled by a power supply box. Power is supplied either by an AC power adapter or by manufacturer specific lithium-ion battery packs. The operation time for the battery packs we used in our setup (with a capacity of approximately 5.4 Ah) is about 3 h. The dimensions of the power control box are approximately $54 \times 47 \times 160\,\mathrm{mm}^3$ and its mass is about 260 g – excluding any battery pack which might be mounted on and connected to the box. For better wearability we mounted the display unit on a light-weight bicycle helmet. Unfortunately this HMD model is not produced any more.

The eMagin Z800 3DVisor incorporates two 800×600 pixels OLED displays and can be driven with up to 85 Hz frame rate as well. The Z800 consists of a head-worn display unit and a control box, similar to the Sony Glasstron. However, there is no optical see-through option for this device. Power must be supplied either by connecting an external power adapter (5 V) or an USB cable.

Stereoscopic output can be a bit troublesome with the Z800. In the case of a wired VGA cable connection to an nVidia graphics card, the Z800 automatically detects frame sequential stereoscopic display signals by inspecting proprietary control signals. However, this is superseded with new graphics cards which do not support this mode anymore. Alternatively, switching into stereoscopic mode can be performed manually but this requires a USB connection. In our wireless solution automatic detection of frame sequential stereoscopic display signals is not possible. Therefore, we utilize certified wireless USB (CWUSB) technology. Our CWUSB setup consists of a pair of USB devices, namely a host and device dongle. The device dongle is connected to the control box and must be externally power supplied, which provides power to the control box as well.

Both HMDs expect VGA signals. However, the WHDI receiver delivers an HDMI video signal, which is incompatible to VGA. Therefore, an HDFury2 device is connected in between in order to perform the required conversion of the video signal.

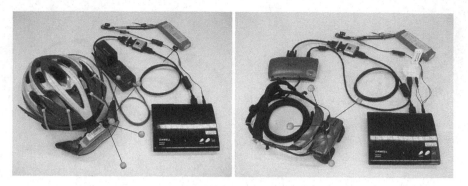

Fig. 6.3 HMD setup assemblies: Sony Glasstron (*left*), eMagin Z800 (*right*)

Unfortunately, the documentation of the WHDI devices does not officially state whether other resolutions than HDTV are supported. Video signal transmission at a resolution of 800×600 pixels and the HMD's maximum frame rate of 85 Hz (approximately 1 Gbps data rate) fails, even though other supported HDTV resolutions require significantly more communication bandwidth. Hence, this is an indication that the problem is caused by technical limitations other than wireless transmission channel bandwidth constraints (approximately 1.5 Gbps as mentioned before). Nevertheless, we were able to demonstrate successful operation of our device setup at a reduced frame rate of 72 Hz (approximately 0.8 Gbps data rate).

The final hardware setup with all components is shown in Fig. 6.3. The interconnecting cables provide power and video signals to the HMD. As mentioned before WHDI devices support wirelessly transmitting stereophonic audio signals as well. In addition to that, both HMD models contain earphones. Providing stereo sound requires an additional cable connection between HMD control box and WHDI receiver.

Power consumption of the WHDI receiver was measured with up to 1.5 A and approximately 1.2 A on average. This means that even a LiPo battery with a low capacity of 1.6 Ah is able to supply power to the receiver for more than 1 h. This figure exceeds the limiting factor of cybersickness symptoms. Various studies (e.g. [5]) recommend limiting the use of HMDs to 20–30 min per session in order to avoid symptoms of cybersickness. Moreover, operating hours can be increased with larger capacities. We used LiPo accumulators with capacities of 3.2 Ah and 5 Ah. All mobile components except for the head-worn display unit fit in a shoulder bag (see Figs. 6.9 and 6.10). This is acceptable for a prototype solution. However, if there is further demand in the future, size and mass of WHDI receiver and HMD control box need to be reduced. Obviously all components could be integrated into a single device. This would eliminate long cables interconnecting subcomponents and would allow for further reduction of size and mass.

Instead of using battery packs, a single LiPo accumulator with a voltage of 11.1 V could supply power to all devices for the Sony Glasstron.

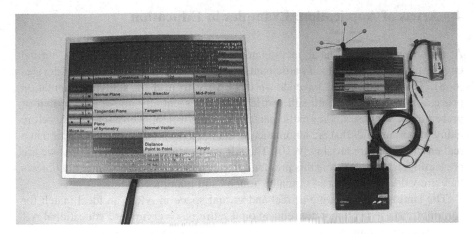

Fig. 6.4 TFT screen (*left*), final setup assembly (*right*)

Furthermore, the CWUSB connection in the eMagin Z800 setup could be eliminated as well, if the necessary signals for the control box were integrated into the WHDI channel. Similar to the unused feature of our WHDI device to transmit remote control signals these signals would occupy only a tiny fraction of transmission bandwidth.

3.2 Wireless Handheld Display

We tested our wireless solution with a commercially available TFT compact module. This kit is an all-in-one display solution containing all necessary components for driving a 12.1 in. TFT screen mounted to a metallic frame (see Fig. 6.4). Its highest resolution is $1,024 \times 768$ pixels. The module must be supplied with power from an external source (12 V) and contains an electrical port for connecting either DVI or VGA sources. Its dimensions of $260.5 \times 204 \times 21\,\mathrm{mm}^3$ are suitable for mobile displaying applications. Due to the metallic frame the mass is approximately 1 kg. However, if there is a demand for reduced weight this could be further reduced in the future.

The display module requires electric current of approximately 1 A. Summing up the power consumption of the display module and the WHDI receiver, a battery capacity of 3.2 Ah is sufficient to supply power to both devices for more than 1 h by using a single LiPo accumulator. If we would increase the capacity to 5 Ah, the operating time would be extended to at least 2 h. The slightly reduced voltage of the mobile power supply (11.1 V) had no negative side effect on operation.

Again due to lack of support, video signal transmission at a resolution of $1,024 \times 768$ pixels using the display's maximum frame rate of 75 Hz failed. However, there was no problem supplying the display with a frame rate of 70 Hz (approximately 1.3 Gbps data rate).

4 Areas of Application: Examples in Education

A number of studies have investigated orientation and navigation in virtual environments through which participants navigate using joysticks or other devices [6–8]. These applications have shown to be very fruitful for studying orientation processes; however they are still restricted to an essentially non-spatial format of presentation. In these studies participants see the environment on a screen. Therefore many important cues that are automatically encoded during real-life locomotion in a real environment are missing [9, 10]. The AR applications and scenarios that we are presenting, try to overcome this problem. Participants can move around the objects they are working on and can virtually "touch" and manipulate them.

The simultaneous sharing of real and virtual space in AR is an ideal match for computer-assisted collaborative educational settings. Overviews of educational AR and VR applications, use cases, requirements and potentials are given in [11–13] (Chap. 2) and [14].

Educational applications are typically characterized by additional specific requirements that are unique to this domain.

- For real applicability in classroom, educational AR applications ideally support a large number of users.
- They allow simultaneous interaction of at least two users, for instance teacher and student.
- They have to be robust and easy to use. Students usually expect technology to work and loose motivation quickly if immature technology negatively affects their work.

In general users do not want to be hindered by cables. Wireless displays seem to assist in fulfilling all of these requirements.

In order to demonstrate maturity, robustness and usefulness of wireless systems as described above, we used these output devices in existing educational applications. In the following we briefly describe educational applications that have been evaluated. Section 5 details teaching scenarios where wireless technologies are beneficial.

4.1 Construct3D

Construct3D [13, 15] is a three dimensional geometric construction tool specifically designed for mathematics and geometry education. A collaborative augmented reality setup is utilized with the main advantage that students actually see three dimensional objects in 3D space which they previously had to calculate and construct with traditional methods. Augmented reality provides them with an almost tangible picture of complex three dimensional objects and scenes. It enhances, enriches and complements the mental images that students form when working with three dimensional objects (Fig. 6.5).

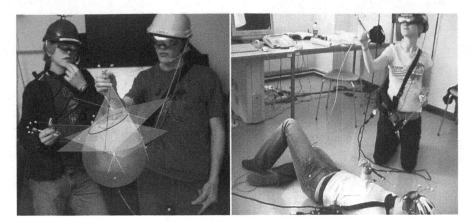

Fig. 6.5 Students working with Construct3D

The application supports multiple collaborating users wearing stereoscopic see-through head mounted displays providing a common, shared virtual construction space. Typically one PC with two graphic ports renders stereoscopic views for both users. Head and hands are tracked with millimeter accuracy using an iotracker [16] optical tracking system. This allows students to walk around objects and to view them from different perspectives.

Construct3D's menu system is mapped to a hand-held pen and panel interface, the Personal Interaction Panel (PIP) [17] (Fig. 6.6). The pen is used for operating the menu on the panel as well as for direct manipulation of the scene in 3D space. Augmented reality enables all users to see the same virtual objects as well as each others' pens and menus, therefore a user can provide help to a colleague if desired. The face-to-face setting allows for traditional pedagogic communication between teacher and students. Other setups for educational use have been reported in [13].

Construct3D is based on the Studierstube software platform [18] as a runtime environment and for multi-user synchronization. The current version of Construct3D offers functions for the construction of 3D points and geometric objects. It provides planar and spatial geometric operations on objects, measurements, and structuring of elements into "3D layers." It supports generation of and operation on points (either freely positioned in space or fixed on curves and surfaces), lines, basic 2D and 3D objects, B-spline curves, NURBS surfaces and surfaces of revolution. To mention just a few, the following geometric operations are implemented: Boolean operations (union, difference, intersection) on 3D objects, intersections between all types of 2D and 3D objects resulting in intersection points and curves, planar slicing of objects, rotational sweeps, helical sweeps, general sweeps along a path, surface normals, tangential planes, tangents and many more. A comprehensive overview of Construct3D is given in [13, 19].

The system features support for 3D *dynamic geometry*. All points can be picked and dragged at any given time. Experiencing what happens under movement allows better insight into a particular construction and geometry in general.

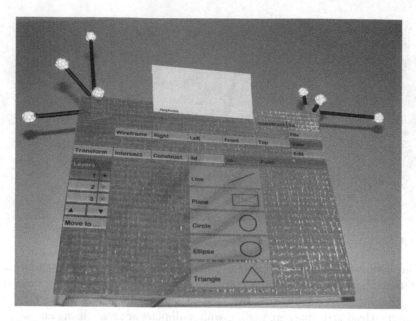

Fig. 6.6 Construct3D's main menu on the PIP seen through an HMD

Construct3D was evaluated multiple times with over 500 users in total (students, teachers and experts) over the course of 5 years and is one of the longest developed educational applications so far. Three usability studies with more than 100 students have been conducted [5] and guidelines have been formulated regarding how to design AR applications for (geometry) education [20]. We studied how ongoing technological improvements can be integrated into an AR system and looked at pedagogical questions such as how to adapt contents of the current high-school curriculum to the new learning environment.

4.2 Physics Playground

PhysicsPlayground [21] is an augmented reality application for mechanics education. Classical mechanics [22, 23] is the oldest discipline in the field of physics. It describes the common motion of objects that humans perceive in everyday life. The three fundamental laws of motion which were formulated by Isaac Newton (1642–1727) are traditionally part of the school curriculum as well as concepts such as force, velocity and acceleration.

It might be that physics in the traditional sense is sometimes taught in an abstract, jejune way and is therefore not very motivating for students. The result is that theoretical models behind physical phenomena are often misunderstood. However, conveying these concepts is of utmost importance since they are fundamental to physics.

Fig. 6.7 *Left*: An experiment simulating the motion of a car crankshaft. *Right*: A centrifugal regulator in PhysicsPlayground

Fig. 6.8 *Left*: Each user is equipped with input devices pen, PIP and head mounted display. *Right*: Example menu on the PIP

PhysicsPlayground utilizes a recent physics engine (nVidia PhysX; survey in [24]) developed for the PC gaming market to simulate physical experiments in the domain of mechanics in real time. Students are enabled to actively build own experiments and to study them in a three-dimensional virtual world (Fig. 6.7). A variety of tools are provided to analyze forces, energy, velocity, paths and other properties of objects before, during and after experiments.

The overall hardware setup is equivalent to the one used in Construct3D. It supports multiple users, allows direct manipulation and free roaming around virtual objects. By using Sony Glasstron see-through head mounted displays students can see each other and their interaction devices. In Fig. 6.8 (right) several menu widgets are shown. Many of them have 3D icons placed on top which are animated when moving the pen over them. This is self-explanatory and clarifies their specific functionality.

Innovative teaching content can be studied to exploit the strengths of this immersive virtual environment. PhysicsPlayground serves as an example of how current technologies can be utilized to deliver a new quality in physics education.

5 Teaching Scenarios

During the work with educational AR applications such as Construct3D and PhysicsPlayground, teachers need to be able to communicate and to establish eye contact with students while interacting with the application. Therefore a teacher's output device of choice might be a mobile (tablet-like) display, a see-through HMD or a (stereo) projector. We pick a few regular teaching situations related to how AR has been used in previous Construct3D evaluations and how it could be used in future classrooms, to explain how wireless displays can be put to use.

In order to provide groups of users with an immersive experience exactly tailored to their point of view, all users (respectively their head and output device) must be tracked in space. Tracking a large number of users in such an environment is a problem on its own. It is obvious that any wireless form of tracking is preferred over a wired alternative because of the number of cables, limited freedom of movement leading to a rather tethered experience and other practical problems that would arise due to the cables. Optical tracking has proved to be an optimal solution in that case.

5.1 Scenario #1: Students Collaborate, Teacher Guides

In evaluations of Construct3D [5] we found that most students liked our standard dual-user setup best, when asked about different teaching scenarios. They had the choice between working together with a tutor (favored by 9.5%), with a second student but without a tutor (4.7%), or with a second student and a tutor (80.9%). The latter scenario consisted of two users wearing HMDs (see Fig. 6.5) and a teacher who guided them.

Ideally students should be able to move freely to foster interaction and engagement. In addition their teacher needs freedom of movement to react to technical or cognitive problems and to communicate freely.

One option would be equipping the teacher with a wireless handheld display such as our TFT module. It is (optically) tracked and serves as a very flexible window into the virtual world. It can be operated single-handedly, frees the other hand for interaction with the application and the display can be put away (or attached to the belt of the teacher for instance) if not needed.

Fig. 6.9 A wireless TFT display serves as a window into the virtual world for the teacher. Two wireless HMDs are used by students

Alternatively the TFT display can be switched to menu mode. In menu mode the display serves as a menu (PIP) which can be used by the teacher to control the application and to help students in case of problems with the menu interface (see Fig. 6.9). We also built a wireless TFT touch screen module. Menu buttons can simply be pushed as known from touch interfaces; if using a pen to select and manipulate objects in 3D space, the pen can also be used to push buttons directly on the touch screen.

In this scenario we suggest that students use wireless HMDs so they can move around freely. In contrast to our work in [2] where wired HMDs hindered interaction and movement, wireless HMDs can be used by a larger group of students providing them with personalized views. This is of great advantage especially in applications such as Construct3D where users are encouraged to choose their own point of view. Some students tend to lie down on the floor (Fig. 6.5 right) or step on a chair to view geometry from different perspectives. They have the absolute freedom of movement within the tracking volume.

5.2 Scenario #2: Teacher Demonstrates and Shares

In this scenario a teacher performs an experiment or construction in 3D space with an output device of his choice (e.g. a see-through HMD). Each student possesses a wireless display module or students share a couple of displays to view and follow the instructions. The displays are tracked.

Fig. 6.10 The student (*right*) has to contribute to a task by using her wireless display while the teacher observes her work

When students are called by their teacher to contribute to an experiment/construction, they are able to interact directly in 3D space. Similar to the capabilities of the teacher's interface in scenario 1, they can switch between a window into the virtual world and menu mode (Fig. 6.10). Their classmates can watch on their own displays.

This scenario allows teaching a group of students, even a whole class in an AR environment.

5.3 Experiences

No formal evaluations have been conducted with the wireless displays yet but experiences from observations can be reported. As soon as we changed our lab setup to reflect scenario 1, users of Construct3D and PhysicsPlayground started to move much more than before in an unconstrained, free way. Suddenly users seemed to have lost their inhibitions. They explored the virtual environment in a more active and natural way.

In the past we always had users who did not dare to move much. They seemed to freeze on the spot as soon as they put on an HMD and didn't even dare to turn their heads. With the introduction of wireless HMDs and a simple shoulder bag containing battery, control box and wireless receiver, there are no visible restrictions of movement anymore. Users do not perceive any limitations in range of movement.

Before starting to work in AR it takes up to a minute until a stable wireless communication channel is established. This is due to initial communication overhead between WHDI transmitter and receiver. In addition to that, as with any wireless technology, power supply of the wireless devices must be guaranteed in order to maintain a stable connection. Consequently, a number of mobile power sources have to be maintained. For intensively used system setups accumulators must be recharged on a frequent basis.

As mentioned before, the form factor of the mobile components could be improved or all mobile components could be integrated into a single device.

Since transmission latency of the chosen wireless transmission technology is very low (1 ms specified) there is no latency noticeable in any of our wireless devices. We do not expect that the described wireless technologies contribute to side effects such as cybersickness in an additional negative way.

Especially students will enjoy this freedom in movement – to lie down on the floor to look at objects from below or to step on a chair. It increases the fun factor and enhances the feeling of immersion.

6 Conclusions

In this chapter we present current wireless technologies to deliver uncompressed video signals at low latency to AR output devices. We have built head mounted and handheld prototype displays to demonstrate their use in educational applications.

In most application areas where head mounted or handheld displays are being used, wireless versions of these displays are favored over wired versions by end users. They allow unconstrained movement within the tracking volume, support untethered interaction and encourage active and natural interaction of multiple users.

At first sight this chapter seems to be targeted to indoor applications only. However, in case of outdoor AR applications, light-weight, flexible mobile devices without computing power could also be used together with wireless technology. The latest fourth generation cellular wireless standard 4G is specified to provide peak data rates of 1 Gbps. Long Term Evolution Advanced (LTE Advanced) is one example. This data rate is most likely not sufficient to continuously supply uncompressed image data to mobile wireless displays at interactive frame rates. However, long term a fifth generation standard is expected which will provide sufficient data rates to stream high resolution uncompressed video data to mobile devices. With the emergence of auto-stereoscopic display modules, stand alone displays could be used for 3D stereo output as well. A future of foldable, bendable, light-weight 3D output devices that receive video signals wirelessly is within reach.

Acknowledgments This work was funded in part by the Austrian Science Fund FWF project P19265, the EU FP7 projects PLAYMANCER (FP7-ICT-215839) and VISION (FP7-211567).

References

1. R. Azuma, "A Survey of Augmented Reality," *Presence - Teleoperators and Virtual Environments,* vol. 6, pp. 355–385, 1997.
2. H. Kaufmann and M. Csisinko, "Multiple Head Mounted Displays in Virtual and Augmented Reality Applications," *International Journal of Virtual Reality,* vol. 6, pp. 43–50, 2007.
3. Y. Boger. (2010, accessed Jan 2011). Cutting the Cord: the 2010 Survey on using Wireless Video with Head-Mounted Displays.
4. M. Feder. (2007, accessed Jan 2011). Enabling wireless uncompressed HDTV connectivity with a unique video-modem approach: A technical overview. *http://www.amimon.com/PDF/tech_article%20final.pdf.*
5. H. Kaufmann and A. Dünser, "Summary of Usability Evaluations of an Educational Augmented Reality Application," in *HCI International Conference (HCII 2007).* vol. 14, LNCS 4563, R. Shumaker, Ed., Beijing, China: Springer-Verlag Berlin Heidelberg, 2007, pp. 660–669.
6. R. P. Darken, *et al.,* "Spatial Orientation and Wayfinding in Large-Scale Virtual Spaces: An Introduction," *Presence: Teleoperators & Virtual Environments,* vol. 7, pp. 101–107, 1998.
7. J. Glück and S. Fitting, "Spatial strategy selection: Interesting incremental information," *International Journal of Testing,* vol. 3, pp. 293–308, 2003.
8. D. Waller, *et al.,* "The transfer of spatial knowledge in virtual environment training," *Presence - Teleoperators and Virtual Environments,* vol. 7, pp. 129–143, 1998.
9. R. L. Klatzky, *et al.,* "Spatial updating of self-position and orientation during ral, imagined, and virtual locomotion," *Psychological science,* vol. 9, p. 1998, 1998.
10. D. H. Shin, *et al.,* "View Changes in Augmented Reality Computer-Aided-Drawing," *ACM Transactions on Applied Perceptions,* vol. 2, pp. 1–14, 2005.
11. F. Mantovani, "VR Learning: Potential and Challenges for the Use of 3D Environments in Education and Training," in *Towards CyberPsychology: Mind, Cognitions and Society in the Internet Age,* G. Riva and C. Galimberti, Eds., Amsterdam: IOS Press, 2001.
12. C. Youngblut, "Educational uses of virtual technology," VA: Institute for Defense Analyses, Alexandria IDA Document D-2128, 1998.
13. H. Kaufmann, "Geometry Education with Augmented Reality," Ph.D. Thesis, Vienna University of Technology, 2004.
14. M. Bricken, "Virtual reality learning environments: potentials and challenges," *SIGGRAPH Computer Graphics,* vol. 25, pp. 178–184, 1991.
15. H. Kaufmann and D. Schmalstieg, "Mathematics and geometry education with collaborative augmented reality," *Computers & Graphics,* vol. 27, pp. 339–345, Jun 2003.
16. T. Pintaric and H. Kaufmann, "Affordable Infrared-Optical Pose-Tracking for Virtual and Augmented Reality," in *Proceedings of "Trends and Issues in Tracking for Virtual Environments" Workshop, IEEE VR 2007,* Charlotte, NC, USA, 2007, pp. 44–51.
17. Z. S. Szalavári and M. Gervautz, "The Personal Interaction Panel - A Two-Handed Interface for Augmented Reality," *Computer Graphics Forum,* vol. 16, pp. 335–346, 1997.
18. D. Schmalstieg, *et al.,* "The Studierstube augmented reality project," *Presence - Teleoperators and Virtual Environments,* vol. 11, pp. 33–54, Feb 2002.
19. H. Kaufmann, "Applications of Mixed Reality," Habilitation Thesis, Faculty of Informatics, Vienna University of Technology, Vienna, 2009.
20. H. Kaufmann and D. Schmalstieg, "Designing Immersive Virtual Reality for Geometry Education," in *Proceedings of IEEE Virtual Reality Conference 2006,* Alexandria, Virginia, USA, 2006, pp. 51–58.
21. H. Kaufmann and B. Meyer, "Simulating Educational Physical Experiments in Augmented Reality," in *Proceedings of ACM SIGGRAPH ASIA 2008 Educators Program,* Singapore, 2008.
22. H. Goldstein, *et al., Classical Mechanics,* 3rd ed. Reading, Massachusetts, USA: Addison Wesley, 2001.

23. L. D. Landau and E. M. Lifshitz, *Course of Theoretical Physics: Mechanics*, 3rd ed.: Butterworth-Heinemann, 1976.
24. A. Seugling and M. Rölin, "Evaluation of physics engines and implementation of a physics module in a 3d-authoring tool," Master thesis, Master thesis. Department of Computing Science, Umea University, Umea, Sweden, 2006.

Chapter 7
Mobile Projection Interfaces for Augmented Reality Applications

Markus Löchtefeld, Antonio Krüger, and Michael Rohs

1 Introduction and Motivation

Nowadays mobile phones are used for a wide range of applications in peoples every day life. Customizable with a variety of applications these mobile phones are becoming the swiss army knife of the generation. With the increase in processing power and memory the only bottleneck left is the small display size and resolution. To keep these devices mobile the size of the screen is restricted and even though the resolution of such displays is increasing, there is a limit to information presentable on the display. One way to overcome these drawbacks is the integration of a projection unit into the mobile phone. Modern projectors have been miniaturized to the size of mobile phones and can be operated using batteries. These projectors are called pico projectors. The next step is to integrate such a projector directly into a mobile phone. These devices are also called projector phones. Up to now several different prototypes both from research and industry exist. First commercial projector phones are available on the mass market [1]. Such phones have the capabilities to overcome the problems that arise when exploring large-scale information on the small display of a present-day mobile phone. With these devices one can explore information like maps or web pages without the need for zooming or panning [2] but up to now the available devices are only projecting a mirror image of the devices display or images and videos. Considering the anticipated widespread availability of phones with integrated cameras and projectors in the future, comparably little research has been conducted so far to investigate the potential of such a mobile unit.

Due to the small size of these new pico projectors the integration into other every day life objects like clothing or accessories is possible.Such projectors hidden in the woodwork can facilitate Augmented Reality (AR) applications like pointing one

M. Löchtefeld (✉)
German Research Center for Artificial Intelligence DFKI, University of Saarland,
Saarbrücken, Germany
e-mail: markus.loechtefeld@dfki.de

B. Furht (ed.), *Handbook of Augmented Reality*, DOI 10.1007/978-1-4614-0064-6_7,
© Springer Science+Business Media, LLC 2011

towards the object one is searching for. The new output capabilities of these pico projectors equipped devices provide a rich design-space for AR applications and games. They have the ability to augment objects through overlaying projection and with that they can overcome the problems that we are facing today when creating AR applications. Projecting a dynamic overlay directly onto a surface of the real world may enhance the possibilities even though it can be hard to identify the projected overlay in bright light. The usage of a head-mounted-display (HMD) provides excellent results in terms of augmentation but it is also cumbersome to use and sometimes straining the users. Furthermore as a consequence of the display being attached to a single user, applications using a head mounted display can only be used in multi-user scenarios when using a large amount of hardware. Another common technique for dynamic AR overlays is to use the screen of the mobile device as a magic lens [3]. But in these scenarios one has to struggle again with the small size of the device. Moreover such a magic lens display is not really enjoyable to use with more than one user at the same time.

To empower pico-projectors to augment the real world around them the projector has to have a clear image of its surroundings. For this several techniques exist. The most suited one for the form factor phone is the usage of computer vision based methods since most modern mobile phones are already equipped with powerful cameras. When using computer-vision based approaches different possible spatial layouts of camera and projector unfold and with that different possible AR applications. In this chapter we identify different application types based on the spatial configuration of the camera and the projector for handheld projector phones. As part of this classification, we derive different application types using of different spatial layouts of cameras and projectors: congruent setups, partially intersecting setups and disjunct setups. Such a classification is useful to structure the design space of projector phone systems, because we think other researchers can categorize their applications to focus on specific problems and topics of each type. The classification presented in this chapter is only reasonable for the form-factor of a mobile phone. Head- or body-worn camera-projector setups provide a higher variety of possible combinations even though they are similar to a certain extend.

With mobile projection also the problems of distorted projection caused by non-orthogonal projection angles or hand jitter arise. Furthermore everyday life objects often have the tendency to have non-planar surfaces that have to be taken into account as well. These problems are out of the scope of this chapter but plenty of research has already focused on these problems, e.g. [4].

The remainder of this chapter is structured as follows. Related work in the field of mobile projection and projector phones as well as the general interaction with mobile devices is presented in Sect. 2. Section 3 describes the different application classes of these interfaces. In this conceptual section we also discuss how the spatial layout of the camera relative to the mobile projection unit can affect the characteristics of applications for this new sort of hardware. How proximity to the object can be used as an input is discussed in Sect. 4 and in Sect. 5 we describe several applications that evolve from the concepts developed in Sects. 3 and 4.

2 Related Work

A lot of research in the past in the field of AR has focused on projection-based applications but most of these applications used stationary or steerable projectors. Bimber et al. distinguish between five spatial areas to create an image-overlay for an AR display starting directly on the retina of the user and ending on the object that should be augmented [5]. To create an AR display directly on an object the one possibility is to use a projector but still it can be located in several different spatial locations. Bimber et al. differentiate between a stationary, a hand-held and a body-/head-worn projector for this. With the miniaturization of projection units the hand-held and body-worn alternatives are not longer limited to research.

Initial research in the field of mobile projection was conducted by Raskar et al. with the iLamps [4]. Their early mobile prototypes focused on how to project on non-planar surfaces and how multiple projectors can be combined to create bigger and brighter projections. Even though the iLamps where capable of augmenting everyday-life objects first interaction techniques for AR applications where developed with the successor of the iLamps the RFIG Lamps [6] which were used to create object adaptive projections. Set in a warehouse scenario, the RFIGLamps could be used for example to mark products where the date of expiry is close to the actual date via projection. To recognize the objects active RFID-tags were used. Blasko et al. [7] explored the interaction with a wrist- worn projection display while web browsing. The wrist-worn projector was simulated with a short-throw projector in a lab and the users were for example able to scroll down a website by tilting their wrist. Mobile projection offers a huge potential for mobile collaborative work since the information can get easily accessible for multiple users through the projection. These possibilities for multiple users were initially examined by Cao et al. [8]. They used an instrumented room to create several information spaces, which could be explored with handheld projectors. It was for example possible to find a spot for a meeting by combining the schedule of multiple users through overlaying the projection of the schedules of each user. That large-scale information are easier to explore when using a projection was shown by Hang et al. in [2]. Their studies outlined that there is a significant increase in speed when searching for points of interest on a map or specific images using the projection compared to the standard display. Furthermore their studies showed that users prefer the projection to the phones display for sharing their content.

A first body-worn projector prototype was demonstrated by Karitsuka et al. [9]. Through the usage of infrared (IR) light it was possible to augment surfaces equipped with IR-retroreflective markers. Additionally it was possible to interact with projection through touch-input. Therefore the fingers of the user had to be equipped with IR-retro-reflective markers as well. However the prototype of Karitsuka et al. was bulky and demanded a steady power-connection. In contrast to that the SixthSense system of Mistry et al. is a lightweight body-worn camera-projector unit that could be operated using batteries [10]. Their application exemplarily showed that mobile projection could be utilized in every day life using gestural interaction. The interaction was realized using colored markers mounted at

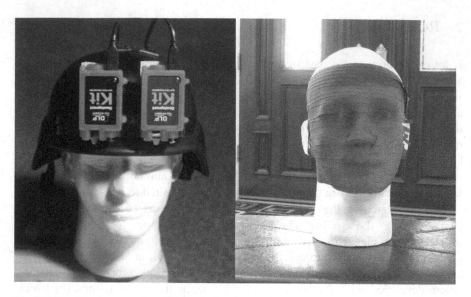

Fig. 7.1 Two head-mounted projectors (*left*) are used to augment a puppet head equipped with retro reflective material (*right*)

the fingers of the user. They claimed that the hardware needed to built their prototype which either could be located in a hat or worn as a necklace costs at the moment around 350$ which is comparable to the price of a current mobile phone. With Cobra, Ye et al. showed how a shoulder mounted pico projector could be used to augment a flexible cardboard interface that uses bends as input [11]. The detection of the cardboard was done with IR light as well. How mobile projection could be used in military training scenarios was demonstrated by Bolas et al. with the REFLECT system [12]. Their head-mounted system allowed user-specific projection onto the surrounding environment by using retroreflective on possible projection surfaces. On such surfaces the projection is only visible when the eyes are near to the projection axis. With that it was possible to augment a puppet face for every user in such a way that the eyes of the face where looking at user. This effect can be seen in Fig. 7.1.

From this development a rich design space for mobile augmented reality applications could emerge. With a built in projector not only the graphical scale of the applications can be increased, also the range of possibilities for developing mobile augmented reality application will widen. In combination with the built-in camera of the mobile device, mobile camera-projector units become a powerful interface for mobile AR applications. To create visual overlays for augmented reality games, in the past often head-mounted displays where used [13, 14]. This retrenched not only the comfort of the user it also limited mobility. Another common technique for dynamic overlays is to use the screen of the mobile device like a magic lens [3]. Therefore the video image taken by the camera of the device is enhanced with additional overlays and shown on the devices screen with the disadvantage to struggle again with the small size of the display. Moreover such a magic lens display is not really scalable when thinking of multi-user settings. Therefore we think that projecting an additional display or augmenting real world objects with additional information can extend the range of possible applications.

3 Classification

Today's projector phones are very limited in the functionality of the projector. Often the projection unit is just used to project a copy of the devices screen or media such as pictures or videos onto any surfaces. The projector is therefore mainly used to explore content that is bigger than the real estate of the mobile devices screen. To fully exploit the potential of mobile projection we classify different spatial layouts of the camera relative to the projector unit and discuss the impact on the AR interaction techniques facilitated by these layouts.

We first want to define the terms camera field of view (FoV) and the term field of projection (FoP) for easier discussion of different layouts. The FoV of the camera is defined, as the area the camera is able to "see." The FoP is the area the projector is able to project on.

Generally one can distinguish between three different spatial layouts: First setups where the FoV and the FoP do not overlap are categorized as "disjunct" because the projection goes to a completely other direction than the visual field of the camera. Setups were the FoV of the camera and the FoP overlap are categorized in two different classes, "partially intersecting" and "congruent." In both setups the direction of camera and projector is the same, they only differ from the configuration of the lens of camera and projector or their distance to each other. If the visual field of the camera overlaps partially with the projected field, then it is categorized as an intersecting projection. In the third category, "congruent," the entire projected field is situated within the image produced by the camera. Due to different hardware specifications of cameras and projectors (different throwing angles, aperture, and others properties) the actual spatial setups could be very different. Today, due to the technical limitations, just disjunct setups exist. This mostly because of the needed size of the projection unit, but keeping in mind that e.g. in the slider part of the Nokia N95 ($\sim$1,5 mm) houses a VGA-camera the integration of such a camera next to a projection unit should be possible. We think the partially intersecting" and "congruent" provide a lot more potential for new interactions as we illustrate in the following paragraphs.

3.1 Disjunct Alignment

In the case of disjunct alignment, camera and projector are often attached to two different sides of the mobile device. As a result, the visual field of the camera and

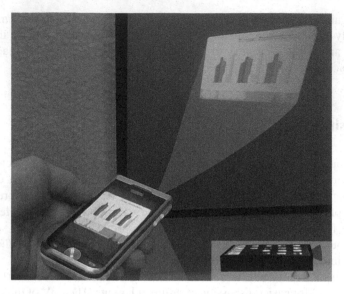

Fig. 7.2 Disjunct alignment of camera and projector. The FoV and the FoP have no shared space

the projected image are not overlapping. This setup is the most common in today's projector phones such as the Samsung W9600 and LG eXpo (compare Fig. 7.2).

The alignment described is rather unsuitable for the augmentation of physical objects. The tracking systems would identify the objects located in the FoV, but the FoP is directed towards a different angle so directly projecting onto the objects in the FoV is not possible. There are two ways of overcoming this problem. The first possibility is determining one's own position in relation to that of an object by means of a digital model of the environment and subsequently being able to augment the whole environment. Again this approach, however, requires the availability of a spatial model of the environment at all times. Furthermore, this procedure causes a considerable restriction of mobility.

The second possibility to create AR application using such a camera and projector setup is adapting objects or taking advantage of the physical structure of the object in order to augment it. For example, an optical marker, which can be identified and interpreted by the camera, could be attached to the first page of a book, resulting in the projection of additional information onto the open cover of the book. This would enable users to quickly and easily access reviews, summaries, and other services.

A benefit of systems that use "disjunct projection" is that they allow for optical flow tracking, which is for the other classes for example possible by sacrificing projection space, as projection within the FoV would impair the tracking process. Optical flow tracking could be used to navigate e.g. in websites, similar to the wrist tilt as Blaskò et al. have described in their work [7]. The movements of the projector phone could be translated to instructions for the browser by the tracking system

Fig. 7.3   Partially intersecting alignment, the FoV and FoP are partially overlapping each other

and navigation through a website or a map which is projected onto a wall would be possible. Such navigation is very similar to the experience of a flashlight or a static peephole: it illuminates a part of an object at a time and the object stays static. This interaction metaphor is also used in Map- and Shelf-Torchlight applications (a partially intersecting setup) described in Sect. 5.

3.2   Partially Intersecting Alignment

In the case of partially intersecting projection the FoV and the FoP are situated on the same level partially overlapping each other as shown on Fig. 7.3. By knowing the angle of aperture of the camera and projector's lens, the size of the FoV and the PoV as well as its misalignment the overlapping area can be calculated. This kind of projection is the most suitable for the augmentation of visual objects. The fact that the FoP just minimally affects or pollutes the image produced by the camera makes the stable use of visual trackers possible. However, this works only for the augmentation of bigger-sized objects. With smaller-sized objects the area that can be used for augmentation can be too small for augmentation and tracking at the same time. The projection would change the appearance of the object to radically such that there are not enough features for the optical tracking.

The Map-Torchlight application uses a partial intersecting setup for the projection of additional Points of Interest (POIs) on a large paper map and Shelf-Torchlight for projecting additional information to products in a retail environment

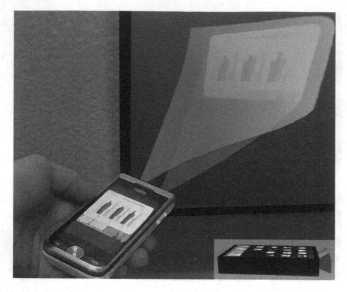

Fig. 7.4 Congruent alignment, the FoP is completly included in the FoV

(compare Fig. 7.6). An application, which assists someone in fixing e.g. the engine of a car, could be realized in a very similar way. By attaching visual markers to the engine compartment the possibility is given to determine the position of the projector phone relative to the engine, so that it can mark for example the screws which shall be removed in a particular step of a procedure which allows to perform a task.

The advantages (or differences) of a partial intersecting setup compared to a congruent setup is that the FoV and the FoP are areas that have just a small effect on each other so that the benefits of both can be exploited. For example the non-overlapped area in the camera field of view can be used to allow gesture-based interaction (as proposed by Baldauf et al. [15]) without interfering with the projection.

3.3 Congruent Alignment

A congruent setup is given when camera and projector are attached on the same side of the mobile phone, as it is in the case with of partially intersecting alignment with the exception that the entire projected image is captured in the camera field of view (see Fig. 7.4). A disadvantage of this spatial configuration is that the projection could influence the processing of the camera image. When an object is augmented the projection changes the visual appearance of the object and by this can interfere with the optical tracking. However, the congruent projection enables the user to interact directly with the projection without any limitation. The application LittleProjectedPlanet, as described in Sect. 5, uses this spatial configuration. It works using direct manipulation and with that enables the user to operate the projection through the modification of the physical objects. Another domain for a synchronous projection setup could be an OCR, which recognizes and marks spelling mistakes. School children would be able to control their homework by holding their mobile phones with the integrated projector upon their exercise books on which the projector could mark the mistakes and give e.g. additional information about them. However, the realization of such a system as an end product for costumers will take considerable research. The main problem is the robustness of the handwriting recognition process.

Generally the effects of the congruent and the partially intersecting alignment can be simulated with both of the hardware types by only using a small part of the FoV and the FoP. In the congruent alignment parts of the camera image and parts of the projection have to be ignored and in the partially intersecting alignment only the part where the FoV and FoP overlap are used. This would result in a loss of resolution and size of FoV and FoP in both cases. But since cameras already provide a high enough resolution for optical trackers and projection units are expected to increase in resolution these workarounds should be kept in mind for future setups.

3.4 Other Alignments and Design Issues

Besides the described alignments no fixed orientations between FoV and FoP are possible. However the design of a projector phone should not be limited to fixed setups. With the FB-04V NTT Docomo presented a projector phone where the projection unit can be removed from the device and is controllable via Bluetooth. Even though such a setup seems promising it is not suitable for vision-based AR applications since the orientation of camera and projector is unknown. Therefore such a system would require a possibility to determine the position of the components relative to each other.

Another possibility is the usage of a mobile steerable projection unit, which was done by Cauchard et al. [16]. A motorized mirror, which could be controlled by a mobile phone, was attached to a mobile projector (compare Fig. 7.5). This mobile setup is very similar to the static Everywhere Display by Pinhanez [17]. Pinhanhez used a static projector with a steerable mirror on top so that it was possible to project on nearly any surface in the room where the projector was set up. Cauchards setup would allow, depending on the possible projection angles, to emulate all discussed alignments without the loss of resolution or size. This would allow keeping the projection steady while moving the device and with that it would be possible to freely interact with the device while at the same time augmenting real world objects.

Besides this classification other issues should be taken into account when designing applications for mobile camera projector systems. The related work

Fig. 7.5 Interaction with a
steerable mobile projector

section provides an overview on the latest research done in this field, e.g. concerning multi-user settings, but some open issues are discussed in the next section.

Not only the spatial configuration of the mobile device camera and the projector play a role when discussing the potential and limitations of mobile camera-projector units. Today, hardware issues still hinder the exploitation of the full impact of projector phones. The effects of environmental light, or energy problems (current projectors need a considerable amount of energy) are problems that have to be solved by the hardware manufactures as well as researcher. Other limitations, such as the physical nature of objects and the projection onto the objects cluttered appearance are still not discussed or investigated. "Am I allowed to project on a stranger passing by?". Many technical challenges still remain and have to be solved by the hardware engineers. Effects of hand shaking and tremor can be overcome utilizing accelerometers and gyroscopes. Moreover, camera-tracking methods have to be improved. All these factors currently have a big impact on the user experience and have to be taken into account when designing applications for the mass market of projector phones.

4   Proxemic Interaction

In AR applications the orientation and distance between the user and the object that should be augmented are always important factors. In most cases these information are only used for the tracking of the object, especially when a mobile device is used as a magic lens [3]. With mobile projection the created AR overlay is significantly different from the magic lens approach since it is visible for everybody. Therefore if personal information is taken into account to create the overlay it is possible that this information is revealed easily. Since this is normally not favored by users applications have to adapt to these situations. We propose to use the knowledge about the spatial relationship between the object that should be augmented and the device as a key indicator for context-aware AR applications.

The concept on how to include spatial relationships (proxemics) as interaction techniques into ubiquitous computing scenarios was introduced by Ballendat et al. [18]. They showed how device movement between discrete proxemic regions can control and influence applications using a prototypical media player. There concepts originated from Edward Hall's theory of interpersonal spatial relationships that he called proxemics [19]. Hall distinguished between three different regions that connect physical distance to social distance, the intimate space, the social and consultative space and the public space. The intimate space is the closest "circle" around a person and the entry into this space is only acceptable for close friends and intimates. As the social and consultative spaces was the space defined in which people feel comfortable conducting routine and social interactions with acquaintances as well as strangers. The public space is the area in which interactions are perceived as impersonal or anonymous. It is difficult to give exact distances for theses regions since they are perceived different depending on the culture.

Since the information about the spatial relationship between the device and the object is already known it is easy to include these proxemic regions into the applications. In a way the projection unit itself already acts according to the proximic since constrained by the distance the possible FoP as well as the possible resolution changes. It should be kept in mind when designing AR applications that demand a high resolution that this only possible when the mobile projector is relatively close to the projection surface. With increasing distance to the projection surface the FoP becomes bigger and easier readable for uninvolved passersby's (Fig. 7.6).

While Ballendat et al. kept the users in the focus for interaction we propose for projection based AR applications to consider the projection as the focus since this is where the information is revealed. General information that are from interest for everybody can be shown in every proxemic region but as more personal the information becomes the more the region should increase to intimate. The following imaginable application exemplifies it more deeply: MuseoLight is an AR application for a projector phone that allows projecting information about a specific exhibit in a museum besides and on the exhibit. When the user is a couple of meters away the projection would show information like date of creation or highlight specific parts

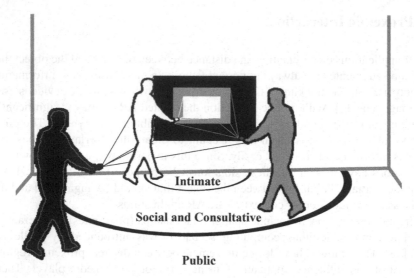

Fig. 7.6 Mobile projection in the three different proxemic regions, initmate (*white*), social and consultative (*grey*) and public (*black*)

of the exhibit that the common sense find interesting. But when the user is only a couple of centimeters away from the exhibit the projection shows a note left by the users partner or highlight a region for a more personal reason. Since the user is closer to the projection surface the projected information is smaller and he is able to shield the projection from uninvolved visitors and with that he can create his small personal sphere.

5   AR Applications Using Mobile Projection

In this section we show the potential of projector phones interfaces for AR applications. On the basis of fully implemented prototypes, covering different alignments of camera and projector and employing different interaction techniques, we present how projector phones can cover a wide range of applications. These reach from mobile recommender systems to mobile games.

5.1   Map Torchlight

5.1.1   Idea

The advantages of paper-based maps have been utilized in the field of mobile AR applications in the last few years. Traditional paper-based maps provide

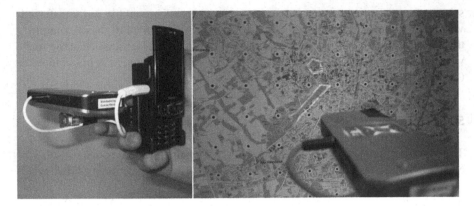

Fig. 7.7 The hardware prototype used for Map Torchlight (*left*) and the augmentation of a paper map using Map Torchlight (*right*)

high-resolution, large-scale information with zero power consumption. There are numerous implementations of magic lens interfaces that combine high-resolution paper maps with dynamic handheld displays [20]. From an HCI perspective, the main challenge of magic lens interfaces is that users have to switch their attention between the magic lens and the information in the background. With the Map Torchlight application [27] we attempt to overcome this problem by augmenting the paper map directly with additional information. The Map Torchlight is an example for a partially intersecting projection and is tracked over a paper map and can precisely highlight points of interest, streets, and areas to give directions or other guidance for interacting with the map.

5.1.2   Interaction Techniques

The general advances of a mobile projection system also show up in our Map Torchlight system: The projection area is larger and the mobile projection can overcome the switching cost of magic lens interfaces. The basic interaction pattern is similar to magic lens interfaces. Sweeping the projector phone over the paper map, the projector will, for instance, highlight different POIs on the map. Because the projection is significantly larger than the device display (around eight times in our setup) more dynamic information can be directly presented on the map (as can be seen in Fig. 7.7). It also provides a higher resolution compared to a standard mobile device display, if the projector is controlled independently from the device display. As shown in Fig. 7.7, larger objects can be highlighted compared to a traditional magic lens interfaces. Using the map as a shared screen can also use the projector to collaboratively interact with a map. For instance, one user can tell another a route through the city by moving a projected crosshair over the map. The waypoints are stored in a Keyhole Markup Language (KML is a is an XML-based language schema for expressing geographic annotation and visualization) file and transferred via Bluetooth to the second user's mobile device. Again, in all of these examples, there are no switching costs for the users. A downside of projection is that the real-world appearance of the map cannot completely be blocked out, as is possible with (video see-through) magic lens interfaces.

5.1.3 Implementation

The Map Torchlight is fully implemented for Nokia mobile camera phones (S60 3rd edition). We use the tracking toolkit by Rohs et al. [21] to track the mobile device with the attached projector in real time relative to the map (6 DoF). The actual prototype is a Nokia N95 mobile phone with an AIPTEK V10 Mobile Projector (640 × 480 pixel) attached to the phone using a standard AV cable. The whole setup weighs about 360 g. Due to technical limitations the mobile phone screen can only be mirrored and not be extended on the projector. Due to this issue, the projector always shows the mobile screen content, even if detailed information is presented on the mobile device screen. The focus and projection size needs to be calibrated manually, because the focus of the projector can only be adjusted manually. The tracking algorithm processes about 12 frames per second.

5.2 Shelf Torchlight

5.2.1 Idea

The search for a certain book in a library that contains many books can be a time-consuming task. Even if one finds the right shelf, one still has to browse an often huge area in the shelf. The same problem occurs when searching for a specific product in a supermarket shelf that fits ones personal preferences (e.g. a allergic or diet profile). With Shelf Torchlight [29] we present a prototype that aims to overcome the problems when searching for a book or a product in a shelf using a projector phone. Furthermore Shelf Torchlight can also act as a mobile recommender system taking the personal profile of the user into account.

5.2.2 Interaction Techniques

The basic interaction concept we apply is similar to the torchlight metaphor that was used in Map Torchlight as well. By sweeping the projector phone over the shelf additional information is projected onto the objects and next to them. As a result of the concept in Sect. 4 we extend this interaction technique with a semantic zoom and with that taking proximity into account. Modjeska describes a semantic zoom in contrast to a physical as follows"A physical zoom, on the one hand, changes the size and visible detail of objects. A semantic zoom, in the other hand, changes the type

Fig. 7.8 Shelf Torchlight in the retail scenario. Projecting dots onto products indicating how suited the product is for the user (*left*) and the semantic zoom revealing detailed information (*right*)

and meaning of information displayed by the object" [22]. In our case a physical movement closer to or away from the object changes the kind of information that gets projected. The closer the user is to the intimate region of the object the more detailed the information becomes. To illustrate the function of the semantic zoom we picked two scenarios for our applications, on the one hand the search for a specific book in a library on the other hand the search for a product that matches the users needs.

In the library scenario the system knows which book the user is looking for and thereby supporting the navigation task at the shelf. When one moves the projector phone over the shelf the desired books are getting highlighted with a white rectangle that matches the spine of the book. If the user draws closer to the shelf and with that activating the semantic zoom, he gets additional information like the average user rating retrieved from amazon.com which gets projected onto the spine. If the user goes one step closer the complete reviews for the book get projected.

In the retail scenario the products get compared to the personal profile of the user, that contains all her allergies, gusto, the shopping list, etc.. And not only the profile of the user but also of her whole family when she does the family shopping. Standing farer away from the shelf and moving the projector phone over the products, Shelf Torchlight projects green, yellow or red circles indicating how suited the product is taking the personal profile into account (see Fig. 7.8). For example a product that contains an ingredient that leads to an allergic reaction by the user or one of her family members gets a red circle projected onto the packaging. The semantic zoom will then reveal an explanation why the product got categorized in this way in this example it will tell the user that the product contains the specific ingredient. Since allergies are private information the semantic zoom show this only when the user is close to the shelf and maybe able to shield the projection. While the projection of the red circle only indicates that the user should not buy this product, uninvolved can not draw con- clusions what reason leads to this advice since it could also be a personal preference.

5.2.3 Implementation

The hardware of the prototype is based on the Map Torchlight prototype and with that a partially intersecting alignment of camera and projector. To track and identify the products and book we use computer vision based methods. In a first attempt we tried to use the feature tracking of the metaio Unifeye Mobile SDK. After the first tests we experienced that the SDK is unsuitable for more than three different markers since the memory of the mo- bile device is to small to process the image data. Therefore we used instead the Visual Codes by Rohs [23]. In our case the codes contain the ISBN of the books respectively the EAN of the products and were positioned on the spine of the books respectively the facing of the product. The projection is aligned on the books and products in such a way that it does not interfere with the markers.

5.3 Little Projected Planet

5.3.1 Idea

With the LittleProjectedPlanet prototype [28] we explore the possibilities of projector phones in a gaming scenario, which was inspired by the Playstation 3^{TM}(PS3) game LittleBigPlanet^{TM}. The projector phone is used to augment the hand drawings of a user with an overlay displaying physical interaction of virtual objects with the real world. Therefore a congruent alignment setup is needed. Players can sketch a 2D world on a sheet of paper or use an existing physical configuration of objects and then simulate physical procedures in this world to achieve game goals. We propose a mobile game combining hand drawn sketches of a user in combination with objects following a physics engine to achieve game goals. With PlayAnywhere [24], Wilson demonstrated initially the possibilities of mobile camera projector units in mobile entertainment. It consisted of an easy to set up camera projector unit allowing the user to play games on any planar surface, which can be used as a projection area, by controlling the games with their hands. Enriching sketching in combination with physical simulation was presented by Davis et al. [25, 26]. The ASSIST system, was a sketch understanding system that allows e.g. an engineer to sketch a mechanical system as she would on paper, and then allows her to interact with the design as a mechanical system, for example by seeing a simulation of her drawing. Interestingly the creators of the game LittleBigPlanet^{TM} bought the ASSIST system and parts of it were integrated into the game play.

In contrast to the ASSIST system we present a game that is designed for mobile projector phones combing real world objects and projected ones utilizing a physics engine. We think that such a projector phone can also be utilized to improve the learning and collaboration in small groups of pupils (cause of the mobile setup of our prototype) in contrast to more teacher-centered teaching e.g. one interactive white board (as shown by Davis et al. [25, 26]).

5.3.2 Game Concept

The slogan of the popular game LittleBigPlanet™ is "play with everything" and that can be taken literally. The player controls a little character that can run, jump and manipulate objects in several ways. A large diversity of pre-build objects is in the game to interact with, and each modification on such an item let them act in a manner physically similar to those they represent. The goal of each level is to bring the character from a starting point to the finish. Therefore it has to overcome several barriers by triggering physical actions. But the main fascination and potential of the game is the feasibility to customize and create levels. Creating new objects is done by starting with a number of basic shapes, such as circles, stars and squares, modify them and then place them in the level. Having done so, the user can decide on how these objects should be connected mechanically.

We took this designing approach as an entry point for a mobile AR game using a projector phone. It allows the user to design a 2D world in reality, which is then detected by a camera. Out of this detection a physical model is being calculated. Into this model the user can place several virtual objects representing items like tennis or bowling balls. These virtual objects then get projected into the real world by the projection unit. When starting the physic engine, the application simulates the interaction of the virtual and the real world objects and projects the results of the virtual objects onto the real world surface.

Just like in LittleBigPlanet™ our application offers the user different ways of playing: One is like the level designer in LittleBigPlanet™; the user can freely manipulate the 2D World within the projected area and place virtual objects in it. Similar to children building tracks for marbles in a sandpit, the player can specify a route and then let the virtual marbles run along it. A different gaming mode is a level based modus, but instead of steering a character as in LittleBigPlanet™, the user designs the world. As a goal the user has to steer a virtual object e.g. a tennis ball from its starting point to a given finish. The game concept uses a direct manipulation approach. Enabling the player to modify the world at runtime let the real world objects become the users tangible interface. But not only the objects are used for the interface, by changing the orientation and position of the projector the user can also modify the physical procedures (e.g. gravity by turning the mobile camera projector unit).

5.3.3 Interaction Techniques

For designing a 2D world the players can use several methods. Basically they have to generate enough contrast that can be detected by using a standard edge recognition algorithm (utilizing the Sobel operator). Sketching on a piece of paper or a white board for example can do this, but simply every corner or edge of a real world object could generate a useful representation in the physics engine. So there is no need for an extra sketching device or other for example IR based input methods. Just requiring the projector phone itself the game is playable nearly anywhere with

Fig. 7.9 LittleProjected-
Planet game screenshot:
A user playing the game with
a postcard (*upper left corner*).
User is sketching a marble
run and projected tennis balls
are bouncing on it (*center*)

nearly everything and it is easy to set up. Figure 7.9 shows how a user is projecting virtual marbles on a track she sketched on a whiteboard. An important problem to allow a smooth and seamless interaction for the user is that the "gravity in the projection" is aligned with the real worlds gravity. Also gravity can be utilized in the game to control some action. A user can take control of the gravity by changing the orientation of the projector. Doing this the user can let virtual objects "fly" through the levels.

5.3.4 Implementation

Due to the unavailability of sophisticated projector phones (with an optimal alignment of camera and built-in projector and e.g. a CPU that is able to process the physics simulation) we used, in contrast to the Map Torchlight application, a Dell M109S, a mobile projector with a maximum resolution of 800 by 600 pixels and a weight of 360 g, in combination with a Logitech QuickCam 9000 Pro. All together our prototype weighs around 500 g and is therefore okay to handle (e.g. compared to the prototype used in Map Torchlight (see above) our prototype is 240 g heavier, but the projector has 50 lm instead of just 10 and also has a higher resolution). We think this prototype provides a good trade-off between mobility and sophisticated projection quality. In contrast to the few mobile devices with built in projectors, our

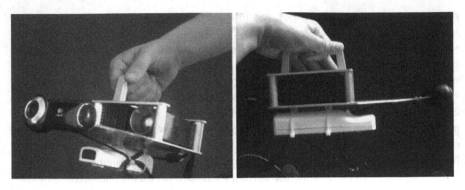

Fig. 7.10 Hardware prototype used for LittleProjectedPlanet, consisting of a Logitech Quickcam 9000 Pro, a Dell M109s and a WiiMote all mounted on a aluminium construction

projector and camera are mounted in such a way that the camera field of view fits the projected area (congruent alignment). But because of the different focal lengths of camera and projector in this setup the camera image is always wider than the projected image. Therefore the camera is installed in front of the projector as can be seen in Fig. 7.10. For controlling the application and to determine the orientation (to set the gravity) a Nintendo Wii remote is attached to the prototype. Today's mobile phones are already equipped with an accelerometer or an electronic compass, so the functionality of the Wii remote can easily be covered using a future projector phone. The application is fully implemented in Java using the QuickTime API to obtain a camera image. As a physics engine Phys2D, an open source, Java based engine is used. WiiRemoteJ handles the communication with the Wii remote. Connected to a standard laptop or PC the camera projector unit has a refresh rate of approximately 15 fps when running the application.

The area of the camera image containing the projected image is processed via an edge recognition algorithm. Every pixel of a detected edge gets a representation as a fixed block in the physics engine. That gives the user total freedom in designing the world. The update of the world in the physics engine is done every 300 ms but the user, for example for editing the sketch, can pause the update. Adapting the gravity of the physical model to the actual orientation of the projector phone is done through calculating the roll (this denotes the angular deviation along the longest axis of the Wii remote) of the Wii remote.

6   Conclusion

We have presented different interface concepts for mobile projection-based AR applications taking hardware issues of future projector phones into account. The interfaces all focus on the augmentation of real word objects in the environment. We showed how the different spatial setups of camera and projector units effect the possible applications and the physical interaction space as well as how proximic interaction can be taken into account. The classification presented can help to structure the design space of mobile projection applications. Of course many open issues still remain. As discussed earlier not only the spatial configuration of the mobile device camera and the projector play a role when discussing the potential and limitations of mobile camera-projector units. Today, hardware issues still hinder the exploitation of the full impact of mobile camera-projector units. Our research tries to make a contribution into the direction that by assuming we will have better hardware of mobile-camera projector units, we will have more powerful applications that go beyond projecting only content like images or videos. The implementations show how researchers can overcome the current hardware problems and investigate the area of mobile camera-projector systems more deeply. With our categorization using different classes based on the spatial configuration we want to establish a first initial framework for AR applications using projector phones. We think that they have a big potential to enrich the usability of mobile devices. They enable larger presentation sizes and are well suited for multi-user settings. In future work we intend to evaluate how mobile projection interfaces are superior to classical AR interfaces such as HMDs and magic lens interfaces.

References

1. E. Rukzio and P. Holleis "Projector Phone Interactions: Design Space and Survey," Proceedings of Workshop on Coupled Display Visual Interfaces at AVI 2010. Rome, Italy, 2010.
2. A. Hang, E. Rukzio, and A. Greaves "Projector phone: a study of using mobile phones with integrated projector for interaction with maps," Proceedings of the 10th international conference on human computer interaction with mobile devices and services, pages 207–216. ACM 2008.
3. E. Bier, M. Stone, K. Pier, W. Buxton and T. DeRose "Toolglass and magic lenses: the see-through interface," Proceedings of the 20th annual conference on Computer graphics and interactive techniques, pages 73–80. ACM New York, NY, USA, 1993.
4. R. Raskar, J. van Baar, P. Beardsley, T. Willwacher, S. Rao and C. Forlines "iLamps: geometrically aware and self-configuring projectors," In ACM SIGGRAPH 2003 Courses, page 5. ACM. 2003.
5. O. Bimber and R. Raskar "Modern approaches to augmented reality," ACM SIGGRAPH 2007 courses (SIGGRAPH '07). Article 1, ACM 2007.
6. R. Raskar, P. Beardsley, J. Van Baar, Y. Wang, P. Dietz, J. Lee, D. Leigh and T. Willwacher "RFIG lamps: interacting with a self-describing world via photosensing wireless tags and projectors," ACM Transactions on Graphics (TOG), 23(3):406–415, 2004.
7. G. Blasko, S. Feiner and F. Coriand "Exploring Interaction with a Simulated Wrist-Worn Projection Display," Proceedings of the Ninth IEEE International Symposium on Wearable Computers (ISWC '05). IEEE Computer Society, Washington, DC, USA, 2–9, 2005.
8. X. Cao, C. Forlines and R. Balakrishnan "Multi-user interaction using handheld projectors," Proceedings of the 20th annual ACM symposium on User interface software and technology, page 43–52. ACM, 2007.
9. T. Karitsuka and K. Sato, K "A Wearable Mixed Reality with an On-Board Projector," Proceedings of the 2nd IEEE/ACM International Symposium on Mixed and Augmented Reality (ISMAR '03). IEEE Computer Society, Washington, DC, USA, 321-. 2003.

10. P. Mistry, P. Maes, and L. Chang "WUW-wear Ur world: a wearable gestural interface," Proceedings of the 27th international conference extended abstracts on human factors in computing systems, pages 4111–4116. ACM, 2010.
11. Z. Ye and H. Khalid "Cobra: flexible displays for mobilegaming scenarios," Proceedings of the 28th of the international conference extended abstracts on Human factors in computing systems (CHI EA '10). ACM, New York, NY, USA, 4363–4368, 2010.
12. M. Bolas and D. Krum "Augmented Reality Applications and User Interfaces Using Head-Coupled Near-Axis Personal Projectors with Novel Retroreflective Props and Surfaces," Proceedings of Ubiprojection 2010 1st Workshop on Personal Projection at Pervasive 2010, 2010.
13. I. Sutherland, I. "A head-mounted three dimensional display," Proceedings of the fall joint computer conference, part I, pages 757–764. ACM, 1968.
14. A. Cheok, S. Fong, K. Goh, X. Yang, W. Liu, F. Farzbiz and Y. Li "Human pacman: A mobile entertainment system with ubiquitous computing and tangible interaction over a wide outdoor area," Lecture notes in computer science, pages 209–223, 2003.
15. M. Baldauf, P. Fröhlich, and P. Reichl "Gestural interfaces for micro projector based mobile phone applications," Adjunct Proceedings of Ubicomp 2009, 2009.
16. J. Cauchard, M. Fraser, J. Alexander and S. Subramanian "Offsetting Displays on Mobile Projector Phones," Proceedings of Ubiprojection 2010 1st Workshop on Personal Projection at Pervasive 2010, 2010.
17. C. Pinhanez, C. "The everywhere displays projector: A device to create ubiquitous graphical interfaces," Lecture Notes in Computer Science, pages 315–331, 2001.
18. T. Ballendat, N. Marquardt and S. Greenberg "Proxemic Interaction: Designing for a Proximity and Orientation-Aware Environment," In Proceedings of the ACM Conference on Interactive Tabletops and Surfaces - ACM ITS'2010. (Saarbruecken, Germany), ACM Press, 10 pages, November 7-10, 2010.
19. E. T. Hall "The Hidden Dimension," Garden City, N.Y.: Doubleday, 1966.
20. M. Rohs, J. Schöning, M. Raubal, G. Essl and A. Krüger "Map navigation with mobile devices: virtual versus physical movement with and without visual context," Proceedings of the 9th international conference on Multimodal interfaces, pages 146–153. ACM, 2007.
21. M. Rohs, J. Schöning, A. Krüger and B. Hecht "Towards real-time markerless tracking of magic lenses on paper maps," Adjunct Proceedings of the 5th Intl. Conference on Pervasive Computing (Pervasive), Late Breaking Results, pages 69–72, 2007.
22. D. Modjeska "Navigation in electronic worlds: Research review," Technical report, Computer Systems Research Group, University of Toronto, 1997.
23. M. Rohs "Real-world interaction with camera phones," In Ubiquitous Computing Systems, Second International Symposium, UCS 2004, Tokyo, Japan, November 8-9, 2004, Revised Selected Papers, pages 74–89, 2004.
24. A. Wilson "PlayAnywhere: a compact interactive tabletop projection-vision system," Proceedings of the 18th annual ACM symposium on User interface software and technology, page 83–92. ACM, 2005.
25. R. Davis "Sketch understanding in design: Overview of work at the MIT AI lab," In Sketch Understanding, Papers from the 2002 AAAI Spring Symposium, pages 24–31, 2002.
26. C. Alvarado and R. Davis "SketchREAD: a multi-domain sketch recognition engine," Proceedings of the 17th annual ACM symposium on user interface software and technology, pages 23–32. ACM New York, NY, USA, 2004.
27. J. Schöning, M. Rohs, S. Kratz, M. Löchtefeld and A. Krüger "Map torchlight: a mobile augmented reality camera projector unit," Proceedings of the 27th international conference extended abstracts on Human factors in computing systems, pages 3841–3846. ACM, 2009.
28. M. Löchtefeld, J. Schöning, M. Rohs and A. Krüger "LittleProjectedPlanet: An Augmented Reality Game for Camera Projector Phones," In Mobile Interaction with the Real World, (MIRW 2009), Mobile HCI Workshop, 2009.
29. M. Löchtefeld, S. Gehring, J. Schöning and A. Krüger "ShelfTorchlight: Augmenting a Shelf using a Camera Projector Unit," Proceedings of Ubiprojection 2010 1st Workshop on Personal Projection at Pervasive 2010, 2010.

Chapter 8
Interactive Volume Segmentation and Visualization in Augmented Reality

Takehiro Tawara

Abstract We propose a two-handed direct manipulation system to achieve complex volume segmentation of CT/MRI data in Augmented Reality with a remote controller attached to a motion tracking cube. At the same time segmented data is displayed by direct volume rendering using a programmable GPU. Our system achieves visualization of real time modification of volume data with complex shading including transparency control by changing transfer functions, displaying any cross section, and rendering multi materials using a local illumination model.

Our goal is to build a system that facilitates direct manipulation of volumetric CT/MRI data for segmentation in Augmented Reality. Volume segmentation is a challenging problem and segmented data has important roles for visualization and analysis.

1 Introduction

Volume segmentation is a challenging problem, and it includes many individually difficult problems: scanning, filtering for noise removal and enhancement, and edge detection. Segmentation is followed by visualization and analysis.

Although many algorithms to automatically extract shapes have been proposed for 2D and 3D datasets [10], existing methods tend to depend only on geometrical features. Moreover existing automatic methods control extraction by parameters, and such parameters often affect its extraction globally. Thus, even for users that are familiar with the algorithm, it is difficult to predict the final shape to be extracted. However the user's decision becomes more important for ambiguous input data which is common for scanned data. Moreover the user may want to perform

T. Tawara (✉)
Riken, 2-1 Hirosawa Wako-Shi, 351-0198 Saitama, Japan
e-mail: takehirotwr@riken.jp

B. Furht (ed.), *Handbook of Augmented Reality*, DOI 10.1007/978-1-4614-0064-6_8,   199
© Springer Science+Business Media, LLC 2011

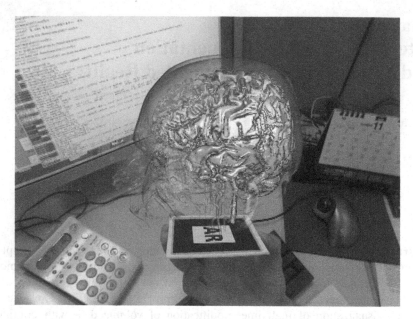

Fig. 8.1 An example of segmentation of a human head. The user can easily extract parts of a human head by the guide of geometric features: cerebrum, cerebellum, spinal cord, and eyes. The cerebrum is further segmented to smaller parts per functionality of a human brain by the user's decision: frontal lobe, parietal lobe, occipital lobe, and temporal lobe. Such semantic segmentation without depending on geometric features can be achieved by an interactive system as we have proposed

semantic segmentation as shown in Fig. 8.1, which shows a functional map of a human brain and doesn't depend on geometric features. Our system allows the user to control shape extraction with intuitive manners.

Though a real anatomical model is often used for explanation in a classroom, direct volume rendering [4] has many advantages comparing to a real model: changing transparency, showing any cross sections, and modifying data. Volume segmentation is necessary for effective visualization.

To achieve this goal, we propose a framework for volume segmentation and visualization using Augmented Reality. Augmented Reality superposes virtual objects on a display with a correct perspective as if they placed in the real world [5]. We develop a two-handed direct manipulation to perform complex segmentation in Augmented Reality with a remote controller attached to a motion tracking cube shown in Fig. 8.3. We exploit Augmented Reality to track the motion of our controller and visualize real time modification of volume data on the user's hand.

Although similar concepts for a two-handed manipulation [3] and segmentation with the haptic device [13] have been proposed, our system can be built by very reasonable, common devices such as a web camera and a wii remote controller.

2   Related Work

Many different approaches have been proposed for automatic segmentation of 2D and 3D datasets including: deformable model methods, level set methods, and graphcut methods. An interested reader can consult to the survey paper [9]. Level set methods and fast marching methods is detailed in the books [7, 10].

Sharf et al. [11] proposed a deformable model to extract a water tight mesh from a point cloud. They built an attraction field which was an unsigned distance field from a point cloud, then deformed an initial mesh to fit to the point cloud. The priority of evolving fronts was concerned in a coarse–to–fine manner. Hence, the approach maintained a better topological interpretation.

Owada et al. [8] proposed a method to extract a volume segment by drawing a 2D free form stroke to indicate the contour of the target. Their algorithm inferred the depth information of the stroke by the idea that the stroke was on the sweep surface. Then a target volume segment was extracted by an existing automatic segmentation method using the acquired 3D path.

Sherbondy et al. [12] proposed an interactive system for volume segmentation and visualization using GPU. They placed seed points and grew homogeneous regions from them by solving the nonlinear diffusion equation. They solved the equation on GPU and further speed up using computational masking. Our system is differ from theirs because their user control is only locating seed points on an axial slice and region growing is automated. Whereas our system directly locates a seed point in the 3D space with the guide of an arbitrary cross section, and our system gives the user the control of the expanding direction.

3   Our Framework

Our system is composed of pre-processing, locating a seed point, and growing a region. In the pre-process, input volume data is filtered, amplified, and binarized by the gradient magnitude of the data. Then a distance function is generated from the binary data. Figure 8.2 visualizes the cross sections of a MRI volume data in the pre-process. The next, the user puts a seed point at the tip of the virtual needle indicated by the controller in the region which the user wants to extract. Then the user can grow the region with the guide of the distance function mentioned above. We locally limit the expansion of a boundary surface by changing a speed function depending on the distance from the tip of the virtual needle. By using this technique, the user can freely expand regions to extract desired shapes. The combination of existing marker based motion tracking and region growing guided by geometrical features makes a success of intuitive and precise volume segmentation.

The following sections explain our framework in detail. Section 3.1 explains the necessary pre-process before segmentation. Section 3.2 introduces our two-handed

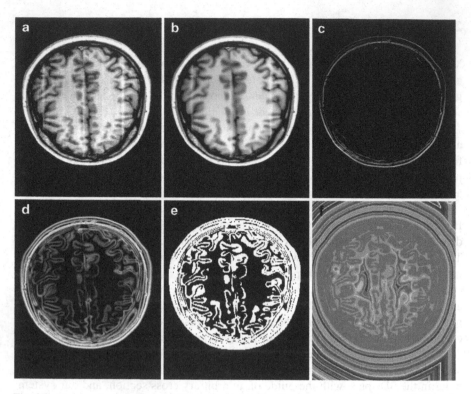

Fig. 8.2 The cross section of a MRI volume data in the pre-process: (**a**) input, (**b**) filtered, (**c**) gradient magnitude, (**d**) gamma, (**e**) binary, and (**f**) the distance function visualized by pseudo colors

controller to handle complex volume segmentation in the 3D space. Precisely locating a seed point is a key of segmentation. This is detailed in Sect. 3.3. Section 3.4 discusses region growing controlled by the user. Section 3.5 explains about multi ID rendering. Section 4 describes results achieved by proposed system. Finally, we conclude the chapter with a discussion of possible future work in Sect. 5.

3.1 Pre-process

Pre-process is a very important stage in our system. This is a key to extract desired shape. First, a filter applies to input raw scanned CT/MRI volume data to remove the noises and smooth. So far many filters have been proposed for 2D and 3D datasets. We use the Non-Local means filter which preserves features of input data. Figure 8.2a is the cross section of an input volume data, and Fig. 8.2b is the image applied the Non-Local means filter.

As mentioned above, because our strategy for extraction is region growing in homogeneous regions, we create walls to stop such growing. To achieve this goal, we compute the gradient magnitude of input volume data shown in Fig. 8.2c. Although it can extract boundaries of homogeneous parts, the gradient magnitude varies depending on the intensity of input data. To increase the value of the low gradient magnitude such as the crease of the brain, we apply a gamma correction like function $f(x) = x^{1/g}$ (Fig. 8.2d). The constant g is a user defined parameter to specify the increasing ratio. Then the user chooses a threshold and creates binary data (Fig. 8.2e).

Finally, we create a distance function from the boundary surface using the fast marching method [10] (Fig. 8.2f). It tells us how far a point in a distance function closes to the nearest boundary surface. This information is used to stop region growing.

3.2   Two-Handed Manipulation

We propose a two-handed manipulation method for volume segmentation and visualization. We use ARToolKit [1] as a motion tracking method. There are several established frameworks to build AR/MR applications including ARToolKit [1, 5, 6] and ARTag [2]. ARToolKit is probably the best known framework, and is widely used in the AR/MR research field. It detects and recognizes printed markers, and returns each transformation matrix from a marker's local coordinate system to a view coordinate system using computer vision based methods. We have built our application based on this framework to estimate the location and pose of our 3D user interface.

The left hand keeps a motion tracking marker to display volume data. The right hand grabs a wii remote controller attached a motion tracking cube. A wii remote controller was introduced by Nintendo for the game console, but it has many useful features as a general 3D user input device: 12 buttons, a three-axis acceleration sensor, an infrared sensor, a vibration motor, four blue LEDs, and bluetooth wireless connection. Although a wii remote controller has a three-axis acceleration sensor, it cannot get the location and pose from only such a sensor. Therefore we attach a motion tracking cube at the top of a wii remote controller. Each side of the cube has a unique AR marker. The tip of the virtual needle is defined as the relative position from each marker. At least one of the markers should be visible from a web camera during operations. If more than one marker are visible, the most well posed marker, which is nearly perpendicular to the viewing direction, is used. Figure 8.3 shows our manipulator. The virtual needle is drawn in the red line. In the figure, the location and pose of a virtual needle is estimated by a detected marker shown in the green square.

Fig. 8.3 Our manipulator;
a motion tracking cube is
attached at the top of a wii
remote controller. The virtual
needle is drawn in the *red
line*. The tip of the virtual
needle is defined as the
relative position from one of
markers. The detected marker
is shown as the *green square*

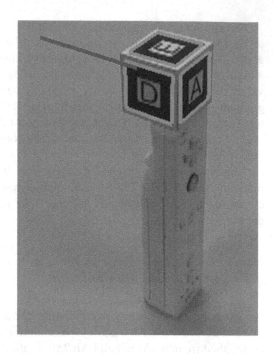

3.3   Locating a Seed Point

The first step of our segmentation framework is locating a seed point. The position
must be carefully chosen. If the position is in the outside of a target homogeneous
region, the following extraction fails. It is difficult to precisely locate the tip of the
virtual needle to the desired position in the 3D space without a guide. On the other
hand it is easy to perform on the 2D space. We decide to display a cross section
and point a seed point on it. We implement two types of a cross section: a plane
($z = 0$) and a quadric surface ($z = x^2 + y^2$). A plane is familiar to people as a use
of radiographic diagnosis. While, a quadric surface can be useful to sense the 3D
structure around the position. Figure 8.4 demonstrates a seed point selection.

During the operation, the user first selects the seed point placing mode. The
color of the virtual needle turns to red for the notification. Then the user selects
the material ID. The user turns the button on to display the cross section. When the
user moves the controller in the 3D space, the cross section follows the movement
of the controller. The z-axis aligns the direction of the virtual needle, and the tip of
the virtual needle always places on the cutting surface. The z-axis of a cross section
can be also fixed, and the user moves a cross section only on the fixed direction.
Hence, the user can lean the controller to be easy to see around the target position
as shown in Fig. 8.4a.

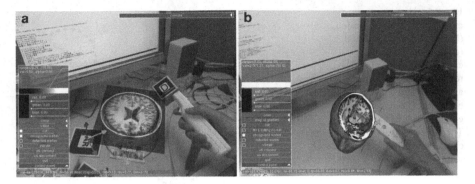

Fig. 8.4 Locating a seed point. We propose two types of a cross section: (**a**) a plane, and (**b**) a quadric surface. When the user moves the controller in the 3D space, the cross section follows the movement of the controller. The tip of the virtual needle always places on the cutting surface, while the z-axis can be aligned to the direction of the virtual needle or fixed to be easy to see around the target position

3.4 Interactive Region Growing

There are several efficient region growing techniques including the fast marching method and the level set method [10]. Such methods define a speed function F which represents the evolution of a boundary surface.

However our motivation is to give the user the control of expansion. So we want to locally modify the extracting shape. Therefore we limit the effective area of expansion by indicating using our controller.

Once a seed point locates in the 3D space, the region is growing from that point. The boundary surface in an effective region centered at the tip of the virtual needle gradually extends toward outside. The user can easily expect the next step of an extending shape, and stop or continue growing until the user satisfies.

Figure 8.5 illustrates the procedure. In Fig. 8.5a, a seed point and an effective area don't overlap at all. Therefore no expansion performs. In Fig. 8.5b, the part of an effective area overlaps to a seed point. In the region inside an effective area, the boundary surface expands toward the normal direction in a fraction of time $\triangle t$.

During regions are overlapping, a boundary surface will expand until the whole area of the effective sphere will fill up. Of course, the user can freely move the controller during expansion, resulting complex shape extraction as shown in Fig. 8.5c. Figure 8.5d shows the final shape of extraction.

3.5 Multi ID Rendering

For efficient and effective volume rendering, we prepare three volumetric textures and corresponding transfer functions: input scalar data, normal data and the gradient

Fig. 8.5 The procedure of expansion: (**a**) no expansion, (**b**) and (**c**) expansion, and (**d**) the final shape to be extracted. The *red line* represents a virtual needle, and the *dotted circle* at the end of the line depicts an effective area of expansion. The *blue region* shows the extracted region

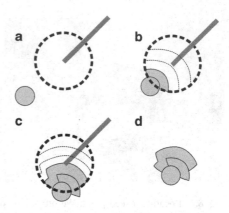

magnitude, and material ID data. To visualize original input data, input scalar data and normal data is used. The normal data is generated as the first derivative of scalar data using the central difference to be easy to see the structure of data. Instead of preparing normal data, we can compute it in real time on GPU. By controlling the transfer function of the gradient magnitude, we suppress the homogeneous region and enhance discontinuity regions to help user's operations. The cross section uses the scalar data with the constant alpha value. It means the constant transfer function. A segmented region is colored by looking up the transfer function of ID data. The user changes the color and opacity by the transfer function. This rendering is done in one-pass using a programmable GPU. Figure 8.6 shows the fragment program for multiple ID volume rendering in NVIDIA Cg language.

4   Results

Using our system, the user can freely extract volumetric shapes such as left and right cerebrums, cerebellums, corpus callosums, medulla and eyes with visualization of a MRI head data on a desktop through a HMD mounted a USB camera. Figure 8.7 shows our devices. Each part of a MRI head data can be extracted in a few seconds to a minutes in real time using Geforce 8800GTX class GPU. The resolution of dataset is $256 \times 256 \times 256$. Figure 8.8 shows the image sequence of the real time demonstration of extraction. The movie can see on YouTube http://www.youtube.com/watch?v=R1cm4WOWO-M.

We implemented a very basic region growing algorithm, which doesn't take into account smoothness of extracting shape and leaking during operations. Such problems are well studied in automatic segmentation algorithms, and we could introduce such sophisticated algorithms in our system.

```
float4 fp_main(
  float3 P : TEXCOORD1,
  float3 texCoord : TEXCOORD2,
  uniform float3 Ka,
  uniform float3 Ks,
  uniform float  Ksh,
  uniform float3 lightColor,
  uniform float3 lightPosition,
  uniform float4 offset,
  uniform sampler3D ScalarData, // scalar data
  uniform sampler3D NormalData, // normal data
  uniform sampler3D IdData,     // material ID data
  uniform sampler1D TF0C, // transfunc0 color
  uniform sampler1D TF0S, // transfunc0 scale
  uniform sampler1D TF1C, // transfunc1 color
  uniform sampler1D TF1S, // transfunc1 scale
  uniform sampler1D TF2C, // transfunc2 color
  uniform sampler1D TF2S, // transfunc2 scale
  uniform float alpha,
  uniform float bothsides,
  uniform float4x4 ModelViewIT
) : COLOR
{
  float len = 0;
  float3 N = normalVectorRT(ScalarData, texCoord,
    ModelViewIT, offset, len);

  float mask = tex3D(IdData, texCoord).x;

  if (mask > 0) {
    float offset_mask = .5/256;
    float3 Kd = tex1D(TF2C, mask+offset_mask).xyz;
    float3 co = phongShading(P, N, lightPosition,
      lightColor, Ka, Kd, Ks, Ksh, bothsides);
    alpha = tex1D(TF2S, mask+offset_mask).x;
    return float4(co, .8*alpha);
  }

  float scalar = tex3D(ScalarData, texCoord).x;
  float alpha0 = tex1D(TF0S, scalar).x;
  float alpha1 = tex1D(TF1S, len).x;

  alpha = alpha * alpha0 * alpha1;

  if (alpha == 0) {
    return float4(0, 0, 0, 0);
  } else if (len == 0) { // emission model
    float3 co = tex1D(TF0C, scalar).xyz;
    return float4(co, alpha);
  } else { // phong model
    float3 Kd = tex1D(TF0C, scalar).xyz;
    float3 co = phongShading(P, N, lightPosition,
      lightColor, Ka, Kd, Ks, Ksh, bothsides);
    return float4(co, alpha);
  }
}
```

Fig. 8.6 The Fragment Program for Multi ID Volume Rendering in NVIDIA Cg Language

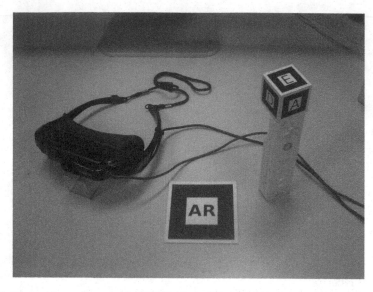

Fig. 8.7 Devices for our framework. HMD is Vuzix iWare VR920 attached to Vuzix CamAR

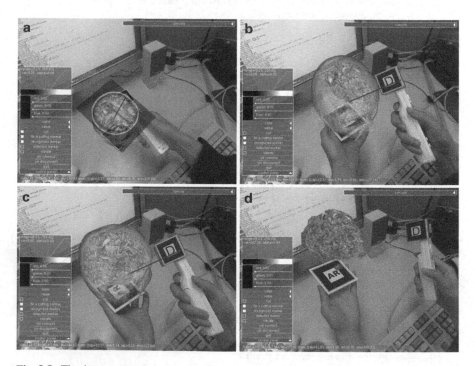

Fig. 8.8 The image sequence of volume segmentation. The image (**a**) shows locating a seed point. The following images represent the extraction of the right brain colored by purple (Movie: http://www.riken.jp/fsi/tawara/)

5 Conclusion

Although many automatic volume segmentation algorithms have been proposed, such algorithms suffer from the try–and–error approach to find the best parameter for desired shape extraction. We proposed an intuitive volume segmentation framework which gives the user a great controllability. Our two-handed interface supports not only volume visualization but also its segmentation comparing to the previous work [3]. Proposed interactive region growing fully works in the 3D space: the seed point selection and the expanding direction. It is impossible to extract an arbitrary 3D shape reflecting the user's intention using existing 2D based segmentation methods. As shown in Fig. 8.1, such semantic segmentation can be handled by only user's interaction. Moreover, our system can be built with very reasonable prices to handle complex volume segmentation exploiting a marker based motion tracking technique [5] and a wii remote controller.

Acknowledgements This work was supported by KAKENHI (a Grant-in-Aid for Young Scientists (B)) (No. 21700126).

References

1. Artoolkit http://www.hitl.washington.edu/artoolkit/.
2. M. Fiala. Artag, a fiducial marker system using digital techniques. In *Proceedings of the 2005 IEEE Computer Society Conference on Computer Vision and Pattern Recognition (CVPR'05)*, pages 590–596, 2005.
3. J. Goble, K. Hinckley, R. Pausch, J. W. Snell, and N. Kassell. Two-handed spatial interface tools for neurosurgical planning. *IEEE Computer*, 28(7):20–26, 1995.
4. M. Ikits, J. Kniss, A. Lefohn, and C. Hansen. Volume rendering techniques. In *GPU Gems*, pages 667–692. 2004.
5. H. Kato and M. Billinghurst. Marker tracking and hmd calibration for a video-based augmented reality conferencing system. In *Proceedings of the 2nd International Workshop on Augmented Reality (IWAR 99)*, pages 85–94, 1999.
6. H. Kato, M. Billinghurst, I. Poupyrev, K. Imamoto, and K. Tachibana. Virtual object manipulation on a table-top ar environment. In *Proceedings of the International Symposium on Augmented Reality (ISAR 2000)*, pages 111–119, 2000.
7. S. Osher and R. Fedkiw. *Level Set Methods and Dynamic Implicit Surfaces*. Springer Verlag New York, 2003.
8. S. Owada, F. Nielsen, and T. Igarashi. Volume catcher. In *ACM Symposium on Interactive 3D Graphics and Games 2005*, pages 111 – 116, 2005.
9. D. L. Pham, C. Xu, and J. L. Prince. A survey of current methods in medical image segmentation. In *Technical Report JHU/ECE 99-01*. The Johns Hopkins University, 1999.
10. J. A. Sethian. *Level Set Methods and Fast Marching Methods*. Cambridge University Press, 1999.
11. A. Sharf, T. Lewiner, A. Shamir, L. Kobbelt, and D. CohenOr. Competing fronts for coarse-to-fine surface reconstruction. In *Eurographics 2006*, 2006.

12. A. Sherbondy, M. Houston, and S. Napel. Fast volume segmentation with simultaneous visualization using programmable graphics hardware. In *VIS '03: Proceedings of the 14th IEEE Visualization 2003 (VIS'03)*, page 23, Washington, DC, USA, 2003. IEEE Computer Society.
13. E. Vidholm, S. Nilsson, and I. Nyström. Fast and robust semi-automatic liver segmentation with haptic interaction. In *MICCAI*, pages 774–781, 2006.

Chapter 9
Virtual Roommates: Sampling and Reconstructing Presence in Multiple Shared Spaces

Andrei Sherstyuk and Marina Gavrilova

Abstract "Virtual Roommates" is a mapping between loosely linked spaces, that allows users to overlay multiple physical and virtual scenes and populate them with physical and/or virtual characters. As the name implies, the Virtual Roommates concept provides continuous ambient presence for multiple disparate groups, similar to people sharing living conditions, but without the boundaries of real space.

This chapter contains updated and extended material, previously presented at the International Conferences on Artificial Reality and Telexistence (ICAT'08) [29] and Advances in Computer Entertainment Technology (ACE'08) [28].

1 Introduction

An ability to communicate is one of the most fundamental human needs. Communication technologies and applications become ubiquitous and cover many modalities: audio, video, tactile. Both volume and nature of information exchanged range immensely. Examples include: a telephone single voice channel; a video stream between a doctor and a patient, with embedded virtual content; a teleconference system, capable of connecting dozens of people in high definition video. Online virtual worlds present a very special case of information exchange between communicating parties. Game servers provide data for planet-size worlds, with geometric details to a single blade of grass. The amount of 3D content available online, now exceeds what can be explored in a single person's lifetime.

It seems likely that virtual worlds will be playing an increasingly important role in society. Evidence for this are numerous academic and commercial conventions on serious games, cyber-worlds, intelligent agents and multitude of similar topics, covering technical and social aspects of this phenomenon. Assuming that this trend

A. Sherstyuk (✉)
Avatar Reality Inc., 55 Merchant Street, Ste 1700, Honolulu HI, USA
e-mail: andrei@avatar-reality.com

B. Furht (ed.), *Handbook of Augmented Reality*, DOI 10.1007/978-1-4614-0064-6_9,   211
© Springer Science+Business Media, LLC 2011

will continue, the following questions come to the front. How one can interact with such virtual worlds and their inhabitants in a more realistic manner? Can virtual worlds be used to enrich person–to–person communications in everyday life?

In the past few years, a number of projects demonstrated examples of meaningful interaction between real and virtual environments: Human Pacman Augmented Reality (AR) game [7], AR Façade [9], AR Second Life [16]. In these projects, life-size virtual characters were brought to real-life environments, both indoors and outdoors. Conversely, techniques were developed that allowed to insert realistic, video-based user avatars into virtual [13] and real scenes [18].

The research project presented below pursues similar goals: provide 'cross-reality' connectivity for multiple spaces and multiple agents. In addition, the solution is sought to be free from spatial constraints imposed by geometric layouts of participating environments. Both goals can be summarized and illustrated with a single metaphor of *Virtual Roommates*, who coexist in loosely coupled environments that can be real, virtual, or mixed, as illustrated in Fig. 9.1.

Virtual roommates, as visible entities, are 3D avatars of remote participants projected and visualized in each one's local space. Functionally, each "roommate" is also an instance of a special-purpose function set for sampling and reconstructing presence of mobile agents in shared spaces. As a whole, the Virtual Roommates system is an extension of conventional telepresence applications into the AR domain.

Before presenting the architecture of Virtual Roommates, we will examine several existing systems, capable of connecting both real and virtual environments. We will demonstrate that despite their seeming flexibility, most telepresence applications put tight restrictions on the geometry of connected spaces and allowed user activities. Removing these restrictions constitutes the goals of this project.

2 Background: From Tele-Collaboration to Augmented Reality Coexistence

Advances in display technologies and growing availability of broadband networks spawned a number of commercial and open-source teleconference systems. The *TelePresence* line of products, launched in 2006 by Cisco Inc., represents the first group [8]. In a TelePresence installation, two dedicated rooms are connected into one shared teleconference environment, using HDTV displays and spatialized sound. TelePresence can accommodate up to 18 people on the "local" side of a conference table. More examples of multi-display collaborative systems may be found in a survey by Ni et al. [23].

The *Access Grid* is an example of a non-commercial system facilitating group–to–group collaboration. It was developed in the USA at Argonne National Laboratory and first deployed by the National Center for Supercomputing Applications in 1999. Access Grid (AG) can connect multiple rooms in arbitrary locations, provided

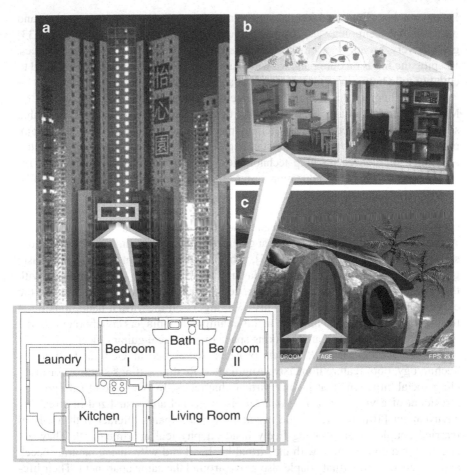

Fig. 9.1 A real apartment in a residential building (**a**, full reality), a dollhouse (**b**, make-belief reality) and a Stone Age cabin from a 3D game (**c**, virtuality) can be linked, populated and shared by virtual roommates

that all participating sites are registered as AG-nodes. During conference sessions, each connected node is represented by its own window, usually projected on a large screen in tiled mode. Because of its flexibility and relatively low operation costs, Access Grid become popular in academic community [27]. Overall, the advent of large displays and broadband networking made tele-collaboration not only possible, but also practical and cost effective [23].

Concurrently, advances in microdisplay and motion tracking technologies made Virtual Reality components available to a wider audience of researchers. The increased availability of VR equipment has stimulated creation of novel interfaces and applications, especially in Augmented Reality field, where virtual content is superimposed onto real scenes. A now classic article by Azuma et al. [1] gives a historic perspective on the scope of traditional AR applications. A recent survey by

Papagiannakis, Singh and Magnenat-Thalmann describes advances in mobile and wearable AR technology [26]. A comprehensive literature review by Yu et al. [33] gives a very broad view on the current state of AR, with over 300 references. Keeping the focus on our goals, we will examine several projects, directly related to collaboration between remote participants and cross-platform communications.

One of them is the HyperMirror telecommunication interface, developed by Morikawa and Maesako [22]. HyperMirror is a video conversation system that superimposes mirrored images of remote participants onto a shared video stream, producing the effect that they are standing side–by–side with the viewer. Taking advantage of modern tracking technologies, the HyperMirror technique was recently used in a distance education system for teaching endoscopic surgery skills, developed by Kumagai et al [15]. Using this system, students are able to watch themselves, standing next to a remotely based instructor. By copying instructor's stances and motions, students learn and practice a variety of surgical procedures.

Another example of employing augmented video for training purposes is described by Motokawa and Saito [21], who created a system for teaching basic guitar skills. Their system captures player's hands on video and overlays it with the rendered 3D model of virtual hands, demonstrating guitar chords. To learn the chords, the player simply overlaps his own fingers on the virtual hand, looking at the mirrored image on the monitor. In this example, real players collaborate with the virtual instructor, using shared working space over the real guitar object.

AR Second Life and *AR Façade* projects, developed at Georgia Institute of Technology, both feature immersive Augmented Reality settings suitable for modeling social situations that involve virtual characters. In AR Second Life project, a resident of a virtual world *Second Life* is projected and visualized in a real lab environment [16]. In AR Façade installation, participants interact with a virtual married couple, while moving freely inside a physical apartment [9]. They get engaged in a conversation with the virtual husband and wife, using natural speech and gestures.[1] The virtual couple also move around the same apartment. Their life-size avatars are visualized with a Head Mounted Display.

Despite the diversity of these projects and systems, all of them require the collaborative spaces to be identical geometrically, for all participants involved, real and virtual. In teleconference systems, such as TelePresence by Cisco [8], the local and remote spaces are usually tiled back–to–back, connected by the surface of display screens. In mirror-based systems [15,21], the virtual or remote environment is overlaid onto a local scene, using reflection transformation. When immersive visual augmentation is used [9, 16], the virtual and physical spaces must coincide precisely. In addition, in video-based systems [8, 15, 21] the feeling of shared presence can only be maintained while a person remains in the camera's field of view. The illusion is broken when participants move too far from their dedicated positions.

---

[1]To avoid errors introduced by automatic speech recognition, user verbal input is manually typed-in in real time by a human operator behind the scene, using a Wizard-of-Oz approach.

These restrictions put severe limitations on types of environments that can be linked and shared and also on range of activities that users can do collaboratively. In the next section, a non-linear mapping between linked spaces will be introduced, which will provide geometry-free persistent connectivity between all participants.

3 Connecting Virtual Roommates Via Feature-Based Spatial Mapping

Sharing objects from different environments requires: (1) localization of the object in its own environment; (2) projecting it into the destination space and (3) visualization of the object.

In this section, the second problem will be addressed, by constructing a meaningful mappings between arbitrary environments, that can be shared by virtual roommates. Without the loss of generality, we will illustrate the main concepts using two fictional characters, Alice and Bob, who reside in physically separate apartments, as shown in Fig. 9.2, and use the Virtual Roommates system for spending time together. For clarity, it is assumed that each participant can be localized in their own space, by using real-time tracking. Also, it is assumed that each participant has all required equipment for visualizing the remote party. In Sect. 4, several solutions will be discussed for tracking and visualization.

The main idea behind the proposed system is to dismiss linear transformations as the means of projecting user paths from one environment to another. A linear transformation is a mapping defined over a vector space, that can be expressed as

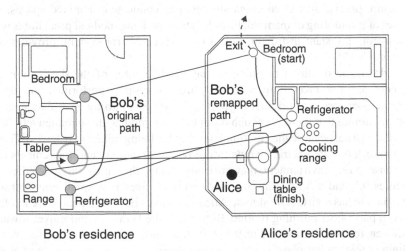

Bob's residence   Alice's residence

Fig. 9.2 Morning activities of two virtual roommates. Bob leaves his bedroom and heads for the kitchen (*left*). His projected avatar is displayed at Alice's place, where she waits for him by the table (*right, solid curve*). A *dashed line* shows the direct mapping of Bob's path, which makes him miss the destination

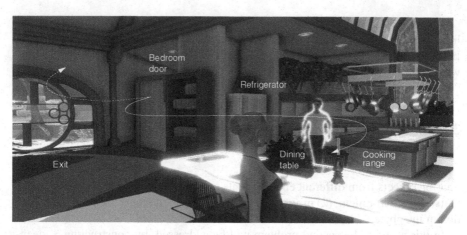

Fig. 9.3 3D reconstruction of the scene, outlined in Fig. 9.2 and described in Sect. 3. The contour of Bob's avatar is high-lighted, to indicate its virtual nature. A *solid curve* shows the correctly resolved path, leading towards the dining table (The scene was staged and rendered in Blue Mars platform [5])

a series of rotations and scaling operations. For the purposes of location mapping, linear transformations are usually complemented with post-translation. With this addition, they are called affine transformations. Affine transformations may be performed by optical devices, when processing visual material captured from real scenes. To process virtual content, affine transformations are expressed and applied in a matrix form.

Linear transformations have two important properties: they preserve collinearity of points and ratios of distances. These features are very important in applications that require precise spatial coordination between connected or mixed spaces, for purposes of monitoring or manipulating objects. Practicing medical procedures with the help from a distant instructor, linked via a HyperMirror system, provides one such example [15].

The downside of direct mapping is that local features of the destination environment are not taken into account. Direct mapping, performed via linear transformations, projects original trajectories of objects into the destination scene "as is", assuming that there is enough room to accommodate these maneuvers. This is not always true, because the environments that are being mixed may have different sizes and different geometric layouts. Moreover, user actions and movements that make sense in one environment, may critically change their meaning in another.

Figures 9.2 and 9.3 illustrate the problem. Bob lives in a small one bedroom apartment. He has a virtual roommate Alice, who lives in a large penthouse in other city. As a part of his morning routine, Bob leaves the bedroom and moves towards the kitchen for breakfast (see Fig. 9.2, left diagram). Alice is waiting for him at the dining table, in her place (right diagram). However, direct projection of Bob's original path onto Alice's room makes him appear to leave the bedroom and then immediately exit the room (right diagram, dashed curve).

In order to project paths correctly, we suggest using local features of the environment as anchors for object localization. With this approach, the original user path (Fig. 9.2, left diagram), is described as a sequence of locations, shown as circles:

```
"bedroom door",
"refrigerator",
"cooking range",
"dining table"
```

As soon as Bob is localized with respect to the closest anchor, this information is transmitted to the receiving end (Alice's place), where the process is run in reverse. For example, when the system receives a "dining table" anchor information, it finds the corresponding feature in the local floor plan and obtains the new coordinates from that map. The new reconstructed path is now based on local features of the destination environment. It leads Bob to his intended target, the dining table, via a series of moves from one anchor to another. The reconstructed path is shown in Fig. 9.2 (right diagram, solid curve), and that is how Alice will see movements of Bob's avatar, projected into her penthouse.

To summarize: the Virtual Roommates system tracks user position and, if possible, orientation, in real or nearly real time. The obtained 3D coordinates are not used or shared immediately in their raw form. Instead, more descriptive albeit less frequent updates are sent to all other parties involved, which can be called *sparse presence samples*. These samples include code names of the local features in the source environment (e.g., dining table, refrigerator, etc.). Every received *presence sample* is then reconstructed into local 3D coordinates in the destination space, according to the local floor plan. Besides user location and orientation, a presence sample may include additional information, such as elapsed time at each location, and guessed activity. One example of a detailed presence sample is shown below:

```
location:          refrigerator,
orientation:       12 o'clock (head-on)
elapsed time:      20 seconds
guessed activity:  accessing content
```

To put it more formally, in our context *a presence-sample* denotes a contextually enriched spatio-temporal data record. By contextually enriched we understand that the preceding or current actions might indicate the intention of a person at that location; spatio means in real or virtual space, and temporal indicates that the time is an added attribute. Furthermore, presence samples can be categorized as strong and weak, depending by the amount of information they convey and/or probability that the guessed activity is correct. The example with the refrigerator above is an example of a strong sample. For convenience, we will also use term "anchor" when referring to spatial attribute of the presence sample, meaning that we are only considering its location.

3.1 Resolving and Optimizing User Path in Destination Space

As illustrated in Figs. 9.2 and 9.3, Bob's avatar completely misses the travel target if he mimics his protagonist's moves and turns verbatim: leave the bedroom, turn right, go straight. This path will lead him to an unexpected exit. Feature-based navigation will help to avoid such mistakes. However, simple jumps from one anchor location to the next is not acceptable, in general case, and the navigation system must deal with at least two issues: (1) obstacle avoidance and (2) path disambiguation and optimization.

A brute force solution for the above tasks would include introducing a high number of dummy anchor locations at regular intervals, covering the whole floor plan, and searching for the shortest path, connecting point A and point B, traversing those anchors. Even for relatively small and confined indoor scenes, this solution might require processing of n^2 anchors, and the search in this space for the shortest path would involve traversing the graph with n^4 edges. Here, n is a number of distinct positions that a person can take while crossing the scene in any direction, in destination space. The room length, measured in steps, may be used as a simple estimate for n. The computational complexity of the path planning process in this case may become prohibitively high.

Luckily, there exist approaches that can be utilized to resolve the problem more elegantly and with less computational resources required. To do this properly, one must resort to computational geometry methods recently introduced in the area of mobile navigation and robotics. Solutions to the path planning problem differ fundamentally, depending on the space representation, the task at hand and the connectivity model of the space. The recent article by Bhattacharya and Gavrilova [3] classifies the main approaches to path planning as: (a) the roadmap method, (b) the cell decomposition method and (c) the potential field method. The roadmap method captures the connectivity of the free space using curves or straight lines. The cell decomposition method partitions free space using grid cells so that the edges of the cells represent the connectivity. The potential field approach fills the free area with a potential field in which a mobile agent (for instance, a robot) is attracted towards its goal position while being repelled from obstacles. Among those methods, the roadmap approach utilizes different kinds of graphs to represent the free space connectivity. Some of the common ones are probabilistic roadmaps which are graphs with vertices that are randomly generated in free space, visibility graph in which the graph vertices are the vertices of the obstacles themselves and Voronoi diagrams, whose edges represent the maximum clearance path among the obstacles. Figure 9.4 shows two types of roadmaps based on visibility graph (left) and Voronoi diagram (right). While the visibility graph based approach creates a complex of inter-connected paths in the environment with triangular-shaped obstacles, the Voronoi diagram based method provides a solution with clearly identified path that can be easily followed by a virtual roommate.

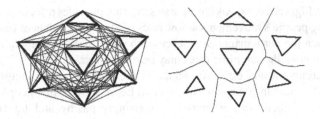

Fig. 9.4 *Left*: roadmap from the visibility graph (includes obstacle edges). *Right*: roadmap from the Voronoi diagram

In order to generate user paths in the destination space correctly and efficiently, we propose to combine the roadmap based Voronoi diagram method for space subdivision with the use of local features of the environment as anchors for object localization.

With this approach, the original user path (Fig. 9.2, left) is described as a sequence of locations: bedroom door, refrigerator, cooking range, kitchen table. In the destination space, these locations (not necessarily all of them) must exist in the local map, used for rebuilding the path within the new environment. The map is represented as the Voronoi diagram, with sites based on local anchor positions. Initially, the direct roadmap method is applied to quickly schedule a collision-free path, but this path is by no means optimal. It may have unnecessary turns and might not be the shortest one. This necessitates some kind of refinement on the path to achieve optimality. We propose to use heuristic based on the Voronoi diagram to obtain the optimal path. Applying a shortest path algorithm on the initial roadmap refines the path iteratively until an optimal path is obtained. The method is guaranteed to converge after $n \log(n)$ steps, where n is the number of anchors. This approach has many advantages aside from fast optimal path planning. For instance, if the topology of underlying space changes, the method can adapt to the new room layout very quickly, without the need to create a new set of dummy features or a new space grid. Also, if we now have to plan the path for a larger moving entity (i.e. a different user or a virtual object with bigger dimensions), we can simply set a new parameter to a proportionately larger value and the heuristic will still find an optimal path.

3.2 Sparse Presence Samples, Additional Remarks

Besides providing a convenient basis for computationally efficient resolution of user paths, the idea of sparse sampling has many other advantages.

Use of sparse sampling follows naturally from an observation that in many collaborative activities, precise real-time tracking is not required. This is even more true in social situations, when people are communicating at close distances. In many cultures, it is considered impolite and even rude to watch people closely and continuously. Figuratively speaking, sparse sampling provides a socially acceptable way of tracing people's movements at low rates of "few direct glances (samples) per minute". When the participants cannot see each other directly (for example, being in different rooms), the sampling rates may be even lower.

Another argument that explicitly supports the idea of sparse sampling comes from the field of human cognition. Simons and Levin showed that people's internal representation of their surroundings is surprisingly patchy and far from being complete [30]. In other words, humans naturally sample reality at rather low rates and then fuse these samples into a single coherent model by mental extrapolation, both in time and space. Therefore, adding a relatively small number of extra visual samples from another environment should suffice for building a continuous description of the augmented scene. Kim and colleagues first suggested [14] and then demonstrated experimentally [17], that people are able to maintain tight association with virtual elements in augmented scenes, without tight spatial and visual registration.

4   System Components

To explain how the system captures and projects user paths from one environment to another, we assumed that both virtual roommates, Alice and Bob, have sufficient means to track their physical movements and visualize themselves as 3D avatars in each other's local environment. In this section, we will discuss technical details and evaluate several possible implementations.

4.1   Tracking

It was shown, that spatial and temporal tracking resolution requirements can be very low during path sampling, when the target object (Bob) is localized and resolved in the destination space, Alice's apartment. A relatively small number of anchors is sufficient for path planning, including obstacle avoidance and path optimization. However, direct immersive visualization of a remote roommate requires, in general, precise registration of its avatar with a local viewer, which calls for real-time tracking of the viewer's head, in six degrees of freedom (DOF).

General-purpose six DOF tracking can be achieved using commercially available high-end systems, such as PPT from WorldViz.[2] PPT is able to capture object position and orientation in a $50 \times 50 \times 3$ m volume, with sub-millimeter precision. PPT tracker is using multiple infrared cameras that entirely cover the working area.

---

[2]Precision Position Tracker. http://www.worldviz.com/products/ppt.

The user must wear a head mounted IR emitter, which is reasonably comfortable and unobtrusive. The only serious issue with this solution is the price of the tracking system.

Combining tracking technologies with multiple sensor fusion provides an alternative solution to the six DOF tracking problem [12, 31]. For example, in a system developed by Tenmoku and colleagues [32], five wearable sensors are used: a head-mounted camera, an inertial InterTrax2 sensor, an IrDA receiver, an RFID tag reader and a pedometer. Combined input from all these devices enables accurate registration of virtual content for current user position and orientation, both in indoors and outdoors scenes. Tracking systems that employ sensor fusion are generally more flexible and customizable than off-the-shelf systems and allow building less expensive applications. However, use of multiple wearable sensors often results in very bulky and uncomfortable sets on interconnected components, including a laptop, PC or ultra-mobile PC, mounted on a special harness.

Presently, video-based tracking technologies experience rapid growth, partly energized by commercial success of EyeToy line of video games by Sony, and much anticipated Kinect system (formerly known as Project Natal) by Microsoft, presented at E3 gaming convention in 2010. In these games, players control their video avatars, using natural body movements, tracked by a TV-mounted camera. Video-based tracking can be used to obtain object position and orientation, in real time. Using adaptive view-base appearance model, Morency and colleagues developed a system for full six DOF tracking of user head [20], with rotational accuracy and resolution of InertiaCube2 sensor from InterSense Inc.,[3] which became a de-facto industry standard in capturing rotation. This technique was demonstrated to be sufficient for real-time tracking and registration of user head at 75 Hz, running on a modest consumer level PC. The main advantage of video-based tracking is its unobtrusiveness: users are not required to wear any devices. The downside is relatively small working range, limited by camera field of view. In order to cover a reasonable working volume (e.g., a living room), multiple cameras are likely to be installed.

In order to build a practical and cost-effective tracking system for Virtual Roommates, we suggest to take advantage of the discrete nature of the tracked space. As discussed before, sampling and reconstruction of user paths assumes and requires that the working volume is partitioned into a set of local features. We suggest to use these features for initial localization of roommates, which can be further refined using video-trackers, installed at these locations.

For initial coarse localization, several techniques may be used. One is *Smart Floor*, a pressure sensitive carpet fit to the floor surface of the tracked room. This device showed good results for indoors environments [25]. However, it has one serious drawback: tracking stops as soon as a person looses contact with the carpet surface, for example, when sitting on a chair or a sofa.

---

[3]InterSense Inc. Inertia Cube2 Manual. http://www.intersense.com.

Fig. 9.5 The iPort display by Tek Gear built into Oakley frame. Weight: 100 g

Radio-frequency identification (RFID) can also be used for tracking a person's location within large areas [2, 4]. As reported by Becker et al. [4], a person wearing a belt-mounted antenna device can be reliably localized in 20 cm range from passive RFID tags, placed in the environment. Their system was successfully tested in a real-life situation, namely, an aircraft maintenance routine. A crew member was detected at every passenger seat in the aircraft cabin. This resolution is quite sufficient for our purposes.

RFID-based approach fits closely to our needs and purposes. Tags can be easily attached to all feature elements in the room, and marked as "kitchen table", "lounge sofa", et cetera. RFID tags are very durable and inexpensive, which makes the whole system scalable and easy to install and maintain. Wearable RFID readers are also getting better and smaller; several commercial and home-made devices are described by Medynskiy et al. [19].

A summary: for Virtual Roommate tracking system, we propose a two-stage approach. First, a person is localized in the environment, using proximity-based techniques, such as RFID, with respect to local features. These sparse positional samples are used for projecting and reconstructing the person's path in remote environment. Also, these samples are subject for further refinement, using locally installed video trackers. The number and density of placements of proximity tags and video-cameras will depend on the size and layout of the physical space and the choice of visualization method. Several options are discussed in the next section.

4.2 Visualization with Wearable Display Devices

Visualization is the most challenging part of the process of reconstruction of user presence. Most commercially available head mounted displays (HMD) are still too bulky and heavy to wear for an extended period of time [6]. Monocle-style displays manufactured by Creative Display Systems and Tek Gear may offer a more comfortable alternative, provided that wireless configurations will eventually appear on the market. The size and weigh of recent near-eye monocular displays allow to attach them onto a pair of conventional sun-glasses, as shown in Fig. 9.5.

A comprehensive review of available wearable headset and discussion of trends in display technologies may be founds in Hainich's book [11].

Recently, Sensics Inc, a manufacturer of high-end panoramic HMDs, announced a new line of products that will provide a high definition wireless video link, compatible with all Sensics' headset models. Their goal is to achieve HD1080p video streaming to battery operated HMDs at 60 Hz frame rate, including the ultra-portable xSight HMD model. This wireless configuration may provide a feasible visualization option for Virtual Roommates, although the price of the whole system may become prohibitive, even for a pilot project, with a single-viewer installation.

4.3 Virtual Mirror

Until light-weight wireless Head Mounted Displays become available and afford-able, we suggest an alternative indirect solution for visualization of 3D avatars, utilizing the concept of a virtual mirror. The display system will contain one or more wall-mounted monitors, operating in a 'mirror' mode. Each monitor will show the interior of the local room, where the viewer is presently located, augmented with rendering of the avatar of a remote roommate. The scene must be rendered as if reflected in a mirror, co-located with the display, and viewed from the current standpoint of the local observer. In other words, virtual roommates can only be seen as reflections in mirrors, but never in the direct view. Reflected views of the local environment may be obtained from live video streams or by using photographs of the room. In order to correctly resolve occlusions with the virtual characters, the rendering system must also have a current 3D geometry model of the local scene. However, in the simplest configuration, the local environment may be approximated by a single cube, textured with high-resolution photographs.

One important feature of Virtual Mirror as a display solution for our system is that it may eliminate the need for full six DOF tracking of user head. Switching from six DOF to three DOF tracking will significantly reduce requirements to system hardware components. In order to render the scene in reflected mode, it is sufficient to obtain position of the viewer in the destination environment. Also, the system must know the current location and orientation of the mirror display. That information is sufficient to render the local environment from the local user position, using standard off-axis rendering technique. The user head rotation will only be needed if stereo-rendering is required and proper stereo-separation of both eyes must be updated, with respect to the mirror location, in real time.

- Virtual Mirror is based on a very familiar device: mirrors have been used for visual augmentation for thousands of years, therefore, no training or suspension of disbelief is needed.
- The display device is unobtrusive, in contrast to monocles and Head Mounted Displays.
- Virtual Mirror provides "viewing on-demand": people will see their roommates only when they want to, by looking into a virtual mirror.

Fig. 9.6 Visualizing roommates as reflections in a virtual mirror: room visibility diagram, for the current Alice's standpoint

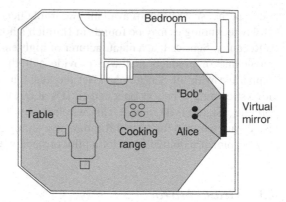

- Virtual Mirror naturally solves the problem of colliding with remote avatars, because reflections are not perceived as tangible objects, they are "see only".
- Is easy to reconfigure at any time, by moving one or more screens to the location of current activities. A prototype for dynamic tracking and reconfiguring of multi-display visualization system, recently presented by Ohta [24], seems suitable for this purpose.

Finally, visualization even with a single virtual mirror screen, may provide a large viewing area, depending on the current position of the viewer. Figures 9.6 and 9.7 show one possible installation of the virtual mirror in Alice's apartment. The shaded part of the diagram in Fig. 9.6 indicates the area where Alice can see her friend while standing close to the mirror. This area covers most of the room.

4.4 Voice Communications

For completeness sake, a few words should be said about voice communications between virtual roommates. Voice communications must be implemented with full spatial localization in the destination space. Fortunately, it is relatively easy to do for indoors environments, using multiple speaker system. Once the position of the remote avatar is resolved in the local space, its voice channel must be redirected to the nearest speaker. The spatial layout of the local environment, such as walls and corridors, will produce all necessary effects automatically, including volume attenuation, reverberation, etc.

5 Building Prototypes in Virtual Reality

In the previous sections, several solutions were discussed for tracking and visualization of connected remote participants. A fully functional Virtual Roommates system requires all these components developed, assembled and installed at two or

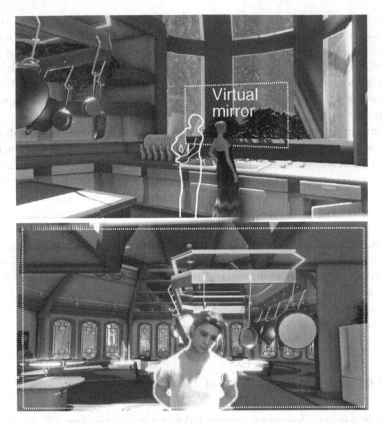

Fig. 9.7 3D reconstruction of the diagram, shown in Fig. 9.6. *Top image*: Alice is looking into a virtual mirror, mounted above the kitchen sink. Bob's avatar is shown as a silhouette, not visible in direct view. The *lower image* shows what Alice sees in the mirror, including fully visible Bob's avatar (Images captured in Blue Mars [5])

more physical locations, which still presents a significant challenge. However, by using Virtual Reality and miniature models, it is possible to implement and test all, or nearly all, aspects of the proposed feature-based spatial mapping that constitutes the core principle of Virtual Roommates.

5.1   Projecting a Real-Life Character into Virtual Reality: Tracking Figurines in a Doll House

The prototype system, described next, took advantage of the fact that a doll house is a perfect example of fully controlled environment, where tracking can be easily implemented. A doll house also has all elements, required for building a feature-based spatial mapping. These elements are miniature furniture models (TV set, table, sofa, etc), that can be rearranged inside the house as desired. For a virtual roommate, a little figurine was used, attached to a Flock of Bird magnetic sensor, for tracking. The doll house and the figurine constituted the source space. The destination space was implemented in a virtual environment, with very different content: a Stone Age village, with one cabin complete with similar furniture items. The room layouts of the doll house and the cabin, shown in Fig. 9.8, were completely different.

During the test, an experimenter was playing with the figurine, "cooking dinner" and "watching TV" inside the doll house, while monitoring evolutions of her 3D avatar in the destination scene, the virtual cabin. The avatar mirrored these actions, moving in the cabin, from one landmark to the next. Two processed were running concurrently, sampling and reconstruction. The sampling process continuously read data from the magnetic tracker and checked for collisions between the geometry model of the figurine and the models of all furniture items. Upon detecting a collision, the name of the colliding object was sent to the reconstruction process, which controlled movements of the avatar in VR. Every new feature elements was checked with the local floor plan, and, if the corresponding item was found, the avatar moved towards the new location. As the result, a meaningful feature based path projection was established and maintained between physical and virtual environments, with different spatial layouts.

5.2 Visualization with a Virtual Mirror Prototype

The virtual mirror prototype was created and tested as a stand-alone VR application. A real office room was approximated in 3D, by a number of boxes, textured with high-resolution photographs. Then, a virtual character was added to the virtual office scene, as shown in Fig. 9.9. The combined scene was rendered on a laptop in a mirror mode, using the laptop screen as a display device. For a reference view, a real physical mirror was attached to the laptop. Both mirrors showed the same room with nearly identical fidelity. The virtual mirror also showed a virtual roommate, moving around the office. For this test, no collision detection was implemented, because the space inside the virtual office was free of occluders.

Both prototypes were developed using Flatland, an open source virtual reality system, developed at the Albuquerque High Performance Computing Center [10].

6 Conclusions

The borderline between real and virtual worlds is getting increasingly fuzzy. People begin to live their alternative lives in VR: make friends and enemies, express themselves creatively and socially, and even earn real money in virtual economies. On the other hand, advances in miniaturization of tracking and display

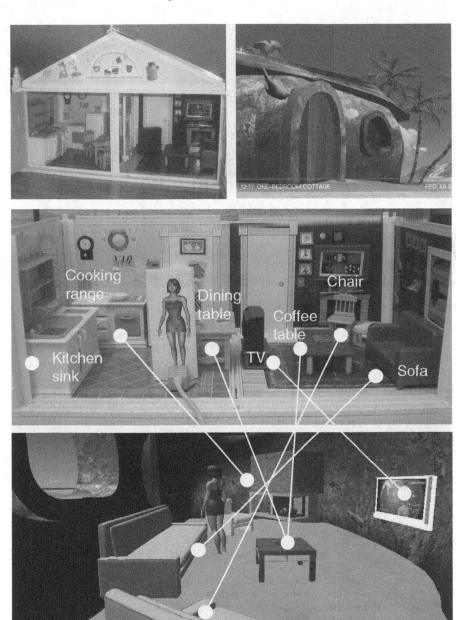

Fig. 9.8 Mixed reality prototype of the virtual roommates. The little paper figurine moves around the doll house, and her locations are mapped and reconstructed inside a virtual Stone Age cabin. Both places are loosely connected via similar elements in their interiors

Fig. 9.9 A virtual mirror: adding a virtual character to a real office scene. High-resolution photographs (*top left*) were used to texture and assemble the office 3D model (*bottom left*). A real mirror is mounted on top of a laptop, providing a reference view. The laptop operates in a virtual mirror mode, showing the same scene, augmented with an animated 3D character

devices allow building systems that effectively insert real people's presence into virtual environments and, reciprocally, bring 3D characters into physical scenes. Further development of online virtual worlds, coupled with continuously improving input/output interface devices will call for new conceptual solutions, aiming to achieve a true fusion between people's real and virtual existence.

The Virtual Roommates system, presented on these pages, describes the first steps towards this goal.

References

1. R. Azuma, Y. Baillot, R. Behringer, S. Feiner, S. Julier, B. MacIntyre. Recent Advances in Augmented Reality. *Computer Graphics & Applications*, 21(6), pp. 34-47, 2001.
2. P. Bahl, V. Padmanabhan. RADAR: An in-building user location and tracking system. *Proceedings of the IEEE INFOCOM 2000*, pp. 775-784, 2000.
3. P. Bhattacharya, M. Gavrilova. Roadmap-based Path Planning – Using the Voronoi Diagram for a Clearance-Based Shortest Path. *IEEE Robotics & Automation Magazine (IEEE RAM)*, Special Issue on Computational Geometry in Robotics. 15(2): 58-66, 2008.
4. B. Becker, M. Huber, G. Klinker. Utilizing RFIDs for Location Aware Computing. *UIC, Lecture Notes in Computer Science*, Springer, vol. 5061, pp. 216-228, 2008.
5. Blue Mars Virtual World, by Avatar-Reality Inc., http://www.bluemars.com
6. Christoph Bungert. HMD Comparison Chart, http://www.stereo3d.com/hmd.htm last updated on Dec. 27, 2006.

7. A. Cheok, S. Fong, K. Goh, X. Yang, W. Liu, F. Farzbiz. Human Pacman: a sensing-based mobile entertainment system with ubiquitous computing and tangible interaction. *Proceedings of Workshop on Network and system support for games*, ACM, New York, NY, USA, 106–117, 2003.

8. TelePresence Conference system, by Cisco Systems, Inc., http://www.cisco.com.

9. S. Dow, B. MacIntyre, M. Mateas. Styles of play in immersive and interactive story: case studies from a gallery installation of AR Façade. *Proceedings of the 2008 International Conference on Advances in Computer Entertainment Technology, ACE'08*, Yokohama, Japan, pp. 373-380, 2008.

10. Flatland: The Homunculus Project at the Albuquerque High Performance Computing Center (AHPCC), http://www.hpc.unm.edu/homunculus, 2002.

11. R. Hainich. *The End of Hardware: a Novel Approach to Augmented Reality. (2nd Ed.)*. BookSurge Publishing. 2006.

12. D. Hallaway, T. Höllerer, S Feiner. Bridging the gaps: Hybrid tracking for adaptive mobile augmented reality. *Applied Artificial Intelligence, Special Edition on Artificial Intelligence in Mobile Systems, 26(5), July 2004.*

13. Y. Kitamura, R. Rong, Y. Hirano, K. Asai, F. Kishino. Video agent: interactive autonomous agents generated from real-world creatures. *Proceedings of the 2008 ACM Symposium on Virtual Reality Software and Technology (Bordeaux, France, October 27-29, 2008). VRST '08.* ACM, New York, NY, pp. 30-38, 2008.

14. G. Kim. Loosely Coupled Mixed Reality. *Proceedings of Mixed Reality Entertainment and Art Workshop*, ISMAR'07, Japan, Nara, 2007.

15. T. Kumagai, J. Yamashita, O. Morikawa, K. Yokoyama, S. Fujimaki, T. Konishi, H. Ishimasa, H. Murata, K. Tomoda. Distance education system for teaching manual skills in endoscopic paranasal sinus surgery using "HyperMirror" telecommunication interface, *Proceedings of IEEE VR Conference*, Reno, Nevada 2008.

16. T. Lang, B. MacIntyre, I. Zugaza. Massively Multiplayer Online Worlds as a Platform for Augmented Reality Experiences. *Proceedings of IEEE Virtual Reality Conference*, Reno, Nevada, pp. 67-70, 2008.

17. M. Lee, M. Lee, G. Kim. Loosely-coupled vs. tightly-coupled mixed reality: using the environment metaphorically. *Proceedings of the 8th International Conference on Virtual Reality Continuum and its Applications in Industry (VRCAI '09)*, Yokohama, Japan, pp. 345-349, 2009.

18. B. MacIntyre, M. Lohse, J. Bolter and E. Moreno. Integrating 2D Video Actors into a 3D AR System. *Presence, Special Issue on Mixed Reality*, 11(2). pp. 189-202, April, 2002.

19. Y. Medynskiy, S. Gov, A. Mazalek, D. Minnen. Wearable RFID for Play. *Proceedings of Tangible Play workshop, Intelligent User Interfaces conference*, January 28, 2007, Honolulu, Hawaii, USA.

20. L.-P. Morency, A. Rahimi, T. Darrell. Adaptive View-based Appearance Model. *Proceedings IEEE Conference on Computer Vision and Pattern Recognition*. 1:803–810, 2003.

21. Y. Motokawa, and H. Saito. Support system for guitar playing using augmented reality display. *Proceedings of the 5th IEEE and ACM international Symposium on Mixed and Augmented Reality (ISMAR'06)*, Washington, DC, October 22-25, pp. 243-244, 2006.

22. O. Morikawa, T. Maesako. HyperMirror: toward pleasant-to-use video mediated communication system. *Proceedings of the ACM Conference on Computer Supported Cooperative Work*. Seattle, Washington, Nov. 14-18, 1998.

23. T. Ni, G. Schmidt, O. Staadt, M. Livingston, R. Ball, R. May. A Survey of Large High-Resolution Display Technologies, Techniques, and Applications. *Proceedings of the IEEE conference on Virtual Reality (VR'06)*, IEEE Computer Society, Washington, DC, March 25-29, 2006.

24. T. Ohta. Dynamically reconfigurable multi-display environment for CG contents. *Proceedings of the 2008 International Conference on Advances in Computer Entertainment Technology, ACE'08*, Yokohama, Japan, p. 416, 2008.

25. R. Orr, G. Abowd. The Smart Floor: A Mechanism for Natural User Identification and Tracking. *Conference on Human Factors in Computing Systems*, Netherlands, April 2000.
26. G. Papagiannakis, G. Singh, N. Magnenat-Thalmann. A survey of mobile and wireless technologies for augmented reality systems. *Computer Animation and Virtual Worlds*, 19, pp. 3-22, 2008.
27. A. Squelch. The Access Grid and Video Conferencing. *Interactive Virtual Environments Centre*, http://www.ivec.org/interactive/docs/AccessGrid_vs_VideoConferencing.pdf
28. A. Sherstyuk, K.Chu, S. Joseph. Virtual Mirror for Augmented Presence Applications. *Proceedings of the 2008 international Conference on Advances in Computer Entertainment Technology (ACM ACE'08)*, Yokohama, Japan, December 3-5, 2008.
29. A. Sherstyuk, K.Chu, S. Joseph. Virtual Roommates in Ambient Telepresence Applications. *Proceedings of the 2008 International Conference on Artificial Reality and Telexistence (ICAT'08)*, Yokohama, Japan, December 1-3, 2008.
30. D. Simons and D. Levin. Change Blindness. *Trends in Cognitive Sciences*, 1(7), pp. 261-267, 1997.
31. D. Pustka, G. Klinker. Dynamic Gyroscope Fusion in Ubiquitous Tracking Environments. *Proceedings of the 7th IEEE International Symposium on Mixed and Augmented Reality, ISMAR*, pp. 13-20, Cambridge, UK, 2008.
32. R. Tenmoku, M. Kanbara, N. Yokoya. A Wearable Augmented Reality System for Navigation Using Positioning Infrastructures and a Pedometer. *Proceedings of IEEE / ACM International Symposium on Mixed and Augmented Reality*, p. 344, 2003.
33. D. Yu, J. Jin, S. Luo, W. Lai, Q. Huang. A Useful Visualization Technique: A Literature Review for Augmented Reality and its Application, Limitation & Future Direction. *Visual Information Communication*, L. Huang et al. (Eds.), Springer, ISBN: 978-1-4419-0311-2, 2010.

Chapter 10
Large Scale Spatial Augmented Reality for Design and Prototyping

Michael R. Marner, Ross T. Smith, Shane R. Porter, Markus M. Broecker, Benjamin Close, and Bruce H. Thomas

Abstract Spatial Augmented Reality allows the appearance of physical objects to be transformed using projected light. Computer controlled light projection systems have become readily available and cost effective for both commercial and personal use. This chapter explores how large Spatial Augmented Reality systems can be applied to enhanced design mock-ups. Unlike traditional appearance altering techniques such as paints and inks, computer controlled projected light can change the color of a prototype at the touch of a button allowing many different appearances to be evaluated. We present the customized physical-virtual tools we have developed such as our hand held virtual spray painting tool that allows designers to create many customized appearances using only projected light. Finally, we also discuss design parameters of building dedicated projection environments including room layout, hardware selection and interaction considerations.

1 Introduction

Spatial Augmented Reality (SAR) projects perspectively correct computer generated images onto physical objects to enhance their appearance and functionality. Most forms of physical matter can have their appearance altered using projected light, allowing familiar looking objects to be instantly transformed to take on a completely new facade. Our research focuses on how this innovative technology can be applied to support industrial designers during prototype development by enhancing the tools available for mock-up creation. We envisage that SAR will revolutionize the industrial design process with two significant features that are not available using traditional mock-up creation techniques. Firstly SAR provides

M.R. Marner (✉)
University of South Australia, Wearable Computer Laboratory, Mawson Lakes, Australia
e-mail: michael.marner@unisa.edu.au

B. Furht (ed.), *Handbook of Augmented Reality*, DOI 10.1007/978-1-4614-0064-6_10, 231
© Springer Science+Business Media, LLC 2011

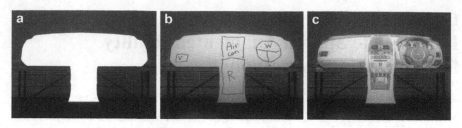

Fig. 10.1 Example of a SAR mock-up stages. (**a**) Simple mock-up prepared for SAR visualization. (**b**) Handwritten annotations projected onto mock-up. (**c**) Enhanced mock-up using SAR to provide appearance and functionality information

a rich fully featured appearance that can be instantly altered at the touch of a button. For example, the layout of a car dashboard can be instantly altered from right to left hand drive without any physical change to the mock-up. Secondly, full functionality of simulated controls, such as a climate control system, can be implemented without the need for physical buttons, lights, displays or electronics to be installed in the prototype. Instead the SAR technology can provide all the functionality using projected light, a tracking system, and customized software. An example of SAR technology in use is shown in Fig. 10.1. Figure 10.1a depicts a SAR prototype mock-up of a car dashboard using cheap, light weight materials for its construction. Figure 10.1b shows the same mock-up with simple annotations and Fig. 10.1c demonstrates a fully featured appearance that leverages SAR technology for its functionality and design visualization.

In 1965 Ivan Sutherland stated that "The ultimate display would, of course, be a room within which the computer can control the existence of matter. A chair displayed in such a room would be good enough to sit in. Handcuffs displayed in such a room would be confining, and a bullet displayed in such a room would be fatal" [31]. While SAR cannot control the existence of matter, we believe the technology is the next step bringing us closer to making his vision a reality. In this chapter we discuss how the powerful new SAR technology can be applied to support industrial designers by expanding the current design methodology.

The chapter begins by defining SAR and explains the differences between common display technologies used for Augmented Reality. Following this, a background presenting the state of the art of SAR systems, applications and the industrial design process is summarized in Sect. 2. A discussion on enhancing the current industrial design methodology by leveraging the features of the SAR technology is presented in Sect. 3. Section 4 demonstrates practical applications, we discuss five case studies that are made possible using a SAR environment. Current tools and applications are discussed in Sect. 5. Design considerations when constructing SAR environments are discussed in Sect. 6. Finally, we conclude with a discussion on future directions of SAR technology in Sect. 7.

1.1 Spatial Augmented Reality

Spatial augmented reality enhances the physical world with computer generated graphics from digital projectors [21]. This is in contrast to other Augmented Reality (AR) display technologies, such as Head Mounted Displays (HMD) which place augmentations on an image plane in front of the user's eyes, and hand-held devices which show augmentations on a hand-held display. SAR requires physical surfaces to project onto. These surfaces can consist of any objects in the environment that are of interest to the user; projections are not limited to walls or purpose built screens.

Unlike CAD and other AR display technologies, SAR allows users to physically touch the virtual information. The surfaces provide passive haptic feedback and all stereoscopic depth cues are naturally provided. Previous virtual reality research has shown that the ability to touch virtual objects and information enhances user experience [9], and can improve users' performance [36]. This physical nature of SAR makes it a compelling choice for industrial design applications since the designers can physically touch the mock-up prototypes and leverage the flexible computer controlled appearance. Hare et al. [8] describe the importance of physical prototypes in the design process. Using SAR, designers can naturally interact with design mock-ups, without having to hold or wear display equipment. As SAR places computer generated information directly onto objects in the real world, groups can view and interact with the system. This makes SAR an ideal choice for collaborative tasks.

SAR also has similarities to the Cave Automatic Virtual Environment (CAVE) [6]. CAVEs are immersive virtual reality environments where perspectively correct graphics are projected onto the walls, floor, and sometimes the ceiling of a four sided room. The user stands in this room and experiences a virtual environment that appears correct from their point of view in the room. CAVEs use the same display equipment and techniques as SAR: calibrated digital projectors. However, for the most part, this is where the similarities end. SAR projections fall onto the physical objects of interest, such as design artifacts. The projection screens of a CAVE are planar surfaces on which to view the virtual images, acting as windows into a virtual world. This virtual window metaphor also affects the types of interaction possible in a CAVE. Interaction is inherently action-at-a-distance, since the objects of interest exist only in the virtual world beyond the projection screens. Physical handles and props can be used to aid interaction, but there is still some disconnection between actions a user performs and the virtual result of these actions. SAR applications are usually interested in the physical objects being projected onto. Therefore, interaction can be much more direct; the user can easily move whole objects around by hand, or manipulate the projections using their hands or physical tools.

CAVEs must project *view dependent* graphics for the system to function. This requirement limits the number of users able to use a CAVE simultaneously, although some systems time-multiplex multiple views by dividing the frames from the projector and using active shutter glasses to ensure each user only sees their correct view. HMD and handheld based AR applications usually also require view-dependent graphics. In contrast, SAR must project *scene dependent* graphics to function. A SAR system works independently from the users, making collaboration with large groups more easily achievable. View dependent projections are only required when view specific effects are desired, such as specular highlights, accurate reflections, and transparency.

2 Background

In this section we give an overview of related spatial augmented reality research, applications of SAR technology, and the industrial design process.

Spatial augmented reality builds on research into digital workspaces, such as Augmented Surfaces [26], which provides a work environment where information is shared between computers, projection screens, and augmentations on desks. This idea is further explored in the Office of the Future [23], which proposes using computer vision techniques to create a model of an entire office, and then using the entire office for augmentations.

Our focus on industrial design applications is inspired by Shader Lamps [24], which uses calibrated projectors to change the appearance of an object. This calibration requires finding the intrinsic parameters of the projector (focal length, field of view, etc.), and its position and orientation relative to objects of interest. This calibration can be automated through the use of structured light [11]. Given a textured 3D virtual model of an object, different materials and lighting conditions can be simulated. In addition, non-photorealistic shading models can be used, to provide effects such as cell-shading on objects in the real world [25]. Shader Lamps has also been extended, allowing users to digitally paint onto movable objects [2], and similar technology has been used to superimpose computer graphics on top of visual art pieces [3]. Shader Lamps style systems project directly onto objects in the environment, extending the size of the augmented environment requires adding more projectors. An alternative to this approach is the Everywhere Displays Projector [16], which uses a rapidly rotating mirror in front of the projector, to redirect projections to anywhere in the room. The main downside to this approach is the projector must be "shared" between areas receiving augmentations, limiting the number of areas that can receive augmentations simultaneously. Another type of SAR display is the Virtual Showcase [5]. Here, objects of interest are placed inside a case of half silvered mirrors. Projectors shine onto the surface of these mirrors, and give the appearance of information being projected onto and around the object. The main downside to the Virtual Showcase is that as objects are inside a case, it is not possible to directly touch and interact with them. This type of display is most suited to museum displays and other situations where the object should not be touched.

SAR user interfaces have similarities to tangible and graspable user interfaces (TUI) [7], where physical objects act as handles to elements of the user interface. Ullmer and Ishii describe how physical counterparts to common user interface controls can be created [33]. Projector based TUI applications have been used for tasks such as landscape analysis [18] and urban planning [34]. The physical nature of SAR makes TUI type user interfaces a compelling choice. Users can interact with the system in the same way they can physically touch and move objects around in the environment.

2.1   SAR Applications

There are several types of applications where SAR has been used in an industrial context. These include training, maintenance, on the job assistance, and design. Providing training through SAR involves projecting instructions for the user to follow. An example of this is the billiard instruction system [30] which instructs the user on how to play billiards by projecting images onto the playing surface. CADcast [17] projects assembly instructions onto a workbench, instructing the user on how to assemble a complex object. SAR can also be used for providing assistance to a user while they are performing a task. Using SAR for assistance may reduce the completion time or amount of errors for the task. An example of this is RFIG Lamps [20] which use handheld mobile projectors to identify important objects that have been marked with radio frequency tags. This technology could be used to identify certain packages from a pile, which would save searching time for a worker in the package delivery business.

Using SAR for maintenance involves projecting onto parts of a complex object that need to be checked or maintained by a user. The requirement for this application is that the projections are correctly registered with the corresponding part of the object. Laser projectors have been used to project onto welding points of a car door [28]. These projections highlight the parts of the car that need to be inspected by the workers. Laser projectors have also been used for programming the motion paths for industrial robots [37]. A tracked stylus is used to draw the motion paths, which are displayed using the projector.

An additional use of SAR in the workplace is for design. The design for an object can be projected directly onto a physical prototype [1]. The projected images displayed on the prototype are changed in real-time to display different designs. WARP [35] allows designers to preview material properties for cars, by projecting onto 3D printed models. A standard desktop user interface is used to select materials and other visual features.

2.2   Industrial Design Process and Concept Mock-ups

Designers select a design methodology according to the requirements of the task at hand. Pugh's Total Design Model [19] and Pahl and Beitz's model of design [15] are two examples of commonly applied methodologies. Whichever design methodology is chosen, concepts need to be generated that provide solutions to the design specification. This phase of design is called the concept stage. The typical process during the concept stage is to: (1) generate ideas, (2) create concepts that embody the ideas, (3) evaluate the concepts, and (4) select the most promising concepts. Using CAD and other design applications to express conceptual ideas is common place. Creating physical mock-ups to assess the viability of a concept is also common during the industrial design process. In practice, a combination of materials is needed to create mock-ups with diverse features. The designer explores different materials, colors, textures and dimensions repeatedly to find the best way to visualize a concept.

3 Industrial Design Process Using SAR

One of our goals is to explore how phases of the modeling methodology used by industrial designers can be enriched by using SAR technologies. The purpose is to allow designers to visualize their concepts with higher detail and be provided with a more flexible modeling environment. The existing industrial design concept phase modeling process is depicted in Fig. 10.2a. This demonstrates how designers are required to rebuild and often restart their prototype designs during the concept development. For example, consider a mock-up of a car dashboard where the

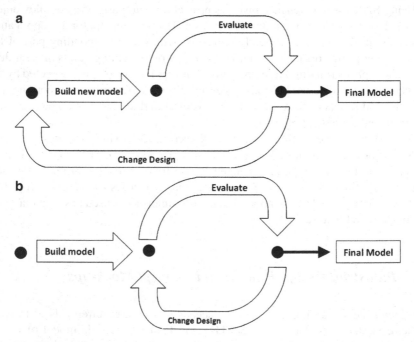

Fig. 10.2 Concept modeling process: (**a**) traditional mock-up flow (**b**) updated mock-up flow using SAR for modeling

designer has constructed a basic right hand drive design. Assume the requirements suddenly change and a left hand drive car is required. This is a significant design change that requires a fundamental feature of the design to be re-developed. Significant changes to the initial mock-up or a new mock-up must be built.

In comparison, when using SAR for development the goal is to allow both the physical model and appearance to be easily altered without requiring a new prototype to be constructed. The basic mock-ups used for projection are very simple and lightweight. Only a simple approximation of the final shape is required to allow the visualization of initial prototypes. The appearance of the mock-up is transformed to present all the fine grained details of the design. This can then be easily changed to move the location of significant features, such as a steering wheel, or change the entire surface color at the touch of a button. This functionality of SAR allows the design methodology shown in Fig. 10.2b to often remove the need to re-construct a prototype mock-up.

We are primarily focused on two aspects of the concept visualization process: the procedures used to augment the visual appearance of the mock-up, and the techniques and materials used to create the physical prototypes.

3.1   Visualizing a Mock-up

The surface appearance is an important aspect of the physical mock-up. Designers use paint and inks to color and annotate their mock-ups. A disadvantage with this approach is when changing a design, either a separate mock-up needs to be constructed or the initial mock-up must be re-painted. Although clay and polymer plasticine are able to have their shape changed continuously, this is not possible once painted, as the painted surfaces become less malleable. We consider these to be limitations of the current practices of mock-up creation in the industrial design process.

An alternate approach we are investigating is to use SAR with Physical-Virtual Tools (PVT) to alter the surface appearance by projecting virtual textures directly onto a physical mock-up [12, 14]. This technology overcomes the second limitation by allowing multiple appearances to be projected in succession onto one mock-up. The designer may digitally paint directly onto the model by interactively modifying the projected texture to alter the appearance. The texture can be saved and recalled later for further evaluation (see Sect. 5.1 for a detailed description).

Although features in the concept stage are created, the actual dimensions are often not well defined. Finding the correct dimensions, shape, and appearance to visualize a concept is therefore an iterative process, moving back and forth between visualizations until the result is satisfactory. A material that facilitates this process is considered a requirement. As previously mentioned, traditional mock-up materials and techniques require a new mock-up to be built after the shape is significantly changed or the visual appearance is changed, adding to the total time and material involved in the concept stage.

SAR can also leverage any preliminary concept sketches, textures and design ideas that are created in the early concept stage. SAR provides the ability not only to generate a new appearance, but also present the initial ideas by projecting them directly onto the physical models. This functionality is inherently provided by the SAR system and intended to maximize the visual information and presentation to the designer.

3.2   Current Mock-up Materials

Industrial designers can utilize several techniques for constructing a physical mock-up and visualizing a concept. In this section we examine three major materials and techniques: rigid materials, 3D printing, and malleable materials. With the exception of very high end color enabled 3D printers, these techniques are used to construct the physical mock-up only, and do not focus on the appearance. Mock-ups need to be painted to provide a finely detailed surface appearance.

Rigid materials such as urethane foam, cardboard, timber, and plastics allow for the quick creation of mock-ups. The level of detail is limited by the skill of the designer and the time spent on the creation of the mock-up. Although the level of detail of the mock-up may be quite high, the shape of the models is difficult to change once created.

3D printing technology is now available to industrial designers for use in mock-up construction. The mock-up design is expressed using CAD software. The design is then printed to create a physical object. 3D printers are a very powerful tool for creating high fidelity mock-ups, however there are a number of limitations. The rigid nature of the material limits physical reworking. Reprinting designs in order to correct mistakes is a common occurrence. Currently, a second limitation is the long printing time, which requires hours before the design can be assessed and further reworked. Finally, CAD modeling is typically limited to keyboard and mouse interaction. The designer is unable to feel the properties of the material during development. With the absence of tactile feedback, designers create their digital models based only on their familiarity with the physical materials. In particular modeling of organic shapes without tactile feedback is difficult, especially early in the product development cycle.

Malleable materials such as clay and polymer plasticine are well suited for the creation of organic shapes by employing free-form modeling techniques. Designers manipulate these materials with their fingers to form the mock-up. The flexibility of the material allows the designer to change the shape of the model after its initial creation. Clay and polymer plasticine overcome the problems of remodeling a design. A drawback to using clay or polymer plasticine is that it is impossible to change the shape after colors have been applied. In addition, clay and polymer plasticine both suffer from a lack of structural strength, limiting their ability to create large flat suspended sheets or large hollow objects. Large clay models are particularly heavy and not appropriate for many prototype mock-ups. To overcome this, a common practice is to use them in conjunction with cardboard or timber to create the underlying structure which the clay or polymer plasticine is applied. However, combining materials further limits the extent to which the shape can be changed afterwards making it difficult to iterate the design without constructing a new model. Combining materials may also cause problems with producing a finish on the prototype that is consistent across the different materials that are used.

4   Practical Considerations for SAR Visualizations

SAR systems can be built to support augmentations onto objects ranging from small hand-held objects through to room, building, and Olympic swimming pool sized objects. There are several issues in implementing SAR systems. Some of these apply to any SAR system, where others depend on the scale of objects being projected onto. This section provides insights into the implementation and operational aspects of SAR systems at varying scales. We discuss technical and theoretical aspects such as the number of projectors required for each case and special requirements for software, hardware, and interaction techniques.

4.1   Tracking

With the exception of extremely large objects, tracking the position and orientation of objects and users in the environment is an important aspect of interactive SAR applications. Tracking objects allows their projections to be updated as users interact with them, and also the user allows view-dependent rendering effects to be implemented. Tracking real-world objects is an active area of AR research. Many factors, such as jitter are important considerations in all applications tracking real world objects. A thorough review of tracking techniques is beyond the scope of this chapter. However, there are several constraints and issues that are unique to tracking in SAR systems.

Latency, the time difference between when a user moves an object and the system registering this change, can be a major problem with tracking systems used with SAR. AR and VR researchers have always had to deal with this problem, which manifests itself in HMD based systems as virtual information appearing to "float" around the physical objects it is registered to. However, this problem is exacerbated in SAR applications, as the virtual information is projected directly onto the surface of the physical objects. High latency will cause projections to appear in the wrong location, or spill onto other objects in the environment.

Another problem unique to SAR involves computer vision based tracking solutions. Many off-the-shelf tracking libraries use fiducial markers, which are detected in camera images in order to obtain the location of objects [10]. The cameras tracking these fiducial markers usually require good, predictable ambient light. However, SAR projections appear better with low ambient light. In addition, SAR projections change the appearance of the fiducial markers themselves. The combination of these two factors make fiducial marker tracking difficult in SAR environments. Ideally, tracking systems employed by SAR systems should avoid markers in the visible spectrum. Alternatives include magnetic tracking, such as systems from Polhemus,[1] or marker based tracking that operates in the infra-red spectrum, such as commercial systems provided by Optitrack[2] and other manufacturers. If visible-spectrum based tracking is to be used in a SAR system, much higher performance can be obtained by using active markers, such as LEDs [29].

4.2 Projector Placement

The relationship between projectors and objects greatly affects the visual quality of the augmentations. For smaller systems, a single projector can be used. However, this limits the number of viewpoints that can view augmentations. Larger systems might allow users to walk around a large object, such as a car. Here, multiple projectors will be needed to project onto all the surfaces of the object. Multiple projectors are also required to compensate for self-shadowing that occurs with complex objects. However, using multiple projectors introduces the problem of *projection overlapping*. Multiple projections may overlap on the model's surface creating a non-uniformly bright surface. Algorithms for blending overlapping projector volumes have been developed for static scenes [22], but remains an open research problem when objects can be moved, as the blending must be recalculated every frame.

Projector placement is a trade-off between a larger distance from objects (and therefore a larger projection volume), and higher spatial resolution. By increasing the distance between projector and projected area, the size of projector pixels grow, while the light intensity declines. In addition, the incident angle of the projected light changes the physical shape of the pixels. If a projector illuminates a surface at an oblique angle, a large area on the physical object will be mapped to only a few projector pixels, severely reducing the visual quality. While the texture resolution of the model can be increased, the final output is limited by the projector resolution. This is an important consideration for hand-held objects, where the projection area available is already very small. Short throw projectors can alleviate this problem, providing a suitable sized projection volume, with the projector-object distance minimized, meaning projections appear bright. If multiple projectors are used, different projectors will create differently sized and shaped pixels on the surface of the object.

---

[1] http://www.polhemus.com.

[2] http://www.naturalpoint.com/optitrack/.

When projecting onto three dimensional objects or a flat surface at an angle, there is no clear focal distance. Therefore, some parts of the augmentations will appear sharp, and others will be out of focus.[3] In practice, a focal distance should be chosen to maximize the area on the object with adequate focus. An alternative is to use several projectors at the same location, but focused at different distances. The rendering system can then choose the best projector for each part of the object [4]. Projector focus is most pronounced when projecting onto large objects, such as a car, or in a large, walk-around environment.

4.3 Interaction

The choice of interaction techniques is a critical design decision for SAR applications. While interaction with desktop software is almost universally accomplished through keyboard and mouse, these are usually not the best choice for SAR applications. The types of interaction techniques possible in a SAR system will depend on the scale of objects projected onto. For smaller table-top systems, direction interaction is most suitable, as the augmented objects are also small, and can be picked up and moved directly by the suer. Passive haptic feedback is a fundamental benefit of SAR systems and small scale SAR systems are ideally suited to interaction involving physical tools and interaction with objects using the hands. The table itself is also a projection area, where information, menus, and other user interface elements can be presented in a non-intrusive way.

As the scale of objects increases, users are no longer able to manually move them. The interaction will therefore focus on the details projected onto the object. For medium sized objects, such as a fridge mock-up or a car prototype, the interaction will focus on the augmentations on the object. For these objects, a combination of direct interaction on the object, and action at a distance techniques will be required. Physical tools could be used to support this. For very large objects, such as the side of a building, the interaction will become more focused on action-at-a-distance, as the user must stand back from the object in order to view and understand the projected information. Here, techniques such as laser pointer interaction may be useful.

5 Tools and Applications

In this section we describe some of the tools and applications we have developed as part of our investigations into using SAR in the design process.

---

[3]This only applies to LCD or similar projectors that use a lens, but not LASER-based projectors as they do not have a focal distance.

Fig. 10.3 Digital airbrushing with SAR. (**a**) The airbrush tool. (**b**) Using a virtual stencil to paint a model car. (**c**) Airbrushing result

5.1 Airbrushing

Digital airbrushing [14] allows a designer to virtually spray paint onto a physical object. The application allows designers to experiment with different finishes for a design mock-up, and shows how SAR can be used in the design process to preview finished products. Digital airbrushing shows how industrial design applications can construct their user interfaces from Physical-Virtual Tools (PVT) [13]. PVT are physical tools the designer works with to interact with the system. The physical nature of these tools means they can be projected onto like any other object in the system. By changing the projections on the tool, a tool can be meaningfully overloaded with several functions.

Three tools are used in this application: the airbrush, the stencil, and the stylus. Airbrushing, shown in Fig. 10.3, works in a similar way to a real airbrush. The amount of paint hitting the surface depends on both the distance and angle between the airbrush tool and the surface of the object. Adding the stencil tool allows a designer to mask out areas from receiving paint. The stencil is a physical board, but the mask shape is digital and projected onto the tool. Designers can select from a library of premade stencil shapes, or draw their own directly onto the board. The stencil also functions as a Personal Interaction Panel [32] for command entry. The stencil shows the benefit of PVT. The physical nature of the tools provide passive haptic feedback against the design artifacts and when drawing the stencil. Rather than using many different stencil tools for each shape, only a single tool is needed. Designers can draw their own stencil for specific needs. The stencil itself can be virtually inverted, either acting as a mask, or as a hole that allows paint to pass through. This functionality could not be replicated easily without PVT.

A 3D virtual model that matches the physical object is required for painting onto movable objects. However, simple stand-in geometry can be used when no virtual model exists, such as early in the design process. In this scenario, a bounding box is used for the virtual geometry. The nature of the projection means that the paint will appear in the correct location on the object, as depicted in Fig. 10.4.

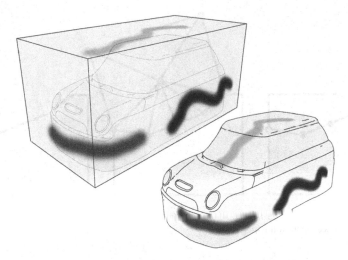

Fig. 10.4 *Left*: The virtual bounding box, drawn from the point of view of the projector. The location of the physical mock-up is shown inside the bounding box. *Right*: The projected textures map correctly onto the physical mock-up

5.2   Augmented Foam Sculpting

The examples we have described so far require 3D virtual models for objects being projected onto. However, such models do not exist early in the design process, as design concepts and forms are still being developed. Augmented foam sculpting [12] bridges the gap between physically sculpting a design mock-up and creating a virtual model in CAD software. A hand-held, hot wire foam cutter is used to carve a block of foam stock into the desired shape. The foam and cutter are both tracked, allowing the system to record the motion of the hot wire through the foam.

Recording the motion of the wire enables the system to replicate the cuts to create a 3D virtual model that matches the physical foam. This eases the transition into the CAD phase of design, since the mock-ups created early on are available for editing digitally. Most importantly, the system fits in with existing industrial design processes, and uses skills designers already have. Foam mock-up creation is already a common part of the design process.

Virtual foam sculpting is implemented internally as a series of constructive solid geometry boolean operations. As each cut is made, representative geometry is constructed, and this is subtracted from a virtual foam blank. This process is illustrated in Fig. 10.5.

The functionality of the system is greatly enhanced through the use of SAR. Since the position and orientation of the foam is tracked and its geometry updated in real time as it is sculpted, perspective correct graphics can be projected onto it. Our initial investigations have used SAR for material previews, and two visualizations for helping designers: cut animation and target.

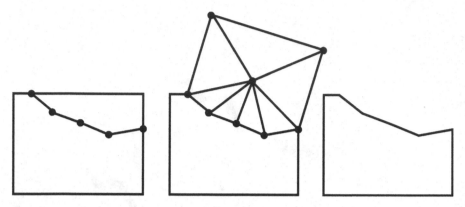

Fig. 10.5 The path the cutter takes through the foam is recorded, geometry is created, and a CSG boolean difference operation is performed

Different material properties are simulated on the foam through the use of 3D textures. 3D textures are ideal for this process as it eliminates the need for a 2D texture atlas, which is important given the geometry is constantly changing. The material appearance also remains consistent as cuts are made onto the foam. We have implemented a procedural 3D wood grain texture using a modified version of the algorithm presented by Rost [27]. Any material that can be represented as a 3D texture be projected onto the foam using this technique. We have also projected the wireframe generated from sculpting onto the foam for verification purposes.

Cut Path (Fig. 10.6) allows designers to recreate a previously sculpted model. The visualization sequentially projects each cut necessary to create a mock-up onto the blank foam. This could be used for instructional purposes. In addition, industrial designers often use foam mock-ups as an inexpensive alternative to 3D printing. A lot of time is invested in deciding on the cuts needed to replicate a model. An algorithm could be developed to calculate the cuts needed to produce a CAD model using this visualization.

Target Visualization (Fig. 10.7) shows the designer which areas of foam need to be removed to produce a target model. This is an alternative to Cut Animation. Here we do not display step-by-step instructions. Instead, the surface of the foam is color coded depending on the amount to be removed form the area. Red indicates a large section of foam should be removed, transitioning to green when the target depth has been reached.

5.3 Virtual Control Panel Design

We envision SAR as being a useful tool for the design of control panels. By projecting components onto a physical mock-up of the control panel, it removes the need to install custom electronics to obtain a functioning control panel. Possible projected

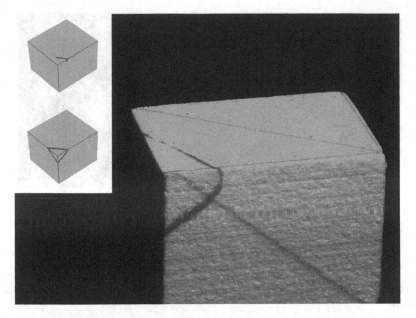

Fig. 10.6 Cut Path projects the cuts to be made onto the foam

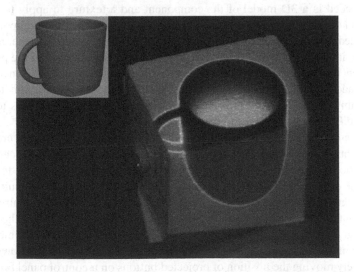

Fig. 10.7 Target Visualization colors the foam based on how much should be removed to produce a target model

components could include buttons, dials, or even simulated displays. Using SAR to assist with this step in the design process can save time and money for designers.

Components that would normally be installed as physical components on a prototype can just be projected onto the prototype. This saves time since the components do not need to be installed. To project a component using SAR, all

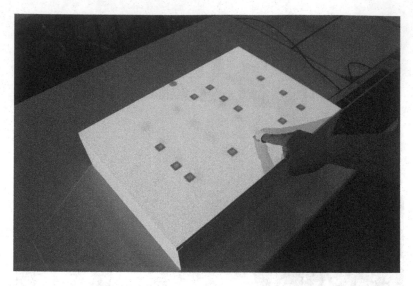

Fig. 10.8 A designer interactively modifies the position of projected buttons on a control panel prototype

that is needed is a 3D model of the component and a texture to apply to that 3D model. When these are projected, it gives the appearance that the component has been placed on the surface of the prototype. Since the projection is generated by a computer, it can be changed in real time. For example, the position of the projected component is not fixed and can be moved to a different position. Also, functionality could be added to the projected components, such as buttons being illuminated. This functionality is programmed into the SAR system and allows designers to define what the different components do when users interact with them.

There are several controls that are ideal for designers to use when creating a virtual control panel. Basic manipulation operations such as moving, scaling and rotating the virtual components are very useful for designers that want to change the layout of a control panel. Additional features such as copying, cutting and pasting components could also reduce the time it takes to design the control panel. Lastly, another important feature is being able to take a snapshot of the current design and compare it with other snapshots. This gives the designer a method of quickly comparing two different control panel designs. Figure 10.8 shows a user interactively moving the position of projected buttons on a control panel prototype.

This tool for creating virtual control panels is designed to be used early in the design process, where the specific positions of components is not finalized. To understand the basic layout of the components, they can be projected onto a low-fidelity model of the control panel. This low-fidelity model can be made out of wood, foam or even cardboard. The components can still be projected onto these surfaces, but if the physical shape of the control panel needs to be changed, then the materials are cheap to replace. This encourages designers to find an optimal physical model for the control panel, since it is quicker and cheaper to replace a low-fidelity prototype than a fully functional prototype where additional time is spent installing the electronic components.

There are two options for projecting components onto a control panel. Firstly, the component can just be projected directly onto the surface of the prototype and appear as a 2D representation of the component. The other option is to create a movable physical model of the component so that it appears in 3D to the user. One difference between these two methods is that the physical model of the component will provide natural haptic feedback to the user, whereas a 2D projection on a surface will not. This can change how some components are controlled, since a projected 2D dial can not be turned like a regular physical dial.

5.4   Control Room Layout

One application of SAR is designing the layout of a room. If each component of the room is tracked, then the projected design for each component can be updated to appear on any moving objects. This allows users to dynamically change the arrangement of several tracked objects. An example application of this is for the design of a control room such as in a submarine or a ship. These rooms contain several work stations that are used to control various parts of the vessel. In the design of these rooms, an optimal layout for the work stations needs to be decided. Using SAR, we can project onto movable work stations that can be reconfigured into the desired layout (Fig. 10.9). This has similar benefits to virtual control panel design such as saving time and money during the design process.

The advantage of this approach is that the physical models can be moved into a custom configuration during the design of the room. Another example application is designing the layout of a kitchen. Physical models of the appliances could be moved into a desired kitchen layout, with the designs for those appliances projected directly onto the models. The material used for each appliance could be changed, so that the user can see what the kitchen will look like with different textured finishes such as wood or metallic.

6   Requirements for a Large Scale SAR Environment

A calibrated projector and computer system are the minimum hardware requirements for a SAR environment. However, to provide a more feature rich environment, additional projectors can be added to increase the volume of augmented space. In addition, object tracking can be used to increase immersive interactions, and customized hardware can be created to support interactions. A large scale SAR environment places further requirements on computer system management, cabling and signal routing, networking, as well as environmental considerations such as air conditioning, projector mounting systems, and lighting.

Fig. 10.9 The SAR system simulating a controlroom, composed of three individual control panels. The user is able to modify the individual instruments on each of the control panels, as well as reposition the panels themselves

This section describes requirements we have found for the development of large scale SAR systems. We base these requirements on lessons learned from building our own forty-projector SAR environment in the Mawson Institute at the University of South Australia. This laboratory is used for investigating how SAR technologies can be leveraged to enhance design aspects of automotive, white goods, free-form modeling, and training devices. Supporting these varied applications has led us to develop a large scale SAR environment that can be easily re-configured.

6.1 Physical Environment

The physical environment determines how many SAR applications can be supported simultaneously, how easily new applications can be deployed, and the maximum possible size available in the environment. Although it is possible to set up a SAR environment in non-dedicated rooms for small applications, we are interested in applications that allow large artifacts to fit in the environment and benefit from the technology.

The size, layout and access to the physical environment are important aspects. The size of the environment should be large enough to cater for the largest object to be used. Additional space is required around projected objects to allow users to comfortably move around while interacting with the SAR visualizations.

The layout of the room, such as the projector positioning, is also important. Objects in-between the projectors and visualization objects cast shadows that interfere with the visualization. To avoid this problem, the projectors can be mounted directly above the objects rather than sitting on the ground or a table. The room design can also be optimized to allow large artefacts, such as a car, by providing large doors and suitable flooring.

Other physical environment issues also need to be considered. To minimize noise and environmental heat build up, the computers used to drive the projectors can be installed in a dedicated room. Heat from the projectors should be considered; this may require changes to air conditioning, or additional cooling capabilities. Many computer systems and projectors also place significant power requirements on the laboratory. For example, assume a generic projector uses 400 W of electricity. In our SAR environment with forty projectors, we therefore require electrical outlets capable of providing 16 kW of electricity. To achieve this, dedicated electrical circuits or multiple circuits are required. Cabling between computers and projectors is a difficult problem, due to the large distances between hardware. Long cable runs can easily exceed the limits of VGA and DVI standards. In practice, repeaters to boost signal strength are required. For projectors to be easily moved and reconfigured, many data points and power outlets can be spread throughout the environment.

Interacting with the SAR environment now needs to be considered. Access to keyboard, mouse, and other peripheral devices is more difficult. One solution to this problem is the use of wireless devices. However, in a large SAR environment, the wireless signals may not reach to the computer room. An alternate approach is a physical conduit, such as a hole in the wall or a trench in the floor, between the room containing the computers and the room containing the projectors.

6.2   Projectors

Projectors in a SAR environment are a critical piece of equipment. Models should be chosen carefully to ensure the best possible visual appearance. The projector technology selected has a large impact on the overall visual performance. Several types of projectors are available, including LCD, DLP, LASER and LED. Each of these technologies have different advantages and disadvantages, which should be evaluated depending on the application. Issues to consider include the grid like effect where black lines are left in-between pixels, dead pixels from LCD projectors, the rainbow effect where the color of fast moving objects does not appear correctly on DLP projectors, and the range of focus of all but laser projectors is limited. Size and weight are also factors that may be important for the final design.

When considering projectors for a SAR environment, the four most important features are the coverage area, brightness, resolution and the contrast. These features are all related to each other. For example, the brightness of a projector is reduced as the coverage area increases. Poor contrast affects projector blending and overall appearance, and low resolution causes poor display quality, due to the increased physical size of projected pixels. The brightness of projectors should be sufficient to illuminate the coverage area in the brightest ambient lighting expected. It is desirable to have the largest resolution available to optimized the sharpness of annotations. The further the projector is away from the display surfaces, the more important this becomes. Pixelation artefacts at long distances become visually noticeable and can partially be reduced using projectors with longer throw lenses at the expense of coverage area. The ability to display fine detail such as text is affected by not only the resolution of the projector, but also the orientation of the projector. Text can be more pixelated or out of focus if displayed across the lower resolution axis.

The orientations supported by the projectors should also be considered. Only some models of projectors can be mounted on any angle. In a SAR environment, the likelihood of these limitations being exceeded needs to be considered, as exceeding the limits may void any warranties and potentially reduce the lifespan of the projector. In a large scale SAR environment, the ability to control individual projectors is also important. Accidentally leaving projectors that are not required to be turned on reduces their lifespan. Ideally, a management system that can be computer controlled should be used where possible.

6.3   Computers, Networking, and Management

Selection of computing equipment for large scale SAR environments must consider graphical outputs, networking, electrical power, computing power, and also the management interface. From our experience, most performance limits have been caused by the graphics card. The type of SAR applications developed require OpenGL shader support, and enough VRAM to load material textures, off screen frame buffer objects and other visual effects. However, performance requirements will vary for different tasks. In general, good all round performance is required, with fast CPU, large amounts of RAM, and high performance graphics cards.

Large scale SAR will often involve multiple projectors illuminating artifacts at the same time. Once the number of projectors used exceeds the graphical outputs on a single computer, network communication will be required between computers to synchronize data used by the SAR application. The network must be fast enough to sustain the required update rate of data between the computers to make the illumination seamless, which can be quite high if camera images are transferred. Multiple machines also introduce management overhead, and an Integrated Lights Out Management System (ILOM) can substantially reduce this. The software installed on the computers must also be considered from a management point of view; management overhead can be reduced by running a shared filesystem across all machines, so that a change in one machine's configuration is instantly available on all the other machines. To further reduce software management overhead, the computers can be run as disk-less clients with the operating system and root filesystem residing on a separate machine. An operating system upgrade then only involves an upgrade of one machine and a reboot of all others. The critical requirement for making disk-less clients work effectively is homogeneous hardware.

6.4   Calibration, Cameras, Interaction, and Tracking

Calibrated projectors are required for SAR to project information and graphics that are registered to objects in the real world. Calibration involves calculating the intrinsic parameters of the projector, and its position and orientation in the environment. For small systems, this calibration can be performed manually by finding projector pixels that align with known points in the environment using a keyboard and mouse to position a crosshair. However, this process quickly becomes cumbersome as the number of projectors increases. Structured light techniques provide an automated calibration solution that more easily scales with the number of projectors.

Cameras are required for automatic projector calibration, and can also be used for tracking objects in the environment. A high resolution is important for both tasks. However, for real-time tracking, a high frame rate is the most important feature. Thus, a balance between resolution and frame rate must be found. In a large scale system, cabling again becomes a factor. The distance between computer and camera may be greater than the maximum length Firewire or USB cable, so repeaters will be required. An alternative is to use IP cameras such as a Point Grey GigE,[4] which transfer images over standard Ethernet. Another advantage of this approach is that through an Ethernet switch, any camera can be accessed by any computer, without the need to reroute cables.

Interactions are an important aspect of SAR environments, at the simplest level this would involve starting the required SAR application, and at the more complex end using custom input devices. Regardless of the interaction techniques required for a specific application, some form of input device for controlling the software will be needed. Keyboards and mice can be used. However, these do not take advantage of the 3D nature of the SAR environment. Often, applications will require tracking objects in the scene, the user's position or the position of their hands, or customized 3D input devices, such as the airbrush shown in Fig. 10.3a. Tracking objects can be accomplished using the same cameras used for projector calibration. The downside to cameras is that objects or the user may occlude the tracking markers. Depending on the required tracking volume, magnetic tracking systems such as those from Polhemus,[5] can also be used. Finally, commercial optical tracking systems, such as those from Vicon[6] can be used to provide robust tracking, but with a higher cost for the equipment.

---

[4]http://www.ptgrey.com/products/grasshopper2.

[5]http://www.polhemus.com.

[6]http://www.vicon.com.

7 Conclusion and Future Applications

To date SAR has shown promising outcomes for supporting applications that require tactile feedback to support computer generated visualizations. This chapter has described current developments in applying large scale SAR visualizations to extend the designers' toolkit when building mock-up prototypes. We believe the co-locating of virtual projected information and a physical object is particularly useful for the industrial designer. It allows the appearance of a mock-up to be instantly changed at the touch of a button. Providing both the designer and the client with the ability to evaluate and compare the different appearances. Additionally, by introducing interactive tools designed to operate with the SAR technology it is possible to provide fully functional prototypes without the need to install expensive electronics, displays, and physical buttons. The goal of these features is to increase flexibility and to reduce the cost involved with incorporating expensive prototype electronics that can be delayed until later stages of the development.

Although the current state-of-the art does not allow matter to be transformed into an arbitrary shape as Sutherland has envisaged, SAR is addressing the visual component of this vision by providing a truly dynamic appearance with fixed haptic feedback. We are currently exploring how deformable materials can be incorporated to further support the dynamic nature of the physical objects. In the future we envisage developments to dynamically controllable physical matter will be possible and this will have a significant impact on how SAR environments are used. In an ideal SAR environment there would be no difference between the simulated design and the final product, however this is currently not possible. The current SAR technology can provide designers with the ability to visualize complex interactive designs to explore many potential concepts before the final development of a product.

References

1. Akaoka, E., Vertegaal, R.: DisplayObjects: prototyping functional physical interfaces on 3D styrofoam, paper or cardboard models. In: ACM Conference on Human Factors in Computing Systems. Boston, Massachusetts (2009)
2. Bandyopadhyay, D., Raskar, R., Fuchs, H.: Dynamic shader lamps: Painting on movable objects. In: IEEE and ACM International Symposium on Mixed and Augmented Reality, pp. 207–216 (2001)
3. Bimber, O., Coriand, F., Kleppe, A., Bruns, E., Zollmann, S., Langlotz, T.: Superimposing pictorial artwork with projected imagery. Multimedia, IEEE 12(1), 16–26 (2005)
4. Bimber, O., Emmerling, A.: Multifocal projection: a multiprojector technique for increasing focal depth. Visualization and Computer Graphics, IEEE Transactions on 12(4), 658–667 (2006)
5. Bimber, O., Frohlich, B., Schmalsteig, D., Encarnacao, L.M.: The virtual showcase. Computer Graphics and Applications, IEEE 21(6), 48–55 (2001)
6. Cruz-Neira, C., Sandin, D.J., DeFanti, T.A.: Surround-screen projection-based virtual reality: the design and implementation of the CAVE. In: Proceedings of the 20th annual conference on Computer graphics and interactive techniques, pp. 135–142. ACM, Anaheim, CA (1993)

7. Fitzmaurice, G.W., Ishii, H., Buxton, W.A.S.: Bricks: Laying the foundations for graspable user interfaces. In: Proceedings of the SIGCHI conference on Human factors in computing systems, pp. 442–449. ACM Press/Addison-Wesley Publishing Co., Denver, Colorado, United States (1995)

8. Hare, J., Gill, S., Loudon, G., Ramduny-Ellis, D., Dix, A.: Physical fidelity: Exploring the importance of physicality on Physical-Digital conceptual prototyping. In: Human-Computer Interaction INTERACT 2009, pp. 217–230 (2009)

9. Hoffman, H., Hollander, A., Schroder, K., Rousseau, S., Furness, T.: Physically touching and tasting virtual objects enhances the realism of virtual experiences. Virtual Reality 3(4), 226–234 (1998). 10.1007/BF01408703

10. Kato, H., Billinghurst, M.: Marker tracking and HMD calibration for a Video-Based augmented reality conferencing system. In: Augmented Reality, International Workshop on, vol. 0, p. 85. IEEE Computer Society, Los Alamitos, CA, USA (1999)

11. Lee, J.C., Dietz, P.H., Maynes-Aminzade, D., Raskar, R., Hudson, S.E.: Automatic projector calibration with embedded light sensors. In: Proceedings of the 17th annual ACM symposium on User interface software and technology, pp. 123–126. ACM, Santa Fe, NM, USA (2004)

12. Marner, M.R., Thomas, B.H.: Augmented foam sculpting for capturing 3D models. In: IEEE Symposium on 3D User Interfaces. Waltham Massachusetts, USA (2010)

13. Marner, M.R., Thomas, B.H.: Tool virtualization and spatial augmented reality. In: Proceedings of the 20th International Conference on Artificial Reality and Telexistence. Adelaide, South Australia (2010)

14. Marner, M.R., Thomas, B.H., Sandor, C.: Physical-Virtual tools for spatial augmented reality user interfaces. In: International Symposium on Mixed and Augmented Reality. Orlando, Florida (2009)

15. Pahl, G., Beitz, W., Wallace, K.: Engineering design: A systematic approach. Springer (1984)

16. Pinhanez, C.: The everywhere displays projector: A device to create ubiquitous graphical interfaces. In: Ubicomp 2001: Ubiquitous Computing, pp. 315–331 (2001)

17. Piper, B., Ishii, H.: CADcast: a method for projecting spatially referenced procedural instructions. Tech. rep., MIT Media Lab (2001)

18. Piper, B., Ratti, C., Ishii, H.: Illuminating clay: a 3-D tangible interface for landscape analysis. In: Proceedings of the SIGCHI conference on Human factors in computing systems: Changing our world, changing ourselves, pp. 355–362. ACM, Minneapolis, Minnesota, USA (2002)

19. Pugh, S.: Total Design: integrated methods for successful product engineering. Addison-Wesley (1991)

20. Raskar, R., Beardsley, P., van Baar, J., Wang, Y., Dietz, P., Lee, J., Leigh, D., Willwacher, T.: RFIG lamps: interacting with a self-describing world via photosensing wireless tags and projectors. ACM Trans. Graph. 23(3), 406–415 (2004)

21. Raskar, R., Low, K.: Interacting with spatially augmented reality. In: Proceedings of the 1st international conference on Computer graphics, virtual reality and visualisation, pp. 101–108. ACM, Camps Bay, Cape Town, South Africa (2001)

22. Raskar, R., Low, K.: Blending multiple views. In: Proceedings of the 10th Pacific Conference on Computer Graphics and Applications, p. 145. IEEE Computer Society (2002)

23. Raskar, R., Welch, G., Cutts, M., Lake, A., Stesin, L., Fuchs, H.: The office of the future: A unified approach to Image-Based modeling and spatially immersive displays. In: SIGGRAPH '98 (1998)

24. Raskar, R., Welch, G., Low, K., Bandyopadhyay, D.: Shader lamps: Animating real objects with Image-Based illumination. In: Rendering Techniques 2001: Proceedings of the Eurographics, pp. 89–102 (2001)

25. Raskar, R., Ziegler, R., Willwacher, T.: Cartoon dioramas in motion. In: NPAR '02: Proceedings of the 2nd international symposium on Non-photorealistic animation and rendering, p. 7ff. ACM, New York, NY, USA (2002). Inproceedings

26. Rekimoto, J., Saitoh, M.: Augmented surfaces: a spatially continuous work space for hybrid computing environments. In: Proceedings of the SIGCHI conference on Human factors in computing systems: the CHI is the limit, pp. 378–385. ACM, Pittsburgh, Pennsylvania, United States (1999)

27. Rost, R.J., Licea-Kane, B., Ginsburg, D., Kessenich, J.M., Lichtenbelt, B., Malan, H., Weiblen, M.: OpenGL Shading Language, 3 edn. Addison-Wesley Professional (2009)
28. Schwerdtfeger, B., Pustka, D., Hofhauser, A., Klinker, G.: Using laser projectors for augmented reality. In: Proceedings of the 2008 ACM symposium on Virtual reality software and technology, pp. 134–137. ACM, Bordeaux, France (2008)
29. Smith, R.T., Marner, M.R., Thomas, B.: Adaptive color marker for SAR environments. In: Poster Sessions: Proceedings of the IEEE Symposium on 3D User Interfaces (to appear). Singapore (2011)
30. Suganuma, A., Ogata, Y., Shimada, A., Arita, D., ichiro Taniguchi, R.: Billiard instruction system for beginners with a projector-camera system. In: Proceedings of the 2008 International Conference on Advances in Computer Entertainment Technology, pp. 3–8. ACM, Yokohama, Japan (2008)
31. Sutherland, I.E.: The ultimate display. In: Proceedings of the IFIP Congress, pp. 506–508 (1965)
32. Szalavri, Z., Gervautz, M.: The personal interaction panel - a two handed interface for augmented reality. pp. 335–346. Budapest, Hungary (1997)
33. Ullmer, B., Ishii, H.: The metaDESK: models and prototypes for tangible user interfaces. In: Proceedings of the 10th annual ACM symposium on User interface software and technology, pp. 223–232. ACM, Banff, Alberta, Canada (1997)
34. Underkoffler, J., Ishii, H.: Urp: a luminous-tangible workbench for urban planning and design. In: Proceedings of the SIGCHI conference on Human factors in computing systems: the CHI is the limit, pp. 386–393. ACM, Pittsburgh, Pennsylvania, United States (1999)
35. Verlinden, J., de Smit, A., Peeters, A., van Gelderen, M.: Development of a flexible augmented prototyping system. Journal of WSCG (2003)
36. Ware, C., Rose, J.: Rotating virtual objects with real handles. ACM Trans. Comput.-Hum. Interact. 6(2), 162–180 (1999). 319102
37. Zaeh, M., Vogl, W.: Interactive laser-projection for programming industrial robots. In: Mixed and Augmented Reality, 2006. ISMAR 2006. IEEE/ACM International Symposium on, pp. 125–128 (2006). DOI 10.1109/ISMAR.2006.297803

Chapter 11
Markerless Tracking for Augmented Reality

Jan Herling and Wolfgang Broll

Abstract Augmented Reality (AR) tries to seamlessly integrate virtual content into the real world of the user. Ideally, the virtual content would behave exactly like real objects. This requires a correct and precise estimation of the user's viewpoint (respectively that of a camera) with respect to the coordinate system of the virtual content. This can be achieved by an appropriate 6-DoF tracking system.

In this chapter we will present a general approach for a computer vision (CV) based tracking system applying an adaptive feature based tracker. We will present in detail the individual steps of the tracking pipeline and discuss a sample implementation based on SURF feature descriptors, allowing for easy understanding of the individual steps necessary upon building your own CV tracker.

1 Introduction

The geometric registration of the virtual content within the real environment of the user is the basis for real Augmented Reality (AR) applications (in contrast to pseudo AR, where the real world content is just superimposed by floating bubbles, arrows and text messages). Correct geometric registration allows the observer to accept virtual content as enhancement of the real environment rather than a separated or overlaid layer of information. The virtual scene is geometrically registered by measuring or estimating the current pose of the user's view point or camera with respect to the coordinate system of the virtual content. This may either be done on a per object basis applying relative transformations, or all or at least several virtual objects share a coordinate system, thus the transformation to that is estimated.

J. Herling (✉)
Department of Virtual Worlds and Digital Games, Ilmenau University of Technology,
Ilmenau, Germany
e-mail: jan.herling@tu-ilmenau.de

B. Furht (ed.), *Handbook of Augmented Reality*, DOI 10.1007/978-1-4614-0064-6_11,   255
© Springer Science+Business Media, LLC 2011

This requires an appropriate tracking system, which either may be sensor based (e.g. applying inertial, gyroscopic or magnetic sensors, using ultrasonic sound, etc.) or computer vision (CV) based.

Computer vision based tracking can roughly be distinguished in marker based tracking and markerless tracking. While marker based tracking applies fiducial markers [8], which can be used to determine the camera pose in relation to each marker, providing a robust tracking mechanism, markers also come along with a couple of drawbacks. The major restriction is that they often cannot be attached to the objects which are supposed to be augmented. While this problem might be overcome by using two or more cameras (one for tracking the markers and one for the image to be augmented) this significantly reduces the overall tracking quality and by that the quality of the geometrical registration. Additionally such an approach is not feasible for most mobile devices like mobile phones. Further, attaching markers in certain environments may be considered as some type of environmental pollution. Finally, applying markers at all locations to be potentially augmented can be quite time-consuming, requiring a very large number of markers, in particular in outdoor scenarios.

Thus, markerless tracking approaches using natural features of the environment to be augmented for tracking is a much more promising approach. However, until recently, performance of suitable algorithms were not sufficient on mobile devices.

In this chapter we will provide an overview of current markerless tracking approaches and explain in detail the mechanisms involved for creating an appropriate computer vision based tracking system. We will also provide a more elaborated example based on the SURF feature descriptor to allow the reader to understand the steps involved and to show possible areas for optimization.

2 Feature Detection

Visual markerless pose trackers mainly rely on natural feature points (often also called interest points or key points) visible in the user's environment. To allow for an accurate pose determination such natural feature points must meet several requirements:

- **Fast computational time**
  It must be possible to calculate a rather large number of features points or even feature points and associated descriptors in real-time in order to allow for a pose estimation at an acceptable frame rate.
- **Robustness with respect to changing lighting conditions and image blurring**
  Set of feature points as well as their calculated descriptors must not vary significantly under different lighting conditions or upon image blurring. Both effects are quite common, in particular in outdoor environments, and thus any susceptibility against those would render the overall approach useless.

- **Robustness against observation from different viewing angles**
  In AR environments users are usually not very much restricted regarding their position and orientation, and by that regarding the viewing angle under which the feature points will be observed. Thus, any vulnerability with respect to the viewing angle will make such feature points pretty useless for AR.
- **Scale invariance**
  In AR, objects providing the necessary feature points are often observed from different distances. Tracking will have to work in a wide range and must not be limited to a certain distance only as users will typically want to spot AR content and approach it if necessary – in particular in outdoor environments. While a closer view will almost always reveal a higher number of feature points on a particular object, scale invariance refers to the fact that feature points visible from a rather large distance will not disappear when getting closer, allowing for a continuous tracking event without applying SLAM-like approaches.

In the last decade numerous feature detectors have been proposed providing different properties concerning e.g. detection robustness or detection speed. However, existing detectors basically can be distinguished into two different classes. First, very efficient corner detectors spotting corner-like features. Second, blob detectors not spotting unique corner positions but image regions covering blob-like structures with a certain size.

On the one hand, it holds that corner detectors are more efficient than blob detectors and allow for a more precise position determination. On the other hand, corner features typically lack of scaling information, resulting in an additional effort within the tracking pipeline.

2.1   Corner Detectors

The Harris detector [6] uses the approximated auto-correlation function for detecting interest point. The auto-correlation function determines the local difference in the image intensity for the direct neighborhood of pixels of interest. For each pixel of a frame an eigenvalue analyses of the auto-correlation matrix is applied to classify the pixel into different feature categories. Thus, strong corners can be distinguished from edges or homogenous image regions.

A different corner detector has been proposed by Rosten and Drummond [16] avoiding the eigenvalue analysis and thus performing significantly faster. The FAST feature detector compares the pixel value of the potential feature point with all pixels lying on a surrounding circle. The circle is selected to have a radius of 3 pixels resulting in 16 pixel values to be considered at most. A FAST feature is detected if the absolute intensity differences between the center pixel and at least 12 adjacent circle pixels are higher than a defined threshold. These intensity differences can be used to calculate the strength of features. Adjacent feature points are erased by a non-maximum-suppression search to determine unique feature positions. Due to the detection algorithm of FAST features, those cannot provide a dimension parameter, but provide a unique pixel position. Thus, FAST features are not scale invariant being a drawback which must be compensated in the tracking pipeline with additional effort. However, the FAST detector is one of the fastest algorithms to find robust natural interest points. Thus, very often the detector is applied on mobile platforms with reduced computational power like e.g. mobile phones.

2.2 Blob Detectors

In contrast to corner detectors, blob detectors search natural feature points with a blob-like shape. Those interest points can be e.g. small dots or large blurred spots with similar color intensity. Most of these features are detected using a Gaussian filtering as bases. It has been shown that the Gaussian kernel performs best under the condition that features have to be scale invariant.

Commonly, blob detectors spot feature candidates within several consecutive scale spaces created by subsequent Gaussian filtering steps. The number of candidates is reduced by a non-maximum-suppression search within the neighborhood of three adjacent scale spaces. Finally, the exact feature position and scale is determined using the information of adjacent scale spaces. Thus, the feature positions between pixels and feature dimensions are characteristics of blob features.

A well-known feature detector has been proposed by Lowe. He proposed the SIFT [13] algorithm to detect scale invariant interest points. SIFT detects feature candidates by Laplacian of Guassian (LoG) filter responses within different scale spaces. Local extremes are extracted using a non-maximum-suppression search providing unique features. Lowe improved the computational performance of SIFT by approximating the LoG by a difference-of-Gaussian approach. Thus, filtered pyramid layers are reused to approximate the exact LoG result. Further, Lowe proposed an algorithm to determine the dominate orientation of a SIFT feature. This orientation can later be used to determine a feature descriptor for feature matching (see Sect. 3.2). In comparison to FAST the SIFT detector needs by far more computational time due to the several filtering iterations to extract the individual scale spaces.

Bay et al. [1] proposed the SURF detector which is in some aspects related to SIFT. Bay also uses different scale spaces to extract scale invariant features. Feature candidates are determined by the determinant of the Hessian matrix of a Gaussian convolution. However, SURF avoids the expensive Gaussian filtering steps to speed up the computational time for feature detection. Bay et al. apply an integral image in combination with rough approximated box filters of the Gaussian derivatives. Thus, the determinant of the Hessian matrix can be approximated with a few look-up operations using the integral image. Further, the computational time is independent from the filter size and thus is constant over all scale spaces. Cheng et al. [3] proved that SURF outperforms e.g. SIFT in performance and robustness.

Figure 11.1 shows a comparison between the FAST corner detector as described in Sect. 2.1 and the SURF feature detector as described in Sect. 2.2. The figure provides the unique characteristics of those detector classes.

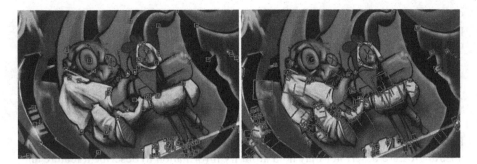

Fig. 11.1 Comparing FAST features without orientation and scale properties (*left*) and SURF features aligned to their dominant orientation (*right*)

3   Feature Matching

Once a set of robust features as been detected, they have to be matched against corresponding features inside a database to extract a respective 6DOF pose. Feature matching is one of the most critical tasks inside the entire tracking pipeline. The high number of potential feature correspondences results in a large computational effort, slowing down the tracking process significantly. Additionally, wrong feature pairs (so called outliers) would result in distorted or even wrong pose calculations and thus have to be handled explicitly. In the following sub-sections three different matching strategies are presented.

3.1   *Image Patches*

Feature matching by image patches is the most intuitive way to find valid correspondences between features inside an image and a huge database. All detected features are surrounded by a small image patch with constant size (e.g. 8×8 pixels) and compared with all patches inside the database. Often the summed square distance function (SSD) or the sum of absolute distance function (SAD) is used to find best matching patches. Especially the SAD computation performs quite efficiently and thus image patches are regularly applied for feature matching on mobile devices. However, image patches are very error-prone with respect to changing light conditions or viewing angles because they are not scale or rotation invariant. Thus, image patches commonly can only be used if enough a-priori information from e.g. a previous tracking iteration is known. Thus, reference image patches from database features may be replaced by image patches of the most recent camera frame to allow an almost perfect matching for the next camera frame. Further, a transformation based on the previous pose is applied to adjust the database patches to the current viewing angle [9, 10]. However, commonly feature patches cannot be applied for pose initialization, e.g. because of the absence of a previous pose. Therefore, image patches often are used for feature matching between two consecutive camera frames only.

3.2 Feature Descriptors

Feature descriptors are designed to compensate the drawbacks of image patches. An abstract feature descriptor may hold arbitrary information to describe a feature and to allow the separation of two different features. Feature descriptors should be scale and orientation invariant, should allow for fast calculation and should describe the concerning interest point as unique as possible while needing as less information as necessary.

Several different feature descriptors have been proposed in the last decade. Additionally, many feature detectors have been suggested with own descriptors like e.g. SIFT or SURF. Most feature descriptors are defined by a vector of up to 128 scalar values defined by the direct neighborhood of the corresponding feature point. Feature matching between camera features and database features then can be applied by seeking the best matching descriptor pairs. The best pair may be found by using any distance function suitable for the specific descriptor (see Fig. 11.2). However, often a simple SSD or SDA search is sufficient to find corresponding descriptors.

One has to distinguish between feature descriptors, which are rotation invariant itself, and descriptors aligned to the dominant orientation of the corresponding feature point allowing for an adequate consideration of the current orientation and by that making the descriptor rotation invariant. The latter category is applied more commonly, although the extra time for orientation determination reduces the overall tracking performance considerably.

3.3 Trees and Ferns

Feature matching also can be solved by a classification problem. Instead of creating scale and orientation invariant descriptors, Lepetit et al. [11, 12] have shown that feature correspondences can be determined by classes specifying the characteristics of feature points. Each feature point represents a class holding all possible appearances of this feature point under changing lighting and viewing conditions. The classification is done by a large number of very simple tests like e.g. an image intensity comparison of two different positions in the direct feature neighborhood. Feature matching than can be formulated as a search for the best matching class traversing a tree-like structure. The advantage of this technique is that the dimension or the orientation of the feature render irrelevant for the matching process. Thus, matching can be performed much faster in particular on mobile devices with reduced

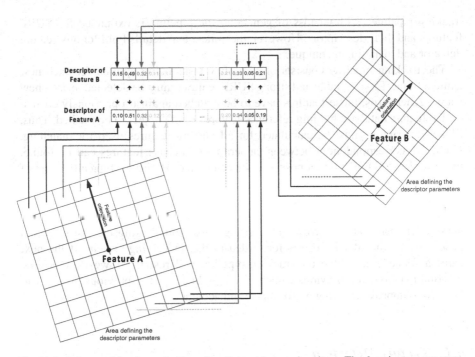

Fig. 11.2 Scheme of the determination of an abstract feature descriptor. The descriptor parameters of two features may be determined as depicted and element wise compared using an arbitrary distance function

computational power. On the other hand this performance speedup has to be paid with an expensive training process of all feature classes in an offline preprocessing step. Further, such classification trees need a huge amount of memory to store all feature classes. Therefore, Özuysal et al. [15] reformulated the problem to a Bayesian classification, grouping the simple tests to several sub classes. They call these groups *ferns* and proved that the memory amount can be reduced significantly while providing comparable classification accuracy as for common trees.

Normally, the feature classes have to be trained with several images of the tracking object from different viewpoints and with different lighting conditions. Although these images can be created automatically, the classification problem leads to significantly more time to setup a tracking system than necessary for trackers applying descriptor matching.

4 Tracking Pipeline

The tracking pipeline covers the entire tracking process starting with camera frame grabbing and ending with the final 6DOF pose. In the following all important pipeline elements are presented in detail necessary to implement a functional feature tracking pipeline. Without loss of generality the pipeline is explained for SURF features and their descriptors. However, the conceptual details hold for any feature detector and matching technique.

The tracking pipeline consists of some few tasks being applied for each new camera frame. First, reliable and strong SURF features must be detected in each new frame. Afterwards, those features have to be matched against a previously created SURF feature database holding reference features of the object to be tracked. Thus, SURF descriptors must be calculated for all camera features used for matching. If enough correspondences between camera and database features can be found, the associated 6DOF camera pose may be calculated. However, typically some of the found feature correspondences are faulty and thus must not be used for pose calculation to guarantee an accurate pose. Therefore, all correspondence outliers must be exposed during the pose determination. Afterwards, the pose can be refined using additional feature correspondences e.g. those found using the just extracted pose. Finally, the 6DOF pose is forwarded to the underlying system. If the next camera frame is available the tracking pipeline will restart. However, this time information from the previous camera frame – like e.g. the previous pose – can be used to improve tracking performance and accuracy.

4.1 Feature Detection

In each new camera frame new feature points have to be detected to be used for pose determination later. Depending on the applied detector this task can be one of the most time consuming parts inside the tracking pipeline. Obviously, the number of detected interest points is directly related to the frame dimension. The bigger the input frame the more feature points will be detected and vice versa. However, often the number of detected feature points can be reduced by a specific strength threshold all features must achieve to count as strong and reliable features. Thus, e.g. very strong corners will be detected while more homogenous regions or blurred corners are discarded as natural features. For SURF features the determinant of the Hessian matrix can directly be used as strength value and allows the separation of strong and robust features from weak and unreliable ones (see Fig. 11.3).

This strength threshold is an important instrument to balance the overall feature number to be considered in each frame and can be used to control the tracking performance and accuracy. Further, features can be sorted according to their strength parameters to use the most robust features for tracking only.

Commonly, available implementations of feature detectors allow for feature detection over the entire input frame only. However, often a-priori information from previous tracking iterations is given, which can be used to predict a small area of interest inside the input image. The exact area of interest can be determined by a projection of all 3D feature points into the camera coordinate system while using the pose of the previous frame for the extrinsic camera parameters. More efficient is an approximation of this area by projecting the 3D feature bounding box only.

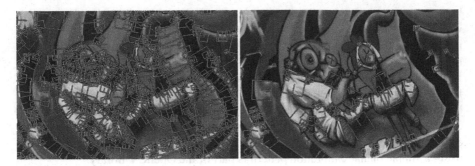

Fig. 11.3 SURF features with different minimal strength detection thresholds; the threshold in the *right* image is four times higher than for the *left* image

If the used implementation supports sub-image feature detection this approximated area of interest can be used to significantly improve the performance of the tracking pipeline. Additionally, the number of invalid interest points can be reduced right from the beginning, speeding up the matching process and reducing the number of matching outliers.

4.2 Feature Map

Apart from SLAM approaches (see Sect. 6), feature tracking needs a predefined set of feature points, which can be used as reference for the real object to be tracked. Thus, the tracking object and its real dimensions should be known in advance. The object then is used to create a corresponding database holding 3D feature points with exact proportions. This database often is referred to as feature map. If feature matching finally is based on descriptors, those have be determined for all features inside the map. Often an image or a bitmap of the tracking object is sufficient to create an appropriate map providing adequate details. Especially, if an image or a poster is used as tracking object, the feature map creation is trivial if the image is also available in digitally. Thus, commonly the creation of a feature map needs approximately the same time as the final tracker for one live camera image. Further, the feature map has to be created only once before tracking starts because the feature map typically does not change while the application is running.

4.3 Camera Distortion

Most camera devices, especially cheap webcams or integrated cameras of mobile phones, provide skewed images due to a weak lens quality resulting in a severe distortion. In contrast to an optimal pinhole camera model, images of real cameras have to be corrected to handle so called *barrel* or *pincushion* distortion. Especially, with raising distance to the principal point, pixel errors can have a substantial influence on the final pose accuracy. Brown [2] has proposed a simple distortion model able to handle radial and tangential lens distortion. A low degree polynomial is appropriate to correct the distortion and provides sufficient accurate results for feature tracking. Thus, before feature tracking can start the used camera should be calibrated and the distortion parameters should be extracted explicitly. Several different calibration methods have been proposed in the last decade needing different types of calibration patterns. An implementation of a calibration method using a simple planar calibration pattern is part of the OpenCV library.

All feature positions should be corrected according to the distortion parameters before using them for pose determination to avoid accuracy errors.

4.4   Feature Description

Once stable features have been detected, SURF descriptors must be calculated for all features actually used for feature matching. Depending on information from previous tracking iterations, feature detectors may be calculated for a subset of the detected features only. Feature description is beside feature detection the most time consuming task in the tracking pipeline. The more SURF descriptors are calculated the more time is necessary for each new frame to proceed. However, obviously feature correspondences can only be found between features providing a calculated descriptor and thus the number of features to be described should be selected carefully.

Tracking systems not using descriptors for feature matching but using ferns instead, can avoid this description task and can directly start searching for correspondences. Therefore, tracking systems not applying descriptors but ferns may perform faster because they shift the expensive descriptor calculations to the training phase of the feature classes before the tracking starts.

4.5   Feature Matching

To extract valid matches between camera and map features, the feature descriptors are used to find feature pairs with nearby similar appearance. SURF features can be matched finding the two SURF descriptors with e.g. smallest summed square distance. Further, the SSD should lie below a specified threshold to ensure a high matching quality with less correspondence outliers. The threshold has to be defined carefully for not rejecting valid feature correspondences on the one hand, while accepting too many wrong feature pairs on the other hand. Each type of feature detector will need its individual threshold to achieve an adequate ratio between accepted and rejected feature correspondences.

If no information can be used to reduce the number of potential feature candidates – e.g. from previous tracking iterations – an initial mapping can be extracted by a brute-force search. Obviously, a brute-force search between n camera features and m map features would need time $O(nm)$ and thus should be applied as rare as possible.

Often a kd-tree is used to speed-up the search for the best matching descriptors. Further, some of the descriptors presented allow for a significant faster matching compared to other descriptor types. All SURF features e.g. can uniquely be categorized into two different kinds of blob-like features. Dark features with brighter environment or bright features with darker environment. Thus, a huge amount of potential correspondence candidates can be discarded very early if two SURF features belong to different categories. In the following more complex culling methods are presented using geometrical information to cull possible correspondence candidates.

4.6   Feature Culling

If the feature tracker can rely on information from previous tracking iterations like e.g. the pose calculated for the previous camera frame, the number of wrong feature correspondences can significantly be reduced by applying culling approaches based on geometrical constraints. We can expect only minor changes in the camera pose for two consecutive frames. Thus, the previous pose can e.g. be used to predict the 2D camera position of all 3D features defined in the feature map.

One efficient culling method is the usage of a culling cone. For each 2D image feature the cone allows to discard all invalid 3D object features upon their 3D position using the previous pose as reference. The implicit form of a cone with apex lying in (m_x, m_y, m_z), having a dihedral angle α and defined along the z-axis is given by the following quadric:

$$F(x,y,z,) = (x - m_x)^2 + (y - m_y)^2 - tan^2\alpha(z - m_z)^2$$

A point $p = (x,y,z)$ is inside the cone if $F(p) < 0$, outside if $F(p) > 0$, and lies on cone surface if $F(p) = 0$. The implicit form of the cone can be expressed in matrix notation:

$$F(p) = p^T \begin{bmatrix} 1 & 0 & 0 & -m_x \\ 0 & 1 & 0 & -m_y \\ 0 & 0 & -tan^2\alpha & m_z tan^2\alpha \\ -m_x & -m_y & m_z tan^2\alpha & m_x^2 + m_z^2 - m_z^2 tan^2\alpha \end{bmatrix} p$$

$$= p^T Q p$$

The cone Q can be transformed by a homogenous transformation matrix M into a new cone Q':

$$F_M(p) = (M^{-1}p)^T Q(M^{-1}p)$$
$$= p^T(M^{-T}QM^{-1})p$$
$$= p^T Q'p$$

Thus, only a single vector-matrix multiplication followed by a vector scalar product is sufficient to determine whether a 3D point lies outside an arbitrary culling cone. The amount of culled 3D features is defined by the cone's dihedral. The angle has to be carefully chosen to handle the difference between the previous pose and the new pose to be determined for the current frame. The smaller the angle the smaller the allowed difference between the two poses and the more 3D features will be discarded.

4.7 Pose Calculation and Pose Refinement

All extracted feature correspondences will be used for determination of the final pose related to the current camera frame. Pose determination from a set of n feature correspondences is known as the *perspective n-point problem (PnP)*. At least three valid feature correspondences between 2D image features and 3D map features are necessary to proceed. The so called *P3P* [5] provides at most four different poses due to geometric ambiguities. Thus, further feature correspondences are necessary to determine the unique pose. Several approaches have been proposed to solve the *P4P,P5P* or even *PnP* [12]. However, the more feature correspondences are known the more accurate the extracted pose. Further, commonly a set of detected feature correspondences contains invalid feature pairs due to matching errors leading to inaccurate or even invalid pose calculations. Thus, invalid features correspondences must be exposed explicitly. The well-known RANSAC [5] algorithm can be used to determine the subset of valid correspondences from a large set of feature pairs containing outliers. RANSAC randomly chooses few feature pairs to create a rough pose using e.g. the *P3P* algorithm and tests this pose geometrically for all remaining pairs. Several iterations are applied using different permutations of feature pairs. This results in the pose where most feature correspondences could be confirmed.

However, RANSAC does not optimize the final pose for all valid feature correspondences. Therefore, the pose should be refined further to reduce the overall error regarding all applied feature correspondences. To optimize the pose with respect to the total projection error, nonlinear models must be applied. Commonly, several iterations of nonlinear least squares algorithms like e.g. the Levenberg-Marquardt (LM) algorithm [14] are sufficient to converge to the final pose. Further, different feature correspondences may be weighted e.g. according to their expected position accuracy to increase the pose quality. Often, an M-estimator [14] is applied automatically neglecting the impact of outliers or inaccurate feature positions.

5 Overall System of an Adaptive Tracker

A naive implementation of a feature tracker would apply the above presented elements of a tracking pipeline simply in a sequential manner. However, the entire tracking pipeline provides space for potential optimizations. As indicated above, a feature tracker may reuse information from previous camera frames to improve tracking performance and accuracy significantly. Further, the tracker should be able to choose the number of necessary features for each new frame in advance to allow a fast tracking iteration, while being as accurate as possible. In the following a SURF tracker adapting to the environment, the current lighting, and the occlusion conditions is presented in detail using the base elements of the above described tracking pipeline as proposed in our previous work [7].

The adaptive tracker provides three different process paths, which are selected depending on the availability of information received from previous tracking iterations. Figure 11.4 shows the overall scheme of the adaptive tracker and its individual paths and the transitions between those paths. The adaptive tracker starts with an initial number of n features to be used and a lower and upper boundary for n.

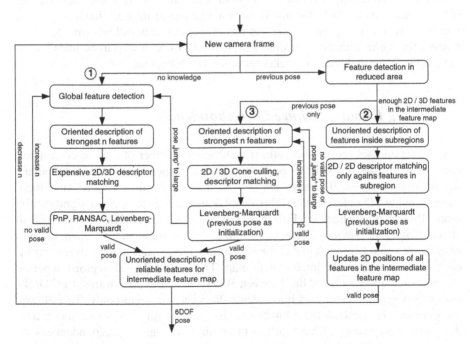

Fig. 11.4 Scheme of an implementation for an adaptive feature tracker

5.1 Tracking without Previous Knowledge

The first path is chosen if the tracker starts for the first time or the tracking has been interrupted in the previous frame. This path needs the most computational effort and therefore is used as rare as possible. The SURF features are detected in the entire image frame and sorted according to their strength (as a result of the hessian determinant) and for the first n strongest features the oriented SURF descriptors are calculated. Afterwards these n features are matched against all features inside the reference feature map of the object to be tracked. Only unidirectional feature correspondences are accepted with a SSD bellow a defined threshold. Additionally, the ratio between best and second best SSD matching must be below a specified ratio e.g. 0.6 to guarantee strong correspondences. Then, the 2D/3D feature correspondences detected are taken to determine the exact camera 6-DOF pose by applying several Perspective-n-Point (PnP) iterations, followed by a pose refinement step with a non-linear-least-square algorithm i.e. the Levenberg-Marquardt algorithm. If a sufficient number of feature correspondences have been detected and validated by the RANSAC iterations, the number of used features n will be decreased as long as it is higher than the lower boundary and the determined 6-DOF pose is returned. Afterwards, the algorithm waits for the next camera frame. If the pose estimation fails, the number of used (oriented and described) features n will be increased and again (better) feature correspondences will be estimated. If n reaches the upper boundary, the object to be tracked is expected to be invisible in the current frame and thus the tracker returns no 6-DOF pose.

5.2 Using Existing Feature Correspondences

The algorithm uses the second path, if a sufficient number of feature correspondences are available from the previous camera frame. Thus, the intermediate feature map contains 2D image features with un-oriented descriptors and their corresponding 3D object points. This enables the tracker to apply a significantly more efficient 2D/2D tracking. First, SURF features are detected inside the smallest area enclosing all previous 2D features with a small extra boundary. Then, the un-oriented descriptors are calculated for all features lying inside small sub regions of each 2D feature from the intermediate map. The size of the sub regions depends on the camera resolution and lies between 30 and 60 pixels. Afterwards, the 2D/2D mapping is applied to features lying inside the same sub region only. This allows for significantly reducing the number of false correspondences, while increasing the overall performance. If an insufficient number of feature correspondences can be recovered or the difference or gap between the previous pose and the new pose is too large, the algorithm proceeds with the third path (see below). However, if a sufficient number of correspondences can be recovered, the exact 6-DOF pose is determined by a Levenberg-Marquardt iteration using the previous pose as initial guess. Afterwards, the intermediate map is updated by the current un-oriented descriptors and the new 2D positions of all successfully recovered correspondences. The remaining features in the intermediate map (those with invalid correspondences in the recent camera frame) receive an updated 2D position by the projection of the known 3D object position and the 6-DOF pose just extracted. Thus, those features are preserved for further usage in forthcoming frames. However, if a feature has not been recovered for several frames, it is removed from the intermediate map. Finally, the 6-DOF pose is returned and the tracker waits for the next frame.

5.3   Using the Previous Pose as Basis

The third path is used if no or an insufficient number of reliable 2D/3D correspondences are available from the previous frame. In this situation the intermediate map is empty and the tracker can use the pose of the previous tracking iteration only. However, a pose from the previous frame still provides a pretty good guess for the current pose, providing a significant advantage compared to a calculation of a pose without any prior knowledge as used by path one. First, the previous pose is used to project the bounding volume of the entire 3D feature map into the current camera image. This bounding box (with a small extra boundary) defines the region of interest. Features useful for tracking may only occur in this region. The reduced 2D tracking area speeds up the detection process and avoids unnecessary descriptor comparison of features not part of the stored object feature map. The feature detection is followed by a feature sorting according to their individual strength. The oriented SURF descriptors are then determined for the strongest n features.

After all geometrically invalid candidates for 3D features have been eliminated feature matching can be applied between the n strongest 2D image features and those having passed the specific *cone culling*. If an insufficient number of correspondences can be determined, n will be increased and the third path restarts with additional features to be matched. On the other side if enough correspondences can be extracted, a Levenberg-Marquardt iteration uses the previous pose as initial guess and uses the new correspondences for the accurate pose determination. Afterwards, the intermediate feature map will be filled with the new reliable correspondences and their un-oriented descriptors (similar to the first path) and n will be decreased. The extracted 6-DOF pose is returned and the tracker starts with a new camera frame.

6   SLAM

Simultaneous localization and mapping (SLAM) approaches explicitly avoid the application of feature maps created before the actual start of the tracking. Rather than using a feature map holding reference features for 6DOF pose determination,

SLAM techniques create and extend their own feature map during the tracking process ad-hoc. Thus, a SLAM based tracking algorithm starts without any previous knowledge of the current environments, gathering all information required – such as the positions of 3D feature points – during the actual tracking process. Commonly, the initialization takes only a few seconds for creating a very rough initial feature map, allowing for an initial pose calculation. Afterwards, this initial feature map is enlarged and improved with new feature points detected in subsequent camera frames.

Originally, SLAM techniques were proposed for autonomous robots for independent exploration of an unknown environment [4]. Typically, robots have access to further sensor input such as odometry or gyro compass data. In contrast to this, handheld single camera Augmented Reality applications completely rely on visual input information. Within the AR context SLAM approaches are also known as Parallel Tracking and Mapping (PTAM) techniques. A well-known PTAM approach has been proposed by Klein et al. [9]. They initialize their tracking system by a stereo image of a small tracking area using a single handheld camera only. Klein et al. apply FAST features in combination with simple image patches for feature tracking. The size of the feature map increases with each new frame and the positions of already found 3D feature points are improved using a global optimization approach. During initialization all found feature points are used to determine the dominant 3D plane. This plane is then used as basis for the virtual objects in the AR application. Due to the high performance when calculating FAST features, PTAM even can be applied on mobile phones as shown by Klein et al. [10]. On the one hand, SLAM approaches do not need any previously created feature maps, on the other hand, the stereo image initialization with a single camera does not allow for an exact definition of the dimensions of the environment. In contrast to this, a unique feature map created previously allows for augmenting the real environment with virtual objects with precise object dimensions.

7   Conclusions and Future Directions

In this chapter we reviewed the current state-of-the-art in feature based tracking for Augmented Reality (Fig. 11.5), providing the reader with the information necessary to decide on the appropriate components of his tracking approach. We investigated into general requirements of feature detectors for real-time capable vision based tracking with a particular focus on corner detectors, such as the Harris or FAST feature detectors, and blob detectors, such as SIFT or SURF detectors. Once, the features detectors have been terminated, matching them against corresponding features for extracting the 6DOF pose is required. We reviewed the three basic approaches: use of image patches, use of feature descriptors and how best matching pairs may be found, and finally the use of trees and ferns. In order to show the functionality of a feature based tracker the individual stages of the tracking pipeline were explained in detail: feature detection, feature mapping, dealing with camera

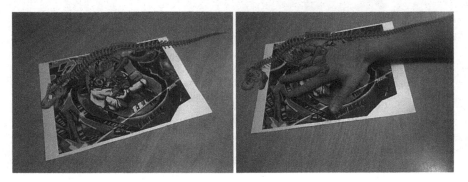

Fig. 11.5 Feature tracking result of the adaptive feature tracker augmenting a virtual dinosaur

distortion, feature description, feature matching, fast feature culling, and finally the calculation of the pose and/or its refinement. We further showed how an adaptive tracker can be realized. The three different tracking approaches applied here were discussed: Firstly, the tracking without any previous knowledge completely based on the information of the current frame. Secondly, tracking using existing feature correspondences from the previous frame, and finally, an approach using the previous pose as a basis for tracking. While the approach presented, relied on SURF feature descriptors, the general architecture may also be applied to other feature descriptors, or may easily be extended to combine several feature descriptors and/or matching approaches.

While selected current approaches may already be used on recent mobile phones and tablets, it can be expected that those mechanisms will become widely used upon availability of multi-core mobile phones and tablets. Further, we expect online 2D and 3D data to be used for this purpose in combination with SLAM like approaches, relying on ad-hoc information from the environment. Combining those will provide a basis for universal mobile tracking.

References

1. H. Bay, A. Ess, T. Tuytelaars, and L. van Gool, "Speeded-up robust Features (SURF)," Computer Vision and Image Understanding (CVIU), Volume 110, No. 3, pages 346–359, 2008
2. D. C. Brown, "Close-range camera calibration," Photogrammetric Engineering, Volume 37, Number 8, pages 855–866, 1971
3. D. Cheng, S. Xie, and E. Hämmerle, "Comparison of local descriptors for image registration of geometrically-complex 3D scenes," 14th International Conference on Mechatronics and Machine Vision in Patrice (M2VIP), pages 140–145, 2007
4. A. J. Davison, and N. Kita, "3D simultaneous localisation and map-building using active vision for a robot moving on undulating terrain," In Proceedings of the IEEE Conference on Computer Vision and Pattern Recognition, Kauai, 2001

5. M. A. Fischler, and R. C. Bolles, "Random sample consensus: a paradigm for model fitting with applications to image analysis and automated cartography," Communications of the ACM 24, Volume 6, 1981
6. C. Harris, and M. Stephens, "A Combined Corner and Edge Detector," Proceedings of the 4th Alvey Vision Conference, pages 147–151, 1988
7. J. Herling and W. Broll, "An Adaptive Training Free Tracker for Mobile Phones", In Proc. of the 17th ACM Conference on Virtual Reality Systems and Technology (VRST 2010), ACM, New York, NY, USA, pages 35–42
8. H. Kato, and M. Billinghurst, "Marker Tracking and HMD Calibration for a Video-based Augmented Reality Conferencing System", *in 2nd IEEE and ACM International Workshop on Augmented Reality*, 1999
9. G. Klein, and D. Murray, "Parallel Tracking and Mapping for Small AR Workspaces", Proc. of IEEE *ISMAR*, 2007
10. G. Klein, and D. Murray, "Parallel Tracking and Mapping on a Camera Phone", Proc. of IEEE *ISMAR*, 2009
11. V. Lepetit, P. Lagger, and P. Fua, "Randomized Trees for Real-Time Keypoint Recognition," Proceedings of the IEEE Computer Society Conference on Computer Vision and Pattern Recognition (CVPR), pages 775–781, 2005
12. V. Lepetit, F. Moreno-Noguer, and P. Fua, "EPnP: An Accurate O(n) Solution to the PnP Problem," International Journal of Computer Vision, Volume 81, Issue 2, 2009
13. D. G. Lowe, "Distinctive Image Features from Scale-Invariant Keypoints," International Journal of Computer Vision. Volume 60 Issue 2, 2004
14. W. H. Press, S. A. Teukolsky, W. T. Vetterling, and B.P. Flannery, "Numerical Recipes: The Art of Scientific Computing," Cambridge University Press, Third Edition, 2007
15. M. Özuysal, P. Fua, and V. Lepetit, "Fast Keypoint Recognition in Ten Lines of Code," Proceedings of IEEE Conference on Computing Vision and Pattern Recognition, pages 1–8, 2007
16. E. Rosten, and T. Drummond, "Fusing Points and Lines for High Performance Tracking," Proceedings of the IEEE International Conference on Computer Vision, pages 1508–1511, 2005

Chapter 12
Enhancing Interactivity in Handheld AR Environments

Masahito Hirakawa, Shu'nsuke Asai, Kengo Sakata, Shuhei Kanagu, Yasuhiro Sota, and Kazuhiro Koyama

Abstract In this paper we present a trial of development of handheld AR supporting two interaction techniques based on the understanding that both real and virtual objects should be compatible in manipulation. One is the ability to contact virtual objects by user's finger, as well as to physical objects in the real world. The virtual objects change their position, shape, and/or other graphical features according to his/her manipulation. The other technique we discuss in the paper concerns pseudo manipulation of virtual objects. The motion such as shake and tilt to a handheld device causes a certain effect to the virtual objects in the AR content.

1 Introduction

One view of the future of computing that has captured our interest is augmented reality (AR), in which computer generated virtual imagery is overlaid on everyday physical objects [1–3]. In fact, AR is not a buzzword anymore and many trials of demonstrating AR systems/applications can be seen in YouTube and other video sharing websites as well as technical publications. This has happened thanks to several reasons.

One is the development of sophisticated algorithms and software libraries that help developers to create augmented reality systems. ARToolKit [4] is the most well-known software library, which provides a capability of calculating the camera position and orientation relative to a square physical marker in real time. Moreover, high performance markerless tracking techniques have been investigated [5–8].

The second key trend in AR is a movement in system platforms. AR systems in the early years run on a PC with highly specialized tools and equipments such as head mounted displays (HMDs), digital gloves and magnetic/ultrasonic sensors

M. Hirakawa (✉)
Shimane University, Shimane, Japan
e-mail: hirakawa@cis.shimane-u.ac.jp

B. Furht (ed.), *Handbook of Augmented Reality*, DOI 10.1007/978-1-4614-0064-6_12,   273
© Springer Science+Business Media, LLC 2011

(e.g. [9]). They are rather expensive and, more seriously, wearing them is an impediment to his/her work. Interestingly, mobile and handheld devices have become powerful lately. While the size of these devices is small, they provide fast processors, full color displays, high quality video cameras, and powerful 3D graphics chips. This can greatly help AR technology spread out in our daily life environments [10]. Actually trials of handheld AR have been increasing. From a user's viewpoint, such mobile and handheld devices are used by novice users and they are acute observers of their functionality and usability. This demands smart interaction facilities with attractive applications in AR environments.

In this paper we present a trial of development of handheld AR supporting two interaction techniques based on the understanding that both real and virtual objects should be compatible in manipulation [11]. One is the ability to contact virtual objects by user's finger, as well as to physical objects in the real world. The virtual objects change their position, shape, and/or other graphical features according to his/her manipulation. The other technique we discuss in the paper concerns pseudo manipulation of virtual objects. The motion such as shake and tilt to a handheld device causes a certain effect to the virtual objects in the AR content. The phenomenon implemented in our application may not be true in the physical space, but seems not unnatural for us since we get used to gizmos which simulate a variety of imaginary events.

The rest of the paper is organized as follows. After discussing related work in Sect. 2, we will present the concept of dual face interaction in handheld AR environments in Sect. 3. Section 4 concerns design issues in dual face interaction. Sections 5 and 6 describe solutions for its implementation. Finally, in Sect. 7, we conclude the paper.

2 Related Work

A great deal of research has been conducted in AR fields. Interaction techniques to AR contents are of great interest. It is reported in [1] that the proportion of the interaction papers is increasing in the ISMAR conference and its predecessors over the last 10 years.

We classify the papers on interaction along two axes: *platform* and *manipulation style*. Platform refers to hardware equipment on which a system runs, which includes *PC* and *handheld device*. Manipulation style concerns how the user specifies his/her demands on manipulating virtual objects which are overlaid on the real world, including *direct* and *indirect*. Direct manipulation allows the user to contact virtual objects directly with his/her finger, hand, or body, while indirect manipulation realizes affecting virtual objects with the aid of a physical prop. Table 12.1 shows a result of the classification.

Reference [12] proposes occlusion-based 2D interaction, where visual occlusion of physical markers is used to provide intuitive 2D interaction in tangible AR

Table 12.1 Classification of interaction studies

Platform		
Manipulation style	PC	Handheld device
Direct	General [12–14]	General [37]
	Planning & design [15–17]	Entertainment [38, 39]
	Authoring [18]	
	Entertainment [19–22]	
	Maintenance [23]	
	Medical care [24]	
	Tabletop [25]	
	Outdoor [26, 27]	
Indirect	General [28–30]	General [37]
	Planning & design [31]	Planning & design [40]
	Authoring [18]	Entertainment [34, 41, 42]
	Entertainment [32–35]	
	Medical care [36]	
	Tabletop [25]	

environments. When the user moves his/her hand or finger on an interaction surface on which a number of markers are attached, the virtual object placed over which the hand/finger lies can be selected.

Reference [17] presents an AR-based re-formable mock-up system for design evaluation, that allows the designer to interactively modify shapes as well as colors, textures, and user interfaces of a prototype. Fingertip tracking algorithm is implemented so that the designer can operate the prototype as if it were a real one.

In [19], application of a gesture-based interface to game content, virtual fishing and Jenga, is demonstrated. User's finger is tracked in a 3D space using a stereo camera, and virtual objects can be picked up and tossed with physical characteristics such as gravity and collisions.

Human Pacman [20] implements a HMD-based mobile game with use of a proximity sensing technology to incorporate player's contextual information into the game context. The player who is taking the role of Pacman physically moves around in a wide-area setting and, if he/she walks across virtual cookies overlaid in the AR world, they can be eaten.

Reference [38] presents a mobile AR application in which the user can interact with a virtual object appearing on a hand by his/her hand motions. In one scenario, when the hand is opened, a virtual flower is opened and a virtual bee comes out and buzzes around it. The flower is close and the bee disappears when the hand is closed. Another scenario is that a virtual character bounces up and down on the hand in response to user's hand movement.

Siemens Business Services C-LAB has realized an AR soccer game for camera phones, named Kick Real [39]. To play, the user aims his/her camera phone down and kicks a virtual ball being superimposed on the display with his/her own foot. Direction and speed are determined by the foot's real movement.

In the trials explained above, the user directly manipulates virtual objects by using his/her finger, hand, foot, or body. On the other hand, there is another approach in which virtual objects are manipulated with the help of an auxiliary device. Trials in this indirect manipulation approach can be divided further into two depending on their system platform. In PC-based ones, the user specifies his/her manipulation requests with aid of a certain prop such as pen, handle, and box. On the other hand, in the case that a handheld device is used, the device is considered itself as a prop. Manipulation of virtual objects is carried out by gesturing with device movements. Some of the trials are explained below.

Reference [29] proposes a new type of 3D Magic Lens which is a way to provide the focus and context concept in information visualization. A lens consists of a flexible visualization surface suspended between two physical handles. The surface changes dynamically in shape and size and is defined implicitly by the location of the two handles.

Reference [40] proposes a technique of editing the geometry of a virtual 3D polygonal mesh. The user is allowed to select one or more vertices in an arbitrary sized polygon mesh and freely translate and rotate them by translating and rotating the camera phone through which the mesh is viewed. That is, the phone acts as a 6 DOF isomorphic interaction device.

AR Tennis [41] is a collaborative AR application. Two players sit across a table from each other with a piece of paper between them that has a set of 2D markers drawn on it. The mobile phones are used as visual rackets to hit the ball back and forth between the players.

Reference [42] presents a gestural interface for a mobile phone maze game, at which the user controls the movement of a ball through a maze. A camera on the phone which is looking at a visual code marker is used to detect tilt and translation of the phone, resulting in the ball movement.

3   Dual Face Interaction in Handheld AR

Though AR systems aim at integration of both real and virtual objects so that they cannot be visually separable, the user is permitted to give actions only to the real objects but not to the virtual objects in some trials, as illustrated in Fig. 12.1a. We say interaction to both of the objects should be compatible.

Meanwhile, as explained in the previous section, most of the existing AR studies assume a PC as their execution platform, in which highly sophisticated or heavy duty equipments such as HMD and data gloves may be attached. We focus our attention on handheld AR systems, since mobile or smart phones are becoming common in our daily activities recently. Here an adequate user interface of handheld AR systems is different from that of PC-based AR systems [41]. The reason is that, when we use a handheld device, one hand is free while the other is occupied to hold the device.

Due to this fact, we consider two different interaction techniques. One is what we called direct manipulation in the previous section, and the other indirect

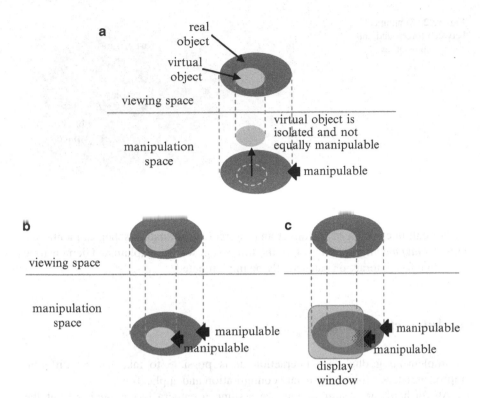

Fig. 12.1 Capabilities in manipulating virtual objects (S. Asai and M. Hirakawa, "Dual Face Interaction in Handheld Augmented Reality Environments," Proceedings of IEEE International Symposium on Multimedia, 2009. © 2009 IEEE)

manipulation. With direct manipulation, the user is allowed to directly manipulate a virtual object which is registered over a target real object by one hand (or finger) which is not occupied, as in Fig. 12.1b. On the other hand, one more hand which holds the handheld device is responsible for control of the area of which the user is viewing through the device. Movement of the handheld device can be considered as a stimulus to make a certain effect to the virtual object (see Fig. 12.1c).

It should be noted here that those two object manipulation schemes of Fig. 12.1a, b cannot be separated. While the user is viewing the AR space where the real and virtual objects are mixed, there exists a rest of the space, or background space, which is not visible on the display but connected to the foreground space he/she is viewing. Those two (sub)spaces form the complete space where the user is located, as illustrated in Fig. 12.2. It is natural to imagine that manipulation of a handheld device belonging to the background space causes effects to computer generated virtual objects in the foreground space.

For example, in a scenario of AR tennis game, a handheld device serves as a racket which is not displayed on a screen. The racket can be swung with a gesture to hit a virtual ball to be seen through the display of the device.

Fig. 12.2 Continuity
between foreground and
background spaces

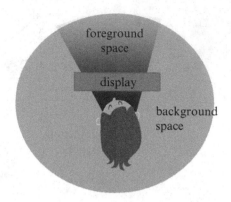

We call integration of the direct and indirect manipulation schemes mentioned above *dual face interaction* [11]. In the following, we will explain and demonstrate how dual face interaction can actually be implemented.

4 Interaction Design

In implementing dual face interaction, it is possible to take several different approaches depending on hardware configuration and application.

As for hardware configuration, we assume a camera is mounted only at the back of a handheld device. Henrysson et al. [37] presents, unlike ours, a technique of interaction by recognizing gestures taken through a front camera of a mobile phone, while the target real world is seen through its rear camera. This means there exist two separate layers for handling of real world situations – one is for viewing the real world and the other for placing commands to manipulate virtual objects. This is cumbersome for the user, and a front camera is not always installed in handheld devices.

Meanwhile, entertainment and marketing are most promising for handheld AR applications [10]. We consider providing facilities which seem interesting and promising in such applications.

The system we propose in this paper is capable of recognizing a finger which is placed at the back of a handheld device, that is, between the device and real physical objects. When the user touches a virtual object with his/her finger, an associated action with it is invoked, as illustrated in Fig. 12.3a.

Moreover, certain changes occur in response to the motion of the device. For example, when the user moves the device quickly, virtual objects appearing on the screen are shaken as if they kept their posture by existence of inertia. This response is not real, but seems acceptable in entertainment applications. It is somewhat related to the idea of illustration- or cartoon-inspired techniques which include speedlines and strobe silhouettes to convey a change of something over time [43, 44]. They

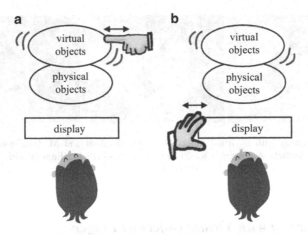

Fig. 12.3 Realization of dual face interaction (**a**) interaction with virtual objects with the finger. (**b**) interaction with virtual objects by motion of the display (handled device)(S. Asai and M. Hirakawa, "Dual Face Interaction in Handheld Augmented Reality Environments," Proceedings of IEEE International Symposium on Multimedia, 2009. © 2009 IEEE)

actually enhance our understanding of the meaning of a thing with non-realistic expressions. A conceptual illustration of this pseudo manipulation scheme is given in Fig. 12.3b.

Illusion which is a distortion of a sensory perception is also worth considering. Our eyes can be tricked into seeing something that is not really happen. It would be nice if visualization functions are designed in consideration of such behavior of our cognitive system [45].

5   Implementation One: Prototyping with PC

Before implementing a system which runs on a smart phone, we built a PC-based prototype for rapid demonstration of the proposed design explained in the previous section. ARToolKit, OpenGL, and OpenCV were used as software libraries for the implementation.

While there exist several modern tracking techniques (e.g., [5–8]), ARToolKit is the most popular software library for AR application development. This is the reason why we chose it as a core library for our system development. Production of 3D graphical objects has been realized with OpenGL. In addition, real-time object tracking is necessary for our system implementation as a particular function. OpenCV is used for this purpose, i.e., tracking of the motion of user's finger and the camera.

Fig. 12.4 Interacting with a virtual object by finger (S. Asai and M. Hirakawa, "Dual Face Interaction in Handheld Augmented Reality Environments," Proceedings of IEEE International Symposium on Multimedia, 2009. © 2009 IEEE)

5.1 Interaction with Virtual Object by Finger

Manipulation of a virtual object by user's finger is done as shown in Fig. 12.4. When the user sees a fiducial marker through a camera, a computer-generated snow man appears on the marker. In response to his/her touch operation to it, the snow man is shaken as in the figure.

Here we assume that, in specification of his/her contact to the virtual object, the finger is inserted in parallel to the display. We ignore the motion in depth direction. This is because, when we assume a handheld device, the user tends to put the device close to the target object due to the small size of its display. If he/she wants to view a different part of the object, it is natural to move the device and change his/her position in relation to the target part. We believe this constraint on finger insertion doesn't lose a generality. Of course this makes system implementation simpler and the processing cost could become lower.

There have been many proposals for detecting and tracking finger (or hand) regions in video streams. In our implementation, finger region detection is carried out simply by skin color. Specifically, for input video frames which are represented in HSV color model, the region whose color is within certain thresholds is considered as a finger. Furthermore, assuming the finger is inserted from a side of the display, rightmost or leftmost point of the region is considered a finger tip.

The system then checks whether a collision of the finger to the virtual object occurs. We considered that a 3D virtual object is composed of simple geometrical models such as sphere and cone. This again makes collision detection simpler.

5.2 Interaction with Virtual Object by Camera Motion

Meanwhile, for realization of indirect manipulation of virtual objects, the system provides a facility to recognize swing motion of the device. In response to the user's motion, the virtual object is shaken as if it tries to keep its posture due to inertia.

Fig. 12.5 Interacting with a virtual object by camera motion (S. Asai and M. Hirakawa, "Dual Face Interaction in Handheld Augmented Reality Environments," Proceedings of IEEE International Symposium on Multimedia, 2009. © 2009 IEEE)

Motion estimation is carried out by using the Lucas and Kanade optical flow function provided in OpenCV. While the motion can take 6 degrees of freedom, we only consider translation at constant distance from the observer in the prototype development. If the rate of acceleration of the motion is greater than a given threshold, the system executes the action of tilting the snow man to the opposite direction of the motion. Figure 12.5 shows a snapshot of the response. The left and right images of the figure correspond to the cases before and after the device motion occurs, respectively.

6   Implementation Two: Targeting at iPhone

6.1   Considerations to iPhone-based Implementation

We have been porting the prototype system into iPhone which is an interesting platform for AR application development. On this phase, we have considered again what necessities for the system are and come to the conclusion that the following should be satisfied.

- The use of fiducial markers which are specially designed for ARToolKit is advantageous to pose recognition but not preferable to practical applications. Markerless tracking in the sense that no specially designed makers are used is indispensable to AR applications in general.
- There is a demand for killer applications or novel interaction scenarios.
- It is expected to prepare software toolkits or libraries to encourage people to develop a variety of fruitful AR applications.

We consider QR codes and natural features such as color and shape as markers for object detection and tracking. QR codes have become more prevalent in marketing and advertising circles. Actually they appear in magazines, on signs, product packages, or business cards. Use of QR codes in AR environments is promising.

Furthermore, detection of a certain color or shape would contribute to the development of novel and enjoyable applications. The traditional applications in most cases realize superimposition of navigation messages or virtual characters playing on real objects. Such behavior is rather direct and straightforward. On the other hand, color and shape are considered to be sensuous. Associating real objects with graphical or patternized expressions may lead us to a new type of AR applications. We will explain more concrete examples later in Sect. 6.3.

The third point in the above list is still an issue to be tackled. We have been working on it to be able to release a software library in the near future.

6.2   Interaction Using QR Code Tracking

Recognition of QR codes is executed in two phases, where pose tracking is executed separately from code identification. The reason is the following: In order to scan a data pattern at the center of a QR code, the camera should be positioned close to it. Otherwise it fails to do scanning. But, this task is required just once and no need to continue anymore after its success. The user would rather like to manipulate the device to change his/her view to the virtual object associated with the QR code. He/she may move the device (or the QR code) away. In this phase, what is needed for the system is to track just where the code is.

Here, for code identification, a certain input image area is recognized as a QR code if three special corner symbols appear within it. Knowing the corner symbol is formed by a black square box with a black square border, the system recognizes one corner symbol if the center of any two black square symbols matches. A square region organized by three corner symbols is finally determined as a QR code.

After identification of the QR code, the coordinate values of its four corner points are registered and updated as their positions move. As noted, the system doesn't continue with QR code identification processing. Rather it tries to find a square or trapezoid region by applying morphological operations. More specifically, dilation and erodation operations in OpenCV are applied to each video frame to execute this processing.

Figure 12.6 shows snapshots of the system. A wireframe box model is positioned on the QR code which is detected. As you see, the code tracking is maintained even though the camera is not close to the code.

Furthermore, the virtual object (i.e., 3D box) overlaid on the QR code is translated by rotating the phone, as shown in Fig. 12.7. Here we use a built-in accelerometer for capturing its posture. While only translation is allowed at this time, we are going to implement a more variety of interaction styles.

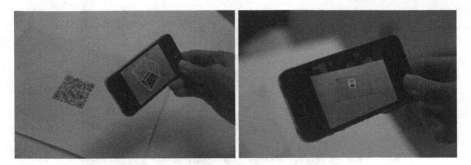

Fig. 12.6 Tracking of a QR code

Fig. 12.7 Placement of an action to translate the box model

6.3   *Interaction Using Color-based Tracking*

The use of QR codes is helpful when the system is applied in marketing since the customer can access to the valuable information associated with a particular physical object to which a QR code is attached. In fact, it is fun to see a virtual character dancing and know discount campaign in an AR environment. But this is not all of possible scenarios for AR. It is a challenge to seek other reasonable and enjoyable application scenarios which, for example, stimulate our emotional experiences. Natural features such as color and shape could serve as possible markers in such scenarios. We explain in this section a graphics-oriented application with a color-based object tracking technique.

Our focus is on color-based interactive AR, so our first implementation is a simple pinwheel content. According to the color selected by the user, a pinwheel is generated and overlaid in the AR content. The shape of its blades can be modified through interaction with the color region at which he/she is viewing.

Fig. 12.8 Selection of a target color

Fig. 12.9 Pinwheel application

Figure 12.8 shows an interface for selection of the color to be tracked. When the system starts execution, a crossing marker appears to allow the user select a target color by keeping its region centered for a few seconds. To initialize the color selection, the user tilts the phone up.

After that, the user may change his/her scope as he/she prefers. A pinwheel appears so that a region having the similar color with the selected one is considered as a wing component of the pinwheel, as shown in Fig. 12.9. When the camera position changes, its view changes accordingly, of course. Here, multiple regions in the real world may be matched for the selected color. The largest one is chosen as the target in the current implementation.

Fig. 12.10 Touching to a pinwheel component

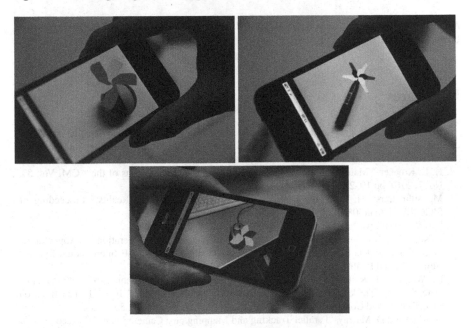

Fig. 12.11 Pinwheels on daily products

Next, consider the user touches the base wing with his/her finger. In truth, he/she places the finger on the physical region. The wing is dented, as shown in Fig. 12.10, resulting in the change of the pinwheel shape.

It may be hard for the user to imagine the shape of the region which is detected by the selected color. This in turn could make a surprise and be fun in application of the system to entertainment and interactive art domains. The capability of directly interacting with the virtual object (or the physical region) enhances it. Figure 12.11 shows some additional snapshots where daily products are chosen as targets.

7 Conclusions

This paper presented the notion of dual face interaction in handheld AR environments, which supports two interaction schemes based on the understanding that both real and virtual objects should be compatible in manipulation.

One of the techniques is to directly manipulate virtual objects by his/her finger. The other concerns indirect manipulation of virtual objects, where the motion to the handheld device (or camera) serves to make a certain change in geometrical and/or spatial properties of the virtual objects. We demonstrated how actually those schemes were implemented. We also presented an idea of using QR codes and color features as a means of object tracking.

Though we have tested the system informally to find how interesting the interaction is and where the bottlenecks are, formal user studies have not been done yet. We should carry out research on this. In addition, we have been working toward preparation of a software library for novel AR applications development.

Acknowledgments This research was funded in part by Shimane Industrial Promotion Foundation.

References

1. F. Zhou, H. B. L. Duh, and M. Billinghurst, "Trends in Augmented Reality Tracking, Interaction and Display: A Review of Ten Years of ISMAR," Proceedings of the IEEE International Symposium on Mixed Reality and Augmented Reality (ISMAR2008), 2008.
2. K. L. Kroeker, "Mainstreaming Augmented Reality," Communications of the ACM, Vol. 53, No. 7, 2010, pp.19–21.
3. M. Billinghurst, H. Kato, and I. Poupyrev, "Tangible Augmented Reality," Proceeding of SIGGRAPH Asia '08, 2008.
4. http://www.hitl.washington.edu/artoolkit/
5. J. Neubert, J. Pretlove and T. Drummond, "Semi-Autonomous Generation of Appearance-based Edge Models from Image Sequences," Proceedings of the IEEE International Symposium on Mixed Reality and Augmented Reality (ISMAR2007), 2007.
6. D. Wagner, G. Reitmayr, A. Mulloni, T. Drummond, and D. Schmalstieg, "Real-Time Detection and Tracking for Augmented Reality on Mobile Phones," IEEE Transactions on Visualization and Computer Graphics, Vol. 16, No. 3, May/June 2010, 355–368.
7. G. Klein and D. Murray, "Parallel Tracking and Mapping on a Camera Phone," Proceedings of IEEE International Symposium on Mixed and Augmented Reality (ISMAR2009), 2009.
8. J. Herling and W. Broll, "An Adaptive Training-free Feature Tracker for Mobile Phones," Proceedings of ACM Symposium on Virtual Reality Software and Technology (VRST2010), 2010.
9. J. Caarls, P. Jonker, Y. Kolstee, J. Rotteveel, and W. van Eck, "Augmented Reality for Art, Design and Cultural Heritage - System Design and Evaluation," EURASIP Journal on Image and Video Processing, Vol. 2009, Article ID 716160, 2009.
10. S. J. Vaughan-Nichols, "Augmeted Reality: No Longer a Novelty," IEEE Computer, Vol. 42, No. 12, 2009, pp.19–22.
11. S. Asai and M. Hirakawa, "Dual Face Interaction in Handheld Augmented Reality Environments," Proceedings of IEEE International Symposium on Multimedia, 2009.

12. G. A. Lee, M. Billinghurst, and G. J. Kim, "Occlusion based Interaction Methods for Tangible Augmented Reality Environments," Proceedings of the 2004 ACM SIGGRAPH International Conference on Virtual Reality Continuum and Its Applications in Industry (VRCAI '04), 2004.
13. G. Heidemann, I. Bax, and H. Bekel, "Multimodal Interaction in an Augmented Reality Scenario," Proceedings of Sixth International Conference on Multimodal Interfaces (ICMI 04), 2004.
14. Y. Kojima, Y. Yasumuro, H. Sasaki, I. Kanaya, O. Oshiro, T. Kuroda, Y. Manabe, and K. Chihara, "Hand Manipulation of Virtual Objects in Wearable Augmented Reality," Proceedings of the Seventh International Conference on Virtual Systems and Multimedia (VSMM'01), 2001.
15. A. D. Cheok, N. W. C. Edmund, and A. W. Eng, "Inexpensive Non-Sensor Based Augmented Reality Modeling of Curves and Surfaces in Physical Space," Proceedings of the International Symposium on Mixed and Augmented Reality (ISMAR'02), 2002.
16. V. Buchmann, S. Violich, M. Billinghurst, and A. Cockburn, "FingARtips – Gesture Based Direct Manipulation in Augmented Reality," Proceedings of the 2nd International Conference on Computer Graphics and Interactive Techniques in Australasia and South East Asia (GRAPHITE '04), 2004.
17. J. Park, "Augmented Reality based Re-formable Mock-up for Design Evaluation," Proceedings of International Symposium on Ubiquitous Virtual Reality (ISUVR2008), 2008.
18. G. A. Lee, C. Nelles, M. Billinghurst, and G. J. Kim, "Immersive Authoring of Tangible Augmented Reality Applications," Proceedings of the Third IEEE and ACM International Symposium on Mixed and Augmented Reality (ISMAR2004), 2004.
19. P. Song, H. Yu, and S. Winkler, "Vision-based 3D Finger Interactions for Mixed Reality Games with Physics Simulation," Proceedings of The 7th ACM SIGGRAPH International Conference on Virtual-Reality Continuum and Its Applications in Industry (VRCAI2008), 2008.
20. A. D. Cheok, S. W. Fong, K. H. Goh, X. Yang, W. Liu, and F. Farbiz, "Human Packman: A Sensing-based Mobile Entertainment System with Ubiquitous Computing and Tangible Interaction," Proceedings of the 2nd Workshop on Network and System Support for Games (NetGame'03), 2003.
21. K. Dorfmüller-Ulhaas and D. Schmalstieg, "Finger Tracking for Interaction in Augmented Environments," Proceedings of the IEEE and ACM International Symposium on Augmented Reality (ISAR'01), 2001.
22. D. Molyneaux and H. Gellersen, "Projected Interfaces: Enabling Serendipitous Interaction with Smart Tangible Objects," Proceedings of the 3rd International Conference on Tangible and Embedded Interaction (TEI'09), 2009.
23. S. Henderson and S. Feiner, "Opportunistic Tangible User Interfaces for Augmented Reality," IEEE Transactions on Visualization and Computer Graphics, Vol. 16, No. 1, January/February 2010, pp. 4–16.
24. D. Zhang, Y. Shen, S. K. Ong, and A. Y. C. Nee, "An Affordable Augmented Reality based Rehabilitation System for Hand Motions," Proceedings of 2010 International Conference on Cyberworlds, 2010.
25. A. Anagnostopoulos and A. Pnevmatikakis, "A Realtime Mixed Reality System for Seamless Interaction between Real and Virtual Objects," Proceedings of Third International Conference on Digital Interactive Media in Entertainment and Arts (DIMEA'08), 2008.
26. T. N. Hoang, S. R. Porter, and B. H. Thomas, "Augmenting Image Plane AR 3D Interactions for Wearable Computers," Proceedings of Tenth Australasian User Interface Conference (AUIC2009), 2009.
27. M. Koelsch, R. Bane, T. Höllerer, and M. Turk, "Multimodal Interaction with a Wearable Augmented Reality System," IEEE Computer Graphics and Applications, Volume 26, Issue 3, May/June 2006.
28. H. Seichter, R. Grasset, J. Looser, and M. Billinghurst, "Multitouch Interaction for Tangible User Interfaces," Proceedings of IEEE International Symposium on Mixed and Augmented Reality (ISMAR2009), 2009.

29. J. Looser, R. Grasset, and M. Billinghurst, "A 3D Flexible and Tangible Magic Lens in Augmented Reality," Proceedings of 6th IEEE and ACM International Symposium on Mixed and Augmented Reality (ISMAR2007), 2007.
30. S. White, D. Feng, and S. Feiner, "Interaction and Presentation Techniques for Shake Menus in Tangible Augmented Reality," Proceedings of IEEE International Symposium on Mixed and Augmented Reality (ISMAR2009), 2009.
31. G. Bianchi, C. Jung, B. Knoerlein, G. Székely, and M. Harders, "High-Fidelity Visuo-Haptic Interaction with Virtual Objects in Multi-Modal AR Systems," Proceedings of IEEE and ACM International Symposium on Mixed and Augmented Reality (ISMAR2006), 2006.
32. D. Calife, J. L. Bernardes, Jr., and R. Tori, "Robot Arena: An Augmented Reality Platform for Game Development," ACM Computers in Entertainment, Vo. 7, Article 11, 2009.
33. H. Kobayashi, T. Osaki, T. Okuyama, J. Gramm, A. Ishino, and A. Shinohara, "Development of an Interactive Augmented Environment and Its Application to Autonomous Learning for Quadruped Robots," IEICE Transactions on Information and Systems, Vol. E92, No. 9, 2009, pp.1752–1761.
34. T. Harviainen, O. Korkalo, and C. Woodward, "Camera-based Interactions for Augmented Reality," Proceedings of International Conference on Advances in Computer Entertainment Technology (ACE2009), 2009.
35. O. Oda, L. J. Lister, S. White, and S. Feiner. "Developing an Augmented Reality Racing Game," Proceedings of the Second International Conference on Intelligent Technologies for Interactive Entertainment (ICST INTETAIN2008), 2008.
36. C. Bichlmeier, F. Wimmer, S. M. Heining, and N. Navab, "Contextual Anatomic Mimesis: Hybrid In-Situ Visualization Method for Improving Multi-Sensory Depth Perception in Medical Augmented Reality," Proceedings of 6th IEEE and ACM International Symposium on Mixed and Augmented Reality (ISMAR2007), 2007.
37. A. Henrysson, J. Marshall, and M. Billinghurst, "Experiments in 3D Interaction for Mobile Phone AR," Proceedings of the 5th International Conference on Computer Graphics and Interactive Techniques in Australasia and South East Asia (GRAPHITE 2007), 2007.
38. B. K. Seo, J. Choi, J. H. Han, H. Park, and J. I. Park, "One-Handed Interaction with Augmented Virtual Objects on Mobile Devices," Proceedings of ACM SIGGRAPH International Conference on Virtual Reality Continuum and Its Applications in Industry (VRCIA 08), 2008.
39. C. Ludwig and C. Reimann, "Augmented Reality: Information at Focus," C-LAB Report, Vol. 4, No. 1, 2005.
40. A. Henrysson and M. Billinghurst, "Using a Mobile Phone for 6 DOF Mesh Editing," Proceedings of the 7th ACM SIGCHI New Zealand Chapter's International Conference on Computer-Human Interaction (CHINZ2007), 2007.
41. A. Henrysson, M. Billinghurst, and M. Ollila, "Face to Face Collaborative AR on Mobile Phones," Proceedings of IEEE International Symposium on Mixed and Augmented Reality (ISMAR 2005), 2005.
42. S. Bucolo, M. Billinghurst, and D. Sickinger, "User Experiences with Mobile Phone Camera Game Interfaces," Proceedings of the 4th International Conference on Mobile and Ubiquitous Multimedia (MUM2005), 2005.
43. A. Joshi and P. Rheingans, "Illustration-Inspired Techniques for Visualizing Time-Varying Data," Proceedings of IEEE Visualization, 2005.
44. A. Joshi, J. Caban, P. Rheingans, and L. Sparling, "Case Study on Visualizing Hurricanes Using Illustration-Inspired Techniques," IEEE Transactions on Visualization and Computer Graphics, Vol. 15, No. 5, September/October, 2009, pp. 709–718.
45. M. Hirakawa, "Going Beyond Completeness in Information Retrieval," International Journal of Computational Science and Engineering, Vol. 5, No.2, 2010, pp. 110–117.

Chapter 13
Evaluating Augmented Reality Systems

Andreas Dünser and Mark Billinghurst

Abstract This Chapter discusses issues with Augmented Reality (AR) systems evaluations. First the role of evaluation and various challenges for evaluating novel AR interfaces and interaction techniques are reviewed. A special focus is then provided on user-based and non-user-based evaluation techniques currently used for evaluating AR systems. The practical application of these methods is demonstrated through different examples from the scientific literature. Various points raised in this chapter provide arguments for the development of more specific frameworks and models for AR-based interfaces and interaction techniques. These will provide researchers with a better basis for developing and applying more suitable evaluation methods that address the specific requirements of evaluating AR-based systems.

1 Introduction

Augmented Reality (AR) research has a long history. Starting from the first early prototypes over forty years ago [1], AR developed into an established field of study in the 1990s and attracted interest from the larger academic community. Most recently, AR technologies also have found their way into a wide range of industrial and commercial applications.

As in most emerging technological fields, AR researchers and developers have had to solve many technological issues to create usable AR applications, such as developing tracking and display systems, authoring tools, and input devices. However, as the field matures and more applications are developed, evaluating these systems with end users will become more important. So far the amount of AR systems formally evaluated is rather small [2]. For example, literature surveys of

A. Dünser (✉)
The Human Interface Technology Laboratory, New Zealand (HIT Lab NZ),
The University of Canterbury, Christchurch, New Zealand
e-mail: andreas.duenser@canterbury.ac.nz

B. Furht (ed.), *Handbook of Augmented Reality*, DOI 10.1007/978-1-4614-0064-6_13,   289
© Springer Science+Business Media, LLC 2011

user evaluation in AR have found that only around 8% of published AR research papers include formal evaluations [3, 4]. One reason for this may be the lack of suitable methods for evaluating AR interfaces. In this chapter we review previous AR studies to give an overview of methods that have successfully been used to evaluate AR systems.

Focusing on user-driven design is an increasingly important aspect of AR system development. As more real world applications are created, developers should adapt a strong user-centered design approach and evaluate the systems with actual users. This is an important step in order to bring the technology out of the research labs and into people's everyday lives. It not only helps provide more insight into the actual usage of new AR systems but also to refine their designs.

Different stages of system development call for a variety of evaluation strategies. However, not all types of evaluations test the systems' usability. Depending on the actual research goal, a user test certainly can help to shed more light on the system's usability, but researchers often have other research questions. In this chapter the term 'user evaluation' is used in a broader sense to reflect user-based studies that have a variety of different goals.

Our aim is to present several issues with AR system evaluation, and so provide researchers with a resource to help them plan and design their evaluations. In this chapter, first the role of evaluation will be described, including a review of work on user and non-user based evaluation in HCI research, and in particular for AR. Then common evaluation techniques that have been used in AR research are examined. We close with a discussion of the issues raised in this chapter.

2   The Role of Usability Testing and User Evaluations

User evaluations are commonly called 'Usability tests'. However, this term can create some confusion. According to Nielsen, usability is associated with five attributes: *Learnability, Efficiency, Memorability, Errors,* and *Satisfaction,* and usability testing involves defining a representative set of tasks against which these attributes can be measured [5]. "Usability testing is an approach that emphasizes the property of being usable [...]" [6], therefore not every evaluation of an AR application is necessarily a usability test.

For example, user evaluations can be used to compare a new interaction technique with regards to user efficiency or accuracy, study user behavior and interaction with a new prototype, or study how a new system supports collaboration, etc. Thus there are many different aims that may be pursued: Is the goal to test the 'usability' of a prototype, to compare how the new technique performs compared to a benchmark system, or to check whether performance with a new interaction technique can be predicted or explained by certain concepts (e.g. Fitt's Law [7])? Usability might not always be the main reason for conducting a user evaluation.

Different evaluation techniques are used at various points in the development cycle. Techniques that are mostly employed in the early stages, such as the think aloud method or heuristic evaluation, are generally concerned with the systems' usability. However, a test conducted after the prototype has been finished is not necessarily a usability test, and may be a verification test instead [8]. Using methods developed for usability testing does not mean that one is performing a usability test. Therefore it is essential to clarify the purpose of an evaluation study.

Small informal tests can be a very valuable way to quickly uncover usability and design problems [9]. They allow for rapid iterative design input and help to ensure that the development is on track. However, they do not provide reliable results that can be generalized. We are mainly interested in finding generalizable results that can answer research questions. Uncovering usability problems of an AR prototype can be one part of a research project but generally is not the final research goal.

Greenberg and Buxton argue that evaluation can be harmful or ineffective if done naively by rule rather than by thought [10]. Academia and end-user testing often have different goals and hence validating a scientific prototype does not necessarily tell us how it is going to be used in everyday life. They also stress that the choice of evaluation method must arise from an actual problem or a research question. The inappropriate application of user evaluation can give meaningless or trivial results, destroy valuable concepts early in the design process, promote poor ideas, or give wrong feedback about how designs will be adapted by end-users.

Thus, evaluating new designs with users can be a very powerful tool in the research process but it should only be done if it employed correctly. User studies can only add value if they are rigorously designed, carried out, and analyzed, and if they help to answer a meaningful research question.

3 AR System Evaluation

There are several challenges for researchers trying to evaluate AR user interfaces. Research on AR systems is still relatively young so there is limited experience with a variety of evaluation design factors. We will discuss some of these challenges including difficulties in applying existing evaluation guidelines, a lack of knowledge about end-users, and the huge variety of software and hardware implementations.

3.1 Applying Traditional Evaluation Approaches

Many authors agree that researchers in emerging interface fields such as Virtual Reality (VR) or AR cannot rely solely on design guidelines for traditional user interfaces [2, 11–14]. New interfaces afford interaction techniques that are often very different from standard WIMP (window, icon, menu, pointing device) based interfaces, but most available guidelines were specifically developed for WIMP interfaces. Sutcliffe and Kaur [15] argue that although traditional usability evaluation methods may be able to uncover some problems with novel interfaces none of the current methods really fit the specific needs of such interfaces.

Stanney and colleagues [14] list limitations of traditional usability methods for assessing virtual environments:

- Traditional point and click interactions vs. multidimensional object selection and manipulation in 3D space
- Multimodal system output (visual, auditory, haptic) is not comprehensively addressed by traditional methods
- Assessing presence and after-effects not covered by traditional methods
- Traditional performance measures (time, accuracy) do not always comprehensively characterize VE system interaction
- Lack of methods to assess collaboration in the same environment

Such limitations apply to AR interfaces as well because they share many characteristics with virtual environments. WIMP inspired heuristics do not always fit the design needs of AR systems. For example Nielsen's well known usability heuristics [16] do not cover issues relating to locating, selecting and manipulating objects in 3D space. Similarly, input and output modalities can be radically different for AR interfaces, requiring different evaluation approaches.

3.2   One off Prototypes

Developing a general evaluation framework for AR systems can be rather challenging. Although we have made great progress in AR research many of the developed systems are one-off prototypes. Researchers often design and create a prototype as a proof of concept, test it, and then move on to the next problem. This leaves us with a collection of interesting ideas and artifacts that generally do not share many common aspects. This complicates the development of common design and evaluation guidelines.

In contrast, WIMP interfaces share many characteristics and therefore have design features in common. These interfaces more established and new developments more likely feature incremental changes rather than radical ones [17].

3.3   Who are the Users?

With many technological developments the key question is who are the end users and what are their needs [18]. This is especially true when products are developed for the consumer market. Until recently there have been very few AR-based consumer products. This changed recently when different mobile and desktop AR applications were brought to market, but few of these have been formally evaluated with users.

If developments are technology driven rather than user-need driven it is not clear who will actually use the AR application. We are therefore often presented with a solution which solves no real problem. If we do not have a clear idea about who the end users will be we do not know with whom we should evaluate the system in order to get representative results. This raises the question about whether a system evaluation would be meaningful in the first place. If it is not obvious how and by whom the system will be used, it is rather difficult to design a meaningful system and evaluation plan. The users may be novices, experts, casual users, frequent users, children, adults, elderly, and so on. All these characteristics affect the ways in which interaction is designed [6].

3.4   Huge Variety of Implementations

Compared to WIMP interfaces that share basic common properties, AR interfaces can be much more diverse. Although we can follow certain definitions, such as Azuma's [19], to determine what constitutes an AR system, this still leaves us with many different types of systems. The digital augmentation can include different senses (sight, hearing, touch, etc.), be realized with an array of different types of input and output hardware (mobile, Head Mounted Display (HMD), desktop, etc.), and allow for a variety of interaction techniques. This makes it challenging to define a common and comprehensive set of evaluation techniques.

One solution could be to create a framework for AR systems as a basis for the development of design and evaluation guidelines. The challenge will be to find an acceptable abstraction level that is necessary to create such a comprehensive framework that would still allow creating practical guidelines.

Another solution would be to narrow down the field of interest to an extent that it permits the definition of common guidelines. For example, creating guidelines for mobile phone AR systems. This would lead to different sets of guidelines for different kinds of AR systems that will share certain characteristics.

4   Expert and Guideline Based Evaluations

In the research literature we can find various classifications of usability evaluation techniques e.g. by Bowman et al. [11]. For simplicity in this chapter we separate evaluation approaches into two rather broad categories; evaluation techniques that do not involve users, and those that do involve users. In this section methods are discussed that do not require users.

Heuristic evaluation is a usability testing method in which experts are asked to comment on and evaluate an interface using a set of design guidelines and principles [16]. After familiarizing themselves with the system the evaluators carry out certain tasks and note the interface problems they found. A limited set of heuristics is then used to interpret and classify these problems [13].

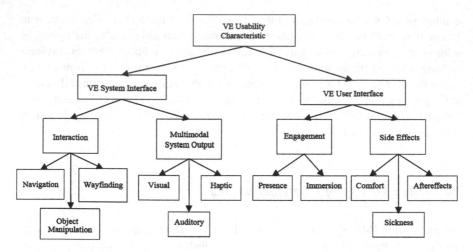

Fig. 13.1 Usability criteria assessed by MAUVE [14]

Some attempts have been made to develop guidelines and heuristics for the evaluation of VE [13,14,20]. These research efforts generally produce very long lists of heuristics that have been extracted from research literature. This reflects some of the problems discussed above. The huge variety of implementation possibilities (hard-/software, interaction devices, etc.) leads to a huge number of guidelines.

Sutcliffe and Gault [13] give a very concise list of 12 heuristics. They include a technology audit stage before the evaluation in order to filter the heuristics and make sure that only relevant ones are applied. They found that some evaluators had difficulty in interpreting some heuristics. To overcome this, the authors suggest giving good and bad examples for each item to better illustrate the heuristics. Some of these heuristics can be applied to AR systems with slight adaptations. 'Natural engagement', 'Compatibility with the user's task and domain', 'Realistic feedback', 'Support for learning', 'Clear turn-taking', and 'Consistent departures' are mostly applicable to AR environments as well. Others heuristics such as 'Natural expression of action', 'Close coordination of action and representation', 'Faithful viewpoints', 'Navigation and orientation support', 'Clear entry and exit points', and 'Sense of presence' might be less applicable for AR because they are mainly concerned with the users' representation or navigation in the VE.

Stanney et al. [14] have created a computerized system to assist in the evaluation of virtual environments. MAUVE (Multi-criteria Assessment of Usability for Virtual Environments) aims at structuring the evaluation process and to help managing the huge amount of guidelines that aid in the VE assessment (the author's list four pages of design considerations/guidelines). The system is based on a hierarchical framework illustrated in Fig. 13.1.

Sutcliffe and Kaur [20] present a walkthrough method for VE user interfaces. This is sensible because it limits the implementation options and therefore the amount of potential guidelines. It also makes the task of defining an interaction framework and creating a concise list of appropriate guidelines more manageable. They specify models of interaction as a basis for the guidelines based on goal-oriented task action, exploration and navigation in VE, and interaction in response to system initiatives. The authors acknowledge that walkthroughs may be more efficient in finding usability problems rather than in helping finding design solutions. They also point out the problem of context and that some general design principles may be inapplicable in different contexts.

Some of these guidelines might be applicable to AR environments as well as guidelines on object selection and manipulation (e.g. Input devices should be easy to use; Object selection points should be obvious, and it should be easy to select multiple objects), multimodal output (e.g. Visual, auditory, and/or haptic should have high frame rate and low latency, and be seamlessly integrated into user activity), and side-effects (e.g. system should be comfortable for long-term use).

One of the few efforts to define design and evaluation guidelines for AR systems was presented by Gabbard (2001). His approach was to collect and synthesize information from many different sources including AR specific research and more general VE based research. The result of this research is an extensive list of 69 statements or guidelines, in several categories, including:

- VE Users and User tasks

    - VE Users (e.g. "Support users with varying degrees of domain knowledge.")
    - VE user tasks (e.g. "Design interaction mechanisms and methods to support user performance of serial tasks and tasks sequences.")
    - Navigation and Locomotion (e.g. "Support appropriate types of user navigation, facilitate user acquisition of survey knowledge.")
    - Object selection (e.g. "Strive for body-centered interaction. Support multimodal interaction.")
    - Object manipulation (e.g. "Support two-handed interaction (especially for manipulation-based tasks).")

- The Virtual Model

    - User Representation and Presentation (e.g. "For AR-based social environments (e.g., games), allow users to create, present, and customize private and group-wide information.")
    - VE Agent Representation and Presentation (e.g. "Include agents that are relevant to user tasks and goals.")
    - Virtual Surrounding and Setting (e.g. "When possible, determine occlusion, dynamically, in real-time (i.e., at every graphics frame).")
    - VE System and Application Information (e.g. "Strive to maintain interface consistency across applications".)

- VE User Interface Input Mechanisms

    - Tracking User Location and Orientation (e.g. "Consider using a Kalman Filter in head tracking data to smooth the motion and decrease lag.")

- Data Gloves and Gesture Recognition (e.g. "Avoid gesture in abstract 3D spaces; instead use relative gesturing.")
- Speech Recognition and Natural Language (e.g. "Allow users to edit, remove, and extract or save annotations.")

• VE User Interface Presentation Components

- Visual Feedback – Graphical Presentation (e.g. "Timing and responsiveness of an AR system are crucial elements (e.g., effect user performance).")

Most of the guidelines listed in Gabbard's work were taken from papers on VE systems and are not necessarily specific to AR systems (such as guidelines on navigation). This again illustrates the challenge of creating a succinct list of AR design guidelines that is easy to apply by practitioners and researchers.

Generally heuristics do not seem to be used very often to evaluate AR systems. Apart from the limited practicality of using extensive lists of heuristics and the limited numbers of experts to do such evaluations, guideline based evaluation is more of a usability evaluation tool rather than a research tool. By using these techniques experts might uncover usability problems with a system, but this hardly permits researchers to answer major research questions. From a research perspective these heuristics might be useful in informing prototype design. Following design guidelines can help reduce time for prototype development and develop more stable systems for user testing. On the other hand, as a testing tool they are more important for industry rather than for researchers. If the goal is to develop an easy to use system for end-users, expert and guideline-based evaluation can be very valuable tools. One of the few AR studies that employed expert based heuristic evaluation was reported by Hix et al. [21] and is discussed in Sect. 5.2.

5 User Based Evaluation

Fjeld [18] argues that researchers still have to find appropriate ways to measure effectiveness and efficiency in AR applications and to define what kind of tasks and with what kind of tools the usability of AR systems can be tested.

Evaluation approaches used in traditional HCI are often applied to AR research, but evaluating AR systems with users sometimes requires slightly different approaches than evaluating traditional GUI based systems. Some issues of evaluating novel user interfaces are discussed by Bowman et al. [11], such as the physical environment in which the interface is used (including interaction issues), evaluator issues (and how they deal with the complexities of VEs), and user issues. For example most users of new systems will be novices because only a few people (e.g. the developers) can be considered as experts. This may produce high variability in the obtained results and therefore require a high number of study participants.

The design space for novel interfaces is generally very large and often more than two competing solutions have to be compared. This requires more complicated study and analysis designs that again call for higher participant numbers. Furthermore, many effects related to simulated environments such as presence or simulator sickness require new methods not considered by GUI evaluation techniques.

Evaluating AR interfaces frequently focuses on somewhat different issues than traditional GUI/WIMP evaluation. With AR systems, increasing the user's effectiveness and efficiency are not always the primary goals. Many WIMP based systems are designed to support users in accomplishing specific tasks effectively (e.g. office work, word processing etc.). While some AR systems pursue similar goals (e.g. AR systems for engineering), most seem to focus more on providing a novel user experience that require different evaluation techniques [22–24].

5.1   AR Evaluation Types and Methods

In previous work [4] we summarized the different evaluation techniques that have been applied in AR user studies. We reviewed evaluation types based on typical tasks that are performed in AR applications and analyzed the evaluation techniques that have been used. In the rest of this section we present these categories and discuss them with examples taken from scientific literature.

5.1.1   Evaluation Types Typically used in AR User Evaluations

Based on work conducted by Swan and Gabbard [3] and from our own survey [4] most AR user evaluations fit into one of four categories:

1. Experiments that study human perception and cognition.
2. Experiments that examine user task performance.
3. Experiments that examine collaboration between users.
4. System usability, system design evaluation.

5.1.2   Evaluation Methods Typically Used in AR User Evaluations

A rough distinction can be made between quantitative methods, qualitative methods, non-user based usability evaluation methods, and informal methods.

1. **Objective measurements**
   These should produce a reliable and repeatable assignment of numbers to quantitative observations. They can be taken automatically or by an experimenter. Typical measures include times (e.g. task completion times), accuracy (e.g. error rates), user or object position, or test scores, etc.
2. **Subjective measurements**
   These rely on the subjective judgment of people and include questionnaires, ratings, rankings, or judgments (e.g. depth judgment).

3. **Qualitative analysis**
   Qualitative analysis is not concerned with putting results in numbers. Data is gathered through structured observations (direct observation, video analysis) or interviews (structured, unstructured).
4. **Non User-Based Usability evaluation techniques**
   This includes non user-based evaluations techniques such as cognitive walk-throughs or heuristic evaluations as well as techniques that involve people who are not end-users (e.g. expert-based usability evaluations).
5. **Informal testing**
   Many published AR papers only report on informal user observations or feedback (e.g. gathered during demonstrations). It is surprising that reporting such limited findings still seems to be very common and accepted in AR contexts. By contrast, in CHI publications informal evaluation has almost disappeared [25].

5.2   Example AR System Evaluations

The following papers provide examples of the different evaluation methods. Studies with more than one evaluation type or method are grouped according to the main focus.

Type: (1) perception; method: (1) objective measurements Gabbard and Swan [26] studied how users perceive text in outdoor AR settings. They tested several hypotheses, such as seeing text on a brick background will result in slower task performance because it is the most visually complex. They tested 24 volunteers who had to identify a pair of letters in a random arrangement (see Fig. 13.2). Independent variables included background texture, text color, drawing style, and drawing algorithm. Dependent variables were response time and error. Results showed that the participants made the least errors with a solid building background and most with a brick background. No main effects of text color were found but the participants were slower with billboard style text.

Type: (1) perception; method: (2) subjective measurements Knörlein et al. [27] investigated the effect of visual and haptic delays on the perception of stiffness in an AR system. Fourteen participants were asked to compress and compare two virtual springs in a visuo-haptic environment and to select the one which they perceived as stiffer (Fig. 13.3).

The metrics used in this study were 'Point of Subjective Equality' and 'Just Noticeable Difference' of the stiffness of the two springs. Results showed that delays for haptic feedback decreased perceived stiffness whereas visual delays increased perceived stiffness. When visual and haptic delays were combined the effects leveled each other out.

Type: (2) user performance; method: (1) objective measurements The goal of Dünser et al. [28] was to evaluate if spatial ability could be improved through

Fig. 13.2 Experimental task used by Gabbard and Swan [26]: participants were asked to identify the pair of identical letters in the upper block ("Vv")

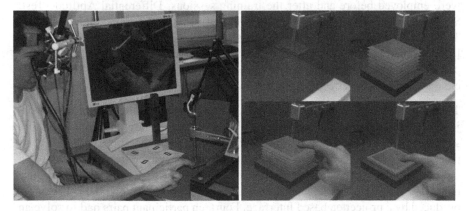

Fig. 13.3 Study setup used by Knörlein et al. [27] to test effects of visual and haptic feedback on perception in an AR system

training with an AR-based geometry education application. The system allows students to collaboratively construct geometry problems in 3D space. The interface consists of optical see-through HMDs and position tracked pens and tablets that allow direct manipulation of the virtual content (see Fig. 13.4).

The study participants were 215 high school students, split into four groups; AR training, traditional computer-based training, control group with geometry classes and control group without geometry classes. Students in the two training groups completed six training sessions in which they worked on a set of geometry tasks.

Fig. 13.4 The Construct3D system, an AR geometry education application [28, 29]

To determine training effects, four tests measuring different aspects of spatial ability were employed before and after the training sessions: Differential Aptitude Test: Space Relations (DAT:SR) [30] (paper folding task; visualization), Mental Cutting Test (MCT) [31]) (object cutting; visualization), Mental Rotation Test (MRT) [32] (speeded mental rotation), Objective Perspective Test (OPT) [33] (change of perspective; orientation). The results showed various gender specific effects but no clear evidence of the effectiveness of AR-based training.

Type: (3) user collaboration; method: (1) objective measurements (and subjective measurement) Billinghurst et. al. [34] evaluated how different interfaces support collaboration. They compared face-to-face collaboration with AR, and projection displays. They were interested how user collaboration differs between these setups. They hypothesized that collaboration with AR technology will produce behaviors that are more like natural face-to-face collaboration than those behaviors produced by a projection based interface. Fourteen participant pairs had to solve an urban design logic puzzle and arrange nine buildings to satisfy ten rules in seven minutes (Fig. 13.5).

A variety of different experimental measures were used; video was captured and transcribed to analyze various communication measures, including the number of gestures, average number of words per phrase, and number turns in the conversation. Although the analysis was based on observation and video analysis, the main focus was on gathering quantities (i.e. numbers of gestures and utterances). Further measures were task completion time and questionnaires.

They found that performance with AR supported collaboration was slower than in the face-to-face and projection conditions. However, pointing and picking gesture behaviors as well as deictic speech patterns were found to be the same in AR and face-to-face and significantly different than in the projection condition.

Fig. 13.5 AR (*left*) and Projection (*right*) conditions used by Billinghurst et al. [34] to study user collaboration

Questionnaire results indicated that users felt that it was easier to work together in the face-to-face condition. Interaction was found to be similar in AR and face-to-face cases, and much easier than in the projection condition.

Type: (2) User interaction (and collaboration); method: (3) qualitative analysis (and subjective measures) Morrison et al. [23] conducted a qualitative analysis of user behavior and complemented this with questionnaire data. They studied user interaction and collaboration using a location-based mobile game. Twenty six participants (in pairs or teams of three) used a mobile AR interface with a paper map, while eleven participants used a traditional 2D mobile phone based map. The application was an environmental awareness game in which the participants had to solve several tasks according to some clues. Researchers followed the participants during the game and took notes, videos, and photographs which were later qualitatively analyzed. This data was complemented with data gathered through an interview as well as presence, flow, and intrinsic motivation questionnaires. The study found that the AR-based system supports collaboration, negotiating, and establishing common ground but was more cumbersome to use. With the 2D mobile phone map the participants completed the game quicker and showed less focus on the interface itself (Fig. 13.6).

Type: (4) system usability, system design evaluation; method: (3) qualitative analysis Nielsson and Johansson [35] investigated how participants experience instructions given by an AR system in a medical environment. They conducted two qualitative user studies to investigate user experience and acceptance of an instructional AR system. This was tested with eight (first study) and twelve (second study) participants respectively. The system included a HMD setup, marker tracking, and a keyboard or microphone and voice recognition for simple command input.

In the experiment, the participants received AR-based instructions on how to activate and prepare medical equipment for surgery. After this they had to assemble a common medical device. The analysis was based on observations and a questionnaire. The questionnaire had an open answer format and questions on

Fig. 13.6 Still shots form experimenter/observer camera taken during Morrison et al.'s [23] user trials

overall impression of the AR system, experienced difficulties, experienced positive aspects, what they would change in the system and whether it was possible to compare receiving AR instructions to receiving instructions from a teacher.

Results showed that the participants were able to complete tasks without assistance but they wished for more interactivity. The instructions and the AR presentation of instructions were rated positively by most users. The study also uncovered several ergonomic issues such as distraction because of marker visibility (Fig. 13.7).

Type: (4) system usability, system design evaluation; method: (4) usability evaluation techniques (and other methods) Finally, Hix et al. [21] provide a nice example of how AR systems can be evaluated with a complete set of usability evaluation techniques. They discuss a model for a cost-effective usability evaluation progression, depicted in Fig. 13.8.

Their paper demonstrates the practical application of this model by describing the interface design and usability evaluation of an outdoor AR system that supports information presentation and entry for situation awareness in an urban war fighting setting. They started with a domain and requirement analysis, followed by six cycles of expert evaluations in which approximately 100 mockups were designed. In a user-based evaluation perceptual issues such as line drawing style and opacity

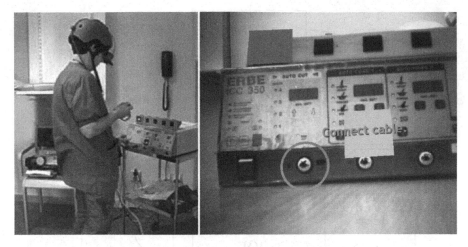

Fig. 13.7 Study setup (*left*) and user view (*right*) of Nielsson and Johansson's instructional AR system [35]

levels were studied. Eight participants had to indicate the location of a target as it moved among different buildings. Task completion time and error rates were analyzed statistically. In the following step the authors conducted what they call a formative usability evaluation. For this they created a formal set of representative tasks which five expert users had to perform. The participants had to find specific task relevant information in the outdoor environment. Analysis was qualitative and focused on system usability issues. The authors did not conduct a summative usability evaluation so there is no available information on this last planned step.

6   Discussion and Conclusion

Many researchers agree that formal evaluation of AR interfaces is an important step in the research process. However many open questions remain. There is no agreement on which are the most appropriate evaluation methods for AR systems, and trying to find 'the best' method(s) might not be a very promising approach. The most suitable evaluation approach always depends on the questions posed.

This chapter gives an overview of the most commonly used evaluation approaches used in AR research literature. First we discussed how non user-based approaches such as heuristic evaluation have not been used very often in AR research. Several challenges complicate the process of defining a comprehensive list of heuristics and guidelines for designing and evaluating AR systems. Initial attempts have been made to derive such guidelines for VE systems. For AR systems there are even fewer available practical heuristic guidelines. The question is whether it is possible to develop a general set of guidelines that are applicable to a broad

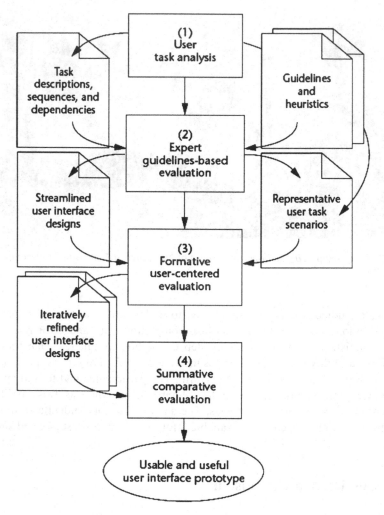

Fig. 13.8 Evaluation methodology for VE user interaction [26]

variety of systems. Some general heuristics can serve as a starting point, but this approach might be limiting because it will only apply to high level design issues.

Evaluations based on measuring user task performance are the most popular in AR evaluations [4]. It is not clear if this is due to a lack of more appropriate methods or if improving user task performance really is the most important research question. As argued in this paper, issues relating to user experience can be very important for many AR systems. However, there are hardly any suitable methods for measuring user experience. If user experience is of interest researchers most generally use qualitative evaluation approaches, but there are still few AR studies using these. In future we should continue exploring a variety of different methods to add to the set of evaluation methods suitable for AR specific research.

Many AR environments afford various interaction possibilities that are to a lesser extend supported by traditional computer interfaces and therefore have gained less attention in these contexts. So researchers have to search in other disciplines for appropriate methods. One example is studying interaction between users. AR interfaces offer different possibilities for collaboration but very few studies aiming at evaluating collaboration in AR environments have been published. Suitable evaluation methods for studying collaboration can be found in fields such as Computer Supported Collaborative Work.

Whether the goal of an AR system evaluation is to find usability problems or to answer a specific research question we will have to adapt current approaches to better fit the specific requirements of AR-based interfaces. In order to derive meaningful heuristics and guidelines we cannot resort to just collecting various guidelines from other scientific publications or through our own experiments. Such guidelines can only be sensibly applied if specific contexts are considered. Therefore we have to begin with setting guidelines in context through developing specific frameworks and models for AR systems and AR interaction techniques. At this stage it is not entirely obvious whether it will be possible to have a single framework that encompass all kinds of AR systems or if there have to be separate, more context specific frameworks. These models would also help to better understand how and where to use the other evaluation methods and how we have to adapt these to be more suitable for testing AR systems.

References

1. I. Sutherland, "A Head-Mounted Three-Dimensional Display," presented at the Fall Joint Computer Conf., Am. Federation of Information Processing Soc. (AFIPS), Washington, D.C., USA, 1968.
2. A. Dünser, R. Grasset, H. Seichter, and M. Billinghurst, "Applying HCI principles to AR systems design," Charlotte, NC, USA, 2007.
3. J. E. Swan and J. L. Gabbard, "Survey of User-Based Experimentation in Augmented Reality," presented at the 1st International Conference on Virtual Reality, HCI International 2005, Las Vegas, USA, 2005.
4. A. Dünser, R. Grasset, and M. Billinghurst, "A survey of evaluation techniques used in augmented reality studies," presented at the ACM SIGGRAPH ASIA 2008 courses, Singapore, 2008.
5. J. Nielsen, Usability Engineering. San Francisco: Morgan Kaufmann, 1993.
6. H. Sharp, Y. Rogers, and J. Preece, Interaction Design: Beyond Human-Computer Interaction: Wiley, 2007.
7. P. M. Fitts, "The information capacity of the human motor system in controlling the amplitude of movement," Journal of Experimental Psychology, vol. 47, pp. 381–391, 1954.
8. R. S. Dicks, "Mis-usability: on the uses and misuses of usability testing," presented at the Proceedings of the 20th annual international conference on Computer documentation, Toronto, Ontario, Canada, 2002.
9. J. Nielsen, Designing Web Usability. Indianapolis, IN, USA: New Rivers, 2000.
10. S. Greenberg and B. Buxton, "Usability evaluation considered harmful (some of the time)," CHI '08: Proceeding of the twenty-sixth annual SIGCHI conference on Human factors in computing systems, 2008.

11. D. A. Bowman, J. L. Gabbard, and D. Hix, "A Survey of Usability Evaluation in Virtual Environments: Classification and Comparison of Methods," Presence – Teleoperators and Virtual Environments, vol. 11, pp. 404–424, 2002.
12. C. Bach and D. L. Scapin, "Adaptation of Ergonomic Criteria to Human-Virtual Environments Interactions," presented at the INTERACT 2003.
13. A. Sutcliffe and B. Gault, "Heuristic evaluation of virtual reality applications," Interacting with Computers, vol. 16, pp. 831–849, 2004.
14. K. M. Stanney, M. Mollaghasemi, L. Reeves, R. Breaux, and D. A. Graeber, "Usability engineering of virtual environments (VEs): identifying multiple criteria that drive effective VE system design," Int. J. Hum.-Comput. Stud., vol. 58, pp. 447–481, 2003.
15. A. Sutcliffe and K. Kaur, "Evaluating the usability of virtual reality user interfaces," Behaviour and Information Technology, vol. 19, 2001.
16. J. Nielsen and R. Molich, "Heuristic evaluation of user interfaces," presented at the Proceedings of the SIGCHI conference on Human factors in computing systems: Empowering people, Seattle, Washington, United States, 1990.
17. W. Newman, "A Preliminary Analysis of the Products of HCI Research, Using Pro Forma Abstracts," presented at the CHI, Boston, MA, 1994.
18. M. Fjeld, "Introduction: Augmented Reality-Usability and Collaborative Aspects," International Journal of Human-Computer Interaction, vol. 16, p. 387–393, 2003.
19. R. T. Azuma, "A Survey of Augmented Reality," Presence – Teleoperators and Virtual Environments, vol. 6, pp. 355–385, 1997.
20. A. Sutcliffe and K. Kaur, "Evaluating the usability of virtual reality user interfaces," Behaviour and Information Technology, vol. 19, 2000.
21. D. Hix, J. L. Gabbard, J. E. S. II, M. A. Livingston, T. H. Höllerer, S. J. Julier, Y. Baillot, and D. Brown, "A Cost-Effective Usability Evaluation Progression for Novel Interactive Systems," presented at the Proceedings of the Proceedings of the 37th Annual Hawaii International Conference on System Sciences (HICSS'04) - Track 9 - Volume 9, 2004.
22. S. W. Gilroy, M. Cavazza, and M. Benayoun, "Using affective trajectories to describe states of flow in interactive art," presented at the Proceedings of the International Conference on Advances in Computer Enterntainment Technology, Athens, Greece, 2009.
23. A. Morrison, A. Oulasvirta, P. Peltonen, S. Lemmela, G. Jacucci, G. Reitmayr, J. Näsänen, and A. Juustila, "Like bees around the hive: a comparative study of a mobile augmented reality map," presented at the Proceedings of the 27th international conference on Human factors in computing systems, Boston, MA, USA, 2009.
24. E. Hughes, E. Smith, C. B. Stapleton, and D. E. Hughes, "Augmenting Museum Experiences with Mixed Reality," presented at the Knowledge Sharing and Collaborative Engineering, St. Thomas, US Virgin Islands, 2004.
25. L. Barkhuus and J. A. Rode, "From Mice to Men – 24 years of Evaluation in CHI," presented at the CHI, San Jose, USA, 2007.
26. J. L. Gabbard and J. E. Swan, "Usability Engineering for Augmented Reality: Employing User-Based Studies to Inform Design," IEEE Transactions on Visualization and Computer Graphics, vol. 14, pp. 513–525, 2008.
27. B. Knörlein, M. D. Luca, and M. Harders, "Influence of visual and haptic delays on stiffness perception in augmented reality," presented at the Proceedings of the 2009 8th IEEE International Symposium on Mixed and Augmented Reality, 2009.
28. A. Dünser, K. Steinbügl, H. Kaufmann, and J. Glück, "Virtual and augmented reality as spatial ability training tools," presented at the Proceedings of the 7th ACM SIGCHI New Zealand chapter's international conference on Computer-human interaction: design centered HCI, Christchurch, New Zealand, 2006.
29. H. Kaufmann, K. Steinbügl, A. Dünser, and J. Glück, "General Training of Spatial Abilities by Geometry Education in Augmented Reality," Annual Review of CyberTherapy and Telemedicine: A Decade of VR, vol. 3, pp. 65–76, 2005.
30. CEEB College Entrance Examination Board, Special Aptitude Test in Spatial Relations MCT: CEEB, 1939.

31. G. K. Bennett, H. G. Seashore, and A. G. Wesman, Differential Aptitude Tests, Forms S and T. New York: The Psychological Corporation, 1973.
32. M. Peters, B. Laeng, K. Latham, M. Jackson, R. Zaiyouna, and C. Richardson, "A redrawn Vandenberg and Kuse mental rotations test: Different versions and factors that affect performance," Brain and Cognition, vol. 28, pp. 39–58, 1995.
33. M. Hegarty and D. Waller, "A dissociation between mental rotation and perspective-taking spatial abilities," Intelligence, vol. 32, pp. 175–191, 2004.
34. M. Billinghurst, H. Kato, K. Kiyokawa, D. Belcher, and I. Poupyrev, "Experiments with Face-To-Face Collaborative AR Interfaces," Virtual Reality, vol. 6, pp. 107–121, 2002.
35. S. Nilsson and B. Johansson, "Acceptance of augmented reality instructions in a real work setting," presented at the CHI '08 extended abstracts on Human factors in computing systems, Florence, Italy, 2008.

Chapter 14
Situated Simulations Between Virtual Reality and Mobile Augmented Reality: Designing a Narrative Space

Gunnar Liestøl

1 Belonging

Theory, terminology and reality often interact in complex and complicated relationships, particularly in disciplines where the material base is evolving rapidly, such as in ICT-related domains. As a consequence, the nomenclature of research in digital design and development is often confusing and contested – the field of Augmented Reality is no exception. This is confirmed by an recent episode from everyday life of Academia.

In the context of a well known conference series on Augmented Reality, the author of this chapter received a rather unexpected comment, stating that the type of mobile Augmented Reality application we have been experimenting with – which we call *situated simulations* – is in fact: "... a mobile VR application (or a mobile MR application at the most), but definitely not AR according to Ron Azumas definition." The utterance was surprising. The project in question has been reported at numerous conference over the last couple of years, but never received any comments questioning its affiliation with the domain of mobile augmented reality.

The question of what should be recognized as inside or outside the field of augmented reality had not been given much attention in our research – until now! For the last five years we had basically followed some key interests and ideas, and tried to explore and solve the potential and problems as we encountered them. 'Augmented Reality' had always been the obvious candidate for a research tradition it made sense to identify with. The comment, however, made us curious and interested in AR definitions as such, and in how our own experiments with 'situated simulations' (sitsims) could in fact be positioned in the context of Augmented and Mixed Reality research and development. A more thorough reflection upon the

G. Liestøl (✉)
Department of Media & Communication, University of Oslo, Norway
e-mail: gunnar.liestol@media.uio.no

B. Furht (ed.), *Handbook of Augmented Reality*, DOI 10.1007/978-1-4614-0064-6_14,   309
© Springer Science+Business Media, LLC 2011

relationship between sitsims and AR might well benefit our own understanding of what we are doing. Such a comparison is also closely related to the method we are practising.

Our experiments with situated simulations have an origin and background that are contrary to most other augmented reality systems. The purpose of our research has been to explore the rhetorical and narrative potential of emerging technological platforms. Rather than following a technological path, we are taking available, off–the–shelf hardware configurations – such as iOS and Android OS devices – as given platforms, and then employ the available software and multimodal assets in order to create innovative solutions at the level of textual expression. Thus, our perspective, in general, is positioned in and dominated by humanistic approaches to digital design and composition [1, 2]. More specifically, our inquiry is part of a practice that attempts to develop a method of design with focus on the potential types and patterns of digital texts. We have tentatively called this 'genre design'. A situated simulation is an eample of such a prototyped potential genre (see: www.inventioproject.no/sitsim).

In this chapter we take the opportunity to dicuss the pertinence of our work on situated simulations in relation to the traditon of augmented reality research and applications. Given our point of departure in the humanities and the question of where sitsims 'belongs', we will take a closer look at some of the most central definitions of augmented and mixed reality over recent decades, and see how they are suited to describe our explorations of situated simulations. At the same time, we would also like to allow some room to present one of the main motivations and purposes behind our research: the attempt to design new narrative spaces in order to generate new rhetorical experiences in the dissemination of knowledge and information linked to a specific space and place. Before we determine whether a situated simulation is AR or not, according to Azuma's taxonomy [3, 4], we need to have a closer look at the defining features and key qualities of sitsims [5, 6].

2 Elucidations

Technically, a situated simulation requires a mobile terminal (smartphone) with broadband networking, high resolution graphics display, and orientation/location capabilities. Semantically, a situated simulation exhibits a multimodal (audiovisual) dynamic 3D environment, which the user can observe, access and explore by moving and interacting with the terminal and the application's interface. The smartphone thus serves as a point of view – a virtual camera – which provides a continually changing perspective into the 3D graphics environment. When using a situated simulation there is then approximate identity between the user's visual perspective and perception of the real physical environment, *and* the user's perspective in(to) the virtual environment as this is audiovisually presented by means of the phone and sitsim's interface. The relative congruity between the 'real' and the 'virtual' is obtained by allowing the camera's position, movement and orientation in the 3D

Fig. 14.1 A situated simulation of Forum Iulium in Rome (see: www.inventioproject.no/sitsim)

environment, to be constrained by the orientation- and location technology of the smartphone: As the user moves the phone in real space the perspective inside the virtual space changes accordingly.

Given these qualities, situated simulations have proved suitable for representing, on a given location, an item or topic (knowledge and information), which is relevant to that specific place or site, but which is some way or another absent or not accessible to the user. These could either be objects that have ceased to exist, that are hidden or have not yet come into being. In our experimental implementations so far, we have primarily focused on the first mode, trying to design situated simulations that reconstruct, on location, historical objects, actions and events that once took place on a particular site. Figure 14.1 depicts an example of a situated simulation in use showing a reconstruction of Forum Iulium on location in Rome.

Azuma's definition of Augmented Reality is quite straight forward: "What is augmented reality? An AR system supplements the real world with virtual (computer-generated) objects that appear to coexist in the same space as the real world." [4] More specifically, his definition of AR is threefold: augmented reality

- combines real and virtual objects in a real environment;
- runs interactively, and in real time; and
- registers (aligns) real and virtual objects with each other

Immediately, it seems that our general description of sitsims above fits with Azuma's definition. (1) In a situated simulation the real and the virtual is combined in a real environment: the actual real environment is combined with the 3D reconstruction of historical objects and events in situ. (2) The sitsim application runs interactively in realtime: the perspective changes as the user moves, and he or she may access information and trigger activity inside the virtual environment with instant feedback. Also, (3) the real and the virtual are aligned with each other: the user's perspective in the real world has approximate identity with the user's perspective into the virtual environment.

One may now interrupt and counter this reasoning by arguing that in augmented reality the real environment is registered by means of certain technologies of tracking: using a digital camera and software for pattern recognition of fiducial markers etc. It thus involves much more advanced computations than the typical location and orientation technologies one finds in current off–the–shelf smartphones. To this objection one may add that in Azuma's discussion it is explicitly stressed that definitions of augmented reality should be general and not limited to particular hardware technologies [3, 4]. Other definitions also seem to support the possibility that situated simulations may be considered a form of augmented reality. Feiner [7] defines augmented reality as follows: "Augmented reality refers to computer displays that add virtual information to a user's sensory perception." There can be little doubt that this general description also is fully consistent with our depiction of situated simulations, despite the fact that it too was conceived long before current smartphones became available.

3   Sitsims as Augmented Reality: *The Temple of Divus Iulius*

Since the launch of the second generation iPhone in 2008 we have implemented and testet six situated simulations with historical topics on location in Norway (Oseberg Viking Ship), San Franscico (Mission Dolores & Earthquake 1906), Athens (The Parthenon) and Rome (Forum Iulium & Temple of Divus Iulius). The latter was evaluated by students of classics at The Norwegian Institute in Rome, first in May 2010, and then a new version in February 2011. The new version of *Temple of Divus Iulius* runs on iOS 4 and the students tested and evaluated it using both the iPhone4 and iPad on location in the Roman Forum. In the following we will take a closer look at this situated simulation by describing its features in accordance with Azuma's three defining criteria of augmented reality [3, 4].

3.1   Combining Virtual and Real in Real Environments

In a sitsim, the virtual environment is brought into the real environment, a specific space and place, and thus combined with it. Ideally, the real and the virtual occupy the same space, that is there is a congruity between the real and the virtual environment, movement and orientation in the one is mapped in the other. Thus the sitsim displays various interpretations of the surroundings in which the user is positioned. In the case of *Divus Iulius,* the site in question is the Republican Forum in Rome. As the user moves around the Forum he or she can

Fig. 14.2 Students in action with iPhone and iPad in the Roman Forum

observe – in parallell – the surroundings at various points in time, from 44 BC, just after the Ides of March and Julius Caesar's murder, to 29 BC, when Octavian consecrated the new Temple to the memory and sacred tribute of his deified grand uncle. As the user navigate this historic site and the various stages in time, the real and the virtual is combined in space by means of the position (GPS), orientation (magnetometer) and movement (accelerometer, gyroscope) of the device (Fig. 14.2).

3.2 Interaction in Real Time

In general (as described above) the sitsim responds in real time to vertical and horizontal movement as well as change of position. More specifically, the user may engage in real time interactions with the virtual environment by means of spatially positioned hypertext links. These links trigger various types of information: verbal audio narrations; written text; photographs; 3D objects of scanned artefacts for detail view, including rotation and scaling based on the touch interface; semi–transparency of larger objects for visual access to hidden inner spaces (rooms in buildings); flying virtual camera (for transcending the user's position in order to visit positions which are physically inaccessible, orientation remains relative to the user); access to external online resources via an internal web browser; in situ link–creation where the user may name, position and compose links and nodes, and add comments to each other's link postings; and switching between temporal episodes containing historical actions and events (Fig. 14.3).

3.3 Registration and Alignment in 3D

The criteria of registration is naturally primarily focused on mixed solution, but alignment is also a necessity in situated simulations where the virtual environment is displayed on a full screen, although it need not be as exact as in a mixed solution, since the comparison and matching is mediated by the user's perceptual

Fig. 14.3 Screenshots from a sitsim reconstructing the Roman Forum in various stages and situations: Temple of Julius Caesar (*left*), and Marc Anthony's Eulogy (*right*)

processes and actions. If the alignment slips, the opportunity to experience the real and the virtual as separate, but parallel, dimensions (interpretations) of the same space disappears, and the virtual environment becomes accidental and irrelevant. In a situated simulation one might say that the digital application and the virtual environment itself is only half of the experience. The real site and surroundings are a necessary context and environment for the system to function according to the design intentions. We strongly believe that it is in this combination of the virtual and the real, that is in their difference and similarity, that incremental information and added value is generated, for instance in the user's reflection upon the relationship (double description) between the reconstructed virtual past and the aura of the historic site in the real present.

4 Situated Simulations as a Narrative Space

One of the key motivations for our research and experiments with digital genre design and situated simulations is to explore the narrative and rhetorical potential of emerging digital platforms. Augmented reality and location–based media certainly present interesting challenges to experimentation with new modes of storytelling. Early experiments with wearable augmented reality suggested the notion of situated documentaries [8] placing multimodal documentation in real locations by means of see–through head–worn display to overlay 3D graphics, imagery and sound to augment the experience of the real world. Our attempts can be viewed as an extension of these endeavours.

Stories have always travelled across media, in prehistoric and ancient times, from orality to literacy. Later, the early 20th century saw rapid development and dissemination of electro–mechanical material markers for new combinations of audio-visual narrative forms, in media such as cinema and television. With digitalization of all the traditional textual types (writing, still images and moving images, and various forms of audio), the computer itself has contributed dynamic

3D environments as a genuinly new form of representation. It presents an integrated text type that has the fascinating feature of being able to include audio-visually and spatio-temporally *all* the traditional analogue text types, thus generating a complex and integrated form of representation with, in principle, enormous potential for expressivity and meaning making.

Just as the novel is the dominant fictional genre of literature and book technology, the feature film is the dominant form of cinema, and the series is the dominant fictional genre of television. When it comes to digital media, neither hypertext fiction nor interactive movies managed to achieve any popular success. In digital media, we may state that computer games are the dominant form of fiction, and today this is most signigicantly expressed in the advanced and innovative uses of the real time 3D environment. How computer games relate to fiction and storytelling has become an extensive and exhausting discussion, but one that we will not address here. In location-based media and mobile augmented reality, fiction and storytelling is still at the experimental level.

In our situated simulation *The Temple of Divus Iulius* we have included a situated documentary as an interpretation of some of the crucial events that led up to the construction of the Temple of the deified Julius Caesar. When the user is positioned in front of the temple near its special altar, as it may have looked in the year 29 BC, one is offered to perform a temporal ellipsis and shift back to the days following the Ides of March in 44 BC. After the temporal transition and by means of sound, the user's attention is directed towards the Northern side of the Forum where Marc Anthony is about to perform his Eulogy. The user may now approach the speaker's platform and witness (an interpretation of) this significant event in western history. Further, the user can observe the following incidents and changes on the site of the later temple.

As a temporal sequence, this narrative combination of actions and events has a traditional structure, combining one flashback with several flash forwards. This is a familiar structure in literary as well as filmic narratives, whether the mode or topic is factual or fictional. In our context the temporal loop is used to provide a significant narrative and informational context to a digitally reconstruction of an historical building. However, what is interesting here is not the fact that a mobile augmented reality application manages to convey a traditional and well-established narrative technique, usually called asynchronous storytelling [9], that was already in advanced use at the time of Homer's *Oddysey*. What is more unique with our simple experiment on the Forum is the fact that the movement in time (the flashback-flash forward loop) is performed and repeated in the *spatial* environment. As the user decides to move back in time, he or she is also triggered to move in space. In this story each point in time has its corresponding point (or position) in space. In this historical case, the effect is given by the circumstances as they are documented and basically follow from that fact. However, it is obvious that this *tempo-spatial parallelism* could also serve as an efficient design technique in the further exploration of mobile augmented reality narratives, whether fictive or factive in character.

The multilinear sequencing of links and nodes in hypertext fiction makes possible complex interrelationships between story level (story told) and discourse level (telling of story) in narratives [10]. In 3D-based computer games the gameplay predominantly takes place in a 'scenic' mode [9] where the time passing inside the game environment is identical with the time played. A situated simulation exploits the 3D modes of games, but the tempo–spatial parallelism and its double descriptions opens new possibilities. We are not limited to the narrative time of the simulation and its relationships to the user: The virtual environment is also *always* placed in a (real) context of present time and space.

5   So, Where do Situated Simulations Belong?

To answer this question we must now return to the definitions. One of the key aspects of a situated simulation, as mentioned, is not in accordance with most augmented reality systems and applications, although interesting exceptions exist [11]. A situated simulation does not mix the graphics of the virtual 3D environment with a live video feed from the phone's camera, thus creating a Mixed Reality solution at the level of the screen. This makes it difficult to position a situated simulation along Milgram's well known Virtual Continuum [12, 13].

In Milgran's diagram, Mixed Reality occupies the middle section of the continuum between Real only and Virtual only environments. Mixed reality is a gradual movement from augmented reality to augmented virtuality depending on which of the two mixed elements is dominant. In this taxonomy augmented reality is a sub category of mixed reality and there is no other option for combining the real and the virtual. So where does a situated simulation belong on this continuum? Or, as our reviewer suggested, does it belong at all?

By aligning a picture of a situated simulation in use with the graphical presentation of Milgram's Virtual Continuum it is easier to see how a situated simulation is related to the continuum (see Fig. 14.4).

The problem with Milgram's virtual continuum is that it is one-dimentional. In its given framing the combinations of real and virtual environments are only possible by means of some form of mixed reality, and the mixing may then only take place at the level of the display, whether it is a screen with a live video feed or a head–mounted display with a see–through solution. This rules out incidents that exploit current smartphones and their location and orientation technology, such as the situated simulations in question, where the real environment is combined and aligned with a virtual environment displayed on a full screen without any direct or integrated mixing. In the early 1990s when Milgram's Virtual Continuum was devised, today's smartphones were not even conceived. The current mobility of hardware features, twenty years ago merely utopian, now demands a revision or an extension of the continuum. The fact that neither Azuma's definitions nor Milgram's continuum account for this form of coupling or combining real and virtual environments does not mean that it is incompatible with the traditional

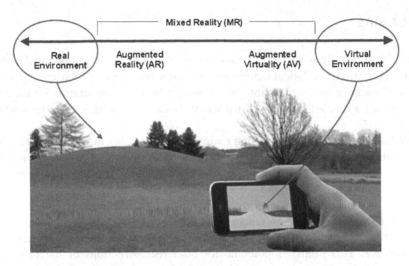

Fig. 14.4 Situated simulation as a combination of real and virtual outside the virtual continuum of mixed realities. The Oseberg Viking Ship burial mound

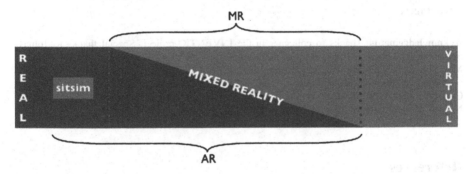

Fig. 14.5 Milgrams's Virtual Continuum revised to include situated simulations

definitions. As we have seen, Azuma's threefold criteria is fully adequate given some clarifiction and interpretation when describing a situated simulation.

Based on the discussion above, it is tempting to suggest a minor revision of Milgram's continuum in order to open up a space where we might position the kind of mobile augmented reality that a situated simulation represents. In this diagram we have substituted the linear continuum with a two-dimentional field. This makes it possible to distinguish between mixed reality and augmented reality and at the same time open up for a space for situated simulations, the variation of mobile augmented reality where the real and the virtual environment is combined independent of mixed reality (Fig. 14.5).

6 Closing

Situated simulations, as we have discussed them here, may not be augmented reality according to strictly technical definitions, particularly when one focuses on certain forms of tracking and registration, but there can be little question about the fact that by using a situated simulation on a specific location you are in fact *augmenting reality*.

AR has been focused on merging reality with additional information provided by graphical layers, which again match the depth, space and texture of reality. Reality is per se what is real. It is the present reality we are concerned with: and that reality which *is* real is the *present*. Consequently, augmented reality, which seeks to mix the real and the virtual in a combined, integrated spatial representation is based necessarily on the presence of the present. As long as augmented reality seeks the mixed reality solution it is always partly representing and anchored in the presence. This limits its potential for both reconstructions of the past, and preconstructions of future scenarios. In our work on situated simulations we have focused on simulating past and future versions of a specific space and place. This is where situated simulations as a variant of mobile augmented reality might have its advantages.

Acknowledgements Thanks to collegues in the INVENTIO-project. Special thanks to Tomas Stenarson for Unity- and Xcode programming and for collaboration on the design; to Andrew Morrison for discussions and copy editing the text; and to Terje Rasmussen for collaboration on the user evaluations. Thanks also to The VERDIKT-programme at the Norwegian Research Council; Department of Media & Communication and Intermedia, University of Oslo; and to Norway Opening Universities and ABM-utvikling.

References

1. A. Morrison (Ed.), *Inside Multimodal Composition*. Hampton Press 2010.
2. I. Wagner, T. Bratteteig, D. Stuedahl (Eds.) *Exploring Digital Design*. Springer Verlag 2010.
3. R. Azuma, "A Survey of Augmented Reality," in *Presence: Teleoperators and Virtual Environments*. vol. 6, no. 4, Aug. 1997, pp. 355–385.
4. R. Azuma, Y. Baillot, R. Behringer, S. Feiner, S. Julier, B. MacIntryre, 'Recent Advances in Augmented Reality' in *IEEE Computer Graphics and Applications*, vol. 21, no. 6, Nov./Dec. 2001, pp. 34–47.
5. G. Liestøl, 'Situated Simulations: A Prototyped Augmented Reality Genre for Learning on the iPhone' in *International Journal of Interactive Mobile Technologies* (iJIM), Vol. 3 (2009) – Open access, available at ⟨http://online-journals.org/i-jim/article/view/963⟩.
6. G. Liestøl, 'Learning through Situated Simulations: Exploring Mobile Augmented Reality.' (Research Bulletin 1, 2011). Boulder, CO: EDUCAUSE Center for Applied Research, 2011, available from ⟨http://www.educause.edu/ecar⟩.
7. S. Feiner, 'Augmented Reality: A New Way of Seeing' in *Scientific American Magazine*, April 2002.

8. T. Hollerer, S. Feiner, J. Pavlik, 'Situated documentaries: embeding multimedia presentations in the real world' in Digest of Papers. The Third International Symposium on Wearable Computers, San Francisco October 1999. Available at IEEE Xplore Digital Library.

9. G. Genette, *Narrative Discourse. An Essay in Method.* Cornell University Press 1990.

10. G. Liestøl, 'Wittgenstein, Genette and the Reader's Narrative in Hypertext' in G. P. Landow (Ed.) *Hyper/Text/Theory*, The Johns Hopkins University Press 1994, pp. 87–120.

11. H. Tarumi et al. (2008) 'Design and Evaluation of a Virtual Mobile Time Machine in Education' in ACM International Conference Proceeding Series; Vol. 352 *Proceedings of the 2008 International Conference on Advances in Computer Entertainment Technology*, Yokohama, Japan.

12. P. Milgram, H. Takemura, A. Utsumi, F. Kishino, 'Augmented Reality: A class of displays on the reality–virtuality continuum, ATR Communication Systems Research Laboratories, Kyoto, Japan 1994. Available at: ⟨http://scholar.google.no/scholar?start=10&q=milgram&hl=no&as_sdt=0,5⟩.

13. P. Milgram and F. Kishino, 'A Taxonomy of Mixed Reality Visual Displays', in IEICE Transactions on Information Systems, Vol E77-D, No. 12, December 1994.

Chapter 15
Referencing Patterns in Collaborative Augmented Reality

Jeff Chastine

1 Introduction

As application domains emerge, they often bring with them a variety of new interaction techniques. Augmented Reality (AR) is a technology that attempts to seamlessly integrate virtual artifacts into the physical world. Though many of the interaction challenges in AR parallel those found in purely virtual environments, the inclusion of the physical world forces us consider new scenarios. This chapter will discuss some of the user interface (UI) challenges in *collaborative* AR environments – or those with more than one participant. For these environments to be successful, it is critical that they support *referential awareness*. The reader may question *why* this is an important item to consider when designing such systems. After all, people collaborate fairly well in the physical world through gestures, such as pointing, and through deictic references (e.g. *"this one"* or *"those"*). One might therefore believe that re-integrating the physical world back into the digital one would make referencing easier. However, consider a multi-user environment that contains hundreds of artifacts that are similar in appearance – with participants geographically separated; one can see that things become complex quickly. Or, consider how one might reference virtual objects that are embedded within physical ones, such as during augmented surgery. References may be made at arbitrary depths, such as physically to the patient's skin or virtually to the volumetric data (e.g. a CAT scan) embedded within.

This chapter will attempt to provide background related to referencing in collaborative augmented reality. It will also summarize the results of previous user studies, and discuss recent advances that have the potential to dramatically impact referencing in augmented reality.

J. Chastine (✉)
Department of Computing and Software Engineering, Southern Polytechnic State University, Marietta, Georgia, USA
e-mail: jchastin@spsu.edu

B. Furht (ed.), *Handbook of Augmented Reality*, DOI 10.1007/978-1-4614-0064-6_15,
© Springer Science+Business Media, LLC 2011

2 Background

Collaborative AR is highly multi-disciplinary, drawing concepts from Computer Supported Cooperative Work (CSCW), Human-Computer Interaction (HCI), virtual environments, computer graphics and computer vision. Though not necessary to address each of these, it is important to provide a brief overview of studies that relate to this discussion. It is also important to distinguish between the acts of *referencing* a set of objects and *selecting* them. While there is certainly a cognitive process to determine which objects will be referenced, this may or may not result in the selection of a set of objects. In fact, references may be made to space alone (e.g. *"Put this object over there"*). It should be noted that selection often *is* used as a form of clarification in ambiguous situations because it is typically accompanied by a visual representation.

2.1 Virtual Interaction Techniques

Human beings are well-equipped to work in the physical world. However, working with non-tactile virtual objects can present interaction challenges. According to Bowman et al. object selection can be affected by target distance, size, number, density of objects and occlusion [1]. Selection techniques can be classified as either *ego-centric* (i.e. from the perspective of the user) or *exo-centric* (e.g. from any other viewpoint). There are numerous ego-centric selection techniques, including the classic "hand", ray-casting, or image plane techniques like (a personal favorite) the "head-crusher" – in which the user frames the objects of interest from their viewpoint between the index finger and thumb. Exo-centric examples include the World-In-Miniature (WIM) where the world is reduced in scale to fit in the palm of your hand – allowing participants to select objects at a distance. In general, Bowman et al. recommend *pointing metaphors* for selection in virtual environments.

2.2 CSCW

Computer-mediated collaborative environments have a long and rich history. In such environments, participants can be *co-located* (i.e they are physically next to one another) or *remotely* located (e.g. a barrier exists between them or they are geographically distant from one another). A common scenario in remote collaboration is that of *expert + technician* – in which a local expert attempts to help a remote technician in the field. The expert receives a channel of communication from the technician, such as a video feed from the technician's viewpoint. Of particular relevance to this scenario is the early work done by Stefik et al. in "What You See Is What I See" (WYSIWIS) interfaces, which provide shared viewports to participants [2].

In their study on pen-based gestures over video stream, Ou et al. noted that participants were unable to make references in the local environment "*without reference to the external spatial environment*" [3]. Further, the authors "*repeatedly observed that remote participants have difficulty communicating because of their inability to gesture or point at objects in the workspace.*" However, when using this technique, annotations become stale once the technician changes his viewpoint. While it is possible to freeze the video frame to keep the reference accurate, the video may no longer match the technician's viewpoint or, even worse, may entirely block his view. Similarly, in their study on the effects of head-mounted and scene-oriented video, Fussell et al. suggest that sharing video is preferable to audio-only conditions [4].

2.3   Collaborative AR

In augmented reality, co-located participants may surround a table-top display or perhaps view the augmented environment through a head-mounted display. Bowman et al. describe the fundamental problem of interacting in AR environments: "*... the user is required to use* different input modalities *for physical and virtual objects: real hands for physical objects and special-purpose input devices for virtual objects. This introduces an* interaction seam *into the natural workflow.*" Bowman et al. [1] as described later, when these environments are extended to support multiple participants, the problem compounds.

Early AR systems were teleconferencing-centric in design and lacked support for shared virtual objects [5]. Later, collaborative mobile systems were designed to help with navigation [6–8]; most often, one participant remained indoors while the second was outdoors. For example, Stafford implemented a "God-like" system where an indoor participant could point to a tabletop with a physical building – allowing for larger-than-life scale references to objects (e.g. a large hand coming down "from heaven") [9].

It can be easily argued that there is an intrinsic requirement to support referencing in any collaborative system. The literature suggests that referencing in collaborative AR is critical [10]. Billinghurst et al. also describe the importance of gesturing to support communication [11]. The literature also suggests that co-located collaboration preserves many non-verbal cues, such as gesturing and eye gaze – and thus can rely on social protocols. The developers of *Studierstube* identified five key characteristics of collaborative augmented reality environments: (1) *Virtuality* – virtual objects can be viewed, (2) *Augmentation* – real objects can be augmented via virtual annotations, (3) *Cooperation* – multiple users can each other and cooperate in a natural way, (4) *Independence* – each user has an independent viewpoint and (5) *Individuality* – the data can be displayed differently to each user [12].

Ostensibly, requirements 4 and 5 are at odds with the recommendation of shared video from the CSCW community. Keep in mind that this is only true if one assumes that participants are co-located. Though remote AR collaboration may at first seem impossible, we have taken a slightly different approach to the characteristics (above), allowing us to explore remote scenarios. Similarly, Krauß et al. have developed distributed collaborative environment for education [13].

3   A Tree in the Forest

In our early research, we designed and implemented a virtual environment for collaborative molecular modeling, which was governed by a molecular mechanics simulator. We noticed that participants had difficulty collaborating (perhaps because they lacked the vocabulary to effectively communicate). Given that the organic molecules were comprised of relatively few atomic types, the environment contained few unique visual cues to aid in identifying areas of interest – analogous to referring to a tree in a forest. Further, the molecules often occluded one another, causing additional referencing difficulty. This problem was eventually alleviated by the use of a transparency shader for molecules that fell outside a 3-dimensional bounding box.

We were curious as to how well this environment would transfer into augmented reality. We imagined that chemists and biologists would sit around a table and *naturally gesture* towards areas of interest. We implemented the system below using an Intersense-900 tracker, which allowed for cross-reality collaboration (i.e. between the AR environment and the previously mentioned virtual environment – see Fig. 15.1). However, we were also interested in how participants would reference artifacts in environments that contain both virtual *and* physical objects.

We therefore conducted a series user studies with the hope of better understanding the referencing behaviors of participants in collaborative AR. The first study was designed to cull down the overall design space – or to better understand which elements are important when supporting referential awareness [14]. The second was a study of the efficacy of pointers in these environments – in how participants

Fig. 15.1 An early AR environment for molecular modeling

Table 15.1 Summary of study configurations

	Physical models	Virtual models	Augmented models
Co-located	*Scenario 1*	*Scenario 3*	*Scenario 5*
	Independent views	Independent views	Independent views
	Physical referencing, only	Physical & Virtual referencing	Physical & Virtual referencing
Remote	*Scenario 2*	*Scenario 4*	*Scenario 6*
	Shared view	Independent views	Shared view
	Physical referencing, only	Physical & Virtual referencing	Physical & Virtual referencing

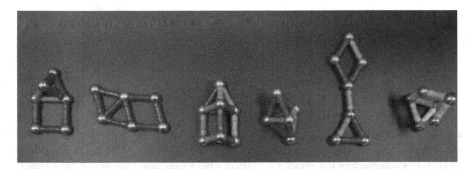

Fig. 15.2 Physical target configurations

both give and interpret references and factors that influence it [15]. This work also contained a follow-up study to better understand how the environment could passively support referencing. The results are summarized here.

3.1   An Exploratory Study

For our first study, we were interested in exploring the kinds of support that participants prefer when referencing physical and digital artifacts. We were also interested in studying how users referenced in co-located and remote environments. There were a total of six configurations – a cross between remote/co-located scenarios and either physical, virtual or augmented objects (see Table 15.1); these were presented in a Latin square design. A WYSIWIS view was provided in remote scenarios when working with physical and augmented models (i.e. those where physical objects were used with virtual referencing support). The environment supported natural hand gestures and multi-modal interactions. While objective data was collected, we were interested in observing referencing behavior between participants and interviewing them about their experiences.

Based on the expert + technician scenario described previously, we divided participants into the roles of *guide* and *builder* and asked them to collaboratively build arbitrary physical and virtual structures (that were very "molecular" in shape – see Fig. 15.2). The guide could view a target configuration and then provide instruction

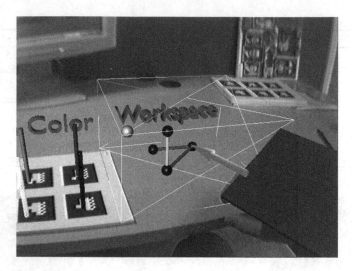

Fig. 15.3 A projected reference

for the builder about how to construct a similar structure. Each participant wore a video-based (non-stereoscopic) HMD and pairs were allowed to talk to one another at all times – including the remote scenarios where they were separated by a small barrier.

We observed that, while each group had their unique method of collaboration, participants made heavy use of deictic speech (e.g. *"this"*, *"that"*, *"here"*) in all scenarios as well as short utterances that served as acknowledgements. Many builders would often clarify a reference by selecting the object if it was not already selected. Participants would also typically begin by establishing common ground since many of them had not previously met one another before this study. Of interest, many participants made use of *referential chaining* – or using the last established reference point to generate a new one – which we assume was because of the sequential nature of the task.

In two of the eight groups, the guides were observed making *projected references*. With this kind of incorrect reference, the tip of the virtual pointer lies approximately half way between (and in line with) the viewpoint of the user and the object of interest (see Fig. 15.3). These became problematic – significantly slowing progress. We assumed that this occurred because the HMD was non-stereoscopic. To help alleviate this, some participants were seen moving their virtual pointer closer and further from themselves in order to use occlusive cues to determine the depth of the object, or were observed repeatedly changing their viewpoint to gain a better understanding of the relative depth of one object when compared to another.

In the co-located/augmented scenario, a majority of the participants made references using their hands, though three of the guides used their virtual pointers. While working in remote scenarios where virtual content was present, the virtual pointer was heavily used. Many guides were observed holding their virtual pointers

Fig. 15.4 A reference from a remote guide (expert)

in position for extended durations when builders did not acknowledge a reference. This behavior occasionally occluded the viewpoint of the builders. Three of them made comments to the guide, such as asking them to *"move your arrow."* This suggests that acknowledgement of a reference is an important social protocol.

In scenarios where the builder and guide shared the builder's view, many builders would often clarify and acknowledge references by holding the model close to their face/camera (or draw in close) and ask the guide for clarification (e.g. *"Like this?"*). They would also adopt a common coordinate system relative to the builder's body – with guides making comments such as *"to your left."* Such behavior suggests that builders and guides alike understood the workspace spatially, and had a "shared body" experience.

Of interest was the relative success of the remote + augmented scenario. In this scenario, participants shared the viewpoint of the builder. The hand of the guide was tracked locally (i.e. the video feed of the guide was used for image tracking only). The guide was provided with a virtual pointer into the remote environment and the coordinate system was adjusted to that of the builder. Though we originally believed that this scenario would present the most challenges for participants (since the guide was not capable of viewing their local environment), when interviewed, the guides suggested that this method of collaboration was intuitive. Further, when rating the remote scenario with and without virtual referencing support, participants overwhelmingly preferred the former (see Fig. 15.4).

During the feedback sessions, we asked participants two very open-ended questions – specifically what they liked and disliked as well as their suggestions on how to make the system better. First, though participants were shown a quick video on how to use the system (and not block the fiducials), the most common complaint was poor tracking. Because our tracking system was image-based, participants would often occlude the view of both the participant *and* the tracker while making references, causing the tracker to fail. Some stated that because of this, the workspace also felt cramped (e.g. they *"kept getting in each other's way."*) One guide became frustrated and abandoned the virtual referencing techniques, instead, using spoken references. Others requested that the visibility of virtual objects (e.g. virtual text) be optional. Though the original intent of this text was to identify parts of the system, it eventually became a referencing obstacle. One participant asked for the virtual pointer to line up with his finger tip, while some participants expressed a desire for virtual reference points within the scene – with two groups explicitly requesting a virtual "grid".

Our observations from this study suggest the following design considerations:

1. Pointing is a fundamental requirement for collaborative augmented reality.
2. Shared video is an effective medium of communication for generating references – as it removes viewpoint asymmetries.
3. The lack of depth cues may lead to projected references.
4. Participants make use of referential chaining.
5. Virtual referencing support can potentially hinder collaboration if it blocks the view of participants.
6. Participants may be reluctant to use virtual references if tracking is poor.

3.2   The Versatile Virtual Pointer

The previous study provided insight into how participants refer to both physical and virtual artifacts in the environment. From this research, we decided to study virtual pointers and the factors that influence its referencing accuracy. While at first such a study may seem unnecessary, consider how fundamental this referencing technique is and how often it appears in collaborative systems. Further, there are many benefits to using virtual pointers. They are registered in three dimensions, are flexible enough to refer to both physical and virtual content, can work in both co-located and remote scenarios, and are analogous to the ways that humans naturally refer to objects – since they are an embodiment of direction. They are trivial to implement, and as we saw in our previous study, can also be used for simple gesturing (e.g. circling around an area of interest) or set into position and remain as long as necessary while still being relevant.

Robinson notes that "The interpretation of what is being pointed at is dependent not just on the act of pointing but on other people being able to perceive what is being pointed at" [16]. We therefore felt it important to separate referencing into two distinct phases – reference generation and reference interpretation – and study each independently. In this way, those who generate poor references (such as the guides who made projected references in the previous study) would not influence the interpretation of the reference. This would also remove any deictic speech that concomitantly supports the reference. We were specifically interested in which factors influence the accuracy of generating and interpreting references – such as

Fig. 15.5 Generating references in perpendicular (with shadows) and in parallel

distance, arrow opacity, spatial configuration, the presence of shadows, viewpoint orientation, and so on – as well as when references became ambiguous. The studies consisted of 22 participants (18 of whom had no AR or VR experience). Each study was presented in a modified Latin square arrangement. Participants wore a HMD equipped with a single camera (with a 40°-wide field of view).

In the first sub-study, participants were asked to point to a small *target sphere*. Once the participant believed they were pointing to the middle of this sphere, they informed the researcher and the next trial began. Accuracy was defined as the distance from the arrow vector to the center of the target sphere (i.e. the minimum distance from the line defined by the arrow vector to the middle of the target sphere). A variably-sized *barrier sphere* enforced a minimum distance between the arrow tip and the inner sphere, though the participant could point from further away if desired. In one configuration, the arrow was perpendicular to the normal of the tracked paddle, while in the second, it was perpendicular. To better understand how to reduce projected references, we included virtual shadows in some configurations (see Fig. 15.5). A total of 4 sets of 15 trials were given to each subject for a total of 1,320 trials.

Overall, we found that participants were most accurate when shadows were present. In the perpendicular scenario, we believe participants leveraged the presence of shadows to align a secondary reference (i.e. the shadow of the virtual pointer could be used to reference the shadow of the target sphere – see Fig. 15.5). Surprisingly, though less pronounced, it could be seen that shadows increased the accuracy of references created in parallel as well (see Fig. 15.6). More research is needed to better understand this, though we know that not all references in the parallel scenario were made directly in parallel.

Most importantly, we found that accuracy increased the more in-line the participant's head was with the arrow vector. Figure 15.7 shows the accuracy of referencing in parallel and perpendicular, compared against the distance of the head to the arrow vector. The cluster in the lower left of Fig. 15.7a shows a tight clustering in the lower-left – where a majority of the references were less than 2 cm off center. Comparing that with Fig. 15.7b, a negative shift "up" in accuracy can be seen.

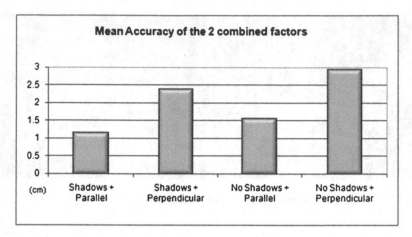

Fig. 15.6 Shadows vs. no shadows

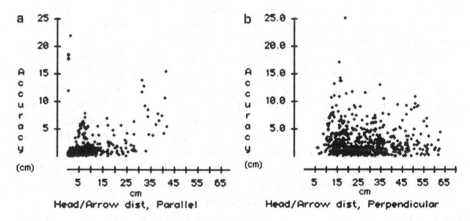

Fig. 15.7 (**a** and **b**) – accuracy of parallel and perpendicular

The shift to the right denotes the enforcement of the orientation of the arrow; it was impossible to reference in parallel in perpendicular scenario without losing tracking. Of interest is the triangular "wedge" that can be seen in both sets of data. It is important to remember that the participants *believed their references to be accurate*. Though there are outliers, this wedge therefore suggests that there is a *cone of inference* – such that the accuracy of generating references is directly proportional to how in-line the participant's view vector is with the arrow vector.

We noticed that, even with the inclusion of shadows, some participants still had difficulty understanding the depth of objects. When shadows were not present, some participants in the perpendicular configuration were observed "poking" the barrier sphere multiple times (from the side) until they were confident the arrow was at the same depth as the barrier sphere. Though this process took significantly longer, participants in post-interviews claimed that this technique provided them

Fig. 15.8 Stationary and moveable configurations

with enough cues to reduce referencing to a 2-dimensional problem. Once they knew the depth, they could leverage proprioception cues to complete the reference. Others were observed trying to create parallel references in the perpendicular configuration. Once they realized this was not possible, they opted for as near to parallel as possible.

When asked their preferences during the follow-up interview, of those who responded, 63% explicitly stated that referencing in parallel was more "natural" than referencing in perpendicular. 32% preferred perpendicular referencing and the remaining 5% believed both techniques to be equivalent. However, when examining the 32%, we found that a majority of these participants were significantly more accurate when referencing in parallel. For the two participants who actually *were* more accurate in perpendicular than parallel, we noticed that they were *considerably* less accurate than most others (i.e. the previously mentioned outliers), regardless of configuration. This also suggests that these participants had difficulty understanding the spatiality of the environment.

In the second sub-study, each trial consisted of a virtual arrow and eight virtual cubes that were embedded below the surface of a tracked, physical plane. The configuration of the cubes changed from trial to trail and each cube was labeled with a number. Participants were asked to identify to which cube the pointer was referring – calling out the cube's number to the research – at which point the next trial began. In the first configuration, the back face of the cone was not rendered, allowing participants to view through the inside of the arrow (i.e. in parallel). In the second configuration, the arrow was opaque. The distance of the arrow varied from trial to trial, yet would always point directly to the middle of one of the cubes – which could be partially, but not totally, occluded by another cube. Finally, participants were allowed to grab and move the physical plane (i.e. the tracker) in some configurations, but could only change their viewpoint in others (see Fig. 15.8). The same participants interpreted 60 references (30 with the moveable workspace and 30 with the stationary workspace) for a total of 1,320 trials.

By recording the distance of the user's head at the beginning and end of each trial, we noticed that participants generally move "in-line" with the arrow vector (i.e. their viewpoint was nearly parallel to the arrow vector, similar to the previous sub-study). When this angle increased, their response times were longer and far less accurate. Larger angles were enforced in the stationary configuration; in some cases, it was impossible to line up with the arrow.

In general, we found that the longer it took for participants to respond, the less accurate the responses were. For example, the mean selection time for a correct response took between 5.1 s and 7.7 s (approximately). Comparatively, incorrect responses took approximately 12.2 s on average. In collaborative pairs, such pauses might indicate confusion or miscommunication. As expected, accuracy decreased in scenarios where cubes were tightly clustered together. Though it was originally hypothesized that the see-through arrow would be more accurate than the opaque one (and 94% of participants *did* prefer the see-through arrow), the results were inconclusive. The dominate factor in referencing accuracy was the distance of the arrow to the cube it was referencing. The data also implies that there is a *cone of inference* during interpretation – with the arrow becoming more ambiguous with distance.

While observing the participants, they overwhelmingly felt the need to line up with the arrow. Much to the paranoia of the researchers, many participants were observed contorting their bodies (and nearly falling out of their chairs) in the stationary configuration in order to line up with the view vector or to gain a better viewpoint. When interviewed, they preferred the moveable workspace over the stationary one because it was easier to move the workspace than themselves. When asked how the system could be improved, many requested an extendable arrow (i.e. a ray); one participant was seen physically tracing the path of the arrow with his finger.

From these two sub-studies, we found:

1. Participants generate more accurate references when in-line with the arrow. Similarly, users who interpret references using this technique prefer to be in-line as well.
2. There is strong evidence for including shared viewpoints (through shared video) in collaborative systems. Not only did this help remove viewpoint asymmetries between collaborators, it also enables both the reference giver and receiver to be in-line. Thus, collaborators can virtually "occupy" the same physical space and have the shared body experience described in the first study. Without shared video, one participant is forced into a less-accurate scenario.
3. Shadows provide additional depth cues to improve the accuracy of generating references.
4. Virtual arrows have a cone of inference, both during reference generation and reference interpretation; referential accuracy decreases with distance.

3.3 A Follow-up Study

During the interview in our first study, many participants requested a virtual grid to appear in the workspace to facilitate referencing. We were therefore interested in how the *environment itself* could passively support references. In a small follow-up study, we focused on remote collaboration containing physical objects – since it presents unique challenges. Because face-to-face non-verbal cues are removed in this scenario, we wanted to examine how they could be mimicked through computer-mediated techniques. Though several factors were measured, we were interested in the perceived support that the environment provided for the pairs.

Similar to our first study, participants were divided into the roles of guide and builder. Knowledge was externalized for the guide in the form of a virtual model and the remote builder was asked to build its physical equivalent using wooden blocks. Sixteen users participated. The configurations of each scenario included:

1. *Video-only*: the guide could toggle between his local view and that of the remote builder.
2. *Video + arrow*: the same as scenario 1, except the hand of the guide was tracked locally. When viewing the local environment, the guide could view the virtual configuration and make references in his own coordinate system; those references were mapped into the coordinate system of the builder yet the viewpoints were independent. When viewing the remote environment of the builder, however, the locally tracked hand acted as a 3D cursor in the remote workspace, appearing as a virtual arrow.
3. *Video + grid*: same as scenario 1, but a virtual grid was present for both participants. There was no virtual arrow.
4. *Video + grid + arrow*: a combination of scenarios 2 and 3.

We observed that there was a significant impact of training on time to complete the task. Over time, guides tended to give better instructions and builders carried them out more efficiently. For example, some pairs started by establishing a common mental coordinate system; for some "up" meant further away from their body while to others it meant increasing in elevation.

Through observation and post-study interviews, we found that participants used the embedded reference points to establish an initial reference point. Once that had been established and the first block was positioned, *referential chaining* took over and the grid was no longer used. Much to our discouragement, some guides (*still!*) gave projected references even though shadows were present in the system. However, guides spent a majority of their time (64%) viewing the remote environment, so *projected references had meaning for both participants*. One guide became frustrated by poor tracking and decided to use spoken references instead. However, when referential chaining failed, he reluctantly returned to using the arrow to establish a new reference point. One (right-handed) guide was observed pointing with his left hand – which, oddly enough, could not be seen by himself or the remote builder.

When asked to rank which environment they preferred (4 = excellent, 1 = poor), participants rated the *video + grid + arrow* configuration the highest (see Fig. 15.9); this was expected, as it provides the most support. We believed that the arrow would provide a much more interactive way of referring to content and that the 2-dimensional nature of the grid would be limiting. However, the *video + grid*

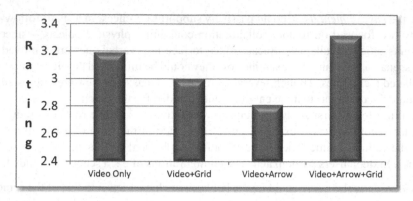

Fig. 15.9 A comparison of scenarios

was rated higher than the *video + arrow* scenario. The results may be an artefact of implementation; when asked how the system could be improved, almost all participants asked for better tracking. Additionally, many groups stated that the arrow was an invaluable tool.

During the course of each trial, we also observed that there was a decline in the use of virtual techniques. Once a point was established, the connectedness of the model facilitated the spoken references. We believe that if the models were disjoint, the virtual referencing techniques would play a more important referencing role. Groups also reiterated their desire for the visibility of virtual referencing support to be toggleable. Because physical objects (e.g. hands and physical blocks) did not occlude virtual ones, the grid began to hinder construction.

Architecturally, it should be noted that shared video was implemented using a subscription model – with each camera becoming a concurrent video server. The first client to connect negotiates video options such as frame rate, resolution, compression and so on. It is during this time that the calibration matrix for the camera is sent as well. A participant typically subscribes to one or more video streams. Using a video-based tracking system that receives multiple streams presents some interesting possibilities. Of interest is *when* tracking and augmentation occur. In our system, augmented video is never sent; thus, when viewing a remote environment, each frame is augmented as if it is the local video feed. However, tracking can occur on multiple video streams – and was required in the scenarios where guides could control a virtual pointer in the remote environment.

Note that when viewing local video feeds, the world coordinate systems are separate. Thus, if a builder rotates the space locally, the guide's arrow rotates as well. However, when the guide switches to the remote view, collaborators share the builder's coordinate system. One benefit in this scenario is that when the guide is receiving low-frame-rate video from the builder, it is still possible have responsive orientation updates for both the participants.

4 Recent Advances

It has been argued that wearable computing is the ideal interface for 3D CSCW because, in addition to being portable, it does not restrict the hands of the user [17]. While this is likely true, portable AR is currently manifesting in the form of mobile phone applications. Many phones now come equipped with the hardware-components to support AR, including a GPU, a camera capable of streaming video, accelerometers, gyros, and GPS. Consequently, there has been a recent surge of companies specializing in developing mobile AR applications, suggesting that AR may finally be making its way out of the lab and into the hands of non-experts. Further, corporate support is now becoming available. For example, Qualcomm has recently released a mobile AR SDK that includes an image-based tracker. It appears that, at least for the time being, phone-based AR will be the common way that the broader population will interact with the augmented world.

However, new HCI challenges exist. On a mobile phone platform, the device acts as a window through which to view the augmented world. Users are therefore required to hold the phone – typically with both hands around the edge of the phone in order to prevent blocking the camera. In doing so, users are no longer able to use their hands to reference artifacts in the environment. Under certain contexts, this can be problematic and we must therefore investigate new methods of referencing for this platform. It is important keep in mind that augmented reality environments contain both virtual *and* physical objects, so we should design multi-modal techniques to support the referencing of both.

One such hands-free technique is to create a skew pair in which two successive rays are cast (see Fig. 15.10). The point of minimum distance between these two rays represents the point of reference. Such an approach does not rely on geometric knowledge of the environment and therefore works with both virtual and physical objects; it also allows for referencing at arbitrary depths, such as virtual objects embedded within physical ones. In the image below, the rays are visualized to demonstrate this concept.

Mathematically, the two viewing vectors l_1 and l_2 create a skew pair (see Fig. 15.11). Taking the cross product of these two generates a third vector that is orthogonal to both. We must find a point on each line such that their distance represents the minimal distance k between the two lines.

Fig. 15.10 (**a, b**, and **c**) – a skew pair technique

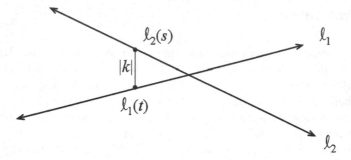

Fig. 15.11 A skew pair

We then have the following equality:

$$l_1(t) - l_2(s) = k(\overrightarrow{V}_1 \times \overrightarrow{V}_2)$$

Replacing with the vector equation of a line yields:

$$a + t\overrightarrow{V}_1 - b - s\overrightarrow{V}_2 = k(\overrightarrow{V}_1 \times \overrightarrow{V}_2)$$

where a and $\overrightarrow{V_1}$ represent the position and viewing direction from the first viewpoint and b and $\overrightarrow{V_2}$ represent the second. It is then possible to solve for k, s and t, where k represents the minimum distance between the skew pair, and s and t are scalars associated with l_1 and l_2.

While the technique above may not be applicable to all scenarios, a promising advance in consumer-grade technology is the *Kinect* by Microsoft®. This device is a small horizontal bar for the Xbox 360 equipped with infrared cameras that provides depth information of physical objects. This (or similar) technology will undoubtedly have an enormous impact on augmented reality. This is especially true in the area of referencing, since such technology enables physical objects to occlude virtual ones. In the previous expert + technician scenario, having occlusive cues would inform the expert about the relative depth of objects in the remote environment and would enable him to generate more accurate references.

5 Closing Remarks and Acknowledgements

The ability to reference is fundamental to successful collaboration. There is little doubt that the concepts and techniques that are currently available in AR, just like other interaction techniques, will improve with time. They depend heavily on the context of the environment and the tasks that the participants are performing. It is hoped that the summary of research presented in this chapter provides the reader with a better understanding of items to consider when implementing collaborative augmented reality systems.

The author would like to thank the many colleagues who helped investigate this subject, including Jeremy Brooks, Maribeth Gandy, Mary Hudachek-Buswell, Blair MacIntyre, Kristine Nagel, G. Scott Owen, Jon A Preston, Luca Yearsovich and Ying Zhu.

References

1. D. Bowman, E. Kruijff, J. LaVoila, and I. Poupyrev, "3D User Interfaces: Theory and Practice", Addison-Wesley Professional, 2004.
2. M. Stefik, D. G. Bobrow, G. Foster, S. Lanning, and D. Tartar, "WYSIWIS revised: Early experiences with multiuser interfaces," ACM Transactions of Office Information Systems vol, 5, pp. 147–186, 1987.
3. J. Ou, S.R. Fussell, X. Chen, L.D. Setlock, J. Yang, "Gestural Communication over Video Stream: Supporting Multimodal Interaction for Remote Collaborative Physical Tasks," in International Conference on Multimodal Interfaces Vancouver, British Columbia, Canada, 2003.
4. S. R. Fussell, L.D. Setlock, R.E. Kraut, "Effects of Head-Mounted and Scene-Oriented Video Systems on Remote Collaboration on Physical Tasks," in Conference on Human Factors in Computing Systems (SIGCHI) Ft. Lauderdale, FL, 2003.
5. M. Billinghurst, J. Bowskill, M. Jessop, and J. Morphett, "A Wearable Spatial Conferencing Space," Proc. of International Symposium on Wearable Computing (ISWC), 1998.
6. T. Höllerer, S. Feiner, T. Terauchi, G. Rashid, D. Hallaway, "Exploring MARS: Developing Indoor and Outdoor User Interfaces to a Mobile Augmented Reality System," *Computers and Graphics,* vol. 23(6), pp. 779–785, 1999.
7. S. Feiner, B. MacIntyre, T. Höllerer, and A. Webster, "A Touring Machine: Prototyping 3D Mobile Augmented Reality System for Exploring the Urban Environment," Proc. of International Symposium on Wearable Computers (ISWC), 1997, p. 74.
8. G. Reitmayr, D. Schmalstieg, "Collaborative Augmented Reality for Outdoor Navigation and Information Browsing," Proc. of Symposium Location Based Services and TeleCartography, 2004.
9. A. Stafford, W. Piekarski, B. H. Thomas, "Implementation of God-like Interaction Techniques for Supporting Collaboration Between Outdoor AR and Indoor Tabletop Users," Proc. of International Symposium on Mixed and Augmented Reality (ISMAR), 2006.
10. H. Slay, M. Phillips, R. Vernik, and B. Thomas, "Interaction Modes for Augmented Reality Visualization", Proc. of Australian Symposium on Information Visualization, Sydney, Australia, 2001.
11. M. Billinghurst, S. Bee, J. Bowskill, H. Kato, "Asymmetries in Collaborative Wearable Interfaces," Proc. of The Third International Symposium on Wearable Computers. Digest of Papers, 1999, pp. 133–140.
12. D. Schmalsteig, Fuhrmann, A., Hessina, G., Szalavari, Z., Encarnacao, L. M., Gervautz, M., Purgathofer, W., "The Studierstube Augmented Reality Project", Presence, vol. II, pp. 33–54, February, 2002.
13. M. Krauß, K. Riege, M. Winter, L. Pemberton., "Remote Hands-On Experience: Distributed Collaboration with Augmented Reality", Proc. of the 4th European Conference on Technology Enhanced Learning: Learning in the Synergy of Multiple Disciplines, Nice, France, 2009.
14. J. W. Chastine, K. Nagel, Y. Zhu, L. Yearsovich, "Understanding the Design Space of Referencing in Collaborative Augmented Reality Environments," Proc. of Graphics Interface (GI), Montreal, Canada, 2007.
15. J. Chastine, K. Nagel, Y. Zhu, M. Hudacheck-Buswell, "Studies on the Effectiveness of Virtual Pointers in Collaborative Augmented Reality". IEEE Symposium on 3D User Interfaces (3DUI), March, 2008.

16. T. Robertson, "Building Bridges: Negotiating the Gap Between Work Practice and Technology Design," International Journal of Human-Computer Studies, pp. 121–146, 2000.
17. M. Billinghurst, S. Weghorst, and T. Furness III, "Wearable Computers for Three Dimensional CSCW," Proc. of International Symposium on Wearable Computers (ISWC), Cambridge, MA, 1997.

Chapter 16
QR Code Based Augmented Reality Applications

Tai-Wei Kan, Chin-Hung Teng, and Mike Y. Chen

The field of Augmented Reality (AR) has grown and progressed remarkably in recent years and many useful AR applications have been developed focusing on different areas such as game, education and advertisement. However, most of these AR systems are designed for closed applications with particular markers, limited number of users and restricted digital contents. Hence, they are inappropriate for public environment with diverse digital contents. In this article we first review a well-known 2D bar code, the QR Code, and then survey a number of marker- or tag-based AR technologies. We then present two applications, including a product demonstration system and a mobile phone application of the OpenID service, by combining these two techniques. For the product demonstration system, a QR Code is pasted on the package of a product and then the content inside the package is displayed on the QR Code in a 3D format. This system allows the customer to visualize the product via a more direct and interactive way. The other system is a simple application that combines QR Code and AR with mobile phones. With this system, users can quickly and easily share their information on social networks. Meanwhile, the information can also be displayed in an AR form on the phones of the users. These two systems demonstrate the success of using QR Code as the AR marker to a particular application and we believe it can bring more convenient to our life in the future.

1 Introduction

Modern technologies are being rapidly developed. With better functions, they are meant to make people's lives more efficient and convenient. Over the last few years, "small and smart" has become the central idea of new inventions, which go in

T.-W. Kan (✉)
Graduate Institute of Networking and Multimedia, National Taiwan University, Taiwan
e-mail: 7533967@gmail.com; d99944001@ntu.edu.tw

B. Furht (ed.), *Handbook of Augmented Reality*, DOI 10.1007/978-1-4614-0064-6_16, 339
© Springer Science+Business Media, LLC 2011

line with "ubiquitous computing." In particular, amazing breakthroughs have been made to mobile devices. Not only do the devices provide more services now, but they are also much smaller in size. They even have built-in operating systems with better CPU performance. This indicates that mobile devices can provide additional services when needed. Moreover, nowadays mobile networks are prevalent and storage media are lighter and smaller. Blessed with all of the above-mentioned factors, smart phones came into our lives. In 2008 alone, 120 million mobile devices were sold globally. Some experts even expect that, by 2012, a total of 180 million cell phones will be sold annually around the world, with 80 million of them as smart phones. It can be inferred that smart phones will be developed quickly and become predominant in the coming years.

2D barcodes were invented during the early 1990s. Compared with 1D barcodes, 2D barcodes can handle a wider range of encodings with larger capacity, and are exploited in a variety of fields. Of more than 30 types of 2D barcodes in the world, QR Code is the most popular. According to a survey conducted in Japan in 2005, nearly 90% of the 7,660 respondents aged under 20 had used QR Code before. Another survey carried out in August 2006 in Japan shows that as many as 187 (82.4%) people out of the 227 respondents, who were randomly selected and interviewed on the streets, used cell phones to read QR Code. Therefore, it can be inferred that QR Code is widely accepted and applied in Japan. The use of QR Code is common in our daily lives, mostly related to digital downloads and information storage. Through open-source software and libraries, programmers can also create computer programs for QR Code applications that support different mobile phone platforms. In fact, creating and decoding QR Codes is an easy task that only a few steps are sufficient to complete the work.

Today, image processing and computer vision technologies have been progressed to a stage that allows us to infer the 3D information of the world directly from the images. Because of the success of these technologies, more and more vision-based AR applications are emerged. Augmented reality refers to the combination of virtual objects and real-world environment, so that users can experience a realistic illusion when using the interactive virtual object to explore the real-world environment. Many technologies have been investigated toward augmented reality, such as the marker tracking techniques and virtual object generation.

Traditionally, in marker-based augmented reality applications, a specific marker is needed for 3D tracking and positioning. This marker is employed to identify the corresponding virtual object that is to be placed in the real-world environment. When the marker is used as a tracking target, it has to be registered in the system in advance, as well as the virtual object it associates with. However, since the registered information is independent for different AR systems, the markers used in one system may not be applied in another system, unless an additional registration procedure is applied. This indicates that traditional AR system is only applicable to private use, not for public domain applications. In light of this, if we can use common 2D barcodes, such as QR Code, as AR markers, it will be much more convenient. First, using QR Code as AR marker can omit the registration procedure, which implies that it can be used in a public domain system. The QR Code can be easily generated by any user and the AR system can track it no matter what the information it embedded. Second, QR Code has considerable information capacity. It allows users to store extra data in QR Code, such as the URLs for augmented contents (e.g., 3D Model). As soon as an URL is read, the system will automatically download the corresponding digital content and show the content to users in 3D format.

This article was therefore organized for establishing a QR Code-based augmented reality system. To achieve this goal, AR markers were replaced with QR Code, and QR Code-based tracking and identification technologies were developed. To demonstrate that a QR Code-based system is feasible, two AR systems were set up for evaluation.

2 QR Code

2D barcodes were invented in the early 1990s. Not only does it hold a wider range of encoding and larger capacity than 1D barcodes, but it is also confidential, anti-counterfeiting and error-correcting in certain cases. Therefore, 2D barcodes have been widely applied to many different fields since their creation. Of the more than 30 types of 2D barcodes currently available in the market, QR Code has the advantages of many different 2D barcodes, and has been widely used for several years in country such as Japan.

QR Code was invented by the Denso Wave Incorporated in 1994, where "QR" refers to "quick response." According to the official website of Denso Wave [1], QR Code not only has high capacity, but can also store many different types of information. It even has a high error-correction rate (see Table 16.3), meaning that even 30% of a symbol is tainted or torn, QR Code can still be read correctly [2]. In the following, the features and applications of QR Code are described.

2.1 Appearance

QR Code, in square shape, is composed of the following five areas (see Fig. 16.1):

1. Finder pattern: Finder pattern refers to the squares on three of the four corners of a QR Code symbol. It is used to facilitate the position detection of a QR Code. By arranging this finder pattern, the position, angle and size of QR Code can be determined.
2. Alignment pattern: Version 2 and higher visions have "alignment pattern," which is used for distortion restoration. The alignment pattern can be used to identify whether the QR Code contains nonlinear distortions. For this purpose, an independent black cell is placed in the alignment pattern.
3. Timing pattern: Timing pattern is composed of black and white cells in horizontal and vertical lines that connect the three finder pattern squares. Timing pattern is used to determine the coordinate of a symbol, so as to make sure a symbol is fixed and can be read correctly without distortion.

Fig. 16.1 Structure of a QR
Code [3]

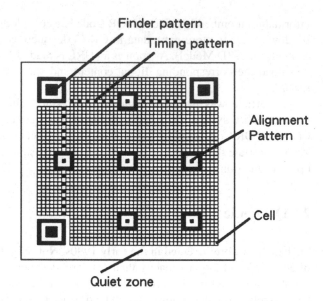

Finder pattern

Timing pattern

Alignment
Pattern

Cell

Quiet zone

4. Quiet zone: This is the blank area around QR Code. An isolated area is necessary for reading the QR Code. The width of quiet zone is usually four or more cells.
5. Data area: The QR Code data will be stored in this area. The data in QR Code will be encoded into the binary numbers of "0" and "1" based on Reed-Solomon codes. As Fig. 16.1 shows, the light grey areas are used to encode the data.

2.2 Advantages

1. Symbol version
   The symbol version of QR Code ranges from Version 1 to Version 40. Each version has a different module configuration and number of modules. (The module refers to the black and white dots that make up QR Code.) "Module configuration" refers to the number of modules contained in a symbol, commencing from Version 1 (21 × 21 modules) up to Version 40 (177 × 177 modules). Increasing the version number by 1 will lead to 4 additional modules per side, which results in the increased symbol size.
2. Data capacity
   Traditional 1D barcodes (often referred to as "barcodes") can carry maximum 20 characters, while QR Code has a much higher capacity of 2,089 characters. The data capacity of QR Code is proportional to its area: the larger its coverage is, the more data it carries. Table 16.1 lists some of the most common 2D barcodes and compares them in terms of appearance, features, usage and capacity.

Table 16.1 Typical 2D barcodes [1]

		QR Code	DataMatrix	Maxi Code
Sample				
Developer (Country)		DENSO (Japen)	RVSI Acuity CiMatrix (USA)	UPS (USA)
Type		Matrix	Matrix	Matrix
Data	Numeric	7,089	3,116	138
Capacity	Alphanumeric	4,296	2,355	93
	Binary	2,953	1,556	Not support
	Kanji	1,017	1,18	Not support
Main Features		Large capacity, small printout size, and high scan speed	Small printout size	High scan speed
Main Usages		All categories	Factory automation	Logistics

Table 16.2 Conversion efficiency of QR Code [3]

Conversion efficiency	Character type	Data Capacity
	Numeric only	3.3 cells/character
	Alphanumeric	5.5 cells/character
	Binary (8 bits)	8 cells/character
	Kanji, full width Kana	13 cells/character
	Chinese (UTF-8)	24.8 cells/character

Table 16.3 QR Code error correction capabilities [1]

Correction level	Error correction capability
Level L	Approx. 7%
Level M	Approx. 15%
Level Q	Approx. 25%
Level H	Approx. 30%

3. Character type

   QR Code is capable of handling English letters, numbers, binary digits, Katakana, Hiragana and Chinese characters. The symbol size of a QR Code varies, depending on the kind of data it contains. For instance, as shown in Table 16.2 Kana takes up four times more space than numbers.

4. Error correction level

   QR Code has error correction functionality for restoring the data encoded in the symbol. Table 16.3 specifies the four error correction levels of QR Code. Level M is the most widely used in general purpose.

5. Module size

The actual size of a QR Code symbol depends on the size of the module. The larger the module is, the more stable and easier it is to be read with a scanner. However, as the QR Code symbol gets larger in size, a larger printing area is required, too. Therefore, before printing a QR Code, one should take into account the available printing area and choose an appropriate module size.

2.3 Summary

Unlike other barcodes, which have to be read with physical scanners, QR Code can be easily detected by a mobile device, provided the gadget is installed with photo-taking functions and decoding software. Thus, QR Code fits perfectly well with mobile devices.

3 Trends in Marker-based Augmented Reality

An extension of virtual reality, augmented reality combines real-world environment and computer-generated image or information so that users can feel more intuitive as they explore in a simulated "real" world. Azuma believed that virtual reality is meant to create computer-generated virtuality, while augmented reality, on the contrary, aims to help users move in a real-world environment.

To display virtual contents in a real-world environment seamlessly, a marker is needed to identify and position the designated graphics. According to previous research on augmented reality, there are three types of marker-based AR systems:

1. Picture/template marker: This is the traditional marker-based AR system. The system will first track a square frame or positioning pattern, match the pattern with pre-stored templates in a database, find out the corresponding virtual object, and finally place the virtual object in the desired position.

2. ID-encoded marker: This is another marker-based AR system. Considering that, in a picture/template marker-based system, it becomes less efficient when there are too many markers to be matched, an ID-encoded marker-based AR system is introduced. ID-encoded marker indicates that markers are comprised by square symbols such as CyberCode [4] and ARTag [5] These markers have been widely adopted by many researchers. The tracking of ID-encoded markers is similar to that of picture/template markers. The only difference is that ID-encoded markers are identified by special decoding algorithm, and each marker is then given a unique ID. Its corresponding virtual object can then be determined when its ID is identified.

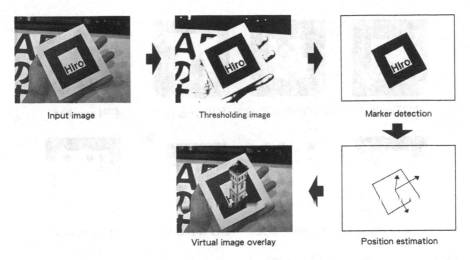

Fig. 16.2 Tracking process of AR technology

3.1   Summary

To place a virtual content in a real-world environment, a marker is needed to identify and position the designated graphics. Owen et al. believed that a pattern with four points/corners can be most easily and accurately identified in a changing configuration. This indicates that a square-shaped framed pattern is most suitable, and the marker used in ARToolKit also resembles a square, which demonstrates this point.

Figure 16.2 shows how marker-based augmented reality systems operate. An image frame is captured through a video device. The captured image is then binarized and a marker pattern is found and matched with the registered markers in the database. Once a registered marker is identified, the system will locate the 3D coordinates of the marker pattern and place the corresponding virtual object on it.

Zhang believed that, of all square symbol-based augmented reality systems, AKT, HOM, IGD and SCR are the four most commonly used markers [6]. AKT refers to the fiducial markers used in ARToolKit (the most widely used AR development kit in the market). HOM was developed in 1994 by C. Hoffman when he worked for Siemens AG [7]. IGD was developed by ARVIKA [8], a research project for commercial AR applications held by the German government. An IGD symbol comprises 6×6 square cells and resembles the appearance of ARTag invented by Fiala. SCR is the acronym of Siemens Corporate Research. It is used in many AR systems for tracking [9, 10]. Figure 16.3 shows a list of commonly used markers in AR systems.

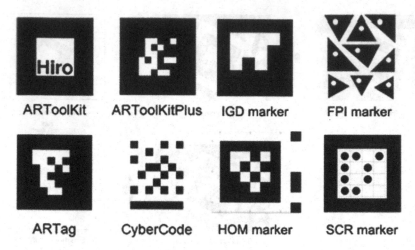

ARToolKit   ARToolKitPlus   IGD marker   FPI marker

ARTag   CyberCode   HOM marker   SCR marker

Fig. 16.3 Some well-known AR markers

3.2   Issues for Marker-based AR

It can be inferred that traditional marker-based AR systems are restricted in applications due to the following issues:

1. They must register markers and the corresponding augmented content before applying them.
2. They only support a limited number of markers.
3. They cannot correct errors or restore information when the markers were blocked or defiled.
4. They often use markers that are not universal. Thus, their markers must be modified or require other additional procedures before being used by other systems.

Above issues can be solved by employing QR Code as a marker. We explore this issue in the following.

3.3   Advantages of the Proposed System

Our AR system is different from others for the following four reasons:

1. In a general AR system, new marker and its corresponding augmented content have to be registered before use, so that the system can identify the markers and display the augmented content. In a QR Code-based system, as soon as QR Code is scanned, the system can decode the information in the QR Code and download the augmented content from the Internet. No any process of registration is required.

2. Considering that matching picture/template markers with the patterns in the database will make AR systems less efficient, Mark Fiala created ARTag, an ID-encoded marker-based system. The system uses robust digital encode techniques, but is still bound by the limited number of markers. To resolve this issue, Fiala further developed Webtag, which is an extension of ARTag. Webtag can handle a maximum number of 4×10^{12} markers, but the number is still much less than the 7,089 characters that QR Code can carry. This means that QR Code-based systems can perform 10^{7089} different encodings. If added with English characters, the quantity may be larger. Thus, QR Code-based markers can resolve the issue of insufficient number of markers.

3. Traditional AR systems use specially designed marker for tracking. To promote these systems to public use, a huge cost is required for constructing the necessary hardware and software. In contrast to this, QR Code has been widely used for several years and the required software tool kits such as encoding and decoding QR Code have been mature. Moreover, QR Code can also be decoded by current cell phones, which indicates that the use of QR Code is quite universal. QR Code has much potential of being an AR marker for public domain use, compared to other specially designed markers.

4. Traditional AR systems are for private use. The marker and augmented content of an AR system are stored in a local machine, and therefore only provide limited access. Because of this, the same marker may be interpreted to generate different contents in different systems. This is not permitted in a commercial or public application. An open AR system should allow more than one users to generate the same augmented content with the same marker, no matter what computer or mobile device they use. Fiala has noticed this problem and included a scheme in his Webtag system, so that Webtag can bring users and service providers together. Webtag works as follows: service providers may register an URL on an "intermediate space," and the URL is linked to an encoded ID marker. Through Webtag, users can download AR content once they send an encoded ID to the intermediate station and obtain the corresponding URL of the content. The advantages of Webtag are that markers can be easily tracked for their encoded IDs. Moreover, their corresponding virtual content can be downloaded rather than retrieved from a local machine, which can reduce the storage space of the local machine. However, a Webtag-based system still requires an intermediate station to bring users and service providers together. This means that some regulations must be made between the intermediate station and the users, as well as between the station and service providers. The QR Code-based AR system that we proposed does not require any intermediate station to read information. The system can directly go to the URL specified in QR Code, download the content, and show it to users. A QR Code-based AR system not only retains the superior points of Webtag, but can remotely edit or manage the virtual content linked to the URLs specified in QR Code. This is beneficial to business promotion and advertising. For instance, when a service provider, i.e. a news agency, wants to update the information to be displayed by a QR Code (i.e. headlines of the day), it

Table 16.4 Comparison between QR Code and general AR markers

	QR Code	Webtag	Regular AR marker
Need to pre-register	No	Yes	Yes
Model storing	Internet	Internet	Local
Limited number of markers	$>10^{7089}$	4×10^{12}	Smaller
Universality	Universal barcode	Stand-alone	Stand-alone

does not have to print new QR Code. It can simply achieve this by modifying the corresponding digital content (i.e. animated news) addressed by a certain URL encoded in the QR Code.

The comparisons of QR Code with other tagging technologies are summarized in Table 16.4.

According to the framework we devised for QR Code-based AR system, users can directly download information without having to go through a third channel. Service providers can also modify AR content in QR Code. Using QR Code for AR system markers will bring many benefits. In Chap. 3, we will specify our process for using QR Code as AR marker in detail.

In fact, we have found that a number of scholars who have similar opinion that use universal code in augmented reality applications.

3.4 Trends

Mark Fiala, a researcher from Canada, introduced ARTag in 2004 based on ARToolKit. ARTag has more sophisticated and efficient graphic processing and identification capability. In particular, ARTag is self-restoring. Even when a symbol gets tainted or blocked, with ARTag, information can still be correctly identified. ARTag is an encoded-ID AR system, which uses a robust digital encoding method to identify markers. Thus users of ARTag can only use the built-in 1,001 markers for tracking and identification.

Fiala emphasized that a marker must be able to correct errors when it is tainted or blocked. He then introduced Webtag [11] in 2007 to enhance his views: to make better use of ARTag and all other AR systems, the number of markers should not be limited, and they should do without registration in advance. On 2009 ACM SIGGRAPH, Carrer suggested using mobile tags in mixed reality for the mobile devices [12]. It is a pity that, while Carrer implemented his idea into a piece of digital artwork, she did not offer a practical framework. Still, Carrer's work showed that if replacing AR markers with standardized 2D barcodes in mobile devices, more practical and diverse AR applications can be developed. It is clear that to further enhance the system, marker-based AR systems must resolve the above-mentioned issues, and QR Code is a solution. In addition, QR Code is becoming more and more common in the world. Therefore, we adopt QR Code in our research for devising a public domain AR system. The system can overcome the issues mentioned above.

4 QR Code Based Augmented Reality

4.1 Our Approach

To preserve the high capacity and adaptability of QR Code, we do not break the structure of QR Code in our system. The system that we established, therefore, can track and read information in a QR Code (marker) as long as the three finder patterns are detected. QR Code makes it possible to link markers and digital content, without registration in advance.

The 3D positioning process of QR Code is shown in Fig. 16.4. The system first identifies the 3D coordinates of QR Code in the frame image captured by camera, and analyzing the information (i.e. URL) encoded in the QR Code. The corresponding digital content is then downloaded and displayed above the QR Code. Specifically, because each QR Code contains three positioning patterns, the system would first identify these three patterns, and compute the coordinates of four corners of the symbol. Based on the coordinates of the four corners, the system then employs ARToolKit to calculate the 3D coordinates of QR Code. In the meantime the QR Code pattern must be rotated to the right position for decoding.

As mentioned above, ARToolKit is the foundation of our system. In operation, we allowed more than one QR Code to be detected. Therefore, in theory, within one single image, it is possible to identify multiple positioning patterns. The question is how to find out the right positioning patterns? In the process of tracking and identification, ARToolKit provides detailed information on each marker, such as the coordinates of the four corners of a certain square marker, the line equations of the four lines of it, and its 3D coordinates. Through the geometry of the three positioning patterns (which in theory should form a right triangle (1:1)), plus information obtained through ARTooklKit, it is possible to identify the correct positioning patterns in QR Code (see Fig. 16.5 P_1, P_2 and P_3). Once the system successfully finds out the three positioning patterns, the coordinates of the fourth corners of the QR Code will be identified.

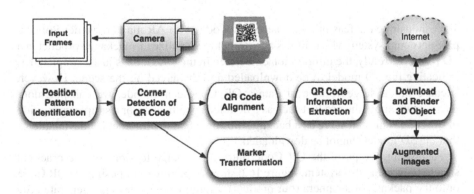

Fig. 16.4 System architecture

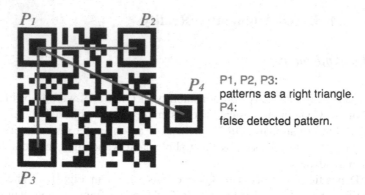

Fig. 16.5 Solving the problem of multi-detection of position detection patterns

After locating the QR Code, we then aim to extract the information embedded in the QR Code. There exists some open software that can be used to decode the information in a QR Code (e.g. libdecodeqr [13]). Some of them require the QR Code to be placed exactly in front of the camera so that the information can be correctly extracted. However, in our system the QR Code is used as an AR marker, thus it is infeasible to demand the user to put the QR Code in a specific position and orientation. Hence, to meet the requirements of these programs and improve the flexibility and accuracy of QR Code decoding, we must align the QR Code to facilitate the information extraction of a QR Code. Since the QR Code is projected from one plane on the camera image plane, we can restore its orientation by the perspective transformation. Finally, we can transform the QR Code to a proper orientation. For a more detailed approach of our QR Code based system, please refer to [14].

In the following, two AR systems are described to demonstrate that a QR Code-based system is feasible.

4.2 Product Demonstration System

To demonstrate the feasibility of using QR Code as an AR marker, we developed a product demo system which allows a customer to visualize the packaged product in a 3D form. Currently, the information embedded in the QR Code is just a simple URL indicating the 3D model to be downloaded and displayed on the scene. However, because of the large volume of data a QR Code can encode, we can put more information about the product such as a detailed specification or a simple user guide in the code. This can serve as a backup solution when the Internet is unavailable so that the 3D model cannot be downloaded.

At present, we paste the QR Code onto the package to simulate the practical situation for using this system. Figure 16.6 shows a picture of imposing the QR Code onto the package of a camera (our product). Figure 16.6 displays the generated 3D visual camera on the QR Code from different viewpoints.

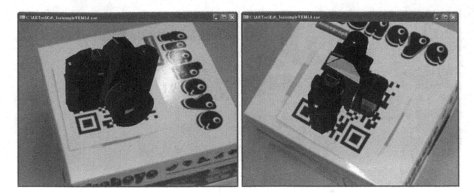

Fig. 16.6 A 3D virtual camera displayed on QR Code

Customer can manipulate the virtual camera by operating the QR Code on the package. Currently, the system is only a prototype thus its functionality is limited. Only a 3D model is shown on the QR Code. However, the system has the flexibility to incorporate more functions into the system, thus enhancing its usability and practicability in the future.

4.3   myID+AR Mobile Application

Online social networks are popular around the world. Nearly all of the websites have their own supporters. Because they are free, many people have one or more personal accounts to access them. However, when people have more accounts than they can handle, problems occur — they may forget the account name or password to a certain online network. "OpenID" is meant to resolve this issue. With just one account and password, users can log in to various social networks through OpenID.

At the moment, OpenID is only applicable on the web browser. We therefore tried to work out a way to make our AR system even more efficient and mobile. We integrated mobile and cloud computing in the "myID+AR" application and used QR Code as the marker of our system. (myID is developed by a research team at Taiwan Academia Sinica. It is a localized OpenID service in Taiwan.) That is, "myID+AR" application has the features of both OpenID and augmented reality. Through this application, users can quickly and easily share their information on social networks. For instance, as long as users capture the QR Code on a certain name card or activity flyer with their phones, social network service account, the contact information of this new contact or activity details will be displayed as augmented digital content on QR Code (Fig. 16.7). Of course, the application also allows users to introduce or to share information of the new contact to his/her other friends (Fig 16.8).

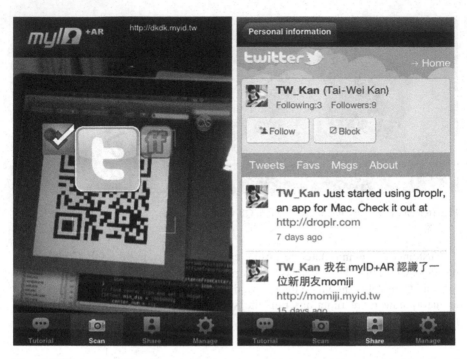

Fig. 16.7 Through myID+AR application, users can retrieve the social network information of new friends easily

5 Conclusions

The development of augmented reality and markers are popular subjects in computer vision and graphics fields. Such studies, however, mostly only focus on the markers specifically used in certain systems. Such markers are not widely available to the public, and as a result cannot be appreciated by most people even if they work well.

In light of this, we think of replacing traditional AR markers with QR Code that people are familiar with and have accessed to. QR Code is a type of 2D barcode that has been widely used in many fields in the world. It is expected to be a standard barcode in the near future (just like the 1D barcode which is being replaced). The goal of this article is to establish a QR Code-based augmented reality with two applications, in which QR Code takes place of traditional AR markers. This new system has the advantages of QR Code and no marker registration is required.

In this article we presented two applications: the product demonstration system and the myID+AR system. The product demonstration system allows users to download digital content through the URLs encoded in QR Code and displays digital content on QR Code-based markers. The myID+AR system allows users to follow friends' activities or make friend with others through capturing QR Code. With its strong adaptability and capacity, QR Code will make AR systems more

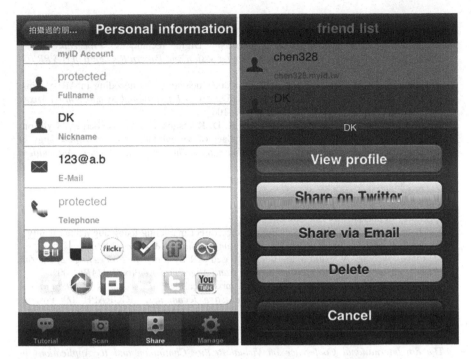

Fig. 16.8 The application allows users introduce his/her new friend to others

flexible for commerce, industry and many others. In fact, our system opens up a new idea for AR systems with 2D barcodes, and we think that in the future, some animations and user interaction can also be included in the QR Code, making the system more attractive and functional. We also believe that the success of this system will trigger many other useful and interesting applications in the future.

Acknowledgement We owe gratitude to many people for the completion of this article. Besides, the "myID+AR" iPhone application is the result of collaboration between National Taiwan University Mobile, Social and HCI Research Lab and the National Digital Archives Program of Academia Sinica of Taiwan. Many people have contributed their efforts to this project, including Momiji Chen and Ilya Li from Academic Sinica, and Meng-Han Li from NTU, among others. We are thankful for their kind instructions, advice and assistance.

References

1. Denso Wave Inc. QR Code features. http://www.qrcode.com, 2002.
2. H. Kato, K. T. Tan, "Pervasive 2D Barcodes for Camera Phone Applications", *IEEE Pervasive Computing*, Vol 6, Issue 4, pp. 76–85, October 2007.
3. T. J. Soon, "QR Code", *Synthesis Journal*, Section 3, pp. 59–78, 2008.

4. J. Rekimoto, Y. Ayatsuka, "CyberCode: designing augmented reality environments with visual tags", *Proceedings of DARE on Designing augmented reality environments*, 2000.
5. M. Fiala, "ARTag, a Fiducial Marker System Using Digital Techniques", *Proceedings of the IEEE Computer Society Conference on Computer Vision and Pattern Recognition (CVPR'05)* Vol. 2, p. 590–596, June 20–26, 2005.
6. X. Zhang, S. Fronz, and N. Navab, "Visual marker detection and decoding in AR systems: A comparative study," In *Proceedings of the IEEE/ACM International Symposium on Mixed and Augmented Reality (ISMAR)*, 2002, pp. 97–106.
7. N. Navab, E. Cubillo, B. Bascle, J. Lockau, K. D. Kamsties, and M. Neuberger, "CyliCon: a software platform for the creation and update of virtual factories." In *Proceedings of the 7th IEEE International Conference on Emerging Technologies and Factory Automation*, pp. 459–463, Barcelona, Spain, 1999.
8. ARVIKA. http://www.arvika.de/www/index.htm.
9. X. Zhang, Y. Genc, and N. Navab. "Mobile computing and industrial augmented reality for real-time data access". *Proceedings of the 7th IEEE International Conference on Emerging Technologies and Factory Automation*, 2001.
10. X. Zhang, N. Navab, and S. Liou, "E-commerce direct marketing using augmented reality", *Proceedings of IEEE International Conference on Multimedia & Expo.*, 2000.
11. M. Fiala, "Webtag: A World Wide Internet Based AR System", In *Proceedings of the 6th IEEE/ACM International Symposium on Mixed and Augmented Reality (ISMAR)*, 2007.
12. M. Carrer, C. Gabriel, "Mobile tagging and mixed realities", *Proceedings of International Conference on Computer Graphics and Interactive Techniques*, SIGGRAPH '09: Posters, 2009.
13. Takao, N., 2007. libdecodeqr. http://trac.koka-in.org/libdecodeqr.
14. T.-W. Kan, C.-H. Teng, W.-S. Chou, "Applying QR Code in Augmented Reality Applications", *The 8th International Conference on Virtual Reality Continuum and Its Applications in Industry*, Tokyo, Japan, 2009.

Chapter 17
Evolution of a Tracking System

Sebastian Lieberknecht, Quintus Stierstorfer, Georg Kuschk, Daniel Ulbricht, Marion Langer, and Selim Benhimane

Abstract This chapter describes the evolution of a feature-based tracking system developed by metaio. One of the reasons that started the development of the system was the first tracking contest at the International Symposium of Mixed and Augmented Reality (ISMAR) in 2008, which was designed to fairly evaluate different tracking systems. We present the toolchain we conceived to solve common problems like referencing to another coordinate system or creating a map of the environment from photos; we also describe the principles of our tracking method which, in contrast to the methods of all other contestants, was robust enough to use exactly the same parameters for all scenarios of the tracking contest held within the German research project AVILUS[1] but at the same time was the most accurate. The ultimate goal of development is its integration into an end consumer product.

1 Introduction

For the effective use of Augmented Reality (AR), the ability to track a camera needed for augmentation with respect to a model of the environment is a prerequisite. To create the required model of the environment, a multitude of options exist featuring different characteristics.

One common approach is to place fiducial markers into the environment. These markers usually consist of a thick black border-frame which contains an unique

---

[1] AVILUS is an acronym from "Angewandte Virtuelle Technologien im Produkt- und Produktionsmittellebenszyklus", meaning "applied virtual technologies inside product and production facility life cycles", see http://avilus.de.

S. Lieberknecht (✉)
Research, metaio GmbH, Munich, Germany
e-mail: Sebastian.Lieberknecht@metaio.com

B. Furht (ed.), *Handbook of Augmented Reality*, DOI 10.1007/978-1-4614-0064-6_17,
© Springer Science+Business Media, LLC 2011

binary-code or picture, designed to be easily detected and identified within a camera image [13, 16]. All AR content is then calculated relative to these fiducials whereas the rest of the environment is not used for tracking. The tracking generally works as long as the fiducials are in the field of view of the camera.

Another class of tracking algorithms, called *extensible tracking*, aims to incorporate a previously unknown environment, starting from (registered) known fiducials. This way, an augmentation is still relative to a fiducial, but tracking will continue even if the fiducial is no longer in the field of view of the camera. This is a very important criterion for real-world AR applications.

Tracking can also be conducted instantly without the need to pre-register the environment at all. Methods following this direction have to construct a *3D map* of the environment and localize the camera either simultaneously or in parallel, which is in general called Simultaneous Localization and Mapping (SLAM [11]) and Parallel Tracking and Mapping (PTAM [17]) respectively. As these methods by definition do not know anything about the environment, the augmentations also cannot be context aware. However, they perfectly suit games or other applications that do not need more than an up-to-scale reconstruction of the environment.

Context-awareness can be introduced to the presented methods by relating the reconstructed map to *a priori* known 3D geometry, to which the augmentations are conceived relatively. For example considering a maintenance scenario in a car, this could mean creating a map of the engine compartment which is later registered via measured 3D coordinates of certain reconstructed objects. The augmentations then could be displayed directly overlaying additional information and highlighting the parts on which a mechanic would have to work on, see Fig. 17.1.

For each of these three classes of tracking algorithms, a variety of methods was presented in the literature. Usually, the authors of the methods evaluate their own algorithms quantitatively on synthetic data and qualitatively on real world scenarios. Unfortunately, until recently there were no widely accepted datasets for evaluating tracking algorithms such as the Middlebury dataset [7] in the multi-view stereo community. Lieberknecht et al. [20] published a dataset suitable for planar template tracking algorithms. For evaluating SLAM methods, there are datasets available from the rawseeds project [4].

Using common datasets is one option to establish a fair comparison of different algorithms. However, based on the results of common datasets alone there is no strong indication on how well a given algorithm could be used in a specific AR-related task, due to the in general unknown speed of an algorithm and the amount of fine-tuning which had to be done by for tracking methods to obtain the published results.

A fair comparison of different tracking methods that also includes the time needed for setting it up has first been established at the International Symposium of Augmented and Mixed Reality (ISMAR) in 2008, it was called the *"Tracking Contest"*. The contest is based on an order picking scenario, i.e. a user should be guided to target-objects using AR only given the 3D coordinates of these objects. The contest was organized by the Technical University of Munich (TUM), as were a

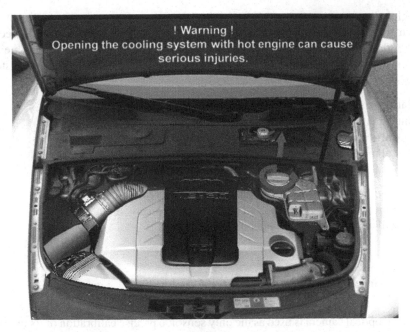

Fig. 17.1 Maintenance scenario using feature-based optical tracking. Augmentations guide the user to correctly maintain the car, in this case how to refill the cooling system

followup at ISMAR 2009 and a contest inside the German research project AVILUS in 2010. The authors developed a feature-based tracking system and according tool chain over the course of the last 3 years. The system was evaluated at each of the tracking contests and is accurate enough to localize points with a worst-case accuracy of 4 cm within the body of an aircraft cabin mockup[2] despite being robust to lighting changes. This chapter presents all steps necessary to create such a map of the environment, registering this map to a predefined reference coordinate system and finally use it for tracking.

2   Proposed Tracking System

In the following, the workflow and the methods we used will be explained in detail. Since the system evolved over 3 years, we will describe this evolution on specific components, including justifications of specific changes.

The general idea behind our approach is to first put a few markers into the scene, then register these with respect to each other and with respect to the reference

---

[2]The mockup consisted of five full rows of business class seats of an Airbus A340, see [25].

(or global) coordinate system. Next, multiple images of the objects of interest are taken, extracted feature points from the images are matched and triangulated directly in the global coordinate system. The resulting map is then used during runtime for tracking and relocalization. From a bird's eye view, the current tracking system consists of the following steps:

1. Intrinsic camera parameter calibration
2. Inter-marker registration
3. Local↔global coordinate system registration
4. Local map creation
5. Relocalization and tracking

where the first three steps are done offline, map creation can be done both offline and online, and (re)localization and tracking are typically online only. Each of these steps will now be described in detail.

2.1 Intrinsic Camera Parameter Calibration

Since an optical camera is used as the only sensor, a precise calibration of its internal parameters is a prerequisite in order to be able to compute any correctly scaled or metric results from its image. In our setup, we usually employ two cameras: One with low resolution and high frame rate for building the map and tracking, typically a webcam, and one with high resolution and low frame rate for the inter-marker registration, typically a digital single-lens reflex camera (DSLR).

The intrinsic camera parameters consist of the horizontal and vertical focal lengths and the principal point of the camera and the skew. The skew is generally assumed to be zero in our cameras. In order to compensate distortion of the camera, also the radial and tangential distortion coefficients up to second order need to be computed. In order to calibrate these, a sufficient amount of 2D–3D correspondences has to be created, this is typically done using a known target like a chessboard. For the calibration of the low resolution camera, we use the calibration method from Zhang [28] from OpenCV [9]. Here the user has to specify the dimension of the chessboard and the dimension of a single cell. Several shots of the chessboard are then captured and its inner corners are detected. A non-linear optimization then iteratively minimizes the squared distance of the reprojection of the chessboard corners to the detected corners by updating the intrinsic and extrinsic parameters of the camera.

A good calibration may be achieved by keeping in mind that on the one hand the chessboard should be covering the whole image sensor to be representative for the whole image. On the other hand using only fronto-planar shots should be avoided as they give rise to ambiguities especially in depth. Empirically, we found out that six images taken as on the left half of Fig. 17.2 give good results. For the calibration of the high resolution camera, we use a professional 3D camera calibration target and

Fig. 17.2 *Left:* For intrinsic camera calibration using OpenCV [9], these six configurations empirically gave good calibration results. They cover the full sensor area and are not fronto-planar. *Right:* The 3D calibration target from AICON [1] used to calibrate the high resolution camera

software from AICON [1] which results in more precise 2D–3D correspondences and thus a better internal calibration. The target is depicted on the right side of Fig. 17.2.

2.2 Inter-Marker Registration

For the creation of the initial map, the proposed system relies on markers to be placed into the scene. While it is conceptually not needed to change the scene to perform feature-based tracking, using fiducials has the benefit that it is a simple way to establish a quite precise estimate of the pose of the camera. Specifically, we apply markers to assign camera poses to keyframes which are in turn used for the initial triangulation, i.e. when the map is empty.

There are multiple ways to use markers in order to create a feature map which needs to be registered to a global coordinate system. One could either register each marker separately to the global coordinate system or form groups of markers registered with respect to each other and then register every group of markers to the global coordinate system. We usually choose the latter way as it makes the registration to the global coordinate system optional, i.e. the creation of the map can be done in a local, independent coordinate system. The map then can be analyzed, maybe rebuilt from different images and just at the end registered to the global coordinate system. Fusing the markers into one coordinate system has also the advantage of a faster registration process in the end.

To register the markers to each other, we use a method that first analyzes a given set of images on the co-visibility of the markers. The user may choose a *reference* marker defining the local coordinate system and to which all other markers should be registered to. This way, the user may only need to register this marker to the coordinate system of the virtual content which may be trivial if accounted for in the design of an AR application. For each detected marker, we compute a quality value based on the size of the marker in the image and the reprojection error. The poses

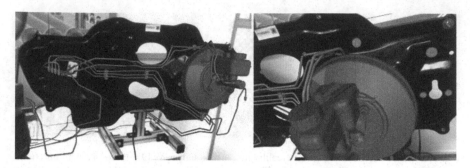

Fig. 17.3 Augmented prototyping: a virtual part is overlayed onto a real part of an engine compartment to check for compatibility at an early stage in development

with the highest quality per marker-pair are used to compute initial poses relative to the reference marker. All observed relative transformations between markers plus the estimation of the camera pose for each image relative to the reference marker are then refined in an non-linear optimization using the overall reprojection error as cost function.

2.3 Registration Local ↔ Global Coordinate Systems

One of the most important steps in industrial augmented reality applications is the registration of the local coordinate system of the sensor to the coordinate system of the content. For example, when using a mechanical measurement arm in automotive prototyping scenarios, the basis of the tracking system is extremely precise – the tip of a mechanical measuring device such as the Faro Arm Platinum [2] is located with an accuracy smaller than 0.013 mm within its working volume. The automotive industry employs these measuring devices traditionally for discrepancy checks between planned and built prototypes, recently also for live virtual integration of planned parts into real prototypes as shown in Fig. 17.3.

However, in this scenario the high accuracy of the measuring device is not paying off in case one of the other registrations/calibrations is inaccurate. In the order picking scenario where we generally deal with less tight accuracy requirement, the registration between local and global coordinate system can be considered as the most critical step.

A naïve approach would be to manually align the coordinate systems by displaying models that refer to real world objects in the global coordinate system, e.g. represent the reference points shown in Fig. 17.4 with small spheres and then align them manually. When doing this, the user has to carefully change the position of the camera as he is only manipulating projections which may perfectly fit in one view, but may be meters away when observed from another perspective.

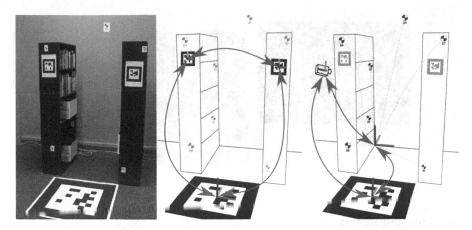

Fig. 17.4 *Left:* One of the stations of the ISMAR 2009 tracking contest. The task was to pick books based on their 3D coordinates in the global coordinate system. *Middle:* Via Inter-marker registration, the distinct marker coordinate systems may be related to each other. *Right:* Local↔global registration is needed to relate the local coordinate system to the global coordinate system which is essential to pick the correct object. This can be done using either 3D–3D or 2D–3D correspondences as described in Sect. 2.3. This figure shows the latter method where the registration is achieved by computing the pose of the camera in both coordinate systems

More elegantly, this problem can be solved semi-automatically with the resulting registration usually being achieved faster and more accurate. There are in general two ways how to do this, using 2D–3D or 3D–3D correspondences. For the contests of 2008 and 2009 we used the 2D–3D method. For this, reference points observed in one image together with one of the markers are necessary which represents a hard constraint. From the correspondences, the pose of the camera can be computed both in the local and global coordinate system using any PnP algorithm such as POSIT [12], thus they may easily be registered to each other by inverting one of the transformations and concatenating it with the other as can be seen from the rightmost scheme of Fig. 17.4. Given three reference points, the 2D–3D algorithms give rise to up to four different solutions, but starting from four points a unique solution can be found.

Unfortunately, two of eight stations at the ISMAR 2009 tracking contest only featured three reference points. In theory, it may still be possible to register the coordinate systems by simply inspecting all possible solutions and from multiple images and then essentially choosing the "correct" one. However, if multiple image are used anyway, then the 3D–3D method can be directly applied, it works fine with a minimum of three correspondences; compared to the 2D–3D method, the hard constraint that every reference point has to be observable on each image is removed, the reference points maybe reconstructed independent of each other.

After the tracking contest, we thus implemented a tool [18] that enables the user to create simple 3D models from sets of images with known camera poses (see Fig. 17.5). The models may also directly use the texture of the object from one of

Fig. 17.5 *Left:* A tool that allows the user to create 3D–3D correspondences intuitively using a model of a real-world object. *Right:* An interactive reconstruction tool integrated into Unifeye that may be used to triangulate 3D points

Table 17.1 Overview of the different requirements of the local↔global registration schemes

Method	Registered images	Correspondences
2D–3D	1	≥4
3D–3D	≥2 per correspondence	≥3

the images. The reconstruction tool is used e.g. for obtaining measurements between the real-world and a virtual model for discrepancy checks or collision analysis. It can also be used to create simple occlusion models, allowing a more realistic augmentation of a scene. However, for registering different coordinate systems, we may also use it to just triangulate points using at least two registered images. These points are then referring to the local coordinate system. Thus, by reconstructing the reference markers in the local coordinate system, we effectively create 3D–3D correspondences. These correspondences are then used to register the coordinate systems via the method of Umeyama [27]. In our case, the method is implemented in a tool displayed in Fig. 17.5 that takes a set of 3D point correspondences as input and outputs the transformation from local to global coordinates. The resulting transformation may directly be applied to a feature map. In case the 3D geometry of a real-world object is available, 3D coordinates can also be intuitively obtained by simply clicking them on the geometry.

Both methods for registering two coordinate systems are briefly characterized in Table 17.1. They were integrated into the Unifeye platform (metaio's end-user software), there the methods are intended to assist the user in registering virtual 3D geometry to the real world within an AR application. This can now be easily done by non-expert users. For example, they just have to click on prominent features on the 3D geometry and their projections in the image which are internally fed into the 2D–3D registration method. This is especially useful for occlusion geometries as they should match the real world closely and thus correspondences may be created straightforward.

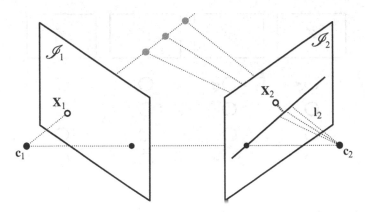

Fig. 17.6 Outlier removal via epipolar geometry/fundamental matrix. When two images $\mathscr{I}_1, \mathscr{I}_2$ are registered, i.e. the position of the camera centers c_1, c_2 and orientations are known, a point x_1 in $\mathscr{I}_1$ has a corresponding (epipolar) line l_2 in $\mathscr{I}_2$. Without reconstructing the 3D point of which both x_1 and x_2 are assumed to be projections, the geometric consistency of the match can be checked by examining the distance of x_2 to the epipolar line l_2

2.4   Local Map Creation

After calibrating the cameras and registering the markers to each other and the global coordinate system, the feature map of the environment is created. This starts by taking a series of images with the low resolution camera that will later be used for tracking, typically images of dimension 640×480 are captured. Ideally, there is a marker visible in every image taken such that the pose of the camera can be accurately computed. From these images, we extract SIFT [21]-like scale-invariant features, i.e. 2D points with scale, orientation and descriptor. Next, we take pairs of images and compute the Euclidean distances for each descriptor in the first image to every descriptor in the second image, keeping only the smallest and second smallest distance. The ratio of these should be below a threshold to accept it as a *match*, typically we use 0.8 as suggested by Lowe [21].

However, using only the ratio as criterion for matched/not matched still leaves a big amount of outliers, especially in scenes that feature repetitive elements. In the proposed reconstruction scheme, we try to eliminate outliers as early as possible, i.e. after each new data association. This is justified as we are interested only in 3D points that are suitable for tracking purposes, we assume that 3D points that were e.g. mismatched during the construction of the map are likely to be mismatched also during tracking. To remove a fair share of outliers after the pair-wise matching, we use the poses assigned to the images and the intrinsic calibration of the camera to compute a fundamental matrix for each image pair. Next, we check for each candidate match the distance to the corresponding epipolar lines. If this is above a threshold (usually 3 pixels), the match is removed. This is also shown in Fig. 17.6.

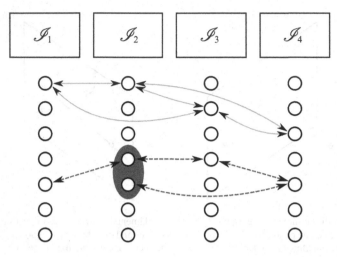

Fig. 17.7 A scenario where features of four images $\mathscr{I}_1,\ldots,\mathscr{I}_4$ are matched pair-wise. From these matches, connected components are created to associate features of more than two images at once. Outliers are detected by removing all components that contain more than one feature of the same image (*dashed component*) and further checking the reprojection error of the reconstruction

The result of this phase are pair-wise consistent matches. To get a globally consistent state, we integrate all pair-wise matches into one graph, using nodes to represent features and an edge for each pair-wise match. This graph is analyzed for connected components of which each node may be an observation of the same 3D point. We analyze the connected components and remove all components in which there is more than one feature from the same image, see Fig. 17.7. Further, components consisting of too few observations are removed, we typically require a minimum of three observations.

After this, we triangulate the observations of each connected component to get the 3D coordinate. Then, we again check for the reprojection error and iteratively remove matches to keep the reconstruction consistent. A linear combination of the feature descriptors is computed and assigned to the reconstructed 3D point.

In case there were images which did not have a pose assigned, i.e. where the marker detection could not find any configured marker, the features of these images are matched against the reconstructed map to obtain a camera pose. This is done for all images previously not included in the map generation and then the map creation is repeated from the 2D–2D match outlier removal phase, giving the "new" features exactly the same status as those already inside the map.

All these steps are integrated into a tool called the "Marker-less tracking map generator", shown in Fig. 17.8. The user gives as input images and a camera calibration, it is assumed that they were all taken with the same resolution and intrinsic camera parameters. Also the dimension of the markers that were placed in the scene has to be specified. The user may change some parameters such as the maximum amount of extracted features per image and parameters for each outlier

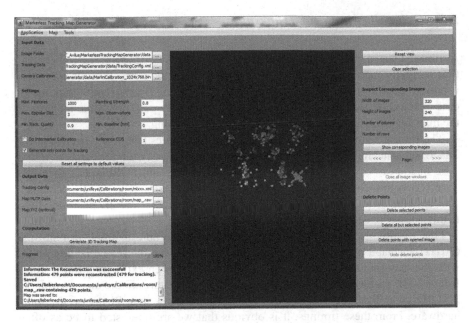

Fig. 17.8 The tool called "Marker-less tracking map generator" which creates a local map from registered images as described in Sect. 2.4. For every reconstructed point, the user is able to display images with highlighted corresponding 2D features and to delete parts of the reconstructed points, e.g. everything that is outside a volume of interest. In this example, an industrial device (displayed in Fig. 17.5) was reconstructed

removal phase. In order to deal with image sequences where consecutive images have very close cameras, we added a simple but effective optional minimum baseline criterion that, if enabled, automatically removes images that were taken from too close positions, which would most likely lead to a suboptimal triangulation anyway due to the high uncertainty in depth.

After the reconstruction is done, the user has the possibility to inspect the created map. He may click on each reconstructed 3D point and the corresponding 2D features will be shown in separate windows. Besides having been a great help while developing the reconstruction algorithm, the user can use this feature to see which features may not belong to the object of interest. There are two ways to remove features from the map, either by selecting their projections ("black list") or by specifying a volume of interest ("white list"). These map manipulating features helped us specifically in the AVILUS tracking contest in a scenario where the camera was fixed and the target to be tracked was attached to a moving robotic arm. Otherwise the relocalization algorithm described in the next subsection, since it assumes a static scene, would not have been able to correctly track as it would not have been clear what is inlier and what outlier. This is exactly what unfortunately happened to one of the other contestants, resulting in either no tracking at all or a static pose in case the background was tracked.

2.5 Relocalization and Tracking

At runtime, the map of the environment is used to obtain the pose of the camera and thus correctly augment the camera image with virtual geometry. For our approach, it makes sense to distinguish between relocalization and (inter-frame) tracking. In case of relocalization, there is no estimate of the camera pose or visible features of the map available while these are given in case of tracking.

The relocalization consists of the extraction of features from the current camera image and matching them against the reconstructed features from the map. An initial pose of the camera is computed using RANSAC [15] and POSIT [12], then this pose is non-linearly refined based on the reprojection error. The same mechanism for obtaining the pose is also used during tracking, however the 2D position of the features are updated using sparse optical flow [22].

One requirement of the tracking system was to be able to track in real-time (30 Hz), to enable AR as defined by Azuma [5]. However, the relocalization scales with the map size and typically takes around 50 ms when extracting 400 features from a VGA frame and matching them against 1,000 features in the map on a single 2.5 GHz core. Tracking 100 features typically takes less than 20 ms on the same hardware. From these timings, it is obvious that we are interested to be as often as possible in the "tracking" state. However, the tracking as described so far is prone to lose features either when they leave the field of view or in case they are classified as outliers by RANSAC. To increase the number of features, we make use of the images used for reconstruction (keyframes). As we know their pose, we may use them to reproject features into the current camera image and add these to the tracking. This change resulted in a major improvement of both accuracy and speed as the relocalization is now used very seldomly when the user is within the known environment.

In case the user explores previously unknown environment, it is also possible to extend the map at runtime (*extensible tracking*). For this, we currently use a minimum baseline requirement as described above. When the current camera position is far enough from the cameras of all keyframes, it is saved as candidate keyframe. When a given number of such candidate keyframes are collected, we apply a reconstruction algorithm similar to the one for local map creation, however we do not re-estimate the previously triangulated 3D points. The new part of the map is computed in a low priority background thread, for five keyframes the thread typically finishes in less than a second. Finally, the new map is merged into the existing map and a new part of the environment can be used for tracking. Of course, the extensible tracking can also be used without a previously reconstructed map. Here, e.g. markers can be used for obtaining the camera pose of the candidate keyframes.

3   Evaluation

The proposed system evolved over the last 3 years. The development was started in August 2008 by Tobias Eble and Sebastian Lieberknecht, later Selim Benhimane and all other co-authors contributed to the system. In the following, we will describe snapshots of the tracking system that participated in the tracking contests of ISMAR and AVILUS.

3.1   ISMAR Tracking Contest 2008

The first iteration of the tracking system contained local outlier removal and matching heuristics, compared to the proposed system of the previous section many global outlier removal steps were missing. The main tracking was based on globally registered markers, the feature-based part was just an extension so that in case no markers were detected the tracking would still continue to work for a small distance. The marker detection developed at metaio has been the core technology of the company in its early years, thus it has received a considerable amount of attention and was continuously improved over a long period of time. Given a good camera calibration its pose estimates are very accurate [23].

Next to each station of the tracking contest, we placed a set of markers which was registered to the global reference coordinate system using the 2D–3D method described in Sect. 2.3. Despite the very early stage of the feature-based part, Tobias Eble was able to correctly pick 15/16 objects from eight stations (see Fig. 17.10). The objects to be picked were varying both in texturedness and size.

Georg Klein from University of Oxford, Harald Wuest and Mario Becker from Fraunhofer Institut für graphische Datenverarbeitung (IGD), Sudeep Sundaram from University of Bristol and Mark Fiala from Millenium 3 Engineering participated in the contest as well. Each team was given 4 h to setup their system including a test run with 3D coordinates from the organizers, then the contest run was conducted in which the contestants had to pick 16 objects from the stations in a specified order. It was allowed to introduce new objects to the scene everywhere but in close proximity of the stations/objects to be picked (marked with blue tape as can be seen e.g. at station **snacks** in Fig. 17.9).

Several technologies have been used, though all were relying on a monocular camera setup. Mark Fiala used ARTag [13] inspired fiducials called "MFD-5", as shown in Fig. 17.10. He planned to use groups of fiducials for each station which would be registered relatively to each other and the given reference coordinate system using bundle adjustment. Sudeep Sundaram planned to use an Extended Kalman filter (EKF) based SLAM system [14] for the tracking contest. Both systems did not succeed to run on time.

Harald Wuest tried to use a method that tightly fuses an inertial sensor and a camera, described in [8]. For this approach, a textured model of the environment is

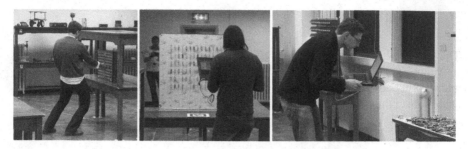

Fig. 17.9 *From left:* Georg Klein at station **shelf**, Tobias Eble at **key rings**, Harald Wuest at **snacks**

Fig. 17.10 Overview of the stations of ISMAR 2008, with Mark Fiala's MFD-5 markers in the foreground. In the very left the theodolite can be seen that was used to create the reference coordinate system of the contest

necessary, but unfortunately the modeling software for creating this textured model did not work as expected. An additional slot in the schedule of the contest was provided, this time a fallback solution was used. It consisted of an ad-hoc method based on directly tracking the reference points of the coordinators with extensible tracking was implemented by using components from the instantVision library [3]. As this method only uses a single reference point, the accuracy was limited. Despite these shortcomings and the fact that the high-level part of the method was developed during the tracking contest, Harald Wuest managed to correctly pick 7/16 objects.

Georg Klein used PTAMM [10], an extension of PTAM [17] dealing with multiple separate maps. Opposed to traditional SLAM, which employs filtering to simultaneously refine the map and pose of the camera using every image, this

Table 17.2 Results of the ISMAR 2008 tracking contest

Rank	Team	Technology	Items	Time
1st	Univ. Oxford	Keyframe-based local maps	16/16	8:48
2nd	metaio	Fiducials and extensible tracking	15/16	10:43
3rd	Fraunhofer IGD	Reference points and extensible tracking (2nd try)	7/16	25:16
–	Univ. Bristol	EKF-based SLAM	–	–
–	Mark Fiala	Fiducial-based local maps	–	–

system is based on the idea of *not* using every camera frame to build up the map. Instead, keyframes are selected from the camera frames and used to build up the map in parallel to the tracking. Thus, the map does not corrupt as easily as in filter-based SLAM, furthermore the split in tracking thread and mapping thread allows the system to track several hundreds of features at frame-rate and perform bundle adjustment in the background, which leads to high mapping accuracy. Klein used multiple local maps and registered each of these to the global coordinate system. At runtime the system switches automatically between maps. He picked 16/16 objects correctly and thus won the tracking contest, detailed results are given in Table 17.2.

A video of the contest can be seen online.[3] A comparison between our system of 2008 and PTAMM is hard since the latter does not use any prior information about the scene when building the map while we use markers of known dimension. Due to the short development time of our system, the feature-based part is less stable and, as outliers may accumulate easily, prone to drift much earlier than PTAM given its sophisticated multi-pass bundle adjustment. All calibration steps seem to have had comparable accuracy nevertheless. On the other hand, such comparisons were exactly the motivation of the tracking contest, so in case both systems are seen as black boxes, the results are in fact comparable, admittedly very much to our favor.

3.2   ISMAR Tracking Contest 2009

The second tracking contest was held at ISMAR 2009 in Orlando, Florida. Harald Wuest, Mario Becker and Folker Wientapper from Fraunhofer IGD as well as Mark Fiala (now from Ryerson University) participated again. Also Peter Keitler and Christian Waechter from TUM joined the contest. The scoring scheme was changed compared to the year before, picking incorrect objects or modifying the environment now resulted in malus points while there were additional bonus points

---

[3] See http://www.ismar08.org/wiki/doku.php?id=program-competition.

Fig. 17.11 *Left:* Station **accuracy test**. Instead of picking an object, the user should draw a mark onto the transparent glass according to a given 3D coordinate. Unless a HMD with proper calibration is used, the user has to triangulate a point-based on the display of the tracking system. *Right:* Peter Keitler from TUM, using a tracking system that employed a modified version of PTAM and sensors of optical computer mice (Courtesy of TUM)

Table 17.3 Results of the ISMAR 2009 tracking contest. In row **items**, the number of picked, correct and total items is displayed

Rank	Team	Technology	Items	Accuracy	Time	Score
1st	Fraunhofer IGD	Local keyframe-based maps	8/8/14	20.7 mm	31:17	11
2nd	metaio	Global descriptor-based map	4/3/14	6.2 mm	23:51	6
3rd	TUM	Keyframe-based local maps and mice	4/0/14	–	25:16	−5
–	Mark Fiala	Fiducial-based local maps	–	–	–	

for speed and accuracy. The accuracy of the tracking systems was determined by requiring the contestants to draw a cross on a transparent surface at specified 3D coordinates, see Fig. 17.11. The average distance between two drawn and corresponding ground truth locations was used as estimate of the accuracy of a system, see Table 17.3. As there was a poster hanging on the wall behind the glass, it was possible to obtain some texture from the background for tracking. Nevertheless, this station also was difficult to handle because, in order to draw the mark precisely, the user had to align his view with the view of the camera to triangulate a point in mid-air using only its projection as seen on the display.

The system used by Sebastian Lieberknecht already embodied the map creation as presented in Sect. 2.4, also the tracking was very similar to the proposed system, however the reprojection of features from keyframes was missing. As already mentioned in Sect. 2.3, the registration of local to global coordinate systems was unfortunately still based on 2D–3D correspondences which directly resulted in two non-registered stations. All locally created maps were integrated into a global map which was used for relocalization and tracking during the contest. Three correct objects and one incorrect object were picked, the mean accuracy was determined to be 6.2 mm.

Mark Fiala followed the approach of ISMAR 2008, using multiple MFD-5 markers to create local maps of each station which afterwards are refined by bundle adjustment. He used an ultra mobile PC (UMPC) for image acquisition and tracking, but for the computationally demanding bundle adjustment he also employed a stationary PC. Markers were added iteratively to the bundle adjustment, this did not work as expected and the contest run was cancelled.

Peter Keitler from TUM modified PTAM [17] such that it has additional map managing capabilities similar to PTAMM [10] (which was not yet publicly available). It was integrated into the Ubitrack Framework [24] and used as main tracking system for the contest. The hardware setup involved a tripod mounted on a movable base as seen in Fig. 17.11. Three modified computer mice were integrated into the base, by exchanging the lenses they were used to provide a coarse relative tracking which acted as a backup in case the main optical tracking would not deliver a camera pose. The camera was rigidly mounted on the tripod, thus the system in essence had to deal with only 3° of freedom while tracking, opposed to 6° the other systems with hand-held cameras had to deal with. During the contest run, the system had problems inside the map switching part.

Harald Wuest from Fraunhofer IGD did not use an extensible tracking approach this time, instead he employed separate tracking and map building phases described in [25] and briefly presented in the following. To build a map of the environment, the user records a video sequence of each station. While recording, the user already gets visual feedback about the quality of the future reconstruction as an initial reconstruction is done online. This part of the algorithm uses Shi-Tomasi [26] extrema for feature detection, for feature tracking a method similar to Lucas-Kanade [22] is used. An initial map is constructed from the epipolar geometry of two frames which are automatically selected according to their baseline, after that it is extended using the same technique. An online refinement of the map is done using an Extended Kalman Filter.

The initial map is created in an arbitrary coordinate frame, in a next step the registration to the coordinate frame of the augmentations is conducted by creating 3D–3D correspondences from reconstructed points and then applying the technique of Umeyama [27]. The registered map is then refined via Bundle Adjustment. To obtain whether a given feature can be used from a given camera pose, visibility information about the features is stochastically generated from the training videos and optional additional videos. This allows that only a reasonable subset of potentially visible features may be used during online tracking, reducing the computational load and improving the quality of the camera pose. The online tracking part of the system then consists of inverse compositional template tracking [6] of the potentially visible features. For relocalization, i.e. in case the camera pose is not known, a learning-based technique from Lepetit et al. [19] is used. Wuest picked eight correct objects in the contest and achieved a mean accuracy of 20.7 mm. As shown in Table 17.3, this made the team from Fraunhofer IGD win the contest.

3.3 AVILUS Tracking Contest (2010)

AVILUS is a German research project focussed on research, development and evaluation of Virtual and Augmented Reality techniques in industrial scenarios in which TUM, metaio and Fraunhofer IGD are involved. Within AVILUS, a tracking contest was organized to evaluate the tracking technologies developed in the AVILUS and AVILUS Plus research projects. Therefore, developers and users were confronted with very realistic scenarios which should be handled in a compact time frame, not only to observe the performance of each technology but also to encourage further improvements and share knowledge. There were five scenarios consisting of 52 sub-scenarios in total, most of them focussed on marker-less tracking. The scenarios were provided by Volkswagen AG, EADS Deutschland GmbH, KUKA Roboter GmbH and Howaldtswerke-Deutsche Werft GmbH who are also AVILUS partners.

Harald Wuest, Mario Becker and Folker Wientapper from Fraunhofer IGD used a tracking system very similar to the setup of ISMAR 2009 with improvements regarding to the relocalization.

The tracking system of Peter Keitler, Christian Waechter, Mahmoud Bahaa and Gudrun Klinker from TUM was also based on the system from ISMAR 2009. They improved the registration of the feature map to the global coordinate system by registering markers to the global coordinate system and aligning these to the reconstructed PTAM maps whenever both were tracked. The mouse sensors were no longer used.

Selim Benhimane, Quintus Stierstorfer and Georg Kuschk from metaio used the system as presented in Sect. 2. Compared to ISMAR 2009, now every part of the tracking system was fully integrated into Unifeye, metaio's technology platform. We tried to make every component productive and also focussed on the usability of our tools regarding to non-experts. Features like merging different maps and clipping parts of the map were added into the tool used for local map creation in order to optimize maps in a postproduction step. Remarkably these efforts seemed to have paid off since the tracking system worked out of the box for all different scenarios. Neither parameter tuning nor coding was necessary in contrast to TUM and IGD.

A detailed overview of each scenario including all results can be found in [25], in the following we will describe two scenarios in detail, please refer to Table 17.4 for the results of all picking contests. All images and data of this section originated from [25].

In the **VW Passat Engine Bay** scenario, the engine compartment of a car should be tracked in order to identify one small (max. dimension <1 cm) and one medium sized object (around 5 cm). It is depicted in Fig. 17.12. The lighting conditions were modified after every team conducted the training of the algorithms to make the scenario more realistic, e.g. with regard to possible future remote-maintenance use-cases. Peter Keitler from TUM did unfortunately not succeed to initialize PTAM due

Table 17.4 Results of the picking scenarios. Three scenarios were based on tracking various parts of a car, the fourth scenario (HDW) consisted in a discrepancy check of a mockup of a submarine component. For details, please refer to [25]

Scenario	Team	Items
VW Passat Engine Bay	Fraunhofer IGD	5/6
	metaio	6/6
	TUM	0/6
VW Passat Interior	Fraunhofer IGD	6/6
	metaio	6/6
	TUM	6/6
VW Passat Exterior	Fraunhofer IGD	2/4
	metaio	2/4
	TUM	2/4
HDW	Fraunhofer IGD	5/9
	metaio	6/9
	TUM	6/9

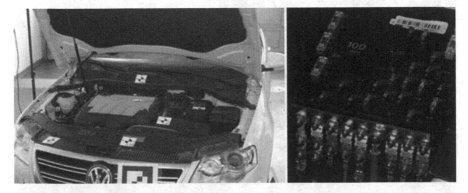

Fig. 17.12 Scenario **VW Passat Engine Bay**. The tracking systems had to be trained using lighting conditions different from the contest run. *Left:* The objects to be picked typically were fuses inside the fuse box (which was closed during training) representing the small objects and e.g. the cap of the windshield wiper system representing the medium sized objects. *Right:* Close-up of the fuse box

to the different lighting conditions. Harald Wuest from IGD at first failed to initialize their tracking system when using wide-baseline matching of features as described in Lepetit et al. [19]. However, a fallback solution was used in which the user has to position the camera close to a known keyframe and then track from there on.

The second scenario described here is the **EADS cabin compartment**. Inside the compartment, there were several reference marks placed using ultra-violet ink. As this is outside of the optical spectrum, the contestants could not see the reference marks. Similar to the accuracy test of ISMAR 2009, the task was to place marks at given 3D reference coordinates. The discrepancy of these marks and the reference masks, which were made visible again using an ultra-violet lamp, was measured and is displayed in Table 17.5. Images of the results of the proposed system are given in Fig. 17.13.

Table 17.5 Results of finding targets inside the aircraft cabin of EADS. Despite not the same items were to be picked, in general the rows of the table embody the same level of difficulty and are thus comparable

Fraunhofer IGD		metaio		TUM	
Item	Discrepancy	Item	Discrepancy	Item	Discrepancy
S3	50.0 cm	S3	4.0 cm	S2	44.0 cm
S5	1.0 cm	S6	2.0 cm	S4	55.0 cm
S8	9.5 cm	S9	0.5 cm	S7	19.0 cm
S12	10.0 cm	S11	2.5 cm	S10	46.0 cm
S13	6.0 cm	S15	2.5 cm	S14	8.5 cm

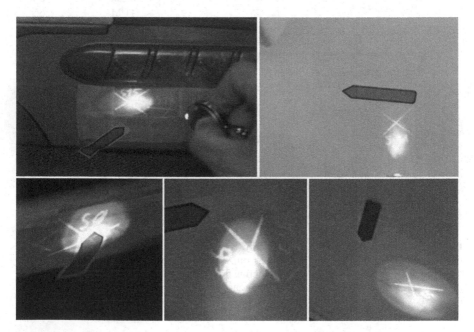

Fig. 17.13 Accuracy test of the AVILUS tracking contest. Inside an aircraft cabin compartment, several marks were placed using invisible ink. The contestants should place *arrows* next to the 3D position shown by their tracking system. These images show the results of the proposed method, please refer to Table 17.5 for detailed results also of the other contestants

4 Discussion

The AVILUS contest also showed a couple of areas in which the proposed tracking system could be improved. As the system depends on feature points, which in turn rely on strong gradients with local extrema, areas with low texture pose a problem. For example, there was one scenario where a toy car should be tracked. The car was unicolored and thus did not give rise to many features. This was a problem for all contestants. After opening the doors of the toy car, it became trackable for the proposed system. However, in absence of *point-based* features, the integration of *edge-based* features into the tracking system looks like a natural next step.

Possible future steps may also take place in the online extension of the map. This is at the moment a scaled-down version of the offline map creation. Instead of using matches from all images for the reconstruction it uses only the n latest (typically 5–10). However, for being productively used in completely unknown environments, further online map refinement steps may be necessary. Strategies as implemented in PTAM [17] may be valuable additions, e.g. using bundle adjustment and advanced feature handling like re-matching candidates, but also removing features after several failed attempts to rematch them, even removing full keyframes in retrospect. These "maintenance" steps are in general suited to run in the background while the system is tracking, which would be a reasonable use of the parallelism found in modern hardware.

5   Conclusion

Tracking contests establish a fair comparison between tracking systems. They take into account all necessary calibrations and registrations, also time constraints and changes in lighting are modeled. These requirements provide feedback to the developers of such tracking systems and, if they are taken into account, the tracking system evolves over time.

We presented a tracking system that was evaluated at international and national tracking contests. All parts of the system were described: the camera calibration, the inter-marker registration, methods for registering local and global coordinate systems, creation of maps of the environment and finally tracking relative to these maps.

We have shown two particular examples where this happened at our system, namely in the map creation and in the local↔global coordinate system registration. The contests also are a good way for potential users of tracking technology to see whether the technology can be readily employed in a specific scenario.

The proposed system is robust and at the same time very accurate. No parameter changes were necessary. During the AVILUS tracking contest, the system ran out of the box. For contests with multiple stations, multiple local maps seem to be the favorable solution. They have the advantage that possible errors stay local and that the size of the maps stays small which positively affects performance.

Future steps may attempt to improve the performance with respect to scenarios featuring low texture. Also a more sophisticated online extension of the map seems to be a reasonable addition.

Acknowledgements Our thank goes to Daniel Pustka and Gudrun Klinker who conceived and organized the ISMAR 2008 and 2009 tracking contests as well as Björn Schwerdfeger who together with Gudrun Klinker mainly organized the AVILUS Tracking contest. Futhermore, we are thankful

to Harald Wuest, Mark Fiala, Peter Keitler and Sudeep Sundaram for disclosing their technology and for valuable discussions about their view on the tracking contests.
This work was partially supported by BMBF grant Avilus / 01 IM08001 P.

References

1. Aicon 3d systems gmbh. http://www.aicon.de, accessed 2010-12-01.
2. Faro europe gmbh & co. kg. http://www.faro.com, accessed 2010-12-01.
3. Instantvision, subproject of instantlabs. http://doc.instantreality.org, accessed 2010-12-01.
4. The rawseeds project. http://www.rawseeds.org, accessed 2010-12-01.
5. Ronald Azuma. A survey of augmented reality. *Presence*, 6(4):355–385, 1997.
6. Simon Baker and Iain Matthews. Lucas-kanade 20 years on: A unifying framework. *IJCV*, 56(3):221–255, 2004.
7. Simon Baker, Daniel Scharstein, J. P. Lewis, Stefan Roth, Michael J. Black, and Richard Szeliski. A database and evaluation methodology for optical flow. In *ICCV*, 2007.
8. Gabriele Bleser and Didier Stricker. Advanced tracking through efficient image processing and visual-inertial sensor fusion. *Computers and Graphics*, 33(1):59–72, 2009.
9. Gary Bradski. The OpenCV Library. *Dr. Dobb's Journal of Software Tools*, 2000.
10. Robert Castle, Georg Klein, and David Murray. Video-rate localization in multiple maps for wearable augmented reality. In *Proc 12th IEEE Int Symp on Wearable Computers, Pittsburgh PA, Sept 28 - Oct 1, 2008*, pages 15–22, 2008.
11. Andrew J. Davison, Ian D. Reid, Nicholas D. Molton, and Olivier Stasse. MonoSLAM: Realtime single camera SLAM. *PAMI*, 26(6):1052–1067, 2007.
12. Daniel DeMenthon and Larry S. David. Model-based object pose in 25 lines of code. *IJCV*, 15:123–141, 1995.
13. Mark Fiala. Designing highly reliable fiducial markers. *PAMI*, 32(7):1317–1324, 2010.
14. Andrew P. Gee, Denis Chekhlov, Walterio Mayol, and Andrew Calway. Discovering planes and collapsing the state space in visual slam. In *BMVC*, 2007.
15. Richard I. Hartley and Andrew Zisserman. *Multiple View Geometry in Computer Vision*. Cambridge University Press, ISBN: 0521540518, second edition, 2004.
16. Hirokazu Kato and Mark Billinghurst. Marker tracking and hmd calibration for a video-based augmented reality conferencing system. In *Proceedings of the 2nd International Workshop on Augmented Reality (IWAR 99)*, San Francisco, USA, October 1999.
17. Georg Klein and David Murray. Parallel tracking and mapping for small AR workspaces. In *ISMAR*, 2007.
18. Marion Langer and Selim Benhimane. An interactive vision-based 3d reconstruction workflow for industrial ar applications. In *ISMAR 2010, Workshop: Augmented Reality Super Models*, 2010.
19. Vincent Lepetit and Pascal Fua. Keypoint Recognition using Randomized Trees. *PAMI*, 28(9):1465–1479, 2006.
20. Sebastian Lieberknecht, Selim Benhimane, Peter Meier, and Nassir Navab. A dataset and evaluation methodology for template-based tracking algorithms. In *ISMAR*, 2009.
21. David G. Lowe. Distinctive image features from scale-invariant keypoints. *IJCV*, 60:91–110, 2004.
22. Bruce D. Lucas and Takeo Kanade. An iterative image registration technique with an application to stereo vision (ijcai). In *Proceedings of the 7th International Joint Conference on Artificial Intelligence (IJCAI '81)*, pages 674–679, April 1981.
23. Katharina Pentenrieder, Peter Meier, and Gudrun Klinker. Analysis of tracking accuracy for single-camera square-marker-based tracking. In *Proc. Dritter Workshop Virtuelle und Erweiterte Realitt der GI-Fachgruppe VR/AR*, 2006.

24. Daniel Pustka, Manuel Huber, Christian Waechter, Florian Echtler, Peter Keitler, Gudrun Klinker, Joseph Newman, and Dieter Schmalstieg. Ubitrack: Automatic Configuration of Pervasive Sensor Networks for Augmented Reality. *to appear in IEEE Pervasive Computing*, 2010.
25. Björn Schwerdtfeger. AVILUS tracking contest 2010 – Abschlussbericht. Technical report, TUM, 2010.
26. Jianbo Shi and Carlo Tomasi. Good features to track. In *CVPR*, 1994.
27. Shinji Umeyama. Least-squares estimation of transformation parameters between two point patterns. *PAMI*, 13(4):376–380, 1991.
28. Zhengyou Zhang. A flexible new technique for camera calibration. *PAMI*, 22(11):1330–1334, 2000.

Chapter 18
Navigation Techniques in Augmented and Mixed Reality: Crossing the Virtuality Continuum

Raphael Grasset, Alessandro Mulloni, Mark Billinghurst, and Dieter Schmalstieg

1 Introduction

Exploring and surveying the world has been an important goal of humankind for thousands of years. Entering the twenty-first century, the Earth has almost been fully digitally mapped. Widespread deployment of GIS (Geographic Information Systems) technology and a tremendous increase of both satellite and street-level mapping over the last decade enables the public to view large portions of the world using computer applications such as Bing Maps[1] or Google Earth[2].

Mobile context-aware applications further enhance the exploration of spatial information, as users have now access to it while on the move. These applications can present a view of the spatial information that is personalised to the user's current context (*context-aware*), such as their physical location and personal interests. For example, a person visiting an unknown city can open a map application on her smartphone to instantly obtain a view of the surrounding points of interest.

Augmented Reality (AR) is one increasingly popular technology that supports the exploration of spatial information. AR merges virtual and real spaces and offers new tools for exploring and navigating through space [1]. AR navigation aims to enhance navigation in the real world or to provide techniques for viewpoint control for other tasks within an AR system.

AR navigation can be naively thought to have a high degree of similarity with real world navigation. However, the fusion of virtual information with the real environment opens a new range of possibilities, and also a significant number

---

[1] Bing Maps, Microsoft Corporation, http://www.bing.com/maps/.

[2] Google Earth, Google Inc., http://earth.google.com.

R. Grasset (✉)
HIT Lab NZ, University of Canterbury, New Zealand
e-mail: raphael.grasset@canterbury.ac.nz

Institute for Computer Graphics and Vision, Graz University of Technology, Austria

---

Fig. 18.1 AR navigation with the World-Wide Signpost application [2] (Image courtesy of Tobias Langlotz)

of challenges. For example, so-called *AR browsers* enable the presentation of large amounts of geo-located digital information (e.g. restaurants, bars, museums, shops) over the real world through a GPS-based AR handheld platform (Fig. 18.1). Nevertheless, efficiently exploring this massive information space and presenting it to the user in a simple way remains an important research topic.

Similarly, finding the shortest path through a multi-floor building using a handheld AR navigation system needs to address specific problems related to the topology, geometry of the building, and the registration of virtual navigation information in the real world. Using a map, directional arrows or wireframe representation of the building are some potential techniques that can be used in this context.

Beyond these standard cases, AR also provides a more seamless way to *bridge* and access other worlds, like 3D Virtual Environments, 2D digital maps, or simply the real world. Accessing or *transitioning* into these worlds using efficient location and navigation cues is still an unresolved and challenging problem.

In this chapter we will introduce some of the benefits, issues and challenges around AR navigation by presenting previous work in this area, and proposing a general navigation framework, addressing future challenges and research topics. The work we present also applies to the broader field of Mixed Reality (MR), where real and virtual information are mixed without a precise definition of which space (virtual or real) is augmented and which space is augmenting.

In the next section, we will first present the general concept of human navigation and location through space. Then we will describe our general model of AR navigation (Sect. 3) before illustrating related work derived from our model. We classify related work by the viewpoint of the user on the spatial information, either considering AR as a primary (Sect. 4) or a secondary (Sect. 5) source of spatial information.

2 Navigation

Navigation is the task of moving within and around an environment, and combines both *travel* and *wayfinding* activities. With travel a user performs low-level motor activities in order to control her position and orientation within the environment. With wayfinding a user performs higher-level cognitive activities such as understanding her position within the environment, planning a path from the current position to another location, and updating a *mental map* of the environment. This last activity requires acquiring spatial knowledge and structuring it into a mental map [3, 4].

Spatial knowledge can be acquired from various sources. Darken and Peterson [3] distinguish between *primary* and *secondary* sources. A primary source of spatial information is the environment itself. As we navigate the environment, we extract information from it which we use for navigational tasks. Secondary sources of spatial information are all other sources such as a map. In the case of a user who acquires information from a secondary source, we also distinguish whether she is immersed in the environment related to the information (e.g., browsing a map of the surroundings) or not (e.g., browsing a map while in a hotel room).

There is still no unique model to detail how spatial knowledge is structured into a mental map. The most established model is the Landmark, Route and Survey (LRS) model of Seigel and White [5], which was later refined by Goldin and Thorndyke [6]. The LRS model defines a classification of spatial knowledge and describes the sources from which the different classes of information can be acquired. *Landmark knowledge* represents the visual appearance of prominent cues and objects in the environment independently from each other. It develops by directly viewing the environment or through indirect exposure to it (e.g., looking at photographs or videos). *Route* (or *procedural*) *knowledge* represents a point-by-point sequence of actions needed to travel a specific route. It provides information on the distance along the route, the turns and actions to be taken at each point in the sequence, and the ordering of landmarks. Route knowledge can be acquired by navigating the route. Finally, *survey knowledge* represents the relationships between landmarks and routes in the environment in a global coordinate system. Survey knowledge can be acquired either by repeated navigation in the environment or by looking at a map.

Lynch [7] classifies the elements of a mental map of a city into five types: *landmarks*, *paths* (or *routes*), *nodes*, *districts* and *edges*. Landmarks are fixed reference points external to the user. They can be either distant prominent elements or local details, and their key feature is singularity. Landmarks are used as clues for the structure of the environment. Paths are channels through which a person can travel. People tend to think of paths in terms of their start and end points. The other elements of the environment are structured along and in relation to the paths. Nodes are strategic points in the environment, typically the convergence of paths. People travel to and from nodes, and wayfinding decisions are often made on nodes. Districts are individual medium-large areas of the environment. Edges are breaks in the continuity of the environment (e.g., a river or a railway), which sometimes inhibit crossing them. The context in which the information is acquired also has an impact on how the information is represented. For example, pedestrians will see a highway as an edge, whereas car drivers will see it as a major path.

As we have seen, the source and the context used for acquiring information impacts on the type of information acquired. Primary sources support landmark and route knowledge, and only after repeated navigation survey knowledge starts developing. In contrast, secondary sources can speed up knowledge acquisition – yet with a loss in quality. For example, maps directly support survey knowledge, yet the knowledge acquired from them is inferior to that obtained from repeated route traversals. This is because knowledge acquired from maps tends to be orientation specific [3]. Goldin and Thondyke [6] show that watching a film of a route can provide substantial landmark and route knowledge.

In general, a user performing navigational tasks uses various types of spatial knowledge and reasons on multiple frames of reference. For example, Goldin and Thondyke [6] show that procedural knowledge supports egocentric tasks – such as estimating the orientation and route distance with respect to their own body – better than survey knowledge. In contrast, survey knowledge better supports exocentric tasks – such as estimating Euclidean distances or the relative position of generic points in the environment. One key element is therefore *resolving the transformation between the frame of reference of the spatial knowledge and the frame of reference of the task to be performed*. The smaller the distance between the two frames of reference, the lower the burden on the user who must mentally transform between the two.

3 Enhancing Navigation Through Augmented and Mixed Reality

Augmented Reality is inherently bound to the frame of reference of the real world scene being perceived. As discussed previously, it is therefore crucial to identify which tasks can be supported from the AR frames of reference.

For example, AR can be used to augment the physical environment in which users are embedded. Users can therefore explore the spatial information just as they would explore the streets and the buildings in the environment. Differently, AR can also be used to overlay a table with a detailed virtual 3D visualisation of a remote location. Users can physically walk around this visualisation, reach closer to it or move further from it. In general, it is crucial to identify which tasks can be supported from the AR frame of reference.

AR and MR can be complemented by other interfaces to better support a broader range of navigational tasks. Interface designers must also consider how to transition between the multiple interfaces. This section presents a generic navigation and transitional model. It details how we can navigate an AR or MR interface and how we can move between different types of interfaces within an MR interface.

3.1   Context and Transition

Our conceptual model encompasses and extends the navigation inside/within an inner space (like AR) to a more generic approach, considering the navigation of multiple spaces and in-between spaces (*transition*). Our model considers space from a mathematical viewpoint, and navigation as motion in this space. In this section we explain our model and how it frames navigation in AR, MR or any composite (multiple spaces) scenarios. Readers can refer to [8] and [9] for more information about the model.

First, we introduce the notion of *Context* related to an environment where users can collaborate and interact within (Fig. 18.2). A context not only defines a *space* (e.g. AR, VR, Reality) but it can define a *scale* (e.g. macro, micro, nano, etc.), a *representation* (e.g. photorealistic, non-photorealistic, symbolic), and any other user parameters (such as *viewpoints* and *navigation mode*). Thus, a context is the collection of values of parameters relevant to the application. For example, one context may be defined as an AR space, on a 1:1 egocentric scale with cartoon rendering and a walking navigation metaphor.

In each context, the user has one (or multiple) *viewpoint(s)* related to the view of a task represented in this context (e.g. viewing a 3D virtual model of a future hospital building). The location of the viewpoint in or out of a task representation defines the egocentric or exocentric viewpoint (e.g. inside the building or "bird's eye view" of the building). Different viewpoints can be spatially multiplexed (e.g. map, WIM, etc), so we consider the *focus view* as the primary view which has the user's attention at a certain time (the other views are defined as *secondary views*).

In a specific context, the user can navigate the environment, and thus has a *viewpoint control* defined by a motion function (navigation technique). To support collaboration and location awareness, we define a user representation (*embodiment*) in each context (*proximal embodiment*) and a proxy representation (*distal embodiment*). A user can navigate and manipulate content within a context but can also *transition* to other contexts (i.e. change in viewpoint, and possibly change in scale, representation and interaction). A *transitional interface* is an interaction technique supporting this concept. Figure 18.3 summarizes our model.

3.2   Transitional Interface: Single-User and Multi-User

We identify two general cases based on the number of users: single-user or multi-users. Three main aspects should be considered for a transitional interface:

- What is a transition?
- How does a transition affect the user perceptually?
- How does a transition affect interaction for the user?

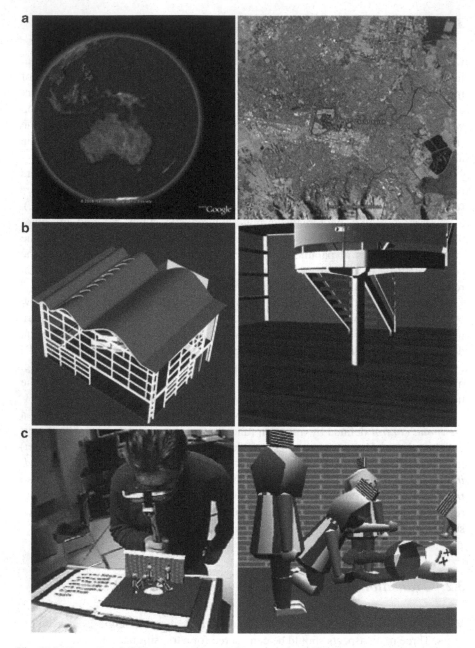

Fig. 18.2 Examples of different contexts: (**a**) different scales, (**b**) different viewpoints (**c**) different spaces

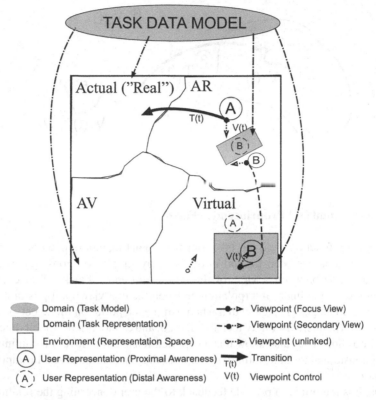

Fig. 18.3 Transitional collaborative model (Contexts are associated here to the notion of Environments)

A transition between two contexts can be decomposed into a succession of different actions. Figure 18.4 describes the steps of navigation and transition between different contexts:

1. The user moves in the first context based on a locomotion function $V(t)$.
2. The user can initiate a transition (e.g. click a position on a map).
3. The user is in a restricted mode where his view "moves" between the two contexts.
4. The user is reaching a new context.
5. The user can navigate in this new context based on a similar or new locomotion function $V(t)$.
6. The user can optionally come back to the first context, by using the same transition function (so we have the notion of 'de-selection') or to another context. The user can therefore come back to his previous state on the other context (e.g. viewpoint) or can also be a new one.

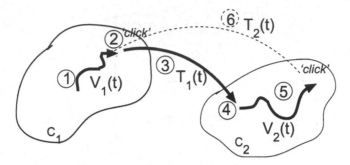

Fig. 18.4 Description of a transitional interface

3.2.1 Perceptual and Proprioceptive Factors

The transition function needs to take user perceptual factors into account. Recent work in this area has been limited to deliberately simple solutions: for example, a sudden switch between a view of the real world and a black VR background or perhaps a simple linear interpolation between the two viewpoint positions [10]. Bowman and Hodges [11] show that when using a teleportation mode between two different viewpoints, a user may feel disoriented, and cannot orient herself quickly in her new position. They also show that an application needs to favour a continuously smooth transitional motion (fading) rather than the discontinuous and fast approach of teleportation.

Thus, it is important to provide feedback to the user concerning the relationship between the two viewpoints. This is most often not merely smoothly interpolating between two viewpoints. It is rather a complex task that requires minimising the user's confusion during the transition while at the same time maximising the user's awareness of the fact that the context is changing. We hypothesize that these concepts need to be applied in the case of the transitional interface from a spatial and visual aspect.

The proprioception factor is thus critical. A user needs not only to be able to identify herself in the different contexts (such as by seeing a virtual hand in a VR space), but also during the transition. Furthermore, if the representation of the user is very different between contexts, she might feel disturbed when transitioning and be disoriented in the new context.

3.2.2 Identified Issues

Brown et al. [12] mention the importance of information representation during a mixed-space collaboration. This was also mentioned by Zhang et al. [13] in a multi-scale application. Coherence must be maintained between the different representations chosen for the application content within the different contexts. Respecting logical spatial relationships, pictorial similarity, articulated dimensionality or topology of the object representations are important criteria. Consequently, we can list the different issues that have been identified:

1. Which interaction techniques are used to initiate a transition?
2. Which transition function is used to maintain a seamless spatial and visual representation between the two contexts?
3. How can a sense of proprioception be maintained during the transition?
4. How can the user come back to the previous context? Does the user need to move back to the same location?
5. How can the application content be coherently maintained between contexts?
6. How can coherence of the proprioception/presence be maintained between contexts?
7. How can coherence be maintained in the interaction between contexts?

In the case of a collaborative application, awareness of other people needs to be provided to the users. In the literature [14], the common parameters cited are:

- Who (presence, identity of users),
- What (their intentions, feedback of their actions),
- Where (location, gaze, view feedback).

A user is generally embodied as a virtual model replicating her behaviour – an avatar [15]. A transitional collaborative interface needs to also provide similar awareness components: between users in a same context (*proximal embodiment*), between users in different contexts (*distal embodiment*), and also during a transition step.

Figure 18.5 illustrates a representative example of transitioning in a collaborative transitional application. In this scenario we have three users: user A and user B are in context 1 (c_1), while user C is in context 2 (c_2). We need to maintain awareness cues between users in the same context (user A and user B), but also a distal embodiment for users in different contexts (user A and user B for user C, user C for user A and user B).

When user A is transitioning between contexts (step 2), other users need to be aware of the transition stage. When the transition is complete, the distal and direct awareness for user A has changed, user B now has a distal embodiment of user A while user C has a proximal embodiment.

We can also list the different new issues identified for the multi-user scenario:

- How to maintain awareness for other users while a user is transitioning between contexts? (from the start, during and at the end of the transition)
- How to illustrate which context the user is transitioning to and from?
- How to modify the proximal embodiment to a distal embodiment of a user transitioning?
- How to maintain co-context and cross-context awareness (co-presence, cross-presence)?
- How to maintain co-context and cross-context information sharing?
- How to maintain co-context and cross-context interaction?

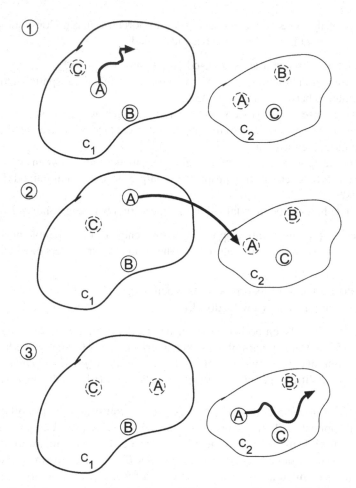

Fig. 18.5 Steps of a user transitioning in a collaborative transitional application (solid circles represent proximal embodiment, dotted circles, distal embodiment)

Our conceptual model supports the human requirements of accessing different representations and different frames of reference in order to perform different types of navigational tasks. Designers of AR navigation systems have the possibility to create advanced systems, considering AR not as the unique context but rather as a component that can enhance a navigation system made up of multiple contexts.

Depending on how AR is used to enhance the system, we distinguish between AR as a primary source or a secondary source of spatial information (Fig. 18.6). In the first case, AR is applied to *augment the environment in which the user is immersed*. In the second case, AR is used to *control a vantage point over a set of spatial information*. In the following sections, we describe first how AR can be used as a primary source and subsequently how it can be used as a secondary source.

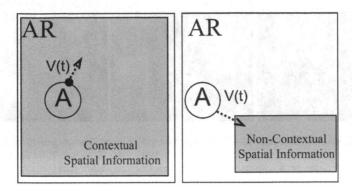

Fig. 18.6 A user (A) using AR as a primary (*left*) or secondary (*right*) source of spatial information

4 AR as a Primary Source of Spatial Information

By fusing the real environment with digital information, AR can be used as a primary source of spatial information. Invisible information becomes visible by superimposing it on physical entities. As the user navigates the environment, digital geo-referenced information augments his or her perception of it.

In this section we discuss the ways in which AR can be used to support navigation. We also analyse the techniques typically used to cope with two limitations of AR – distant or occluded augmentations, and off-screen augmentations. Finally, we look at which other interfaces are usually combined with AR and the types of tasks they are intended to support.

To date, most of the work on AR as a primary source of spatial information has been performed either on wearable setups or on handheld devices. This section will look at the work on both types of platform.

4.1 Supporting Navigation with AR

AR can support both exploratory and goal-oriented navigation. Examples of support for exploratory navigation are annotations that provide information regarding the nearby buildings or the surrounding streets. Such annotations do not explicitly provide wayfinding instructions but they support users in understanding the environment. In contrast, an example of supporting goal-oriented navigation is an arrow or a path superimposed on the street to inform the user about the turns to take. In this case AR supports the user by explicitly embedding wayfinding instructions in the physical environment.

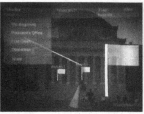

Fig. 18.7 Exploratory (*left* and *middle*) and goal-oriented (*right*) navigation support in the Touring Machine [17] (Images courtesy of Tobias Höllerer. © 1997–2003, S. Feiner, T. Höllerer, E. Gagas, D. Hallaway, T. Terauchi, S. Güven, and B. MacIntyre, Columbia University)

4.1.1 Exploratory Navigation

AR supports exploratory navigation through annotations in the environment. The environment becomes an anchor for geo-referenced hypermedia databases. Users can browse the information by physically navigating the environment and looking at the various annotated objects.

One pioneering work in this field is the Touring Machine by Feiner et al. [16]. This allowed users to browse a geo-referenced hypermedia database related to the Columbia University campus. Users can navigate the campus and interact with the digital content overlaid on the physical buildings. Physical buildings are labelled with virtual information shown through a head-worn display. The authors intentionally label whole buildings and not smaller building features: this high-grain labelling means that tracker inaccuracies do not affect the usability of the application (Fig. 18.7).

One advantage of digital technology is that annotations can be personalized and filtered based on the user's needs and interests. Further, the annotations can present dynamic content and the physical anchors can have a mutable position.

Julier et al. [18] developed the Battlefield Augmented Reality System (BARS) focused on supporting situation awareness for soldiers, and informing them about the location of personnel, vehicles and other occluded objects in the soldiers' view. In BARS, AR is used for three reasons: the urban environment is inherently 3D, accessing secondary sources of information requires the soldiers to switch attention from the environment, and the information to be displayed is often dynamic (e.g., the position of snipers). Julier et al. [19] also discuss methods for reducing information overload by filtering the visual information based on the mission, the soldier's goal and physical proximity.

The MARA project by Kähäri and Murphy [20] implements the first sensor-based AR system running on a mobile phone. MARA provides annotations related to the points of interest in the surroundings of a mobile user. Points of interest are marked with squares and their distance is written as a text label. Clicking a button on the phone while pointing the camera towards a point of interest shows further information about the point. A similar concept is implemented by the many AR

Fig. 18.8 Goal-oriented navigation support in AR, outdoors [22] (*left*) and indoors [23] (*right*) (Image courtesy of Gerhard Reitmayr and Daniel Wagner)

browsers recently appeared in the smartphone market (e.g., Junaio[3]). AR browsers are typically applications that retrieve geo-referenced content from online databases and present it to a mobile user on their phone through an AR interface (see also Fig. 18.1).

4.1.2   Goal-oriented Navigation

AR supports goal-oriented navigation by visualizing the path from one location to another directly in the frame of reference of the physical environment. An advantage of digital technology is that paths can be personalised on the fly.

A pioneering work in the field is Tinmith [21] where a user explicitly defines a desired path as a finite sequence of waypoints. Tinmith then shows the position of the next waypoint through a head-worn display. A diamond-shaped cursor is overlaid on the physical location of the waypoint. The waypoints are also labelled with textual information. More recently, Reitmayr and Schmalstieg [22] show an AR system for outdoor navigation in a tourist scenario. Once the user selects a desired target location the system calculates a series of waypoints from the current location to the target. All waypoints are visualized as cylinders in the environment connected to each other by arrows (Fig. 18.8, left). The authors use a 3D model of the city to correctly calculate occlusions between the rendered path and the physical environment. The system also supports three types of collaborative navigation between users. A user can decide to *follow* another user, to *guide* her or to *meet* her halfway between their current positions. The application also implements a browsing modality for exploratory navigation.

Reitmayr and Schmalstieg [24] also use the same wearable setup for a system called Signpost that supports indoor goal-oriented navigation, by using a directional arrow that shows the directions to the next waypoint. Wagner and Schmalstieg [23]

---

[3]Junaio Augmented Reality browser: http://www.junaio.com.

pioneered handheld indoor navigation systems based on AR and implemented the Signpost system on a personal digital assistant. Similar to the wearable interface, the handheld interface also uses arrows to indicate the direction of a next waypoint.

4.2   Occluded and Distant Augmentations

Annotations are merged with live images from a video camera. AR is therefore bound to the frame of reference of the video camera. The augmentations are constrained to the field of view of the camera and restricted to the viewpoints that are physically reachable by it. In most cases, these viewpoints coincide with the locations physically reachable by the user herself. The amount of information visible from the viewpoint of the camera can be insufficient due to occlusions or large distances between the camera and the information.

4.2.1   Depth and Occlusion Cues

Various navigation systems employ transparency and x-ray vision to communicate depth and occlusion of annotations. Livingston et al. [25] conducted an experiment to evaluate various transparency cues to communicate multiple levels of occlusion. They found that a ground plane seems to be the most powerful cue. Yet, in the absence of a ground plane users are accurate in understanding occlusions when occluding objects are rendered in wireframe and filled with a semi-transparent colour with decreasing opacity and intensity the further they are from the user. Bane and Höllerer [26] discuss a technique for x-ray vision in a mobile context. A tunnel metaphor is used to browse the rooms of a building from the outside. Semantics of the building are used, so that a user can select the rooms one by one rather than using a continuous cursor. A wireframe rendering of the tunnel provides cues about the depth of the various rooms. Avery et al. [27] show a similar x-ray vision technique that employs transparency and cut-outs to communicate multiple layers of occlusion. More recently, the authors also add a rendering of the edges of the occluding objects [28] to better communicate depth relations.

Another approach is to warp or transform virtual information interactively in order to make it more legible. For example, Bane and Höllerer [26] allow selected objects to be enlarged. This zooming technique causes the AR registration to be no longer valid because the object becomes much larger than it should be in the camera view. Yet, as the user's task is the exploration of a specific object, this solution provides a much closer view on it.

Güven and Feiner [29] discuss three methods to ease the browsing of distant and occluded hypermedia objects in MARS. A *tilting* technique tilts all the virtual content upwards in order to see hidden objects. A *lifting* technique translates a virtual representation of the environment up from the ground. This makes it possible to view otherwise occluded objects. A *shifting* technique moves far objects closer to the user to explore them from a shorter distance. These techniques also break the AR registration, yet they allow for a much closer look at information that cannot be browsed with conventional AR. The authors conducted a formal evaluation of the tilting and lifting techniques compared to a transparency-based technique, and they found that they were slower than the transparency-based interface but were more accurate.

Sandor et al. [30] suggest using a 3D model of the city to virtually melt the closest buildings to show the occluded content behind them. Aside from the content directly visible in the camera view, the remaining content is rendered from the textured virtual models.

4.3 Off-screen Augmentations

Information can be outside the field of view of the camera and not directly visible in the augmented visualization. AR systems therefore often integrate special interface elements that hint at the location of off-screen augmentations.

4.3.1 Graphic Overlays

Graphic overlays can hint at the direction of off-screen augmentations. Such overlays are typically bi-dimensional and therefore operate in a frame of reference different from the three-dimensional frame of AR. These overlays hint at the direction in which a user should turn to bring the augmentation into view.

In the Touring Machine [16], a conical compass pointer is overlaid on the AR view and always points towards a selected label. A visualization element in Tinmith also hints at the location of off-screen waypoints [30]. When the waypoint is not in view, a diamond-shaped cursor appears on the left or the right side of the screen, showing the user the way to turn their head to bring the waypoint into view. AR browsers often employ radar-shaped like overlays to show the horizontal orientation of all the surrounding annotations.

The Context Compass [34] uses a more complex graphic overlay, that shows the horizontal orientation of annotations with respect to the user. It is a linear indicator of orientation: icons in the centre of the overlay represent annotations currently visible by the user, whereas icons to the side of the overlay represent annotations outside the field of view of the user. The Context Compass is designed to have minimal impact on the screen space while providing key context information.

4.3.2 AR Graphics

AR graphics can also be used to hint at off-screen annotations. In this case, the hints are three-dimensional and embedded in the frame of reference of AR.

Biocca et al. [31] present the *attention funnel*, an AR visualization element shaped as a tunnel which guides the attention of a user towards a specific object in the environment. The authors evaluate the technique in a head-worn setup, comparing it against visual highlighting (a 3D bounding box) and a verbal description of the object. Results show that the attention funnel reduces visual search time and mental workload. However, the interface also provides visual clutter, so the user should be able to disable the tunnel when needed, or the transparency of the tunnel can be increased as the view direction approaches the direction of the object.

Schinke et al. [32] uses 3D arrows to hint at off-screen annotations. The authors conduct a comparative evaluation of their 3D arrows versus a radar-shaped graphic overlay. Participants were asked to memorize the direction of all annotations from the visualization without turning their body. The evaluation showed that 3D arrows outperformed the radar overlay and users were more accurate in estimating the physical direction of off-screen annotations.

4.4   Combining AR with other Interfaces

As different interfaces and frames of reference are needed for various tasks, AR is often combined with other non-AR interface elements to support tasks that are more easily performed outside the AR frame of reference. In this section we will detail both *what* interfaces are combined with AR, and *how* they are combined with AR. Interfaces are sometimes separated spatially. In this case a certain screen space is allocated to each interface, or a separate device is provided for accessing the non-AR interface. In other cases the interfaces are separated temporally by animations and transitions that allow moving between AR and the other interfaces.

4.4.1   Web Browser

One simple addition to a mobile AR system is a web browser. AR can be used as an interface to select the content of a geo-referenced hypermedia by looking (or pointing a handheld device) towards points of interest. A web browser can then be used as an interface for viewing multimedia content in a web page.

In the Touring Machine [16, 17], the wearable setup is used in combination with a handheld device which provides contextual information as a web page. The AR context is used for intuitive selection of the labels, by simply looking at the corresponding physical building in the campus through the head-worn display. Users were provided with further information about the labels in a web page on the handheld device. Most AR browsers also adopt this approach. The environment is augmented with annotations and selecting an annotation often opens a web page or a textual description that provides further details.

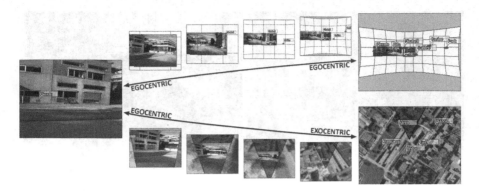

Fig. 18.9 Smoothly moving between an AR view, and a map or a panoramic view [33]

4.4.2   Maps

Many AR systems for navigation also allow browsing a map of the environment. MARS, for example, provides a map view on a separate handheld device [17] that can be brought into view whenever needed. The AR and map contexts are synchronised, so that an object selected in one context is also automatically highlighted in the other. On handheld devices, Signpost [23] provides a semi-transparent map overlay that is superimposed on the AR view on request. Graphic overlays were also employed in Tinmith [34] to show a 2D outlook of the user and the objects in the environment from a top-down frame of reference. AR browsers also usually provide a map view that users can select from the application's menu.

MARA [20] also integrates a map view centred and oriented accordingly to the user's position and orientation. It uses the phone's orientation to move between representations: when the phone lies flat the map view is shown; when the phone is tilted upwards the AR view becomes visible.

In a recent work [33], Mulloni et al. look at a transitional interface that moves between AR and map views. In their case, the transition is achieved by smoothly moving between the viewpoint of the camera and a top-down viewpoint. They compare this transitional interface with a graphic overlay that hints at off-screen objects – similar to the Context Compass [34]. They evaluate the interface on a set of spatial search tasks: finding a highlighted café, finding a café with a given name and finding the closest café. They found that task performance with the graphic overlay is better than with the transitional interface if the system highlights the target object. In contrast, task performance with the transitional interface scales better with increasing task complexity. In real-world applications this suggests that hinting at off-screen objects is sufficient if the system knows what the user is looking for (e.g., as a result of a search query). For exploratory browsing, transitioning from AR to a map interface improves task performance (Fig. 18.9).

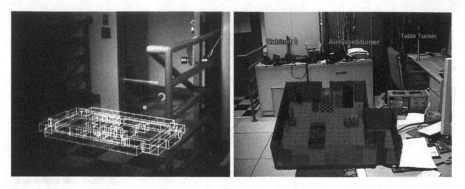

Fig. 18.10 Supporting overview on the environment by moving between AR and World-in-Miniature representations (Images courtesy of Tobias Höllerer. © 2001–2002, T. Höllerer, D. Hallaway, N. Tinna, S. Feiner, B. Bell, Columbia University)

4.4.3 Worlds in Miniature

Some AR navigation systems provide a World in Miniature (WIM) view [35], which extends the 2D map to the third dimension and represents a 3D miniaturized version of the surrounding environment.

Bell et al. [36] combine AR with a World-in-Miniature (WIM) to support situation awareness (Fig. 18.10, right). The WIM acts as a miniature bird's eye view on the environment in which the user is immersed. Head tilting triggers the movement between WIM and AR views: tilting the head down magnifies the WIM, whereas tilting it up minimizes it. The view angle on the WIM is also updated accordingly to the head movements. Looking slightly downwards shows a bird's eye view on the model while looking straight down provides a top-down view. The position of the user is highlighted within the WIM. Finally, the representations in AR and in the WIM are tightly connected to each other. Labels are shared between the WIM and AR views. Objects can be selected either in the WIM or in AR to show further information. Bane and Höllerer [26] use a similar approach to provide a preview of a selected room in a building. Users of their system can exploit AR and x-ray vision to explore the rooms of a nearby building. Once they identify a room of interest they can trigger a "Rooms in Miniature" interface, providing an exocentric view on a virtual model of the selected room. To avoid loss of context, the room is smoothly animated from its real-world position to the virtual position.

Höllerer et al. [37] use a WIM representation (Fig. 18.10, left) that transitions between AR and WIM views depending on the quality of the tracking. When the tracking is sufficiently accurate annotations and route arrows are superimposed on the environment. When the tracking accuracy degrades, the interface smoothly transitions to a WIM view. An avatar representation is used to indicate the current position of the user in the WIM. Rather than inaccurately placing the augmentations – which could potentially confuse users – the authors transition the system to a WIM interface that is more robust to tracking inaccuracies.

Reitmayr and Schmalstieg [24] also support their indoor navigation system with a WIM. In this case the WIM is virtually located on an arm-worn pad. Users can therefore access the WIM view at any time by lifting their arm into view. Further, users can click on a room in the WIM to select it as the target location for navigation. Path, and current target locations are all highlighted on the WIM. In this case, the WIM is used as an exocentric view to select target destinations in the real environment.

4.4.4   Distorted Camera Views

Maps and WIMs allow the user to gain an exocentric view on the surrounding environment. In contrast, some work proposes virtually modifying the field of view of the camera while maintaining an egocentric view on the environment.

Sandor et al. [30] uses a 3D virtual model of the environment to provide a distorted view of the surroundings with a much larger field of view. In recent work [33], Mulloni et al. virtually change the field of view of the AR camera by exploiting an online-generated panorama. As for the transition to the 2D map, evaluations show that when search tasks require an overview on the information, transitioning to a virtual wide-angle lens improves task performance.

4.4.5   Virtual Environments

Finally, some AR navigation systems combine AR and VR. Virtual Reality can be useful to support users in browsing an environment that is not available. The situated documentaries [38] use 360° omni-directional images to immerse the users in such an environment. When viewing these images, the interface switches from AR to VR. In the VR interface the omni-directional images are mapped to a virtual sphere that surrounds the head-worn display. The user can thus physically turn their head in order to explore the image.

Virtual Environments (VEs) can also support collaboration between users immersed in the environment and users that do not have physical access to the environment. Piekarski et al. [39] explore interconnecting AR and VR representations to support collaboration in military settings. The system supports collaboration between the outdoor users and a base station equipped with a PC. Users at the base station can visualize the battlefield environment in a VE. The VE can be freely explored or watched from the exact position and orientation of one of the outdoor users. Users of the base station can support the awareness of outdoor users from advantageous virtual viewpoints and outdoor users can update the elements in the virtual environment based on their experience of the real environment. MARS [17] also supports collaboration between outdoor and indoor users with two different interfaces. On a desktop PC indoor users can access 2D and 3D visualizations of the environment as multiple windows on the screen. Indoor users can also access a tabletop AR view. A head-worn display allows browsing a virtual model of the campus augmented on a physical table. Virtual objects can be added, modified and highlighted by both indoor and outdoor users. All users can see the modifications. Finally, paths can be drawn in the environment to support collaborative navigation.

5 AR as a Secondary Source of Spatial Information

The previous section presents the use of AR in the context of a spatial fusion between real and virtual space in an egocentric viewpoint environment. Another approach is to consider restricting part of the real environment to a limited space, and representing virtual spatial information that can be observed with an exocentric viewpoint.

Using a table (overlaid with a virtual map), a room (augmented with a 3D virtual map that floats above the ground) or real spatial source of information like a real map are some of the most widely used approaches. In this case, the physical space is acting only as a frame of reference to position and contain the virtual information. The spatial knowledge is generally dissociated from the location of the users, presenting, for example, cartography from a different building, landscape or city.

As the exocentric viewpoint restricts the spatial knowledge, different research works have explored the access to the other spatial contexts of information such as a virtual reality world or superposing multiple spaces of information in the real world (e.g. projecting on a wall). We describe in this section some of the major work done in both of these areas.

5.1 Virtual Map in the Physical Space

The first category of augmentation is to consider the existence of a physical source of spatial information like a printed map. The printed map generally furnishes a high-resolution version of contextual information, which can be enhanced with live, dynamic, and focused virtual information. Navigation and interaction with the content is generally supported through a tangible user interface or gesture interaction. The map also provides a shared and common tangible artefact for collaboration, supporting communication or physical annotations.

Different AR display technologies have been explored for this purpose. We can cite three major approaches for viewing the AR content: projection-based, HMD-based/screen-based or handheld devices.

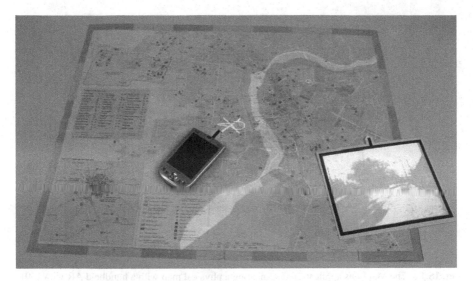

Fig. 18.11 An augmented map using projection technology and supporting tracking of physical objects (Image Courtesy of Gerhard Reitmayr [40])

5.1.1   Projection-Based AR Maps

Reitmayr et al. [40] present a projection-based system coupled with a camera, allowing tracking of different physical elements over a map. A user of their application is able to select different region of interest with a tangible user interface or handheld device (see Fig. 18.11).

5.1.2   HMD and Screen-Based AR Maps

Different projects explore the use of HMD-based or screen-based AR to show 3D information directly above the map. Hedley et al. [41] developed a collaborative HMD-setup where users can overlay a printed map with different type of 3D GIS datasets (e.g topology, soil) by manipulating and positioning encoded tangible markers over the map. A similar idea is explored by Bobrich [42] using a paddle interface to query information on the map. Asai et al. [43] introduce a screen-based solution for lunar surface navigation using a pad to control navigation and displaying elevation information above the map. Jung [44] proposes a similar system for military applications.

Tangible User Interface methods are often used for interacting with an augmented map. Moore and Regenbrecht [45] push the boundaries of the concept further, using a physical cube with a virtual map wrapped around it. Interaction and navigation are supported through different natural gestures with the cube (e.g. rotating on the left face to go west). Using a different approach, Martedi et al. consider the materiality of the map as a support for interaction, introducing some initial ideas for interacting with a *foldable augmented map* [46].

Fig. 18.12 The MapLens application: augmenting a physical map with a handheld AR view [50]

Only a few works have used a room space as a frame reference for navigating virtual information. Kiyokawa et al. [47] explore this concept with the MR Square system where multiple users can see and observe a 3D virtual landscape displayed floating in the centre of a room and naturally navigate through it by physically moving around the landscape.

5.1.3 Handheld-Based AR Maps

Finally, a handheld device can provide a lens view over an existing map, the device acting as a focus (and individual) viewpoint to navigate the map [48]. For example, Olwal presents the LUMAR system [49], using a cell phone as a way to present 3D information above a floor map.

Rohs et al. [51] present a comparative study between a standard 2D virtual map on handheld vs. an augmented map. Their results demonstrate the superiority of the augmented approach for exploration of the map. Similarly, Morrison et al. [50] (Fig. 18.12) found that an augmented map, in contrast to a virtual 2D map, facilitates place making and collaborative problem solving in a team-based outdoor game.

5.2 Multiple Contexts and Transitional Interface

Extending spatial information using additional contexts can be realized with two main approaches: *spatially* (showing more viewpoints from the view of the user) or *temporally* (switching successively between different viewpoints). Below we present some of the contributions based on both of these methods.

5.2.1   Spatially Multiplexed Contexts

One of the seminal works using a projection-based system is the BUILD-IT system [52], developed for collaborative navigation and interaction with a floor map of a building. The authors develop different techniques for navigating with the map and changing viewpoint (using a tangible user interface), including both an augmented exocentric view of a building, and a 3D VR egocentric view.

The concept is extended in 3D through the SCAPE system [53] which combines both an egocentric viewpoint (projected on a wall) and an exocentric viewpoint (projected on a table) with a Head-Mounted Projection Display (HMPD) to display the spatial information. Navigation is supported in both contexts: physically moving in the room to change locally the viewpoint, and moving a token on a table to change exocentric viewpoint location or displace the egocentric viewpoint.

Navigation can also be considered for different users navigating in two different contexts. The MARS system [17] illustrates this concept, where an indoor user has only an exocentric view on a 3D virtual map. Another example is the 3D Live! System [54] that demonstrates how a user with a VR egocentric viewpoint can move in a virtual space whilst a second user with an AR exocentric viewpoint can navigate the same virtual scene, seeing the distal embodiment of the first user (polygonal model reconstructed with a visual hull technique).

Relatively few works empirically evaluate multiple-context navigation. A noticeable work is [55] comparing the impact of different modalities as navigation cues for an egocentric HMD-based AR context and an exocentric projection-based AR context for a cooperative navigational task. The results point out that using visual guidance cues (such as the representation of a virtual hand for indicating directions to a mobile user) is more efficient than audio cues (only). Grasset et al. [8] evaluate cooperative navigation for a mixed-reality space collaboration between a VR egocentric user and a secondary user in different spatial conditions (AR exocentric, VR exocentric). The study shows that combining VR egocentric navigation with AR exocentric navigation benefits from using an adapted distal embodiment of the egocentric user (for the exocentric user) to increase location awareness. Additionally, the usefulness of an AR approach (see Fig. 18.13) depends on whether the application can take full potential of gestural and tangible interaction in the real world and also on the choice of the display to support the navigation.

5.2.2   Time-Multiplexed Contexts

A time-multiplexed AR navigation system was introduced by Billinghurst et al. with the MagicBook Application [56]. This is an interface for navigating between different contexts (AR egocentric, VR exocentric or real world) which also supports transitions between these different contexts (viewpoint interpolation). Using a novel type of handheld device, the system allows the user to trigger the transition step and accesses different virtual worlds, each of them associated with a page of a book.

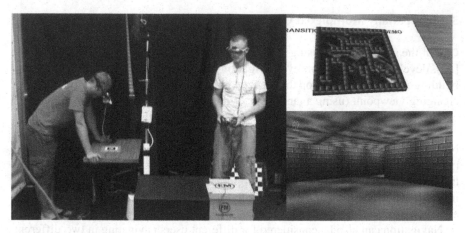

Fig. 18.13 *Left*: Navigation in a Mixed-Reality collaboration, left user has an AR exocentric viewpoint, the right user has a VR egocentric viewpoint. *Right*: AR and VR view

Fig. 18.14 A time-multiplexed transitional interface

This innovative concept has been evaluated in [57], considering transition for a single-user and different type of transition techniques (e.g. using a MagicLens metaphor to select a location in a new context, see Fig. 18.14). In their paper, the authors demonstrate that participants easily understood the metaphor, but the design of the navigation and transition techniques for the contexts where highly connected. An importance observation was related to the perception of the presence in the contexts: The AR context had really low perceived presence, concluding that proposing navigation between multiple contexts reduces the perceptual discrepancy between them (in this latter case the perception was leaning towards "everything is VR").

6 Conclusion and Future Directions

In this chapter, we presented an overview of navigation techniques in AR and MR. We introduced a model for navigation in AR/MR and a generalization of the problem to multiple spaces and contexts. Finally, we categorised previous work based on whether AR is used as a primary or a secondary source of spatial information. As shown by the broad list of previous work, AR can support various spatial tasks and cover various application areas. Yet, a number of future research directions for AR navigation are still open: we present a few of them below.

Augmented Reality Navigation relies heavily on registration and tracking. While it was not the focus of this chapter, the need for temporally and spatially accurate tracking and a correct registration is primordial to support a usable and efficient navigation in AR. Taking into consideration the current inaccuracy of tracking technologies and registration algorithms is one of the first potential research direction in this area. Developing navigation techniques that model the inaccuracy of the system and integrate it into a navigation model (*uncertainty model*) to adapt the presentation of visual guidance information is one potential approach, as shown by Höllerer et al. [37].

In addition, there is no tracking system sufficiently robust and reliable to work in a large range of spatial locations such as in an office, a whole building and outdoors. This implies the need to develop different navigation modalities as a function of the tracking availability. Creating adapted and adaptive models, navigation patterns and tools will help to develop more systematic integration of multiple tracking technologies and facilitate navigation in and between these different locations.

Another major aspect of AR navigation is its dependency on the existence of a spatial model per se, thus including the different objects of the real and virtual environment. Significant progress is currently being made on reconstructing and acquiring real environments (i.e. position, geometry and topology of real artefacts), but the possible challenges induced by error in this process or the scalability of the system (city, country) can potentially lead to more hybrid navigation models (i.e. using different representations of the real environment in different areas).

Other types of visual interfaces can be combined with AR and can complement it. For example, several other interfaces are employed in location-based services (based for example on 2D maps, 3D maps and 360° panoramic images) and could be integrated with AR to build more flexible navigation systems. Furthermore, other modalities can also be explored in addition to visual information, such as audio navigation or haptic guidance. More longitudinal and empirical studies of the viability of these concepts need to be conducted.

In general, the role of AR for supporting navigation is still not fully clear. More experimental work will be needed in the future to identify which navigation tasks are best supported by AR interfaces and which are not. Furthermore, as we are now observing a tremendous increase of digital devices, social applications and spatial information, defining more advanced models to support natural transition between the context of tools simultaneously used by the public will also need further user studies.

Information spaces (e.g., *cyberspace*[4], *hypermedia*[5], Internet) and contexts (e.g., AR, VR, real world) that were once disconnected are now slowly converging towards a unified model. Concepts such as context and transition are now paramount,

---

[4]http://en.wikipedia.org/wiki/Cyberspace.

[5]http://en.wikipedia.org/wiki/Hypermedia.

as users who are embedded in the information space need moving from one context to another. AR will surely play a major role in this model, offering us a solid and direct connection to the physical world that we still navigate in our everyday life.

References

1. R. Azuma, "A Survey of Augmented Reality," *Presence*, vol. 6, no. 4, pp. 355–385, 1997.
2. T. Langlotz, D. Wagner, A. Mulloni, and D. Schmalstieg, "Online Creation of Panoramic Augmented Reality Annotations on Mobile Phones," *IEEE Pervasive Computing*, 2010.
3. R. P. Darken, B. Peterson, and B. S. Orientation, "Spatial Orientation, Wayfinding, and Representation," *In K. M. Stanney (Ed.), Handbook of Virtual Environments: Design, Implementation, and Applications*, p. 493–518, 2001.
4. D. A. Bowman, E. Kruijff, and J. LaViola, *3D User Interfaces: Theory and Practice*, 1st ed. Addison Wesley, 2004.
5. A. W. Siegel and S. H. White, "The development of spatial representations of large-scale environments," *Advances in Child Development and Behavior*, vol. 10, pp. 9–55, 1975.
6. S. E. Goldin and P. W. Thorndyke, *Spatial Learning and Reasoning Skill*. 1981.
7. K. Lynch, *The Image of the City*. The MIT Press, 1960.
8. R. Grasset, P. Lamb, and M. Billinghurst, "Evaluation of Mixed-Space Collaboration," in *Proceedings of the 4th IEEE/ACM International Symposium on Mixed and Augmented Reality*, Washington, DC, USA, 2005, p. 90–99.
9. R. Grasset, J. Looser, and M. Billinghurst, "Transitional interface: concept, issues and framework," in *Proceedings of the 5th IEEE and ACM International Symposium on Mixed and Augmented Reality*, Washington, DC, USA, 2006, p. 231–232.
10. K. Kiyokawa, M. Billinghurst, S. E. Hayes, A. Gupta, Y. Sannohe, and H. Kato, "Communication Behaviors of Co-Located Users in Collaborative AR Interfaces," in *Mixed and Augmented Reality, IEEE/ACM International Symposium on*, Los Alamitos, CA, USA, 2002, p. 139.
11. D. A. Bowman and L. F. Hodges, "An evaluation of techniques for grabbing and manipulating remote objects in immersive virtual environments," in *Proceedings of the 1997 symposium on Interactive 3D graphics*, New York, NY, USA, 1997, p. 35–38.
12. B. Brown, I. MacColl, M. Chalmers, A. Galani, C. Randell, and A. Steed, "Lessons from the lighthouse: collaboration in a shared mixed reality system," in *Proceedings of the SIGCHI conference on Human factors in computing systems*, New York, NY, USA, 2003, p. 577–584.
13. X. Zhang and G. W. Furnas, "Social interactions in multiscale CVEs," in *Proceedings of the 4th international conference on Collaborative virtual environments*, New York, NY, USA, 2002, p. 31–38.
14. C. Gutwin and S. Greenberg, "A Descriptive Framework of Workspace Awareness for Real-Time Groupware," *Computer Supported Cooperative Work*, vol. 11, p. 411–446, Nov. 2002.
15. S. Benford, J. Bowers, L. E. Fahlén, C. Greenhalgh, and D. Snowdon, "User embodiment in collaborative virtual environments," in *Proceedings of the SIGCHI conference on Human factors in computing systems*, New York, NY, USA, 1995, p. 242–249.
16. S. Feiner, B. MacIntyre, T. Hollerer, and A. Webster, "A touring machine: prototyping 3D mobile augmented reality systems for exploring the urban environment," in *Digest of Papers. First International Symposium on Wearable Computers*, Cambridge, MA, USA, pp. 74–81.
17. T. Höllerer, S. Feiner, T. Terauchi, G. Rashid, and D. Hallaway, "Exploring MARS: developing indoor and outdoor user interfaces to a mobile augmented reality system," *Computers & Graphics*, vol. 23, no. 6, pp. 779–785, Dec. 1999.
18. S. Julier, Y. Baillot, M. Lanzagorta, D. Brown, and L. Rosenblum, "BARS: Battlefield Augmented Reality System," *In NATO Symposium on Information Processing Techniques for Military Systems*, p. 9–11, 2000.

19. S. Julier et al., "Information filtering for mobile augmented reality," in *Proceedings IEEE and ACM International Symposium on Augmented Reality (ISAR 2000)*, Munich, Germany, pp. 3–11.

20. M. Kähäri and D. J. Murphy, "MARA – Sensor Based Augmented Reality System for Mobile Imaging," 2006.

21. B. Thomas, V. Demczuk, W. Piekarski, D. Hepworth, and B. Gunther, "A wearable computer system with augmented reality to support terrestrial navigation," in *Digest of Papers. Second International Symposium on Wearable Computers (Cat. No.98EX215)*, Pittsburgh, PA, USA, pp. 168–171.

22. G. Reitmayr and D. Schmalstieg, "Scalable Techniques for Collaborative Outdoor Augmented Reality," in *ISMAR*, 2004.

23. D. Wagner and D. Schmalstieg, "First steps towards handheld augmented reality," in *Seventh IEEE International Symposium on Wearable Computers, 2003. Proceedings.*, White Plains, NY, USA, pp. 127–135.

24. G. Reitmayr and D. Schmalstieg, "Location based applications for mobile augmented reality," in *Proceedings of the 4th Australian user interface conference on User interfaces 2003*, 2003, pp. 65–73.

25. M. A. Livingston et al., "Resolving Multiple Occluded Layers in Augmented Reality," in *Mixed and Augmented Reality, IEEE/ACM International Symposium on*, Los Alamitos, CA, USA, 2003, p. 56.

26. R. Bane and T. Hollerer, "Interactive Tools for Virtual X-Ray Vision in Mobile Augmented Reality," in *Proceedings of the 3rd IEEE/ACM International Symposium on Mixed and Augmented Reality*, Washington, DC, USA, 2004, p. 231–239.

27. B. Avery, B. H. Thomas, and W. Piekarski, "User evaluation of see-through vision for mobile outdoor augmented reality," in *Proceedings of the 7th IEEE/ACM International Symposium on Mixed and Augmented Reality*, Washington, DC, USA, 2008, p. 69–72.

28. B. Avery, C. Sandor, and B. H. Thomas, "Improving Spatial Perception for Augmented Reality X-Ray Vision," in *2009 IEEE Virtual Reality Conference*, Lafayette, LA, 2009, pp. 79–82.

29. S. Guven and S. Feiner, "Visualizing and navigating complex situated hypermedia in augmented and virtual reality," in *2006 IEEE/ACM International Symposium on Mixed and Augmented Reality*, Santa Barbara, CA, USA, 2006, pp. 155–158.

30. C. Sandor et al., "Egocentric space-distorting visualizations for rapid environment exploration in mobile mixed reality," in *Proceedings of the 2009 8th IEEE International Symposium on Mixed and Augmented Reality*, Washington, DC, USA, 2009, p. 211–212.

31. F. Biocca, A. Tang, C. Owen, and F. Xiao, "Attention funnel: omnidirectional 3D cursor for mobile augmented reality platforms," in *Proceedings of the SIGCHI conference on Human Factors in computing systems*, New York, NY, USA, 2006, p. 1115–1122.

32. T. Schinke, N. Henze, and S. Boll, "Visualization of off-screen objects in mobile augmented reality," in *Proceedings of the 12th international conference on Human computer interaction with mobile devices and services*, New York, NY, USA, 2010, p. 313–316.

33. A. Mulloni, A. Dünser, and D. Schmalstieg, "Zooming interfaces for augmented reality browsers," in *Proceedings of the 12th international conference on Human computer interaction with mobile devices and services*, New York, NY, USA, 2010, p. 161–170.

34. J. Lehikoinen and R. Suomela, "Accessing Context in Wearable Computers," *Personal and Ubiquitous Computing*, vol. 6, p. 64–74, 2002.

35. R. Stoakley, M. J. Conway, and R. Pausch, "Virtual reality on a WIM: interactive worlds in miniature," in *Proceedings of the SIGCHI conference on Human factors in computing systems*, New York, NY, USA, 1995, p. 265–272.

36. B. Bell, T. Höllerer, and S. Feiner, "An annotated situation-awareness aid for augmented reality," in *Proceedings of the 15th annual ACM symposium on User interface software and technology*, New York, NY, USA, 2002, p. 213–216.

37. T. Höllerer, D. Hallaway, N. Tinna, and S. Feiner, "Steps Toward Accommodating Variable Position Tracking Accuracy in a Mobile Augmented Reality System," in *In Proceedings of AIMS 2001: Second Int. Workshop on Artificial Intelligence in Mobile Systems*, 2001, vol. 1, p. 31–37.

38. T. Hollerer, S. Feiner, and J. Pavlik, "Situated documentaries: embedding multimedia presentations in the real world," in *Digest of Papers. Third International Symposium on Wearable Computers*, San Francisco, CA, USA, pp. 79–86.

39. W. Piekarski, B. Gunther, and B. Thomas, "Integrating virtual and augmented realities in an outdoor application," in *Proceedings 2nd IEEE and ACM International Workshop on Augmented Reality (IWAR'99)*, San Francisco, CA, USA, pp. 45–54.

40. G. Reitmayr, E. Eade, and T. Drummond, "Localisation and Interaction for Augmented Maps," in *Proceedings of the 4th IEEE/ACM International Symposium on Mixed and Augmented Reality*, Washington, DC, USA, 2005, p. 120–129.

41. N. R. Hedley, M. Billinghurst, L. Postner, R. May, and H. Kato, "Explorations in the use of augmented reality for geographic visualization," *Presence: Teleoperators and Virtual Environments*, vol. 11, p. 119–133, Apr. 2002.

42. J. Bobrich, "An Immersive Environment Based on Paper Maps," in *Proceedings of ICC 2003*, Durban, South Africa, 2003.

43. K. Asai, T. Kondo, H. Kobayashi, and A. Mizuki, "A Geographic Surface Browsing Tool Using Map-Based Augmented Reality," in *Visualisation, International Conference on*, Los Alamitos, CA, USA, 2008, pp. 93–98.

44. K. Jung, S. Lee, S. Jeong, and B.-U. Choi, "Virtual Tactical Map with Tangible Augmented Reality Interface," in *Computer Science and Software Engineering, International Conference on*, Los Alamitos, CA, USA, 2008, vol. 2, pp. 1170–1173.

45. A. Moore and H. Regenbrecht, "The tangible augmented street map," in *Proceedings of the 2005 international conference on Augmented tele-existence*, New York, NY, USA, 2005, p. 249–250.

46. S. Martedi, H. Uchiyama, G. Enriquez, H. Saito, T. Miyashita, and T. Hara, "Foldable augmented maps," in *Mixed and Augmented Reality (ISMAR), 2010 9th IEEE International Symposium on*, 2010, pp. 65–72.

47. K. Kiyokawa, M. Niimi, T. Ebina, and H. Ohno, "MR2 (MR Square): A Mixed-Reality Meeting Room," in *Augmented Reality, International Symposium on*, Los Alamitos, CA, USA, 2001, p. 169.

48. V. Paelke and M. Sester, "Augmented paper maps: Exploring the design space of a mixed reality system," *ISPRS Journal of Photogrammetry and Remote Sensing*, vol. 65, no. 3, pp. 256–265, May 2010.

49. A. Olwal and A. Henrys, "LUMAR: A Hybrid Spatial Display System for 2D and 3D Handheld Augmented Reality," in *Artificial Reality and Telexistence, 17th International Conference on*, 2007, pp. 63–70.

50. A. Morrison, A. Mulloni, S. Lemmela, A. Oulasvirta, G. Jacucci, P. Peltonen, D. Schmalstieg, and H. Regenbrecht, "Collaborative use of mobile augmented reality with paper maps," *Computers & Graphics*, vol. 35, no. 4, pp. 789–799, Aug. 2011.

51. M. Rohs, J. Schöning, M. Raubal, G. Essl, and A. Krüger, "Map navigation with mobile devices: virtual versus physical movement with and without visual context," in *Proceedings of the 9th international conference on Multimodal interfaces*, New York, NY, USA, 2007, p. 146–153.

52. M. Fjeld, M. Fjeld, M. Bichsel, and M. Rauterberg, "BUILD-IT: an intuitive design tool based on direct object manipulation," 1998.

53. H. Hua, L. D. Brown, C. Gao, and N. Ahuja, "A new collaborative infrastructure: SCAPE," in *IEEE Virtual Reality, 2003. Proceedings.*, Los Angeles, CA, USA, pp. 171–179.

54. S. Prince et al., "3-D live: real time interaction for mixed reality," in *Proceedings of the 2002 ACM conference on Computer supported cooperative work*, New York, NY, USA, 2002, p. 364–371.

55. A. Stafford, B. H. Thomas, and W. Piekarski, "Comparison of techniques for mixed-space collaborative navigation," in *Proceedings of the Tenth Australasian Conference on User Interfaces-Volume 93*, 2009, p. 61–70.
56. M. Billinghurst, H. Kato, and I. Poupyrev, "The MagicBook: a transitional AR interface," *Computers & Graphics*, vol. 25, no. 5, pp. 745–753, Oct. 2001.
57. R. Grasset, A. Duenser, and M. Billinghurst, "Moving Between Contexts - A User Evaluation of a Transitional Interface," in *ICAT*, 2008.

Chapter 19
Survey of Use Cases for Mobile Augmented Reality Browsers

Tia Jackson, Frank Angermann, and Peter Meier

1 Introduction

A fully augmented world, visible through the live-view of a smartphone's camera, is taking shape. Bringing virtual, web based content to mobile users as a preliminary stage for the Internet of things is becoming a reality. The paradigm shift that began with Kooper and MacIntyre's **"RWWW Browser"** is categorically shifting the organization and accessibility of information in our world through modern mobile augmented reality (AR) browsers. Though many "single usage" mobile AR applications already exist, the following chapter will instead focus on mobile AR *Browsers, which* aggregate functionality rather than divide it. The industry refers to these programs as "browsers" because they allow the user to access a network of web-based information, not unlike the traditional internet browser. With the abundance of mobile applications available today, a standard, multipurpose mobile AR browser will allow the mobile user to access augmented information and functionality far more efficiently than thousands of specialized applications used one at a time. The authors of this article therefore believe that widespread adoption of mobile AR will take place if and only if users can access multiple functionalities and a wide range of content within a single application: an AR browser that allows the user to explore information in the same fashion that an internet browser already offers.

Recent advancements in technology and major consumer brand participation have been instrumental in the success of a variety of Augmented Reality Browser use cases: camera-equipped smartphones can now present users with physically interactive web-based information and location-based consumer services. Web-browsers such as Google Chrome or Mozilla Firefox, depend on a strong and consistent internet connection. However, as communication networks grow stronger

T. Jackson (✉)
Metaio, Munich, Germany
e-mail: tia.jackson@metaio.com

B. Furht (ed.), *Handbook of Augmented Reality*, DOI 10.1007/978-1-4614-0064-6_19,   409
© Springer Science+Business Media, LLC 2011

and Wi-Fi becomes more readily available to a larger demographic, so too will Augmented Reality capable devices and use cases proliferate. In addition, the majority of existing mobile AR browsers have publicly released their respective APIs (Application Programming Interfaces) in order to encourage user-generated content and overall adoption of AR browsers as a new communicative medium.

Mobile browsers are optimized to display web content most effectively for small screens on portable devices. As consumers rely more and more on smartphones, everyday activities are becoming integrated with mobile browsing. In order to counter the diminished hardware capabilities of mobile devices (relative to current laptops or desktops), access to information and user interface therefore need to be designed efficiently to maintain user engagement. Mobile AR browsers can provide convenient real-time processing of web-based information that the user perceives *through* the phone, rather than *on* it. Rather than surf the world's information via mouse and keyboard, mobile graphical overlays allow the user to walk *through* the world's information and interact with it in a more intuitive way.

In order to participate in a given AR experience, the user must point his or her camera-equipped device towards either a geo-located point of interest or a registered two dimensional marker. In this way, event locations, product packages or even newspapers can be supplemented with web-based data. By measuring the user's viewing angle relative to the physical world (GPS location, Accelerometer Data, Computer Vision and 3D Tracking Sensor Fusion) mobile AR applications allow developers to anchor digital graphics and objects onto different physical locations or objects. Current popular mobile browsers include but are not limited to: Wikitude, junaio, Layar and Accrossair. Most of these browsers provide an interface for developers to add content to theses Browsers. These "AR Websites" are called differently for each browser, whether it is a *World*, a *Channel* or a *Layer.*

When using a mobile AR browser, information and content can be accessed by three means:

- Through Geo-location data (Lat/Long, Compass, Accelerometer and other on-board sensors)
- Through image/object recognition (recognition via computer vision)
- Through dynamic physical interaction with a viewed object (tracking via computer vision)

This chapter gives an overview of the capabilities of available mobile AR browsers and introduces several use cases that have already been successfully realized. Throughout the course of this discussion we will examine different technical approaches such as sensor and image based tracking, navigation, marketing, mCommerce, edutainment and interactive gaming. Furthermore, an outlook into the future of mobile AR and possible next steps will be presented.

2 Technical Capabilities of AR Browsers

When mobile AR browsers were first introduced, their overlay capabilities were limited to displaying location-based, textual information over a given camera direction using mobile accelerometers or onboard compasses. Most mobile AR browsers available today, such as Wikitude, Layar and Sekai Camera, still depend on internal sensors to display geo-referenced information, but with the added ability to integrate images, sounds and links to external websites. The mobile AR browser junaio is currently the only available application that reconciles textual, navigational AR with image recognition and tracking, allowing the user to access Augmented Reality content using all three methods listed above. Most other AR browsers remain capable only of location-based experiences, examples of which are detailed in the following section.

2.1 Location Based Augmented Reality

Accessing location-based information is still the most common use of available mobile AR browsers. A smartphone utilizes its available hardware, like internal gyro sensors, accelerometers, compasses etc. in order to display virtual information layered over the perceivable camera image of the users surrounding environment. Because location-based AR relies almost exclusively on these internal sensors, it is limited by the available hardware specifications of current mobile devices. This can lead to inaccuracies in GPS data, compass malfunctions, and poor location tracking. As mobile devices like smartphones become more advanced, smooth and accurate AR experiences will be the standard, allowing for seamless indoor and outdoor experiences.

Within the outdoor AR experience, the mobile device identifies the user's current position and contextualizes it in relation to the information being accessed. More often than not, if the user is in an outdoor setting he or she is using AR in some sort of navigational manner: directions from two discreet points; hyper- local information like the locations of nearby assets: parks, bookstores, movie theaters, ATMs, available public transportation, parks, public restrooms, hospitals; or even more specific information like which Laundromats in a surrounding area are open 24 h and/or happen to have extra capacity washers and dryers. Outdoor mobile AR browsers can already aid the user in navigating to all sorts of places, or more commonly known as, "Points of Interest" (POIs). In most cases, the user can access real-time information regarding the POI, (store hours, phone number, associated website, address etc.) all while "viewing" the location from miles away.

Though mobile can be limited by the hardware issues listed above, a combination of advanced image/object tracking and more precise calibration of smartphone sensors has overcome the position inaccuracies of GPS to allow very accurate overlaying of outdoor geo-location information. Since GPS has not yet become

Fig. 19.1 LLA marker

precise enough to use in indoor navigation, image/object recognition and tracking become necessary in order to create these types of outdoor experiences, indoors.

For indoor use cases, junaio uses so called LLA Markers. These have a geo referenced position encoded, which overrides the GPS signal.Hence, once the marker is scanned, the user's position can be determined and information can be provided very accurately (Fig. 19.1).

2.2 Image Based Augmented Reality

Currently only junaio is capable of recognizing images to provide marker based as well as 2D image tracking by analyzing the camera image. This can be used to display virtual 3D objects on image references such as products, pieces of art, advertisements, billboards, print news and in the near future for the world as it stands (Fig. 19.2).

3 Use Cases

3.1 Navigation

Navigation within the AR sphere is carried out in real-time within real world settings. When compared to existing navigational technologies such as printed or virtual maps, orientation and navigation within the AR spectrum is intuitive and allows the user to constantly perceive reality through their device, rather than consulting an abstract graphic and trying to reconcile its perspective relative to the users respective physical location. Showcased below are several use cases

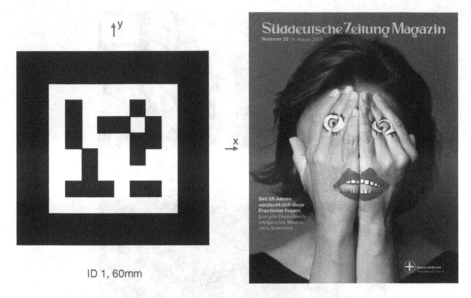

Fig. 19.2 Marker based recognition // Markerless recognition (SZ Magazine case)

that explain the benefits of AR in the field of navigation. These navigational use cases include: Intel Developer Forum (IDF) Guide, BART, Kino, Campus Tour and Wikitude Drive.

3.1.1 Bay Area Rapid Transit (BART), Geo-Location

The Bay Area Rapid Transit (BART) of San Francisco desired an alternative way for users to access their transit information. This channel is dedicated to geo-location data gathered from the BART system. It grants the user access to the location of the nearest BART station and to up-to-the-minute information for incoming trains and estimated arrival times. Figure 19.3 pictured above is an example of the display screen used to deliver the channel. Similar information has been provided for several other cities, such as Portland.

3.1.2 Kino.de, Geo Location for Nearby Theatres Show Times

The Kino.de junaio channel allows users to conveniently access theater information relevant to their location, including showtimes, theater locations, and trailers of movies currently being played. One of the most successful aspects of Kino.de is the user's ability to reserve movie tickets with one click. It shows possibilities of mobile AR browsers today to integrate location and time sensitive information in combination with video and textual information to give users a one step interface to navigate to relevant information efficiently (Fig. 19.4).

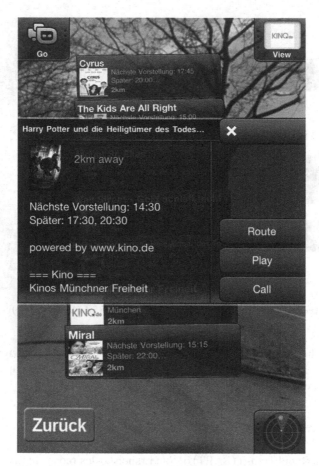

Movie theaters with upcoming movies and trailers in your real world

3.1.3 Wikitude Drive, World's First AR Navigation System

Wikitude Drive is a mobile AR navigation system with global coverage (available for Android 2.1 and above). It distinguishes itself from other navigation systems in two ways: first, the overlaying of the route onto the live video stream of the surroundings, the driver can easily recognize and follow the suggested route. Second, instead of looking at an abstract map the user is more able to remain looking at the real world. The navigation system leads the driver through unfamiliar territory in a natural, real and intuitive way.

This navigational application works by attaching a mobile phone to the top of a dashboard with its external camera oriented toward the road. Next, the application overlays real-time directions and instructions *over the camera feed of the road itself*. This allows drivers to safely examine and heed their GPS coordinates without completely losing sight of the road, possible obstacles or sudden occurrences that could easily occur while looking at a normal GPS navigational system.

Fig. 19.3 Mobile AR Browser with public transportation information

Fig. 19.4 Wikitude for in-car AR navigation

Fig. 19.5 Indoor Navigation at Intel Developer Forum

3.1.4 Intel Developer Forum (IDF) Augmented Reality, Indoor Navigation and Information Display

Through the use of the mobile AR browser junaio and its capability to provide accurate indoor tracking via LLA markers, Intel was able to create an innovative and appealing way to help attendees get around their "Intel Developer Forum". Intel's IDF 2010 Augmented Reality channel provided users with real-time information about conference locations, speaker sessions, floor vendors and POIs throughout the facility. Because of the sheer volume of information on the IDF channel, the people at junaio added a filter capability which allowed users to conveniently and efficiently decide which information they wanted to access at a given time by searching with key words (Fig. 19.5).

The metrics showed that approx. 9% of all visitors visited the IDF channel. The average visitor navigated back to the channel 5 times.

3.1.5 Kiosk Europe Expo 2010

The Kiosk Europe Expo wanted to find an innovative yet entertaining way to help the attendees get around the conference (Fig. 19.6).

The Kiosk Europe Expo's Augmented Reality channel enabled users to find up-to-the-minute-information about speaking sessions and facility locations.

Fig. 19.6 Indoor Navigation at Kiosk Europe Expo

By combining compass-based information with the LLA-marker-technology, users could experience augmented reality inside a building within which reliable GPS was unavailable. This is ideal for situations like trade fairs, such as Kiosk Europe Expo 2010, shopping malls or museums. In this way junaio helped users find their way around the facility and directly benefit from information displayed directly onto their surroundings. The Kiosk Europe Expo 2010 Channel was the first implementation of advanced indoor navigation on a smartphone.

3.1.6   AcrossAir, Stella Artois, Bar Finder

Another example of outdoor location-based AR is the AcrossAir mobile application. Stella Artois, a Belgian brewery, teamed up with mobile augmented reality firm AcrossAir to launch a mobile app that allows fans of the Stella Artois brand to find the nearest Stella-dispensing bar. Figure 19.7 pictured above displays how the app is used. The names and addresses of the designated bars are displayed on the screen of a user's smartphone.

3.2   Tourism and Culture

Thanks to recent advances in mobile AR technology there are now several different ways to discover location-related information about the world in which we live. Instead of searching for information in a book, city guide, search engine or an

Fig. 19.7 Outdoor Navigation Barfinder

internet database, there are existing applications that allow any tourist or newcomer to a given geographic location to access useful or interesting information about their respective area *while they navigate through it*. Photographs have defined limits of user experience: the subject of a photo that is taken during the winter will most likely not appear as it does in the summer, and vice versa. A person looking at a photograph in a book or guide, or in some cases even online, cannot manipulate the subject of the photo to see what it would look like in the dark, in the morning, in the rain, or even from a different angle. What the following AR applications and channels allow the user to do is remove this stationary nature from the art of the photograph and open up visual experiences for the subject in real-time, from any angle, during almost any time of day. Examples of these include the Wikipedia and Lonely Planet information.

3.2.1   Wikipedia

Wikipedia's data is used to display information about sights and points of interest around you. Depending on your location the Wiki channel delivers exploratory information. If you are lost in the city and would like know more about it you can utilize the Wiki channel to become more informed about your surroundings. The end goal was to publish the online encyclopedia in the real world.

The target demographic for this channel is tourists, consumers, and even local people who want to discover different parts of the city. Through the use of this channel people can discover location related information instantly, instead of combing through the pages of a book or a city guide (Fig. 19.8).

Fig. 19.8 Outdoor Wikipedia
Encyclopedia

3.2.2   Lonely Planet

Lonely Planet provides travel content to North and South America. They are also
responsible for producing travel books and guidebooks for almost every corner
of the world. The travel information produced consists of content from renowned
travel editors and use cases for guide book content that targets first time visitors.
Lonely Planet, a popular travel content provider, provided their information via an
Application Programming Interface (API) for developers to create a comprehensive
channel with great geo located travel information.

3.3   Mobile Social Networking

A relatively new method of staying connected with friends and family is via mobile
social networking. Social networks such as Twitter and Facebook are now available
for use on a user's smartphone.

Fig. 19.9 Integration
of Tweets in AR view

3.3.1 TwittAround

Location based services have joined forces with overwhelmingly popular social sites. A prime example of this social interaction is the information channel TwittARound, available for Layar browser. This application uses the GPS, compass and camera to show where different Tweets are coming from. The Tweets are overlaid on the landscape, virtually augmenting a user's view of the world (Fig. 19.9).

3.3.2 Facebook

The newest addition to Facebook, called "places", is a location based functionality that allows users to "check-in" to their current location. The Guidepost channel on junaio utilizes Facebook Places API to display a 3D representation of the location of your friends and their latest check-ins overlaid on top of the live view on your camera phone. Additionally, it is important to create an interface to social media sites, so users are able to not only view, but also post from their mobile AR browser.

Fig. 19.10 Review based
social media in AR view

Fig. 19.10 Review based
social media in AR view

Although relatively new, geo-tagging is becoming the next social tool for users
to leave virtual tags in specific locations in the real world.

3.3.3   Yelp Monocle

Yelp, an online review service helped pioneer social augmented reality integration
with its popular iPhone application. Known as the Yelp "Monocle", the application's
AR overlay feature places restaurant reviews and ratings on top of the perceived
location. Users can easily access user-authored reviews of nearby venues while
shopping, exploring new neighborhoods, or lazing in a park- all the user needs is
to orient his or her smartphone in a given direction and each restaurant that has a
listing on Yelp that exists in that area will conveniently appear. For UK augmented
reality users, another review-based site, Qype, has launched a similar mobile AR
application that allows simple accessing of restaurant reviews, ratings, and locations
in the United Kingdom (Fig. 19.10).

Fig. 19.11 Available coupons by Valpak

3.4   mCommerce

mCommerce, or mobile Shopping has been taken to a other level through mobile Augmented Reality technology. Coupons are now instantly sent to users mobile phones. Items that are "for sale" in your vicinity are now overlaid on top of your view of the neighborhood. The following mobile shopping use cases are as follows: Valpaks, mobile coupons, Virtual Shopping with goCatalogue and eBay Classifieds.

3.4.1   Valpak, Mobile Coupons

Mobile coupons have become a recent trend amongst consumers. The idea of walking into the grocery store and having all the coupon deals automatically sent to your phone was once an unrealistic dream. Now the mobile coupon is a great tool and with the advancements in AR technology, users are able to discover local deals around their specific locations (Fig. 19.11).

By launching the Valpak channel on junaio, a user can point their phone around and see coupons and deals around them based on their location. The virtual coupon displayed on the live view shows the details of the coupon and the location of the offer. With mobile augmented reality, the coupons are now tied to the GPS location of the user to offer more location relevant coupons directly targeted to the user.

Fig. 19.12 eBay classifieds
offers

3.4.2   eBay Classifieds, Geo-location Channel

eBay Classifieds has now enabled U.S. smartphone users to quickly discover local listings in their designated area. By scanning the area with the smartphone camera, users discover eBay Classifieds listings around them through an augmented reality viewer.

For example, when a user points the camera at an apartment building, he/she will see eBay Classifieds listings for the apartments for rent in that particular building. Also, if a user points the camera down the street, they will see items such as furniture, vehicles and even pets available for adoption right in your own neighborhood (Fig. 19.12).

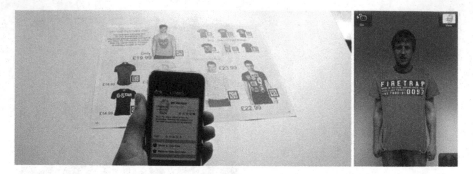

Fig. 19.13 Virtual shooing catalogue

3.4.3 Virtual Shopping- goCatalogue

Virtual Shopping is considered to be one of the most practical uses for AR mobile applications. Displaying context sensitive products in the user's own and real environment helps to make buying decisions more confident and understand products better. The UK based junaio Certified Developer "goAugmented" allows the user to see what clothes would look like dressed on without the need to pay for the clothing item beforehand. The idea of overlaying the clothing item on top of the user's image is certain to be a favorite amongst consumers all over the world. Although this example is only a prototype, it is destined to become productive with high-end retail brands in the near future (Fig. 19.13).

3.5 Advertisement

Ad placements within a consumer's mobile phone are quickly becoming the best way to target the everyday consumer. Large companies such as Google have adapted to the recent changes in the advertising industry. Google Admob is now bridging the gap and transforming the world of traditional advertising by allowing brands to reach the mobile consumer (Fig. 19.14).

As more and more consumers purchase smartphones this will quickly become the go-to method for targeting the average consumer. Google admob is a leading mobile advertising company, offering company's an easy to use advertising platform. They are able to specifically target their designated end-consumer and effectively measure the results.

Fig. 19.14 Banner apps on mobile devices

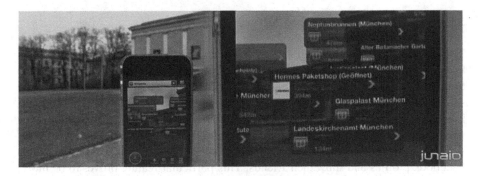

Fig. 19.15 Test run of location based advertisement

3.5.1   Location Based Advertisement- Ad-Inject

Junaio's "Ad inject"mobile advertising service allows major brands and sponsors
to inject location and context sensitive messages into relevant information channels
within junaio. Another similar Location based advertisement medium is Google's
Ad Sense program on the internet. Just as webmasters of public websites may show
Google supplied ads on their pages suitable for their audience, the same is possible
for junaio channels. When a channel owner allows to receive ads with a simple
tick mark, junaio will inject location based ads into his channel. Whenever a user
subscribes to this channel they can view points of interests and see miniature ad
bubbles which can be expanded with one click (Fig. 19.15).

Fig. 19.16 Coca Cola Light ad in bar magazine

The German parcel service Hermes, launched a first time, nationwide pilot with the new Ad-inject mobile advertising medium. When a junaio user accesses the Wikipedia channel to view points of interest, ads corresponding to the nearest Hermes parcel shop are augmented in the camera's view.

3.5.2 Goldrun, Location Based Advertising

The mobile platform GoldRun, uses AR to rejuvenate the traditional scavenger hunt. With the GoldRun app, the user becomes engaged in a virtual scavenger hunt. Specifically implemented to drive sales, boost brand awareness and increase product sales, Goldrun aims to modernize the advertising industry. GoldRun provides an interactive and customizable approach to location-based advertising. Within the app, users are given special offers, including an option to create photos that picture users virtually trying on products. The users could then share these photos through their Facebook profiles and show their friends. This particular feature proves to be most valuable to brands because their products are being marketed via word of mouth.

3.5.3 Print Advertisement- Sausalitos Magazine

Print advertisements for the mobile consumer aim to provide not only informational content but also emotionally enhanced experiences. The special offers lead to increased customer visits which, in turn, equals an increase in revenue for that particular brand. The advantage for the consumer is the emotionally enhanced experience. Interacting with a particular print ad the customer is actively engaged in the brand. Real-time, moving 3D experiences make viewing the information much more fun and provides non-traditional insights (Fig. 19.16).

For example the Sausalitos bar and restaurant channel within the junaio browser, called "SAUSALITOS FINDER", provides smart phone users with directions to the nearest locations as well as Happy Hour times and special offers.

Sausalitos Magazine features an ad, which when viewed through the "SAUSAL-ITOS MAG" channel on junaio provides an animation and a coupon for a free Coke Zero at any Sausalitos restaurant locations.

3.6   Entertainment

AR has the ability to visually place gamers in the virtual world of their favorite games. The traditional couch potatoes are no longer confined to their living rooms, and can play games anywhere and at any time.

Augmented Reality can be used to entertain as well as educate users.

This section highlights the popular AR Games; Zombie Shooter and Parallel Kingdom.

3.6.1   Zombie Shooter, First Mobile AR Shooter Game

Augmented Reality gaming is a relatively new genre. Zombie ShootAR, is the best example of how AR technology is revolutionizing the gaming industry. The game utilizes the camera in real time live-stream for optical tracking to create an exciting, interactive experience for the user. Players can explore the real world around them through the display of their mobile phones. Whether a user is in the kitchen or in the streets, zombies will start to crawl out of the ground. The object is to use the shotgun and the targeting radar view there to fend off the zombies and stay alive (Fig. 19.17).

3.6.2   Parallel Kingdom, AR Mobile Game

The geo-location, mobile AR game Parallel Kingdom, uses google maps to place players in a virtual world on top of the real world setting. A unique feature is that you can instant message other players, bartering and trading items with them as you are fight your way around the mythical dungeons and dragons within the game (Fig. 19.18).

3.6.3   Süddeutsche Zeitung Magazine

Süddeutsche Magazine (SZ) is a magazine supplement, placed inside of Germany's most prominent, print newspaper. The entire magazine was filled with stunning AR content which comes to life when a user scans the pages with their mobile

Fig. 19.17 AR Game Zombie ShootAR on Symbian platform

Fig. 19.18 Parallel kingdom

phone. The user could experience five different interactive elements including; stop-motion animations, interactive speech bubbles, 3D content and virtual solutions to a crossword puzzle.

The results for this use case showed, that within 6 days of the launch, 20,000 unique users and 84,000 application starts were registered, counting for more than 1% of all German iPhone users.

3.6.4   South by Southwest (SXSW) Conference, Interactive Mobile Game

The South by Southwest (SXSW) Conferences & Festivals are a comprehensive blend of original music, independent films, and emerging technologies. The word "Edutainment" aims to educate and entertain people of all audiences. SXSW along with metaio and Porter Novelli partnered to bring to attendees a non-traditional scavenger hunt using augmented reality. The scavenger hunt contained virtual clues and physical markers were hidden throughout the conference center and the city of Austin, Texas. There were people at specific locations with markers on their T-shirts. Users were encouraged to use the T-shirt clad clues to unlock 3D experiences and score points. At the end of the conference the winner received a $1000.00 cash prize (Fig. 19.19).

3.6.5   Galileo TV Quiz

Through a media experiment of a German TV show, the potential of Augmented Reality to have viewers actively participate in the show by answering the quiz questions live during the show was researched. The slogan "Turn your TV into a touch screen" explains the idea of this experiment.

During the approximately 10 min lasting quiz, about 40,000 users participated by answering about 100,000 questions. Users were given their direct stats as well as a comparison with other users.

Fig. 19.19 Reward of
finding a marker at SXSW

4   Conclusions and Future Possibilities

Several use cases and scenarios with mobile browsers have shown that mobile AR is majoring. Nowadays, mobile AR browsers go beyond simply displaying textual, geo referenced Points of Interest, but provide scenarios and information from multiple fields. Also, cross medial integration of content and more user interaction show how mobile Augmented Reality browsers push to become an everyday useful tool for consumers. However, the ongoing technological growth of mobile Augmented Reality and Augmented Reality in general, will help AR browsers to overcome currently existing obstacles like GPS inaccuracies or screen sizes.

For instance, projective augmented reality might become more and more available in the near future. Projective AR is a system that visualizes 3D design data directly onto the exterior surface of a vehicle for example. A projective AR system combined with pico projectors, miniature components that will soon be embedded into your mobile phones, comprise the perfect AR-projector to share enhanced visions of the world. More future possibilities for mobile AR include; using real-time image recognition to differentiate in mobile AR – while there are hundreds of POI-only based applications. Mobile AR will become even more popular in gaming, indoor navigation and mobile advertising. Also smart tracking algorithms will soon be able to adopt features in unknown environments in first applications. As for devices, the arrival of the next generation of the iPad and other tablets will help AR's popularity, especially for guided tours in museums/exhibitions and for sales presentations.

Part II
Applications

Chapter 20
Augmented Reality for Nano Manipulation

Ning Xi, Bo Song, Ruiguo Yang, and King Lai

1 Introduction

In recent research in nano and micro world, the Atomic Force Microscope (AFM) [1] plays more and more important role because of high resolution image [2] and vacuum free working environment. With the help of AFM, it makes people more convenience to get high quality live cell or fixed cell image. The AFM also has the ability to test and measure the mechanical characteristic of sample such as force curve, Young's modulus and roughness [3–7], therefore, some researchers [8–10] focus on the subject of measuring the mechanical property of living cell or using functionalized tip to stimulate the cell by means of electric or chemical solution [11–13]. The vacuum free working environment makes AFM much more flexible in various working conditions both in air and liquid.

The augmented reality interface with visual feedback for AFM-based nano-robotic system makes AFM available for nano-particle manipulation. Because of the sharp AFM tip, it can be used for nano-particle pushing, lithography, surface cutting and scribing in very tiny area. Although these nano-manipulations might also be done in other devices such as the Scanning Tunneling Microscope (STM) [14], the constrain and limitation of these devices are obvious, for example, the vacuum working condition or conductivity sample and so forth. For AFM based manipulation, there nothing depends on the working atmosphere and the conductivity of sample. Moreover, it can be used in liquid for chemical or biology experiment. The AFM tips have been employed as an end effector of robot to do the manipulation of nano-particle or modify sample surface for several years [15, 16]. The main challenge is the lack of the real time feedback during manipulation [17]. Inconveniently it takes several minutes to get another AFM image in order

N. Xi (✉)
Department of Electrical and Computer Engineering, Michigan State University,
East Lansing, MI, USA
e-mail: xin@egr.msu.edu

B. Furht (ed.), *Handbook of Augmented Reality*, DOI 10.1007/978-1-4614-0064-6_20,   435
© Springer Science+Business Media, LLC 2011

to see the manipulation results. Therefore it is a time consuming work for the nano-manipulation without visual feedback. Recently, the research focuses on scanning locally in the surface to find where is the particle and updates its current position after the manipulation [15,16]. That is a big step for building up AFM based nano-manipulation augmented reality system with visual feedback. It provides the opportunity for doing the manipulation simultaneously seeing the manipulation results with the help of visual feedback. This new technology promotes the operation efficiency and accuracy for AFM based manipulation system. However the negative point is that this technique needs previous knowledge about the feature of nano-particle which would be pushed during the manipulation. For an instance, the system must have already built a model for detecting and recognizing that special shape of particle [18]. If the sample changed, it need manually rebuild another detection and reorganization model for the new sample. Therefore it lacks something like "flexible", because each particle needs each special pattern to recognize. In addition, for the manipulation of modify the surface of sample, to get its feedback of surface appearance is more complicate and difficult. The surface of sample would change much and more complicate [19]. It is hard to use some pattern to measure and depict the surface change. There is increasingly demand on some new approaches for the visual feedback system without previous knowledge on sample and also could real-time update surface change during cutting or lithography process.

In this work, we have developed a new approach for building up a real time augmented reality system with visual feedback for cutting fixed cell surface. For the visual feedback part, there are two ways to achieve. One is using a model to describe and update the change in surface; the other one is using local scan to update the entire local surface which might change. Here we are more interested in the latter one. The reason for that is the surface change is too complicated to be described by a build-in mathematic model in cell cutting experiment. Instead of that, we designed a proper local scan method to update the changes in cutting trajectory. In Sect. 2 a new online sensing and visual feedback system are introduced. Firstly a cutting force calculation and detection modulus is provided, and it undercover the relationship between the cutting depth and force afforded by AFM tip. Secondly, it shows the implantation of nano-manipulation system, and finally the online sensing method is introduced. Here an active local scan strategy is provided to get the real-time topography of the local cutting area. Section 3 shows the experiment setup and results. Finally a display model would be discussed, and with this model, the system could update the sample surface during cutting.

2 Augmented Reality with Visual Feedback System

Augmented reality with visual feedback system provides both visual display and force feedback during manipulation. The visual feedback could be seen in a simulation window in this system. Inside the simulation window an AFM image like real-time video is shown as a monitor of sample surface. Besides, this sample surface in visual feedback is always being update by scanning locally while manipulation. Therefore with this visual feedback the nano-manipulation process would be guided under both the tip position and the sample surface change. A force calculation modulus is developed for measuring and calculating the force between the AFM tip and sample surface. For AFM, the force could be calculated through the voltage change of photodiode which receives the laser signal reflected by cantilever. With the help of laser signal we can get the force information simultaneously doing the manipulation. The force and visual display offer our system the ability of accurate manipulation on sample surface. People could operate the movement of AFM tip during manipulation and simultaneously see the manipulation result – the change of surface without scanning another AFM image which will take several minutes.

2.1   Augmented Reality with Visual Feedback System Implantation

Augmented reality with visual feedback system based on online sensing has been set up as Fig. 20.1. An AFM named Bioscope (Veeco Inc.) with the scan range of 90 microns in X and Y directions. A computer with haptic joystick is used here as the main computer to run the nano-manipulation software. Also a real-time (RT) Linux system with DAQ cards is used for control the movement of AFM tip. We also develop a box named Signal Access & Control Box and with that we can put the control voltage into the AFM controller as well as read the feedback of each sensor inside the scanner. These three computers could communicate with others through internet. At the time when system desire update the surface change of the sample, through the RT-Linux system we can control the scanner of the AFM to scan follow some patterns in local area where the surface modified happen during manipulation. This online sensing system provides the way to do manipulation on nano-particle and modify the surface of sample with the visual feedback.

2.2   Force Measurement and Calculation Modulus

For most nano-manipulations, the force between manipulator and nano-particle is a very essential feedback. With the force feedback it is easy to infer the contact condition between AFM tip and sample surface. In this system the force suffered by AFM tip and cantilever could be detected by means of processing the voltage change of photodiode that received laser reflection signal. The force could be decomposed into three directions spatially. Here we are more interesting in the vertical force, because the force mainly depends on the deflection of the cantilever. This deflection has relationship of real cutting depth during manipulation.

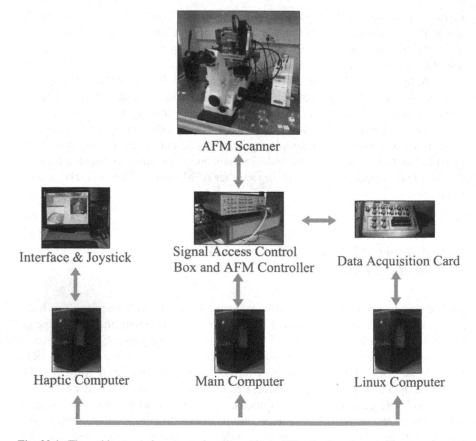

Fig. 20.1 The architecture of augmented reality with visual feedback system

Figure 20.2 shows the process of cutting using AFM tip. In this figure upper cantilever denotes the condition of non-contact condition of AFM tip and sample surface. In this moment there is no deformation happened to cantilever. So the tip position could be known if we know the scanner position. However when the tip get close to the sample and finally touch it (as the middle and bending one in Fig. 20.2), the cantilever starts to surfer the force from sample and form the deformation. Now the position of tip is hard to denote by using scanner position. Fortunately we can calculate the deflection of cantilever by means of calculate the force between the AFM tip and sample surface. Also the force information could be calculated using laser signal. Therefore, a relationship between the force suffered by tip and the cutting depth should be found. Because the cantilever is very thin, here we can use the deflection equation to solve this problem.

$$y = px^2(x - 3l)/6EI \tag{20.1}$$

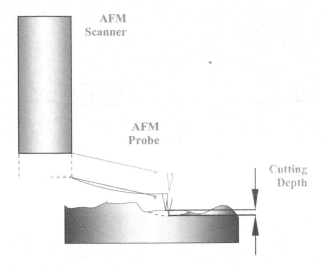

Fig. 20.2 AFM scanner and probe positions during manipulation

where y is the cantilever deflection which could be seemed as cutting depth, P means the force which is perpendicular with the cantilever, x means the distance from the point suffered force to the end of cantilever, l is the length of cantilever, E is the elastic modulus and I is the moment of inertia of cantilever. Usually the tip locates at the end of cantilever, so here we get

$$x = l \qquad (20.2)$$

Then the (20.1) could be expressed as

$$y = -px^3/6EI \qquad (20.3)$$

For AFM probe, the elastic modulus E could be calculated using force curve function of AFM and I could be calculated by the shape and size of cantilever. As long as obtaining the parameters value (20.3), the cutting depth y could be calculated.

Cutting depth is an important marker in the cutting process. For instance (as shown in Fig. 20.2), the cantilever in middle and bending is the condition of cutting. If it cut through in some certain depth, the deformation of cantilever would change into lower cantilever shown in Fig. 20.2. With the help of cantilever deflection we could know its cutting depth. It is useful if the sample is an elastic one such as cell which is hard to judge that whether it has been cut through or not. With the help of cutting depth value, it would be much easier if it is lower than some threshold and stays stable. It means the AFM tip has cut through the surface material and the surface has been modified. Then local scan is performed.

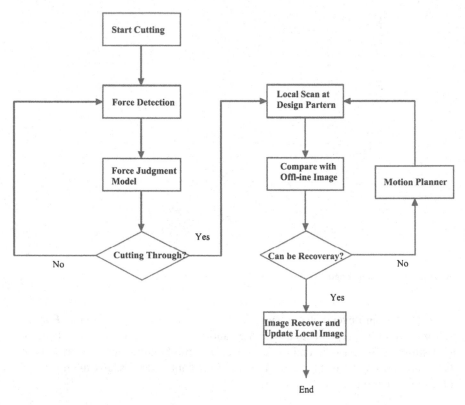

Fig. 20.3 Strategy of online sensing for cell cutting

2.3 *Online Sensing Approach*

The core technique for this augmented reality with visual feedback system is online sensing. Online sensing provides the visual feedback part of this system. It could update the sample surface with visual feedback by means of using AFM tip scan locally to get the topography of sample surface. Online sensing approach includes several steps just as shown in Fig. 20.3. Firstly a force detection and calculation modulus is used here for calculating the force suffered by AFM tip. After that, just as previous mentioned the force and depth judgment part would judge whether the tip has cut through the sample surface or not. Until the AFM tip has cut through the sample surface the local scan start to work. This is because at that moment the surface has been modified and the system needs update the sample surface in visual feedback window. In this step, the local scan pattern is just based on the off-line image scan size. Moreover at this time the AFM tip just scans in a fixed pattern such as couple lines which are perpendicular with the cutting trajectory.

All these useful information will be transferred into the display model and motion planer. Motion planner would compare the topography got by local scan with the one acquire by off-line AFM image before manipulation. With this information, it is easy

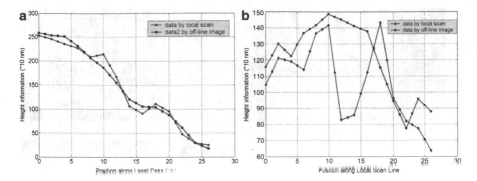

Fig. 20.4 Local scan height information compared with off line image. (**a**) condition of does not cut through; (**b**) condition of cut through

to tell where the cutting trench is and where the biggest change happens in surface. This is because we use the off-line image to compare with the data got by local scan. Figure 20.4a shows one time local scan data and the same points of off-line image. In this moment the AFM tip has not cut through the sample surface, so the local scan data seems like the one with off-line image. But in Fig. 20.4b, it shows another time of local scan, and from that it is clear to find the biggest surface change happened in the center of this local scan line. So the motion planner would control where and how long the next local scan line is. It would make sure the biggest change area would scan more than one line to obtain more accurate topography in that area, the scan pattern could be changed depend on whether it collect enough information about the local area. If not, it would scan more lines in that local area. Finally the displace model is now using for translate the height information got by local scan into each pixel's color information which would display in the simulation window.

As shown in Fig. 20.5, for the person who operates this online sensing AFM based nano-manipulation system, the first thing is to get an off-line AFM image. This process might take couples minutes because the way an AFM obtaining an image is scanning line by line. After that, the orginal image (off-line image) is loaded into the online sensing mainipulation system and the operaters could see both the tip position and surface topography through the visual feedback window. With the help of joystick, the AFM tip could be moved in three directions spatially.

Consequently, we can control the AFM tip get close to the sample surface and start cutting. When the tip start to cut, the motion planner would save the trajectory of the cutting and design a proper local scan trace for AFM tip. The direction of local scan is just perpendicular with the cutting trajectory curve. The length and frequency of local scan depend on the AFM image scan size. The movement of AFM tip during cutting is that cutting some certain distance then stepping back to scan one or two lines rapidly and then get back to cutting position and continue cutting. Therefore what the local scan got is height information along couple lines, and last step is using these lines' height information to recover the local area image covered by local scan. A simple method is to do the color interpolation between these lines.

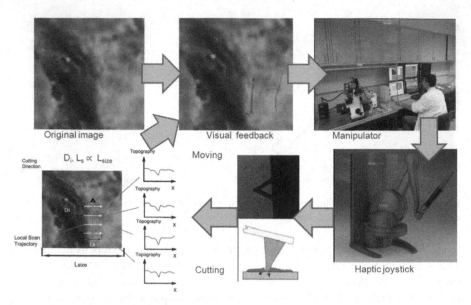

Fig. 20.5 Online sensing approach

Through the visual feedback system, the operator is easy to control the movement of AFM tip and see what happens in the sample surface. Just as shown in Fig. 20.5, through the visual feedback window, the cutting channels or trenches are truly updated by local scan without taking time to get another AFM image.

3   Experimental Results

3.1   Sample Preparation

In order to test the performance of this augmented reality with visual feedback system, a fixed human skin cell was used as the cutting sample. This cell was immortalized human keratinocytes cell line HacaT cells. We used this special kind of cell because many recent researches are based on this cell for investigation the cell adhesion structures and mechanical property. Therefore there was an increased demand on the nano-manipulation on this cell, especially for cutting the adhesion part between cells to study the single cell's property [3–7].

The HaCaT cells were grown in DMEM (Gibco-Invitrogen, Carlsbad, CA USA.) medium, and supplemented with 10% fetal calf serum (Gemini Bio-products, Wesr Sacramento, CA USA.). After cell matured, we used the process of Paraformaldehyde- Triton Fixation to make the fixed cell. In this process, first we fix the cells in 3–4% Paraformaldehyde for 15 min, and then rinse briefly with PBS (Phosphate-Buffered Saline) [20].

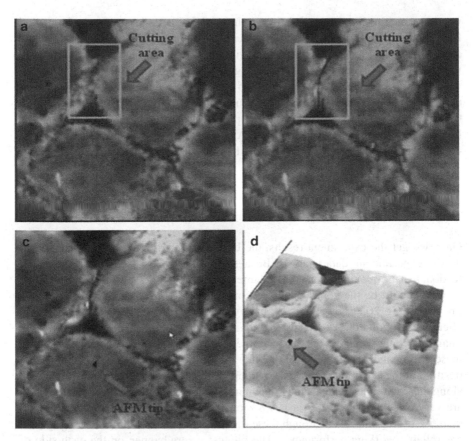

Fig. 20.6 AFM off-line image and online sensing visual feedback window. (**a**) AFM image before cutting (scan size: 35 micron); (**b**) AFM image after cutting (scan size: 35 micron); (**c**) visual feedback interface; (**d**) visual feedback interface (3-D)

3.2   Experiment Setup and Result

An AFM off-line image was first obtained as shown in Fig. 20.6a, before we do the nano-manipulation in this fixed cell sample. The scan size of this off-line image is 35 microns. Then we load this image into our online sensing visual feedback manipulation system and use it as our initial visual image in our system. Then, we use the phantom joystick to move the AFM tip to the area where we want to cut through and begin cutting.

The rectangle parts in Fig. 20.6a and b are the areas we want to cut through. They are the adhesion parts of the cells. What we want to do is to separate these two cells, so we choose here as the cutting area. Figure 20.6b is the AFM image about the same area after cutting. It is clear to see the trench made by AFM tip and that is the cutting result. During the cutting we can see the surface change in our visual feedback windows such as Fig. 20.6c. This is very helpful for us to do the manipulation and from that we can see the tip position (black triangle in Fig. 20.6c and d) during the cutting process. Figure 20.6d is the 3-D view in our visual feedback window from which it is easy to see the relative cutting depth during manipulation. During the whole process of experiment, the cutting is under the guide of this visual feedback and force feedback. The cutting force would transfer through the phantom joystick to the people's hand. This is a real-time process, and the topography information has been update by adaptive local scan. Also, here the tip velocity of local scan is 45 µm/s and the scan angle is just perpendicular with the cutting direction.

3.3 Experiment Data Analysis

Once we get the experiment results, the best way for improving the system is to do the experimental data analysis. Because this system is used for online visual feedback nano-manipulation, the judgment of whether its performance is good enough should be the contrast between off-line AFM image and visual feedback image. As Fig. 20.7 shown, here we use an off-line AFM image which is obtained after the manipulation. The scan area is the same with online sensing visual feedback image. The other image is the one in online sensing visual feedback window. Within these two image, random choose one line along the cutting trajectory in the same position of these two images and then compare the topography (height information) along these two lines. The result is shown in Fig. 20.7. These two topography curves are very close and biggest error is 9.8% of the total range. The mean error is less than 5% during this test. Through these data, it testifies this online sensing system has reliable working performance. The biggest errors happen on the each side of the channel or trench generated by cutting, and the reason for that might be the parameter setting such as the gain value setting not proper enough. That would make the scanner cannot follow the topography very well while the surface changes rapidly such as the each side of the trench in Fig. 20.7.

4 Summary

AFM is very popular in imaging and manipulating in micron and nanometer-size particle, because of its high resolution and vacuum free working environment. However, because of lacking visual feedback, it is very inconvenience and time consuming for doing manipulation using AFM. Moreover, some existed augmented reality system for AFM also needs the previous knowledge and mathematic model about the sample. In this chapter it proposes a new augmented reality with visual feedback system based online sensing. It is nothing demanded on previous information about sample feature. First, a force calculation model has been used here to judge both the cutting depth and when to start local scan. Then, the

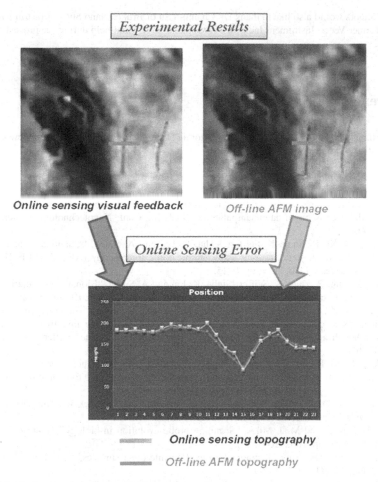

Fig. 20.7 Online sensing error analysis

online sensing would identify the actual surface topography during the process of manipulation. The surface changed during manipulation could be real-time updated by local scan. Finally a fixed cell cutting experiment and data analysis show that the visual feedback system based on online sensing has the ability of identifying the actual surface topography during the process of nano-manipulation.

In the future work, we are more interesting in live cell manipulation and local scan parameter optimization such as the best scan speed and gain setting. For the live cell manipulation, it is much more complicate because of the effect of liquid flow, cells elastic deformation and so forth.

Acknowledgements This research work is partially supported under NSF Grants IIS-0713346 and DMI-0500372; ONR Grants N00014-04-1-0799 and N00014-07-1-0935; NIH Grant: R43 GM084520 (Angelo).

The authors would also like to thank Dr. Chanmin Su of Bruker Nano Surface Instrumentation Group (former Veeco Instrument Inc.) for his technical advice and help during the process of this research.

References

1. G. Binning, C. F. Quate, and C. Gerber. "Atomic force microscope", Physical Review Letters, vol. 56–9, 1986, pp. 930–933.
2. D. M. Schaefer, R. Reifenberger, A. Patil and R. P. Andres. "Fabrication of two-dimensional arrays of nanometer-size clusters with the atomic force microscope". Applied Physics Letters, vol. 66, 1995, pp. 1012–1014.
3. R. Yang, et al., "Analysis of keratinocytes stiffness after desmosome disruption using Atomic Force Microscopy based nanomanipulation," IEEE Int. Conf. Nanotechnology, Genoa, Italy, July 2009.
4. C. Fung, N. Xi, R. Yang, K. Seiffert-Sinha, K. Lai and A. Sinha, "Quantitative analysis of human keratinocyte cell elasticity using atomic force microscopy (AFM)," IEEE Trans on Nanobioscience, vol. 10, 2011, pp. 9–15.
5. N. Xi, C. Fung, R. Yang, K. Seiffert-Sinha, K. Lai and A. Sinha, "Bionanomanipulation using atomic force microscopy," IEEE Nanotechnology Magazine, vol. 4, 2010, pp. 9–12.
6. R. Yang, N. Xi, C. Fung, K. Seiffert-Sinha, K. Lai and A. Sinha, "The emergence of AFM applications to cell biology: how new technologies are facilitating investigation of human cells in health and disease at the nanoscale," Journal of Nanoscience Letters, vol. 1, 2011, pp. 81–101.
7. R. Yang, N. Xi, K. Lai, B. Zhong, C. Fung, C. Qu and D. Wang, "Nanomechanical analysis of insulinoma cells after glucose and capsaicin stimulation using atomic force microscopy," Acta Pharmacologica Sinica, vol. 32, 2011, pp. 853–860.
8. A. Engel and D. J. Müller, "Observing single biomolecules at work with the atomic force microscope," Nat. Struct. Biol., vol. 7, no. 9, 2000, pp. 715–718.
9. J. K. H. Hörber and M. J. Miles, "Scanning probe evolution in biology," Science, vol. 302, no. 5647, 2003, pp. 1002–1005.
10. Y. F. Dufrêne, "Using nanotechniques to explore microbial surfaces," Nat. Rev. Microbiol., vol. 2, no. 6, 2004, pp. 451–460.
11. A. Pelling, F. Veraitch, C. Chu, C. Mason and M. Horton, "Mechanical dynamics of single cells during early apoptosis," Cell motility and the cytoskeleton, vol. 646, 2009, pp. 409–422.
12. C. K. M. Fung, K. Seiffert-Sinha, et al., "Investigation of human keratinocyte cell adhesion using atomic force microscopy." Nanomedicine-Nanotechnology Biology and Medicine vol. 6(1), 2010, pp. 191–200.
13. DE. Discher, N. Mohandas, EA. Evans "Molecular maps of red cell deformation: hidden elasticity and in situ connectivity," Science, vol. 266–5187, 1994, pp. 1032–1035.
14. J. Stroscio and D. M. Eigler, "Atomic and molecular manipulation with the scanning tunneling microscope," Science, vol. 254, no. 5036, Nov, 1991, pp. 1319–1326.
15. G. Li, N. Xi, and D. H. Wang, "In situ sensing and manipulation of molecules in biological samples using a nano robotic system," Nanomedicine, vol. 1, no. 1, 2005, pp. 31–40.
16. G. Li, N. Xi, M. Yu, and W. Feng, "Development of augmented reality system for AFM-based nanomanipulation," Mechatronics, IEEE/ASME Transactions on Mechatronics, vol. 9, 2004, pp. 358–365.
17. D.J. Muller and Yves F. Dufrene, "Atomic force microscopy as a multifunctional molecular toolbox in nanobiotechnology," Nat. Nanotechnol, vol. 3, May 2008, pp. 261–269.
18. L. Liu, N. Xi, Y. Luo, J. Zhang, G. Li, "Sensor referenced guidance and control for robotic nanomanipulation," IEEE International Conference on Intelligent Robots and Systems, 2007, pp. 578–583.

19. G. Li, N. Xi, and D. H. Wang, "Probing membrane proteins using atomic force microscopy," J. Cellular Biochem., vol. 97, no. 6, 2006, pp. 1191–1197.
20. B. Song, N. Xi, R. Yang, K. W. C. Lai and C. Qu, "On-line sensing and visual feedback for atomic force microscopy (afm) based nano-manipulations," IEEE Int. Conf. Nanotechnology Materials and Devices (NMDC), Oct 2010, pp. 71–74.

Chapter 21
Augmented Reality in Psychology

M. Carmen Juan and David Pérez

Abstract Psychology is a field in which Virtual Reality has already successfully been applied. Augmented Reality (AR) has started to be applied as a new technology. In this paper, we introduce several AR works for being used in psychology. We also present a study of an AR system for the treatment of acrophobia using immersive photography in which participated expert computer science engineers. From the results and related to the sense of presence, all statistical tests applied showed significant differences between the two environments (real and AR) for all measures. The order of the visit did not influence the users' scores on presence. Comparing the sense of presence experienced by the expert group and a non-expert group, it is possible to observe that there is not significant difference in the sense of presence between both groups.

1 Introduction

Psychology is a field in which Virtual Reality (VR) has already successfully been applied. For example, for acrophobia [1,2], or for arachnophobia [3,4]. Augmented Reality (AR) has started to be applied as a new technology (e.g. [5–7]). In this paper, we introduce several AR works for being used in psychology. We also present a second study of our AR system for the treatment of acrophobia using immersive photography. In this second study participated expert computer science engineers.

Acrophobia is an intense fear of heights and consequent avoidance of situations related to heights (e.g., balconies, terraces, elevators, skyscrapers, bridges, planes, etc.). People who suffer from acrophobia know this fear is excessive or unreasonable, but they fear any situation that involves heights, even when other people are

M.C. Juan (✉)
Instituto Universitario de Automática e Informática Industrial, Universitat Politècnica de València, C/Camino de Vera, s/n, 46022-Valencia, Spain
e-mail: mcarmen@dsic.upv.es

B. Furht (ed.), *Handbook of Augmented Reality*, DOI 10.1007/978-1-4614-0064-6_21,
© Springer Science+Business Media, LLC 2011

in those situations. The greatest fear is falling. A common treatment for acrophobia is "graded in vivo exposure". In this treatment, the avoidance behavior is broken by exposing the patient to a hierarchy of stimuli. After a time, habituation occurs and the fear gradually diminishes.

For the treatment of phobia to small animals [5, 8] presented the first AR system for the treatment of phobias of cockroaches and spiders. This system only used a marker and the center of this marker was used as origin for the appearance of animals. The system showed a different number of animals depending on the selection of the user. Five different menu options/keys could be used for selecting: one animal appear; three animals appear/disappear; 20 animals appear/disappear. The system could also increase or reduce the size of the selected animals. The visualization system that participants used was a video see-through Head-Mounted Display (HMD). In these works, they demonstrated that, with a single one-hour session, patients significantly reduced their fear and avoidance. Initially, the system was tested in a case study [8], and then it was tested on nine patients suffering from phobia towards small animals [5]. In all cases, the patients reduced their fear and avoidance of the feared animal in only one session of treatment using the AR system [9]. Moreover, all of them were able to interact with the real animal after the treatment. Before the treatment, none of them were able to approach or interact with the live animal without fear. A second version of this system used invisible markers instead of using visible markers [10]. This second system was a marker-based system, but the markers were invisible. The functionality of both systems was the same. The invisible markers were drawn with a special ink. The ink used fell into the near-IR spectrum. For detecting the marker, an infrared camera was used (an IR bullet camera with an IR filter of 715 nm.). To capture the colour scene, a colour camera was also used (a Dragonfly camera, Drag-Col-40, Point Grey Research). The augmented scene was shown to participants using a HMD. The visible and invisible systems were compared for the level of presence and anxiety. In a third version, an optical see-through HMD (LitEye-500 monocular) was used as a visualization system [11]. In this case, the same IR bullet camera that was used in the invisible marker system was also used. The functionality of this third system was the same as the two previous versions. Twenty-four non-phobic adults participated in a comparative study of the sense of presence and anxiety using this third version and the equivalent first system. The results indicated that if all participants were analyzed, the first system induced greater sense of presence than the third system. If the participants who had more fear were analyzed, the two systems induced a similar sense of presence. For the anxiety level, the two systems provoked similar and significant anxiety during the experiment.

For the treatment of acrophobia, Juan et al. [12] proposed the use of immersive photography in an AR system for the treatment of this phobia. This system is the system used in the second study presented in this chapter. In this second study participated expert computer science engineers. In the first study [12], 41 participants without acrophobia walked around at the top of a staircase in both a real environment and in an immersive photography environment. Immediately after their experience, the participants were given the SUS questionnaire to assess their subjective sense of presence. The users' scores in the immersive photography environment were very high. From the results, statistically significant differences were found between the real and immersive photography environments. In a second work, Juan and Pérez [6] presented the development of an AR system and a VR system that recreated the same virtual scene. The virtual scene that the two systems recreated was a room in which there was a square brown mat. This mat was used for placing the virtual elements, which were in charge of "augmenting" the scene that produced the acrophobic situation. A hole appeared in the center of the mat, the blocks of the floor fell away, and the user was at the edge of the hole; the user could also have the sensation of falling with the blocks (elevator effect). The view was stereoscopic. A study involving both those systems and 21 non-phobic users was carried out in order to compare the levels of presence and anxiety. For the sense of presence and anxiety levels, no differences between the systems were found. For the anxiety level, the results showed a significant difference between the level of anxiety felt at the moment before starting the experiment and the level felt during the different stages of the experiment using both systems. In a third work, Gandy et al. [7] presented an AR experiment in which presence, performance, and physiological measurement were analyzed. The results indicated that users experienced a high feeling of presence. Behavior, performance, and interview results indicated the participants felt anxiety in the AR environment. However, the physiological data did not reflect that anxiety.

2 Description of the AR System

In this section the characteristics of the AR system are briefly explained. For a detailed explanation of the system, consult [12]. Immersive photography is a technique in which the entirety of a space is captured from a single point and digitally processed to create a 360-degree photograph. When an immersive photograph is viewed, it appears to be a standard two dimensional photograph, but when manipulated by users, it spins 360 degrees in any direction. This allows users to look around an space in any direction that they choose. They can turn all the way around and look at all the details.

The steps that were followed to create a 360-degree photograph that was suitable to be mapped as texture into the development tool were:

1. Taking a 180-degree photograph. A digital color Coolpix 4500 Nikon Camera and a FC-E8 Fisheye converter were used. The digital camera together with the Fisheye converter covers a field of view of over 180 degrees and is capable of capturing a full spherical panorama. Photographs of different locations were taken. In each location, we took three parallel photographs for each eye. Figure 21.1 shows two images captured by the Coolpix camera and the Fisheye converter.

Fig. 21.1 Captured images. (**a**) Image for the left eye. (**b**) Image for the right eye

Fig. 21.2 Image after processing and ready for being used

2. Retouching the photograph. In this step, undesirable information was removed from the image.
3. Creating a 360-degree photograph. Because the photograph was 180 degrees, a new 360-degree image had to be created. We created a 360-degree image by sewing together the 180-degree photograph and a transparent 180-degree image.
4. Assigning a transparency to the 180-degree white image. The 180-degree white image had to be converted into a transparent image. Otherwise, the white 180-degree image would cover the users' positions and they would not see their bodies. The system maps this new image as a 360-degree texture. Figure 21.2 shows an image after processing and ready for being used. The image shown on Fig. 21.2 is horizontally flip respect to the original. This is because the sphere over which it has to be mapped will see from inside. If this flip is not done, the user will see the other side of the scene.

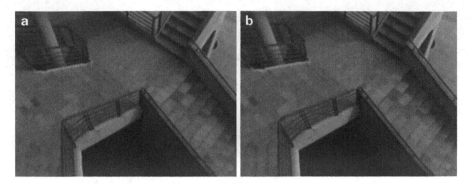

Fig. 21.3 Images to be shown for the left eye (a) and the right eye (b)

The system uses five different markers that ARToolKit recognizes. If the camera focuses on the central marker, the system shows the central photograph of the selected level on this central marker. If the camera is focused to the left of this central marker (left markers), the system will show the left photograph of the selected level. The same occurs for the right photograph. The immersive photograph is mapped as a spherical texture on a sphere. The appropriate image of this sphere is determined by the orientation of the user (information given by the tracker) and is shown over the marker. Therefore, the marker the camera focuses on determines the immersive photograph that must be shown at the selected level. The part of this photograph to be shown is determined by the tracker. If the user rotates his/her head 90 degrees up or down, the user will see part of the immersive photograph. If the user rotates his/her head more than 90 degrees up or less than −90 degrees down, the user will see part of the immersive photograph and part of the image taken by the Firewire camera (real image). Figure 21.3 shows an example of user' view when s/he is focusing only on immersive photography. Figure 21.4 shows another example of user's view when s/he is focusing part of the immersive photography and part of the real environment.

With regard to the development tool, Brainstorm eStudio (www.brainstorm.es) was used to develop the application. Brainstorm eStudio is an advanced, multiplatform real time 3D graphics presentation tool. We included ARToolKit [13] into Brainstorm as a plugin which was programmed in C++. With this plugin, we had AR options in a 3D graphic presentation tool. ARToolKit recognizes the markers and obtains the position and orientation where virtual 3D objects must be placed. Brainstorm eStudio uses this information to draw the virtual 3D objects. This plugin can work with more than one marker. The position and orientation of each marker is assigned to as many different 3D objects in Brainstorm eStudio as needed.

With regard to the hardware, the immersive photographs were taken using a digital color Coolpix 4500 Nikon Camera and the FC-E8 Fisheye converter (Fig. 21.5). The system can run on a typical PC, without any special requirements. The real world was captured using a Dragonfly camera (Drag-Col-40, Point Grey Research), Fig. 21.6a. The AR image was shown in a HMD and on a monitor. Thus, the therapist or the person in charge of the experiment had the same

Fig. 21.4 A user is partly inside and partly outside of the immersive photograph of a dam

Fig. 21.5 (**a**) Coolpix 4500 camera. (**b**) FC-E8 Fisheye converter (**c**) Camera+ Fisheye converter

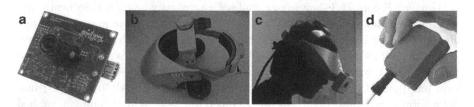

Fig. 21.6 (**a**) Dragonfly camera. (**b**) 5DT HMD (**c**) HMD + camera + tracker. (**d**) Mtx tracker

visualization as the patient/participant. We used 5DT HMD (5DT Inc., 800 H ×
600 V, High 40° FOV), Fig. 21.6b. The camera was attached to the HMD so that
it focused wherever the user looked (Fig. 21.6c). The system also had to know the
position of the user's head in order to spin the immersive photograph according to
the user's head movements. We used a MTx tracker (Xsens Motion Technologies),
Fig. 21.6d, to detect the user's head rotation, which was attached to the HMD.

3 Study

The aim of this study was at first to test the efficacy of immersive photography to induce sense of presence in expert computer science engineers and, second, compare those scores with the scores given by non-experts in computer science. For the first purpose, subjective presence measurements collected after exposure to a real environment and in an immersive photography environment were compared. For the second purpose, subjective presence measurements collected after exposure to an immersive photography environment gave by the two groups of participants were also compared.

The expert group (computer science engineers) included 25 participants, 20 males and five females. They were professors, lecturers and Computer Graphics PhD students at the Technical University of Valencia (age range from 24 to 61). All participants filled out the Acrophobia Questionnaire [14] in order to exclude people suffering from acrophobia. The non-expert group was composed of 41 participants, 28 males and 13 females (age range from 17 to 45). A detailed analysis for this group was presented at [12].

The scenario was a staircase. There were two versions of this space: the real space and the immersive photograph of this space. The space was a terrace of the Applied Computer Science Superior Technical School building, from which a staircase could be seen. Participants using the AR system wore the camera, the tracker and the HMD.

Participants were counterbalanced and assigned to one of two conditions:

1. Participant first visited the real space and later the immersive photography environment.
2. Participant first visited the immersive photography environment space and later the real one.

Before starting to walk in the real or immersive photography environment, a narrative was introduced so that the experience had more meaning and interest for them. The narrative was: "You are going to be in a place where there is a staircase. You are a security guard at the Technical University and you are on duty. You have to pay full attention to all details of the location because later we will ask you some questions about it. You are here to watch out for burglars who may enter or leave the building and to notify the security center". Participants stayed at about seven minutes in both the immersive photography environment and the real place. After visiting each place (real or virtual), participants were asked to fill out the Slater et al. questionnaire [15] (SUS). Table 21.1 shows the SUS questionnaire used. Therefore, the same questionnaire was used for both environments (real and immersive photography) and participants filled it out twice (after visiting each place). The presence score is taken as the number of answers that have a score of 6 or 7.

Table 21.1 Presence questionnaire

Question ID	Questions
P1	Please rate *your sense of being in this* space within a staircase, on the following scale from 1 to 7, where 7 represents your *normal experience of being in a place*.
	I had a sense of "being there" in the space within a staircase: 1. Not at all... 7. Very much.
P2	To what extent were there times during the experience when the space within a staircase was the reality for you?
	There were times during the experience when the space within a staircase was the reality for me:
	1. At no time... 7. Almost all the time.
P3	When you think back about your experience, do you think of the space within a staircase more as *images that you saw*, or more as *somewhere that you visited*?
	The space within a staircase seems to me to be more like:
	1. Images that I saw... 7. Somewhere that I visited.
P4	During the time of the experience, which was strongest on the whole, your sense of being in the space within a staircase, or your sense of being elsewhere?
	I had a stronger sense of: 1. Being elsewhere... 7. Being in the space within a staircase.
P5	Consider your memory of being in the space within a staircase. How similar in terms of the *structure of the memory* is this to your memory structure of other *places* you have been today? By "memory structure" consider things like the extent to which you have a visual memory of the space within a staircase, whether that memory is in color, the extent to which the memory seems vivid or realistic, its size, location in your imagination, the extent to which it is panoramic in your imagination, and other such *structural* elements.
	I think of the space within a staircase as a place in a similar way to other places that I've been today:
	1. Not at all... 7. Very much.
P6	During the time of the experience, did you often think to yourself that you were actually in the space within a staircase ?
	During the experience I often thought that I was really standing in the space within a staircase:
	1. Not very often... 7. Very much.
P7	Please write down any further comments that you wish to make about your experience

4 Results

For the sense of presence, Table 21.2 shows the results related to presence measures. The significance level was set to 0.05 in all tests. All of the experts' participants were considered. Paired t-tests were applied to the scores given to all of the questions. The SUS Count column shows the mean of the SUS count of 6 or 7 scores amongst the 6 questions. The SUS Mean column uses the mean score across the 6 questions

Table 21.2 Means (SD) of the real environment and the immersive photography environment, and paired t-test of the presence questionnaire, d.f. 24

GROUP	SUS Count	SUS Mean	Q1	Q2	Q3	Q4	Q5	Q6
Real environment	5.76(0.88)	6.9(0.35)	7.0(0.00)	6.96(0.20)	6.84(0.55)	6.84(0.55)	6.88(0.44)	6.88(0.44)
Immersive photography environment	2.4(2.08)	4.94(1.14)	5.3(1.22)	4.64(1.47)	4.96(1.90)	5.44(.58)	4.8(1.35)	4.48(1.50)
t	8.16[a]	8.33[a]	6.94[a]	7.77[a]	5.07[a]	4.16[a]	7.22[a]	7.59[a]
p	<0.001[a]	<0.001[a]	<0.001[a]	<0.001[a]	<0.001[a]	<0.001[a]	<0.001[a]	<0.001[a]

[a] indicates significant differences

instead. The remaining columns show mean results for the individual questions. The results obtained in this study indicate that users achieved a high degree of presence in the immersive photography environment (mean scores near 5 in a scale from 1 to 7). However, all statistical tests applied (paired t-tests) showed significant differences between the two environments for all measures: each of the individual responses, the mean total score obtained in the SUS, and the SUS Count score. From these results, it is possible to assure that the immersive photography environment was not confused with reality since data show that SUS distinguished between the real and immersive photography experiences.

We have performed a second analysis in order to know whether previously visiting one of the two environments had some effect on the presence measurement in the second environment. With this aim, the sample was divided into two groups (participants who had first visited the real space and participants who had first visited the immersive photography environment) and Student t tests assuming equal variances for the scores given to all questions were applied. No significant statistical differences were found (see Table 21.3) and from this, it is possible to say that the order of the visit did not influence the users' scores on presence.

For comparing the sense of presence experienced by the expert group and a non-expert group, Table 21.4 shows the results related to presence measures. The significance level was set to 0.05 in all tests. Student t tests assuming equal variances were applied to the scores given to all of the questions. From these results, it is possible to observe that there is not significant difference in the sense of presence between both groups.

Figures 21.7 and 21.8 show a participant visiting the real and the immersive photography environments, respectively.

5   Conclusions

In this chapter, we have presented a second study of our AR system for the treatment of acrophobia using immersive photography. In this second study, the participants were expert computer science engineers. From the results and related to the sense of presence, all statistical tests applied showed significant differences between the two environments (real and AR) for all measures. Therefore, we can conclude that the immersive photography environment was not confused with reality by this group of participants. The order of the visit did not influence the users' scores on presence. Comparing the sense of presence experienced by the expert group and a non-expert group, from the results, it is possible to observe that there is not significant difference in the sense of presence between both groups.

With regard to future works, first, the immersive photography is directly mixed with the real scene without considering any possible transition. It would be possible to add transitions in order to the scene looks more natural and no two different images. Second, it would be possible to add physical elements in order to add more realism. For example, a balustrade of a balcony, that would be in the real

Table 21.3 Means (SD) of the scores obtained in the presence questionnaire (Comparison according to the order of presentation)

	Presentation	Q1	Q2	Q3	Q4	Q5	Q6
Real Environment	1real-2AR	7.00(0.00)	7.00(0.00)	7.00(0.00)	7.00(0.00)	7.00(0.00)	7.00(0.00)
	1AR-2real	7.00(0.00)	6.92(0.28)	6.69(0.775)	6.69(0.75)	6.77(0.60)	6.77(0.60)
Immersive photography	1real-2AR	4.92(1.38)	4.08(1.51)	4.17(2.08)	5.33(1.72)	4.42(1.68)	4.17(1.64)
environment	1AR-2real	5.65(0.99)	5.15(1.28)	5.69(1.44)	5.54(1.1)	5.15(0.90)	4.77(1.36)

Table 21.4 Means (SD) of the scores obtained in the presence questionnaire using the immersive photography environment (Comparison according to the group of participant using Student t tests assuming equal variances, d.f. 64)

GROUP	Q1	Q2	Q3	Q4	Q5	Q6
Non-experts	5.56(1.23)	5.24(1.24)	5.12(1.60)	5.54(1.40)	5.05(1.18)	5.10(1.40)
Experts	5.3(1.22)	4.64(1.47)	4.96(1.90)	5.44(1.58)	4.80(1.35)	4.48(1.50)
t	0.84	1.79	0.37	0.26	0.79	1.68
p	0.40	0.08	0.71	0.80	0.44	0.10

Fig. 21.7 Participant in the real place

Fig. 21.8 Same participant of Fig. 21.1 using the AR system

scene, the user can touch it and the immersive image could be just as s/he was putting his/her head out. Third, the jitter should be reduced. For achieving it, other AR libraries could be used. Fourth, the user interfaces used by the person in charge of the experiment are very simple, but not always intuitive or comfortable to use. More intuitive and comfortable interfaces could be designed, and also wireless technologies could be taken into account. Fourth, a system with less equipment could be studied. Fifth, for the sound, surrounding sound could also be considered. Sixth, in this study only questionnaires are used. Presence is a subjective condition and the use of self-reports could give rise to some errors if the user does not give the correct score. It could possible to use physiological measures for measuring presence [16]. A possible future work could be made regarding the use of these measures and including a contrast of the results obtained with questionnaire responses. Seventh, immersive photography shows some advantages over VR, it offers more versatility and can be more economical. With immersive photographs it is possible to create as many environments as the therapist desires on demand with a high level of realism at a very low cost. This system or an improved version of it could be tested for the treatment of real patients. Finally, we firmly believe that AR is an interesting technology for its use in psychology.

Acknowledgments We would like to thank:

- The people and institutions that helped in this work.
- The volunteers that participated in this study.

References

1. M. M. North, S.M. North, J.R. Coble, "Effectiveness of virtual environment desensitization in the treatment of agoraphobia", Presence: Teleoperators and Virtual Environments, Vol. 5, 1996, pp. 346–352.
2. D.P. Jang, J.H. Ku, Y.H. Choi, B.K. Wiederhold, S.W. Nam, I.Y. Kim, S.I. Kim, "The development of virtual reality therapy (VRT) system for the treatment of acrophobia and therapeutic case", IEEE Transactions on Information Technology in Biomedicine, Vol. 6, No. 3, 2002, pp. 213–217.
3. A. Carlin, H. Hoffman, S. Weghorst, "Virtual reality and tactile augmentation in the treatment of spider phobia: a case study", Behaviour Research and Therapy, Vol. 35, No. 2, 1997, pp. 153–158.
4. A. Garcia-Palacios, H.G. Hoffman, A. Carlin, T. Furness, C. Botella, "Virtual reality in the treatment of spider phobia: A controlled study", Behaviour Research and Therapy, Vol. 9, 2002, pp. 983–993.
5. M.C. Juan, M. Alcañiz, C. Monserrat, C. Botella, R.M. Baños, B. Guerrero, "Using augmented reality to treat phobias", IEEE Computer Graphics and Applications. Vol. 25, No. 6, 2005, pp. 31–37.
6. M.C. Juan, D. Pérez, "Using augmented and virtual reality for the development of acrophobic scenarios. Comparison of the levels of presence and anxiety", Computers & Graphics, Vol. 34, 2010, pp. 756–766.

7. M. Gandy, R. Catrambone, B. MacIntyre, C. Alvarez, E. Eiriksdottir, M. Hilimire, B. Davidson, A.C. McLaughli, "Experiences with an AR evaluation test bed: Presence, performance, and physiological measurement", IEEE International Symposium on Mixed and Augmented Reality, 2010, pp. 127–136.

8. C. Botella, M.C. Juan, R.M. Baños, M. Alcañiz, V. Guillen, B. Rey. "Mixing realities? An Application of Augmented Reality for the Treatment of Cockroach phobia", Cyberpsychology & Behavior, Vol. 8, 2005, pp. 162–171.

9. L. Öst, P. Salkovskis, K. Hellstroöm, "One-session therapist directed exposure vs. self-exposure in the treatment of spider phobia", Behavior Therapy, Vol. 22, 1991, pp. 407–422.

10. M.C. Juan, D. Joele, "A comparative study of the sense of presence and anxiety in an invisible marker versus a marker augmented reality system for the treatment of phobia towards small animals", International Journal of Human-Computer Studies, Vol. 69, No. 6, 2011, pp. 440–453.

11. M.C. Juan, J. Calatrava, "An Augmented Reality system for the treatment of phobia to small animals viewed via an optical see-through HMD. Comparison with a similar system viewed via a video see-through", International Journal of Human-Computer Interaction, Vol. 27, No. 5, 2011, pp. 436–449.

12. M.C. Juan, R. Baños, C. Botella, D. Pérez, M. Alcañiz, C. Monserrat, "An Augmented Reality System for acrophobia: The sense of presence using immersive photography", Presence: Teleoperators & Virtual Environments, Vol, 15, 2006, pp. 393–402.

13. H. Kato, M. Billinghurst, "Marker tracking and HMD calibration for a video-based augmented reality", 2nd IEEE and ACM International Workshop on Augmented Reality (IWAR'99), 1999, pp. 85–94.

14. D.C. Cohen, "Comparison of self-report and behavioral procedures for assessing acrophobia". Behavior Therapy, Vol. 8, 1977, pp. 17–23.

15. M. Slater, M. Usoh, A. Steed, Depth of presence in virtual environments. Presence: Teleoperators and Virtual Environments, Vol. 3, 1994, pp. 130–144.

16. M. Meehand, B. Insko, M. Whitton, F.P. Boorks, Physiological measures of presence in stressful virtual environment, ACM Transactions on Graphics, Vol. 21, No. 3, 2002, pp. 645–652.

Chapter 22
Environmental Planning Using Augmented Reality

Jie Shen

1 Introduction

Before a large project is carried out, it is difficult to know the resulting view of the project accurately and realistically. Even though you invite specialists to look up blue prints or data, the results obtained cannot be perceived directly through this sense. Moreover, a large project affects environments greatly, it is necessary to develop a new powerful visualization-tool that assesses environmental impact accurately from the esthetics and ecology points of view before engineering is constructed. Clearly, this is of great importance for avoidance of negative effects on environment. In recent years, the virtual reality (VR) has been rather popular for project planning. It provides us with a new means for visual assessment. As known, virtual reality needs to use three-dimensional (3D) computer graphics to model and render virtual environments in real-time. This approach usually requires laborious modeling and expensive 3D graphic accelerator for fast rendering of more complicated scenes. The rendering quality and scene complexity are often limited because of the real-time constraint. Consequently, it is difficult to obtain a satisfactory solution. However, augmented reality [1, 2] method can overcome the above limitations. Augmented Reality (AR) is a technology that incorporates the rich information available in the real world into the virtual reality. The AR can be realized by overlaying 3D graphical objects with image without camera parameters pre-calibrated. Because of being a video-image approach, fewer virtual objects that will be fused into real environment need to be drawn, and so the cost of rendering is independent of the scene complexity. As a result, the AR system does not require specialized graphics accelerators. On the other hand, the amount of realism in the

J. Shen (✉)
School of Computer Science and Engineering, University of Electronic Science
and Technology of China, Chengdu, China
e-mail: zeropoint17@hotmail.com

B. Furht (ed.), *Handbook of Augmented Reality*, DOI 10.1007/978-1-4614-0064-6_22,   463
© Springer Science+Business Media, LLC 2011

AR system depends on the quality of the input images. It is easy to make the AR systems more realistic than many VR systems. In the following, the main idea of the AR based on vision for environmental planning is presented.

In this chapter, a more practical AR approach based on affine invariant, calibration-free augmented reality on mobile phones is formulated. The weak perspective projection model is assumed for camera-to-image transformation. This approach does not use the calibration parameters of the camera and the 3D locations of the environment's object, and can realize the augmentation of virtual objects. Moreover, we present a contour-based approach to resolving occlusion problem in AR. First, the key points of occluding contours between virtual and real objects may be specified interactively according to epipolar and other constraints in the first two frames. Second, the arm-optimized implementation of SIFT [3] and RANSAC algorithm [4] are applied to search for the correct point correspondences in any two views [5]. With these points, the points of the occluding contour C are transferred to any views by the invariant for two views. Finally, it is feasible to track the occluding contours in any views, so the virtual objects can be drawn behind the contour. Since this approach is based on mobile phones, it is convenient to apply AR to environmental planning. In the following, we briefly present some of the research literature related to augmented reality.

In the past several years, model-based [6, 7] and structure-and-motion methods [8] are widely used in augmented reality. However, these methods require a priori knowledge of 3D models or a limitation to motion. With the development of computer vision, the application of AR has been promoted, and the new models have become more practical. These models include that when 3D location and calibration parameters of camera are unknown, several images are used to restore the structure of objects to complete reprojection. Through the recognition of fiducial in the scene and by means of affine representation, the virtual objects produced by computer will be seamlessly synthesized into the video images of the real scene. This method is different from the camera calibration technology [9, 10]. In this chapter, the weak perspective projection model is assumed firstly for the camera-to-image transformation, and the calibration-free augmented reality based on four points is formulated by the tensor method, and then image augmentation is realized. However, this method is not effective when occlusions exist between virtual and real objects [11]. This occlusion problem could easily be solved on condition that the model of 3D scene is given. Since little is usually known about the real world to be augmented, it becomes challenging to resolve occlusion in augmented reality. Theoretically, a dense map [12] may be inferred from a stereo pair, so the depth between virtual and real objects can be compared. As a matter of fact, this method lacks accuracy, and is difficult to use. A contour based approach with 3D reconstruction has been developed by shen [13]. However, four or more fiducial points from frame to frame have to be tracked. The proposed approach in [14] is based on background subtraction. It needs to model the background using two uncalibrated views, and displacements of the camera must be small in order to fit with the initial background model. More recently, an approach using deepness calculation [15] to accelerate processing speed, but it only judge occluding or occluded relation between whole virtual object and whole real object.

2   Augmented Reality Based on Affine Invariants

2.1   Affine Structure Based on Four Point

Based on the results of Koenderink and van Doorn [16], the affine representations of virtual objects can be formulated by the tensor method. As known, the affine frame is constructed by four noncoplanar points. Let $\mathbf{O}$, $\mathbf{P}_1$, $\mathbf{P}_2$, $\mathbf{P}_3$ be four noncoplanar points in the 3D world, and $\mathbf{O}$', $\mathbf{P}_1$', $\mathbf{P}_2$', $\mathbf{P}_3$' the corresponding coordinates from the second camera position. An object point of interest $\mathbf{P}$ with respect to the basis $\mathbf{OP}_1$, $\mathbf{OP}_2$, $\mathbf{OP}_3$ is shown as follows:

$$\mathbf{P} - \mathbf{b}^i \, \mathbf{g}_i. \tag{22.1}$$

Where $\mathbf{g}_i$ is $\mathbf{OP}_i$, and b^i is the affine coordinate of the point $\mathbf{P}$. In order to make the deduction convenient, the two-dimensional question is shown by Greece letters such as α, β, and the three-dimensional question by Latin letters such as i, j.

Under parallel projection, the viewing transformation between two scene-cameras can be represented by an arbitrary affine transformation, i.e. $\mathbf{O}'\mathbf{P}' = T(\mathbf{OP})$, where T is a linear transformation. Therefore, the coordinates b^i of $\mathbf{P}$ remain fixed under the viewing transformation. At the second camera position, the corresponding $\mathbf{P}'$ of the point $\mathbf{P}$ may be written as follows:

$$T(\mathbf{P}) = T(b^i \, \mathbf{g}_i).$$

i.e.:

$$\mathbf{P}' = b^i \, \mathbf{g}_i'. \tag{22.2}$$

Since the depth is lost under affine transformation, we have a similar relation in image coordinates (using lower case):

$$\mathbf{p} = b^i \, \mathbf{g}_i \tag{22.3}$$

$$\mathbf{p}' = b^i \, \mathbf{g}_i'. \tag{22.4}$$

Let $\mathbf{g}_i$ and $\mathbf{p}$ be divided in image coordinate, and substitute them into (22.3):

$$p_\alpha = b^i u_{i\alpha}. \tag{22.5}$$

According to (22.5), if the coordinates of the point $\mathbf{P}$ in two images are known, the affine coordinates of the point $\mathbf{P}$ can be derived from the affine basis. Finally, the position of the point $\mathbf{P}$ in any frame may be reprojected according to (22.4).

2.2   Virtual Object Rendering

Under affine coordinate, the locations of virtual objects are determined by the affine basis. At the same time, the rendering operation like Z-buffering is allowed, and thus the hidden-surfaces may be processed. Let ξ be the direction of optical axis, which is given by the cross product:

$$\xi = \varphi \times \psi \tag{22.6}$$

where φ, ψ are the corresponding vector of row value of basis vector. Thus, the transformation of the point $\mathbf{P}$ can be achieved:

$$P^T = [\varphi, \psi, \xi] b^T. \tag{22.7}$$

Where $\mathbf{P} = [p^1, p^2, p^3]$ is the reprojection of the point $\mathbf{P}$ and depth value, and $[\varphi, \psi, \xi]$ is the mix product.

2.3 Location of Virtual Object

Before virtual objects can be augmented into a three-dimensional environment, the geometrical relationship between these objects and the environment must be established. From the result of stereo vision the three-dimensional location of a point in the environment can be derived from two images taken by the different locations of a camera. The main questions are how many point projections need to be specified, and how the user specifies the projections of these points. According to the result of affine geometry, if y_1, y_2, y_3, y_4 are the coordinates of four noncoplanar points on virtual object expressed in the object's coordinate frame and y_1', y_2', y_3', y_4' are their corresponding coordinates in the affine frame. There is an invertible and homogeneous object-to-affine transformation $\mathbf{A}$ such that:

$$[y_1' \ y_2' \ y_3' \ y_4'] = \mathbf{A} \ [y_1 \ y_2 \ y_3 \ y_4] \tag{22.8}$$

Therefore, the affine coordinate of any point on the objects can be determined, when the affine coordinates of four points on the objects are known, and the transformation $\mathbf{A}$ can be derived from the affine coordinates of four points.

To determine the locations of a point on the virtual object in two images, interactive method may be adopted. If the locations of a point $\mathbf{Y}$ are determined in two images, its affine coordinate can be computed, and thus reprojection can be realized. The locations of point $\mathbf{Y}$ in two images are constrained each other. If the location of point $\mathbf{Y}$ in first image is determined, the corresponding location in second image is certain to be determined through epipolar and other constraints.

As shown in Fig. 22.1, $\mathbf{Y}$ is a point of 3D space, and $\mathbf{X}_1$, $\mathbf{X}_2$, $\mathbf{X}_3$ are coplanar with images x_1, x_2, x_3 and x_1', x_2', x_3' in the first and second images respectively. The epipolar plane defined by the optical centers $\mathbf{O}, \mathbf{O}'$ and point $\mathbf{Y}$ intersects the plane $\mathbf{\Pi}$ which is determined by the lines $\mathbf{YO}$ and $\mathbf{YO}'$ respectively. From the result of affine geometry, three points determine a plane affine transformation such that $x_i' = \mathbf{T} x_i$, $i = 1, 2, 3$. This transformation is used to transfer the point y to $y_1' = \mathbf{T}y$, and so a point y_1' on the epipolar line can be determined. Under affine transformation, all epipolar lines are parallel. The direction of any epipolar line is simply determined by making the global affine coordinate frame aligned with the first image [17].

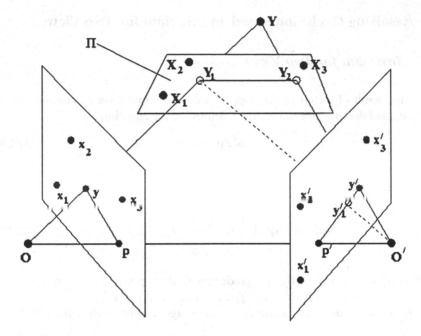

Fig. 22.1 Epipolar geometry relationship

If **B** is the projection matrix of the first image, there is a non-singular 3×3 matrix **S** satisfying:

$$\mathbf{BS} = \begin{bmatrix} 1 & 0 & 0 \\ 0 & 1 & 0 \end{bmatrix}.$$

A simple solution for **S** is:

$$\mathbf{S} = \begin{bmatrix} \mathbf{A}_1^{-1} & -\mathbf{A}_1^{-1}\mathbf{d}_1 \\ 0 & 0 & 1 \end{bmatrix}$$

Where $\mathbf{A}_1$ is 2×2 and $\mathbf{d}_1$ is 2×1. If **B** is divided into $\mathbf{B} = [\mathbf{A}_1 \,|\, \mathbf{d}_1]$, and $\mathbf{B}_i = [\mathbf{A}_i \,|\, \mathbf{d}_i]$, $\mathbf{d}_i$ is the direction of the epipolar line. To get $\mathbf{d}_i$, we must make each projection matrix post-multiplying matrix **S**.

Once a point and the direction of epipolar line are determined, the epipolar line can be drawn in images. For a point **Y** of 3D space, not only is there epipolar constraint, but also collinearity or coplanarity constraint. Through these constraints the location of point **Y** in the second image can be determined.

3   Resolving Occlusion Based on Invariant for Two Views

3.1   Invariant for Two Views

From the result of stereo vision, suppose we have found a set of matched points $\mathbf{u}_l \leftrightarrow \mathbf{u}_r$, and the fundamental matrix is defined by the equation

$$\mathbf{u}_l^T \mathbf{F} \mathbf{u}_r = 0 \qquad (22.9)$$

for the pair of matching points. In particular, writing $\mathbf{u}_l = (x_l, y_l, 1)^T$ and $\mathbf{u}_r = (x_r, y_r, 1)^T$, the above equation will be

$$\mathbf{u}_l^T \mathbf{F} \mathbf{u}_r = [x_l y_l 1] \begin{bmatrix} f_{11} & f_{12} & f_{13} \\ f_{21} & f_{22} & f_{23} \\ f_{31} & f_{32} & f_{33} \end{bmatrix} [x_r y_r 1]^T . \qquad (22.10)$$

This equation is written by a dot product, $\mathbf{p} \cdot \mathbf{f}$, where $\mathbf{p} = (x_l x_r, x_l y_r, x_l, y_l x_r, y_l y_r, y_l, x_r, y_r, 1)^T$ and $\mathbf{f} = (f_{11}, f_{12}, f_{13}, f_{21}, f_{22}, f_{23}, f_{31}, f_{32}, f_{33})^T$.

Given nine points correspondences in two images can be constructed as follows,

$$\mathbf{P} = \begin{bmatrix} \mathbf{p}_1 \\ \cdots \\ \mathbf{p}_9 \end{bmatrix} . \qquad (22.11)$$

From the nine points correspondences, we obtain a set of linear equations of the form

$$\mathbf{P} \mathbf{f} = \mathbf{0}. \qquad (22.12)$$

To avoid a trivial solution $\mathbf{f}$, the determinant of $\mathbf{P}$ must be identically zero. Since the condition $|\mathbf{P}| = 0$ is satisfied in any position of the cameras, the $|\mathbf{P}| = 0$ is an invariant for any two views. This invariant can be used to transfer any ninth point.

If the ninth vector $\mathbf{p}_9$ is written by the notation $\mathbf{p}(\mathbf{u}_l, \mathbf{u}_i)$, $\mathbf{P}$ between views 1 and 2 can be expressed as,

$$\mathbf{P} = \begin{bmatrix} \mathbf{p}_1 \\ \cdots \\ \mathbf{p}(\mathbf{u}_1, \mathbf{u}_i) \end{bmatrix} \qquad (22.13)$$

where $\mathbf{u}_i$ denotes the position of the ninth point in view i. The invariant $|\mathbf{P}| = 0$ leads to a linear expression about the coordinates of $\mathbf{u}_i$. That is

$$\alpha x_i + \beta y_i + \gamma = 0 \qquad (22.14)$$

If eight point correspondences are given between 1 and i, the position of $\mathbf{u}_i$ lies on a line in image i. Similarly, we can determine another line by this invariant between views 2 and i. Thus, the position of the ninth point in view i is given by the intersection of these two lines.

3.2 Feature Detection and Matching

Epipolar geometry defines the geometry between the two cameras creating a stereoscopic system, but all the epipolar geometry is contained in the so called fundamental matrix. Hartley did a lot of work about fundamental matrix [18]. However, in the computation of the fundamental matrix, outliers typically arising from gross errors such as correspondence mismatch result in estimation error. In this chapter, a method based on the RANSAC algorithm for fundamental matrix estimation is put forward. Thus, the estimation error due to the mismatching points is eliminated. At the same time, the matching points are obtained. The flow scheme based on robust RANSAC method is as followed.

Step 1. Find interesting points in scale space.
In this work we use Lowe's [3] SIFT features, which are geometrically invariant under similarity transforms and invariant under affine changes in intensity. The SIFT algorithm may be decomposed into four stages: feature point detection, feature point localization, orientation assignment and feature descriptor generation. The resulting 128 element feature vectors are called SIFT descriptor.

However, the traditional SIFT computation and matching algorithms do not work very well on low-end embedded platforms. Some improvements have been proposed to speed up the SIFT computation. The SIFT's runtime is dominated by the computation of the Gaussian pyramid and descriptors. First, based on the experimental results in [3], the number of orientations and size of the descriptor can be used to vary the complexity of the SIFT computation. We use a 3×3 descriptor with 4 orientations, resulting in feature vectors with 36 dimensions, which lead to only $\sim 10\%$ worse than the best variant with 128 dimensions. Second, a 2D gaussian kernel is a separable convolution. In other words, it may be decomposed into two successive 1D blurs. This means that instead of a RxR(R is the radius of the kernel) convolution kernel, you have a $1 \times R$ kernel and a $R \times 1$ kernel. Obviously this is quite a improvement. Finally, the memory access optimizing techniques are applied in our system. Since ARM compiler uses four registers, namely R0–R3 to pass parameter to a function, we limit the parameters of a function no more than four to eliminate unnecessary memory accesses. At the same time, the C library functions memset and memcpy are designed for all type data size, and thus they include a number of checks for different cases and sizes. However, these checks will cause processing time increasing. We can customize these functions to exactly suit specific requirements. Due to space limitations, we will only discuss these optimization approaches.

Step 2. Find feature matching and its consistent set.
Now all features have been detected and described, this step is to mach them. The original SIFT uses a k-d Tree with the BBF strategy. This paper adopts the hybrid SP-Tree search approach [19] which has been shown to outperform other existing approaches. Since this approach may properly set an overlapping buffer, the computational load of back-tracking can be greatly reduced. Next, we use RANSAC to reject additional outliers.

Step 3. Do $J++$

Step 3.1 Choose a set of seven points from candidate matches.

Step 3.2 Compute fundamental matrix using seven points method.

Step 3.3 Compute median M_J. The M_J is given by

$$M_j = \text{median}_i \left| r_i^2 \right| \tag{22.15}$$

$$r_i^2 = d(\mathbf{x}_i', \mathbf{Fx}_i)^2 + d(\mathbf{x}_i, \mathbf{F}^\mathbf{T}\mathbf{x}_i')^2$$

$$= \mathbf{x}'^T\mathbf{Fx}\left(\frac{1}{(\mathbf{x}'^T\mathbf{F})_1^2 + (\mathbf{x}'^T\mathbf{F})_2^2} + \frac{1}{(\mathbf{Fx})_1^2 + (\mathbf{Fx})_2^2}\right) \tag{22.16}$$

Where r_i^2 is the distance from matches point to its epipolar lines.

Step 3.4 Compute weight function and number of inliers.

The weight function is proposed by Torr [20] is the following:

$$w_i = \begin{cases} 1, r_i^2 < T^2 \\ 0, r_i^2 \geq T^2 \end{cases} \quad (T = 1.96\sigma) \tag{22.17}$$

$$\sigma = 1.4826\left(1 + \frac{5}{n-7}\right)M_J. \tag{22.18}$$

Where n is the number of data. Once the w_i is obtained, the number of inliers is given by

$$I_J = \sum w_i \tag{22.19}$$

Step 3.5 until $J > n$

Step 3.6 Calculate the number of inliers for each $\mathbf{F}$, and the chosen $\mathbf{F}$ is the one that maximizes it. Once the inliers are obtained, $\mathbf{F}$ is recalculated using the normalized 8-point algorithm.

3.3 Resolving Occlusion Based on Invariant

When a virtual object is added into the scene, the user needs to specify the relationship between them. For instance, we want to add the virtual house A behind the real house B (Fig. 22.1). In order to resolve occlusion, if it is feasible to track the contours consisted of key points 1, 2, 3, 4, the virtual house A can be drawn behind the contour. If the scene is complicated, we may label each contour point as being "behind" or "in front of", this idea depending on whether it is in front of or behind the virtual object.

According to the above invariant, if position of a point on occluding contours is determined in stereo images, the position of the point in any images may be calculated using the intersection of two lines. The main question is, after the position of a point in the first frame is determined, how to fix its position in the second frame.

As known, if projection of point **P** in a 3D world is specified in one image, its projection in the second image must lie on a line satisfying the epipolar constraint. At the same time, through point collinearity or coplanarity constraint, the position of any point in the second frame can be determined.

4 Interactive Algorithm

Step 1. Select four fiducial points in the first image to establish the affine basis, and four noncoplanar points on the virtual object s as well as the key points of occluding contours between virtual object s and the real scene.

Step 2. Select four corresponding fiducial points in the second image to obtain the projection matrix, and compute the epipolar lines of four points on the virtual objects and the key points of the occluding contours in the second image.

Step 3. Specify the locations of four points on the virtual objects and the key points of the occluding contours in the second image according to epipolar and other constraints.

Step 4. Compute the affine coordinates of four points on the virtual objects from (22.5) as well as the object-to-affine transformation matrix **A** in (22.8), and determine the affine coordinate of any point on the virtual objects.

Step 5. Detect and track the four fiducial points in any images to construct affine basis, and implement the reprojection of the virtual objects. At the same time, based on the invariant for two views, the occluding contours are tracked in any images, and so the virtual objects can be drawn behind the occluding contours.

5 Experiments

In order to demonstrate the effectiveness of this method, two typical examples were selected and briefly described in the following. The target device at client is a ASUS mobile phone with an Intel XSCALE CPU works at 520 MHz.

5.1 Experiment 1

The first experiment is to fuse the virtual building into real 3D scene which is based on affine structure for calibration-free augmented reality. Figure 22.2 is the experiment environment. Now, suppose that a high building will be constructed. In Fig. 22.2a, a set of salient points are extracted using SIFT algorithm. The black lines show all correct correspondences based on RANSAC. In Fig. 22.2b and c, the affine frame is constructed from the image coordinates of cross-center in Fig. 22.2b, which are acquired by interactive method. Similarly, the image coordinates of key

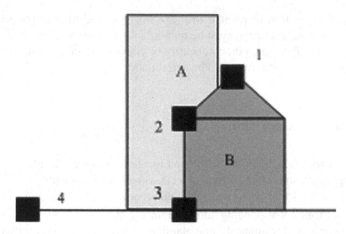

Fig. 22.2 The occlusion between real and virtual objects

points on the occluding contour are obtained in the first image (see the four small black squares in Fig. 22.2b). The epipolar lines of these points are computed and drawn in the second image (see the four black lines in Fig. 22.2c). Then, according to epipolar and collinearity or coplanarity constraints, the image coordinates of key points on the occluding contour in Fig. 22.2c are obtained with interactive method. Furthermore, according to the invariant for two views and point correspondences, the positions of the occluding contour in other frames are determined. In Fig. 22.2d and e the virtual building is fused into the 3D scene very well.

5.2 Experiment 2

The second experiment in Fig. 22.3 is to fuse building group into a scenic spot. The process of resolving the occlusion problem is similar to that in experiment 1. The difference between these two experiments is that this occluding contour between virtual and real objects (see the two black circles in Fig. 22.3b) is relatively complicated. Of course, the more accurate the occluding contours tracked are, the more key points on contours which should be interactively marked in the first two frames are needed (Fig. 22.4).

6 Shadow Algorithm

Since shadows to provide what is essentially a second view of an object convey a large amount of information, it is necessary to model lighting conditions and shadows. However, they are difficult to compute in most augmented reality environments on mobile phones. Currently, no algorithm is known that renders physically correct

Extracted salient feature-points and correct correspondences

The first view of the scene   The second view of the scene

Augmented virtual building   Augmented virtual building

Fig. 22.3 Resolving occlusion with a simple occluding contour. (**a**) Extracted salient feature-points and correct correspondences. (**b**) The first view of the scene. (**c**) The second view of the scene. (**d**) Augmented virtual building. (**e**) Augmented virtual building

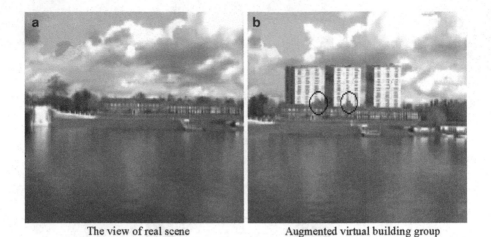

The view of real scene   Augmented virtual building group

Fig. 22.4 Relatively complicated occluding contour. (**a**) The view of real scene. (**b**) Augmented virtual building group

and dynamically updated shadows in arbitrary scenes, and so shadow algorithm requires simplifications to meet the physical limitation needs of mobile phones. In our augmented reality system, a single algorithm is chosen for shadow calculations. As depicted in Fig. 22.5, a light source at infinity is modeled. Because of the light being from infinity, we may assume that all the rays reaching the object are parallel. According to the geometric relationship of the light source and polygons, each polygon's projection on $z = 0$ plane is calculated. Given that the point-vectors of light direction and vertex point are (x_l, y_l, z_l) and (x_p, y_p, z_p) respectively, the shadow point (x_s, y_s, z_s). The projection **S** of any polygon vertex **P** is shown as follows:

$$\mathbf{S} = \mathbf{P} \bullet \mathbf{M}_{shadow} \qquad (22.20)$$

Where

$$\mathbf{M}_{shadow} = \begin{bmatrix} 1 & 0 & 0 & 0 \\ 0 & 1 & 0 & 0 \\ -\frac{x_l}{z_l} & -\frac{y_l}{z_l} & 0 & 0 \\ 0 & 0 & 0 & 1 \end{bmatrix}$$

6.1 Experiment1

This example for demonstrating our shadow algorithm is to fuse a virtual building with shadow into a real scene. As depicted in Fig. 22.6, the process added is similar to the experiment 1. After the virtual building is added into the real scene (Fig. 22.6a and b), we can know how the proposed new virtual building with shadow would change people's view and environment.

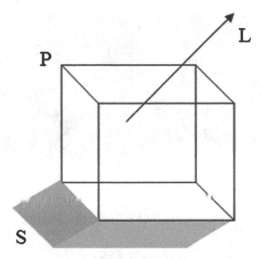

Fig. 22.5 Lighting model

Augmented building with shadow   Augmented building with shadow

Fig. 22.6 The building with shadow fused into a 3D real scene. (**a**) Augmented building with shadow. (**b**) Augmented building with shadow

6.2   Experiment2

In order to demonstrate the feasibility of this method, a typical civil engineering example is given in the following. By means of the above method, a virtual concrete-filled steel tube arch-bridge is fused into the 3D real scene in Fig. 22.1. Figure 22.1a shows the original scene. Figure 1b and c give the views of the different viewpoints of the augmented scene, which is the result needed by practicing engineers. If such result is realized by virtual reality, we have to model and draw more buildings, rivers,

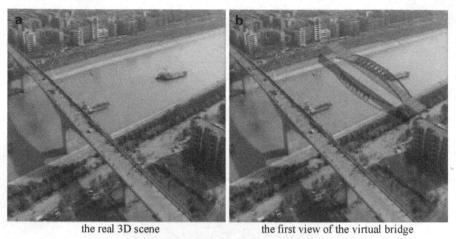

the real 3D scene   the first view of the virtual bridge

the second view of the virtual bridge

Fig. 22.7 A virtual arch-bridge fused into a 3D real scene based on affine method. (**a**) the real 3D scene. (**b**) the first view of the virtual bridge. (**c**) the second view of the virtual bridge

trees, and so on. Further, the details available in the real scene are so many that we must make a choice between realism and real-time. However, using the AR method, all details in the real scene come from the input images. Thus, one of the advantages of the AR is to save the constructing of complicated scenes, which usually takes planners more time, especially in producing highly real virtual reality systems. At the same time, the average error of this method may be less than 1.0 pixel [2]. In summary, this method can meet the needs for visualization of civil engineering (Fig. 22.7).

7 Conclusions and Future Directions

This chapter proposed a contour-based approach without 3D reconstruction which can be used to calculate correct occlusion. The experiments in this chapter have demonstrated that this algorithm is feasible for augmented reality. We compare our approach to previous work by zhu [15] and Shahidan [11], and the contribution of this work includes that there is not the occluding or occluded limit-relation between virtual object and real object, and there is not any marker. Moreover, virtual objects can be mobile or even deformable. However, our approach is not able to deal with partial occlusion problem when there are some movable real objects on occluding contour, which is still the important future work. To our knowledge, no methods can successfully handle all the cases of occlusion problem in augmented reality. The algorithm in this article has greatly enriched the tools for resolving the occlusion problem.

At the same time, the augmented reality system that is based on affine representation is presented in this chapter. Using this system, users only need a mobile phone to realize a richer presentation of information. Through these examples, it has been demonstrated that augmented reality is a powerful visualization tool for environmental planning. It is easy to construct a photo-quality virtual world, and can present more realistic results. Since there is no need to model all the scenes, thus save more time than the traditional VR and raise the efficiency greatly.

References

1. Ohta,Y, "Mixed Reality-merging real and virtual worlds," Tokyo: ohmsha/Springer-Verlag, 1999.
2. Azuma, R.T, "A survey of augmented reality," Presence: Teleoperators and Virtual Environments, Vol. 6, no. 4, 1997, pp. 355–385.
3. D. Lowe, "Distinctive Image Features from Scale-Invariant Key-points", Int'l J. Computer Vision, Vol. 60, no. 2, November, 2004, pp. 91–110.
4. M. Fischler, and R. Bolles, "Random Sample Consensus: A Paradigm for Model Fitting with Applications to Image Analysis and Automated Cartography," CACM, vol. 24, no. 6, June, 1981, pp. 381–395.
5. Johnny Park, and Avinash C. Kak, "3D modeling of optically challenging objects", IEEE Trans. On Visualization and Computer Graphics, vol. 14, no. 2, March, 2008, pp. 246–262.
6. Behringer R, Park J, and Sundareswaran V, "Model-Based Visual Tracking for Outdoor Augmented Reality," Proceedings of the Int' 1 Symp on Mixed and Augmented Reality, Germany, October, 2002, pp. 277.
7. Drummond T, and Cipolla R, "Real-Time Visual Tracking of Complex Structures," IEEE Trans on Pattern Analysis and Machine Intelligence, vol. 24, no. 7, July, 2002, pp. 932–946.
8. Hartely R, and Zisserman A, Multiple View Geometry in Computer Vision, Second ed., Cambridge University Press, 2004.
9. Zhu Miao-liang, Yao Yuan, and Jiang Yun-liang, "A Survey on Augmented Reality," Chinese Journal of Image and Graphics, vol. 9, no. 7, July, 2004, pp. 767–774.
10. Shi Qi, Wang Yong-tian, and Cheng Jing, "Vision-Based Algorithm for Augmented Reality Registration," Journal of Image and Graphics, vol. 7, no. 7, July, 2002, pp. 679–683.

11. M.S. Shahidan, N. Ibrahim, M.H.M. Zabil, and A. Yusof. An implementation review of occlusion-based interaction in augmented reality environment. 2nd International Conference on Computing & Informatics, Kuala Lumpur, Malaysia, June, 2009, pp. 24–25.

12. Wloka M, and Anderson B. Resolving occlusions in augmented reality. In Symposium on Interactive 3D Graphics Proceedings,(New Your), August, 1995, pp. 5–12.

13. Jie Shen, and Haowu Liu, "Solving occlusion problem in augmented reality," Chinese Journal of UEST, vol. 30, no. 3, March, 2001, pp. 236–240.

14. H. Wang, K. Sengupta, P. Kumar, and R. Sharma, "Occlusion handling in augmented reality using background-foreground segmentation and projective geometry," Presence: Teleoperators & Virtual Environments, vol. 14, no. 3, June, 2005, pp. 264–277.

15. Zhu Jiejie, and Pan Zhigen, "Computer Vision Based Occlusion Handling Algorithm for Video-Based Augmented Reality," Chinese Journal Of Computer-Aided Design & Computer Graphics, vol. 19, no. 12, December, 2007, pp. 1624–1628.

16. J.J. Koenderink, and A.J. van Doorn, "Affine structure from Motion," J.Opt.Soc.Am.A, vol. 8, no. 2, February, 1991, pp. 377–385.

17. M. Seitz, and C.R. Dyer, "Complete Scene Structure From Four Point Correspondences," Proc. Fifth Int'l Computer Vision, Cambridge, MA, June, 1995, pp. 330–337.

18. Hartley, R.I, "In defence of the 8-point algorithm", Proceedings of the fifth International Conference on Computer Vision, Cambridge, Massachusetts, USA, June, 1995, pp. 1064–1070.

19. T. Liu, A.W. Moore, A. Gray, and K. Yang, "An Investigation of Practical Approximate Nearest Neighbor Algorithms", Advances in Neural Information Processing Systems, Vancouver, BC, Canada, 2005, pp. 825–832.

20. P.H.S. Torr, and D.W. Murray, "The Development and Comparison of Robust Methods for Estimating the Fundamental Matrix", International Journaxl of Computer Vision, vol. 24, no. 3, October, 1997, pp. 271–300.

Chapter 23
Mixed Reality Manikins for Medical Education

Andrei Sherstyuk, Dale Vincent, Benjamin Berg, and Anton Treskunov

Abstract In medical education, human patient simulators, or manikins, are a well established method of teaching medical skills. The current state of the art manikins are limited in their functions by a fixed number of in-built hardware devices, such as pressure sensors and motor actuators that control the manikin behaviors and responses.

In this work, we review several research projects, where applied techniques from the fields of Augmented and Mixed Reality allowed to significantly expand manikin functionality. We will pay special attention to tactile augmentation, and describe in detail a fully functional "touch-enabled" human manikin, developed at SimTiki Medical Simulation Center, University of Hawaii. Also, we will outline possible extensions of the proposed touch-augmented human patient simulator and share our thoughts on the future directions in use of Augmented Reality in medical education.

1 Introduction

Medical manikins are realistic looking life-size replicas of a human body, equipped with a large number of electronic, pneumatic and mechanical devices, controlled from a host computer. Manikins can be programmed to simulate a variety of conditions. The level of visual realism and physiological fidelity varies between models, but in general, manikins can provide a range of convincingly accurate responses to medical interventions. One medical manikin is shown in Fig. 23.1.

Most of manikins capabilities for interaction, including physical examination are implemented in hardware. All interactions between a human and a manikin are mediated by dedicated mechanical or electronic devices, installed in the manikin. For example, a SimMan line of products by Laerdal Medical Corporation

A. Sherstyuk (✉)
Avatar Reality Inc., Honolulu HI, USA
e-mail: andrei@avatar-reality.com

B. Furht (ed.), *Handbook of Augmented Reality*, DOI 10.1007/978-1-4614-0064-6_23,
© Springer Science+Business Media, LLC 2011

Fig. 23.1 *Resusci Anne*, a realistic life-size cardiopulmonary resuscitation (CPR) simulator, manufactured by Laerdal Medical Corporation (Image from the simulator manual, available online[1])

(see footnote 1) have touch sensitive elements installed at both wrists. These sensors allow a person doing examination to check a manikin's pulse by physically touching its wrists. The manikin "feels" that its pulse is being felt and responds by providing the pulse data to the host computer.

In addition to checking pulses, healthcare persons in training are expected to learn how to collect other data using physical examination techniques. Manual examination may be as simple as touching the patient at different locations and asking whether it hurts. Nevertheless, these techniques are not supported even in advanced manikins, because user hands are not part of the system. Figuratively speaking, manikins are not aware of their own bodies as tangible objects. To compensate for the absence of feedback from the manikins, it is a common teaching practice for an instructor to observe student examination techniques from behind a one-way mirror. If a student is palpating a simulated appendicitis and presses on the tender location, the instructor can provide a cry of pain using a microphone.

The need for such continuous and close human facilitation during the course of the exercise has many disadvantages. First, it requires undivided attention from the instructor, which makes it difficult to supervise more than one student at a time. As a result, manikin-based training is very resource intensive. Secondly, visual monitoring, even with video recording equipment, may not always capture all student actions, which reduces the quality of debriefing and performance evaluations. Finally, examination techniques may be subtle and require precise positioning of the student's hands on the patient's body. Such details are also easy to miss in visual observation alone.

All of these issues can be solved by making manikins sense where and how they are touched, allowing them to respond autonomously and keep logs of these events. We suggest filling this gap in manikin functionality by employing methods known from Mixed Reality (MR) and Augmented Reality (AR) fields. Briefly, to make a

---

[1]Laerdal Medical Corporation, http://www.laerdal.com.

manikin touch-sensitive at arbitrary locations on their bodies, we reproduce real physical examination procedures in the 3D domain. The geometry surface model of the manikin and user hands are checked for collisions, which gives the location of points of contact. A gesture recognition process, running in real time, determines which examination procedure is currently being applied. With this information, the simulation software that controls the manikin's behavior is able to trigger an appropriate response function, such as a cry of pain in the appendicitis scenario.

In this chapter, we review the current state of the art in applying AR and MR methods to medical education. In Sect. 3, a detailed description of the manikin with tactile augmentation will be presented, developed in the SimTiki Medical Simulation Center, University of Hawaii. A special attention will be given to implementation and calibration of virtual hands. One complete training scenario will be presented in Sect. 5. Finally, we will explain our novel method for creating high-fidelity manikin geometry surface model in Sect. 6 and conclude with a discussion of possible extensions and applications of tactile augmentation. Material presented in Sects. 3–7 is largely based on our previously published work [23, 24]; that material was revised and updated.

2 Augmented Reality in Medical Education

Medicine and medical education are a fertile ground for Augmented Reality techniques to grow, for an important reason: the cost of human error is high. In the last few years, medical AR applications experienced a rapid expansion, driven by advances in hardware (tracking, haptics, displays [2]), new concepts in user interface design, such as Tangible User Interface (TUI) [25] and a palette of new interface metaphors and display techniques, including *MagicLens* [18] and *Virtual Mirror* [20]. These advances made it possible to visualize invisible, obscured or abstract objects and data, such as a flow of gases in a Mixed Reality anesthesia machine simulator [21].

Visual overlay of medical imaging data obtained from living patients received much attention from the research community as early as in 1992. From Bajura, Fuchs and Ohbuchi [3]:

> ...Of special interest are recent efforts to apply such AR displays to medical imaging, by superimposing data acquired via imaging techniques such as ultrasound, CT scanning, etc. conformally onto the actual patient. (1992)

In 2007, using a Head Mounted Display and direct volume rendering of CT scans, Bichlmeier and colleagues presented a system, that allowed surgeons literally see into a living human patient [4].

In addition to visual augmentation, other input modalities were explored, including the sense of touch [10]. SpiderWorld VR system for treating arachnophobia, described by Carlin, Hoffman and Weghorst [7], is one of the earliest examples of using tactile augmentation for medical purposes. In SpiderWorld, immersed VR

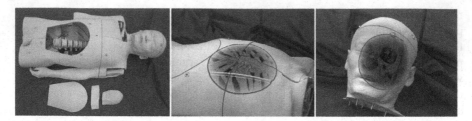

Fig. 23.2 *The visible Korean human Phantom,* direct view (*left*) augmented view (*middle and right*) (Images courtesy of Christoph Bichlmeier, Technical University of Munich)

patients interacted with a virtual spider, which was co-located and synchronized in movements with a replica of a palm-sized tarantula, made of a furry material. During contact with a user hand, the visual input was receiving strong reinforcement from the tactile feedback. With a certain stretch of imagination, the SpiderWorld system may be considered as a very special case of augmented medical manikins.

2.1 Examples of Augmented Human Manikins

Human manikins with augmented sensory input for medical education have been developed in several research centers. We review three systems, which exemplify the most advanced visualization and interaction techniques to date.

2.1.1 The Visible Korean Human Phantom

Phantom is another word for a life-size anatomically correct replica of a human body, or one of its parts. The Visible Korean Human Phantom was developed by Bichlmeier and colleagues at the Technical University of Munich. The team created a method for fast direct volume rendering of CT data [16], which was applied for in-situ visualization of Visible Korean dataset, using a see-through Head Mounted Display [5]. As illustrated in Fig. 23.2, direct volume rendering allows to achieve correct depth perception of inner organs: they appear to be inside the body, rather than painted onto the surface of the phantom. Infrared camera tracking system provides accurate registration.

2.1.2 Free Form Projection Display Applications

As the name implies, the Free Form Projection Display (FFPD) technology allows to project virtual content onto curved surfaces, adjusting the image according to viewer's position [14]. Using FFPD, a research team at Gifu University, Japan, created Virtual Anatomical Model (VAM) [13], where virtual content (internal

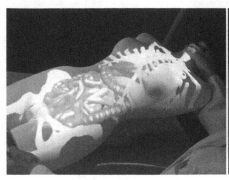

Fig. 23.3 The virtual anatomical model uses real-time adjusted projection of internal organs onto human-shaped surface. Both the viewer's head and the manikin object are tracked in real time, which allows students to handle the display and examine if from different angles (Images courtesy of Ryugo Kijima and Yuzo Takahashi, Gifu University, Japan)

human organs) is rendered and projected onto a human-shaped screen. Electro-magnetic motion sensor attached to the screen detects changes in its position and orientation, therefore, when the viewer tilts the screen, the image is also adjusted accordingly. Although the projection is monoscopic, motion parallax provides viewers depth cues, and the projected organs appear as if they lie inside the transparent manikin, as shown in Fig. 23.3.

In addition, the internal organs, stored in VAM as 3D geometry models, can be marked as fixed (bones) and movable (stomach and small intestine). When a viewer tilts the manikin, locations and shapes of movable organs are recalculated dynamically, using simulated gravity. As the result, the viewer can see how organs move inside the torso, interactively responding to direct manipulation of the tangible torso object. The improved VAM-based Dynamic Anatomical Model is described by Kondo, Kijima and Takahashi [12]. As the original VAM system [13], the Dynamic Anatomical Model uses FFPD for visual augmentation. A common term in AR community for Free Form Projection Display is Spatial AR [6].

2.1.3 Mixed Reality Humans

Mixed Reality Humans (MRH), developed by Kotranza and colleagues [17], incorporate tactile modality into student-patient interactions, by means of using tangible user interface technology. MRH system was designed for teaching breast cancer examination techniques, focusing on improving student communication skills. An MRH combines a physical tangible object, in this case, a realistic replica of human breast, equipped with force sensors, with a virtual human patient. The breast object is mounted on a passive manikin, lying on a table. Students observe the scene through a Head Mounted Display, where the rendered image of the virtual patient is composed with video stream from a web camera, directed at the breast object, as shown in Fig. 23.4.

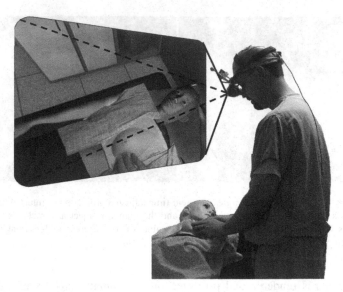

Fig. 23.4 *The mixed reality human patient* undergoing breast examination (Image © 2009 Aaron Kotranza, used with permission)

During examination, the MRH system processes student's motions and gestures applied to the breast tangible object, and the virtual patient provides appropriate responses, sometimes showing signs of distress and anxiety. User studies demonstrated that most students readily accepted the tactile modality in their interactions with the Mixed Reality Humans [15, 17]. Students naturally used gentle stroking and touching motions to calm the "patient." Following the positive results for breast cancer examination, the developers announced plans to extend the MRH patients to additional types of intimate examinations, where interpersonal doctor–patient communications play the most important role [15].

2.2   Industrial Medical Simulators

Conventional (i.e., non-augmented) medical simulators, including human manikins, are becoming a "golden standard" in medical education, especially in training first responders. Manikins become more sophisticated and begin to take advantage of methods from the AR field. For example, the 3G model of SimMan line of manikins by Laerdal Medical Corporation (see footnote 1), uses RFID tags for identifying syringes for the virtual administration of pharmaceuticals. This is done by attaching a labeled syringe to an IV-port on one of his arms. The dedicated IV-arm has an RFID antenna installed under the skin surface, which allows the manikin to detect the presence of the labeled drug and measure the administered amount, by capturing elapsed time while in contact.

However, new generations of manikins show trends in favoring hardware solutions, by installing more structural elements, such as pressure sensors and response actuators. As the result, use of dedicated devices inevitably increases production costs and does not provide enough flexibility for programming new teaching scenarios. For example, the Dynamic Anatomical Model simulator, the successor of VAM [12], is equipped with two additional pressure sensors for simulated appendicitis and cholecystitis, installed in lower and upper abdominal areas, respectively. These two sensors can recognize palpation actions in two locations only. Everywhere else, the manikin remains "touch-blind."

Similarly, Resusci Anne CPR trainer, shown in Fig. 23.1, can only detect and count chest compression actions performed by a person in training. The rest of her body does not respond to any other physical intervention, which limits this particular model to simulating comatose or unconscious conditions. In general, limited capabilities for detecting and processing hand-to-body contacts, make even advanced manikins less useful in scenarios that require manual examination and immediate responses from the patient.

3   "Awakening" Manikins to Human Touch

The research project that will be described next, was carried out at the SimTiki Medical Simulation Center, University of Hawaii. SimTiki teaching curriculum is mostly based on Resusci Anne and SimMan lines of manikins, manufactured by Laerdal Medical Corporation (see Fig. 23.1). We set it our goal to improve the response from the available units by enabling their global "sense of touch," in every part of their bodies.

The core idea is to make the examiner's hands a part of the manikin system, by replicating the physical examination procedures in a virtual 3D space, co-located and aligned with the real manikin object. Within this approach, the manikin's role is reduced to providing visual, tactile and audio sensory input, reacting to hand-surface collisions that are processed in software. The shape of the manikin and the examiner's hands are modeled with required precision. Using motion tracking of the examiner's hands, the system performs gesture recognition, and determines which procedure is being applied. Examples are: palpation, percussion, deep-press-and-release procedure, which all have characteristic motion signatures that can be reliably captured and recognized. Once the hand activity and location on the body are obtained, the system triggers audio responses from the manikin, according to the simulated medical condition. These responses are pre-recorded and can be easily re-programmed for each new teaching scenario.

A fully assembled touch-augmented manikin is shown in Fig. 23.5. It includes an Anne Torso module (the top part of Resusci Anne), and a Flock of Birds motion tracking system from Ascension [1], with four feet tracking range. That area reliably covers the whole body of a human adult, by placing the transmitter unit in the center of the working space. For this project, two motion sensors were used, one

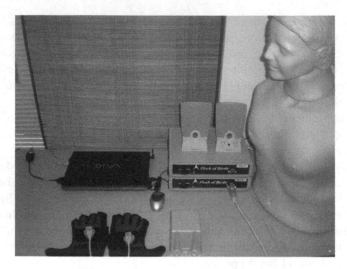

Fig. 23.5 Touch-augmented *Anne Torso* manikin, augmented with a tangible user interface. System components: the manikin object, laptop PC, Flock of Birds tracking system, speakers

for each hand, Velcroed onto sports gloves. The software module is implemented in Flatland, an open source VR engine [9], with added gesture-recognition capabilities, developed earlier for VR-Triage training system [22]. The system runs on a medium grade Vaio laptop, with Linux OS, 1.86 GHz CPU, and 1G RAM.

4   Virtual Hands

A virtual hand is one of the oldest metaphors developed for immersive VR applications [11]. It remains by far the most popular technique for direct interactions with objects in close proximity, which is exactly the case with human manikins.

Virtual hands are the most important and delicate part of the touch-augmented manikin, because users expect the manikins to be as sensitive and responsive as their own hands. High-end manikins have very realistic looking surface made of elastic skin-like material. Some models even mimic distribution of human soft and hard tissues under the skin. Thus, when a user touches the manikin, the sensation is very rich and life-like. As a result, users involuntary expect the manikin to reciprocate and "feel-back" the hand-surface contact event, with the same level of tactile fidelity and spatial resolution.

A carefully designed and implemented system for virtual hands control can create and maintain this illusion, by recognizing stereotypical physical examination gestures and making the manikin react promptly. As discussed by Navab et al [19], reliable recognition of user activity is a very important component of a successful medical training system. Below, we describe our implementation of virtual hands, focusing on features that are specific to our application.

4.1 Spatial Resolution Requirements for Hand-Surface Contact

During physical examination, the requirements for spatial resolution for hand positioning vary between simulated conditions and techniques used for their detection. In many cases, these requirements are surprisingly low.

For some cases, the area of hand localization may be as big as the whole abdomen (e.g., simulated peritonitis); for others, one quadrant of the abdomen (e.g., left upper quadrant for splenic rupture, right lower quadrant for appendicitis). These conditions are commonly diagnosed using palpation techniques, consisting of applying gentle pressure on the areas of interest. During palpation, the hands move in unison and are held in a crossed position. Palpation action can be captured in VR by placing a motion sensor close to the center of the user hand, and monitoring the mutual proximity of both hands and their collisions with the surface. In pilot tests, contact spheres the size of a tennis ball yielded reliable three-way collision detection (hand-hand-surface) for virtual palpation.

Other examination techniques need higher precision in localization of contact area. For example, when applying percussion, a non-dominant hand is placed palm down on the designated area, while the other hand taps over that area. The tip of the middle finger on the moving hand must hit the center of the middle finger on the resting hand. Thus, in order to detect percussion in VR, the system must be able to locate not only the user hands, but fingers as well.

This may be achieved by direct tracking of user fingertips with miniature sensors, such as used in Ascension Mini Bird 800 system [1]; their sensors are the size of a fingernail and weigh 1.2 g only. The tracking range is 76 cm in any direction, which is more than enough for our purposes, provided that the hand is tracked separately with the standard Flock of Birds system, running in four-foot tracking range. The fingertips locations may also be obtained with a CyberGlove.[2] This configuration, however, may be very expensive.

Instead of direct finger tracking, a simpler solution was chosen, based on an observation that each individual finger does not require tracking in full six degrees of freedom. During physical examination, fingers always (or almost always) move along with the hand and their individual range of motions is practically zero. In addition, only few fingers are actively used in direct hand-body contacts.

We implemented a two-step finger tracking solution. Each hand is tracked with a single motion sensor, attached with Velcro onto a sports glove (see Fig. 23.5). Magnetic tracking gives the general hand position and orientation, covering an area of four feet in each direction from the center of the manikin. By using an anatomically correct skeletal model of a human hand, the system infers locations of all virtual fingers needed to process the current hand activity. The virtual fingers are represented by small invisible cubic shapes, attached to strategically important joints of the hand skeleton such as end joints of each finger.

---

[2]CyberGlove, by Immersion Corporation, http://www.immersion.com.

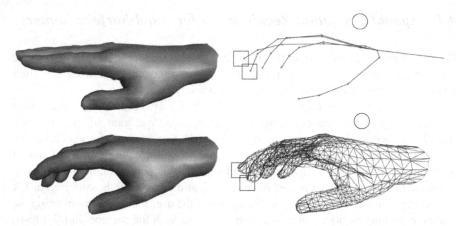

Fig. 23.6 Virtual hands in flat and neutral poses. *Left*: skin surface. *Right*: skeleton and wireframe views. *Small cubes* represent virtual fingertips, attached to hand joints for precise localization of contact points. *The circles* show where motion sensors are attached

Thus, our hand tracking is implemented partially in hardware, using magnetic sensors, and then refined in software, using a hierarchical skeletal model of human hand. The skeletal hand model is also used for posing the virtual hands into different shapes, as shown in Fig. 23.6.

4.2 Activity Recognition and Hand Processing Loop

The key element in our "real-hand, virtual-finger" solution is based upon real-time activity recognition. The system analyzes user hand location, orientation and velocity, as reported by the Flock of Birds, and checks for collisions with the 3D geometry model of the manikin. With this information, the system infers the current user activity and updates the hand pose accordingly. For example, when one of the hands is found to be resting on the manikin's abdomen (the hand collides with the surface and its velocity is close to zero), the corresponding virtual hand assumes a flat pose (Fig. 23.6, top left). When the user hand is moving freely, its virtual counterpart is set to neutral pose (Fig. 23.6, bottom left).

Presently, the system recognizes the following examination procedures: percussion, shallow and deep palpation, pulse check, press-and-sudden-release gesture. On every cycle of the main simulation loop, the system goes through the following routine:

1. For each hand, check for collisions between its bounding sphere and the 3D model of the manikin; if no collisions are detected, set hand pose to neutral and return.

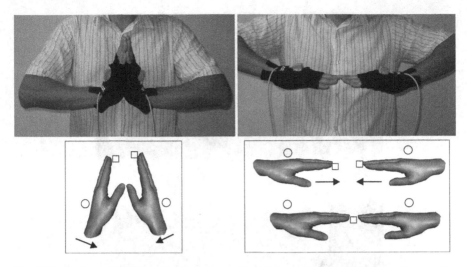

Fig. 23.7 During calibration, virtual hands are adjusted to accommodate thickness of user palms (*left*) and the length of their fingers (*right*)

2. Check the hand orientation and velocity (both relative and absolute); determine the intended action and update the hand pose accordingly; update location of all virtual fingers;
3. For each virtual finger, involved in the current activity, check for collisions between the manikin surface model and the finger shape; if no collisions are detected, return;
4. Process collisions and evoke appropriate functions to simulate manikin response.

In Sect. 5, one complete example will be described in detail, including a code sample for the simulated abdominal pain.

4.3   Hand Calibration and Alignment with Manikin Model

Hand calibration is performed for each new user, after he or she puts on the gloves and straps the motion sensors onto them. During calibration, users are asked to put their hands in a "praying" position and keep them in this pose for 5 s (Fig. 23.7, left). During that time, the system measures the distance between the tips of virtual middle fingers, shown as little cubes, and translates the virtual hands in Y position until these two points coincide. This step accommodates users with different palm thickness. During the next step (Fig. 23.7, right), virtual hands are translated along Z-direction, adjusting for finger length. Translations are performed for both hands, in the coordinate system of the corresponding motion sensor. The calibration process takes a few seconds and is fully automated. A 5 s long interval ensures that the system collects enough samples for a specific hand positions and computes a useful average value.

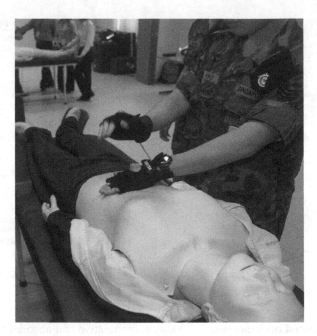

Fig. 23.8 The touch-augmented manikin was first presented at medical simulation workshop held in Singapore Medical Training Institute, April 16th, 2008. A young cadet is performing percussion of Anne Torso manikin, searching for sore spots

Hands-to-model alignment is performed once per system installation, after the manikin is placed in a working position and the magnetic transmitter is installed in its close proximity, as shown in Fig. 23.8. In this particular case, the transmitter is placed under the examination table. The alignment procedure registers the virtual hands with physical location of the manikin and the magnetic transmitter, which defines the origin of the tracked space. In order to align the hands with the manikin model, the user must touch a dedicated spot on the manikin surface with one of the motion sensors, making a physical contact. The system captures the offset between the current location of the sensor and that virtual landmark. Then, both hands are translated by that offset, making contact in 3D space. If the visual monitor is used, users can see their hands "snap" onto that dedicated location. For that purpose, we use the manikin's navel, an easy-to-find and centrally located feature.

5 A Pilot Study: Simulated Abdominal Pain

The first functional touch-augmented manikin was presented to public at the Medical Simulation Workshop organized by SimTiki Center at Asia Pacific Military

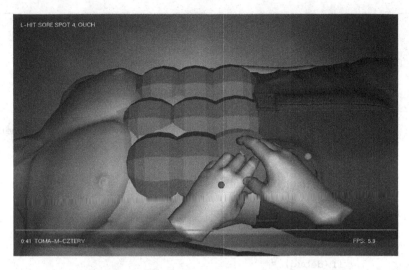

Fig. 23.9 Simulated abdominal pain scenario. A tapping event detected, at the *lower right zone* in the abdominal area. The human male shape is displayed for reference only

Medicine Conference held in Singapore in April 2008.[3] The audience of the workshop were mostly medical educators and health-care providers. The simulated patient was programmed to have abdominal pain, randomly assigned to different locations. In some cases, the simulated patient was pain free. Workshop attendees were invited to examine the patient, using percussion technique, and decide whether the patient was non-tender (healthy) or tender (had abdominal pain). One of the sessions is shown in Fig. 23.8. For that scenario, we used a very simple model of the manikin abdominal surface, a union of nine spheres, shown in Fig. 23.9; simplified code is listed in Fig. 23.10. The tender zone was randomly assigned to one of the spheres. When a user tapped on a non-tender location, the system responded with a neutral "knock" sound, indicating that the tapping event was detected, but the location is not sore. When a painful zone was encountered, the program played back one of the prerecorded sounds of pain. At this moment, most participants stopped and declared the examination complete.

Informal observations of the participants gave us very useful feedback:

The concept of touch-enabled manikins was well received. Over thirty medical professionals participated in the exercise. Practically all of them accepted the "magic" of performing live percussion on a plastic inanimate object. Only one person lost interest during the exercise and quit; the remaining participants continued with the examination until they were able to decide on the patient's condition.

---

[3]Workshop on Medical Simulation Systems at the 18th Annual Asia Pacific Military Medicine Conference, Singapore, April 2008, http://www.apmmc.org/.

```
OBJECT   *LH;        // left hand object (tracked)
OBJECT   *RH;        // right hand object (tracked)
OBJECT   *AO;        // abdomen object: union of zones
boolean  tapping;    // are hands tapping now?
OBJECT   *zone;      // current zone being probed
boolean  sore;       // is current zone painful to touch?

if(in_collision(LH, AO) && in_collision(RH, AO)) {
    //  both hands are touching the abdomen, check movements
    tapping = detect_percussion_gesture(LH, RH);
    if(tapping) {
        zone = find_closest_object(AO, LH, RH);
        //  touching sensitive zone, provide audio response
        if(sore = is_sore(zone)) {
          play_painful_sound();
        } else {
          play_neutral_sound();
        }
        if(debug) {
            // provide visual responses
            if(sore) {
              high_light_object(zone, RED);
            } else {
              high_light_object(zone, GREEN);
            }
        }
    }
}
```

Fig. 23.10 Simulated abdominal pain case algorithm

Calibration must be done for all users. The default placements of virtual hands on the tracker may work adequately for the developers, but for most other users, these settings need adjustment, as described in Sect. 4.3.

Variability of motion. The percussion technique apparently allows for certain variations in hand movements. Some users tapped very fast and their motions failed to register with the system, which expected the hitting hand to stay within a certain speed range. This suggests that the gesture recognition system could benefit from a training phase, when each new user gives a few sample strokes. These samples can be captured, measured and memorized by the system.

6   Creating Manikin Surface Model

Anne Torso touch-augmented manikin is a successor of our first appendicitis simulator prototype, based on SimMan human manikin. The 3D surface model

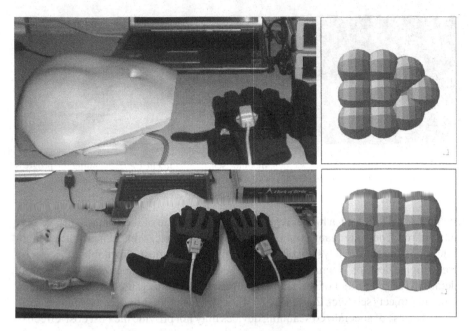

Fig. 23.11 3D surface models of SimMan abdomen module (*top*) and Anne Torso (*bottom*), approximated by spheres

for the SimMan abdomen module, shown in Fig. 23.11, upper right corner, was constructed using the following steps:

1. Measure the physical extent of the abdomen module;
2. Approximate its surface by spheres, using Maya 3D authoring tool;
3. Export the spheres from Maya into the simulator;
4. Run the simulator, detecting hand-spheres collisions using the motion tracker.

Steps 2–4 were repeated, varying the number, locations and sizes of the spheres, until reported collisions with the virtual hand matched the physical contacts between user hands and the abdomen module closely. The whole process didn't take a very long time. However, when we had to go through the same routine again, building a surface model for our second manikin, Anne Torso, it became clear that this process must be improved.

6.1 Improved Manikin Surface Model

A simple union of contact spheres appeared quite sufficient for simulated abdominal pain scenario. However, other medical conditions and examination techniques may require higher precision in localization of hand-surface contact points, as discussed

Fig. 23.12 Scanning SimMan abdomen module: sensor alignment (*left*), scanning in progress (*middle*), completed mesh (*right*) Grid size 40 × 40 cm, 20 × 20 points. Scanning time: under 2 min

in Sect. 4.1. Therefore, a higher resolution representation of the contact surface may be required. There are many commercially available devices that can produce a high-fidelity 3D mesh of a physical object. Examples of the most affordable devices are: NextEngine desktop scanner and DeltaSphere 3D Laser Scanner (see [8] for more details). The 3D model of the tangible human breast object, used in Mixed Reality Human project (see Sect. 2.1.3, Fig. 23.4), was also created by a laser scanner [15]. However, use of specialized scanning devices may not provide the best cost-effective solution.

In order to optimize and automate the process of manikin surface modeling, we developed a new technique, which effectively turned the motion tracking equipment into a home-made surface scanner. The main idea behind our method is to approximate the working area of the manikin by a heightfield over a plane. In order to build the heightfield in 3D, a user moves one of the motion sensors over the area of interest, such as the manikin's torso. The tracker finds the closest vertex on the heightfield grid and snaps this vertex vertically to the current location of the motion sensor. The process happens in real-time and is monitored visually. To improve the positional sensitivity of the motion sensor, which has a roughly cubical shape of 25 × 25 × 20 mm, we placed it at the center of a Ping-Pong ball, as shown in Fig. 23.12. This new enclosure allows tracing of surface features smaller than the original footprint of the sensor. The scanning process is described below step by step.

1. *Grid generation.* A regular grid of quadrilaterals is created in Maya and is used as a template to build the height-field. The dimensions and density of the grid are adjusted to match the size of the object to be scanned.
2. *Sensor-grid alignment.* The motion sensor is placed on top of the object that must be scanned (Fig. 23.12, left); the system captures the sensor location and shifts its rest position to and above the center of the grid. This calibration procedure is implemented as a single key-stroke command. This step is identical to hand-to-model alignment, described in Sect. 4.3. At this moment, scanning is initiated.
3. *Surface scanning.* The user moves the sensor along the surface of the object in continuous sweeping motions and the system updates the height-field interactively, at the frequency of the graphics loop. On each cycle, the closest

vertex is found and snapped vertically to the current sensor position. The process continues, until all vertices are elevated and the height-field is complete.

4. *Run-time operations on the mesh.* During scanning, the mesh can be saved, reset and convolved with a low-pass filter.

Using this technique, we were able to create a 3D scan of the SimMan abdomen module in less than 2 min, using 20 × 20 grid.

The second model scanned with this technique was the Anne Torso manikin, shown in Fig. 23.13. For Anne Torso, the density of the base grid was doubled (40 × 40 points) and an enhanced plastic Easter egg sensor enclosure (5 × 3 cm) was used. The eggshell shaped sensor enclosure naturally conforms to high, medium and low precision scanning modes illustrated in Fig. 23.14. Users can switch between resolution modes simply by touching the surface with the appropriate side of the egg. The motion tracking system detects the changes in orientation of the sensor, and scanning modes are toggled as directed.

Multi-resolution scanning permits dynamic adjustment of both speed and accuracy to match the local geometric detail of the surface. This method requires each vertex in the grid to have a list of its neighbors. Such lists are commonly created during initialization of the grid. If all neighbors of a certain vertex are snapped to the same height, as shown in Fig. 23.14, scanning speed can be further improved by skipping recently snapped neighbors in the main search loop. In our implementation, we did not use this optimization, as the search time was not an issue. The system was able to update grids of sizes 20 × 20, 40 × 40 and 80 × 80 points at 25 frames per second, which was adequate to our purposes.

Using multi-resolution scanning, a detailed surface model of Anne Torso module was created under 10 min, as shown in Fig. 23.13. Besides its speed, our semi-automatic surface scanner has the following features: it is cost-effective, requires no special skills nor equipment and is easy to learn and use.

In addition, the scanner naturally addresses the long-standing problem of distortions in the magnetic environment, that plagues many applications that use magnetic tracking. During scanning, these distortions are imprinted into vertex positions of the surface. Normally, these tracking artifacts are not welcome and may invalidate the resulting mesh, if used elsewhere (i.e., under different magnetic environment). However, if the mesh is known to be used with the same simulator at the same location, the distorted shape is perfectly preprocessed for correct hand/surface collision detections. The shape produced with our scanner is a reflection of the true surface of the physical object (a manikin) in the magnetic environment of the lab and its own inner "organs." Creating a perfect surface model under distorted magnetic conditions would require complicated calibration of the tracker, to take magnetic distortion into account. Utilizing the same tracking equipment for surface acquisition effectively mitigates this problem.

In fact, we expected this feature to manifest itself in our system. Eventually, distortions were encountered while scanning the Anne Torso object, caused by magnetically active inner "organs," asymmetrically located inside the manikin, as shown in Fig. 23.15. Distortions in the mesh are denoted by a circle. However,

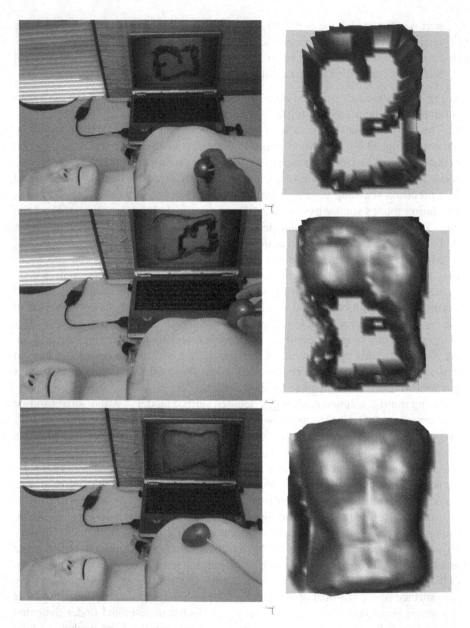

Fig. 23.13 Scanning Anne Torso: initial contour (*top*), intermediate shape (*middle*), and final mesh (*bottom*). The 3D mesh snapshots are shown as produced by the scanner, without retouching (see also Fig. 23.15). Grid size 40 × 40 cm, 40 × 40 points. Scanning time: about 8 min

during model use, these distortions are not noticed by the tracker, because the sensor's path in 3D space is also distorted in exactly same way. Full details on this technique, including the source code and discussion of possible extensions and limitations, were recently published [24].

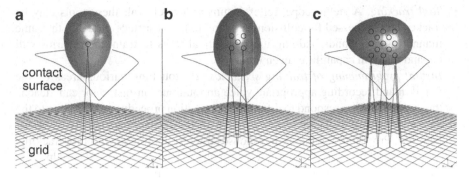

Fig. 23.14 A plastic eggshell provides three intuitive scanning positions: (a) contact with the sharp end moves one vertex; (b) the obtuse end moves the vertex and its closest neighbors (5 vertices per move); (c) contact with the elongated area makes the system to iterate on vertex neighbors twice (13 vertices per move)

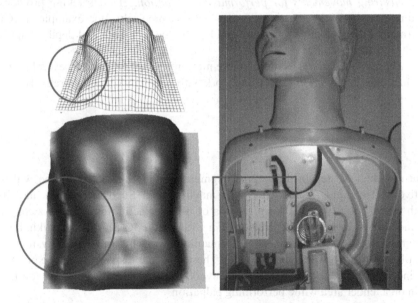

Fig. 23.15 Distorted area in the scanned surface, denoted by a circle. A "postmortem" examination revealed that Anne was engineered asymmetrically: a large metal switchbox installed in her upper right abdominal area, caused distortions in the magnetic field

7 Applications and Extensions

Mixing real and virtual elements in medical simulators, equipped with a motion tracker, yields a multitude of interesting extensions. Below, we list a few that immediately follow from the basic technique.

- *Tool tracking.* A stethoscope, reflex hammer, scalpel – all these tools may be tracked and processed for collisions with the manikin surface model in the same manner as user hands. Adding use of medical tools to training scenarios will expand manikin capabilities even more.
- *Instant programming of training scenarios.* By touching various areas on the manikin and recording appropriate voice annotations, an instructor can "teach" the manikin how to respond to different examination procedures, according to the simulated condition. These *location-action-response* mappings may be saved for later use. Programming manikin responses may be combined with tool-tracking, making manikin react differently when touched by a bare hand and a scalpel.
- *Non-contact interaction.* Tracking of user hands and hand-held instruments allows to process non-contact examination techniques also. Examples include: clapping hands to check hearing; make the patient's eyes follow a moving object; simulate pupil contraction as a response to a tracked penlight.
- *Measuring movements for performance evaluation.* Hand tracking provides a unique opportunity to measure user actions precisely. For example, in CPR training, the system can measure and log the location, rate and depth of applied chest compressions.
- *Multi-user capabilities.* Adding more motion sensors will allow several users to share the same working space and work with one manikin collaboratively.

8 Future

The next logical step in developing augmented manikins is integration with the native host computer, supplied by the manufacturer. Such integration may start with sharing log files that keep records of all user activities. Further steps may include access to manikin's actuators. For example, a 3G SimMan manikin has an "aggressive patient" behavior, when the manikin moves his arms violently, imitating hostile intentions towards the examiner. These extreme responses may be provoked by incorrect or clumsy user hand maneuvers, for example, by inflicting too much pain on a tender area while performing palpation.

Further exploration of video augmentation may open new possibilities in teaching medical science. Projecting pre-recorded didactic video material on the manikin's surface can show, for example, how fast a wound will heal, depending on the depth of a virtual incision made with a tracked scalpel tool.

We believe that advances in Augmented Reality, human-computer interaction techniques and medical human simulators will evolve together into highly realistic, multi-modal interactive system, capable of delivering life-like training experiences. We hope that the work described here will give researchers and practitioners some food for thought in their road towards this goal.

References

1. Ascension Technology Corporation, http://www.ascension-tech.com.
2. R. Azuma, Y. Baillot, R. Behringer, S. Feiner, S. Julier and B. MacIntyre. Recent Advances in Augmented Reality. *IEEE Computer Graphics And Applications*, Vol. 21, No. 6, pp. 34-47, 2001.
3. M. Bajura, H. Fuchs, and R. Ohbuchi. Merging virtual objects with the real world: Seeing ultrasound imagery within the patient. *Computer Graphics*, 26(2), 1992.
4. C. Bichlmeier, F. Wimmer, S.M. Heining, N. Navab. Contextual Anatomic Mimesis: Hybrid In-Situ Visualization Method for Improving Multi-Sensory Depth Perception in Medical Augmented Reality *Proceedings of The Sixth IEEE and ACM International Symposium on Mixed and Augmented Reality ISMAR '07*, Nara, Japan, Nov. 13-16, 2007.
5. C. Bichlmeier, B. Ockert, O. Kutter, M. Rustaee, S.M. Heining, N. Navab The Visible Korean Human Phantom. Realistic Test & Development Environments for Medical Augmented Reality. *Proceedings of the International Workshop on Augmented environments for Medical Imaging including Augmented Reality in Computer-aided Surgery (AMI-ARCS 2008)*, USA, New York, September 2008.
6. O. Bimber and R. Raskar. *Spatial Augmented Reality: Merging Real and Virtual Worlds*. A. K. Peters, Ltd., Natick, MA, 2005.
7. A. Carlin, H. Hoffman, S. Weghorst. Virtual reality and tactile augmentation in the treatment of spider phobia: A case study. *Behaviour Research and Therapy*, 35, pp. 153-158, 1997.
8. A. Cracknell and L. Hayes. *Introduction to Remote Sensing*, (2 ed.), London: Taylor and Francis, 2007.
9. Flatland, open source VR engine. *The Homunculus Project at the Albuquerque High Performance Computing Center (AHPCC)*, http://www.hpc.unm.edu/homunculus, 2000.
10. H. Hoffman. Physically touching virtual objects using tactile augmentation enhances the realism of virtual environments. *Proceedings of the IEEE Virtual Reality Annual International Symposium*, Atlanta GA, p. 59-63. IEEE Computer Society, Los Alamitos, California, 1998.
11. R. Jacoby, M. Ferneau and J. Humphries. Gestural Interaction in a Virtual Environment. *Stereoscopic Displays and Virtual Reality Systems*, SPIE 2177, pp. 355-364, 1994.
12. D. Kondo, R. Kijima, Y. Takahashi. Dynamic Anatomical Model for Medical Education using Free Form Projection Display. *Proceedings of the 13th International Conference on Virtual Systems and Multimedia*, Brisbane, Australia, Sept. 23-26, 2007.
13. D. Kondo, T. Goto, M. Kouno, R. Kijima and Y. Takahashi. A Virtual Anatomical Torso for Medical Education using Free Form Image Projection, *Proceedings of 10th International Conference on Virtual Systems and MultiMedia (VSMM2004)*, pp. 678-685, 2004.
14. D. Kondo and R. Kijima. Proposal of a Free Form Projection Display Using the Principle of Duality Rendering. *Proceedings of 9th International Conference on Virtual Systems and MultiMedia*, pp. 346-352, 2002.
15. A. Kotranza, B. Lok, A. Deladisma, CM. Pugh, DS. Lind. Mixed Reality Humans: Evaluating Behavior, Usability, and Acceptability. *IEEE Transactions on Visualization and Computer Graphics*, vol. 15, no. 3, May/June 2009.
16. O. Kutter, A. Aichert, C. Bichlmeier, J. Traub, S.M. Heining, B. Ockert, E. Euler, N. Navab. Real-time Volume Rendering for High Quality Visualization in Augmented Reality. *International Workshop on Augmented environments for Medical Imaging including Augmented Reality in Computer-aided Surgery (AMI-ARCS 2008)*, USA, New York, September 2008.
17. B. Lok and A. Kotranza. Virtual Human + Tangible Interface = Mixed Reality Human: An Initial Exploration with a Virtual Breast Exam Patient. *Proceedings of IEEE VR Conference*, Reno, Nevada 2008, pp. 99-106.
18. J. Looser, M. Billinghurst and A. Cockburn. Through the looking glass: the use of lenses as an interface tool for Augmented Reality interfaces. *Proceedings of the 2nd International Conference on Computer Graphics and Interactive Techniques in Australasia and SouthEast Asia*, June 15-18, Singapore, 2004.

19. N. Navab, J. Traub, T. Sielhorst, M. Feuerstein, C. Bichlmeier. Action- and Workflow-Driven Augmented Reality for Computer-Aided Medical Procedures. *IEEE Computer Graphics and Applications*, vol. 27, no. 5, pp. 10-14, Sept/Oct, 2007.

20. N. Navab, M. Feuerstein, C. Bichlmeier. Laparoscopic Virtual Mirror – New Interaction Paradigm for Monitor Based Augmented Reality. *Proceedings of IEEE VR Conference*, Charlotte, North Carolina, USA, March 10-14, 2007.

21. J. Quarles, S. Lampotang, I. Fischler, P. Fishwick, B. Lok. A Mixed Reality Approach for Merging Abstract and Concrete Knowledge. *Proceedings of IEEE VR Conference*, Reno, Nevada, pp. 27-34, 2008.

22. A. Sherstyuk, D. Vincent, J. Hwa Lui, K. Connolly, K. Wang, S. Saiki, T. Caudell. Design and Development of a Pose-Based Command Language for Triage Training in Virtual Reality, *Proceedings of IEEE Symposium on 3D User Interfaces*, March 10-14, 2007.

23. A. Sherstyuk, D. Vincent, B. Berg. Creating Mixed Reality Manikins for Medical Education *Proceedings of the 2008 International Conference on Artificial Reality and Telexistence (ICAT'08)*, Yokohama, Japan, December 01-03, 2008.

24. A. Sherstyuk, A. Treskunov, B. Berg. Semi-Automatic Surface Scanner for Medical Tangible User Interfaces *International Journal on Imaging and Graphics*, vol. 10, issue 2, pp. 219-233, 2010.

25. B. Ullmer and H. Ishii. Emerging frameworks for tangible user interfaces. *IBM Systems Journal*, Vol. 39, No. 3&4, pp. 915-931, 2000.

Chapter 24
Augmented Reality Applied To Edutainment

M. Carmen Juan and Francesca Beatrice

Abstract Edutainment is a field in which AR is being applied. Edutainment point out the connections and the positive correlations between the educational field and the entertainment one. In this chapter, several edutainment applications are introduced and an AR application for learning the interior of the human body is presented. For the visualization, a HMD and a monitor were used. For the interaction, two physical zips and the keyboard were also used. We have performed a study with 36 children in which we have considered the introduction using an avatar or a video, and aspects related to the application itself. From the introduction using AR and an avatar or a video, children did not found differences between the two types of introduction for several aspects. However, the children considered funniest the introduction using the avatar, and 86.11% of children liked the most the introduction using the avatar. From the results with the game using a HMD+zips or a Monitor+keyboard, none of the statistical analyses except one (related to easiness of selection) showed significant differences between the two systems. However, 86.11% of children liked the most the HMD+zips system. The children considered that the selection using the keyboard was easier. 91.67% of children preferred to be asked instead of reading the questions. Related to the perception of learning, 97.22% of children considered they have learnt using the games.

1 Introduction

Augmented Reality (AR) can be applied to all type of sectors as an innovative technology that has not been widely exploited. It is consolidated on PCs and with a boom on mobile devices. Its applications are diverse. For example, AR can be

M.C. Juan (✉)
Instituto Universitario de Automática e Informática Industrial, Universitat Politècnica de València, C/Camino de Vera, s/n, 46022-Valencia, Spain
e-mail: mcarmen@dsic.upv.es

B. Furht (ed.), *Handbook of Augmented Reality*, DOI 10.1007/978-1-4614-0064-6_24,   501
© Springer Science+Business Media, LLC 2011

applied to the car sector for maintenance (e.g. companies such as BMW) or for guidance (e.g. companies such as General Motors). Another field in which AR has been applied is edutainment. Edutainment point out the connections and the positive correlations between the educational field and the entertainment one. In this chapter, several edutainment applications are introduced and an AR application for learning the interior of the human body is presented. Other examples applied to other areas can be found in this book.

AR has already been used for learning applications. For example, The Virtual Showcase [1] placed virtual objects on real artefacts. One of the most outstanding applications was to place skin and bones on the skull of a Raptor dinosaur. Construct3D [2] was designed for learning mathematics and geometry. With ARVolcano, the children can learn about volcanoes, which included details on subduction, rifts, the Ring of Fire, volcano formation, eruptions and tectonic plates [3]. It is also possible to learn organic chemistry using AR [4] or inorganic chemistry [5]. With PlantStory is possible to learn how the plants germinate, disperse, reproduce and perform photosynthesis [6].

At the Technical University of Valencia several AR applications for edutainment have been developed. First, a story telling game in which the children can choose how evolves the story and its end. In this application, a story based on the Lion King story was created. The story had eight different ends and it was composed of videos of lions that allow the child to follow a modified Lion King story [7]. The game was visualized using a Head-Mounted Display (HMD) and a typical monitor. Twenty-two children participated in the study. The results did not offer statistical significant differences using both visualization devices. Second, an AR game for finding and learning about animals in a fun way and using magnet cubes. This game was tested with adults for finding exotic animals that are not very well-known [8] and with children for finding endangered animals [9]. With regard to the test with adults, 20 adult participants played the AR game and the equivalent real game. All the participants liked the AR game the most. With regard to the test with children, 46 children played the AR game and the equivalent real game. Sixty-five percent of children who played the AR first preferred the AR game. If AR is played second, 83% of children also preferred the AR game. The children seemed to learn about the subject of endangered animals. Third, an AR game for finding matching pairs to learn about endangered animals [10]. Thirty-one children participated in a study. These children played the AR game and the equivalent real game. Forty-five percent of children aged from 6 to 7 years old preferred the AR game. Seventy-three percent of children aged from 8 to 12 years old preferred the AR game. Children also seemed to learn about the subject of endangered animals. Fourth, an AR game for learning words [11]. This application contained the following options: (1) Spell the word. (2) Start with… (3) End with… (4) Complete the word, and (5) Look for the intruder. As the options indicate, in the spell the word option, the children have to spell the word asked by a virtual pet. In the start with option, the children have to complete the word asked by a virtual pet with the initial letter. The end with option works as similar as the start with option does. The complete the word option is a different version of the two previous options where the child has to find the missing letter. With regard to the look for the intruder option, the children have to look for the letter that does not belong to the word pronounced by a virtual pet. Thirty-two children played the AR game and the equivalent real game. Eighty-one percent of the children liked most the AR game. Fifth, an AR mobile phone game for learning how to recycle. In this game, the player only has to pick up objects that appear over the objects' marker and place them in the correct recycling bin. The recycling bins appear over four different markers. There are three different levels within the game. It depends on the level, the number of objects is different. When players correctly place the residue they are rewarded by the game showing two hands applauding over the recycling bin. If participants wrongly place the object, the game shows a red cross over the recycling bin. The game applies the usual rules for games A player gains/loses points for correctly/incorrectly recycling or leaving the residue outside the recycling bins. A collaborative version of this game has also been developed in which players can play in pairs. Each player plays with his partner, there is no competition, just collaboration. Each player while playing can see his team performance and at end of game can see his team performance in relation with other teams performance on his Nokia screen. A competitive version has also been developed in which players compete against other groups. There is both competition and collaboration. Each player while he is playing can see his team performance and his opponent team performance on his Nokia screen. At the end of the game he can see his team performance in relation with other teams performance on his Nokia screen. The AR basic version was compared with a "team" version in which players played the basic version in pairs [12]. Forty-five children participated in this study. Analysis of the results showed significant differences between the basic AR game and the "team" AR basic game with higher means for the "team" version. A majority of children (59.1%) expressed a preference for the "team" version.

This chapter is organized as follow. Section 2 presents the AR game and includes the software and hardware requirements as well as a description of the game. Section 3 presents the results of the game. Finally, in Sect. 4, we present our conclusions, our suggestions for improvements and future work.

2 Description of the Game

In the AR game for learning anatomical structures in a human body, users are able to "open" the abdomen of a virtual human body, using their own hands. They could see inside the human body, the areas where the stomach and the intestine are placed. Tangible interfaces have been used to interact with the game. The image of a human body and its interior organs are shown over a squared structure in wood. This squared structure is covered with a white fabric. Two cuts have been made in the fabric in the zones where intestine (low part of the abdomen) and stomach (high part of the abdomen) are localized. These zones can be opened and closed by two white zips. Two colored papers (orange and blue) have been placed under these two zones. This facilitates the identification of the two different zones.

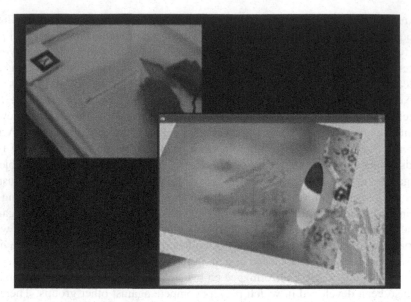

Fig. 24.1 *Left-upper* area shows a picture of the physical elements. *Right-lower* area shows the hands over the female body

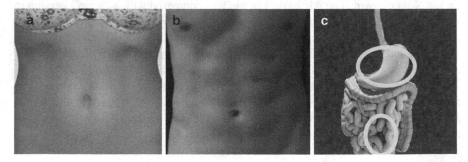

Fig. 24.2 (**a**) The used female body. (**b**) The used male body. (**c**) The image chosen for the selected anatomical structures

The game requires establishing the origin of the coordinate system where all these elements have to be placed. This is achieved placing a marker is one corner of the squared structure. Figure 24.1 (left-upper area) shows a picture of these physical components. Figure 24.1 (right-lower area) shows the hands over the female body.

The game works as follow:

1. At first the game asks the children if they want to see a body of a male or a female. Later, the desired body is shown. Figure 24.2a and b show the used female and male bodies.

Fig. 24.3 (a) Avatar given instructions about the game (b) Child receiving the instructions given by the avatar

2. Users are seeing the chosen body and the game ask them to open the zip where the indicated organ is, for example, please, indicates where is the stomach. Figure 24.2c shows the image chosen for the selected anatomical structures (intestine and stomach).
3. Children open the zip and the game recognizes if the right organ has been chosen. In this case, the game shows: Congratulations!!. You have found the right organ!! and it shows the organ in the hole opened by the user. If not, the game shows: Sorry. You have chosen a wrong organ. Please, try again. This step is repeated meanwhile the child does not found the right organ.
4. Steps two and three are repeated for the two organs included in this first version of the game.

In order to make the game as interesting as possible for children, the presentation of the game was listening meanwhile a moving person/avatar appeared over a marker. For achieving this, we used 3D Live [13]. 3DLive is an AR system for capturing a real person from many viewpoints, then re-generating and superimposing the 3D image of that person onto a real marker in real time. This process has two steps. In the first step, the 3DLive Capturing, is responsible for receiving captured images of the real object from many cameras, and subtracting the background scene to get the foreground images from different viewpoints. In the second step, 3DLive Rendering, calculates the virtual viewpoint, generates and renders the 3D image from that viewpoint onto the markers. For capturing the person, we used a recording-room with nine cameras capturing the person from nine point of views. During the introduction, every child had to take a little palette in his/her hand and when the marker was detected, the avatar began talking to them explicating what they were going to do. Figure 24.3 shows an example of this type of presentation where a person is presenting the system. Figure 24.4 shows a child that participate in the study using the HMD+zips system.

With regard to the hardware, the game requires a camera to capture the real world in order to determine where the virtual elements will exactly have to be drawn. We

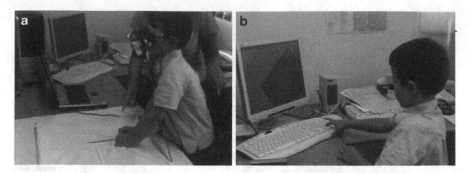

Fig. 24.4 (**a**) Child using the HMD+zips system. (**b**) The same child as in figure (**a**), but using the Monitor + keyboard system

Fig. 24.5 (**a**) Dragonfly camera. (**b**) Dragonfly camera attached to the i-Visor HMD

used a FireWire camera (a Dragonfly with a frame rate of 30 frames per second at 640 × 480). Figure 24.5a shows an image of this camera. After processing the captured image, the game obtains the real camera position and orientation relative to physical markers, and determines where the virtual elements have to be drawn. A HMD was used as visualization system. We have used an i-Visor HMD from Daeyang that provides a full, true color, SVGA resolution at 800 × 600. The camera has been attached to the HMD. In this way, users see what they would see if they did not wear any device. Figure 24.5b shows the camera attached to the HMD. The image that appears on the HMD also appears on the computer screen. This allows the person in charge of the test to see what exactly participants are seeing and this facilitates to help them.

With regard to the software, we developed the game using ARToolKit 2.65 version with VRML support [14]. The virtual elements are the picture of a male or a female and two possible organs: the intestine or the stomach.

3   Study and Results

3.1   Participants and Procedure

Thirty-six children ranges from 8 to 10 years old took part in the study (mean = 8.86, SD = 0.68), with more boys than girls (52.8%, 19 boys and 17 girls). They were children that attended to the Summer School program of the Technical University of Valencia.

The children were counterbalanced and randomly assigned to one of two conditions:

1. The introduction was made using the 3DLive application (avatar version). Later, children used a HMD as visualization system and used the tangible interface to interact with the system first and then the monitor option.
2. The introduction was made using a "simple" video in which a person is given the instructions. Children used a typical monitor as visualization system and used the computer keyboard to interact with the system first and then the HMD option. In this case the organs are selected pressing 1 for choosing the intestine, and 2 for choosing the stomach.

The protocol was the following. Before the child played with the game, he or she received instructions about how to interact with the systems during the experiment. This introduction was done using the avatar or the video versions. The duration of the complete experiment was at about 20 min. After the introduction, children were asked to fill out a questionnaire (Table 24.1). After the exposure, children were also asked to fill out a questionnaire (Table 24.2). At the end of the experiment, children were asked to fill out a final questionnaire (Table 24.3). The scoring was on a scale of 1–5 (1-Completely disagree, 5-Completely Agree) in nearly all questions. If the scale was different, it was indicated in the questions. We tried that the games were as less boring as possible for children when they had to answer to questions. For achieving this, we recorded all questions and they were played back each time. Not

	Question ID	Questions
Table 24.1 Questions after the introduction	Q1	Have you had the sensation of seeing a person that told you how to play? (where 1 represents "For sure, not," and 5 represents for "For sure, yes")
	Q2	This game was fun
	Q3	Do you like to use this system for other purposes such as a teacher explaining you a concept?
	Q4	Have you had the sensation it was real? (only avatar)
	Q5	I think my friends would like to use it
	Q6	I would like to use it again
	Q7	Has it been easy to use it? (only avatar)

Table 24.2 Questions after playing

Question ID	Questions
Q1	Have you had the sensation of playing with and educational game that allows you to see two organs of the interior of the human body? (where 1 represents "For sure, not," and 5 represents for "For sure, yes")
Q2	This game was fun
Q3	Do you like to learn more organs of the human body or other subjects?
Q4	I think my friends would like to play this game
Q5	I would like to play it again
Q6	Has it been easy to play?
Q7	Has it been easy to select the parts of the human body? (in each group the selection was different)
Q8	Have you feel comfortable wearing the HMD? (only for the HMD)

Table 24.3 Final questions after playing both games

Question ID	Questions
Q1	Which game did you like the most? (Monitor or HMD)
Q2	Have you leant or remember (if you already known) where are the stomach and the intestine?
Q3	Have you liked the images and colours? (where 1 represents "For sure, not," and 5 represents for "For sure, yes")
Q4	What introduction have you liked the most? (Avatar or Video)
Q5	Related to questions, have you liked that we ask you the questions or you have preferred to read? (Ask or Read)
Q6	What have you liked the most?

all children at that age can read easily and with enough agility in order to answer to all questions. In order to facilitate the selection, the page shown in Figure 24.6 was presented to children in each answer. Therefore, children listened to the questions, chose the right image for their answer and the person in charge of the experiment noted down the score to the question.

3.2 Results

To investigate if the children prefer the introduction using an avatar or a video, we have analyzed the answers to the questionnaire of Table 24.1 using one-way ANOVA analyses. The significance level was set to 0.05. The results are shown

Completely Disagree   Disagree   Indifferent   Agree   Completely Agree

Fig. 24.6 Score scale

Table 24.4 Means (SD) of the Avatar and the Video versions, and one-way ANOVA analyses of questions after using both introductions. d.f. 1, 34

	Avatar	Video	F	η
Q1	4.44(0.51)	4.22(1.00)	0.70	0.41
Q2	4.67(0.59)	4.11(0.90)	4.78[a]	0.04[a]
Q3	4.33(1.08)	4.67(0.49)	1.42	0.24
Q4	4.06(1.39)			
Q5	4.67(0.59)	3.44(1.29)	13.27[a]	< 0.01[a]
Q6	4.67(0.59)	4.50(0.79)	0.52	0.48
Q7	3.56(1.54)			

[a]Indicates significant differences

Table 24.5 Means (SD) of the HMD+zips and the Monitor+ keyboard systems, and one-way ANOVA analyses of questions after using both systems. d.f. 1, 34

	HMD+zips	Monitor+keyboard	F	p
Q1	4.89(0.32)	4.67(0.59)	1.94	0.17
Q2	4.72(0.67)	4.56(0.62)	0.61	0.44
Q3	4.61(0.61)	4.67(0.77)	0.06	0.81
Q4	4.28(0.89)	3.78(0.94)	2.66	0.11
Q5	4.50(0.86)	4.56(0.62)	0.05	0.83
Q6	4.39(0.98)	4.56(0.70)	0.34	0.56
Q7	4.00(1.14)	4.67(0.49)	5.23[a]	0.03[a]
Q8	4.89(0.32)			

[a]Indicates significant differences

in Table 24.4. The results from questions 1, 3 and 6 did not showed significant statistical differences between the two introductions (avatar or video). However, the results from questions 2 and 5 showed statistical significant differences between the two introductions. In these two questions (2 and 5) children showed their preference for the introduction using the avatar. For questions 4 and 7, and considering scores 4 and 5 as yes, 36.11% of children considered the avatar as real. 27.78% of children considered easy to use the introduction with the avatar.

To investigate if the children prefer the HMD+zips or the Monitor+keyboard in order to play with the system, we have analyzed the answers to the questionnaire of Table 24.2 using one-way ANOVA analyses. The significance level was set to 0.05. The results are shown in Table 24.5. None of the statistical one-way ANOVA analyses that were applied to the results except one showed significant differences between the two systems. The results from question 7 showed significant statistical differences between the two systems when tests were applied. Question 7 refers to the easiness of selection using the two different possibilities (zips or keyboard). The children considered that the selection using the keyboard was easier. For Q8 and considering scores 4 and 5 as yes. Hundred percent of children felt comfortable wearing the HMD.

Related to final questionnaire, 86.11% of children liked the most the HMD+zips system (Q1). 86.11% of children liked the most the introduction using the avatar (Q4). 91.67% of children preferred to be asked instead of reading the questions (Q5). Related to Q2 (perception of learning and considering scores 4 and 5 as the child considers he/she has learnt), 97.22% of children considered they have learnt using the games. Related to Q3 ("Have you liked the images and colours," and considering scores 4 and 5 as yes), 91.67% of children liked the images and colours.

Related to the answer about what they have liked the most. Some of the answers were:

- To use the HMD (55.56%)
- The introduction using the avatar (19.44%)

4 Conclusions and Future Directions

This article describes an AR system for learning the interior of the human body. We have performed a study with 36 children of the Summer School of the Technical University of Valencia. From the introduction using AR and an avatar, or a video for receiving the instructions about how to play, children did not found differences between the two types of introduction for: the sensation of seeing a person, using the system for other purposes, or using it again. However, the children considered funniest the introduction using the avatar and also that their friends would like to use it. Moreover, 36.11% of children considered the avatar as real, and 27.78% of children considered the avatar version easy to use.

From the results with the game using the HMD+zips or the Monitor+keyboard, none of the statistical one-way ANOVA analyses except one (related to easiness of selection) showed significant differences between the two systems. The children considered that the selection using the keyboard was easier. Hundred percent of children felt comfortable wearing the HMD. Related to final questionnaire, 86.11% of children liked the most the HMD+zips system. 86.11% of children liked the most the introduction using the avatar. 91.67% of children preferred to be asked instead of reading the questions. Related to the perception of learning, 97.22% of children considered they have learnt using the games. 91.67% of children liked the images and colours. Finally, in the open question "what you have liked the most?," 55.56% of the children expressed their preference for the use of the HMD and 19.44% for the introduction using the avatar.

With regard to future works, first, in this work we have evaluated different aspects that can be evaluated in this type of studies, but a more exhaustive evaluation could be performed. Special attention could be paid to the learning aspect. In our work, we have asked children if they have learnt, but a more objective evaluation could be used (e.g. evaluating the children about their improvement in knowledge). Second, in this game only two organs of the digestive system have been used, but the addition of new organs would improve the experience of learning and the interaction with a human body (e.g. oesophagus). Finally, using this game it could be possible to learn other subjects, such as the circulatory system or the respiratory system.

References

1. O. Bimber, D. Fröhlich, D. Schmalstieg, L.M. Encarnaçao, "The virtual Showcase", IEEE Computer Graphics & Applications, Vol. 21, No. 6, 2001, pp. 48–55.
2. H. Kaufmann, "Geometry Education with Augmented Reality", PhD Dissertation thesis, Vienna University of Technology, 2004.
3. E. Woods, M. Billinghurst, J. Looser, G. Aldridge, D. Brown, B. Garrie, C. Nelles, "Augmenting the science centre and museum experience", GRAPHITE, 2004, pp. 230–236.
4. M. Fjeld, J. Fredriksson, M. Ejdestig, F. Duca, K. Bötschi, B.M. Voegtli, P. Juchli, "Tangible User Interface for Chemistry Education: Comparative Evaluation and Re-Design", CHI 2007, 2007, pp. 805–808.
5. M. Nuñez, R. Quirós, I. Nuñez, J.B. Cardá, E. Camahort, "Collaborative augmented reality for inorganic chemistry education. New aspects of engineering education", 5th WSEAS, 2008, pp. 271–277.
6. C.L. Mei-Ling, Y. Theng, W. Liu, A. Cheok, "A User Acceptance Study on a Plant Mixed Reality System for Primary School Children", Ubiquitous Computing, Design, Implementation and Usability, Ed. IGI Global, 2008, pp. 87–98.
7. M.C. Juan, R. Canu, J. Cano, M. Gimenez, "Augmented Reality Interactive Storytelling systems using tangible cubes for edutainment", IEEE International Conference on Advanced Learning Technologies Learning technologies in the Information society (ICALT'08), 2008, pp. 233–235.
8. M.C. Juan, "Chapter 10: Augmented Reality and Tangible interfaces for learning", Advanced Learning, Ed. In-teh, 2009, pp.153–166.
9. M.C. Juan, G. Toffetti, F. Abad, J. Cano, "Tangible cubes used as the user interface in an Augmented Reality game for edutainment", The 10th IEEE International Conference on Advanced Learning Technologies (ICALT'2010), 2010, pp. 599–603.
10. M.C. Juan, M. Carrizo, M. Giménez, F. Abad, "Using an Augmented Reality game to find matching pairs", WSCG'11, Session: SH-5. Paper code: I13, 8 pages, http://wscg.zcu.cz/WSCG2011/!_2011_WSCG-Short_Papers.pdf.
11. M.C. Juan, E. Llop, F. Abad, J. Lluch, "Learning words using Augmented Reality", The 10th IEEE International Conference on Advanced Learning Technologies (ICALT'2010), 2010, pp. 422–426.
12. M.C. Juan, D. Furió, L. Alem, P. Ashworth, M. Giménez, "Chapter 9: An Augmented Reality Library for Mobile Phones and its Application for Recycling", Open Source Mobile Learning: Mobile Linux Applications, Ed. IGI Global, 2011, pp. 124–139.

13. T.H.D. Nguyen, T.C.T. Qui, K. Xu, A.D. Cheok, S.L. Teo, Z.Y. Zhou, A. Mallawaarachchi, S.P. Lee, W. Liu, H.S. Teo, L.N. Thang, Li, Y., Kato, H., "Real-Time 3D Human Capture System for Mixed-Reality Art and Entertainment", IEEE Transactions on Visualization and Computer Graphics, Vol. 11, No. 6, 2005, pp. 706–721, http://dx.doi.org/10.1109/TVCG.2005.105.
14. H. Kato, M. Billinghurst, "Marker tracking and HMD calibration for a video-based augmented reality", 2nd IEEE and ACM International Workshop on Augmented Reality (IWAR'99), 1999, pp. 85–94, http://www.hitl.washington.edu/artoolkit.

Chapter 25
Designing Mobile Augmented Reality Games

Richard Wetzel, Lisa Blum, Wolfgang Broll, and Leif Oppermann

1 Introduction

In the gaming area, augmented reality (AR) and especially mobile augmented reality provides unique opportunities. Unlike traditional video games, mobile augmented reality games are not imprisoned in the screen-space but provide for interaction with the world that surrounds us. They incorporate real locations and objects into the game, therefore tapping into a set of pre-existing thoughts, emotions and real-life experiences of its players, which in turn provides the material for a much richer gaming world and user experience. In mobile augmented reality games the playing area becomes borderless and they can be played literally anywhere and anytime. The current advancement of modern cell phone technology is finally giving more people than ever the hardware necessary to participate and experience such games.

However, game design considerations that explicitly cater for the affordances of mobile augmented reality games have often been considered of secondary importance when compared to the technical aspects. Furthermore, the technological aspect arguably tends to overwhelm first-time players, with them often responding to the novelty of the situation rather than the underlying gaming experience. While this problem makes it difficult to evaluate such games, this may also be considered the main reason for the absence of appropriate game design guidelines for mobile AR games.

In order to address these issues this chapter focuses on the game design aspects of mobile AR games: What constitutes a truly "good" mobile augmented reality game? What kinds of design mistakes are easy to make and how can they be avoided? How is augmented reality best utilized in a mobile game? In trying to answer these questions this chapter will start with an overview of AR games developed in both

R. Wetzel (✉)
Collaborative Virtual and Augmented Environments, Fraunhofer FIT, Schloss Birlinghoven,
53754 Sankt Augustin, Germany
e-mail: richard.wetzel@fit.fraunhofer.de

B. Furht (ed.), *Handbook of Augmented Reality*, DOI 10.1007/978-1-4614-0064-6_25,
© Springer Science+Business Media, LLC 2011

the commercial as well as in the research domain. This is followed by an in-depth look on a mobile augmented reality game called *TimeWarp*, whose theme is strongly coupled to the folklore of the city it is hosted in. The chapter closes with a set of game design guidelines that were mainly derived from the evaluation of *TimeWarp* to be helpful when designing such games.

2   An Overview of Augmented Reality Games

As the main focus of this chapter should lie on mobile augmented reality games, it is necessary to define what we mean by that and how we would categorize it. The first separation one can make is rather easy: differentiating between stationary and mobile devices. Stationary devices are usually tied to a specific space (often literally through power-cords and other cables) and often requiring their users to be in their vicinity and adopt a certain pose while using them. Mobile devices, on the contrary, are usually cords-free and not tied to a specific space for interaction. With regards to the video augmented reality specific requirement of having a camera and a display linked to a computer, this usually means that with mobile devices the users can select the viewing angle by naturally positioning the device rather than trying to bring something to the computer.

The second separation that we use in this document is how space is used for content placement – near vs. far, or also: local vs. remote – and how a change to the user's location context changes the presentation of the content. In one extreme group of AR applications the content is always placed locally near the user (think of a marker-based example). In this group the main AR experience is often limited to seeing the effects of positioning a marker with respect to a camera (when using a stationary device) or a camera with respect to a marker (when using a mobile device). In a second extreme group, the content is always placed remotely and can only be viewed from a distance (think of an AR telescope). In both groups, the mobility of the user does not have a positive effect on the user experience, as the design does not lead towards roaming the space. In our sense of mobile augmented reality we demand that the user's mobility has an influence on the location context which alters the presentation of content.

Figure 25.1 summarizes those two separations into a two-dimensional taxonomy for augmented reality games, with device mobility depicted on the x-axis and content locality depicted on the y-axis. Mobile augmented reality gaming is located on the right side of the diagram. When examining this side more closely however, one can split it one into two subgroups: faux mobile AR games and true mobile AR games. While the first group is only played on a mobile device but otherwise mostly local on the content side, the latter is forcing the players to physically move around the real world while playing.

Finally, a third separation that we apply is about how strongly the content is semantically coupled to locations. Depending on the degree of coupling with the real world, these games can be separated into location independent, loosely coupled AR

Fig. 25.1 Classification of AR games based on device mobility and use of content space

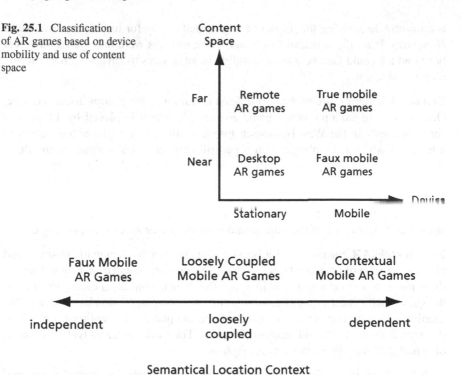

Content Space

	Far	Remote AR games	True mobile AR games
	Near	Desktop AR games	Faux mobile AR games
		Stationary	Mobile

Device

Faux Mobile AR Games   Loosely Coupled Mobile AR Games   Contextual Mobile AR Games

independent   loosely coupled   dependent

Semantical Location Context

Fig. 25.2 Classification of mobile AR games based on their semantical location context

games and contextual AR games, as depicted in Fig. 25.2. This separation helps to further distinguish mobile augmented reality games. Typically, completely location indepent mobile AR games fall into the bigger group of faux mobile augmented reality games.

The following categories of augmented reality games are based on these three dimensions of classification.

Desktop AR games are played on a PC (laptop or desktop) or a gaming console. The graphics are output on a large screen and the user usually interacts with the game via a webcam which is in a fixed position. Tracking is done by means of computer vision. This can either be marker-based or based on visual feature tracking.

One of the most popular desktop AR games is the *EyePet* for Sony's PlayStation [1]. The player can interact and play with a virtual gremlin-like creature and solve different tasks. The camera recognizes objects and some gestures in the image and the virtual creature reacts accordingly. An earlier, but less successful PlayStation game is *Eye Of Judgement* [2] which is played with cards containing markers that were used to position virtual armed forces of different strength on a board. The user could then visually follow the fights between the different forces on the screen. While these two examples are commercial games, the advertising industry is currently discovering the impact of augmented reality for its purpose. In case of *Honeyway Train* [3], artificial black-and-white markers were distributed on cereal boxes which could then be used as tangible input devices to navigate a bee through a virtual landscape.

Remote AR games are probably the least common of the groups discussed here. One interesting example is the game *Flypad* [4] which is played by 11 players simultaneously in the West Bromwich Public Gallery. Every player has access to a terminal which is combined with a pan-tilt camera and a footpad on the floor. With it each player can control an avatar that is flying around in the atrium.

Another interesting example is *AR.Pursuit* [5] which is played with the Parrot AR Drone, a flying quadcopter equipped with two webcams and ultra-sonic sensors which can be controlled remotely by iOS devices. In the game the players see the augmented viewscreen of their drone and have to race or shoot the opposing drone.

Faux mobile AR games make it possible for the user to change his position and also the position of the output device. However, this movement primarily influences the camera view of the augmented image, rather than having any meaning in terms of the game itself. These types of games are usually computer vision based or employ inertial sensors to create a game space around the player's current position, where the overall location is not relevant for the game. The game content is typically output on a mobile device like a modern smartphone.

Invisible Train [6] is played with a PDA and lets the players control trains and junctions. The playing field is a wooden board on which the virtual trains are travelling, tracking is done via markers on the board. A popular example of the computer vision based type of faux mobile AR games is the augmented reality shooter *Arhrrrr* [7]. The player has to point the device at the map of a city in which a zombie outbreak is taking place. The map is at the same time used to track the device's position and the camera image of the smartphone is then overlaid with virtual buildings and zombies. The player now has to aim and shoot at the virtual creatures to save the day. Similar marker-based games are *ARDefender* for iPhone [8] and *Splatter Bug* [9] in which players have to shoot hostile forces and crawling bugs respectively.

A slightly different approach applies built-in accelerators and magnetometers to display visual effects on top of the camera image and assumes that the user is only rotating around him/herself. A typical game of this type is *Firefighter360* [10] for the iPhone in which the player has to move the phone around to aim at the fires and extinguish them with a water hose. The player can also move forward and backward, however this is not done via actual physical movement but by pressing the movement buttons on the screen. A similar iPhone game from a technical point of view is *AR Monster* [11]. Like in a typical role playing game, the player controls a character that develops over time: e.g. getting stronger or learning new magic. The game itself revolves around killing monsters that appear around the player. The player first has to locate the monster by moving the phone around. Once the monster is found, it engages the player in a simple round-based fight. Like in *Firefighter360*, the player's physical movement is not reflected in the game but only the orientation change from moving the phone around. Other similar games are *Arcade Reality* [12] in which the player is attacked by alien spaceships that have to be shot, *Zombie ShootAR* [13] in which zombies have to be eliminated and *Mosquitoes* [14] in which the corresponding annoying little insects have to be killed.

True mobile AR games depend heavily on the user moving about the game space. Here, this spatial movement is crucial for playing the game. Most often a combination of GPS and inertial sensors is used, but computer vision tracking is also possible. The game is experienced by the player on the screen of a mobile device or by using head-mounted displays. For this group we distinguish between loosely coupled mobile AR games and contextual (strongly location dependent) mobile AR games.

Loosely coupled mobile AR games are actually played without or very little relation to enclosing places. Due to this they can easily be played at different locations. Sometimes they have specific constraints like e.g. playing in streets or on side-walks, but can still be replaced with reasonable adjustment as the constraint is found in many similar locations. Currently most true mobile AR games remain loosely coupled as the following examples that can be played virtually almost everywhere.

One of the oldest mobile AR games of this category is *Human Pacman* [15]. The players are equipped with a laptop and a head-mounted display and have to walk along the city streets to collect virtual pills known from the arcade classic *Pacman*. Other players take on the role of ghosts moving in the same game space trying to catch the player. Another mobile augmented reality game with a popular regular computer game archetype is the first person shooter *ARQuake* [16]. Like in *Human Pacman* players are equipped with GPS, inertial sensors, laptop and a head-mounted display. The players are then confronted with the same virtual enemies as in the desktop version of the game *Quake* and have to shoot those down.

NetAttack [17] also has similarities to a first-person shooter. Players are wearing giant markers which makes it possible for other players to shoot at them, although a hit only effects the player's communication abilities. Combining several elements of the aforementioned games, *Epidemic Menace* [18] adds strong storytelling elements to the game, and also allows switching between several mobile and stationary modes of play. Players have to solve the mystery of who released a deadly virus by finding clues in the form of video snippets and interaction with a real actor. At the same time the deadly viruses have to be neutralized by using similar AR equipment as in *Human Pacman* as shown in Fig. 25.4.

In contrast to the previously mentioned, the AR game *Cows* vs. *Aliens* [19] uses visual markers placed at several locations for tracking. Goal of the game is to save the own cows from alien attacks. Therefore, players walk around and point their devices at these markers to interact with the game. On the markers, the cows as well as the aliens come to live as animated 3D models. *Interference* [20] combines markers that are distributed in the urban playing area of the game using simpler

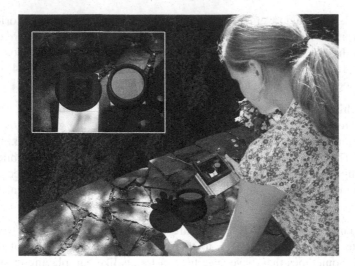

Fig. 25.3 The Alchemists

Fig. 25.4 Epidemic Menace

mechanics of location-based games: The players discover audio and video snippets that advance the game story while they have to follow tracks of a mysterious network that is made visible by AR on the aforementioned markers.

Another marker-tracking-based mobile AR game is *The Alchemists* [21] in which players have to search for ingredients and then cook different magical potions (see Fig. 25.3). As the game does not rely on a specific game area, the markers can be placed literally anywhere.

Recently, mobile augmented reality software platforms like *LayAR* [22], *Wikitude* [23] or *Junaio* [24] have made a stong impression on the mobile augmented reality market in providing a development environment for today's smartphones. One of the earliest examples of such a mobile game is *Hoppala Goes Easter* [25] in which the players encounter virtual Easter eggs all around the world that can be collected. *iButterfly* [26] is a similar example: Players can catch different types of butterflies by quickly moving their phone like a butterfly net. Later they can be exchanged for shopping coupons. Like the Easter eggs, the butterflies are distributed in the real environment.

One thing to keep in mind when looking at these smartphone-based games however is the fact that although they have *mobile* qualities they might not be fully-developed *augmented reality* games as the virtual game objects only have binary appearance attributes: They do not grow visually bigger when a player walks closer to them but are always displayed at the same size (or not at all when out of sight). We have included these games here for completeness sake nevertheless.

Contextual mobile AR games have a strong relation to the game area they are played in. This can be a real place, highlighting the storyline of a game visually, acoustically or olfactory and therefore indeed creating a mixed reality experience. Due to their strong relation to the surroundings, these games are typically hard to move to different places.

The marker-based game *Eduventure* [27] is played in the medieval Marksburg castle from the twelfth century, situated in the Middle-Rhine valley in Germany. Equipped with a tablet PC the player takes on the role of a scientist and walks to different places on the castle terrain in order to solve tasks in a scavenger hunt style and find a captive. Here the story line is based on the old historic location.

Lastly, *TimeWarp* [28, 29] is a mobile augmented reality game that is played at the banks of the river Rhine in Cologne. Similar to *Eduventure*, the content of the game is rather strongly coupled to the real environment. Players use GPS, inertial sensors and Ultra-mobile PCs to explore different time periods of Cologne solving different tasks. *TimeWarp* will be presented in more detail in the next section of this chapter.

Table 25.1 summarizes the discussed games and their characteristics including genre, hardware, tracking mechanism and whether the game is played collaboratively, competitively orsingle.

3   *TimeWarp* – Successive Study of a Contextual AR Game

Currently the game *TimeWarp* in its different incarnations is one of very few mobile augmented reality games that puts emphasis on the environment in which it is played, therefore belonging to the contextual games section. The game was developed during the 4-year European project IPCity [30] and was evaluated by extensive user tests leading to several substantial redesigns. Central idea of the game

Table 25.1 Overview of augmented reality games

Game	Genre	Hardware	Tracking	Players
Desktop AR games				
EyePet (move edition)	Casual	Playstation (+movecontroller)	Marker	Variable
Honeyway train	Racing	Computer	Marker	Single
Eye of judgement	Strategy	Playstation	Marker	2-Player
Remote AR games				
FlyPad	Casual	Terminal, camera, footpad	Camera movement	Collaborative
AR.Pursuit	Action	Parrot AR drone	Marker	2-player
Faux mobile AR games				
Invisible train	Strategy	PDA	Marker	2-Player
ARDefender	Action	Smartphone	Marker	Single
Splatter bug	Action	Smartphone	Marker	Single
Arhrrrr	Action	Smartphone	Natural feature	Single
Firefighter360	Action	Smartphone	Inertial	Single
AR Monster	Action	Smartphone	Inertial	Single
Arcade reality	Action	Smartphone	Inertial	Single
Mosquitoes	Action	Smartphone	Inertial	Single
Zombie ShootAR	Action	Smartphone	Inertial	Single
True mobile AR games (loosely coupled)				
Cows vs. Aliens	Strategy	PDA	Marker	Collaborative, competitive
The Al-chemists	Action	UMPC/Tablet PC	Marker	Variable
Human Pacman	Action	Laptop + HMD	GPS + inertial	Multiplayer
ARQuake	Action	Laptop + HMD	GPS + inertial	Single
Epidemic Menace	Action	Laptop + HMD	GPS + inertial	Collaborative, Competitive
Interference	Adventure	UMPC	Marker	Collaborative
NetAttack	Action-Adventure	Laptop + HMD	GPS + marker	Collaborative, Competitive
Hoppala goes Easter	Casual	Smartphone	GPS + inertial	Single
iButterfly	Casual	Smartphone	GPS + inertial	Single
True mobile AR games (contextual)				
Eduventure	Adventure	Tablet PC	Marker	Single
TimeWarp	Adventure	UMPC	GPS + inertial	Collaborative

staged in the old part of Cologne is the tale of the *Heinzelmännchen*. According to the legend these small gnomes, which used to help the citizens of Cologne during the night, suddenly disappeared due to the nosy tailor's wife which trapped them. The game picks up the city's legend and extends it by spreading the rumor that the gnomes are still around but living in different time periods. Therefore, the goal of the game is to travel through the different time periods, find the gnomes in historical and future Cologne and bring them back into their time. In order to rescue the gnomes, the players have to solve challenges presented by the gnomes.

In this section *TimeWarp*, its core game design elements and the process from the first prototype (referred to as *TimeWarp 1*) to the last prototype (*TimeWarp 2*) are described to illustrate a sophisticated example of a contextualized mobile augmented reality game that takes surrounding places into account, but nevertheless covers many of the problems loosely coupled mobile games have to face as well. The challenges the players have to solve in the game are also diverse enough to give insight into a variety of different playmodes for mobile augmented reality games. The game involves the players intellectually, emotionally and physically and can therefore serve as a basis for many different design guidelines.

3.1 Technological Concept and Interaction

TimeWarp 1 was conceived as a single player game. The user was equipped with a see-through visor to augment the real city with the virtual gnomes and historic buildings and a handheld-based information device (Dell Axim x51v running Windows Mobile 2005) showing an interaction map. The position and orientation of the user was tracked by a GPS receiver and a 3-DOF orientation sensor attached to the visor. For interaction a standard Bluetooth mouse or a gyroscopic mouse were used. User tests showed that the AR visor (as seen in Fig. 25.5) led to severe problems in sunny weather conditions as virtual elements were nearly invisible. Remedies such as self-constructed parasols helped temporarily but used to distract the users from the actual game play and had a negative impact on the experience. Additionally the even more bulky equipment resulted in strange responses from other pedestrians. Interaction with the mouse was experienced as problematic. Partly this was due to confusing interaction techniques and the lack of any former user familiarization with the technologies.

TimeWarp 2 makes use of ultra mobile PCs (UMPCs, see Fig. 25.6) as opposed to an AR visor and therefore overcomes one of the weaknesses of the previous approach. It applies a collaborative style of gaming as opposed to being only single player. The two players have different user interfaces on their UMPCs and perform slightly different roles in the game. In that way the new technologies are less complex for each individual player and they are encouraged to collaborate. The device of player 1 (AR player) provides an augmented reality view of the environment. This is created by using data gathered from a GPS unit and an

Fig. 25.5 HMD
in *TimeWarp 1*

Fig. 25.6 Ultra Mobile PCs in *TimeWarp 2*

orientation sensor to create the so-called "magic lens" effect [31]: Virtual objects
and characters are overlaid on the live camera image of the UMPC. The AR player
can furthermore interact with the augmented content. From a game play perspective
the interaction approach was significantly simplified by applying a point and click
style approach on the UMPC rather than an external mouse. A crosshair changes
its color when pointed at an object or character ready for interaction, which can

then be performed by pressing a button. The interaction can take various forms like starting to talk to a character, picking up an object or repairing something. Player 2 (the navigator) is in control of a map overview of the game area. The players can see their current position as well as interesting places that are marked on the map as soon as the players get in range. This player is also able to control dialogues with virtual characters by selecting one of typically three pre-defined statements. Furthermore, the screen of the device shows the remaining time and the state of progress that the players have made so far. The devices of both players are connected via an ad-hoc wireless network and continuously exchange data to keep the game state synchronized. The conceptual design as a collaborative game was rated as very positive by the majority of players. They often stated that it is much more fun to play in pairs and several players also found it helpful to have somebody who might know what to do when discovering a new technology like augmented reality. The video analysis also revealed that team partners were often quite preoccupied with the personal security of their game partners e.g. warning them about upcoming obstacles or quickly passing pedestrians.

3.2 Game Content

In *TimeWarp 1* the players had to solve challenges in virtual four time periods ranging from Roman times to the future. Traveling from one time period to another was realized by physically walking into virtual time portals that were placed at specific places of the city (Fig. 25.9). The main virtual characters in the game were the Heinzelmännchen, but other characters supported the feeling of being in different time periods. The look of the virtual gnomes resembled the visual appearance many people imagine when they think of the Cologne Heinzelmännchen (see Fig. 25.7). Each time period was depicted by several virtual objects that were also important for the different challenges the players had to solve. The challenges consisted of tasks like e.g. identifying the correct coat of arms of Cologne. In addition to graphical augmentation, *TimeWarp 1* featured spatial sound. The purpose of sound was firstly to support the sense of temporal presence, and secondly to guide the user through the non-linear game play.

TimeWarp 2 contained fewer challenges and time periods (Roman, medieval and future) and was reduced to the area of the banks of the river Rhine close to the old part of Cologne. In this game area neither busy streets nor too many pedestrians distracted the users from the actual game play. Significant changes to the game content were also undertaken with the story being changed to a more science-fiction-like one. Both players are now hired by the ChronoGuard, an agency which deals with anomalies in the space time continuum. Their supervisor is Agent Morgan who appears throughout the game in short video clips that are seemingly live broadcast from his headquarter in the thirty-second century. According to him, a group of newly manufactured household robots has developed conscience and escaped from the factory by time travelling. It is now the task of the players to follow

Fig. 25.7 Traditional gnomes in *TimeWarp 1*

Fig. 25.8 Gnome-like robots in *TimeWarp 2*

them into three different time periods, locate them and send them back to their original time as otherwise they would create anomalies that endanger the universe itself. The appearance of the Heinzelmännchen has been altered to a robot-like variation matching the science-fiction character of the new storyline (see Fig. 25.8). Besides, moral dilemmas have been introduced and the use of music and strong

Fig. 25.9 Time portal in *TimeWarp 1* and *2*

stories has been increased. Each time period holds a challenge for the users and consists of a variety of typical buildings and objects that appear in the environment like an archway, tents, fountains or a radar station. In comparison to *TimeWarp 1* much more scenic virtual objects were used to create a time-specific atmosphere. Additionally, when placing the virtual content into the real world, the underlying structure of the real world was considered. Thus, both would complement each other nicely whenever possible (e.g. staging a virtual wedding at a real church or placing the Roman content in an area where there arc still remains of the real Roman period of Cologne). Time travelling was again realized by the same virtual time portals but in *TimeWarp 2* the players could create their own time portals nearby. Thus, the navigator player had to create a time portal by selecting a certain time period as target period and then place the time portal on the map. It then appeared as a large wobbly sphere in the augmented view of the other player (see Fig. 25.9), and both players had to physically walk through the time portal before it collapsed (after 30 s). The players had to perform the same actions again each time they wanted to a switch time periods. For most players this process worked fine and players experienced this time-critical activity as an action-packed task that amused them. Often the players had to walk faster or run to reach the time portal resulting in a higher involvement in the game.

Another new game design element was a virtual character that followed the players around for a while. In the medieval time period the players have to reunite a Heinzelmännchen-robot wedding couple by finding the groom that has gone lost. The players first meet the bride that emotionally describes its situation and asks them to find her fiancé and bring it back. In order to do this, the players have to find the groom robot and convince it to come with them. It then indeed follows the path of the players, which can be visually observed by the players until they get back to the bride. Most players intuitively looked behind them to verify if the virtual Heinzelmännchen was really following and were fascinated that it did. Many players frequently turned around to check if the virtual character was still there following them.

4 Discussion

A common misconception about augmented reality is that everything is improved by augmented reality. Sometimes developers and marketing people are very enthusiastic about this new technology (new in the sense that is has not yet been widely used in game development) and do not question their decision to use augmented reality technology in the first place. This is a very dangerous attitude as although players might be astonished the first couple of times they play such an augmented reality game, the novelty factor will wear off sooner or later.

Augmented reality does not necessarily add anything meaningful to the game play. Players will not have "more fun" just because some 3D objects are placed in the environment! Game designers and developers should think hard before incorporating AR into their designs to assure that the game truly benefits from it.

In the following section we will present a variety of game design guidelines that should help with making this initial decision, offer useful insight when employing them and give tips that reach beyond pure technical implementation. The guidelines are based on work done in the authors' own research projects and by analyzing other existing augmented reality games.

We have put a clear focus on the third group of games that we presented in the previous section: true mobile augmented reality games. We think that this category of games provide the richest possibilities for game developers to create truly unique gaming experiences by fully utilizing the potential of augmented reality. In desktop augmented reality games, AR is mostly used to present the user with an intuitive way to control the virtual camera of the game space, or rather: the relation between the virtual space and the fixed camera. Take a look back at our examples, and try to envision the game played completely on a computer screen with the possibility to change your point of view with a mouse or the keyboard. How is this game different from the AR version? Does AR make it a better game? The main advantage here in most cases is probably just the intuitive control, something that shows the inherent weaknesses of games like *The Eye of Judgment*.

In the category of faux mobile games similar problems exist. Although the usage of a mobile device as the gaming platform gives the illusion of a mobile game, in reality it is not – at least when talking about the used content space in the game. The mobile device only gives the player a more intuitive control and makes it possible to turn around in the game – something a desktop based system would not be able to achieve. For such games it is important that they go beyond using AR as a gimmick.

When investigating such a game, think about what would happen if the camera of the device would be switched off. Does this affect the game play at all or the way the players perceive the game world? This is something that easily happens in inertial-sensor based games as opposed to marker-based games that are played on a nicely designed board like *The Invisible Train*.

True mobile augmented reality games however get you really "out there." The real environment is much more influential on the game play as you are completely surrounded by it and it has an effect on how you behave and move in the game. Walking along the city streets collecting pills in *Human Pacman* is therefore a much richer experience for all senses than for example in faux mobile AR games like *Firefighter360*, which have no relation to the real environment.

However, as said in the beginning of this section, it is not enough to just place 3D objects in the environment to create an engaging game. A look at location-based games can be helpful in this respect as they often provide exactly the same game play. Instead of seeing an augmented view of the environment, these games typically utilize a 2D map or no visualization at all. This can be done when not relying on GPS but instead incorporating RFID tags or WLAN and Bluetooth signatures like in the location-based games *Feeding Yoshi* [32] and *Insectopia* [33]. True mobile augmented reality games really need to distinguish themselves from such location-based games and justify the usage of AR. On the other hand such games often offer valuable insight that is also relevant for mobile augmented reality games.

In the end, true mobile augmented reality games can really shine, when they embrace both aspects of "augmented reality."

Augmented refers to the virtual part of the game. The 3D content must bear more meaning in the context of the game than a simple icon on a 2D map can convey. In order to achieve this, for example technical limitations need to be considered such as faulty tracking as well as usability issues involved when interacting with the device used in the game.

Reality however, is often underestimated in augmented reality games. During the game design, people focus too much on the virtual part and as a result the game loses much of the inherent potential of augmented reality. Instead, the real environment needs to be embraced by such games and brought into the context of the game, thus creating a contextual mobile augmented reality game. If the game is closely tied to the reality, players become much more engaged in the game, than if the actual location of the game is completely meaningless in game terms.

Of course it is easier to create loosely coupled augmented reality games, as they can be played anywhere without much additional effort in adjusting it. This might explain why most truly mobile augmented reality games have been developed as part of research work. However, there lies a huge potential also for commercial games in embracing true mobile augmented reality games or even contextual mobile reality games. Again however, mobile augmented reality games can learn from location-based games that often manage to create strong location dependency with comparably little effort like in *Tidy City* [34]. In the game players have to solve riddles that deal with physical places in a city and then find the location in question. This creates a unique gaming experience for every city the game is staged, as all objects in the game are likewise unique. As the game is supported by a dedicated authoring system, creating a new set of riddles for a new city becomes rather easy.

5 Game Design Guidelines

We will use the game *TimeWarp* presented in detail, as well as other games listed in Sect. 2 to come up with guidelines that should help when designing mobile AR games in the future. Some of the guidelines are further refinements of those found within prior work [29, 35], which were drawn from extensive user studies. It is acknowledged that not all of them are relevant to every mobile augmented reality game. Some of the guidelines presented here may also not seem specific for mobile AR games, but are stated here as they deal with weaknesses that these games often suffer from.

While this chapter focuses on guidelines that are specific for mobile augmented reality games, many of the guidelines for regular (video) games can also be applied in addition to the ones mentioned in this section [36–38].

There are also already many lessons learned from location-based games and pervasive games, which are extremely relevant to mobile AR games [39–46].

5.1 General

The first two guidelines deal with one common danger when deciding to create an AR game, and also with one very important potential that all AR games have intrinsically.

Justify the use of AR. Many times, AR games are only a conversion of an already existing computer or board game. Examples for this approach are *The Eye of Judgement* (which is a simple trading card game) and *Human Pacman* that follows the game play of successful video game. At a closer look at both games, one can realize that *The Eye of Judgement* does not add anything to the original game concept except an intuitive interface and nice looking graphics and animations. The question becomes, how quickly the novelty factor wears off after the initial excitement. In *Human Pacman* however, transporting the game into the real city streets has enhanced the feeling of the original game as it creates a new look and atmosphere. Especially with addition of human players as ghosts, the game succeeds in becoming a unique version of the original.

Engage players physically. One big advantage of mobile augmented reality games set in the outside world is the fact that players have to physically move around to explore the game area. Try to create situations where they not only have to casually stroll along, but have to walk faster or even run. Giving the players time-critical tasks can greatly increase their involvement within the game. In the *TimeWarp* games the players had only 30 s to reach a virtual time portal that could appear at different places in order to travel through time. Often the players had to run to make it, which was experienced as engaging and got them physically more involved. The video game market is following this trend for physicality (and the connected intuitive control) that was started with the *Wii* [47] and is now followed up by *PlayStation Move* [48] and *Microsoft Kinect* [49]. Another aspect to incite the players to get physical is the creation of competition. Especially with children as players this can speed up games like *The Alchemists* and results in a more exciting game experience. This on the other hand bears the danger that the player "who can run the fastest" will also be the winner of the game. For even chances the competitive character should not be limited to physical action so that no player feels disadvantaged by design.

5.2 Virtual Elements

Only by the combination of real world elements and virtual elements can one create an augmented reality game. As the virtual content is under full control of the game designer, special care should be taken that the potential is utilized in the right way.

Create meaningful AR content. The visual features that augmented content brings into the real world need to live up to their potential. Consider if there is anything gained by using an AR placement in comparison to just displaying it on the screen and enabling the player to pan and zoom as desired. One way to achieve this is spatial meaning like showcased in *Interference*. Here, the players can inspect virtual power lines with the help of their devices. These lines have a distinct direction and therefore are anchored in reality in an essential way. Having virtual characters follow players around like in *TimeWarp 2*, leading the way or trying to escape from them (like the viruses in *Epidemic Menace*) are ways of employing this guideline.

Furthermore, overly large objects are also a prime example for engaging AR content. If players encounter such objects, they cannot just "zoom out" to view the whole object. Instead they need to lean back and hold the device up high, walk several steps to the side and might even be able to enter a virtual building. This is well illustrated in the *TimeWarp* games, where players encounter a life-size model of the Stapelhaus (a trading hall) and can investigate and walk underneath a Roman archway. This adds interesting physical engagement to the interaction of the players.

Create fully-fledged characters. While players might expect the same high-end graphics in an augmented reality game as in the latest commercial game for their desktop PC or game console (which often is difficult to achieve due to lack of computing power of mobile devices), you can easily make up for it by enhancing different attributes of your characters. By choosing professional sounding voice actors and emotionally engaging dialogue, you can create convincing characters nonetheless. Equip your characters with believable personalities and emotions, and get the players involved with these emotions. This extends them also to non-verbal social behavior like characters that actively follow the players instead of just transporting themselves to the final destination are a simple but easy example. When trying to create convincing virtual characters, give them (possibly unsuspected) social behavior. One other danger with the creation of extremely realistic looking virtual characters is the so-called "uncanny valley" [50] which means that too convincing artificial characters might create revulsion in people they interact with.

Create a rich scenery. When creating virtual content, it is appreciated by the players if there is a considerable amount of it. While players should not be overwhelmed by creating so much virtual content that they lose complete sight of reality, do not save on the wrong side. Atmospheric scenery objects help the players to immerse themselves into a place. In *TimeWarp 2* the impressive aqueduct and archway for example helped to visualize the Roman time period although they were not necessary for solving the task at hand. Nevertheless, for the players the atmosphere of the time period was increased.

Go beyond the visual. While the visual augmentation of the real world is the central aspect of every AR game, don't forget that there are other ways to augment the reality as well. Audio for example is always a great choice to emphasize a specific ambience. This can be sound effects to support the believability of interactions, feedback sounds, or atmospheric background music. In *TimeWarp 2* every time zone had a specific underlying audio theme to support the atmosphere of each one.

5.3   Real World Elements

Going out in the real world creates a rather high degree of uncertainty into any gaming or application scenario. Being in an uncontrollable environment can easily have negative effects on literally every aspect of the experience. Therefore, it is necessary to be well aware of the potential problems that might arise at any time. On the other hand, true mobile augmented reality games become much stronger, if real world elements are incorporated into the game so that the game feels like it is being played also in the real world and not just the virtual one.

Make the journey interesting. The paths the players walk along should be designed to fit the theme of the game and narrative structure. This could be a street where the buildings give a heightened sense of interest at specific points. Additionally clear start and end points (and perhaps middle point) should be chosen for placing content in order to create a dramatic build up and a reward for the players. When plotting routes for the players to follow and locations to visit, try to keep everything new without the players having to walk back the same way they came. This is something that players easily find unexciting – especially if there are large distances between different virtual elements – and therefore reduces their immersion and sense or presence. One way to overcome this problem, if there are no other solutions, might be to provide new and exciting virtual elements for the second visit.

Comprise atmospheric elements from the reality. Location scouting should not be limited to only look for visually interesting places. Although this is an obvious and important quality to look for, other aspects are also worth investigating. Every place can also have certain audible, olfactory or other features that can greatly affect your game and are worth exploiting. This could for example be traffic noise, rock music always playing in the evening, church bells ringing (that can coincidentally ring like during the wedding ceremony of *TimeWarp 2*), the smell of flowers, a windy and cold bridge, freshly baked bread near a bakery, . . .

Include other (non-digital) media. Augmented reality games do not necessarily have to focus entirely on digital technology and the utilization of real life props creates a more encompassing game experience. A very good example for this kind of design comes from *Interference*. Although the players find and analyze the network with the help of the UMPC, they still need to make use of a real paper map in order to orient themselves. This concept can also be extended to include support for real elements such as cups, glasses and other objects within the game, for example using computer vision to detect when users have collected such items.

Think about security. Walking around while being immersed in an AR environment greatly inhibits the user's abilities to correctly judge dangers or notice them in the first place. This includes obvious ones like roads as well as less obvious ones such as stairs, especially when only consisting of very few steps so that they are easily overlooked. If players do not pay enough attention, they are in serious danger. But if they take care of e.g. the traffic, this greatly limits their immersion into the game. Therefore, it is recommended to be very cautious, when placing the virtual content and deciding where the players will walk along. In *TimeWarp* several challenges had to be relocated as pilot studies proved the original locations as too dangerous. Also pay attention in action-oriented games where players can easily stumble when they are moving too fast while focusing on the game play.

Plan ahead. Scouting the game locations in advance is a crucial step to make sure that the conditions are suitable for the game in terms of mobile phone connectivity, ambience, crowds etc. Besides, it is always wise to also check the calendar for events taking place that can completely change the chosen space. This may be ongoing construction work but also festivities or other urban events. At this point in time it is typically too late to change anything, and postponements might also not be possible. In *TimeWarp* one challenge of the game had to be removed from the game as a Christmas market was occupying the whole square where the challenge had to take place (as it was closely tied to the real location). Another seemingly suitable space for a challenge only proved unusable after a few test runs during the pilot studies: Underneath the area is the concert hall of the Cologne Harmonic Orchestra and during shows and rehearsal it is forbidden to walk on it. Test runs of a modified version of the game in Christchurch, New Zealand, on the other hand coincided with the Busker's Festival – a giant street artist festival taking place all over the city with 300,000 visitors, occupying many of the spaces that were selected for gaming content. Therefore, not only check the physical suitability for your chosen locations, but also the temporal one.

5.4   Social Elements

While single-player experiences can be fun, we found that enabling and encouraging collaboration between users has direct benefits for their engagement and is therefore desirable. Good player-player interactions are crucial for a satisfying gaming experience. Social interactions are not limited to players between themselves, but include also actors that are part of the game and strangers that are not.

Use complementing roles. To foster collaboration it helps if players perform different tasks with their devices as this way each player is needed. Not all players necessarily need to be equipped identically therefore. In *TimeWarp 2* one player had the navigator role with a map view displayed on the UMPC and the power over any decisions of the game while the other player was able to see the augmented reality view. It is however a good idea to encourage device sharing or showing the screen to the other player. This brings the players physically close together and creates collaboration when they jointly work on a problem. When players are fulfilling different roles in the game, make sure however that all roles are equally important or exciting. This prevents players from feeling less useful and creates a more balanced teamwork between two (or more) equal partners. In *TimeWarp 2* the split into navigator and augmented reality part was reportedly unbalanced for some of the players as the augmented reality view was valued as more exciting.

Use non-player characters. One of the most rewarding experiences in mobile augmented reality games can be the inclusion of other people in the game. This creates an element in the game that is not part of the virtual game space and allows natural interaction with the players. This could be competing or collaborating players, but actors are also an option with immense potential. In *Epidemic Menace* and *Interference* large parts of the story are conveyed by real actors. They can react with improvisation to requests or problems of players, and can also steer them into certain direction. Of course this involves more effort for staging the game, but the effort is well worth it. In *TimeWarp 2*, the main character of the game Agent Morgan was only relayed to the players via pre-recorded video clips – something that makes it near to impossible for the players to truly interact with. The game experience would have arguably profited from a real life Agent Morgan leading the players through the game.

Encourage discussions. Engagement into a game can be increased when a player has to voice his thoughts and discuss them with fellow players. One possible topic can be strategic discussions in action-oriented games, another way is presenting a dilemma to the players where they are forced to make a decision. While players will not argue much about questions like "How much is five plus three?" meaningful decisions evoke discussions between them that engage them on different and potentially much richer levels. It is very valuable to confront the players with moral questions or other important story dilemmas where there is neither a clear nor a correct solution. For example in *TimeWarp 2* upon completing a quest, the players were asked to send the virtual creatures to another time period in order to save the space-time-continuum. While doing so, players had the choice between fulfilling their mission and sending the gnomes book to the headquarter for disintegration or setting the heart-breakingly begging Heinzelmännchen free. Often this decision preoccupied players a lot and resulted in detailed discussions between them. In *Epidemic Menace*, player teams on the one hand needed to find out the identity of the game's villain and were speculating about it. On the other hand they were relying on tactical orders from the headquarter when some were out hunting viruses.

Avoid crowded areas. People are one very unreliable element for mobile AR games. It is hard to foresee how strangers will react when they see the players equipped with (possibly strange looking) devices. However, this especially becomes a problem when there happen to be crowds. Technically, it is nearly impossible to incorporate them into the game (i.e. concerning occlusion problems), and they are also very distracting for the players. If you cannot incorporate them into your game play on a social level, it is best to avoid heavily populated areas. This guideline can be subverted when the game encourages interaction between the players and non-players. As people are getting more and more used to smartphones being used in the public, the level of curiosity will be less dramatic if such devices are used. As *Interference* had strong roleplaying elements, it was possible for the players to interact with local strangers without leaving the game story.

5.5   Technology and Usability

This set of guidelines deals with rather mundane topics, which are still unavoidable when creating a heavily technologically supported augmented reality game or application. In many of the games described earlier, one of the main focuses was on the technology side, rather than using technology for supporting the underlying game structure. When designing such games, care should be taken to avoid a pre-selection of the technologies to be used. The game format should always be developed first, and only then appropriate technologies should be selected and one should be aware of their strengths and weaknesses.

Make the technology part of the game. Augmented reality games require technology to be played. However, not all games are having a theme that corresponds to this. *The Alchemists* presents itself as a game about mythical ingredients and magic, similarly to *TimeWarp 1*. Having to deal with such modern technologies without them fitting to the theme of the game can create a contrasting experience, which reduces the immersion of disbelief. The story for *TimeWarp 2* was adjusted so that now all technology became a natural part of the new science fiction setting. The devices were now part of the game and not an artificial addition to it. The same concept has been used in *Interference* where there was even a dedicated technology support team that helped the players with their problems without them having to mentally leave the game. This guideline also applies when utilizing visual markers in the game. In *Interference* they were once again part of the game story as they were interpreted as physical stations which allowed one to connect to the virtual network.

Keep the interaction simple. As augmented reality games are still new to most players, the technology itself typically occupies a lot of their attention already. This should not be made more difficult by employing complicated means of interaction during the game. Although this is typically true for all games, this needs to be explicitly emphasized again for AR games. Especially, when they are played in the real world, players are often on their own without access to playing aids for example. This was a major weakness of *TimeWarp 1* and remedied in *TimeWarp 2* by simplifying the interactions drastically. Augmented reality often offers intuitive ways of interaction as illustrated in *Eye Pet*, which is a strength that should not be undermined by difficult user interfaces.

Take display properties into account. Similar to computer vision tracking and GPS, there are two main options for merging the real world with the virtual content and creating an augmented reality. Head-mounted displays are one option, but they are far from being perfect: having a limited field-of-view, being hardly usable in bright sunlight, and often showing a lack of long-time wearing comfort are just a few aspects to be taken into account before utilizing them in AR games. In *TimeWarp 1* these problems became so severe that *TimeWarp 2* employed UMPCs instead. However, they together with tablets and smartphones are also far from being perfect devices for mobile AR. Reflections in the sunlight easily render games unplayable if they were not taken into account beforehand when designing the user interface. Although they are designed to be carried around and do not seem to be too heavy, this changes quickly if they are used as a see-through device for mobile AR games. Players need to hold up the device in front of their face when walking around the area and looking at the virtual scenery, characters and objects. They can certainly do this for a short time, but if the game or application forces them to do this for a longer time, their arms will tire easily. Therefore the game design should avoid that the users have to hold up the device "the whole time," but instead provide them with breaks, where they do not have to use the device at all or at least can point it at the ground instead of in front of them. Smartphones also have the problem of rather small screens on which the game will come to live which might negatively affect the overall level of immersion.

Take tracking characteristics into account. All tracking approaches that can be currently applied in mobile augmented reality come with inherent weaknesses (and strengths). Marker tracking or using natural feature tracking on images will provide a very stable and precise tracking, as long as the camera points in the right direction and can recognize the target. With inertial sensors one can extend the range of this tracking method, but it will not be possible for players to freely walk around in the game space and experience AR fluidly and constantly. Instead, such games tend to become "hunts for new markers" where players are only on the lookout for new visual clues so they know where to point the camera. In *The Alchemists* which is susceptible to this problem, the game experience can be increased by placing the markers so that the real world and the virtual content complement each other (e.g. a virtual spider in a dusty corner of the basement). Another problem of visual markers is of course the fact that they require decent lighting conditions. This was cleverly circumvented in *Interference*. As the game was set to be played after dark, the players used flashlights to solve the resulting lighting problems. Whenever they now encountered a marker they would use these and thus creating a more intense atmosphere.

The other common option is to use a combination of GPS and orientation sensors to calculate the player's position and direction. With this approach one can achieve constant tracking in the complete game area (unless the players enter a building) and therefore create a continuous AR experience. The main drawback is of course the rather limited quality if the positioning which leads to virtual objects that jitter and float around. The problem becomes even more sever when using standard smartphones that use less advanced sensor technology than dedicated devices. This can be very distracting for the players. Therefore, objects should be used where this imprecision is not harmful for their believability. Good examples in *TimeWarp 2* are the time portals and the UFO in the future challenge. The time portal only has a very vague shape and a ghostlike appearance. Furthermore, it is very easy for the players to suspend disbelieve when a time portal is moving around as this can be called an expected behavior of such a scientific phenomenon (see Fig. 25.9). The UFO on the other hand has no problems with bad GPS reception while it is flying around in the sky above the players. First of all the players can never get very close to the object thus negating some of the imprecision, but on the other hand the UFO is moving around by itself. The animation of the movement hides many of the undesirably effects you get when employing GPS. Game areas should be scouted out beforehand to avoid negative surprises. It might also be a good idea to supply players with information about the quality of the GPS signal so they are aware of the problem. In *TimeWarp 2* players had the possibility to stop updating the GPS data and "freeze" their position. This enabled them to interact with objects and characters when precision was important or they wanted to inspect something more closely and the GPS quality made it impossible.

Avoid occlusion-rich areas. Mutual occlusion between real objects and their virtual counterparts is a common issue within AR applications. If a virtual character moves around the corner of a real house, the house should hide the character from sight. If an accurate virtual model of the real environment (and accurate tracking) is available, it can be used as a stand-in object to achieve the desired visual effect as done in *ARQuake*. But what about trees? Cars? People? Temporary construction sites? Scout out the locations in advance and be aware of these real life obstacles, and if it is not possible to solve the occlusion technically in a convincing manner, the virtual objects should rather be placed elsewhere.

Design seamfully and for disconnection. When playing mobile games in the real world, technology can often malfunction. There might be areas without GPS signals or mobile reception. Make sure that the game does not break in such instance, and never expect perfect conditions for network communication. Another way of dealing with these issues is to embrace them and to make them part of the game. Such seamful design [51] can for example declare connectivity problems or GPS shadows as areas that have special meaning in the game world and thus might become desirable for the players to find. A good example for such design is the location-based game *Tycoon* [52] in which can award clever players that make active use of areas without connectivity.

6 Outlook

In this chapter an overview of the current state of the art in the design of mobile augmented reality games was provided. From the experience of previous user studies and tests we shaped a set of game design guidelines covering important aspects such as sense of place, usability, technological aspects and real world implications.

In the future, we expect games to benefit more and more from the rapid progress of current smart phones, tablet PCs and other portable devices. While more powerful devices with a faster CPU will help to increase the quality of graphics, new sensors might also improve tracking technologies and add new game design potential. Furthermore the constantly increasing market share of such devices finally enables the development of games for a wide base of potential players.

In the past, true mobile augmented reality games were created mainly as research projects. Producing such games still is a complex and demanding task, especially when one is aiming for games that are extremely closely coupled between the virtual and the real world. Such games are not easily relocated as the context of the environment has a strong meaning in the game itself and is crucial for its success. Porting such a game – which is necessary to make it economically feasible as only then one can reach a sufficiently large audience – adds a lot of extra work to the production pipeline. The development of similar easy-to-use tools for the creation and also modification of mobile augmented reality games seems to be one important next step to overcome this problem. Making it easier to produce such games decreases the cost of failure, and also will enable a variety of people with different backgrounds to become game designers and developers in this area. Only with an increased quantity of true mobile augmented reality games those games may become better, as the understanding of such games increases likewise.

Acknowledgements We thank our colleagues at the Collaborative Virtual and Augmented Environments Department at Fraunhofer FIT and our former colleague Rod McCall for their comments and contributions.

Furthermore we gratefully acknowledge the support of the following projects:

IPerG, the European Project on Pervasive Gaming, project FP6-004457 under the European Commission's IST Programme (www.pervasive-gaming.org).

IPCity, the European Project on Interaction and Presence in Urban Environments, project FP-2004-IST-4-27571 under the European Commission's IST Programme (www.ipcity.eu).

TOTEM, the German-French project on Theories and Tools for Distributed Authoring of Mobile Mixed Reality Games under the Programme Inter Carnot Fraunhofer from BMBF (Grant 01SF0804) and ANR (http://www.totem-games.org).

References

1. "EyePet. http://www.eyepet.com/ (Accessed 2 February 2011)."
2. "Eye of Judgment. http://www.eyeofjudgment.com/ (Accessed 2 February 2011)."
3. "Honeyway Train. http://www.honeydefender.millsberry.com/augmentedreality/#/home (Accessed 2 February 2011)."
4. "Flypad. http://www.blasttheory.co.uk/bt/work_flypad.html (Accessed 2 February 2011)."
5. "AR.Drone Parrot. http://ardrone.parrot.com/parrot-ar-drone/usa/ar-games (Accessed 2 February 2011)."
6. Wagner, Daniel, Pintaric, Thomas, and Schmalstieg, Dieter, "The invisible train: a collaborative handheld augmented reality demonstrator.," *SIGGRAPH '04 ACM SIGGRAPH 2004 Emerging technologies*, Los Angeles, California: ACM New York, NY, USA © 2004, 2004.
7. "ARhrrrr! http://www.augmentedenvironments.org/lab/research/handheld-ar/arhrrrr/ (Accessed 2 February 2011)."
8. "ARDefender. http://www.ardefender.com/ (Accessed 2 February 2011)."
9. "Splatter Bugs. http://www.slapdowngames.net/slapdowngames_splatterBugs_iphone_game.html (Accessed 2 February 2011)."
10. "Firefighter 360. http://www.firefighter360.com/ (Accessed 2 February 2011)."
11. "AR Monster. http://dothehudson.net/en/app/armonster/catalog.html (Accessed 2 February 2011)."
12. "Arcade Reality. http://www.toyspring.com/arcade/ (Accessed 2 February 2011)."
13. "ShootAR. http://www.metaio.com/media-press/press-release/press-release-metaio-delivers-first-mobile-augmented-reality-shooter-game-to-ovi-store/ (Accessed 2 February 2011)."
14. "Mosquitoes. http://www.makayama.com/mosquitoes.html (Accessed 2 February 2011)."
15. A.D. Cheok, S.W. Fong, K.H. Goh, X. Yang, W. Liu, and F. Farzbiz, "Human Pacman: a sensing-based mobile entertainment system with ubiquitous computing and tangible interaction," *Proceedings of the 2nd workshop on Network and system support for games*, Redwood City, California: ACM New York, NY, USA ©2003, 2003, pp. 106–117.
16. B. Thomas, B. Close, J. Donoghue, J. Squires, P.D. Bondi, M. Morris, and W. Piekarski, "ARQuake: An Outdoor/Indoor Augmented Reality First Person Application," *IEEE International Symposium on Wearable Computers*, Atlanta, GA: 2000, pp. 139–146.
17. I. Lindt and W. Broll, "NetAttack - First Steps Towards Pervasive Gaming," *ERCIM NEWS Special Issue on Games Technology*, vol. 57, Apr. 2004, pp. 49–50.

18. I. Lindt, J. Ohlenburg, U. Pankoke-Babatz, W. Prinz, and S. Ghellal, "Combining Multiple Gaming Interfaces in Epidemic Menace," *CHI*, Montreal, Quebec, Canada: 2006.

19. A. Mulloni, "A collaborative and location-aware application based on augmented reality for mobile devices," Master Thesis, Universita degli Studi di Udine, 2007.

20. J. Bichard and A. Waern, "Pervasive Play, Immersion and Story: designing Interference," *3rd International Conference on Digital Interactive Media in Entertainment and Arts (DIMEA)*, Athens, Greece: 2008.

21. R. Wetzel, I. Lindt, A. Waern, and S. Johnson, "The Magic Lens Box: Simplifying the Development of Mixed Reality Games," *3rd International Conference on Digital Interactive Media in Entertainment and Arts (DIMEA)*, Athens, Greece: 2008.

22. "Layar Reality Browser. http://www.layar.com/ (Accessed 2 February 2011)."

23. "Wikitude. http://www.wikitude.org/ (Accessed 2 February 2011)."

24. "junaio. http://www.junaio.com/ (Accessed 2 February 2011)."

25. "Hoppala goes Easter. http://www.hoppala-agency.com/article/hoppala-goes-easter/ (Accessed 2 February 2011)."

26. "iButterfly. http://www.mobileart.jp/ibutterfly_en.html (Accessed 2 February 2011)."

27. P. Ferdinand, S. Müller, T. Ritschel, and U. Wechselberger, "The Eduventure - A New Approach of Digital Game Based Learning Combining Virtual and Mobile Augmented Reality Game Episodes," *Pre-Conference Workshop Game based Learning*, Rostock, Germany: 2005.

28. I. Herbst, A. Braun, R. McCall, and W. Broll, "TimeWarp: interactive time travel with a mobile mixed reality game," 2008.

29. R. Wetzel, L. Blum, R. McCall, L. Opperman, S.T. Broeke, and Z. Szalavari, *IPCity Deliverable D8.4: Final Prototype of TimeWarp application*, http://bit.ly/timewarpcologne2010 (Accessed 10 June 2011).

30. "IPCity. http://www.ipcity.eu/ (Accessed 2 February 2011)."

31. E. Bier, M. Stone, K. Pier, W. Buxton, and T. DeRose, "Toolglass and magic lenses: the see-through interface," 1993.

32. M. Bell, M. Chalmers, L. Barkhuus, M. Hall, S. Sherwood, P. Tennent, B. Brown, D. Rowland, S. Benford, A. Hampshire, and M. Capra, "Interweaving Mobile Games With Everyday Life," *CHI*, Montréal, Québec, Canada: 2006, pp. 417–426.

33. J. Peitz, "IPerG Deliverable D9.8B: Game Design Document – "Insectopia"," Aug. 2009.

34. R. Wetzel, L. Blum, F. Feng, L. Oppermann, and M. Straeubig, "Tidy City: A location-based game for city exploration based on user-created content," *Proceedings of Mensch & Computer*, 2011.

35. R. Wetzel, R. McCall, A. Braun, and W. Broll, "Guidelines for Designing Augmented Reality Games," *Proceedings of the 2008 Conference on Future Play*, Toronto, Canada: ACM, New York, NY, 2008.

36. S. Björk and J. Holopainen, *Patterns in Game Design*, Charles River Media, 2005.

37. K. Salen and E. Zimmerman, *Rules of Play: Game Design Fundamentals*, MIT Press, 2003.

38. C. Crawford, *The Art of Computer Game Design*, 1982.

39. M. Montola, J. Stenros, and A. Waern, *Pervasive Games: Theory and Design*, Morgan Kaufmann, 2009.

40. S. Matyas, C. Matyas, C. Schlieder, P. Kiefer, H. Mitarai, and M. Kamata, "Designing location-based mobile games with a purpose: collecting geospatial data with CityExplorer," *Advances in Computer Entertainment Technology (ACE)*, Yokohama, Japan: 2008.

41. J. Reid, K. Cater, C. Fleuriot, and R. Hull, "Experience Design Guidelines for Creating Situated Mediascapes," Aug. 2009.

42. R. Ballagas, A. Kuntze, and S.P. Walz, "Gaming Tourism: Lessons from Evaluating REXplorer, a Pervasive Game for Tourists," *Pervasive Computing*, Sydney, Australia: 2008.

43. T. Söderlund, "Stories from the Frontier of Mobile Gaming," Aug. 2009.

44. S. Benford, D. Rowland, M. Flintham, A. Drozd, R. Hull, J. Reid, J. Morrison, and K. Facer, "Life on the Edge: Supporting Collaboration in Location-Based Experiences," *CHI*, Portland, Oregon: 2005, pp. 721–730.

45. R. Gilbert, "Why Adventure Games Suck And What We Can Do About It," Aug. 2009.

46. S. Benford, M. Flintham, A. Drozd, R. Anastasi, D. Rowland, N. Tandavanitj, M. Adams, J. Row-Farr, A. Oldroyd, and J. Sutton, "Uncle Roy All Around You: Implicating the City in a Location-Based Performance," ACE, Singapore: 2004.
47. "Wii. http://wii.com// (Accessed 2 February 2011)."
48. "PlayStation Move Motion Controller. http://us.playstation.com/ps3/playstation-move/ (Accessed 2 February 2011)."
49. "XBox Kinect.http://www.xbox.com/en-US/kinect (Accessed 2 February 2011)."
50. M. Mori, "Bukimi no tani [The uncanny valley]," *Energy*, vol. 7, 1970, pp. 33–35.
51. M. Chalmers, L. Barkhuus, M. Bell, B. Brown, M. Hall, S. Sherwood, and P. Tennent, "Gaming on the Edge: Using Seams in Ubicomp Games," *Advances in Computer Entertainment (ACE)*, Valencia, Spain: 2005, pp. 306–309.
52. G. Broll and S. Benford, "Seamful Design for Location-Bases Mobile Games," *ICEC*, 2005, pp. 155–166.

Chapter 26
Network Middleware for Large Scale Mobile and Pervasive Augmented Reality Games

Pedro Ferreira and Fernando Boavida

1 Introduction

According to Mark Weiser in [1], "The most profound technologies are those that disappear. They weave themselves into the fabric of everyday life until they are indistinguishable from it."

According yet to Mark Weiser in [1], and his colleagues at Palo Alto Research some time ago, the idea of The Personal Computer itself is misplaced and the and that the vision of laptop machines, "dynabooks" and "knowledge navigators" is only a transitional step towards achieving the real potential of information technology.

In the same article Weiser continues to argue that such machines can now truly make computing an integral, invisible part of people's lives, and they were trying at Palo Alto Research to conceive a new way of thinking about computers, one that takes into account the human world and allows the computers themselves to vanish in the background.

Augmented reality tries to extend the real world with virtual objects while maintaining the computer in an assistive, unobtrusive role, thus trying to keep in line with the pervasive computing objective of invisibility [2].

Augmented Reality is a sub concept of Mixed Reality [35]. AR augments the real world with synthetic electronic data. Augmented Virtuality (AV) enhances the virtual world with data from the physical (real) world. Mixed reality is a term that covers a continuum from AR to AV.

An example project of Mixed Reality is exposed in [3] by the Mixed Reality Systems Laboratory.

Both Mixed Reality and Augmented Reality are different than Virtual Reality, which is not pervasive at all (as we discussed in the previous section), and just deprives the user from the real world, completely evolving it in a virtual world.

P. Ferreira (✉)
Centre for Informatics and Systems, University of Coimbra, Portugal
e-mail: pmferr@dei.uc.pt

B. Furht (ed.), *Handbook of Augmented Reality*, DOI 10.1007/978-1-4614-0064-6_26,   541
© Springer Science+Business Media, LLC 2011

It is quickly becoming clear that entertainment will be one of the killer applications of future wireless networks [5]. More specifically mobile gaming was predicted to be worth more than 1.2 billions of American dollars in 2006 in the United States market alone. However mobile applications faces issues that are different from fixed network applications, including fluctuating connectivity, network Quality of Service and host mobility.

In the times before computers existed, the games people played were designed and played out in the physical world with the use of real world properties, such as physical objects, our sense of space, and spatial relations [4].

Pre-computer day's game interactions consisted of two elements: human to human interaction and human to physical world interaction. In the current times, due to their higher level of attractiveness to game players, computer games have become the dominant form of entertainment.

Computer games motivate the players by bringing them more challenge, curiosity and fantasy, which are the three main elements contributing to fun in games. They provoke curiosity because they are usually designed with an optimal level of information complexity, they create fantasy by creating the illusion of the player being immersed in an imaginative virtual world with computer sound and graphics, and they create challenge by having goals typically more interactive than traditional games.

However, there is a also a new tendency in gaming called pervasive games, where the real world is coming back to the computer entertainment field stressing the pervasive and ubiquitous nature of these games: Pervasive games are no longer confined to the domain of the computer (the virtual domain), but integrate the physical and social aspects of the real world.

Pervasive gaming is a relatively new field but we can already identify several unique types of pervasive games, each focusing on different aspects of the gaming experience.

To our knowledge, there is no specialized network middleware solution for large-scale mobile and pervasive augmented reality games, and we feel this is a field worth exploring. Not only pervasive technology is becoming more and more important and its use widespread, but also pervasive games are beginning to be built and used by gamers all around the world. Augmented reality is an interesting concept for games and pervasive computing, bringing together the real world with a virtual world that exists only in the game. Enabling it in large scale brings true mobility to the solution, enabling the players to play alone or against one another wherever they are, as long as they are covered by the system. Building a network middleware to help build this pervasive and mobile large scale augmented reality game applications is important because in this way we hope to contribute with a solution that solves most of the problems these applications face in terms of software, excluding the ones related to graphic presentation.

2 Architecture

2.1 Introduction

This work had its focus on the creation of network middleware for mobile and pervasive entertainment, applied to the area of large scale augmented reality games. There is a tremendous opportunity for research and development in the area of massive multiplayer pervasive games applied to augmented reality, from the point of view of multimedia and communications. The installed infrastructure of mobile operators makes it possible to install distributed solutions directly linked to geographical locations bounded by its transmission cells. Solutions extending the work envisioned in [5] and applying map subdivision like in [6] may be useful. The need for killer applications to justify the overwhelming investments made is another important factor to consider. But the difficulties exist, because of the current characteristics of the mobile networks. Bandwidth on mobile networks, though increasing, is a scarce resource when compared to fixed networks. Adding to this, both transient and persistent storage spaces on the mobile host are very limited. There are also the problems of mobility handling and disconnected operation.

The middleware that we created incorporated experiences and results obtained from previous work from the candidate in the area of interactive distributed multimedia, more specifically in state transmission for a collaborative virtual environment middleware platform, the Status Transmission Framework (STF) [7,8]. This platform extended another platform, called ARMS – Augmented Reliable CORBA Multicast System [7], for event distribution. Knowledge will be used from areas as diversified as peer–to-peer computing, mobile and wireless networks, pervasive computing, embedded systems, multimedia protocols and systems, interactive distributed multimedia, and network gaming theory and protocols.

We may consider that distributed collaborative virtual environments have network requirements that will in its majority be common to augmented reality environments. The fundamental problem for collaborative virtual environments is how to maintain a consistent shared state of the virtual reality world [7,8]. Another research topic is, from a quality of service point of view, how to efficiently transmit update messages so as to provide scalability, minimized delay, consistency and reliability. Collaborative virtual environments also have the requirement of being able to handle multiple types of data, which may be multimedia data, state update and control data.

The system that targeted by the middleware is composed of three levels, depicted in (Fig. 26.1): the back-office central level, the large scale network level, and the personal area network level.

The back-office central consists of one or more of a series of parallel servers and will serve as the main controlling station of the game administrator: The person responsible for starting, stopping and managing game performance and general maintenance tasks. This may be done for every specific game running on the system.

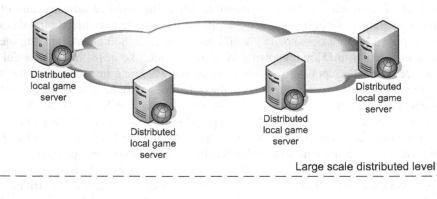

Central level

Large scale distributed level

Personal area network level

Fig. 26.1 High level system view

The large-scale network is the 3GPP network as it is being built by the specifications, where servers will be distributed according to some logic of spatial distribution and linkage of its location with specific geographic locations. These may be, in the extreme, the cells of the mobile communications network.

The personal area network level consists of the network of pervasive devices dedicated to personal communications and to augmenting reality that the person carries with it. These may be sensors, actuators, and other devices that can communicate under Bluetooth or other means of communication. All those communicate

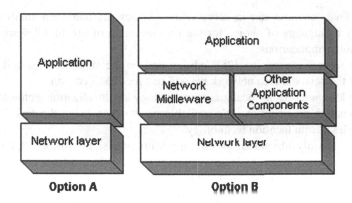

Fig. 26.2 Opting for network middleware architecture

to the mobile host, probably just a cell phone or specialized device connected to the large scale network, the 3GPP network. The player is so enabled to play games of augmented reality wherever it is.

Targeting this architecture allows the study, evaluation and proposal of mechanisms to deal with issues of scalability, multimedia data heterogeneity, data distribution and replication, consistency, security, geospatial location and orientation, mobility, quality of service, management of networks and services, discovery, ad-hoc networking and dynamic configuration.

We can consider that building the augmented reality applications using the network middleware (option B of Fig. 26.2) is better that building them standalone (option A of Fig. 26.2). This is because with option B many games applications may then use the same application programming interface (API) to leverage network resources, giving it much faster service development and deployment.

The middleware produced is built according to the characteristics of agile pervasive middleware [9], such as application – awareness, mobility, integration, interoperability, scalability, portability, adaptability, robustness and simplicity of evolution.

2.2   Requirements Specification

Is important to establish first the requirements needed to run our system. We are building a middleware for mobile and pervasive large scale augmented reality gaming, targeting the three levels described on the previous section.

The first thing we need to do is to establish the kind of devices, servers, programming languages and platforms the system will run on.

Today, mobile devices and gadgets come with more than just a cool and cutting-edge design. They come equipped with small brains and a common language, which makes them smarter and more powerful than ever before [10]. That language is Java.

Since Java can now run in servers, mobile devices and even small devices it's clearly a language of choice for the programming of our middleware and its corresponding applications.

On the servers we use the J2SE edition and on the small devices and mobile devices of the personal area network we will use the J2ME edition.

The middleware uses as localization technology any localization technology that provides enough precision and it's available on the spot, using the Java Location API to abstract from location technology.

To provide truly ubiquitous positioning with precision, outdoors GPS would be used with carrier based techniques (which are already available commercially, thought at a price) and differential GPS techniques (such as Assisted GPS), while indoors some other solution would be needed, like acoustic tracking devices that employ ultrasonic sound waves that measure the position and orientation of the entity being tracked (This can be done through time-of-flight tracking and phase-coherence tracking). Galileu, because of the abstraction provided by the Java Location API, will be automatically used if it provides the needed precision when it becomes available. Orientation (see state of the art chapter) can also be obtained through the use of a digital compass and/or orientation sensors. Through the use of the Java Location API is possible to the middleware to obtain both location and orientation, if available. We require its availability in the main game device. So, we require both J2ME and Java LAPI and the existence of both an orientation and location technologies of sufficient precision on the main game device.

On the main game device, we feel we must demand an existing J2ME profile, and that profile is the MIDP 2.0, that runs on the CLDC 1.1 [36] configuration of J2ME, which provides us with the capability to do floating point arithmetic. The main game device will be, preferably, a specialized device for the management of a personal area network of devices dedicated to augmented reality gaming. However, due to these specifications, there is nothing stopping it from being a common advanced mobile phone.

For the sensors and actuators, the requirements must not be so demanding, so we only require the CLDC 1.1 configuration, and we do not require any profile at all. We just require the possibility to use JSR-82 APIs (Bluetooth for Java) [11]. This for a sensor. For an actuator, optionally, it may have also the JSR-184 API (Mobile Media API) [12] and JSR-135 API (Mobile 3D API) [13]. This for it to be possible to build a multimedia actuator such as an augmented reality glasses device. An actuator that does not need these APIs may live without them.

For the servers, central and distributed, we will use J2SE, and demand simply enough processing power, memory capacity and disk capacity for the databases and the middleware and application that will run the game, for the probable load of the system. Obviously, there should be enough distributed servers for the dimension of the game area and the expected load of the game.

A basic requirement is the existence of a 3GPP (UMTS) network supporting IMS (IP Multimedia Service) where to run the central and distributed servers and where the main game device connects wirelessly, that will be the main game network for the whole system.

2.3 General Architecture

The system targeted by the proposed middleware is composed of three levels: the back-office central level, the large scale network level, and the personal area network level.

The back-office central level consists of one or more of a series of parallel servers and serves as the main controlling station of the game administrator, the person responsible for starting, stopping and managing game performance and general maintenance tasks.

The large-scale network is the standard 3GPP network, where servers are distributed according to some logic of spatial distribution, typically corresponding to aggregations of cells of the mobile communications network.

The personal area network level consists of the network of pervasive devices dedicated to personal communications and to augmenting reality, which the person carries. These may be sensors, actuators, and other devices that can communicate using Bluetooth or other means of communication. All these communicate with the mobile host, probably just a cell phone or specialized device connected to the large-scale 3GPP network. In this way, the player is so enabled to play games of augmented reality irrespective of his/her location.

Targeting this architecture allows the study, evaluation and proposal of mechanisms to deal with issues of scalability, multimedia data heterogeneity, data distribution and replication, consistency, security, geospatial location and orientation, mobility, quality of service, management of networks and services, discovery, ad-hoc networking and dynamic configuration.

We consider that building augmented reality applications using a network middleware is better that building them standalone. This is because then many games applications may then use the same application programming interface (API) to leverage network resources, giving it much faster service development and deployment.

The middleware here presented is built according to the characteristics of agile pervasive middleware [14], such as application-awareness, mobility, integration, interoperability, scalability, portability, adaptability, robustness and simplicity of evolution.

2.3.1 Central Level

At the central level, there is one server, which may be constituted by more than one parallel server, running Java Standard Edition 1.5.0. There will also be database servers, which may or may not be integrated with the same server.

This server or collection of servers will be connected to the HSS (Home Subscriber Server) of the 3GPP Network by the DIAMETER protocol SH application and are, together, an IMS (IP Multimedia Subsystem) application server.

All authentication, accounting, and authorization will happen through this interface. All management of the game servers will happen through this server.

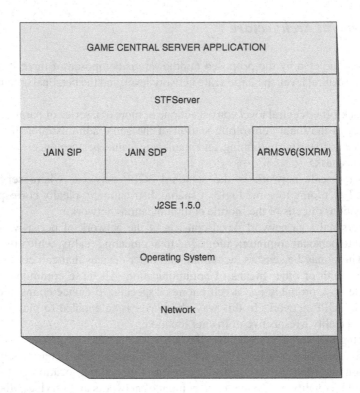

Fig. 26.3 Central level architecture

Status Transmission Framework version 2.0 APIs for the server side include a DIAMETER [15] API which includes the base protocol, the CX and DX [16] applications and the SH application [17] of 3GPP. This would communicate preferably through SCTP [18] (we also developed a java SCTP API that presently only works under Linux, but can be easily extended to other platforms, as soon as those platforms support SCTP natively) if available. If not, TCP will be chosen. The DIAMETER API implementation supports TLS and works over IPSec.

The terminal (UE) from the personal area network will communicate with the central server through SIP [19] to initiate the session, authenticate itself and get the details for the session through SDP [20] negotiation.

The SIP and SDP exchanges include enough information to choose a distributed server to communicate with, according to the terminal's geographical location. The terminal geographical location is acquired through the use of the J2ME Location API (JSR 179) [21] on the mobile terminal.

The Status Transmission Framework Middleware on this level is called the STFSERVER API, which includes ARMS communications APIs, works above ARMSV6 itself and Sixrm multicast.

The schematics of the middleware architecture the central level are represented in Fig. 26.3.

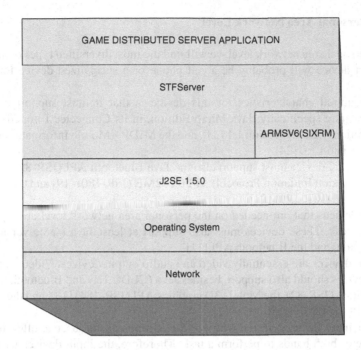

Fig. 26.4 Large scale distributed level architecture

2.3.2   Large Scale Distributed Level

At the distributed server level, there are multiple distributed servers, linked to geographical coverage areas which in the extreme may even be linked to the cells of the mobile network, which will distribute the load off the main server.

These servers run Java Standard Edition 1.5.0, also. They will have integrated database servers running on the same or different computers.

These servers will be interconnected by a reliable multicast protocol capable of working in an IPv6 network, without the support of network elements, capable of working in the many-to-many scenario, without the nak implosion problem but nak based, source ordered and avoiding duplicates: The Sixrm Protocol [22]. This protocol will also connect these servers with the central server.

The Status Transmission Framework Middleware on this level is the STFSERVER API, which includes ARMS communications APIs, works above ARMSV6 itself and Sixrm multicast.

The schematic of each of the distributed servers on the large scale distributed level is presented in Fig. 26.4.

2.3.3 Personal Area Network Level

At the personal area network level we will find the most diversified types of devices. The main device will probably be a cell phone or a specialized device for game playing.

The required characteristics for this device is that it must support the Java language, more specifically, Java Micro Edition, in its Connected Limited Device Configuration (CLDC) version 1.1 [23], and the MIDP – Mobile Information Device Profile – version 2.0 [24].

This central device must support also the Java Bluetooth API (JSR-82) [11], the Java SIP (Session Initiation Protocol) API for J2ME (JSR-180) [19] and the location API for J2ME (JSR-179) [21].

Other devices that are needed on the personal area network level are input and output devices. These devices must also support at least Java (same version and configuration) and the Bluetooth API [11].

Output devices are essentially video and audio output devices. Video and audio output devices should also support, besides Java (CLDC 1.1) and Bluetooth for Java Micro edition (JSR-82), the Mobile 3D graphics API (JSR-184) [13], and the Mobile Media API for J2ME (JSR-135) [12].

As for input devices, in the real world environment, the user is often used to using one or both hands to perform a task. Therefore, the input devices used with wearable computers need to be designed with this requirement in mind. Appropriate input devices need to be utilized to allow the user to efficiently manipulate and interact with objects. For data entry or text input, body mounted keyboards, speech recognition software, or hand held keyboards are often used. Devices such as IBM's Intellipoint, trackballs, data gloves, etc., are used to take the place of a mouse to move a cursor to select options or to manipulate data. One of the main advantages of using a wearable computer is that it allows the option of hands free use.

Common factors in the design of input devices are that they all must be unobtrusive, accurate, and easy to use on the job.

In order for any digital system to have an awareness of and be able to react to events in its environment, it must be able to sense the environment.

This can be accomplished by incorporating sensors, or arrays of various sensors (sensor fusion) into the system. Sensors are devices that are able to take an analogue stimulus from the environment and convert it into electrical signals that can be interpreted by a digital device with a microprocessor.

For a sensor or array of sensors to be supported by the Status Transmission Framework version 2.0, it must be accompanied by hardware that translates its electrical impulses to digital signals transmitted over Bluetooth communications over the personal area network to the central device.

The central device will coordinate all the augmented reality experience for the user, using all the multimedia capacities of the other devices and eventually, even own multimedia capacities of the central personal area network device.

Here, we have developed the Status Transmission Framework version 2.0 PAN API and the SENSACT API [24].

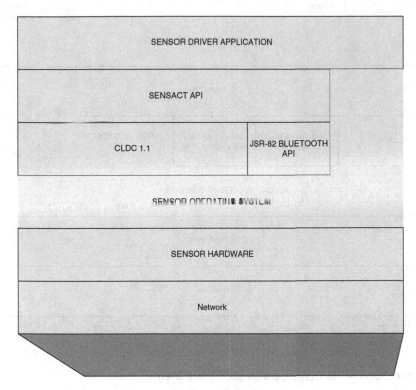

Fig. 26.5 Sensor architecture (personal area network level)

Figure 26.5 shows the minimum required architecture for a sensor, Fig. 26.6 shows the minimum required architecture for an actuator, and Fig. 26.7 shows the minimum required architecture for the central game playing device.

3 Experimental Development

3.1 The SENSACT API

The SENSACT API, which was introduced in [24], is the part of the system which enables the sensors and actuators to be deployed with the help of java CLDC 1.1 and communicate by Bluetooth with the help of JSR-82. This API and correspondent protocols make part of the personal area network level of the system.

The SENSACT API is a small footprint set of classes occupying less than 60 kB, constituted by 5 java packages.

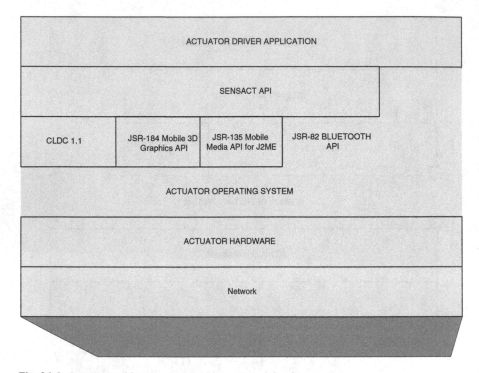

Fig. 26.6 Actuator architecture (personal area network level)

In order to deploy one sensor/actuator, one has to have the respective hardware, a CLDC 1.1 implementation that runs on the hardware, a Bluetooth API (JSR-82) implementation for that hardware and platform, and the SENSACT API.

The SENSACT API on the sensors and actuators and the STF PAN API (see below) on the main game device work as a whole to organize an ad-hoc network of sensors and actuators around a main game device in a way that the main game device works as a coordinator for the sensors and actuators.

The SENSACT API contains classes that allow us to build sensors and actuators, to control a network of sensors and actuators and interact with these sensors and actuators, all through a Bluetooth network.

3.2 The STF PAN API

The STF – Status Transmission Framework – version 2.0 PAN – Personal Area Network level API is the correspondent API on the central game device of the user that communicates with the SENSACT API on the sensors and actuators and that communicates with the distributed and central servers.

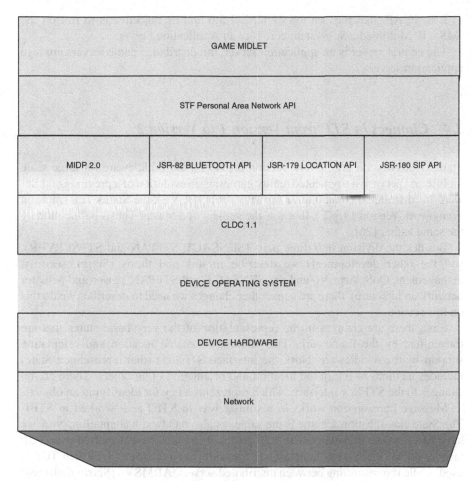

Fig. 26.7 Central game device architecture (personal area network level)

Session Description Protocol [20] is used in SIP [19] messaging to the central server and to the IMS – IP Multimedia Subsystem of 3GPP to negotiate session parameters and QoS. For this, we make use of Java SIP-API (JSR-180) [25] and the help of our developed SDP helper classes in pt.uc.dei.lcst.stf.pan.sdp.

3.3 The STF SERVER API

The middleware that runs on the central level and on the large scale distributed server level is the STFServer API. This API makes use of ARMSV6 (and so, Sixrm).

It is an API that runs on top of J2SE 1.5.0 and its objective is to run on the IMS – IP Multimedia Subsystem core – as an Application Server.

The central server is an application server, the distributed game servers are also application servers.

3.4 Changes in STF from Version 1 to Version 2

Status Transmission Framework version 2 (STF2), our middleware for large scale mobile and pervasive augmented reality games, is an evolution of a previous middleware for distributed collaborative virtual worlds (DCVE), the Status Transmission Framework Version 1 (STF), that was the subject of a Master Thesis publication by the same author [26].

Besides the division into three parts (SENSACT, STFPAN and STFSERVER), and the other developments we describe in this phd thesis (Sixrm, security, management, QoS, ArmsV6 and the SENSACT and STFPAN sensor and actuator network architecture), there are some other changes we need to describe. We do this on this section.

First, there are changes in the representation of the very basic states that are transmitted by the framework. This is done to enable location and orientation support by the middleware. Now, the interface STFState (that represents a State) includes methods to return the location and orientation of an object. There are no changes to the STFKey interface, which represents a key for identifying an object.

Message transmission works in a similar way in STF2 as it worked in STF1. The State classification scheme is the same, as also bandwidth adaptation. Now we have two possible transports. The STF protocol can now be transported over TCP or over ARMSV6 (Sixrm multicast). If transmitting to or from a UE, then TCP is used, while if transmitting between distributed servers, ARMSV6 (Sixrm multicast) is used.

That means that while doing SDP negotiation, the media protocol negotiated is STF (our own media protocol), which must be appropriately authorized by the network. Of course any other media can be used additionally to this, such as media for audio and video, additionally to state and virtual 3D information.

The partitioning method also has changed. While in STF version 1 we had to specify the STFKey set we defined as the partition that was active for each node, now that is not necessary. This has various consequences. The first is that a particular partitioning method is always chosen for us, and the second is that this method is always available and optimized by the middleware.

The partitioning method is spatial partitioning. We choose only to enable partitioning and choose a particular partitioning radius, beyond which no state messages will be considered or transmitted. This works for STFPAN or STFSERVER, and the adequate changes are done on the methods of the STFPartitioner interface.

The latejoining method has changed a little to improve scalability. The change was to include the consideration of spatial partitioning. Now, if spatial partitioning is active, latejoining takes that into account and only includes states coming from users and servers in the spatial partitioning area.

The optional time synchronization method (which is active by default in STFPAN and STFSERVER), has some changes to accommodate the architectural differences between STF and STF2. When active on STFPAN, the method to vote for a new main time server is never activated. This is because in this case the main time server is always considered to be the current distributed server. So, a voting process is never required. All the other mechanisms function the same way as STF.

When working in STFSERVER, the time synchronization mechanism, if active, works the same way as STF, a main time server is automatically choosed. If the main time server fails, a new one is choosed by distributed voting. The system maintains a common virtual time synchronized by all servers. This virtual time is also sent to the UEs running STFPAN. The system takes into account network delay the same way as STF1 would.

3.5 The Sixrm Reliable Multicast Protocol

We felt it was necessary to create a protocol capable of working in the many-to-many scenario, without the nak implosion problem but nak based, source ordered and that avoided duplicates. We also needed a protocol that could work in ipv6, and that does not require the support of network elements. So, we created Sixrm.

The Sixrm protocol consists of six types of packets. These are: Data packets (TYPE_DATA), Open packets (TYPE_OPEN), Close packets (TYPE_CLOSE), nak packets (TYPE_NAK), information packets (TYPE_INFO), and error packets (TYPE_ERROR). It is a nak based protocol, in which the destinations, when they detect that they did not received a packet from certain source, transmit a nak for the group that only that source will listen to and repeat the transmission of the lost packet. If that is not possible, an error packet will be transmitted for the destination. A source first opens the channel for communication sending a packet for all destinations in the multicast group, an open packet (TYPE_OPEN), that all currently listening destinations will receive. This corresponds to the Open operation on the Sixrm node. The packet contains the source identity and source ip address. All currently open destinations (those that already have executed the Open operation), when receiving the open packet, perform initialization for that source, and respond to the open packet with an information packet containing the destination (and possible source) identity and ip address. The source (or destination) identities are Java long data types. When receiving the information packets, the source performs the same initialization that the destinations did when they received the open packet.

For the close operation, the source transmits the close packet and removes itself from the group. All destinations, when they receive the close packet, perform cleanup operations for that source.

As for data transmission, data is transmitted sequentially. Each new byte buffer that is handled to the Sixrm protocol for transmission is buffered for transmission and subsequently transmitted, in the next available time slot. When the data is transmitted, it is given a monotonically increasing sequence number, packed in a packet of type data (TYPE_DATA) and send to the group for all destinations to listen.

It must be mentioned by now that every packet transmitted by Sixrm contains the source transmit memory buffer state (send window), which includes all messages since the last one memorized until the newest one that was sent (the biggest sequence number). The newest and oldest sequence numbers are transmitted with each message.

Each destination maintains a receiving window, for each source, that is smaller than the source transmit window and which has is greatest sequence number always equal to the source transmit window newest sequence number and its oldest sequence number adjusted to be that number minus some minimum value.

Each time a source transmits a value, it puts that value in its sent buffer (transmit window), and if necessary, if the buffer cannot grow anymore, discards the oldest message that was in the buffer. The value is transmitted and stored in the buffer in a packet of type data (TYPE_DATA).

Each time a destination receives a packet, it verifies witch kind of packet it is. Depending on the kind of packet, the destination acts differently.

3.5.1 Packets of Type NAK

When a destination (which is also a source) receives a Nak packet, it means someone did not receive a packet. The Nak packet contains the source address, the source identity, the sequence number, the target address, and the target identity.

We can tell if the nak packet is for us by comparing the target address and target identity with our ip address and identity. If equal, it was our packet that was not received, if not equal, it was someone else's packet that was not received, but we still need to memorize the nak. Our answer will depend on the fact that the nak was direct to us or not.

NAK Directed to Us

If the Nak was directed to us, then we must try to resend the packet that was lost. Unfortunately, that may not always be possible. Given the sequence number of the nak, we access the sent memory (transmit window), and verify if we have the packet.

If we have the packet, then, we resend the packet to the group. We do not memorize the nak.

If we do not have the packet, then we cannot recover from the error and must send an error packet to the destination informing the destination that we do not have the packet with that sequence number. We also send an error packet to the application telling the application that a data packet with a determined sequence number did not reach all destinations.

NAK Directed to Someone Else

If the nak was directed to some other destination (and source) then we must memorize the nak to prevent us from, in the near future, transmitting a nak for the same packet. For this effect, we memorize the nak and a time value that is equal to the current time plus a random back off time value during which we cannot transmit a nak for this packet, We do not prevent the transmission forever because even naks can be lost. In this way, probably we will receive the packet related to the nak if it is missing and clear the nak before the need to transmit it again arises.

3.5.2 Packets of Type ERROR

When a destination (which is also a source) receives an error packet, it means a source could not retransmit a packet for a destination. The error packet contains the source address, the source identity, the sequence number of the packet that generated the error, and the target address and target identity.

We can tell if the error packet is for us by comparing the target address and target identity with our ip address and identity. If equal, it was our packet that wasn't available, if not equal, it was someone else's packet that wasn't available. Only if the error is for us do we deliver it to the application.

3.5.3 Packets of Type DATA

When receiving a packet of type data, the destination first verifies if it did already initialize the memory structures for that source.

Then, if the packet sequence number is within the receiving window, it buffers the data packet. It also removes from memory any naks for that data packet that may exist.

A data packet contains the source address, the source identity, the sequence number, the data buffer, the transmit window newest sequence and the transmit window oldest sequence.

Taking for granted that the memory structures were already initialized, they are altered by the data packet, namely the receiving window. The newest element in the receiving window is always the transmit window newest sequence number.

After buffering the data packet, the destination verifies that the receiving window oldest sequence number is below the minimum difference with the newest and a packet with that sequence number exists. In that case, the packet is handed to the application. The process repeats while possible until the receiving window oldest sequence number aligns with the minimum configured difference from the newest sequence number.

After this, the receiving buffer is verified for missing packets in between the receiving window. Naks are transmitted for each missing packet if is not forbidden to do so. It is forbidden to do so if the nak is memorized and its associated time value is greater than the current system time.

3.5.4   Packets of Type OPEN

Packets of type open means a source has executed the open operation and expects us to execute initialization of internal memory structures and respond with information packets with our information (source address and identity).

Open packets contain the source address and the source identity. When receiving an open packet, the destination (and source) will initialize its memory structures for that source, and send an information packet containing its information (that would be sent on an open packet) on an information packet.

3.5.5   Packets of Type CLOSE

Packets of type close means a source has executed the close operation and will not be sending or receiving more packets with sequence numbers bigger than the latest.

3.5.6   Packets of Type INFORMATION

Packets of type information means a destination (and source) is responding to a request from a source open packet. It expects us to execute initialization of internal memory structures, if we did not that already for it.

Information packets contain the source address and identity. When receiving an information packet, the destination (and source) will initialize its memory structures for that source, if it did not already did so.

3.6   The Sixrm API

The Sixrm API is a simple API with only four classes, all on the package pt.uc.dei.lcst.stf.sixrm.These classes are the following: SixrmEntity, SixrmFileKey, SixrmListener and SixrmPacket. We now describe in more detail each of these classes.

3.6.1 Class SIXRMENTITY

This class SixrmEntity takes care of communication for a Sixrm node (entity). A Sixrm node acts simultaneously as a source and destination of Sixrm packets.

A Sixrm entity is constructed from the identifier (long), the address (ip address – Java InetAddress), the group (ip address – Java InetAddress), the port (int), the ttl (time to live – int), the profile (Java Properties), and the listener (SixrmListener).

When the SixrmEntity receives data packets or error packets, methods of SixrmListener are called.

3.6.2 Class SIXRMPACKET

The class SixrmPacket represents a Sixrm packet. A Sixrm packet may contain a data buffer, a source ip address, a sequence number, a packet type, a source identity, a target identity, a target ip address, a source transmit window newest sequence number and a source transmit window oldest sequence number.

Basically, this class has constructors for the various types of packets that exist (TYPE_DATA, TYPE_OPEN, TYPE_INFO, TYPE_CLOSE, TYPE_NAK and TYPE_ERROR), and getter and setter methods for the data fields it contains.

3.6.3 Class SIXRMLISTENER

The class SixrmListener contains only one method, to receive a SixrmPacket.
This is the interface that applications must implement.

3.6.4 Class SIXRMFILEKEY

The Class SixrmFileKey is a helper class used to uniquely identify a source by its address and identity. A SixrmFileKey contains an ip address and an identity (long).

A SixrmFileKey instance identifies a source or destination of Sixrm packets (a Sixrm node).

3.7 The ARMSV6 System

ARMS – The Augmented Reliable corba Multicast System [8,27] – was extended to work in IPV6 in large scale networks by substituting, in its new version ARMSV6, the reliable multicast protocol it used by the Sixrm protocol.

Now, the distributed servers communicate using ARMSV6, and so, the Sixrm reliable multicast protocol.

ARMS [8, 27] is a improvement for the corba event service that, maintaining compatibility with the standard corba event service, adds reliable multicast communication to it. ARMSV6 does the same thing but now supporting ipv6 through Sixrm reliable multicast protocol.

3.8   The QoS APIs

We now discuss the general architecture of the Status Transmission Framework version 2 QoS API on J2ME (that is, on the UE, the central coordinating device of the personal area network).

3.8.1   General Architecture

The general architecture is based on two APIs for QOS: The PDP Context Handler API and the RSVP API. Both are used at the same time to guarantee quality of service on a 3GPP network with RSVP support (witch is optional) and that may or may not use uses Service Based Local Policy between the PDF (Policy Decision Function) and the GGSN as specified on [28].

3.8.2   The PDP Context Handler Architecture

The PDP Context handler API is an Application Programming Interface that allows us to activate and deactivate PDP contexts with all its characteristics including QoS characteristics.

3.8.3   The RSVP API

The RSVP API on the UE (J2ME) is based on the RSVP specifications [29–33] and is used to alter the way the GGSN in particular (if it supports RSVP) and other routers on the way to the distributed servers (which are located on the IP Multimedia Subsystem) allocate resources to the connection in question.

The GGSN affects, if supporting RSVP, the PDP context traffic handling.

3.8.4   General Architecture of the STF QoS APIs on the Distributed Servers

On the distributed servers, we use RSVP (Resource Reservation Protocol) and related standards [29–33].

3.8.5   The RSVP Architecture

The RSVP architecture on the distributed servers is very similar to the architecture on the UE clients, with differences in implementation and in configuration of course. But the list of classes is the same except that the package is now part of the bigger STFServer API.

3.9   The Security Architecture

Security and privacy are issues of significant importance on our middleware architecture for mobile and pervasive large scale augmented reality games.

Many times the information that is passed on the system should be kept secret for any other purpose other than gaming, and for anyone else than the appropriate other players.

A striking example of this information is the location and orientation context information of the central device on the personal area network.

Of course this information needs to circulate on the system, but needs to be kept secure from outside attack.

So, we need encryption on the system. We also need authorization and authentication, to know which players and which devices can be connected.

It's all that architecture we be discussing in this section, for all the levels of the system.

We have built architecture of security on our system that goes a step beyond and effectively extends the 3GPP security architecture (it is meant to work alongside with it).

3.9.1   Personal Area Network Level Security

In the personal area network level of the system, we have a network of sensors and actuators that is connected to the central device through Bluetooth and a central device that is connected to a large scale distributed level server through the use of TLS/SSL over TCP.

So, the security we apply here is the following, we demand that all the Bluetooth connections be authenticated and encrypted. We apply security certificates do ensure authentication and authorization in TLS/SSL over TCP and the encryption itself (witch is RSA).

This is all possible without using nothing more than Java capacities in J2ME and J2SE, including the capacity to install security certificates.

In doing so, we secure communications in the personal area network and in the communications between the personal area network and the large scale distributed server level.

3.9.2   Large Scale Distributed Level Security

On the large scale distributed server level, we communicate between servers using Sixrm reliable multicast using ipv6, trough the use of our updated ARMSV6 corba event system using multicast, that evolved from previous work in ARMS – Augmented reliable corba Multicast System [8, 27].

To be secure, we now symmetrically encrypt all communications that go through ARMSV6 (and Sixrm), in RCA5.

Communications are symmetrically encrypted (and not asymmetrically) because Sixrm is an any-to-any multicast protocol and so there is no direct correspondence between the sender and the receiver.

The key of encryption is distributed by the central server to the distributed servers in the authentication process.

3.9.3   Central Level Security

The central level is responsible for distributed server authentication and authorization.

Every distributed server must know a login and password to the distributed server so that it can access this server trough TLS/SLL over TCP so it can receive the encryption key to use on symmetric encryption.

The key is passed encrypted over the secure channel. Certificates for this are pre-installed on the Java Virtual Machines the servers run on (J2SE).

3.10   Managing the System

3.10.1   Objectives of Managing the System

The main objective of building a managing subsystem and management application for our middleware for mobile and pervasive large scale augmented reality gaming is, primarily, a system that is able to work in the most autonomous way possible and at the same time able to get its management orders from outside the system.

In this way, in our system, we want the system to generate and report statistics automatically, but only report the statistics to the outside application when it requests them.

In the same way, the system must be able to do all that is necessary to authorize users and revoke user's authorization, including stopping users running in a clean way, automatically, but only when requested by the management application.

The management application must be able to enable, disable statistics, and to re-set statistics, and have the middleware do that on the complete system automatically.

In this way, we have the maximum of self-management combined with the most controllability.

3.10.2 The Management Architecture

The management architecture is based on a distributed way of passing messages and on a direct way of passing messages. The distributed way is used for communication between the central server and the distributed servers and between these and the UE, and the direct way is used for communication between the central or distributed server and the management application.

All communication is message based and uses on the direct way, SSL over TCP, and on the distributed way, ARMSV6 (which uses Sixrm reliable multicast) between central server and distributed servers, and SSL over TCP between these and UE.

The management architecture supports the collecting of statistics of the UE, the distributed server, and the central server, and also supports aggregating the statistics of all the UEs of one distributed server, aggregating the statistics of all distributed servers, aggregating the statistics of all UEs of all distributed servers, and aggregating the statistics of all UEs and all distributed servers (global aggregation). Aggregation of central server statistics with those is not supported because they are fundamentally different.

Because of maintaining the scalability, it is not possible to get a specific UE statistics. Only aggregated statistics of all UE of a distributed server are possible to get.

This kind of statistics generation is done in the UEs by the middleware in its various tasks, and communicated periodically to the currently connected to distributed server.

As for authorization of user and revoking the authorization of users, this can also be handled by the central servers and distributed servers in a coordinated fashion.

This requires not only the central server and distributed server coordination, but communication with the UEs, and that the central application server communicates with the HSS (Home Subscriber Server) of the 3GPP network to see if it can authorize the user.

So, to authorize a user to use the system, the application tries to do so by sending a message UserAuth to the central server containing the SIP identity to authorize. If the server, for any reason, cannot authorize this user, it returns an error code in the resulting response message UserAuthError, else it returns a code in that message indicating that all is right.

To revoke a user authorization it is not needed for the central server to consult the HSS, but may be needed to the system to disconnect a running user of the system (emitting a SIP BYE message and terminating the session).

To revoke a user authorization, the manager application tries to do so by sending a message UserRevokeAuth to the central server, containing the SIP identity to revoke authorization to, to which the server verifies if it exists and if it is running. If it does not exist, it returns an error in the message of response, UserRevokeAuthError, else it returns a code in that message that says all is ok. If the user was running a BYE SIP message is emitted to the UE, and the session is terminated, along with all open communication channels and QoS reservations.

For the communication between central server and HSS, the 3GPP SH DIAMETER [17] application protocol is used.

3.10.3 The Management Application

The management application is a Java 2 Standard Edition Application that runs with the help of the STFSERVER middleware and that connects by SSL over TCP to a known port of the central server, and may also connect to a known port again by SSL over TCP, to any of the distributed servers, the addresses and ports of witch it gets from the central server.

The interface of the application is based on the Swing framework of J2SE and has a system of menus that we can choose to do the manager work.

4 Evaluation

To evaluate our network middleware for mobile and pervasive large scale augmented reality games, we first evaluate its scalability analytically considering all levels of its architecture, and then evaluate first the SENSACT and STFPAN technologies (personal area network), the SIXRM protocol (on the distributed and central server level), the QoS APIs (both on the personal area and on the distributed server level), the management architecture (present on all levels of the system) and the security architecture (present on all levels of the system) and also evaluate a common API (persistence). Finally to evaluate the middleware in general we demonstrate building and executing a concept application.

4.1 Evaluating Scalability

To analyse the scalability of our architecture, we are going to analyse the network traffic that is probably going to be generated in an analytical way. The network traffic generated also affects the processing time at the nodes so all aspects of scalability are affected in this way. To do this, we must analyse all levels of the system and the way they work together.

4.1.1 The Personal Area Network Level

The first level that is analysed is the personal area network level. Within this level are sensors, actuators and the main game device. All sensors and actuators communicate with the game device that communicates with the large scale distributed level servers of the system. The API for sensor and actuator communication with the central game device is the SENSACT API on the sensors and actuators and the API on the game device is the STF PAN API. The STF PAN API coordinates all sensors and actuators and sends and receives only one stream of data to the current distributed server.

If we note by A_i and S_i the messages (its size in bytes) sent from a sensor i to the central game device on the PAN and the messages sent to actuator i from the central game device, and we suppose that set of actuators and sensors the central game device can process that data so that only the minimal messages M_k, in bytes, get transmitted or received from the distributed servers, we get that Tm, the total maximum number of messages (its size in bytes) handled by the central game device on a period of time between instants t_0 and t_1 is:

$$Tm = \sum_{i=1..N} A_i + \sum_{j=1..M} S_j + \sum_{k=1..L} M_k. \tag{26.1}$$

Where N is the number of sensors active, M is the number of actuators active and L is the number of messages received from the distributed server on that period of time, which depends on the number of objects we are getting updates from, which is limited by partitioning. So we can consider L approximately equal to the number of objects in a period of time sufficiently small between t_0 and t_1 multiplied by 2, because we both send and receive.

So we have that:

1. The maximum number of messages from the sensors increases linearly with the number of sensors active;
2. The number of messages to the actuators increases linearly with the number of messages relevant received from the distributed servers (objects in view that trigger the activators) and the number of sensors active.
3. The number of messages to the distributed servers increases not with sensor number, but with the number of objects in view, and this is limited by partitioning the virtual world.

4.1.2 The Large Scale Distributed Server Level

At the large scale distributed server level each distributed server, at the same time interval, will be responsible for the users in its area and only minimal communication will be maintained between the servers. We can denote that minimal communication by MC_i, in bytes. We can denote the user communication at each server by M_k, in bytes, as we did on the personal area network level. Note that this user communication depends on the number of objects in its view, but that largely is limited, due to partitioning that is made by the system of the virtual world. So the messages are even further minimized in that way in a location oriented dependent manner. As we communicate through ARMSV6 and Sixrm reliable multicast, the

formula for the maximum number of messages TDm (its size in bytes), which each
distributed server will handle, will be approximated by:

$$TDm = \sum_{i=1..N} M_i + \sum_{j=1..M} MC_j. \qquad (26.2)$$

Where N is the number of users and M is the number of distributed servers. We have
that the total number of messages handled by the distributed server will:

1. Increase linearly with the number of users on that distributed server.
2. Increase linearly but in a much slower rhythm with the number of distributed
   servers (because MC_j is really a small amount).

4.1.3   The Back Office Central Level

The back office central level will be handling management and session initiation and
termination. In management, messages exchanged depend linearly on the number of
distributed servers on the network. In session initiation and termination messages,
as also mobility handling messages, the total number of messages also depends
linearly on the total number of users on the system. But these kinds of messages
happen infrequently, only when users join or leave the system, or when the manager
wants to look, examine data or change things.

4.1.4   Analysing the Scalability of Possible Alternate Architectures

The Totally Centralized Architecture

We assume that by the totally centralized architecture we mean that the central game
device on the PAN will do no processing on sensors and activator messages and send
all to a central server to do all processing related to the user and send the result back
to this user sensors and activators.

   This would be of course a situation where the server would be a major bottleneck,
as the equation for the total number of messages on the server clearly shows, for the
time between instants t_0 and t_1:

$$Tm = \left(\sum_{i=1..N} \left(\sum_{j=1..M} S_j + \sum_{k=1..L} A_k \right) \right) x2. \qquad (26.3)$$

We use here the same notation used until now with Tm being the total maximum
number of messages, in bytes, handled by the central server. We multiply the sum
by 2 because we both receive and send messages. N is the number of users, M the
number of sensors per user and L the number of actuators per user.

We now have the entire load on one component, and loose the benefits of distributing the load for more than one component.

Here we are not counting with session initiation, session termination, mobility handling, and management messages. These tend to happen infrequently.

The Totally Distributed Architecture

In the total distributed architecture, we would have only the large scale distributed level of the system doing all the processing. There would be no processing on the PAN and no processing on the Central BackOffice Level.

This leads to problems of finding the correct server to connect to in the first place, we would have to build a list of servers in each user central device. And these lists must be maintained synchronized with the configuration of the network, which would be no easy task.

Mobility and management will also be moved to the distributed level completely, complicating things a little more. On our architecture mobility and management have a distributed component, but are centrally coordinated, which does not happen in this scenario.

But, seeing things in number of messages transmitted and using the same notation we have in each distributed server, between instants t_0 and t_1, taking that the PAN central device does not do any processing, TDm the total maximum number of messages (its size in bytes) processed in one distributed server is:

$$TDm = \left(\sum_{i=1..N} \left(\sum_{j=1..M} S_j + \sum_{k=1..L} A_k \right) \right) x2 + \sum_{l=1..O} MC_l \qquad (26.4)$$

Where N is the number of users on this distributed server, M is the number of sensors by user, L is the number of actuators per user and O is the number of distributed servers on the system.

We have that the total number of messages handled by the distributed server will:

1. Increase linearly with the number of distributed servers
2. Not increase linearly but in a faster rhythm with the number of users, sensors, and actuators on the users of this distributed server.

So we have that the solution is more scalable than the totally centralized one, but less scalable than our solution, because the load on the distributed servers is much more.

The Pure Peer-to-peer Architecture

By the peer-to-peer architecture, we aim to analyse a situation where the central game device has all the work of the system, communicating only with other central game devices through the 3GPP network. It has processing capabilities and processes the sensor and actuator messages. It only sends and receives messages from all other nodes on the system. We denote by Si the sensor messages, Ai the actuator messages and Mi the node messages to and from other nodes. We have that TPm, the total maximum number of messages (it's size in bytes), on the main game device, the main device on the personal area network, is, on the time between t0 and t1:

$$TPm = \sum_{i=1..O} A_i + \sum_{j=1..N} S_j + \sum_{k=1..M-1} M_k. \qquad (26.5)$$

Where N is the number of sensors active on the PAN, M is the number of users on the system and O is the number of actuators active on the PAN. We see that this formula is very similar to our formula in our three levels system for the PAN level, but now the M_k factor depends on the number of users and not on the number of distributed servers, which clearly is worse than in our case. So, the totally peer-to-peer architecture is not as scalable as ours.

4.1.5 Graphical Case Study of the Alternate Architectures

For a more visually appealing comparison, we will do a graphical comparison between de various alternatives. For this, we will fix the number of sensors in 5 and the number of actuators in 3. We will start with 100,000 users and work our way up to 3,000,000 users in steps of 100,000. We will analyse a network, in our case, with 100 distributed servers uniformly distributed and with users uniformly distributed, on the three levels architecture and on the totally distributed architecture. We will analyse output variables. We will fix the size of messages in 50 bytes for the sensors, 300 bytes for the actuators (in reality this maybe more depending on the kind of actuator but for our study this will do), 300 bytes for MCi and Mk. We will fix the number of objects in view to 10. We will build a program to run the simulation and output the results to a CSV file that then gets analysed by Microsoft Excel to output the graphs shown here (Figs. 26.8–26.12).

Notice how the PAN level on our architecture does not depend on the number of users, contrary to what happens on the totally peer to peer architecture. Notice on how on the totally distributed architecture when the users go up to 3,000,000, we go exponentially to $6E + 11$ bytes in each server (corresponding to 30,000 users on each server), contrary to only 214,560,000 bytes linearly in our solution in each of the distributed servers. In the fully centralized architecture, the maximum number of messages linearly increases to a maximum of 6,900,060,000 bytes, when we have a maximum of 3,000,000 users, which is much more than any of our distributed servers on our large scale network.

We may have had better results yet if we had allowed our distributed servers to grow to accommodate the ever growing user base, but that was not the scenario envisioned. In reality, probably we will have more distributed servers with a growing

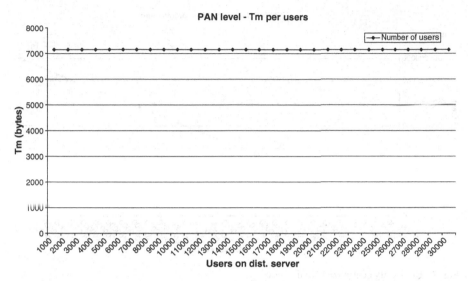

Fig. 26.8 Personal area network level

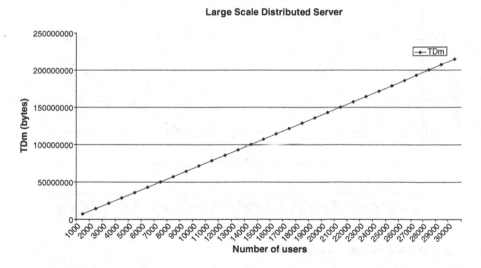

Fig. 26.9 Large scale distributed server level

user base. Even so, when comparing our solution to the totally distributed one, our solution has linear increase with the number of users and the totally distributed solution has exponential increase with the number of users. Our solution would be better none the less.

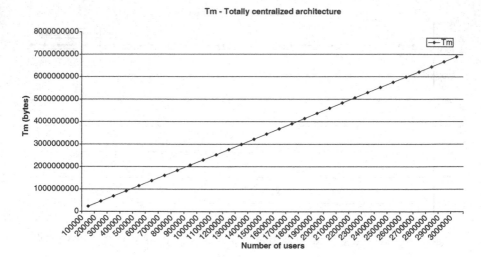

Fig. 26.10 Totally centralized architecture

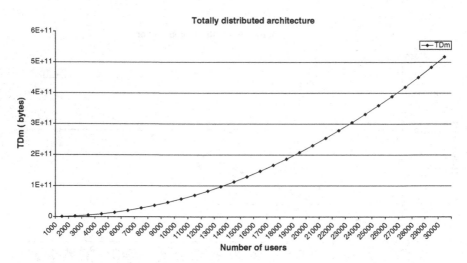

Fig. 26.11 Totally distributed architecture

4.2 Evaluating SENSACT and STFPAN

The SENSACT API combined with the STF API were subject to extensive functional and performance tests, with various kinds of simulated sensors and actuators and a simulated reading and actuating application using Java Wireless Toolkit from Sun Microsystems running in a series of emulators in a Pentium 4 3.6 GHz System with 1 Gb Memory (Figs. 26.13–26.16).

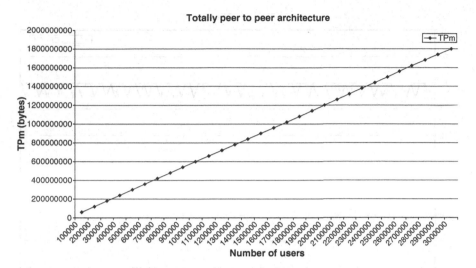

Fig. 26.12 Totally peer-to-peer architecture

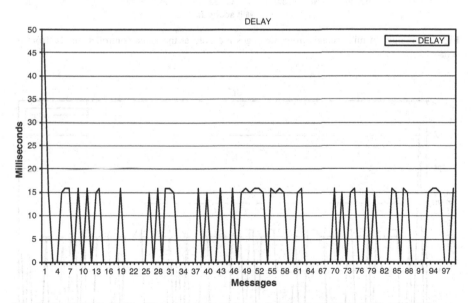

Fig. 26.13 Delay in milliseconds from messages received at the game controller device from a sensor

We present here extracts from the results for delay and jitter for two of those tests, one for a simple simulated position sensor, and another for a simple force actuator.

The tests show that the combined sensor-middleware delay varies from 0 to 16 ms with jitter from 0 to 16 ms, while the combined actuator-middleware delay varies

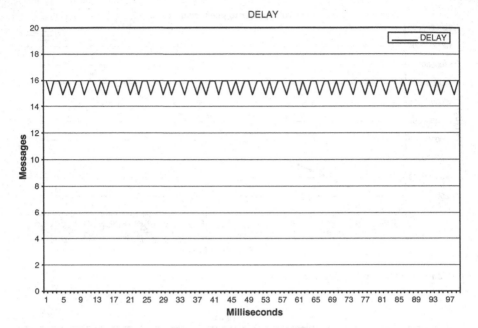

Fig. 26.14 Jitter in milliseconds from messages received at the game controller device from a sensor

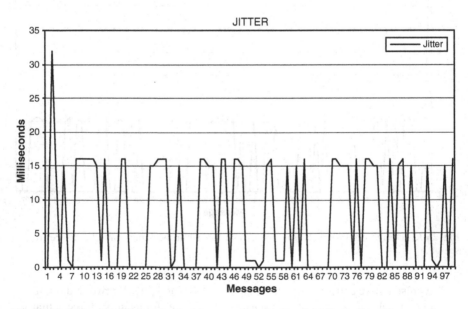

Fig. 26.15 Delay in milliseconds from messages received at the actuator from the main game controller device

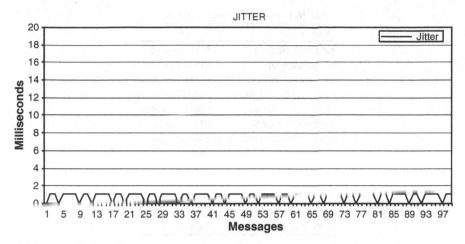

Fig. 26.16 Jitter in milliseconds from messages received at the actuator from the main controller game device

from 15 to 16 ms with jitter from 0 to 1 ms. These values prove that the solution is adequate for small sensor and actuator networks around a central coordinating device, such as the ones found in mobile and pervasive augmented reality scenarios.

4.3 Evaluating the Sixrm Protocol

The Sixrm protocol API as it is implemented was subject to various functional and stress tests, with several profile settings. It was demonstrated that, according to the profile settings, one can have many instances of Sixrm running on the same computer (over 10 instances, if the settings are right). It was demonstrated also, that according to the settings, many more instances could be run on different computers. This is because they will not consume all CPU time, like we did on these stress tests, but only a minimum, and the sources will try to adapt to the slowest computer and weakest link (because of nak throughput adaptation, and error throughput adaptation, within the limits set forth in the profile).

We did tests on two computers connected by a 100 Mbit full duplex switch configured in a IPv6 network, and tests in one only computer configured to run in a ipv6 network.

Those were real tests, not simulated tests. The test results presented here are extracts from the tests with one computer, because they show the delay and jitter introduced solely by the responsibility of the Sixrm protocol.

We present here graphics for delay and jitter for one of the nodes (received at the first node) of a Sixrm network witch achieved 12 nodes in the same computer without errors. When the thirteen's node was added, there were briefly some errors

Table 26.1 Profile settings for the tests

Profile value	Setting
maxOutBufferSize	3,000 messages
maxInBufferSize	3,000 messages
maxSentBufferSize	1,000 messages
maxQueuedBufferSize	5 messages
maxRecvBufferSize	1,000 messages
minRecvWindowSize	10 messages
maxRecvWindowSize	250 messages
minRandomBackoff	10 ms
maxRandomBackoff	50 ms
minIntervalTime	25 ms
maxIntervalTime	250 ms
intervalSteppingDown	1 ms
intervalSteppingUp	16 ms

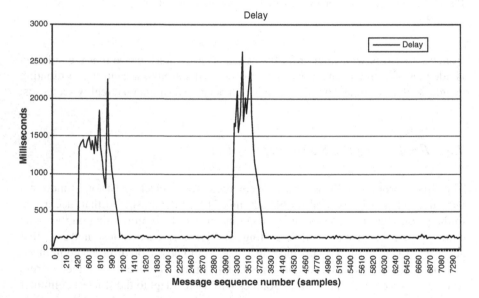

Fig. 26.17 Delay from second node on first node

that were handed to the test application by the Sixrm protocol, in a period when the computer's processor was at a peak load of 100% and availability was arriving at its physical limits, which we believed were the causes of the inability of the node to handle processing data.

The profile settings for these tests are described in Table 26.1.

The Fig. 26.17 represents delay for the second node on the system as received on the first node. The Fig. 26.18 represents jitter for the same situation.

We do not show here results from more nodes because the results are in all cases similar to these.

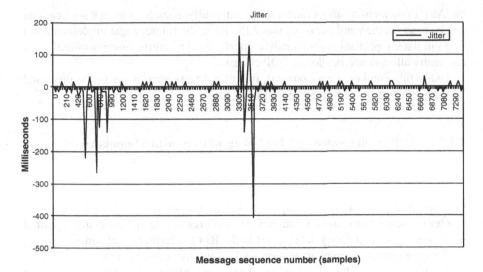

Fig. 26.18 Jitter from second node on first node

From these results we can conclude that the delay is normally always approximately 150 ms and that the jitter normally varies between 0 and approximately 17 ms. This happens consistently except some exceptions, which occur exactly on the moments where we were adding nodes to the Sixrm network and the network was adjusting itself. We can see that in these moments the delay and jitter briefly increase and then stabilise in acceptable values again. In fact, they stabilize in the same values as the number of nodes increases.

These numbers for delay and jitter (the stable ones) are adequate for most interactive delay sensitive applications.

As the server network will mostly be a stable one, as probably all nodes will be functioning since the first few minutes when integrated into the large scale network, the Sixrm protocol is, we think, adequate for the purpose we create it for.

4.4 Evaluating the QoS APIs

To test our architecture we have made some functional tests, on a simulated implementation of the PDP context Handler architecture and on a protocol implementation of RSVP.

4.4.1 Emulation of the PDP Context Handler Architecture

We did not have access to a platform where we could implement real PDP context activation and deactivation, in a way that we could test it, in Java. So, we emulated the API, implementing all its functionality internally in such a way that applications can be made in the emulator using this API and in the future, a real implementation (not emulated), probably using a native interface to the native features of real UEs, can really allocate and deallocate PDP contexts.

Using this emulation environment, functional tests were made to the proposed API, enabling us to confirm its operational capabilities.

4.4.2 RSVP Implemented by UDP Encapsulation with a Simulated Router in Between

As for RSVP, we implemented RSVP, both on the emulated UE and on the distributed server using UDP encapsulation, which is a feature of the protocol [27].

Our implementation does not support the features of integrity checking (optional in all messages), and policy data (stated in the RFC as further study item).

A future alternative implementation could implement these items.

For testing, we built a program that simulated a router with UDP encapsulation support and tested in an isolated fashion the communications of the RSVP protocol between a program that sent and received data (so it needed reservations), an RSVP simulated router, and a similar program (actually the same program) running on another machine.

The functional tests consisted of, considering both computers as senders and receivers at the same time, setting up reservations in RSVP having a router in between the two (actually, the simulated router).

The tests only targeted the protocol, no real reservations at the network layer were made.

The tests were successful and we proceeded with the integration of the API with the rest of the Status Transmission Framework Middleware.

4.5   Evaluating the Security Architecture

To test our security architecture, we are going to test its usability for our target middleware objectives, which are mobile and pervasive large scale augmented reality games.

These objectives put scalability constraints on security architecture and also QoS constraints such as delay and jitter.

We can test the security architecture for delay and jitter targets, and we can analyse it to derive conclusions about its scalability.

We can divide these tests into the various parts of the system, namely in the personal area network, on the link between the personal area network on the large scale network level, and in the large scale network level itself.

This is because the central level works essentially as a key distribution level and so does not get itself involved in any real-time communications.

4.5.1 Personal Area Network Level Security Testing

The personal area network part of the system, both the STF PAN API and the STF SENSACT API, was subject to extensive functional and performance tests, with various kinds of simulated sensors and actuators and a simulated reading and actuating application using Java Wireless Toolkit 2.5 Beta from Sun Microsystems running in a series of emulators in a Pentium 4 3.6 GHz System with 1 Gb Memory. These tests give the same results as the tests run in [34] as nothing has changed, we still use Bluetooth encryption and authentication. So, we do not present graphics here due to the fact that the results are the same as presented before. So, we did not add any delay or jitter to the previous architecture.

4.5.2 Testing the Communications Between the PAN and the Large Scale Distributed Level Architecture

Between the personal area network central device, that runs Java 2 Micro edition Mobile Information Device Profile 2.0 over the Connected Limited Device Configuration 1.1 (MIDP 2.0 and CLDC 1.1), and the distributed server where it happens to be connected there is a TLS connection over TCP where STF messages are exchanged according to our protocol.

To be able to test for delay and jitter on this connection, which is handled by specialized classes of STFPAN (the library of classes for the central device of the personal area network) and STFServer (the library of classes for the distributed servers and central server), we implemented time stamping of messages with the current time when sending the message, and automatically calculating the delay based on that timestamp and the current time on the receiving machine when receiving the messages. For the test to be meaningful, both machines must be synchronized through NTP, preferably to a common timeserver.

We also implemented logging to a file both on STFPAN and STFServer of the received delay values so that we can calculate the delay and jitter values for the various UE (mobile terminals or central devices of the personal area network), and elaborate graphics (Figs. 26.19–26.21).

We then made the tests with only one UE connected to one distributed server working in connection to one central server. In this situation, even if we do not have a working application to test messaging, there are messages exchanged between the distributed server and the central device of the personal area network, between the central device of the personal area network and the central server and between the distributed server and the central server (Fig. 26.22).

The messages we are interested in are the messages between the central device of the personal area network and the distributed server. At this stage, those messages are only messages of virtual time synchronization of STF's internal virtual time synchronization mechanism, which keeps a virtual clock synchronized between the central device of the personal area network and the distributed server. Is the delay and jitter of those messages that is evaluated in the graphics shown on this section.

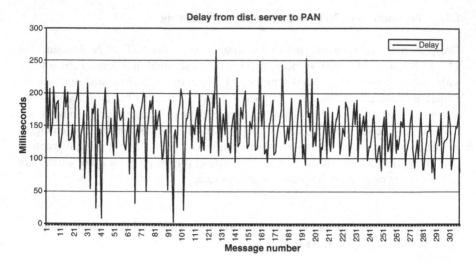

Fig. 26.19 Delay received at PAN from distributed server

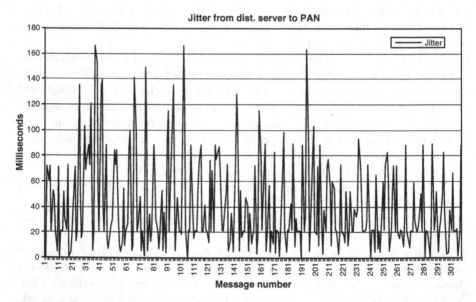

Fig. 26.20 Jitter received at PAN from distributed server

Figure 26.13 shows the delays for all the messages received at the central personal area network device that were sent from the distributed server, and Figure 26.14 shows the jitters for the same messages, calculated as the difference between current and previous delay.

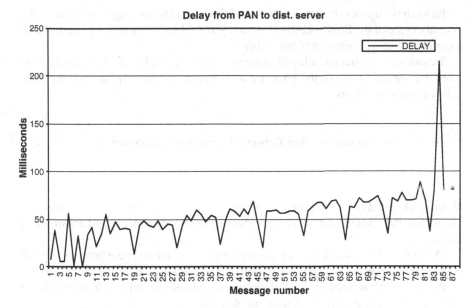

Fig. 26.21 Delay received at the distributed server from the PAN

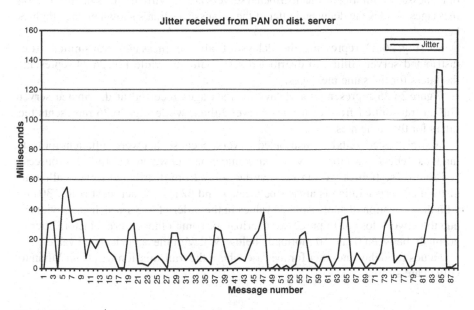

Fig. 26.22 Jitter received on the distributed server from the PAN

Figure 26.15 shows the delays for all the messages received at the distributed server that were sent from the central personal area device, and Fig. 26.16 shows the jitters from the same messages.

From these figures we can see that the delay from the messages received at the central device of the PAN is always between 9 and 218 ms. The Jitter from the same messages is always between 0 and 160 ms.

We can also see that the delay from the messages received at the distributed server from the central device of the PAN is always between 7 and 215 ms and the jitter varies from 0 to 134 ms.

4.5.3 Testing Communication Between Large Scale Distributed Level Servers

For testing communications between the large scale distributed level servers, we also implemented time stamping of messages the same way we implemented on the connection between the central device of the personal area network and a distributed server.

The message is marked with a timestamp equal to current time when sending and is marked again with the delay when receiving the message at the receiving end.

We also implemented logging of the received message delays (from which we can also derive the jitter), on the distributed servers.

Because we still do not have a concept application to run on the architecture, the only messages running on the distributed servers are the virtual time synchronization messages. And is the delay and jitter of these messages that's shown on the graphics below.

So, Fig. 26.23 represents the delays of all the messages transmitted from distributed server Gillian to distributed server Julian, while Fig. 26.24 represents the jitters for the same messages.

Figure 26.25 represents the delays for messages received at distributed server Gillian transmitted from distributed server Julian, while Fig. 26.26 represents the jitters for the same messages.

We only tested with two distributed servers, because that were sufficient for testing the effects of cryptography on communication and we are not full of resources.

From these figures we can see that the delay from distributed server Gillian to distributed server Julian is always between 7 and 62 ms, in fact most below 30 ms, with the exception of some isolated values in the order of 4–5 s which are obviously due to network loss or to processor overload or some other external factor. Jitter is normally between 0 and 50 (normally below 30), with the same isolated values.

Values for delay and jitter for the case where the transmission was from Julian to Gillian are similar.

4.6   Evaluating Common APIs

We have also tested the persistence sub-package on its own in order to estimate network bandwidth usage. For this, we designed a program to compare the savings

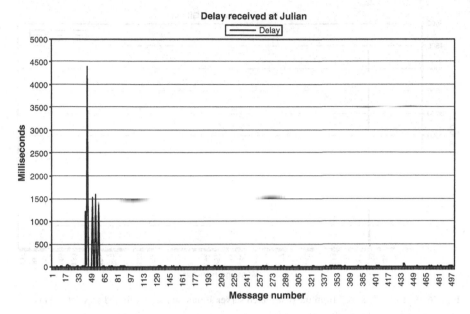

Fig. 26.23   Delays received from the distributed server Gillian on distributed server Julian

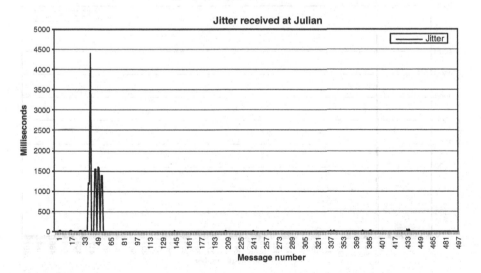

Fig. 26.24   Jitter received from the distributed server Gillian on the distributed server Julian

made in relation to java Serialization and Externalization mechanisms and to allow us to calculate the size of a message for a common case. This common case was chosen to be the transmission of a position update (position sensor, for example). Then we ran a program to evaluate the size of the message that is produced applying

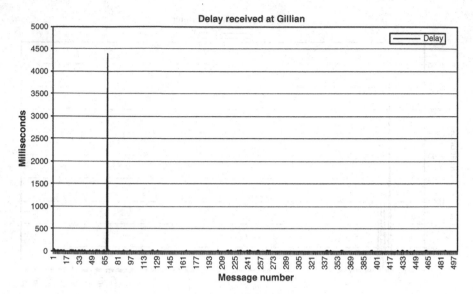

Fig. 26.25 Delay received from the distributed server Julian on the distributed server Gillian

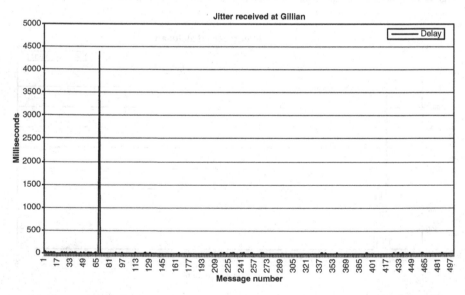

Fig. 26.26 Jitter received from the distributed server Julian on the distributed server Gillian

each of the three methods, and printed the results. The obtained results were 92 bytes for Serialization, 83 bytes for externalization and only 22 bytes for SENSACT persistence.

4.7 Evaluating the Management Architecture

For the testing phase of the management architecture, we configured the system with one UE (emulated with a program made over the middleware STFPAN on Java Wireless Toolkit 2.5), one central server (running on another computer), and one distributed server (running in the same computer as the central server). The HSS was emulated by one program of ours, that makes part of our middleware and that emulates essential function of the HSS that our application servers need. This is the minimum configuration.

First we started the central server, then the distributed server, then the UE. The UE connected to the central server by SIP and by SSL over TCP to the distributed server, after it had negotiated the session and the respective QoS properties.

We then, after some time, started the management application on the same computer where the servers were running.

First we connected to the central server. Then we connected to the distributed server (the only one). Then we tested every menu option. The results were acceptable for the scenario.

4.7.1 Scalability Analysis

As for scalability, we can analyze it in the following way. When the statistics are disabled, there are no messages going around in the system. Scalability is not a problem. Authorization of users only involves the central server and management application. Revoking of authorization only involves the central server and management application. Scalability is not a problem.

When generating statistics, the various UE (can be many of them per distributed server) periodically send their reports to the distributed server, which aggregates it into one only report and sends it periodically to the central server. Therefore, the central server only receives each aggregated UE report from the distributed server and each distributed server report. The number of reports received by the central server depends on the number of distributed servers, not on the number of UEs (i.e. the number of users on the system). Generated reports from the central server are generated and kept on the central server. The management application connects to the central server and possibly to a distributed server. The system is therefore scalable.

As for resetting statistics, only one message is diffused only one time for the entire system. As for checking if the user is running, only the central server and management application are involved. As for enabling statistics and disabling statistics, only one message is diffused by the entire system one only time. So the system is kept scalable.

Of course there is a performance penalty in enabling statistics generating and collecting over not having the system generating statistics generation and collecting, but this is unavoidable, and tells the manager that he should use this capacity sparingly, mostly to test the system while still in alpha or beta testing and occasionally, to track some bugs that may exist.

5 Conclusions and Future Directions

In this work we have built and evaluated a network middleware for large-scale mobile and pervasive augmented reality games, which works over a 3GPP network.

This middleware has evolved from previous work in the area of interactive distributed multimedia, more specifically in state transmission for a collaborative virtual environment middleware platform, the Status Transmission Framework (STF) [7, 8]. This platform extended ARMS – Augmented Reliable corba Multicast System [27] – with capabilities for the handling of state transmission for distributed collaborative virtual environments.

As with any work, we can never say the work is complete. It is always possible to make improvements. It is the case with this work also.

Future work in the Status Transmission Framework possibly will include new kinds of sensors and actuators included by default on the SENSACT API and the STF PAN equivalent API, and further testing of this API on real devices (not simulated ones) if that becomes possible.

Also in the SENSACT API and correspondent communication layer on the STFPAN API, it would also be interesting to implement support for other personal area network communication technologies like ZIGBEE, for example, which is a direct contender of Bluetooth, but not so much implemented on the mobile world.

We also should, of course optimize and extend the API as required as future research is made.

A bottleneck which in the future, if possible, we should investigate ways to remove is the fact that we use TCP to make the communications between the UE (STFPAN API) and the current allocated distributed server (STFSERVER API), though through a message oriented protocol we created especially designed for augmented reality and that utilizes available bandwidth adaptively.

The fact that we use TCP and not any form of multicast protocol on these connections is a fact that hinders performance of the whole system, but that is justified that is impossible, due to current J2ME specifications, which do not give us the possibility to use multicast for mobile network connections.

As for mobility support, the system supports mobility through the moving of the user, besides at the level of the UMTS network, between the various cells using the UMTS network technology and related methods, at the distributed game application server level through switching the gaming server that is currently communicating with the user. Each gaming server is responsible for a different gaming area.

Currently, there is no direct connection between the two levels. It would probably be beneficial to the system if we find a way in the future to integrate these two levels.

For example, instead of managing a rectangular area, the application server could manage a group of cell coverage areas. Communication between the 3GPP(UMTS) layer and the middleware layer should make that operation simpler.

As for system security, we could research ways to further improve the security architecture of the middleware. If we, as already mentioned, implemented other communication technologies into SENSACT and STFPAN we would need to integrate security also with these technologies. We could also introduce new encryption algorithms into STFPAN and STFSERVER, but, because of maintaining high software compatibility, we should maintain J2SE compatibility, so, it is better to wait for J2SE support for these algorithms before actually supporting them.

For system manageability, in the future we could research ways in which to integrate closer the management architecture of our middleware for mobile and pervasive large scale augmented reality with the management architecture of UMTS.

Future work on the QoS APIs will include implementing, testing and evaluating those APIs on real devices and not on emulated or simulated ones.

References

1. M. Weiser, "The Computer for the Twenty – First Century", Scientific American, pages 94–104, Sept. 1991.
2. Pedro Miguel da Fonseca Marques Ferreira, "Network Middleware for Mobile and Pervasive Large Scale Augmented Reality Games", Phd Thesis, Coimbra University, September 2008.
3. Keith Mitchell, Duncan McCaffery, George Metaxas, Joe Finney, Stefan Schmid and Andrew Scott, "Six in the City: Introducing Real Tournament – A Mobile IPv6 Based Context-Aware Multiplayer Game", Proceedings of NetGames'03, May 22–23, 2003, Redwood City, California, USA, pp. 91–100, ACM Press.
4. Cartsten Magerkurth, Adrian David Cheok, Regan L. Mandrik, Trond Nilsen, "Pervasive Games: Bringing Computer Entertainment Back to the Real World", ACM Computers in Entertainment, Vol. 3, No. 3, July 2005, Article 4A.
5. Tino Pissysalo, Petri Pulli, "A Picocell-Based Architecture for a Real-Time Mobile Virtual Reality", Proceedings of the 9th Euromicro Workshop on Real Time Systems (EUROMICRO-RTS '97), pp. 144–151, 1997, IEEE.
6. Stefan Fiedler, Michael Wallner, Michael Weber, "A Communication Architecture for Massive Multiplayer Games", Proceedings of NetGames2002, April 16–17, 2002, Braunschweig, Germany.
7. João Gilberto de Matos Orvalho, "ARMS – Uma plataforma para aplicações multimédia distribuídas, com qualidade de serviço", Phd Thesis, December 2000, DEI-FCTUC.
8. Pedro Ferreira, "Transmissão de estados em ambientes de realidade virtual distribuídos e colaborativos", M.Sc. thesis, Universidade de Coimbra - FCTUC - Departamento de Engenharia Informática, October-2002.
9. Bruce Thomas, Ben Close, John Donoghue, John Squires, Phillip De Bondi and Wayne Piekarski, "First Person Indoor/Outdoor Augmented Reality Application: ARQuake", Personal and Ubiquitous Computing (2002), No. 6, pp. 75–86, Springer-Verlag London Ltd, 2002.
10. Sumi Helal, "Pervasive Java", IEEE Pervasive Computing, January-March 2002, pp. 82–85.
11. Java APIs for Bluetooth (JSR-82), http://jcp.org/en/jsr/detail?id=82.
12. Mobile Media API, http://jcp.org/en/jsr/detail?id=135.
13. Mobile 3D Graphics API for J2ME, http://jcp.org/en/jsr/detail?id=184.

14. Eila Niemelä, Teemu Vaskivuo, "Agile Middleware of Pervasive Computing Environments", Proceedings of the Second IEEE Annual Conference on Pervasive Computing and Communications Workshops (PERCOMW'04), IEEE, 2004.
15. P. Calhoun, J. Loughney, E. Guttman, G. Zorn, J. Arkko, "Diameter Base Protocol", RFC 3588, Network Working Group, IETF, September 2003.
16. 3GPP TS 29.229 v7.0.0, "3rd Generation Partnership Project; Technical Specification Group Core Networks and Terminals; Cx and Dx interfaces based on Diameter protocol; Protocol details (Release 7)", January 2006.
17. 3GPP TS 29.329 V7.0.0, "3RD generation Partnership Project; Technical Specification Group Core Network and Terminals; Sh interface based on the Diameter protocol; Protocol details (Release 7)", December 2005.
18. R. Stewart, Q. Xie, K. Morneault, C. Sharp, H. Swarzbauer, T. Taylor, I. Rytina, M. Kalla, L. Zhang, V. Paxson, "Stream Control Transmission Protocol", RFC 2960, Network Working Group, IETF, October 2000.
19. J. Rosenberg, H. Schulzrinne, G. Camarillo, A. Johnston, J. Peterson, R. Sparks, M. Handley, E. Shooler, "SIP: Session Initiation Protocol", RFC 3261, Network Working Group, IETF, June 2002.
20. M. Handley, V. Jacobson, C. Perkins, "SDP: Session Description Protocol", RFC 4566, Network Working Group, IETF, July 2006.
21. Java Community Process, "Location API for J2ME", http://www.jcp.org/en/jsr/detail?id=179.
22. Pedro Ferreira, João Orvalho and Fernando Boavida, "Sixrm: Full Mesh Reliable Source Ordered Multicast", in Proc. of the SoftCom2006 - 14th International Conference on Software, Tellecommunications & Computer Networks, SoftCom2006 - 14th International Conference on Software, Tellecommunications & Computer Networks, Split, Croatia, September 2006.
23. MIDP – Mobile Information Device Profile 2.0, http://jcp.org/en/jsr/detail?id=118.
24. Pedro Ferreira, João Orvalho and Fernando Boavida, "Middleware for embedded sensors and actuators in mobile pervasive augmented reality", in Proc. of the INFOCOM 2006 (IEEE XPLORE), INFOCOM 2006 Student Workshop, Barcelona, April 2006.
25. SIP API for J2ME, http://jcp.org/en/jsr/detail?id=180.
26. João Orvalho, Pedro Ferreira and Fernando Boavida, "State Transmission Mechanisms for a Collaborative Virtual Environment Middleware Platform", Springer-Verlag, Berlin Heidelberg New York, 2001, pp. 138–153, ISBN 3-540-42530-6 (Proceedings of the 8th International Workshop on Interactive Distributed Multimedia Systems – IDMS 2001,Lancaster, UK, September 2001).
27. João Orvalho, Fernando Boavida, "Augmented Reliable Multicast CORBA Event Service (ARMS): a QoS-Adaptive Middleware", in Lecture Notes in Computer Science, Vol. 1905: Hans Scholten, Marten J. van Sinderen (editors), Interactive Distributed Multimedia Systems and Telecommunication Services, Springer-Verlag, Berlin Heidelberg, 2000, pp. 144–157. (Proceedings of IDMS 2000 – 7th International Workshop on Interactive Distributed Multimedia Systems and Telecommunication Services, CTIT/University of Twente, Enschede, The Netherlands, October 17–20, 2000).
28. 3GPP TS23.207 V6.0.0, "3rd Generation Partnership Project; Technical Specification Group Services and System Aspects; End to End Quality of Service (QoS) concept and architecture (Release 6)", September 2005.
29. R. Braden (Ed.), L. Zhang, S. Berson, S. Herzog, S. Jamin, "Resource Reservation Protocol – version 1 Fuctional Specification", RFC 2205, IETF Network Working Group, September 1997.
30. J. Wroclawski, "The Use of RSVP with IETF Integrated Services", RFC 2210, IETF Network Working Group, September 1997.
31. S. Shenker, J. Wroclawski, "General Characterization Parameters for Integrated Service Network Elelements", RFC 2215, IETF Network Working Group, September 1997.
32. J. Wroclawski, "Specification of the Controlled-Load Network Element Service", RFC 2211, IETF Network Working Group, September 1997.

33. S. Shenker, C. Partridge, R. Guerin, "Specification of Guaranteed Quality of Service", RFC 2212, IETF Network Working Group, September 1997.
34. Pedro Ferreira, João Orvalho and Fernando Boavida, "Middleware for embedded sensors and actuators in mobile pervasive augmented reality", in Proc. of the INFOCOM 2006 (IEEE XPLORE), INFOCOM 2006 Student Workshop, Barcelona, April 2006.
35. Hideyuki Tamura, Hiroyuki Yamamoto, and Akihiro Katayama, "Mixed Reality:Future Dreams Seen at the Border between Real and Virtual Worlds", Virtual Reality, November/December 2001, pp. 64–70, IEEE.
36. CLDC – Common Limited Device Configuration 1.1, http://jcp.org/en/jsr/detail?id=139.

Chapter 27
3D Medical Imaging and Augmented Reality for Image-Guided Surgery

Hongen Liao

Abstract Rapid advances in medical imaging, including its growing application in diagnosis, have attracted interest in the integration of research in the life sciences, medicine, chemical & physical sciences, and engineering. The goals of future biomedicine are to develop minimally invasive precision diagnostic and therapeutic techniques for human diseases by means of bio-medical imaging, bio-robotic, and precision and control engineering. This chapter introduces a variety of augmented reality techniques that were integrated into image-guided diagnostic and therapeutic system, including multi-disciplinary researches of medical imaging and augmented reality for image-guided intervention and medical implementation.

1 Introduction

Rapid advances in medical imaging, including its growing application in diagnosis, have attracted interest in the integration of research in the life sciences, medicine, chemical & physical sciences, and engineering. The goals of future biomedicine are to develop minimally invasive precision diagnostic and therapeutic techniques for human diseases by means of bio-medical imaging, bio-robotic, and precision and control engineering.

Image-guided surgery is a general term used for surgical procedure with image visualization to realize the minimally invasive operation. The procedure is carried out by inserting surgical instrument into the body through a small incision. By localizing the targeted lesion and the critical area that should be avoided, the guidance images help to decrease the invasiveness of surgical procedures and increase their accuracy and safety in treatment. The traditional medical image used in the minimally invasive diagnostic and therapeutic system is often displayed as

H. Liao (✉)
The University of Tokyo, Tokyo, Japan
e-mail: liao@bmpe.t.u-tokyo.ac.jp

B. Furht (ed.), *Handbook of Augmented Reality*, DOI 10.1007/978-1-4614-0064-6_27,   589
© Springer Science+Business Media, LLC 2011

a set of two-dimensional (2D) sectional images or computer reconstructed three-dimensional (3D) models and placed in a nonsterile field from the surgical area. This forces the surgeon to take extra steps to match pre-/intra-operative information on the display with the actual anatomy of the patient [1,2]. Such hand-eye coordination problem is possible cause of the interruption of surgical flow [3]. To overcome this problem, augmented reality (AR) techniques have been developed to merge images or models into real-world views in a natural and unconstrained method.

AR refers to displays that add visualizing information to an observer's perceptions. The techniques of AR have been widely used in medical field, such as surgical simulation, planning, training, and implementation [4]. Most of these AR applications based on binocular stereoscopic imaging and image fusion techniques. Previous works of AR focused on the development of "see-through" devices, which were usually worn on the head with overlay images and extended information on the observer's view of surroundings. Head mounted display (HMD) is a typical device [5, 6], which can display a computer generated image, show live images from the real world or a combination of both. The HMDs have been used in various forms to support and improve visualization of the working area.

The use of half-silvered mirror for image overlay enables the viewing fusion of computer-generated image and the real object [7, 8]. The images can be superimposed over the observer's direct view of the real world. For clinical application, the medical image can be overlaid over the organ of the patient and the surgical area. These image overlay techniques including 2D slice image overlay [9] and stereoscopic image overlay [10] can provide a see through view. Projection overlay technique for surgical microscopic and laser beam guidance can also be used for enhancing the reality of surgical area [11, 12].

One interesting field of medical imaging technology is naked-eye stereoscopy, which displays 3D autostereoscopic images without the need for special viewing glasses or tracking device. Integral Videography (IV) is an idea technique for autostereoscopic medical imaging [13]. Using IV, the 3D image can be observed from a wide area in front of the display by several viewers at the same time. The use of semi-transparent display devices makes it appear that the 3-D image is inside the patient's body.

This chapter introduces a variety of augmented reality techniques that were integrated into image-guided diagnostic and therapeutic system, including multi-disciplinary researches of medical imaging and augmented reality for image-guided intervention and medical implementation. Section 2 briefly introduces the conventional 2D image-based AR windows, including binocular stereoscopic image based augmented reality and its medical applications. Section 3 describes the 3D autostereoscopic IV imaging technique and IV image overlay system. Section 4 describes the feasibility study of AR with IV image overlay and related applications for oral and knee surgeries. Section 5 introduces a combination system of IV image overlay and laser guidance. Section 6 summery the merit of 3D medical imaging technique and its advantage in image-guided surgery.

2   Conventional AR Techniques and Medical Applications

2.1   Slice Image Overlay Based AR Windows for Image-Guided Surgery

There are various techniques for producing AR windows for image-guided surgery. Several groups have investigated slice image overlay AR systems for image-guided intervention. The use of a half-silvered mirror for merging computer-generated images with a direct view enables an image overlay that displays image slices in-situ. Masamune et al. investigated 2D slice image reflection produced in a half-silvered mirror to aid needle insertion procedures [9]. This technique requires only a simple preoperative alignment. Fichtinger et al. integrated the system to computed tomography (CT) scanners. The system can provide the physician with 2D slice vision to guide needle insertions, and reduce faulty insertion attempts [14].

George et al. developed a direct visual technique of ultrasound image by merging the visual outer surface of a patient with a simultaneous ultrasound scan of the patient's interior [15]. A flat panel monitor is combined with a half-silvered mirror so that the image on the monitor can be reflected precisely at the proper location within the patient. The technique enables in situ visualization of ultrasound images during invasive procedures. The ultrasound image is superimposed in real time on the patient, merging with the operator's hands and surgical tools.

2.2   Binocular Stereoscopic Image Based Augmented Reality

Binocular stereoscopic display can reproduce depth of projected objects by using fixed binoculars. Blackwell et al. introduced an image overlay system that uses a binocular stereoscopic vision display and describes an image overlay prototype with initial experimental results [10]. By using image overlay with 3-D medical images reconstructed via CT or MRI, a surgeon can visualize the data "in-vivo" when it is aligned exactly to the patient's anatomy. Using this image overlay with reconstructed 3D medical images, a surgeon can see through the patient's body while being exactly positioned within the patient's anatomy. This system potentially enhances the surgeon's visual perception ability to perform a complex procedure.

Although conventional augmented reality systems can adequately handle depth cues based on geometry (for instance, relative size, motion parallax, and stereo disparity), incorrect visualization of interposition between real and virtual objects has already been identified as a serious issue [16, 17]. Furthermore, when real and virtual images are merged, relative position and information in terms of depth may not be perceived correctly, even though all positions are computed correctly. Because the images for the left and right eyes are formed separately, there is a disparity in the reproduced image. Therefore, different viewers can have inconsistent depth perception [18].

2.3   Head-Mounted Display for Medical Augmented Reality

Various head-mounted displays including optical see-though, video see-though, and projective display HMD have been widely used in image-guided surgery. These devices augment the surgeon's view of the surgical field with computer-generated medical images and models [19]. Typical HMD has either one or two small displays with lenses and semi-transparent mirrors embedded in a helmet, eye-glasses, or visor. Recent technical advances in high-resolution displaying, various see-through designing, and light device manufacturing have significantly increased the benefits of HMD for the medical use [6]. For example, a 3-D visualization system with an HMD for use in laparoscopic surgical procedures was reported by Fuchs et al. [20]. The HMD is tracked to compute an appropriate perspective. Birkfellner et al. presented a modified HMD to increase the clinical acceptance of augmented reality [21]. However, these systems still have a problem of lag for motion parallax and cannot provide a natural view for multiple observers.

3   Augmented Reality of 3D Autostereoscopic Image for Image-Guided Surgery

To overcome the issues of AR that uses 2D images or binocular stereoscopic images, a novel 3D medical autostereoscopic IV image and corresponding image overlay techniques have been developed for image-guided surgery [8, 13, 22]. IV is an animated extension of Integral Photography (IP) [23]. Compared with conventional 3D image techniques, IP can provide geometrically accurate 3D spatial images and reproduces motion parallax without using any supplementary eye glasses or tracking devices. Because IP projects a 3D image into space, it has advantages over the traditional stereoscopic method, where different images are displayed for the viewer's left and right eyes. IV uses a fast image rendering algorithm to project a computer-generated graphical object through a micro convex lens array. Each point shown in the 3-D space is reconstructed at the same position as the actual object through the convergence of rays from the pixels of the elemental images on the computer display after they pass through the lenses of array. Switching to "scene" mode enables IV to display animated objects (Fig. 27.1). This technique could revolutionize real-time, autostereoscopic, in vivo imaging.

The IV imaging technique can be integrated into a surgical navigation system by superimposing the real autostereoscopic image onto the patient via a half-silvered mirror. The augmented reality navigation system with IV image overlay can increase the surgical instrument placement accuracy and reduce the procedure time as a result of intuitive 3D viewing. Furthermore, this intriguing technology not only has applications in medicine, but is being studied as a practical technology for a variety of professional applications.

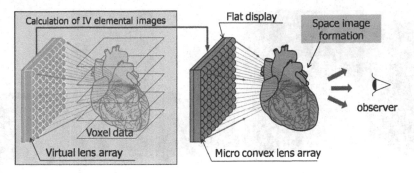

Fig. 27.1   Principle of integral videography (IV)

3.1   High-Quality and High-Speed IV Imaging Techniques

IV records and reproduces 3-D images by using a micro convex lens array and a high-pixel-density display. The screen of the display is usually placed at the focal plane of the lens array so that light rays from the corresponding pixels will converge and form a single dot in physical space (Fig. 27.1). Medical imaging modalities such as MRI, CT, and Ultrasound can be processed to produce corresponding IV images. The 3D object can be rendered using ray-casting, surface rendering, and similar image rendering algorithm. The elemental images of the IV can be reconstructed by pixel distribution method. A high-speed image processing algorithm that renders high-quality IV images from the surface model in real time and allows interactions like rotating and scaling to be done smoothly has been developed [24].

The volume ray-casting method directly processes the volume data (CT, MRI, US). It is basically an extended volume rendering method in which a light ray goes through a micro lens before intersecting with the screen. This method enables a fast image processing, which can be used in intra-operative real-time IV image generation. A sample of high-quality IV image using ray-casting rendering in shown in Fig. 27.2a. The image could be viewed from different directions, and motion parallax could be generated (Fig. 27.2b).

The pixel distribution method constructs IV image from a set of multi-view images acquired by geometrically based surface rendering [25]. This method processes computer graphics (CG) surface models, and therefore, it can produce high-quality images with many visualization effects. In addition, peripheral devices such as surgical instruments can be visualized in the IV image as a simple CG model. For these reasons, the system uses pixel distribution as the primary method for rendering IV images. A 3D IV imaging system has been developed instead of 2D display for pre-operative diagnosis and surgical planning. The IV display and corresponding IV images are shown in Fig. 27.3. GPU-accelerated IV image rendering method is used to realize real-time user interactivity. Furthermore, the system is also combined with a direct volume rendering based on ray-tracing method on NVIDIA Compute Unified Device Architecture (CUDA) as GPU programming platform [26].

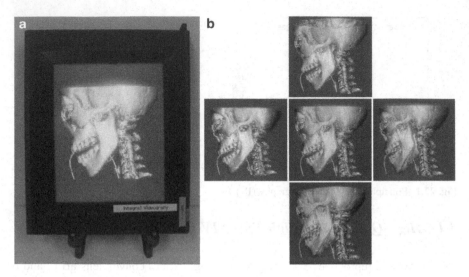

Fig. 27.2 (**a**) High-quality 3D autostereoscopic IV image device. (**b**) Motion parallax of IV autostereoscopic skull images taken from various directions

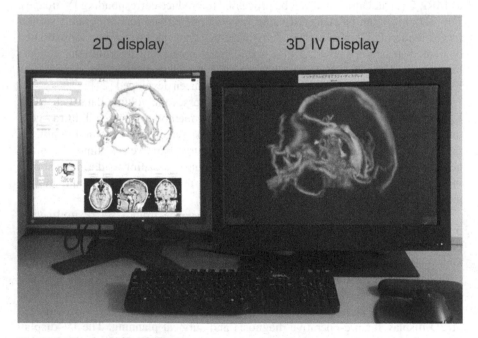

Fig. 27.3 Developed 3D IV display and conventional 2D display

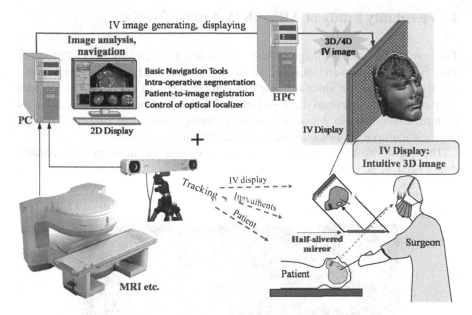

Fig. 27.4 Configuration of IV image overlay navigation system (From Liao et al. 2010.)

3.2   IV Autostereoscopic Image Overlay Navigation System

The IV autostereoscopic image can be integrated into 3D augmented reality surgical navigation system. The system consists of an IV overlay device, a 3D position tracking device, a medical imaging scanner, and computers for IV image rendering and display (Fig. 27.4). The IV overlay device combined with an IV display aligned with a half-silvered mirror. The device is mounted on a robotic arm or movable mechanism that can manipulate the overlay device to the required position and posture. Spatially projected 3D images are superimposed onto the patient and appear via the half-silvered mirror. A fast and accurate spatial image registration method is developed for intra-operative IV image-guided therapy. The navigation information of the segmented data and the spatial coordinate transformation matrix is calculated, and the resulting IV images are displayed on the IV image overlay device [27].

Preliminary experiments showed that the total system error in patient-to-image registration was about 1 mm, and the procedure time for guiding a needle toward a target was shortened. The feasibility studies using animal experiment showed that augmented reality of the image overlay system could increase the surgical instrument placement accuracy and reduce the procedure time as a result of intuitive 3D viewing.

4 Feasibility Study of AR with IV Image Overlay

The feasibility of the IV image overlay system was evaluated by a set of phantom tests. Figure 27.5 shows an image of the surgical instrument, brain tumor, and ventricle directly overlaid on a human model [27]. The IV image of the surgical instrument inserted into the model was displayed and updated according to the changing of its position and orientation. A fast IV algorithm developed for calculating the 3D image of surgical instruments enabled the real-time imaging.

The feasibility of the system was also evaluated by an animal experiment (Fig. 27.6a). A set of markers was attached to the skin of the surgical area. The surgical area was scanned by an MR device. Using IV image overlay to display

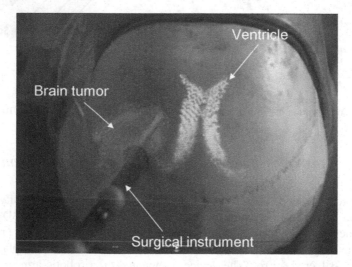

Fig. 27.5 IV images overlay of tumor, ventricle, and surgical tool onto the model of the human brain (From Liao et al. 2010)

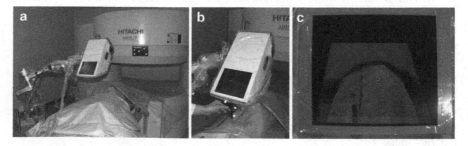

Fig. 27.6 In-vivo experiment: (**a**) experiment scene of IV image overlay device, (**b**) optical tracking device for measuring spatial location of a surgical instrument, and (**c**) targeting implementation (From Liao et al. 2010)

Fig. 27.7 Clinical trial of oral surgery with IV image overlay intervention

the 3D location of fiducial markers, target, and critical areas, the surgeon plans the approach to minimize the surgical exposure. An optical tracking device was used to measure the spatial location of the surgical instrument by tracking a probe fixed to the instrument (Fig. 27.6b). The position data were used to create an intra-operative IV image of the instrument. The targeting experiment was performed by a medical doctor. The surgical area was scanned again to confirm the instrument had reached the target after finishing the targeting test (Fig. 27.6c). The post-operative checkup showed that the instrument successfully reached the target.

Figure 27.7 shows another set of IV image overlay device and its application in oral surgery. During the oral surgery, the complexity of the anatomical structures involved often makes it difficult to directly visualize the operation site. A simplified IV image overlay device is integrated into the computer-aided oral surgical navigation system. The effectiveness of the system was evaluated by a volunteer experiment. The jaw and peripheral organ were scanned by a CT scanner, and the resulted 3D data were segmented and reconstructed to 3D surface models. IV images were generated and projected onto the volunteer's mouth through a half-silvered mirror. The movement of the volunteer was detected and the images were updated in real time. Evaluation experiments show that the system could provide a real-time, in situ, autostereoscopic visualization of the internal structures of the body, allowing visualization of the surgical site with the naked eye.

Figure 27.8 shows another test of overlaid IV image for the knee joint surgery. The images could be viewed from different directions, and motion parallax could be generated as if it were fixed in the body. The IV images combined with the volunteer's knee was taken from various directions. The motion parallax of the IV image are shown in Fig. 27.9.

5 Integration System of Laser Guidance and 3D Autostereoscopic Image Overlay

Several groups have introduced the use of lasers for CT-guided procedures and percutaneous musculoskeletal procedures in the 1990s [28]. These techniques enable needle placement to be more accurate, thus saving time compared to a

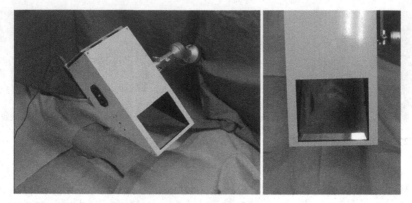

Fig. 27.8 IV image overlay device for knee joint surgery

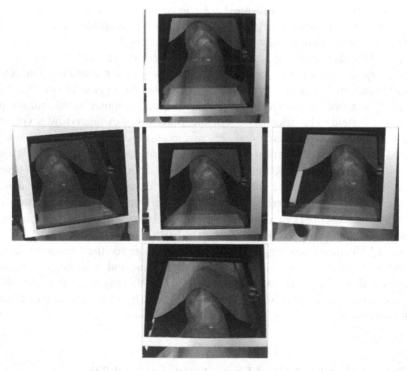

Fig. 27.9 Registration of IV image and volunteer's knee. Motion parallax of IV autostereoscopic images combined with the volunteer's knee is taken from various directions

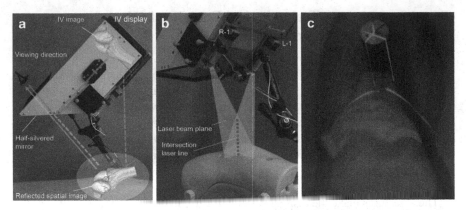

Fig. 27.10 Laser guidance system with autostereoscopic image overlay: (**a**) IV image overlay device and reflected spatial IV image; (**b**) Laser guidance device and laser planes intersect to form a line; (**c**) image-patient registration results and surgical path guidance of laser beams (From Liao et al. 2010)

freehand approach by minimizing the need for repositioning. The desired puncture angle of the surgical instrument is defined by the laser beam. Sasama et al. developed a laser guidance system that was monolithically integrated with an optical tracker [29]. The laser beams are projected onto the surgical field so that the surgeon can obtain guidance information directly. Glossop et al. used scanned infrared and visible lasers to project computer generated information onto the patient by moving a laser beam in arbitrary directions by means of controlled mirrors [30]. However, these systems still can't provide intuitive visualization of complex anatomical structures of inside the patient's body.

A precision-guided surgical instrument navigation combined with IV image overlay (Fig. 27.10a) is developed to extend the abilities of image-guided minimally invasive surgery [31]. The laser guidance device is mounted at the bottom of the IV image overlay device for alignment of the surgical instrument and better visualization of patient's internal structure (Fig. 27.10b). The projection directions of the laser planes are adjusted by a set of motors rotating corresponding mirror axes. The relationship between the reflection direction of the mirror and the rotation of the motor is calculated for properly projecting the laser beams at the position and orientation. Experimental evaluations showed that the system could guide a linear surgical instrument toward a target with a small error and standard deviation. Figure 27.10c shows the procedure of alignment of the surgical instrument and the image-patient registration results. Further improvement to the design of the laser guidance device and the patient-image registration procedure would make this system practical.

6   Advantages and Technological Benefits of IV Autostereoscopic Image Based AR

A unique autostereoscopic image overlay technique has been developed for surgical navigation and image-guided surgery. Compared with conventional stereoscopy and holography, the IV-based autostereoscopic display has several significant features as listed follows: Geometrical accuracy in the vicinity of projected objects, especially in showing depth; Visibility of motion parallax over a wide area; No need to track the surgeon's head and no special glasses for 3-D vision is necessary; Simultaneous viewing by several people; Freedom from visual fatigue in theory; Possibility of displaying an animated image in real-time.

These features make the display suitable for use in operating theaters, where the wearing of glasses may restrict vision and surgical maneuvers. Intra-operatively, IV images can help with the navigation of instruments by providing a broader view of the operating field. The actual 3D image is superimposed onto the patient by using a semi-transparent display based on an adaptation of autostereoscopic IV to image overlay. The IV image overlay system has the following significant features compared to traditional AR techniques. First, autostereoscopic images can be observed without special glasses for 3-D vision or a tracking device to track the surgeon's head. Second, the patient, IV image, and surgical instrument are displayed in a single window. Third, the overlaid image provides an intuitive augmented reality environment that can be shared by multiple observers. Fourth, the spatial formation 3-D image provides visibility of motion parallax over a wide area. Fifth, geometrically accurate IV images are overlaid onto the patient to enable the surgeon to see through the patient's body.

A key difference between the images created by IV and those created by other 3D imaging techniques is that the IV image is a real 3D image. Although the image reflected through a half-silvered mirror and viewed by the observer is a virtual one, our image-overlay system is different from that using binocular stereoscopic image-based augmented reality, such as optical and video see-through HMD, because it merges a real 3D IV image into a real object. The reflected spatial IV image is fixed at the required position although the IV screen cannot be placed at the position of the projected images (i.e., inside the patient's body). That means the position of the reflected IV image will not be changed even if the observer moves their eyes. Moreover, the IV image can provide depth perception and allow multiple viewers to have different perspectives from different directions. Geometrical accuracy of the stereo cues is important because it provides the observer with a 3D image with precision spatial information [26].

Due to the simplicity and accuracy of real-time projected point location, the developed IV imaging technique and corresponding IV image overlay devices should be of practical use in image-guided surgery and surgical navigation, which enables a safe, easy, and accurate surgical diagnosis and therapy.

References

1. P. Breedveld and M. Wentink, "Eye-hand coordination in laparoscopy - an overview of experiments and supporting aids," Minim. Invasiv. Ther., vol. 10, No. 3, pp. 155–162, 2001.
2. E. Kobayashi, K. Masamune, I. Sakuma, T. Dohi, and D. Hashimoto, "A new safe laparoscopic manipulator system with a five-bar linkage mechanism and an optical zoom," Computer Aided Surgery, vol. 4, pp. 182–192, 1999.
3. P. Breedveld, H. G. Stassen, D. W. Meijer, and L. P. S. Stassen, "Theoretical background and conceptual solution for depth perception and eye-hand coordination problems in laparoscopic surgery," Minim. Invasiv. Ther., vol. 8, pp. 227–234, 1999.
4. J. Traub, T. Sielhorst, S. M.l Heining, and N. Navab, "Advanced Display and Visualization Concepts for Image Guided Surgery," J. Display Tech., Vol. 4, No. 4, pp. 483–490, 2008.
5. I. Sutherland, "A head-mounted three dimensional display," in Proc. Fall Joint Computer Conf. pp. 757–764, 1968
6. K. Keller, A. State, and H. Fuchs, "Head Mounted Displays for Medical Use," Journal of Display Technology, Vol. 4, No. 4, pp. 468–472, 2008.
7. Y. Masutani, M. Iwahara, O. Samuta, Y. Nishi, N. Suzuki, M. Suzuki, T. Dohi, H. Iseki, and K. Takakura, "Development of integral photography-based enhanced reality visualization system for surgical support," Proc. ISCAS, vol. 95, pp. 16–17, 1995.
8. H. Liao, N. Hata, S. Nakajima, M. Iwahara, I. Sakuma, and T. Dohi, "Surgical navigation by autostereoscopic image overlay of integral videography," IEEE Trans. Int. Technol. Biomed., Vol. 8, No. 2, pp. 114–121, 2004.
9. K. Masamune, Y. Masutani, S. Nakajima, I. Sakuma, T. Dohi, H. Iseki, and K. Takakura, "Three-dimensional slice image overlay system with accurate depth perception for surgery," in Proc. Int. Conf. Medical Image Computing and Computer Assisted Intervention (MICCAI), Lecture Notes in Computer Science, Vol. 1935, pp. 395–402, 2000.
10. M. Blackwell, C. Nikou, A. M. Digioia, and T. Kanade, "An image overlay system for medical data visualization," Medical Image Analysis, Vol. 4, pp. 67–72, 2000.
11. P. J. Edwards, A.P. King, C. R. Maurer, Jr., et al., "Design and evaluation of a system for microscope-assisted guided interventions (MAGI)," IEEE Trans. Med. Imag., vol. 19, pp. 1082–1093, Nov. 2000.
12. Y. Miaux, A. Guermazi, D. Gossot, P. Bourrier, D. Angoulvant, A. Khairoune, C. Turki, and E. Bouche, "Laser guidance system for CT-guided procedures," Radiology, Vol. 194, No. 1, pp. 282–284, 1995.
13. H. Liao, M. Iwahara, E. Kobayashi, I. Sakuma, N. Yahagi, T. Dohi: Development of Real-Time Navigation System with intra-operative Information by Integral Videography; 9th Annual Conference of Japan Society of Computer Aided Surgery, pp. 91–92, 2000.
14. G. Fichtinger, A. Deguet, K. Masamune, E. Balogh, G. S. Fischer, H. Mathieu, R. H. Taylor, S. J. Zinreich, L. M. Fayad, "Image Overlay Guidance for Needle Insertion in CT Scanner," IEEE Trans. on Biomedical Engineering, Vol. 52, No. 8, pp. 1415–1422, 2005.
15. George D. Stetten, Vikram S. Chib, "Overlaying ultrasonographic images on direct visio," J Ultrasound Med Vol. 20, pp. 235–240, 2001.
16. M. Bajura, H. Fuchs, and R. Ohbuchi, "Merging Virtual Objects with the Real World: Seeing Ultrasound Imagery within the Patient," Computer Graphics, Vol. 26, No. 2, pp. 203–210, July 1992.
17. L. G. Johnson, P. Edwards, and D. Hawkes, "Surface transparency makes stereo overlays unpredictable: The implications for augmented reality," in Medicine Meets Virtual Reality (MMVR), Vol. 94 of Studies in Health Int. Technol. and Inf., J. D. Westwood, Ed.: IOS Press, 2003, pp. 131–136.
18. B. T. Backus, M. S. Banks, R. van Ee, and J. A. Crowell: "Horizontal and vertical disparity, eye position, and stereoscopic slant perception," Vision Research, vol. 39, pp. 1143–1170, 1999.
19. K. Keller, A. State, H. Fuchs, "Head Mounted Displays for Medical Use," Journal of Display Technology, Vol. 4, No. 4, pp. 468–472, 2008.

20. H. Fuchs, M.A. Livingston, R. Raskar, D. Colucci. K. Keller, A. State, J. R. Crawford, P. Rademacher, S. H. Drake, and A. A. Meyer, "Augmented Reality Visualization for Laparoscopic Surgery," in Medical Image Computing and Computer-Assisted Intervention (MICCAI) 1998, LNCS 1496, pp. 934–943, 1998.

21. W. Birkfellner M. Figl, K. Huber, F. Watzinger, F. Wanschitz, J. Hummel, R. Hanel, W. Greimel, P. Homolka, R. Ewers and H. Bergmann, "A head-mounted operating binocular for augmented reality visualization in medicine - Design and initial evaluation," IEEE Trans. Med. Imag., vol. 21, pp. 991–997, Aug. 2002.

22. H. Liao, S. Nakajima, M. Iwahara, E. Kobayashi, I. Sakuma, N. Yahagi, and T. Dohi, "Intra-operative real-time 3-D information display system based on integral videography," The 4th International Conference on Medical Image Computing and Computer assisted Intervention – MICCAI 2001, LNCS 2208, pp. 392–400, 2001.

23. M. G. Lippmann. Epreuves reversibles donnant la sensation du relief, J. de Phys., vol. 7, pp. 821–825, 1908.

24. H. H. Tran, K. Matsumiya, K. Masamune, I. Sakuma, T. Dohi, and H. Liao: Interactive 3D Navigation System for Image-guided Surgery, The International Journal of Virtual Reality, Vol. 8 No. 1, pp. 9–16, 2009.

25. H. Liao, K. Nomura, T. Dohi: Autostereoscopic Integral Photography Imaging using Pixel Distribution of Computer Graphics Generated Image; ACM SIGGRAPH 2005, CD-ROM, Los Angeles, USA, July-August 2005.

26. N. Herlambang, H. Liao, K. Matsumiya, K. Masamune, T. Dohi: Interactive autostereoscopic medical image visualization system using GPU-accelerated integral videography direct volume rendering, International Journal of Computer Assisted Radiology and Surgery, Vol. 3 supp. 1, pp. 110–111, 2008.

27. H. Liao, T. Inomata, I. Sakuma, and T. Dohi: 3-D Augmented Reality for MRI-guided Surgery using Integral Videography Autostereoscopic Image Overlay, IEEE Transactions on Biomedical Engineering, Vol. 57, No. 6, pp. 1476–1486, 2010.

28. F.S. Pereles, H.T. Ozgur, P.J. Lund, E.C. Unger, Potentials of laser guidance system for percutaneous musculoskeletal procedures, Skeletal Radiology, Vol. 26, No. 11, pp. 650–653, 1997.

29. T. Sasama, N. Sugano, Y. Sato, Y. Momoi, Y. Nakajima, T. Koyama, Y. Nakajima, I. Sakuma, M. Fujie, K. Yonenobu, T. Ochi, S. Tamura, "A Novel Laser Guidance System for Alignment of Linear Surgical Tool: Its Principles and Performanve Evaluation as a Man-Machine System," MICCAI 2002, pp. 125–132, 2002.

30. N. Glossop, C. Wedlake, J. Moore, T. Peters, and Z. Wang, "Laser projection augmented reality system for computer assisted surgery," in Proc. Int. Conf. Medical Image Computing and Computer Assisted Intervention (MICCAI), 2003, Lecture Notes in Computer Science, vol. 2879, pp. 239–246, 2003.

31. H. Liao, H. Ishihara, H. H. Tran, K. Masamune, I. Sakuma, T. Dohi, "Precision-guided Surgical Navigation System using Laser Guidance and 3-D Autostereoscopic Image Overlay," Computerized Medical Imaging and Graphics, Vol. 34, No. 1, pp. 46–54, 2010.

Chapter 28
Augmented Reality in Assistive Technology and Rehabilitation Engineering

S.K. Ong, Y. Shen, J. Zhang, and A.Y.C. Nee

1 Introduction

With increasing life expectancy and declining fertility, the ageing population continues to increase worldwide while the population of younger people decreases [1]. The change in the demographic structure would bring greater pressure on long-term health services with increasing population of people who need healthcare and decreasing population of people who can be part of the work force. It is expected that the proportion of people aged above 60 years old would reach 19% by 2050 [2], and there would be a growing proportion of individuals who suffer from disabilities due to illnesses related to ageing. Therefore, there is increasing demand for Assistive Technology (AT) devices and Rehabilitation Engineering (RE) applications and researches in AT and RE have received more attention.

AT devices facilitate the elderly and the people with disabilities to perform tasks that they have difficulties to accomplish. Such devices can partially solve the problems caused by the increasing population of the aged persons. RE devices and applications allow the elderly and physically disabled individuals to perform rehabilitation therapies to recover certain capabilities. With AT and RE, the independent living ability of the aged persons can be enhanced and the cost in healthcare can be reduced. With low-cost portable AT and RE devices, the elderly individuals can live in their present residence independently without relocating to different care facilities and leaving their familiar communities. This would further improve the quality of life of the elderly.

With the developments in computer science and information technology, new and emerging technologies have been applied in AT and RE to provide better solutions and improve the end-user experience. Augmented Reality (AR) is a technology which superimposes computer generated virtual objects onto the physical world in

S.K. Ong (✉)
Department of Mechanical Engineering, National University of Singapore, Singapore
e-mail: mpeongsk@nus.edu.sg

B. Furht (ed.), *Handbook of Augmented Reality*, DOI 10.1007/978-1-4614-0064-6_28,   603
© Springer Science+Business Media, LLC 2011

real time [3]. Different from Virtual Reality (VR) in which the user is fully immersed in a virtual environment, AR does not replace the real world but augments a user's view of the real world with virtual objects. In an AR environment, the real and virtual objects coexist in the real world and the user can interact with the real/virtual objects. Applying AR technology in AT and RE is a new paradigm for the research in AT and RE. AR-based AT and RE devices provide a more controllable augmented environment, where the users can have more realism feeling and interact in a more intuitive way. With these characteristics, AR-based AT and RE devices are potential solutions for providing more effective caring services and recovery treatments.

There is increasing research interest in the application of AR in AT and RE fields. This research is multi-disciplinary fusing technologies of sensors, computer vision, wireless communication, etc. To date, there is no survey on the applications of AR in AT and RE fields. This chapter is prepared to fill this gap and provide a general introduction of the current studies. This chapter firstly presents the applications of AR in the AT and RE fields focusing on the methods and application aspects. After this, the advantages and limitations of applying AR technology in these applications are discussed.

2 Applications of AR in AT and RE

Many AT and RE systems have been developed in the last decade, and it has been proven that AT and RE systems can greatly improve the quality of life of the people with disabilities [4]. Several different schemes have been used to classify assistive and rehabilitative devices; one common classification scheme is based on the functions provided by these devices, such as in learning, walking or eating. This classification scheme is especially useful for the end users with specific requirements during the purchasing process. O'Brien and Ruairí [5] categorized the AT devices based on the device and application types. With this scheme, devices may be classified in the same category based on the device types and in different categories based on the applications types. The advantage of this scheme is that both the technologies and application contexts of these devices can be introduced logically, and the relationships between these devices can be clearly illustrated.

This review focuses on the application of AR in AT and RE, where there are different types of augmentations provided to the users to enhance the performance of these services. AR-based AT devices are mainly devices that would ease the independent living of the users, and AR-based RE devices and applications would concentrate on the methods to recover the mental or motor functions. Based on the applications of existing studies, research in AR-based AT can be classified into systems for (1) visually impaired persons, (2) hearing impaired persons, (3) facilitating the learning process of physically disabled persons and (4) computer interaction. Research in AR-based RE can be classified into the recovery of motor functions and the recovery of mental functions.

Previously, systems designed without augmenting the real world in the sense of sight cannot be classified as AR applications [3]. However, nowadays the definition of AR is not limited to the sense of sight and has been extended to include other senses such as hearing and touching [6].

2.1 AR in AT

Table 28.1 summarizes most of the existing researches in the application of AR in AT.

2.1.1 Visually Impaired Persons

The lack of sight would cause a lot of challenges in the tasks of daily living, such as information access, way-finding and interaction with other people. The traditional AT systems are mainly in three areas, namely information access, navigation and computer access [7], in which information access mainly refers to accessing information from printed materials.

Table 28.2 shows the applications and related devices of traditional AT systems used by visually impaired persons. These systems share the same working principle: they collect information from the environment and display the information in other senses, such as hearing and touching.

The limitation in the AT systems designed for navigation is that the users will stand out from ordinary people as blind persons. AT systems which are inconspicuous or non-intrusive are highly desired by the blind. Another problem with these AT systems for navigation is the unavailability of the route selection function. Nowadays, with the development of GPS and computer vision technologies, more advanced navigation systems have been designed for the vision impaired persons. The concept of AR has been implemented in some of these systems.

NAVIG is a multidisciplinary project designed for individuals with low vision to support navigation and object localization [8, 9]. In this project, an Ultra Mobile PC is used and video images are captured using a webcam with a resolution of 320×240. A bio-inspired image processing algorithm is designed to support robust and rapid recognition of selected objects in the images. This algorithm can calculate the optic flow in real-time based on neurobiological principles to support the grasping of desired objects without attaching any sensors to the objects. This method determines the motion between two image frames at every pixel by calculating the edge energy and luminance change. The audio feedbacks are augmented through headphones. This project allows the users with impaired vision to navigate indoor and outdoor, in known and unknown environment with the functions of object recognition, obstacle detection and route selection.

In the project by Toledo et al. [10], the Field Programmable Gate Array (FPGA) based AR application has been developed for people affected by tunnel vision in

Table 28.1 Applications of AR in AT

Applications	User groups	Functions	Methodologies	Characteristics	Limitations
NAVIG [8, 9]	Visually impaired persons	Support daily activities, e.g., navigation and object localization	• Bio-inspired image processing algorithm • Route selection algorithm • Audio feedback	• Real-time data gathering • Feedbacks augmentation	• Heavy stereoscopic camera mounted on the head
Toledo et al. [10]	People affected by tunnel vision	Enable visualization of image patches positioned around the peripheral vision	• Display minified images at the center • Augment the contours	• Contours to enhance the contrast • Light weight devices	• Special hardware configuration
LookTel [11]	Visually impaired persons	Support daily tasks, e.g., object recognition and navigation	• Object recognition through image matching on the server • Remote sighted assistance	• Recognize all objects through training • Remote monitoring to support complicated tasks • Smartphone	• Lack of personal privacy
NSVI [12, 13]	Visually impaired persons	Provide orientation information to approach user-defined destinations	• Marker detection using computer vision • ZigBee for wireless communication	• Map-less • Invisible markers	• Prepared environment • Dynamic information cannot be detected
Zhang et al. [14]	Visually impaired persons	Detect the road surface reflectance and obstacles	• Two IR proximity sensors and a long range distance sensor • Vibration feedback	• Shoe-mounted device • Hand-free configuration • Low cost	• Wired data communication • Not suitable for everyday wear

AudioNav [15]	Visually impaired persons	Indoor navigation	• 3D model of the building • Dead reckoning approach • Probabilistic localization scheme	• Infrastructure-free • Low cost • Portable device • Augment audio and haptic feedback	• Cannot be used for outdoor navigation due to the accumulated errors
Nishioka [16]	Hearing impaired persons	Guarantee the perception of acoustic information	• Augment the text or movie on a HMD	• Hand-free • No viewpoint shifting	• Rich contents cannot be displayed
BabelFisk [17]	Hearing impaired persons	Facilitate the translation of speech	• Designed as a pair of glasses	• Hand-free • No viewpoint shifting • Fashionable design	• Only text information can be projected
CONNECT [20]	Physically disabled persons	Facilitate their learning	• Mobile augmented environment • Web-based streaming	• Interactive learning environment • User-centered learning experience	• Uncomfortable backpack
Lin and Chao [21]	Physically disabled children	Facilitate their learning	• Virtual object rendered on markers • Sounds augmentation	• Interactive media • User-centered learning experience • Low cost	• Only simple learning activities are supported
Chi et al. [22]	Physically disabled with neck movements	Facilitate interaction with computers and electrical appliances	• An inertial sensor to detect head movements • An eyebrow switch	• Wearable devices • Slight body movements are needed	• Training is needed to control the sensors
Gao et al. [23]	Physically disabled with speech	Facilitate interaction with computers and electrical appliances	• Speech recognition • Virtual interface is augmented	• Body movements are not required	• Easily affected by the noises

Table 28.2 Traditional AT
systems for visually impaired
persons

Applications	Related technologies
Information access	Braillers, magnifiers, large-print books
Navigation	White cane, seeing-dog
Computer access	Screen reader, voice synthesizer

which the central vision is clear while the peripheral vision is lost. The working principle is to display minified images to the user at the position around the central vision. To ensure the minified image is still visible, image processing technology is used to extract the contour information from the environment and augment this contour information onto the user's view. The contours of the captured images are extracted using the Canny edge detection algorithm. With the FPGA chip and the cellular neural network, the performance of the system can be real-time ensuring that the user's perception of the environment can be improved effectively. In this project, a Sony Glasstron PLM S700E Head-Mounted Display (HMD) is used to display the augmented videos and a monochrome digital camera is used to capture the images.

LookTel [11] is an AR scanning service provided through mobile phones. This service can recognize everyday objects with image recognition technology. AR is used in this application service as a media to augment audio feedback to the users. Through this application, a remote assistant can monitor the images captured by the cell phone camera in real-time and guide the navigation of the user using descriptions. In this way, the vision impaired user can interact with everyday objects and navigate safely.

Zhang et al. [12] presented a survey on the navigation systems for the visual impaired (NSVI) and categorized these systems into those based on the positioning-based method, Radio Frequency Identification (RFID) tag-based method and vision-based method. They [13] proposed an AR-based map-less NSVI system for indoor and outdoor navigation based on vision-based methods. In this system, an infrared emission material is used to make invisible markers for detecting the orientation of the objects in the surrounding of the users. This system fuses infrared, computer vision and inertial technologies to provided user-centric orientation information for approaching user-defined destinations. During navigation, navigational information is only provided at decision-making locations indicated by invisible markers, as shown in Fig. 28.1. ZigBee technology is used for wireless communication between the location nodes and the user.

Zhang et al. [14] have developed a shoe-mounted device to facilitate the navigation of visually impaired individuals. This device consists of a sensor unit and a feedback unit, as shown in Fig. 28.2. The shoe-mounted device detects the road surface reflectance and obstacles using two Infrared (IR) proximity sensors and a long range distance sensor. Vibration feedback is augmented on the user when these different contexts are detected. This device is designed to be a hand-free configuration to supplement the functions provided by the white cane during navigation.

AudioNav [15] is a low-cost indoor navigation system for visually impaired individuals without embedding any expensive sensors into the environment, such

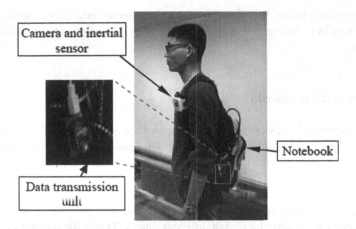

Fig. 28.1 The backpack worn by a user [13]

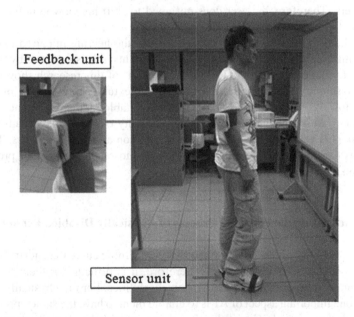

Fig. 28.2 Illustration by a subject [14]

as infrared, Bluetooth, ultrasonic sensors or radio frequency identifier tags. This system is implemented on an Android phone. Dead reckoning approach is employed to estimate the current position based on a previously determined position with the speed, time and course estimated using a 3D model of the building and the information detected using the inertial sensors. The feedbacks provided by the user about the presence of landmarks are used with a probabilistic localization scheme to obtain better path planning by minimizing uncertainties. The system will provide step-by-step instructions to approach the destination using voice or haptic feedback.

2.1.2 Hearing Impaired Persons

The conventional AT devices for hearing impaired persons are usually to amplify the auditory signals or transform speech to text. These existing devices include hearing aids, phone amplifiers, etc. The alerts or alarms are usually sent to the users using flashing lights.

In the conventional AT devices designed for persons whose hearing is seriously impaired, the textual information provided to these users and the contexts that the users perceive are always located in different places. This is the motivation to apply AR technology in AT devices designed for hearing impaired persons. Using HMD, information in the forms of text, image or video can be augmented onto the view of the users. Therefore, the user does not need to shift his viewpoint between the objects and information augmented.

Nishioka [16] introduced an approach to help the hearing impaired understand acoustic information without shifting their viewpoints; this is achieved by augmenting the information through the HMDs. The results of this research show that it is difficult to support rich contents, such as movie or textural captions for a long period of time. However, the AR-based AT devices are suitable for displaying the signaling information. This is mainly because of the visibility of the displayed information. BabelFisk [17] is designed with the same motivation as a pair of glasses. This pair of glasses can take spoken speech, translate it into readable text and project the translation onto the glasses instantly.

2.1.3 Facilitating the Learning Process of Physically Disabled Persons

Physically disabled children always have longer learning curve than normal children and require more technical support. Therefore, it is difficult for them to join the mainstream education facilities due to their disabilities. For the physically disabled persons, one important aspect of AT is to enable them to have the same opportunities as the normal individuals. Currently, AT services provided in the schools are mainly to facilitate the communication, information access and navigation, which are almost the same as the AT services provided to facilitate the daily living at home. The only difference is that the special requirements in school are considered, such as the training of the teachers and the layout of the classrooms.

VR has been proven to be effective for educational purposes with its high interactivity and the ability to present a virtual environment in which the learners can be immersed [18]. With VR, a user-centered learning experience can be provided. Integrating VR technology and Internet, novel e-Learning systems have been developed to provide good social environments and enable the students with disabilities to participate in some social activities, such as going for a walk or climbing a mountain, in the virtual environment [19]. The limitation in these VR-based learning environments is that the users are immersed in a virtual environment and personal interaction is reduced.

With virtual objects augmented onto the physical world, AR can also provide an interactive and user-centered environment, while more realism feeling can be provided in AR systems. In these AR-based systems, the users can visualize the real world and interact with people around them. In an AR environment, real objects can be used to facilitate the interaction.

The CONNECT project [20] aims to create a learning environment in which students with physical disabilities can interact physically and virtually with the materials they are learning. In CONNECT, the learners can remotely visit museums through web streaming as there is a network setup between museums, science centers and schools. A wearable system is designed to support the augmentation of graphics and videos in real time. In the wearable system, a DELL Precision M60 notebook is included, and the HMD used is an i-glass SVGA 3D Pro. The evaluation results demonstrated that although the CONNECT system is helpful in learning for handicapped and normal students, they may feel uncomfortable wearing the CONNECT system and the perception of discomfort can be observed in almost all subjects due to the design of the HMD.

The system reported by Lin and Chao [21] aims to offer new teaching aids in special education by providing real-time assistance using AR technology. AR tags are designed as picture cards, and these tags are tracked and recognized using the ARToolkit library. Once an AR tag is recognized, the system will retrieve the corresponding ID component in the database and play the corresponding sound file in real time. Based on the user experience, the researchers concluded that this system makes learning easier and more interesting for children with special needs by providing a user-centered learning experience.

2.1.4 Computer Interactions

Computers and information technology are becoming increasingly more important in improving the quality of life of the disabled. With computer and information technologies, the disabled are able to maintain their integration with the society, reinforce their ability of independent living and have control over their environment. The major barrier to the use of computers and information technologies by the elderly or people with disabilities is the lack of good interfaces which can be manipulated easily

Chi et al. [22] have developed a wearable system to emulate the mouse and keyboard, facilitating the disabled to interact with the computer and control home appliances. This configuration of the system is shown in Fig. 28.3. In this system, an inertial sensor, InterTrax2, is attached to the head of the user to measure the

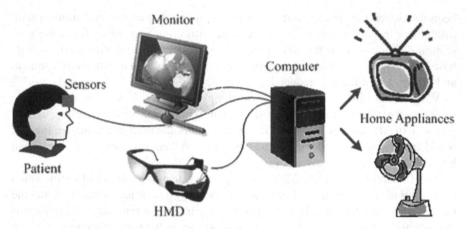

Fig. 28.3 System configuration [22]

head movements. Head movements are mapped to the pixels displayed on the monitor to control the movements of the cursor. An eyebrow switch is attached to a lightweight, adjustable head worn visor, and it can be activated by the user raising his eyebrow. With the inertial sensor, the interface is robust and would not be affected by changes in the environment. Another advantage of this system is that very slight body movements are needed to control the movements of the cursor. The developed system is especially useful for individuals who can only control slight movements of his body.

Gao et al. [23] proposed an interface to facilitate communication between the computers and the disabled based on speech recognition. In this system, the disabled can control home appliances, e.g., TV and fan, using voice commands. A mouse and keyboard emulator has also been developed to help the disabled individuals to access computer applications. A virtual interface designed to access the computer application or control the appliances is augmented into the view of the user and the cursor is controlled by voice to interact with the buttons on the virtual interface (Fig. 28.4). This system is especially useful for the disabled who have difficulties in controlling body movements but the speech ability is not impaired.

2.2 AR in RE

Rehabilitation engineering applications are specially designed to recover certain impaired functions of individuals with disabilities. The applications of AR in RE can be briefly classified into two classes, namely systems to recover motor functions and systems to recover mental functions. Table 28.3 summarises researches in the application of AR technology in developing rehabilitation systems.

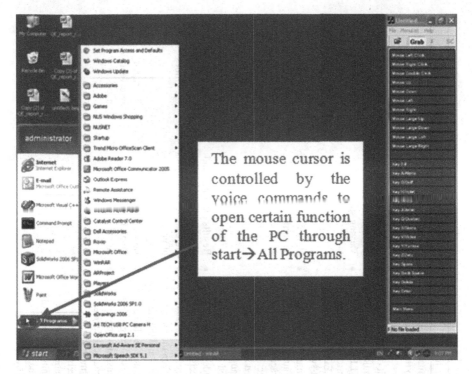

The mouse cursor is controlled by the voice commands to open certain function of the PC through start→All Programs.

Fig. 28.4 AR interface with mouse emulator [23]

2.2.1 Related Technologies

The traditional rehabilitation processes to recover motor functions are usually carried out with external devices, such as the nine-hole pegboards and the exercise hand skate, and repetitive practices. Traditional rehabilitation to treat mental problems is usually done with *in-vivo* exposure. In these systems, the exercises are closely monitored by the therapist assistants. The first limitation in the traditional RE systems is boredom. This limitation is usually observed in rehabilitation systems requiring intensive practice. Tedious practices without fun and entertainment tend to reduce the motivation of the patients. The second limitation is these rehabilitation systems are expensive. A one-to-one rehabilitation program would impose considerable financial burden on the patients and makes it difficult for them to undergo the practices needed to effect neural and functional changes. The third limitation is there is no data collection function in these systems. In conventional rehabilitation systems, the simple exercising devices are designed without sensors and cannot collect digital information about the performance.

VR-based rehabilitation systems have been explored and developed to address these limitations. The earliest applications of VR in therapy are to treat psychological problems, such as flying phobia [24], driving phobia [25], spider phobia

Table 28.3 Applications of AR in RE

Applications	User groups	Functions	Methodologies	Characteristics	Limitations
Weghorst [37]	Patients with Parkinson's disease	Facilitate a more normal gait pattern	• Augment visual cues onto the real scene	• Virtual objects augmented	• Extra expense due to HMD
Ferrarin et al. [38]			• Emit optical stimulation using two LED matrices • Control the flashing of LEDs using foot-switches	• Designed as a pair of glasses • Varying stimulus	• Position of stimulus is not where the feet are
Espay et al. [39]			• Augment optical flow and auditory cues • Use accelerometer to detect the walking speed and control the augmentation speed	• Virtual floor appears to be earth-stationary	• Extra expense due to the see-through HMD
David [40]	Stroke survivors	Improve their walking	• Render virtual objects • Detect the collision between the virtual objects and the feet	• Results recording and analysis • Adjustable dimensions of virtual obstacles	• The exercises have to be conducted in the clinics
Luo et al. [41, 42]	Stroke survivors	Hand opening and finger extension	• Measure the force and assist finger extension using mechanical devices • Augment virtual objects and dynamic feedbacks • Monitor and control by the therapist locally or remotely	• Low cost • Small in size • Home or clinics use	• Therapist intervention is necessary

Sucar et al. [43]	Stroke survivors	Improve hand movements	• Web-based system • Detect arm movements in 3D using computer vision	• Low cost • Reduced therapist intervention	• Cannot detect finger movements • Simple exercising scenarios
AR-REHAB [44–46]	Stroke survivors	Improve hand movements	• Use markers to render virtual objects and track hand movements • Support the training of daily activity	• Tangible-object concept • Minimized therapist intervention	• Everyday objects used in the training are virtual
Burke et al. [47]	Stroke survivors	Upper-limb rehabilitation	• Use markers to render everyday objects • Develop two game prototypes	• Considering the principles in game designs • Low cost	• Everyday objects used in the training are virtual
King et al. [49]	Stroke survivors	Upper-limb rehabilitation	• Use markers for rendering and interaction • Develop a reaching task	• Entertaining computer games • Adjustable forces	• More games are desired
Wang et al. [50]	Patients with hand muscle problems	Hand rehabilitation	• Use an air pressure detecting device to detect the physical condition of patients • Use a real entity to support the interaction	• High interactivity • High entertainment • Tactile feedback	• No data recording
Correa et al. [52, 53]	Patients with physical problems in hands	Hand rehabilitation	• Use color cards with musical symbols as markers • Occlusion based interaction	• Low cost • Adjustable keys • Home use	• Little effect for individual with low mobility

(continued)

Table 28.3 (continued)

Applications	User groups	Functions	Methodologies	Characteristics	Limitations
Zhang et al. [56]	Stroke survivors	Recover the motor functions of upper limb	• Use self-designed data-glove to measure the flexing of fingers • Marker-based rendering and interaction	• Low cost • High interactivity • High entertainment • Home use	• The movements of the thumb cannot be detected
Shen et al. [57]	Patients with impairments in hands	Improve the moving range of the hand	• Computer vision based interaction with bare hand	• Low cost • No external devices	• A specific gesture needs to be maintained
Hoffman et al. [58]	Patients with spider phobia	Treat the spider phobia	• Provide tactile feedback using a tracked toy spider	• Tactile augmentation • Enhanced realism feeling	• The lack of convincing user studies
Juan et al. [59–61]	Patients with phobia to small animals	Threat the phobia to small animals	• Display virtual small animals • Expose the patient in the augmented environment	• Low cost	• The lack of convincing user studies
Richard et al. [63]	Cognitive disabled children	Train the ability of object matching	• Markers based rendering and interaction • Visual, olfactory or auditory cues	• Simple and intuitive interaction	• Complex hardware set-up
O'Neill et al. [64]	Amputees	Alleviate phantom limb pain	• Augment the virtual arm • Use commercial data-glove to detect the movements of intact arm	• Able to display all types of phantom limbs • Support more general movements	• Do not support patients with two amputated limbs • More expensive than traditional mirror box

[26], acrophobia [27], agoraphobia [28], claustrophobia [29], etc. Besides these applications in removing phobias, Jo et al. [30] demonstrated that VR is also useful in treating public speaking anxiety. In this study, the Virtual Environment (VE) is a seminar room with a virtual audience consisting of six persons. The virtual audience would respond with some motions to the speaker and the responses are controlled by the therapist. From these works, it can be concluded that the principle to remove phobia using VR therapy is to simulate the real situations which would bring fears to the patients and to expose these patients to this environment gradually. The main advantages of VR therapy over the traditional therapy in phobia management are: (1) the therapy can be performed in the therapist's office; (2) the features of VE, such as the difficulty levels and contexts are totally controllable by the patient or the therapist; and (3) it is possible to create situations which are impossible or nonexistent in the real world. VR therapy has also been used to distract patients and work as a virtual pain relief.

Another important application of VR is in the field of cognitive rehabilitation for people with brain injury and neurological disorders. It has been used for the enhancement of functional ability, improving sensory, motor and cognitive functions. Most of the existing research focuses on investigating the use of VR in the assessment of cognitive abilities. However, there are increasing studies concentrating on the use of VR training in rehabilitation nowadays [31].

Virtual Classroom [32] was developed for the assessment and rehabilitation of students with attention deficits. In this system, the patients with HMDs are immersed in the VE of a classroom scenario with typical distractions. The study by Brooks et al. [33] sought to use VR to train a patient with amnesia in route finding around a hospital rehabilitation unit for memory impairing rehabilitation.

Besides these applications on mental disorder, VR has also been successfully applied for motor disorder. In the study of treating Parkinson's Disease (PD) with VR [34], the gait of PD patients is maintained by presenting virtual stepping stones in their views using a head-up display.

Robot training using a VE has recently been shown to enhance stroke rehabilitation [35]. The motor function of the affected arm can be improved following a robot-assisted sensorimotor activity of that arm. Jack et al. [36] have developed a VR system for rehabilitation of hand functions of stroke patients. The patients can interact in a VE using two input devices, i.e., a cyber-glove and a Rutgers master II-ND force feedback glove. In this system, several simple games in a VE are designed according to the training targets to motivate the users to do more exercises. The main advantage of VR-based rehabilitation over traditional therapy in motor disorder is that in VE, the intensity of feedback and training is totally controllable by the patients or therapists to fit the patients' current physical situations. In addition, patients are motivated by the novel and entertaining nature of the experience.

One disadvantage of VR-based rehabilitation would be that the movement of the body parts and the interaction with the virtual objects are in independent coordinate references. The patients have to map the movements of the hand to the movements of the avatars themselves, which would affect the effectiveness of these rehabilitation systems. In addition, in VR-based rehabilitation, the extent to which people experience this feeling of "presence" is limited as they are immersed in a computer-generated environment.

Compared with VR-based rehabilitation, AR-based rehabilitation is still in the exploratory stage and there are fewer known studies in this field. AR and VR share some common advantages with respect to traditional rehabilitation treatment. However, AR also presents additional advantages compared to VR. The prominent advantage of AR over VR therapy is that in an AR environment, the user can view the real world and real objects can be used as stimuli for the therapy. In the AR environment, it is possible to keep the physical movements and interacting activities consistent.

2.2.2 Recovery of Motor Functions

There are several applications of AR in the rehabilitation of motor disorder. AR has been applied as a tool to facilitate a more normal gait pattern for the patients with Parkinson's disease (PD) [37]. In this system, AR is used to present visual cues overlapping the real visual scene during the walking of the patients using HMDs. Ferrarin et al. [38] have also reported a microprocessor-controlled device that is designed as a pair of portable glasses to improve the gait of patients with PD. This device can augment optical stimulations to the views of subjects with PD to prevent freezing episodes and improve their gait pattern. These glasses are equipped with two Light-Emitting Diode (LED) matrices, one on each side and controlled using a microcontroller. Foot-switches are used to synchronize the flashing of the LEDs with the gait patterns. The research by Espay et al. [39] to improve gait pattern of patients with PD is based on similar working principles [37, 38]. The optical flow and the auditory cues are augmented at a speed that is proportional to the walking speed of the user. The walking speed is measured in real time by the accelerometer which is worn by the patient. Therefore, the augmented visual cues appear to be stationary with reference to the Earth.

David [40] has investigated the application of AR in improving the walking of stroke survivors. Virtual objects are presented to the patients walking on a treadmill. These patients have to step over the virtual objects without colliding with these virtual objects. The training results are recorded and analyzed. From the training results, it was concluded that the improvements of the patients receiving AR training is better than those who trained using real objects. In addition, AR training is potentially more beneficial as the virtual obstacles' height and length can be adjusted at anytime.

A few AR-based hand motion rehabilitation systems have been reported in which the user can view the real world and real objects can be used as stimuli for the therapeutic exercises. Luo et al. [41] have developed a rehabilitation system integrating AR and assistive devices for hand opening actions of stroke survivors. In this system, repetitive practice in an AR environment is supported with mechanical devices, i.e., a body-powered orthosis and a pneumatic-powered device. Dynamic feedbacks of the subject performance are provided in the form of force record and waveform on the computer screen. The devices are relatively low-cost and small in size to be used in clinics and at home. With the same system configuration, Luo et al. [42] have also designed a rehabilitation system to facilitate the performance of the grasp-and-release tasks. With this system, a user without muscle strength can move virtual objects without difficulties. At the same time, the user can see his real hand existing in the virtual environment.

Sucar et al. [43] have proposed a web-based gesture therapy system using AR technology to provide intensive motion training at low cost. Two inexpensive cameras are used to track the 3D movements of the user's hand. The hand region is represented as a rectangle and tracked using the skin color. Visual feedback of the patient's performance is provided and the practice progress is illustrated through a simple statistical chart. Due to the tracking method employed, the system can only track the movement of the hand and cannot detect the flexing of the fingers. In addition, the designed exercising scenarios are only for the upward and downward movements of the user's hand.

AR-REHAB [44–46] is a rehabilitation system based on AR to increase the immersive feeling of the post-stroke patients. A tangible-object concept is implemented to provide interaction with everyday objects. Fiducial markers are used to render the virtual objects seamlessly onto the real environment and track the hand movements of the patient. These movements will be analyzed subsequently to evaluate the performance progress of the patient. A usability study based on two exercises which were designed based on daily activities has been conducted. The two exercises are a shelf exercise, which aims to recover the user's ability of placing and removing objects on a shelf, and a cup exercise, which is to evaluate the ability of the user to follow a predefined visual path. The recorded parameters include the completion time, compactness of the completion and the speed of the hand movements. In this rehabilitation system, seven performance measurements are used to design a decision model to monitor the progress of the patient automatically. The progress of the patient is monitored continuously and alerts are sent to the remote therapist only under several scenarios. In this way, the supervision of the therapist can be minimized.

AR-based games have been reported to support the rehabilitation of the upper limb [47]. In this project, AR markers are used to augment everyday objects and track the movements of these objects. This project takes into consideration the principles in game designs to enhance the user engagement. Two game prototypes were developed to provide treatment. Several issues, such as the mounting position of the camera, the depth perception, marker occlusion and illumination in the environment are identified, as the problems to be addressed in future research to produce a user-friendly rehabilitation interface. There are other rehabilitation systems based on fiducial markers [48,49]. The working principle of these systems is similar and they detect the interaction between the body parts and the virtual objects using markers. The system designed by King et al. [49] is for stroke survivors and it is a table-based system. A reaching task is motivated by a computer game to catch flying butterflies. A computer mouse/arm skate with variable resistance is developed in this system to provide intensified exercises.

Wang et al. [50] have developed a system based on AR and an air pressure detecting device. A real entity is held by the user to interact with a fish tank computer game which can promote hand joint activity and enhance muscle strength. Based on the physical condition of the user, which is measured using pressure sensing devices, the parameters of the game are adjusted to ensure that patients with different extents of hand impairments can interact with the game.

Music therapy has been established as one of the clinical-therapeutic methods with its ability to promote positive cognitive and physical changes in individuals with health problems [51]. Correa et al. [52,53] have created a system based on AR to facilitate the music access of disabled individuals. In this system, the users can compose, edit and play music. Markers from ARToolkit are used to simulate virtual music instruments and the users can play the instruments by occluding the markers using fingers. Different instrument sounds and pitches are recorded in the system. The advantages of the system are that patients without muscle strength can use this system, there is no external devices attached to the user hands and this system can be used easily at home. A child with cerebral palsy has used the system and the results are promising, which show that the system can offer therapeutic interventions.

The AR Piano Tutor is an AR application involving virtual objects augmented onto a real MIDI keyboard in a video captured scene which represents the user's viewpoint [54]. The keyboard is connected to a computer via a MIDI interface which captures the order and timing of the piano key strokes. In this way, the programme can check how well a user is doing and give instant visual feedback using graphics superimposed over the keyboard. Since the user is playing directly on a real keyboard, this application offers the same features as the PianoVR system [55] without the disconnection feeling. However, the disadvantage is that a real keyboard would have to be used and thus the portability of the application is limited. In addition, with regards to the rehabilitation purposes of the AR Piano Tutor, a patient with limited finger strength and control may not be able to depress the physical keys.

A similar project has been reported by Zhang et al. [56] in which a virtual piano is augmented onto the real environment and a self-designed data-glove with flex sensors is used to measure the flexing angles of the fingers. By measuring the flexing angles of the fingers, the movements of the virtual hand augmented onto the view are kept consistent with those of the real hand. Based on the tracking methods provided by ARToolkit, the spatial relationship between the virtual piano and fingers can be detected. Monitoring the position of the real hands and the flexing of the fingers, the corresponding key under the flexed finger will be depressed and the corresponding sound file played. Two difficulty levels are designed in the recovery programs to provide suitable challenges to the patients. A view of the project is illustrated in Fig. 28.5.

Shen et al. [57] have developed a bare hand interaction method for rehabilitation. In the rehabilitation system, the user is required to move his hand to catch a falling ball. When the distance between the hand and the ball is shorter than a threshold,

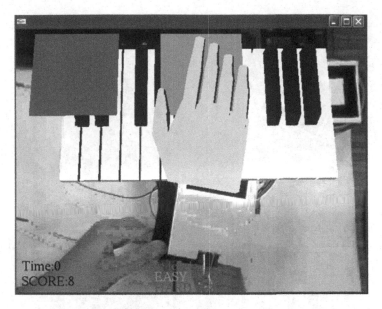

Fig. 28.5   Rendering a piano in real environment [56]

the system will determine that the ball has been caught and the color of the ball will be changed. Figure 28.6 illustrates the process to catch a falling ball using bare hand. The rehabilitation system based on bare hand has many advantages, such as low cost, no external device and easy setup. However in the current system, the user needs to maintain a specific gesture which is recognized by the system to interact with the virtual objects. This may make the user feel tired and frustrated. Advanced gesture recognition algorithms to recognize everyday living activities are expected to put the rehabilitation system based on bare hand into practice.

From these existing works, it can be concluded that an effective rehabilitation system for motor functions recovery should (1) provide intensive practice at low cost, (2) provide salient feedbacks with respect to the physical actions of the users, and (3) provide an intuitive interface to the patient or therapist.

2.2.3   Recovery of Mental Functions

Rehabilitation applications have been developed for recovery of psychological conditions. An AR therapy system has been developed for the treatment of spider phobia [58]. In this study, they used tactile augmentation by presenting a tracked toy spider in the scene to enhance the user's presence and realism during the therapy. The results of the three treatment conditions, i.e., no therapy, VR therapy and AR therapy, demonstrate that patients who received the AR therapy have the greatest improvement.

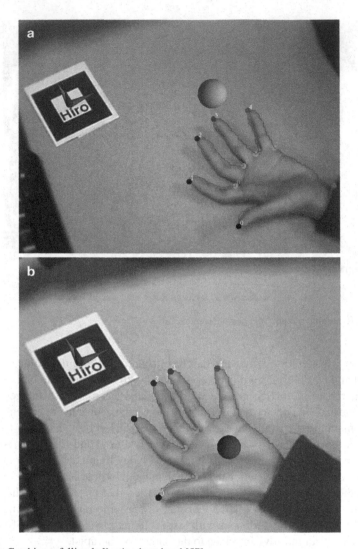

Fig. 28.6 Catching a falling ball using bare hand [57]

Juan et al. have developed a prototype to use AR for treatment of phobia to cockroaches [59] and acrophobia [60]. It is believed that AR can provide a higher level of realism at a lower cost than VR. Juan et al. [61] reported another system designed to treat phobia to small animals using an optical see-through (OST) approach and an infra-red camera. The virtual small animals rendered are spiders and cockroaches whose 3D models were modeled using Autodesk 3D Studio Max. In this research, they carried out an experiment to compare the effectiveness of the systems based on the OST approach and the video see-through approach (VST). The comparison results show that an OST AR system performs slightly better than the VST AR system in provoking the anxiety. In this project, the LiteEye-500 monocular OST HMD is used. One of the limitations in the above studies on the treatment of phobia is the lack of convincing good user studies. Botella et al. [62] conducted long-term and short-term user studies to evaluate the usability of an AR system in the treatment of cockroach phobia with six subjects. The results are promising and there are prominent improvements for all subjects after the treatment.

Rechard et al. [63] reported an educational AR system named ARVe which allows children with cognitive problems to handle plant entities. The plant entities are virtually rendered onto fiducial markers. The children have to complete the matching task based on the visual, olfactory or auditory cues provided by the system. A video projector is used to render the augmented scene. The completion time of the task at each stage is recorded. The results with the disabled children are very encouraging

U Neill et al. [64] used AR to treat phantom limb pain in amputees. Using AR, the amputees can view and control the motion of their phantom limb to relieve the pain. Their work has demonstrated that AR has the ability to change a person's sensory experience. Compared with traditional therapy, AR therapy has the advantage of providing all types of phantom limbs to resemble the phantom limb of a patient. In addition, AR therapy would give the amputees the feeling that the limbs are under control by providing more general movements of the phantom limbs.

3 Discussions

In this section, the advantages and limitations of the application of AR in AT and RE system are discussed.

3.1 Advantages in the Application of AR in AT and RE

There are several advantages of applying AR in AT and RE systems due mainly to the characteristics of the AR technology. These advantages are discussed with respect to AT and RE systems in the following sections.

3.1.1 Programmable Augmented Environment

Systems based on AR technology provide a programmable environment that can be controlled and adjusted easily. Therefore, the RE systems based on AR technology can provide salient feedbacks easily, which is helpful in promoting more intensive practices and enhancing the effectiveness of the recovering systems. In addition, the AR applications designed for AT and RE can be customized easily to meet the requirements of patients with different physical conditions. Considering the continuous changes in the physical conditions of the patients, which may be due to intensive recovery exercises, an adjusted system is especially important.

Compared to VR-based AT and RE systems, there are real objects and virtual objects coexisting in AR systems. Therefore, AR systems can retain the advantages of VR systems, such as controllable environment and salient feedbacks with less modeling time in the environment [65].

3.1.2 Intuitive Interface

With virtual objects augmenting over the real objects, a more intuitive and engaging experience can be provided in an AR environment. In some systems discussed [44–46], it has been observed that the patients can manipulate virtual objects in a natural way to learn daily living activities.

With real objects in their view, the patients would have more realism feeling and the real objects can be used to provide tactile feedback [44]. The haptic feeling provided by real objects is more natural. In addition, there are no cumbersome external devices attached to the hand.

In an AR environment, the spatial relationships between the augmented information and the real objects can be indicated clearly using visual cues. This property has been applied to design AT devices for the hearing impaired [16, 17].

3.2 Limitations in the Application of AR in AT and RE

There are a few limitations in the applications of AR in AT and RE due mainly to the challenges in the supporting technologies.

3.2.1 Haptic Feedback

Haptic feedback generally refers to the vibrations or forces that are experienced by an individual through touch. There are three reasons to provide haptic feedback during the recovering treatment [66], which are namely, (1) haptic feedback is important for specific patients, such as when the patients need to strengthen muscle and blind children need to receive the perceptual training; (2) higher level of realism feeling can be provided with haptic feedback; and (3) multimodal feedbacks would enhance the recovery performance. In some rehabilitation systems, real objects are used to provide tactile feedback [44, 53]. Some specific haptic feedbacks cannot be simulated without external devices, such as the stretching force.

3.2.2 Depth Perception

In AR systems, it is difficult to perceive depth in the scene. This would decrease the performance of the rehabilitation systems, which are designed to train the movements of the patients in the 3D space. When patients cannot perceive the depth of the view, it is difficult for them to reach the desired positions in the 3D space. In some systems [47], shadows or visual aids are augmented to improve depth perception.

3.2.3 Tracking in Unprepared Environment

Accurate tracking is required in AR systems to superimpose the virtual objects seamlessly onto the real world. Tracking in an unprepared environment still remains a challenge in AR technology as the environment cannot be controlled and various factors need to be considered [67]. All existing AR applications in AT and RE are based on the tracking methods for a prepared environment. This may be a limitation for AT devices that are designed to support navigation.

3.2.4 Social Acceptance

Social acceptance remains a challenge for most of the AT and RE systems based on AR. The sizes of most existing HMDs are relatively large and cannot be accepted socially. Nowadays, more fashionable HMDs with smaller sizes have been produced. In another aspect, the peripheral devices for used with these systems should be minimized and hidden from the people around. Arvanitis et al. [20] have observed that some of the subjects felt embarrassed and uneasy with the bulky wearable systems while visiting the museum.

4 Conclusion

Studies in the research and application of AR in AT and RE have attracted increasing interest in the recent years. In this chapter, the current state-of-the-art research in AR-based AT and RE devices and systems has been surveyed. The working principles of these systems are detailed and the related works are compared. Although the prominent advantages of AR technologies have made these systems promising to the therapists and patients, many technical challenges must be addressed before they will be useful to people with special needs.

From the reported studies, it can be observed that the research in the application of AR in AT and RE systems is relatively new. One of the potential areas for future research is to develop rehabilitation systems to train daily living activities. Most of the existing research studies focus on the training of one function of the body parts, such as extending or reaching of the upper limb. The purpose of RE is to enable independent living in which the ability to perform daily living activities is important. The rehabilitation systems targeting daily living activities, such as eating, drinking and pouring water are deemed desirable by the patients and their families.

To support the training of daily living activities, more intuitive and natural interaction methods are required in which the interactions involved in daily living activities can be supported. In most of the existing studies, the interaction between the body parts and the virtual objects are supported with sensors, which are used to detect the movements of the body parts. With the external devices attached to the body parts, the setup of the systems becomes cumbersome and the usage of these systems would be reduced. More non-intrusive methods should be developed to detect the body movements and support intuitive human-computer interaction. With the intuitive interaction methods, AR-based RE and AT systems can be used to facilitate the interactions in daily living.

There is also a need to augment haptic feedback without bulky equipments in the rehabilitation systems, especially for systems used by the patients needing to recover their muscle strength. With haptic feedback, multimodal feedback can improve the effectiveness of the rehabilitation systems, and the haptic feedback would make the interaction process more realistic.

Nowadays, the computing units in mobile phones have become more powerful. It becomes possible to develop portable systems to provide greater convenience to the users. With the integration of GPS, inertial sensors and wireless communication devices, portable AR-based AT and RE systems would be able to provide various services. The wide use of mobile phone would further promote the usage of these portable systems.

References

1. W. Lutz, W. Sanderson and S. Scherbov, "The coming acceleration of global population ageing," Nature, 451, 7 February 2008, pp. 716–719. doi:10.1038/nature06516.
2. Population Division, DESA, United Nations. United Nations (UN), "World Population Ageing: 1950–2050," Available from:http://www.un.org/esa/population/publications/worldageing19502050/ [last access date: 12 December, 2010].
3. R. Azuma, "A Survey of Augmented Reality", Presence: Teleoperators and Virtual Environments, 6(4), 1997, pp. 355–385.
4. National Council on Disability: Study on the financing of assistive technology devices and services for individuals with disabilities: a report to the president and the congress of the United States, Washington, DC, 1993, National Council on Disability. Available from: http://www.ncd.gov/newsroom/publications/1993/assistive.htm#10 [last access date: 25 December 2010].
5. A. O'Brien and R. Mac Ruairi, "Survey of Assistive Technology Devices and Applications for Aging in Place", Second International Conference on Advances in Human-Oriented and Personalized Mechanisms, Technologies, and Services, 2009, pp. 7–12.
6. D. W. F. van Krevelen and R. Poelman, "A survey of augmented reality technologies, applications and limitations", The International Journal of Virtual Reality, 9(2), 2010, pp. 1–20.
7. R. Velázquez, "Wearable Assistive Devices for the Blind", Chapter 17 in A. Lay-Ekuakille & S. C. Mukhopadhyay (Eds.), Wearable and Autonomous Biomedical Devices and Systems for Smart Environment: Issues and Characterization, LNEE 75, Springer, 2010, pp. 331–349.
8. F. Dramas, S. Thorpe, C. Jouffrais, "Artificial vision for the blind: a bio-inspired algorithm for objects and obstacles detection", International Journal of Image and Graphics, World Scientific, 10(4), November 2010, pp. 531–544.

9. S. Kammoun, F. Dramas, B. Oriola, C. Jouffrais, "Route selection algorithm for blind pedestrian", International Conference on Control, Automation and Systems (ICCAS 2010), Gyeonggi-do, Korea, October 27–30 2010, pp. 2223–2228.

10. E. J. Toledo, J. J. Martinez, E. J. Garrigos and J. M. Ferrandez, "FPGA implementation of an augmented reality application for visually impaired people", International conference on field programmable logic and applications, 24–26 August 2005, pp. 723–724.

11. LookTel, Available from: http://www.looktel.com/ [last access date: 15 December, 2010].

12. J. Zhang, S. K. Ong and A. Y. C. Nee, "Navigation Systems for Individuals with Visual Impairment: A Survey", International convention on rehabilitation engineering & assistive technology, i-CREATe, Bangkok, Thailand from 13–15 May 2008, 159–162.

13. J. Zhang, S. K. Ong and A. Y. C. Nee, "Design and development of a navigation assistance system for visually impaired individuals", International Convention for Rehabilitation Engineering and Assistive Technology, i-CREATe, 22–26 April, Singapore 2009, CDROM.

14. J. Zhang, C. W. Lip, S. K. Ong and A. Y. C. Nee, "Development of a Shoe-mounted Assistive User Interface for Navigation", International Journal of Sensor Networks, 9(1), 2011, pp. 3–12.

15. N. Fallah, "AudioNav: a mixed reality navigation system for individuals who are visually impaired", ACM SIGACCESS Accessibility and Computing Newsletter, 96, January 2010, pp. 24–27.

16. T. Nishioka, "Head mounted display as a information guarantee device for hearing impaired students", Lecture Notes in Computer Science, 3118/2004, K. Miesenberger et al. (Eds.): ICCHP 2004, pp. 1167–1171.

17. BabelFisk, Available from: http://www.gearlog.com/2010/09/speech-to-text_glasses_use_aug.php [last access date: 15 December, 2010].

18. E. A. L. Lee and K. W. Wong, "A review of using virtual reality for learning", Lecture Notes in Computer Science, 5080/2008, DOI: 10.1007/978-3-540-69744-2_18, 2008, pp. 231–241.

19. E. Araujo, P. Morais, S. Kasola, "e-Learning 2.0, collaborative tools for people with disabilities", Research, Reflections and Innovations in Integrating ICT in Education, 2009, pp. 1153–1155.

20. T. N. Arvanitis, A. Petrou, J. F. Knight, S. Savas, S. Sotiriou, M. Gargalakos and E. Gialouri, "Human factors and qualitative pedagogical evaluation of a mobile augmented reality system for science education used by learners with physical disabilities", Personal and ubiquitous computing, 13(3), 2009, pp. 243–250.

21. C.-Y. Lin and Chao J.-T., "Augmented Reality-Based Assistive Technology for Handicapped Children", 2010 International Symposium on Computer, Communication, Control and Automation, 5–7 May 2010, pp. 61–64.

22. Y. L. Chi, S. K. Ong, M. L. Yuan and A. Y. C. Nee, "Wearable Interface for the Physically Disabled", International Convention for Rehabilitation Engineering and Assistive Technology, i-CREATe, 23–26 April 2007, Singapore, pp. 28–32.

23. X. T. Gao, S. K. Ong, M. L. Yuan and A. Y. C. Nee, "Assist Disabled to Control Electronic Devices and Access Computer Functions by Voice Commands", International Convention for Rehabilitation Engineering and Assistive Technology, i-CREATe, 23–26 April 2007, Singapore, pp. 37–42.

24. L. F. Hodges, B. Watson, G. D. Kessler, D. Opdyke, and B. O. Rothbaum, "A virtual airplane for fear of flying therapy", In Proceedings of the 1996 Virtual Reality Annual International Symposium (VRAIS 96) (Santa Clara, California, 30 March-3 April, 1996). IEEE Computer Society, Washington, DC, USA, 1996, pp. 86–91.

25. J. Wald and S. Taylor, "Preliminary research on the efficacy of virtual reality exposure therapy to treat driving phobia", CyberPsychology & Behavior, 6(5), 2003, pp. 459–465.

26. A. Garcia-Palacios, H. G. Hoffman, A. Carlin, T. A. Furness and C. Botella, "Virtual reality in the treatment of spider phobia: a controlled study", Behaviour Research and Therapy, 40(9), Sep. 2002, pp. 983–993.

27. P. M. G. Emmelkamp, M. Bruynzeel, L. Drost, C. A. P. G. van der Mast, "Virtual reality treatment in acrophobia: a comparison with exposure in vivo", CyberPsychology & Behavior, 4(3), Jan. 2001, pp. 335–339.

28. M. M. North, S. M. North and J. R. Coble, "Effectiveness of virtual environment desensitization in the treatment of agoraphobia", Presence: Teleoperators and Virtual Environments, 5(4), 1996, pp. 346–352.

29. C. Botella, R. M. Baños, C. Perpiñá, H. Villa, M. Alcañiz and A. Rey, "Virtual reality treatment of claustrophobia: a case report", Behaviour Research and Therapy, 36, 2, Feb. 1998, pp. 239–246.

30. H. J. Jo, J. H. Ku, D. P. Jang, B. H. Cho, H. B. Ahn, J. M. Lee, Y. H. Choi, I. Y. Kim and S. I. Kim, "Movie-based VR therapy system for treatment of anthropophobia", Engineering in Medicine and Biology Society, 2001. Proceedings of the 23rd Annual International Conference of the IEEE (Istanbul, Turkey, 25–28 Oc. 2001), Vol. 4, 3788–3791.

31. F. D. Rose, B. M. Brooks and A. A. Rizzo, "Virtual Reality in Brain Damage Rehabilitation: Reivew", CyberPsychology & Behavior, 8(3), 2005, pp. 241–262.

32. A. A. Rizzo, J. G. Buckwalter, M. S. Bowerly, C. van der Zaag, L. Humphrey, U. Neumann, C. Chua, C. Kyriakakis, A. van Rooyen, and D. Sisemore, "The virtual classroom: a virtual reality environment for the assessment and rehabilitation of attention deficits", CyberPsychology & Behavior, 3(3), 2003, pp. 483–499.

33. B. M. Brooks, J. E. McNeil, F. D. Rose, R. J. Greenwood, E. A. Atree, and A. G. Leadbetter, "Route learning in a case of amnesia: a preliminary investigation into the efficacy of training in a virtual environment", Neuropsychological rehabilitation, 9(1), 1999, pp. 63–76.

34. J. D. Prothero, "The treatment of akinesia using virtual images", Master thesis, Industrial Engineering, University of Washington, Seattle, WA, 1993.

35. B. T. Volpe, H. I. Krebs, N. Hogan, O. L. Edelstein, C. Diels and M. Aisen, "A novel approach to stroke rehabilitation: robot-aided sensori-motor simulation", Neurology, 54, 2000, pp. 1938–1944.

36. D. Jack, R. Boian, A. S. Merians, M. Tremaine, G. C. Burdea, S. V. Adamovich, M. Recce and H. Poizner, "Virtual reality-enhanced stroke rehabilitation", IEEE transactions on neural systems and rehabilitation engineering, 9(3), Sep. 2001, pp. 308–318.

37. S. Weghorst, "Augmented reality and Parkinson's disease", Communications of the ACM, 40(8), 1997, pp. 47–48.

38. M. Ferrarin, M. Brambilla, L. Garavello, A. Di Candia, A. Pedotti and M. Rabuffetti, "Microprocessor-controlled optical stimulating device to improve the gait of patients with Parkinson's disease", Medical & Biological Engineering & Computing 42(3), pp. 328–332.

39. A. J. Espay, Y. Baram, A. K. Dwivedi, R. Shukla, M. Gartner, L. Gaines, A. P. Duker and F. J. Revilla, "At-home training with closed-loop augmented-reality cueing device for improving gait in patients with Parkinson disease", Journal of Rehabilitation Research & Development, 47(6), 2010, pp. 573–582.

40. L. J. David, "Using Augmented Reality to improve walking in stroke survivors", In Proceedings of the 2003 IEEE international workshop on Robot and Human Interactive Communication, California, USA, Oct. 31-Nov. 2 2003, pp. 79–83.

41. X. Luo, T. Kline, H. C. Fischer, K. A. Stubblefield, R. V. Kenyon and D. G. Kamper, "Integration of Augmented Reality and Assistive Devices for Post-Stroke Hand Opening Rehabilitation", In Proceedings of the 2005 IEEE, Engineering in Medicine and Biology 27th Annual Conference, Shanghai, China, September 1–4, 2005, pp. 6855–6858.

42. X. Luo, R. V. Kenyon, T. Kline, H. C. Waldinger and D. G. Kamper, "An augmented reality training environment for post-stroke finger extension rehabilitation", IEEE the 9th International Conference on Rehabilitation Robotics. New York, 2005, pp. 329–332.

43. L. E. Sucar, R. S. Leder, D. Reinkensmeyer, J. Hernández, G. Azcárate, N. Casteñeda and P. Saucedo, "Gesture Therapy - A Low-Cost Vision-Based System for Rehabilitation after Stroke", HEALTHINF 2008, Funchal, Madeira, Portugal, January 28–31, 2008, pp.107–111.

44. A. Alamri, J. Cha, M. Eid and A. E. Saddik, "Evaluating the Post-Stroke Patients Progress Using an Augmented Reality Rehabilitation System", 2009 IEEE International Workshop on Medical Measurements and Applications, 29–30 May 2009, Cetraro, Italy, pp. 89–94.

45. A. Alamri, J. Cha and A. E. Saddik, "AR-REHAB: An augmented reality framework for poststroke-patient rehabilitation", IEEE Transactions on Instrumentation and Measurement, 59(10), 2010, pp. 2554–2563.

46. A. Alamri, K. Heung-Nam and A. E. Saddik, "A decision model of stroke patient rehabilitation with augmented reality-based games", 2010 International Conference on Autonomous and Intelligent Systems, 21–23 June 2010, Povoa de Varzim, pp. 1–6.

47. J. W. Burke, M. D. J. McNeill, D. K. Charles, P. J. Morrow, J. H. Crosbie and S. M. Mc-Donough, "Augmented reality games for upper-limb stroke rehabilitation", Second International Conference on Games and Virtual Worlds for Serious Applications, 2010, pp. 75–78.

48. S. J. Gaukrodger and A. Lintott, "Augmented reality and applications for assistive technology", 1st International Convention on Rehabilitation Engineering & Assistive Technology: in conjunction with 1st Tan Tock Seng Hospital Neurorehabilitation Meeting, Singapore, 26–23 April 2007, pp. 47–51.

49. M. King, L. Hale, A. Pekkari and M. Persson, "An affordable, computerized, table-based exercise system for stroke survivors", International Convention for Rehabilitation Engineering and Assistive Technology, i-CREATe, 22–26 April, Singapore 2009, CDROM.

50. H. Wang, C. Hsu, D. Chiu and S. Tsai, "Using augmented reality gaming system to enhance hand rehabilitation", 2nd International Conference on Education Technology and Computer, Shanghai, China, 22–24 June 2010, V3–243–V3–246.

51. N. A. Jackson, "Professional Music Therapy Supervision: A Survey", Journal of Music Therapy, 45, 2008, pp. 192–216.

52. A. G. D. Correa, G. A. de Assis, M. do Nascimento, I. Ficheman and R. de Deus Lopes, "GenVirtual: An Augmented Reality Musical Game for Cognitive and Motor Rehabilitation", Proceedings of the International Workshop on Virtual Rehabilitation, 27–20 September 2007, Venice, Italy, pp. 1–6.

53. A. G. D. Correa, I. K. Ficheman, M. do Nascimento and R. de Deus Lopes, "Computer Assisted Music Therapy: a Case Study of an Augmented Reality Musical System for Children with Cerebral Palsy Rehabilitation", 2009 Ninth IEEE International Conference on Advanced Learning Technologies, New York, pp. 218–220.

54. I. Barakonyi and D. Schmalstieg., "Augmented reality agents in the development pipeline of computer entertainment", In Proceedings of the 4th International Conference on Entertainment Computer, Sanda, Japan, 2005 September 19–21, pp. 345–356.

55. R. Aguiar, Piano VR, 2007. Available from: http://www.youtube.com/watch?v=wdDxXdMO-KX0 [Last access date: 16th December, 2010].

56. D. Zhang, Y. Shen, S.K. Ong and A.Y.C. Nee, "An Affordable Augmented Reality Based Rehabilitation System for Hand Motions", International Conference on CYBERWORLDS, 20–22 October 2010, Nanyang Technological University, Singapore, pp. 346–353.

57. Y. Shen, S.K. Ong and A.Y.C. Nee, "Vision-based Hand Interaction in Augmented Reality Environment", International Journal of Human-Computer Interaction, 27(6), May 2011, pp. 523–544.

58. H. Hoffman, A. Garcia-Palacios, C. Carlin, T. Furness and C. Botella-Arbona, "Interfaces that heal: Coupling real and virtual objects to cure spider phobia", International Journal of Human-Computer Interaction, 16(2), 2003, pp. 283–300.

59. M. C. Juan, C. Botella, M. Alcañiz, R. Baños, C. Carrion, M. Melero and J. A. Lozano, "An augmented reality system for treating psychological disorders: Application to phobia to cockroaches", The Third IEEE and ACM International Symposium on Mixed and Augmented Reality (ISMAR'04), Arlington, VA, USA, Nov. 2–5, 2004, pp. 256–257.

60. M. C. Juan, D. Pérez, D. Tomás, B. Rey, M. Alcañiz, C. Botella and R. Baños, "An augmented Reality system for the treatment of acrophobia", The 8th International Workshop on Presence, London, England, Sep. 21–23, 2005, pp. 315–317.

61. M. C. Juan, M. Alcañiz, J. Calatrava, I. Zaragozá, R. Baños and C. Botella, "An optical see-through augmented reality system for the treatment of phobia to small animals", Lecture Notes in Computer Science, 4563/2007, 2007, pp. 651–659.

62. C. Botella, J. Bretn-Lpez, S. Quero, R. Baños and A. García-Palacios, "Treating cockroach phobia with augmented reality", Behavior Therapy, 41(3), September 2010, pp. 401–413.
63. E. Richard, V. Billaudeau, P. Richard and G. Gaudin, "Augmented reality for rehabilitation of cognitive disabled children: a preliminary study", Proceedings of International Workshop on Virtual Rehabilitation, 27–29 September 2007, Venice, Italy, pp. 102–108.
64. K. O'Neill, A. dePaor, M. MacLachlan, and G. McDarby, "An investigation into the performance of a virtual mirror box for the treatment of phantom limb pain in amputees, using augmented reality technology", In Proceedings of HCI International 2003 (Crete, Greece, Jun. 22–27, 2003). Universal access in HCI: Inclusive design in the information society, 4, pp. 236–240.
65. Y. Shen, S. K. Ong and A. Y. C. Nee, "Hand Rehabilitation based on Augmented Reality", International Convention for Rehabilitation Engineering and Assistive Technology, i-CREATe, 22–26 April, Singapore 2009, CDROM.
66. U. Feintuch, L. Raz, J. Hwang, N. Josman, N. Katz, R. Kizony, D. Rand, A. S. Rizzo, M. Shahar, J. Yongseok and P. L. Weiss, "Integrating haptic-tactile feedback into a video capture based VE for rehabilitation", CyberPsychology Behavior, 9(2), April 2006, pp. 129–132.
67. G. Cagalaban and S. Kim, "Projective illumination technique in unprepared environments for augmented reality applications", International Journal of Database Theory and Application, 3(3), September 2010, pp. 29–38.

Chapter 29
Using Augmentation Techniques
for Performance Evaluation in Automotive
Safety

Jonas Nilsson, Anders C.E. Ödblom, Jonas Fredriksson, and Adeel Zafar

Abstract This chapter describes a framework which uses augmentation techniques for performance evaluation of mobile computer vision systems. Computer vision systems use primarily image data to interpret the surrounding world, e.g. to detect, classify and track objects. The performance of mobile computer vision systems acting in unknown environments is inherently difficult to evaluate since, often, obtaining ground truth data is problematic. The proposed novel framework exploits the possibility to add new agents into a real data sequence collected in an unknown environment, thus making it possible to efficiently create augmented data sequences, including ground truth, to be used for performance evaluation. Varying the content in the data sequence by adding different agents or changing the behavior of an agent is straightforward, making the proposed framework very flexible. A key driver for using augmentation techniques to address computer vision performance is that the vision system output may be sensitive to the background data content. The method has been implemented and tested on a pedestrian detection system used for automotive collision avoidance. Results show that the method has potential to replace and complement physical testing, for instance by creating collision scenarios, which are difficult to test in reality, in particular in a real traffic environment.

1 Evaluation Challenges in Active Safety

In recent years automotive Active Safety (AS) systems have become increasingly common in road vehicles since they provide an opportunity to significantly reduce traffic fatalities by active vehicle control. The first systems introduced to the market

J. Nilsson (✉)
Vehicle Dynamics and Active Safety Centre, Volvo Car Corporation, Gothenburg, Sweden

Department of Signals and Systems, Chalmers University of Technology, Gothenburg, Sweden
e-mail: jnilss94@volvocars.com

B. Furht (ed.), *Handbook of Augmented Reality*, DOI 10.1007/978-1-4614-0064-6_29,
© Springer Science+Business Media, LLC 2011

Fig. 29.1 Collision warning with full autobrake

were Anti-lock Braking Systems (ABS) and Electronic Stability Programs (ESP). These systems utilize sensor information on the current vehicle state, such as wheel speeds and yaw rate, to detect if the vehicle is in an unsafe state, e.g. with locked wheels or unstable. In case an unsafe state is detected the AS system will intervene to bring the *host* vehicle, i.e. the vehicle equipped with the AS system, back to a safe state. In the ESP case this could mean braking the wheels independently to reduce understeer or oversteer, i.e. to increase stability. Stability alone does not guarantee safety as safe operation of a vehicle also requires that the vehicle stays on the road and avoids contact with other road users and obstacles. Advances in sensor technology have made it possible to develop AS systems which consider not only the host vehicle state, but also the surrounding environment. Examples of such sensors are cameras, radars and laser scanners. Examples of AS systems based on these sensor technologies include stay-in-lane types of systems, such as Lane Departure Warning (LDW) [22], and Lane Keeping Aid (LKA) [33], where the system helps the driver to stay in the current lane, either by warnings or by actively steering the vehicle. Collision Warning/Mitigation/Avoidance systems (CW/CM/CA) [21] and [24], use sensors to detect possible collision threats and issue warnings to the driver. If the driver does not respond, the system can autonomously intervene by braking or steering to mitigate the consequences of, or completely avoid, a collision, as illustrated in Fig. 29.1.

A key challenge when developing an AS system is to verify that the system meets the function requirements, e.g. makes correct decisions at the right time. For the system to be effective, the number of missed interventions, i.e. when the system does not intervene when supposed to, must be minimized. Also unnecessary interventions must be avoided since they can be a nuisance to, or unacceptable for, the driver. As AS systems evolve to support the driver in an increased number of complex traffic situations, see e.g. [5], to further save lives [24], by avoiding severe traffic accidents, the interventions will become more intrusive which in turn puts stricter requirements on the acceptable rate of unnecessary interventions. This implies that AS performance evaluation methods must cover large sets of possible scenarios to verify that the system performance is correct.

System performance evaluation can be done using either theoretical or experimental methods. Theoretical methods require models of the system and its surrounding environment on such a level that performance can be described mathematically. As AS systems are developed for more and more complex traffic situations/scenarios this becomes increasingly challenging. A novel framework for worst case performance analysis of collision mitigation and avoidance systems was recently presented [28] based on a theoretical approach to identify worst case intervention timing and the corresponding scenario to guide further in-vehicle testing. Numerical simulations including production intent controller hardware is used to verify correct implementation of compiled code [29]. For in-vehicle physical experiments, the system's performance can be evaluated in a selected set of scenarios on test tracks and in uncontrolled scenarios in field tests in real traffic environments, see e.g. [23] and [9]. For a complex product or process such as vehicles in traffic, the set of scenarios that needs to be evaluated is extremely large and this makes evaluation of all possible scenarios unrealistic. In other words, there is a need to develop more efficient test methods, theoretical or experimental, to enable future development of AS systems.

The remainder of this chapter describes a novel framework for performance evaluation of camera based AS systems acting in unknown environments. The key idea is to combine the inherent realism of real world data collected in field tests with the efficiency and flexibility offered by computer generated images. The outline of the chapter is as follows; since many AS systems are camera based and relies on computer vision, Sect. 2 gives an introduction to the various verification approaches used for computer vision systems. Section 3 presents the proposed method and also introduces the notation used in the chapter. Section 4 presents a case study to illustrate that augmentation techniques provide a viable method. Also, preliminary results are presented and the method as well as the results are discussed. Finally, Sect. 5 summarizes the work presented in the chapter.

2   Performance Evaluation of Computer Vision Based Systems

Image analysis methods which extract information regarding depicted items in images are often referred to as Computer Vision (CV). CV technologies have become widely used in AS applications, largely due to the availability of cost efficient camera technologies. CV techniques are used for many purposes, e.g. detecting, classifying and tracking objects such as vehicles, pedestrians, lane markings and traffic signs, see e.g. [15]. Often CV algorithms exploit not exclusively image data, but also data from additional sensors.

Performance evaluation of CV algorithms can be divided into several different categories according to [8], *Mathematical analysis, Simulation using data with/without noise, Empirical testing using real data with full control, Empirical testing using partially controlled real data* and *Empirical testing in an uncontrolled environment*. This categorization fits well into the evaluation process of an AS-CV system. First the system is evaluated using simulation, this can be based on simulated or virtually generated data, so called Virtual Reality (VR). VR require models that describe relevant scenarios and sensor behavior. In VR a complete computer generated representation of the scenario is created, this means that all objects and the background in the scenario can be independently controlled, i.e. it corresponds to the category *Simulation using data with/without noise*. In [6], a VR solution is proposed to generate image data for the purpose of evaluating *mobile* CV systems. More recent VR work, focused on the evaluation of CV systems using networks of distributed stationary cameras, is presented in [34] and [35].

The next phase in the evaluation process is empirical testing, starting with dedicated tests on test tracks, corresponding to *Empirical testing using real data with full control* and *Empirical testing using partially controlled real data*. Verifying the performance of an AS-CV system requires collection of image data, as well as additional sensor data, for a representative set of traffic scenarios. Since traffic environments have unlimited variability, large field tests are conducted in addition to dedicated tests on test tracks for the purpose of collecting enough data to be able to certify the results, see e.g. [9]. Field tests correspond to *Empirical testing in an uncontrolled environment*. Since physical test methods are both expensive and time consuming complementary methods are needed for future active safety applications. Furthermore, in real data, ground truth is often problematic to acquire and some scenarios are dangerous or difficult to reproduce on demand, e.g. for AS applications different weather conditions, animals crossing the road or scenarios where vehicles collide or nearly collide.

Compared to physical tests, VR test methods are cheap and efficient, enabling repeatable and reproducible evaluation of large input sets in early phases of system development. Furthermore, VR test methods are flexible in the sense that once a VR environment has been created, variations in the scenario, such as multiple trajectories, motion patterns and appearance, can be created with relatively small effort including ground truth data. An alternative method often used in television and movie industries is to combine virtually generated data with real image data. This is known as Augmented Reality (AR). AR supplements reality, rather than completely replacing it as VR does. As a consequence, fewer virtual objects need to be developed in AR, but at the same time the desired properties from VR remain such as repeatability, reproducibility and test scenario variability. In [4], a *static* CV system is evaluated using the two complementary approaches VR and AR.

The drawback compared to physical testing is that AR/VR test results are merely a prediction of the system performance. The quality, in terms of *realism*, of the generated images defines with what confidence the test results can be used to draw conclusions on the system performance in real operating conditions. A challenge for both AR and VR based performance evaluation methods is to ensure that the CV system produces the same output for an augmented/virtual scenario as it would for an equivalent real scenario, i.e. to validate that the generated data set is sufficiently realistic. Outdoor real world system validation experiments, including CV algorithms, are challenging to arrange since two equivalent recordings, with and without target validation objects, are required. In order to guarantee scenario equivalence, control of the external environment such as weather and light conditions, are needed along with control of the camera trajectory, image exposure timing and additional sensors.

Modeling complex 3D environments with a high degree of realism is challenging as well as time consuming, including for instance lighting effects, motion patterns geometries and materials. When comparing AR to VR methods, this challenge is in one sense reduced significantly, as fewer virtual objects need to be developed. Also, the background image is taken from real data and is therefore representative, both with respect to the camera hardware used and the scenario from which the image sequence originates. When compared to VR methods, a limitation with AR methods is that the camera trajectory cannot be modified without recording a new image sequence. When evaluating the performance of a CV system which influences the future path of the camera, this may be a major limitation. When verifying that unnecessary interventions are not made by an AS system, this is usually not the case since the system has no influence on the motion of the vehicle prior to the intervention.

The proposed performance evaluation framework uses augmentation techniques, i.e. augmented imagery in combination with augmented sensor data from additional sensors, to enlarge the set of analyzed traffic scenarios. In the present work the aim of using augmentation techniques is to determine sensor errors and to make sure that such errors do not lead to system failures. In order to ensure that the system performs well when exposed to those errors, for the large scenario variations present in real traffic, extensive testing is required as pointed out in [17] and [20] for CV algorithms. Furthermore, the approach extends the category *Empirical testing in an uncontrolled environment* by using AR based methods.

The key driver for using data augmentation techniques for system performance evaluations is the inherent realism of the data backgrounds. With real background data, collision scenarios can be tested in real traffic environments. The challenges to overcome are to correctly insert augmentations which are consistent with the recorded data set. For images this means that the augmentation object is added in the correct place with the correct size and observation angle. It also requires the augmented image data to be consistent with the corresponding real scenario in terms of material properties such as reflections and granularities as well as blending of the object with the image background. Furthermore, the appearance of the object in the image is affected by the optical characteristics of the imaging system.

3 Framework for Performance Evaluation

The idea of augmented imagery goes back to the early 1990s, see e.g. [31]. The novelty of this work is the use of augmentation techniques for performance evaluation of mobile computer vision systems. In order to be able to do performance evaluation an augmented scenario needs to be developed.

Consider a camera moving along a trajectory $C = [c_1\ c_2\ ...\ c_n]$, as shown in Fig. 29.2, where c_j describes the position and orientation, i.e. pose, of the camera at time t_j in a three-dimensional (3D) world-fixed coordinate system. At each time t_j the image i_j is recorded by the camera and forms the image sequence $I = [i_1\ i_2\ ...\ i_n]$. Let a *data set* sampled from the *scenario S* be defined as $D = \{I, X\}$, where X is sensor data from additional sensors, e.g. laser, radar, gyro, GPS. Each image frame, together with additional sensor input, is processed by a CV algorithm forming the output $Y = [y_1\ y_2\ ...\ y_n]$, which contains detected, classified and tracked objects.

The proposed method is visualized in Fig. 29.3. Consider a set of agents $A = [A_1\ A_2\ ...\ A_k]$, with k being the number of agents. Each agent A_i is represented by a state trajectory defined as $a_i = [a_{i,1}\ a_{i,2}\ ...\ a_{i,n}]$, where $a_{i,j}$ is the agent's state at time t_j. By using techniques developed for augmented reality, A can be added to a real data set D and a new augmented data set $D_A = \{I_A, X_A\}$, corresponding to the augmented scenario S_A, can be created. The augmented data set D_A is processed by the CV algorithm, delivering the output Y_A which can be compared to a ground truth Y_{GT} for performance evaluation of the CV system. The method is flexible in the sense that multiple object trajectories and motion patterns, a_i, can be created with relatively small effort, making it suitable for extensive testing of critical scenarios.

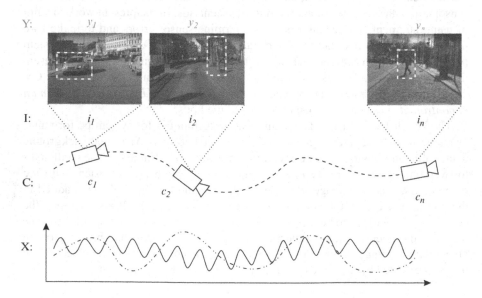

Fig. 29.2 Definitions

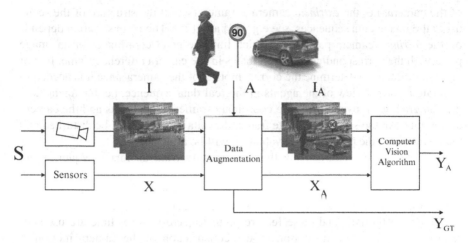

Fig. 29.3 Performance evaluation framework

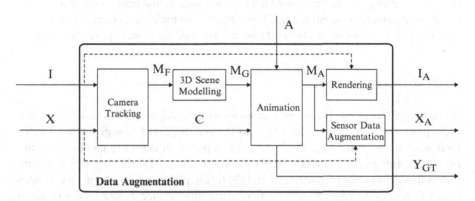

Fig. 29.4 Data augmentation process

3.1 Data Augmentation

The data augmentation process is described in more detail in Fig. 29.4. In the following subsections the process for developing an augmented scenario will be presented.

3.1.1 Camera Tracking

Camera tracking is the first step in the data augmentation process and the first basic step in transforming a sequence of 2D images into a 3D world. For a camera moving in an unknown environment, the problem is to reconstruct both the motion of the camera, i.e. the *extrinsic* camera parameters, and the structure of the scene using the image data sequences, see e.g. [14] and [25]. The reconstruction depends on the *intrinsic* camera parameters which link the pixel coordinates of an image point with the corresponding 3D coordinates in the camera reference frame. It is of great importance to determine the correct motion of the camera since it is needed to generate a correct view of the agents in the real data sequence, i.e. the agents and the camera must move in the same coordinate frame. If the agents and the camera do not move in the same coordinate frame, the data sequence will be disturbed and the results from the performance evaluation will be affected.

The process of reconstructing the 3D structure from an image sequence can be divided into two parts, feature point tracking and camera parameter estimation or calibration. [18] provides a comprehensive treatment of the subject. The main idea is that feature points in the image, such as corner points etc, are tracked from one image to the next and these feature point trajectories over time are used for reconstructing the camera motion. The reconstruction of the camera motion is usually done in several steps, from image to image, but also from a set of images or the complete image sequence, so-called bundle block adjustment, in order to reduce the error in camera pose estimation. The output from the camera tracking process is a set of 3D feature points located in the scene, M_F, and the camera pose trajectory, C.

3.1.2 3D Scene Modeling

Since the feature points in M_F are located around the edges of objects, it is possible to fit planes or other geometric shapes to the points [27]. These geometric shapes form a 3D scene model M_G, which is used as a playground for the agents. There are two main problems associated with 3D scene modeling: (1) selecting which feature points that belong to the same object and (2) fitting planes or other geometric shapes to the feature points. The problems are of equal importance, because both relate to the reality level of the final augmented image sequence and therefore the final result of the proposed method. If for example the "ground plane" is not correctly fitted, it could result in that the agents either "fly" or "move underground". There exist methods to do this automatically, as mentioned in [7].

3.1.3 Animation

Given the 3D scene model, M_G, it is possible to add agents A into the scene. For each agent, a state trajectory a_i is created. Once the state trajectories are created in the scene, the agents, e.g. humans, animals, vehicles or road signs, can be placed and animated in the scene using the trajectories as reference. In most cases for ground vehicles the state trajectories of the agents are aligned with the planes in M_G. The outcome is an animated 3D model M_A. The ground truth Y_{GT} can be obtained from the state trajectories of the agents A_i.

3.1.4 Rendering

In the rendering step the original image sequence I is joined together with the animated 3D scene model M_A, to produce the final augmented image sequence I_A. In order to make I_A realistic several steps are needed, such as material matching, environment setting and rendering, see e.g. [16] for a comprehensive overview on the topic. The needed realism is difficult to quantify for the general case due to its dependence on the choice of CV algorithm and camera hardware. However, the required level of realism of the virtual images is bounded since it does not need to exceed the resolution of the real image data used by the system.

Material matching of the agents is an important but challenging task. It is important that the agents do not stand out in the image. The texture of the agents should be adjusted according to the background of I, the same goes for their color, brightness, glossiness and diffusion. This step might be very time consuming, depending on for instance the number of agents added to the scene and the length of the data sequence. Making the scene close to reality also requires environment settings such as lighting, reflections of the environment in the agents and projection of shadows, see e.g. [19]. The lighting effects should be in the same directions as in the real scene. This includes also the sky light effects covering the whole scene. When material adjustments and lighting effects are completed, the animated 3D scene is subjected to the rendering which generates the augmented image sequence I_A.

3.1.5 Sensor Data Augmentation

If the CV system does not rely exclusively on image data, it may also use information from additional sensors, such as lasers, radars or gyros. As I_A contains information originating from the agents, some of the sensors used must also be augmented with the corresponding information. By combining information in M_A with the original sensor data sequence X, the augmented sensor data sequence X_A is generated. Especially the state trajectories of the agents, a_i, are of importance when creating additional sensor data. Depending on sensor type the information needs to be processed in different ways, meaning that the process of generating X_A must be customized for each individual sensor type, see e.g. [10], [13] and [30].

3.2 Validation

Validating the complete performance evaluation framework including vision algorithms requires a scenario with two data sets, one with real objects D and one with added agents D_A. The two data sets are to be equivalent, meaning that identical outputs, $Y \equiv Y_A$, are expected for the two input data sets, D and D_A. If the outputs are equal it means the augmentation process is sufficiently realistic.

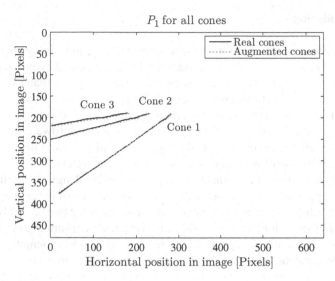

Fig. 29.5 Coordinates of augmented cones and corresponding real traffic cones, in a real world image sequence

The accuracy of the various subsystems building up the evaluation framework can be analyzed sequentially. Subsystem validation might be needed to ensure that two errors do not cancel. Of particular importance, is the accuracy of the camera tracking algorithm (M_F and C) and the 3D scene model M_G since they affect where the added agents will be placed in the images. On the other hand, validating the details of animation and rendering aspects are not needed provided vision algorithms are insensitive to such variations. This is most easily determined by direct experiments for unknown black-box vision algorithms.

A camera parameter error or 3D scene model error, may result in a discrepancy between the expected and actual 2D pixel position of the agents A in an image frame i_j. Such discrepancies may be ignorable if they are small compared to pixel size, or not noticeable if small compared to either the agent's size or translational distance between subsequent images. Anyway, such errors represent errors in ground truth and in agent position in the image frame. To make sure that these errors are ignorable the process of placing agents in the image requires validation.

A preliminary result for validating the positioning of agents in the image is presented in Fig. 29.5. Here, a vehicle is driven on a test track towards three traffic cones placed along a line perpendicular to the vehicle path. By augmentation techniques virtual traffic cones with the same size as the real cones are added to the 3D position of the real world cones in the 3D scene model. The pixel coordinates of a characteristic point (P_1) on the cones is determined by visual inspection for each image frame. Preliminary results shows good agreement between augmented and real cone pixel coordinates, see Fig. 29.5.

The experiment presented in Fig. 29.5 evaluates the resulting position error for the added agents A (the three traffic cones) in the augmented image sequence I_A. The positioning of agents is done by multiple subsystems in the augmentation process and, as mentioned above, individual validation of these subsystems may be needed to ensure that two errors do not cancel. The 2D position of the agents in the image is determined by the 3D position of the agent and the camera parameters. There are well established procedures to determine the intrinsic and extrinsic camera parameters of the imaging system, see e.g. [14] and [38]. The true value of the extrinsic camera parameters, i.e. the camera pose C, needs to be determined with the use of accurate reference measurements. Often, the accuracy of the relative position between the agent and real objects in the scene is of importance, for instance when agents are placed onto the ground surface or occluded by real objects. Therefore the 2D position error of the agents in the image is also subjected to the accuracy of the 3D scene model M_G, which similarly can be validated using accurate reference measurements.

4   Case Study

The purpose of the present case study is to illustrate that augmentation techniques provide a viable method for addressing performance evaluation of mobile CV systems. An augmented scenario is compared to a similar real traffic scenario to show that they produce similar results for detection, classification and tracking of a crossing pedestrian.

4.1   System Description

A collision avoidance (CA) prototype system under development is used as test subject. A forward looking camera is mounted behind the windshield of a test vehicle. A CV system use image data I from the camera to detect, classify and track objects. Additional inputs X are data from a forward looking radar and sensors measuring the state of the vehicle, e.g. wheel speeds and accelerations. The CA system use radar and CV system outputs to identify situations when the vehicle is close to colliding with detected objects. When judged necessary, the CA system will warn the driver and if the driver does not respond, autonomously brake the vehicle to avoid the impending collision. The CV algorithm is not public, but can be executed offline on recorded or augmented image sequences using [11].

Fig. 29.6 Image frames from the reference image sequence I^1. For privacy reasons, the face of the pedestrian has been blurred

4.2   Scenario Description

Two scenarios are addressed in this case study. In the first scenario S^1 a pedestrian is initially occluded at the side of the road and then crosses the road in front of the moving vehicle. This is chosen as it is a common scenario in real traffic. A subset of the images from I^1 is displayed in Fig. 29.6. The second scenario S^2 is used as a basis to create augmented scenarios. S^2 is recorded in the same day and at the same location as S^1, but without a pedestrian crossing the road. The absence of moving objects makes it ideal for adding agents. To be able to compare the augmented scenario S_A^2 with the real scenario S^1, the set of agents A^2 is chosen to be a single crossing pedestrian. Adding A^2 to the empty scene in S^2 means that S^1 and S_A^2 are qualitatively similar.

4.3   Implementation

This section briefly describes how the data augmentation process shown in Fig. 29.4 is implemented to create the augmented data sequence $D_A^2 = \{I_A^2, X_A^2\}$. Two

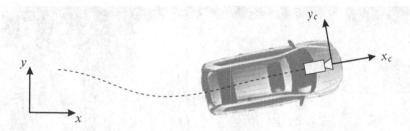

Fig. 29.7 Coordinate systems

coordinate systems will be used for the remainder of this chapter. The first one is a world-fixed Cartesian coordinate system and the second one is a coordinate system with the origin placed at the forward looking camera, see Fig. 29.7.

4.3.1 Camera Tracking

There exist a number of tools that can estimate camera parameters and track feature points automatically from an image sequence, e.g. Voodoo Camera Tracker [12], 3D-Equalizer [37], SynthEyes [1], PFTrack [32], or VooCAT, [36]. In this case study, 3D features M_F^2 and camera pose C^2 are estimated using the software tool Voodoo Camera Tracker (VCT) [12]. The intrinsic camera parameters are known and provided to VCT. The size of the 3D models is inferred from vehicle velocity data obtained from on board wheel speed sensors. For more information regarding VCT, see [38] and [26].

4.3.2 3D Scene Modeling

The software tool Autodesk 3ds Max [2] is used for the geometric modeling of the 3D scene M_G. This modeling is done by manually fitting planes to clusters of feature points obtained from M_F. The ground surface is modeled for the purpose of adding agents at a correct position in the scene as well as creating realistic agent shadows. Also, planes are added to simulate agent occlusions. Figure 29.8 show examples of feature points and modeled planes.

4.3.3 Animation

The geometry and motion pattern of the agent are obtained from Metropoly 3D Humans [3], which is a human model library. The animation is performed in the scene by manually setting a reference trajectory for the agent. The world-fixed position of the agent in the animated 3D scene model M_A^2 can be directly used as ground truth data Y_{GT}^2. Finally, the augmented image sequence I_A^2 has been rendered from M_A^2 using 3ds Max.

Fig. 29.8 3D feature points and 3D scene model

4.3.4 Rendering

In order to make I_A^2 realistic, light sources and virtual side planes need to be created to produce the effect of reflections from the environment. Reflections from the environment are added by projecting the environment from the virtual side planes

Fig. 29.9 Image frames from the augmented image sequence I_A^2

onto the agents. The projection of shadows is done on the virtual planes in M_G^2. Since these planes, with the exception of the agent shadows, are made invisible during rendering, the shadows are projected on the "real" objects in the augmented image sequence I_A^2. Finally, the augmented image sequence I_A^2 has been rendered from M_A^2 using 3ds Max.

4.3.5 Sensor Data Augmentation

As the CV system utilize information from a forward looking radar, which is capable of detecting a real pedestrian, augmented sensor data X_A^2 needs to be generated. The radar response of the agent is assumed ideal, meaning that the agent is detected without measurement errors, given that the agent is within the sensor field of view.

4.4 Results

A subset of the augmented image sequence I_A^2 is shown in Fig. 29.9. When compared to I^1, shown in Fig. 29.6, it can be noted that the pedestrians in S^1 and S_A^2 are both initially occluded by the commercial sign on the right side of the road and then

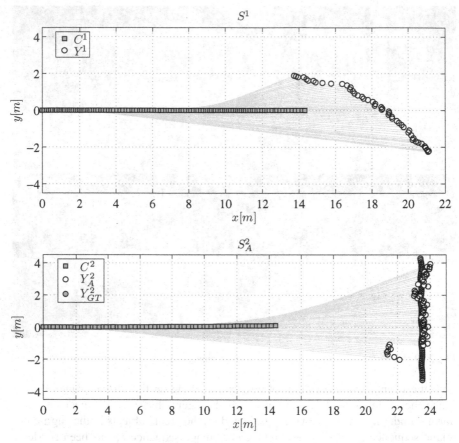

Fig. 29.10 Camera position, CV detections and ground truth agent positions. Data originating from the same time instance are linked with *gray line*

cross the road in front of the moving vehicle. The pedestrian in S^1 has a different direction when crossing the road than the pedestrian in S_A^2. Also, the appearances of the pedestrians are different with regards to clothing and size.

Figure 29.10 illustrates the camera and object position estimates, for each detection, in world-fixed coordinates for S^1 and S_A^2. For S^1, all detections shown in the figure have been classified by the CV system as pedestrian detections. The world-fixed camera trajectory C^1 is estimated by integrating host vehicle velocity data obtained from on board wheel speed sensors. There is no ground truth data Y_{GT}^1 available for this scenario. By visual inspection of I^1 and Y^1, the *initial detection* delay T_{det}^1, which is defined as the time between the visual appearance of the pedestrian from behind the occlusion and the first detection, can be determined. An object is termed *visible* when the complete object is visible in the image. The time for the visual appearance is defined as the first time instance where the object is visible. Starting at the initial detection, the pedestrian is tracked in every image frame, until the pedestrian is no longer visible, i.e. the pedestrian is tracked as he crosses the road.

For S_A^2, all detections shown in Fig. 29.10 have been classified by the CV system as pedestrian detections. C^2 is obtained by camera tracking. By visual inspection of I_A^2 and Y_A^2, it can be concluded that the agent is tracked in every image frame until no longer visible, with an initial detection delay $T_{det}^2 = T_{det}^1$. As pointed out in Sect. 4.2, the scenarios S^1 and S_A^2 are similar but not identical. Differences in for instance vehicle speed, pedestrian trajectory, motion pattern and clothing between the two scenarios imply that differences between the CV system outputs Y^1 and Y_A^2 are expected. The similar augmented and real crossing pedestrian scenarios yield qualitatively similar results for CV detection, classification and tracking. Regarding quantitative positioning, Fig. 29.10 illustrates deviations in the estimates of the agent position, in the initial part of S_A^2, as compared to ground truth. These position discrepancies may be due to incorrect matching between image-based and radar detections. The sign initially occluding the pedestrian is detected by the radar and could potentially be matched with the detection of the pedestrian in the image.

5 Conclusions

In this chapter, a framework has been proposed which uses augmentation techniques for evaluating the performance of mobile computer vision systems. Varying the scenario by adding different agents such as pedestrians, bicyclists, animals, vehicles or traffic signs is straightforward, making the proposed framework very flexible. The performance of a computer vision system is not only affected by what objects are present in a scene but possibly also details like clothing, lighting conditions and background data. An inherent strength of the proposed evaluation framework is that it is based on real recorded data backgrounds.

In automotive active safety applications, the number of parameters which can be varied in real scenarios is essentially unlimited meaning that an efficient method which can evaluate large sets of scenarios could complement or even replace parts of real data evaluations. Also, some situations are difficult to reproduce on demand, e.g. different weather conditions or animals crossing the road. Another type of scenario which could be problematic to collect real data from is collision situations, in particular in real traffic environments. Some active safety systems must be verified in scenarios where the host vehicle collides or nearly collides with an object. Safety concerns make this kind of testing very problematic or in some cases even impossible to arrange. The methods proposed in this chapter do not have these limitations.

The proposed method has been applied to an automotive collision avoidance application. Comparison of two similar crossing pedestrian scenarios, one real and one augmented, yield qualitatively similar CV results for detection, classification and tracking. Further studies are needed to validate that the realism of the augmented data is sufficient for its purpose.

Acknowledgements Financial supports from the Swedish Automotive Research Program (FFP contract Dnr 2007-01733 and FFI contract Dnr 2008-04110 at VINNOVA) and the Vehicle and Traffic Safety Centre (SAFER) are gratefully acknowledged. Furthermore, the authors wish to thank Gunnar Bergström and Henrik Moren at Xdin, Gothenburg, Sweden, for initial discussions on augmented reality techniques, and Robert Jacobson at VCC for 3ds Max support.

References

1. Andersson Technologies LLC. SynthEyes. http://www.ssontech.com/, June 2011.
2. Autodesk. Autodesk 3ds Max 2008. http://usa.autodesk.com/, June 2011.
3. aXYZ design. Metropoly 3D Humans. http://www.axyz-design.com/, June 2011.
4. P. Baiget, X. Roca, and J. Gonzalez. Autonomous virtual agents for performance evaluation of tracking algorithms. Articulated Motion and Deformable Objects. 5th International Conference, AMDO 2008, pages 299–308, Berlin, Germany, 2008. Springer-Verlag.
5. M. Brannstrom, E. Coelingh, and J. Sjoberg. Threat assessment for avoiding collisions with turning vehicles. 2009 IEEE Intelligent Vehicles Symposium (IV), pages 663–668, Piscataway, NJ, USA, 2009.
6. W. Burger, M. J. Barth, and W. Strzlinger. Immersive simulation for computer vision. In K. Solina, editor, *joint 19th AGM and 1st SDRV workshop Visual Modules*, pages 160–168, Maribor, Slovenia, 1995. Oldenbourg Press.
7. D. Chekhlov, A. Ge, A. Calway, and W. Mayol-Cuevas. Ninja on a plane: Automatic discovery of physical planes for augmented reality using visual slam. In *International Symposium on Mixed and Augmented Reality (ISMAR)*, 2007.
8. H. Christensen and W. Förstner. Performance characteristics of vision algorithms. *Machine Vision and Applications*, (9):215–218, 1997.
9. E. Coelingh, H. Lind, W. Birk, and D. Wetterberg. Collision warning with auto brake. In *FISITA World Congress, F2006VI30*, 2006.
10. L. Danielsson. *Tracking and radar sensor modelling for automotive safety systems*. PhD thesis, Chalmers University of Technology, 2010.
11. Delphi Corporation. Cwm2 resimulator, 2008.
12. Digilab. Voodoo Camera Tracker. University of Hannover, http://www.digilab.uni-hannover.de/docs/manual.html, June 2011.
13. L. France, A. Girault, J.-D. Gascuel, and B. Espiau. Sensor modeling for a walking robot simulation. In *Eurographics Workshop on Computer Animation and Simulation*, Sep 1999.
14. A. Fusiello. Uncalibrated euclidean reconstruction: a review. *Image and Vision Computing*, 18:555–563, 2000.
15. D. M. Gavrila and V. Philomin. Real-time object detection for 'smart' vehicles. In *Proceedings of the IEEE International Conference on Computer Vision*, volume 1, pages 87–93, 1999.
16. A. Glassner. *Principles of Digital Image Synthesis*. Morgan Kaufmann, 1st edition, 1995.
17. R. Haralick. Computer vision theory: The lack thereof. *Computer Vision, Graphics, and Image Processing*, (36):372–386, 1986.
18. R. Hartley and A. Zisserman. *Multiple view geometry in computer vision*. Cambridge University Press, Cambridge, 2003. 2nd ed.
19. K. Jacobs, J.-D. Nahmias, C. Angus, A. Reche, C. Loscos, and A. Steed. Automatic generation of consistent shadows for augmented reality. In *GI '05: Proceedings of Graphics Interface 2005*, pages 113–120, School of Computer Science, University of Waterloo, Waterloo, Ontario, Canada, 2005. Canadian Human-Computer Communications Society.
20. T. Jain and R. Binford. Ignorance, myopia, and naivet in computer vision systems. CVGIP: Image Understanding, 1991.
21. J. Jansson. *Collision Avoidance Theory with Application to Automotive Collision Mitigation*. Dissertation No 950, Dept. of Electrical Enginering, Linköping University, Linköping, 2005.

22. D. J. LeBlanc, G. E. Johnson, P. J. T. Venhovens, G. Gerber, R. DeSonia, R. D. Ervin, C. F. Lin, A. G. Ulsoy, and T. E. Pilutti. Capc: A road-departure prevention system. *IEEE Control Systems Magazine*, 16(6):61–71, 1996.
23. K. Lee and H.Peng. Evaluation of automotive forward collision warning and collision avoidance algorithms. *Vehicle System Dynamics*, 43(10):735–751, October 2005.
24. M. Lindman, A. Ödblom, E. Bergvall, A. Eidehall, B. Svanberg, and T. Lukaszewicz. Benefit estimation model for pedestrian auto brake functionality. In *Proceedings of the 4th International Conference Expert Symposium on Accident Research*, Hannover, Germany, September 2010.
25. Q.-T. Luong and O. D. Faugeras. Camera calibration, scene motion and structure recovery from point correspondences and fundamental matrices. *IJCV*, 22:261–289, 1997.
26. P. Mikulastik, H. Broszio, T. Thormaehlen, and O. Urfalioglu. Error analysis of feature based disparity estimation. In *First Pacific Rim Symposium on Advances in Image and Video Technology*, volume 0, pages 1–12, dez 2006. ISSN 0302-9743, ISBN 978-3-540-68297-4.
27. N. J. Mitra and A. Nguyen. Estimating surface normals in noisy point cloud data. In *SCG '03: Proceedings of the nineteenth annual symposium on Computational geometry*, pages 322–328, New York, NY, USA, 2003. ACM.
28. J. Nilsson and A. Ödblom. On worst case performance of collision avoidance systems. In *Proceedings of the IEEE Intelligent Vehicles Symposium*, San Diego, California, USA, 2010.
29. P. Olsson. Testing and verification of adaptive cruise control and collision warning with brake support by using hil simulations. *SAE 2008-01-0728*, 2008.
30. Z. Papp, K. Labibes, A. Thean, and M. van Elk. Multi-agent based hil simulator with high fidelity virtual sensors. In *Intelligent Vehicles Symposium, 2003. Proceedings. IEEE*, pages 213 – 218, 2003.
31. K. Pimentel and K. Teixeira. *Virtual Reality: Through the New Looking Glass*. McGraw-Hill, 2nd edition, 1995.
32. Pixel Farm. PFTrack. http://www.thepixelfarm.co.uk/, June 2011.
33. J. Pohl, W. Birk, and L. Westervall. A driver-distraction-based lane-keeping assistance system. *Proceedings of the Institution of Mechanical Engineers. Part I: Journal of Systems and Control Engineering*, 221(4):541–552, 2007.
34. F. Z. Qureshi and D. Terzopoulos. Towards intelligent camera networks: a virtual vision approach. In *Visual Surveillance and Performance Evaluation of Tracking and Surveillance. 2nd Joint IEEE International Workshop on*, pages 177–184, 2005.
35. A. Santuari, O. Lanz, and R. Brunelli. Synthetic movies for computer vision applications. *Proceedings of the 3rd IASTED International Conference: Visualization, Imaging, and Image Processing (VHP 2003)*, 1:1–6, 2003.
36. Scenespector Systems. VooCAT. http://www.scenespector.com/, June 2011.
37. Science-D-Visions. 3D-Equalizer. http://www.sci-d-vis.com/, June 2011.
38. T. Thormählen, H. Broszio, and P. Mikulastik. Robust linear auto-calibration of a moving camera from image sequences. In *Proceedings of the 7th Asian Conference on Computer Vision (ACCV), Hyderabad, India, Springer, LNCS 3852, Part II, ISSN 0302-9743*, volume 0, jan 2006.

Chapter 30
Augmented Reality in Product Development and Manufacturing

S.K. Ong, J. Zhang, Y. Shen, and A.Y.C. Nee

1 Introduction

Augmented Reality (AR) is a technology that provides intuitive interaction experience to the users by combining the real world seamlessly with computer-generated texts, images, animations, etc. An augmented world with functions designed for the intended application as well as the end user interaction experience is rendered to the user, resulting in efficient perception and creation for them. AR technology has evolved from one that only appears in science fiction movies to one that has been applied broadly in industries. A review paper published in 2008 discussed the application of AR in industries [1]. In this chapter, research papers focused on the development of industrial applications that were published from 2006 to 2010 are reviewed. These papers are categorized according to the product development cycle shown in Fig. 30.1.

Traditionally, the product development cycle and the manufacturing processes have been assisted with computer-based software, namely the computer-aided design (CAD), computer aided manufacturing (CAM), computer aided assembly planning (CAAP), etc. Virtual reality (VR) technologies were applied to enhance the CAD/CAM processes. However, a few common limitations of the computer-based and VR-based systems can be observed. Firstly, the availability of accurate solid models of the industrial objects, facilities and the surrounding environment is an issue. Secondly, dynamic rendering of all the solid models is vital but it imposes high computation loads.

Although AR has been frequently discussed together with VR, the characteristics of VR and AR enable them to be applied to applications with different foci. At the current stage, due to the presence of tracking errors, VR-based systems may outperform AR-based systems for those applications where process simulation and

S.K. Ong (✉)
Department of Mechanical Engineering, National University of Singapore, Singapore
e-mail: mpeongsk@nus.edu.sg

B. Furht (ed.), *Handbook of Augmented Reality*, DOI 10.1007/978-1-4614-0064-6_30, 651
© Springer Science+Business Media, LLC 2011

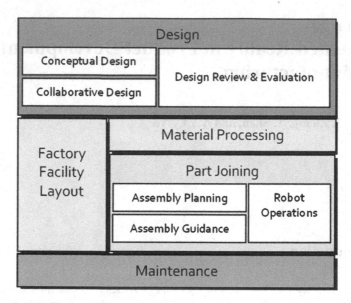

Fig. 30.1 Product development cycle

interactions using highly accurate models are vital, while little intervention from the users is needed. On the other hand, AR has advantages over VR in applications where manipulations and interactions with tangible objects are important. In addition, AR eliminates the necessity of user tracking and avatar modeling in some industrial applications, such as during the evaluation of car models [2]. Limitations of applying VR technology and the advantages of using AR technology in different research areas will be discussed in the following respective sections.

The remainder of this chapter is organized as follows. Sections 2 and 3 review the AR approaches applied in the product development cycle and in rapid and flexible manufacturing, respectively, with the focus on the implementation of the applications and the contributions of these AR-based approaches to solving problems encountered using traditional computer-based and/or VR-based approaches. Section 4 reviews and analyzes the fundamental AR-related methods and approaches applied in the manufacturing applications. Section 5 summarizes the trends in AR-based industrial applications.

2 AR Approaches in Product Development Cycle

2.1 Design

Current research status in the area of product design can be summarized as follows. Firstly, researchers aim to develop design spaces with integrated functions, including product design, analysis based on product simulation, etc. Secondly, collaborative design is encouraged so that experts and even customers can provide feedbacks to the designers during the early design stage. However, CAD-based and VR-based design and collaborative design spaces lack the intuitiveness for the experts and customers to participate in the design process without having been trained first. AR-based design spaces address these problems by introducing input devices and multimodal input approaches to promote natural, efficient geometry creation and manipulation using hands, speeches and gestures.

The intuitive interaction methods provided by AR facilitate conceptual design or intuitive sketch-based design to be achieved in an effective and efficient way. Chen et al. [3] developed a 3D sketching system based on computer vision technology for product design. The system enables the user to draw wireframes consisting of straight lines and curves using a color-tipped wand together with keyboard operations. Planar surfaces and curved surfaces using Bezier representation can be generated based on wireframes. A tablet PC-based sketching tool was developed as a design platform [4], where 3D designs are facilitated by restricting the strokes in 2D frames, which can be generated as a plane perpendicular to the current frame by default or the designer can further rotate the plane to meet his requirement. The 3D design space is defined based on the "napkin," a virtual plane rendered on a set of ARTag markers. Saakes and Stappers [5] applied AR technologies using the spatial AR (SAR) configuration during the early design stage. Textures captured from real objects can be mixed with digital images, and this new texture can be projected onto a physical shape model to inspect the design.

A design space developed in an AR environment enables the user to generate designs based on the characteristics of real objects in the physical surroundings. Anabuki and Ishii [6] implemented the design of 3D digital form using a tangible user interface (TUI), which consists of a jig and an in-line array of motor-driven pins. This TUI can help the user design from a primitive 3D form, e.g., a cylinder in several ways, namely, by manipulating the pin array manually or capturing 2D profiles from real objects to re-define the surfaces of the designed workpiece, and by removing materials from or adding volumes to the workpiece according to the profile of the pin array.

Implementation of collaborative design spaces has been carried out in AR environment for two reasons. Firstly, group discussion and brainstorming among a number of designers are needed during the early design stage. Secondly, the designers benefit, especially in the earlier stage, from the reviews from the planners and engineers based on their experience on the following production steps. Research has focused on both hardware development and information manipulation to enhance the intuitive interaction between designers, experts, and the design space. Haller et al. [7] developed an AR tabletop system for meetings and discussions for idea creation purposes. The Anoto digital pen [8] was applied for the designer to use as a normal pen to draw sketches from given colors and patterns. The digital pen was also used as an interaction tool to manipulate menus, to facilitate data transmission and transfer between the table and the wall or between the personal laptop of the designer and the system. A collaborative product design and development environment was developed by Ong and Shen [9] (Fig. 30.2). Intuitive

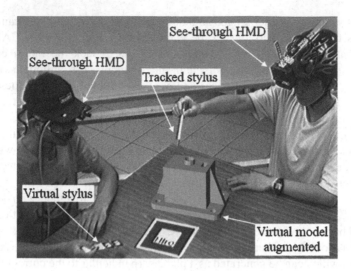

Fig. 30.2 A multiple view collaborative design and development system [9]

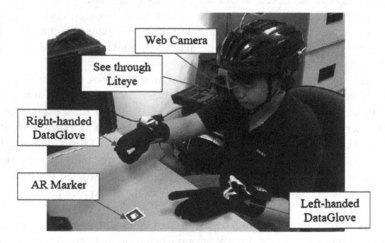

Fig. 30.3 The ARCADE system for product design [10]

interaction and modeling methods were developed in the AR environment to help the designers and experts design and review the CAD model of a product. Online model generation and modification was achieved by using API functions provided by SolidWorks. An AR computer-aided design environment (ARCADE) has been developed to facilitate interactive design for a layman [10] (Fig. 30.3). The user can generate and modify solid models using marker-based interaction methods. Solid models can also be generated from everyday objects for the user to modify and to combine with other models.

Researchers have carried out qualitative evaluation experiments to measure the effectiveness and/or performance of interaction methods developed for AR applications. The effect of using a virtual pointer as an interaction tool in a collaborative design space has been studied [11]. Experiments were designed to evaluate the selection and representation of the virtual artifacts that are selected by the user. Lee and Hua [12] carried out the experiments to measure the effectiveness of the viewing methods and the rotation methods applied in a collaborative AR environment. According to the experimental results, the viewing conditions implemented in the tabletop AR environment to fulfill synchronous tasks need to be implemented according to the applications.

2.2 Design Review and Design Evaluation

Traditionally, the evaluation of a design is performed using physical mock-ups. Some mock-ups are developed to enable the review of the physical appearance of a product by the designer, while some are developed with partially realized functions for usability evaluation purposes. Rapid prototyping (RP) technology has been applied to building physical mock-ups. However, RP technology has the disadvantages of high cost and long lead time. Hence, researchers have applied VR and AR technologies to enable efficient design evaluation in terms of physical design and usability. VR-based design systems may show superiority when evaluations based on the simulation of functionalities are needed due to the well-established integration of simulation modules. However, physical properties of the design, such as weight and texture, are not easy for the user to perceive in VR-based design systems. To address this problem, AR-based design systems were developed for the designers and experts to evaluate the designs based on tangible mock-ups.

Park [13] developed an AR application for the evaluation of Portable Multimedia Player (PMP). Physical mock-ups were developed with one main body and several parts that can be installed onto the main body to simulate the physical appearance of different products. Various colors and textures can be rendered onto the physical mock-up using AR technology. The user can move his fingertip on the mock-up and activate virtual buttons to test certain functions of the design. Computer vision based techniques, namely edge detection, skin color segmentation, etc., have been applied to facilitate intuitive interaction experience. A preliminary user test with 10 subjects was performed with highly satisfactory feedbacks. Another product usability evaluation application [14] applied a handheld device emulator to facilitate the AR-based evaluation process where the user can see the emulated responses from the device as if he is manipulating a real product. A touch sensor is applied in one fingertip to emulate the manipulation of touch screens that have been widely applied in handheld devices nowadays.

Caruso and Re [15] focused on the development of visualization and interaction methods in a design review system. A video see-through (VST) head mounted display (HMD) was designed with two motor-driven video cameras that can adjust the camera convergence automatically. This self-adjusting mechanism solves the problem encountered in common VST HMD that the visualization of a virtual prototype (VP) may distort if it is too close to the designer. The researchers also focused on utilizing a commercial user interaction tool, the WiiMote, to facilitate the designer's operation on the VP, such as panning, rotating, zooming, and pointing operations. A hybrid marker (H-marker) was designed incorporating an image pattern and four infrared (IR) LEDs for VP rendering and manipulating using a common video camera and the IR camera in the WiiMote. Aoyama and Kimishima [16] applied an ARToolKit marker and magnetic sensors on the physical mock-up to facilitate the rendering of the product appearance and the responses of the product triggered when the thumb touches the buttons. An immersive modeling system (IMMS) was developed for the evaluation of personal electronic devices [17]. Multi-modal interactions were considered in IMMS, namely the rendering of visual, tactile, auditory sensory and the interactive rendering of the functions of the device.

Simulation technologies have been applied in the design review application to facilitate the evaluation of the product. A design review (DR) system was developed [18, 19] with various integrated and rendered technical data to the reviewers under network communication. The technical data includes the 3D CAD model of the product, finite element method (FEM) based simulation, and annotations from peer reviewers, web content, etc. In the work by Bordegoni et al. [20], computational fluid dynamics (CFD) analysis and haptic interaction were integrated in an AR environment during the early design stage so that these tools can be used to refine the design based on the analysis of an engineer.

2.3 Manufacturing

2.3.1 Material Processing

Material processing procedures, such as molding, casting, machining, etc., refer to the machine-controlled or machine-assisted procedures that are performed to generate parts before the part joining procedures, such as assembly, welding, etc. VR technologies have been applied in the simulation of these material processing procedures, such as the simulation of casting process [21], tunnel boring machine simulation [22], etc. Comparatively fewer applications have been developed that apply AR technology in material processing. This is probably due to the fact that the processing procedures are machine-centric and fewer human factors are involved during this stage. However, researchers have investigated the application of AR technology for training and process condition monitoring purposes. The advantages of applying AR in these applications are that the user can accumulate knowledge and information when operating on real machines, and the switching of context with the use of computer-based and VR-based simulation systems can be avoided.

A metal casting process simulation was developed in an AR environment for training purposes [23]. A rigid fluid particle model was applied to simulate the pouring process of the metal fluid. The movement direction of each particle was

Fig. 30.4 An in situ CNC machining simulation system [27]

calculated based on the analysis of the particle-to-particle collision and particle-to-wall collision. A blueprint of the respective cast design was used as the marker where the virtual pouring process will be rendered onto.

Few research studies have been conducted on CNC machining applications using AR technology. An ASTOR system [24, 25] has been developed to facilitate the real-time visualization of machining conditions on real machining scenes using SAR configuration. Machining process data obtained using sensors was rendered on a holographic optical element (HOE) window, which was installed on the sliding door of a lathe. The user will see the machining process data being aligned with the machining process in real time on the 2D window. This research focused on the exploitation of AR display mechanism for machining process inspection. Weinert et al. [26] developed a CNC machining simulation system for 5-axis CNC machines. In the system, an ARToolKit marker was applied to track the movement of the cutter with respect to the machine table, and dexel boards were applied to model the workpiece. The simulation module in the system can estimate the cutting forces using the Kienzle equation, and predict collision between the head stock and the workpiece. An in situ CNC machining simulation system, namely the ARCNC system, has been developed [27] for machining operations on a 3-axis CNC machine. To achieve in situ CNC simulation, the position of the cutter is registered in the machining coordinate system using a hybrid tracking method and constraints extracted from given NC codes. The system was designed to be used by novice machinists, who can use the system to alter NC codes and observe responses from the CNC machine without possible tool breakage and machine breakdowns. According to the simulation results, alarms can be rendered to the user to notify dangers and errors (Fig. 30.4).

2.3.2 Assembly Planning and Verification

Given a set of assembly components, an optimal assembly sequence needs to be achieved to reduce the assembly completion time and effort. CAAP systems and

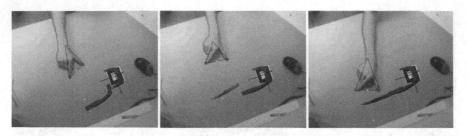

Fig. 30.5 A bare-hand interaction-based assembly design system [31]

CAD-based assembly planning systems are applied traditionally. More recently, VR-based virtual assembly systems have been investigated so that the human motions can be considered during planning [28]. However, intuitive assembly operations cannot be achieved in VR-based assembly planning systems as the planner is not able to have a realistic feel in handling the parts As a result, the effort that is needed to handle certain assembly components cannot be estimated and considered as one of the parameters in solving the optimization problem.

AR technology facilitates the assembly sequence planning and verification as it saves the time and material needed to produce the real assembly components to test the sequences. In addition, the user can handle real objects directly and assemble virtual components with real parts, which facilitates the assembly sequence design for product re-use or reverse engineering. To achieve this, CAD models of real objects must be reconstructed in real-time. Park et al. [29] proposed an AR browser architecture to be applied in an assembly planning application for the assembly planner to visualize the assembly tasks performed in the real assembly station. The researchers addressed the issues of collision, rendering, camera calibration, etc., and the architecture was tested using a scaled cockpit module assembly station. Li et al. [30] developed a prototype system for assembly verification and training using VR and mixed reality (MR) technologies. To verify the assembly process, datagloves and inertial tracking technology were applied in the prototype system to map the movement of the user's hand to the virtual assembly part that he is holding. The orientation of the virtual part can be adjusted automatically according to the inter-part constraints extracted from the CAD models to ensure the assembly features can be matched. An assembly model in tree structure was applied to manage the rendering of assembly information. Wang et al. [31] developed an assembly design system where bare-hand interaction was developed using the fingertip detection method. Virtual parts can be displayed and controlled by the movement of the fingertips, and thus the simulation of assembly operations can be achieved (Fig. 30.5).

It should be noted that challenges in VR-based assembly sequence planning systems are similar in AR-based systems, such as collision detection. AR-based systems are even more difficult to achieve due to the fact that accurate real-time reconstruction of real objects is still an open research topic.

2.3.3   Assembly Training and Guidance

Traditionally, assembly operations are guided using 2D blueprints for the operator's reference. Boud et al. [32] investigated the performance of training approaches using traditional 2D blueprints, VR, and AR approaches. Based on the comparison of the task completion times using these three approaches, it was concluded that both VR and AR approaches can outperform the traditional approach. Their investigation also shows that the VR approach has better flexibility in that the assembly training can be performed anywhere, but AR approach improves the training performance.

AR in assembly guidance can help improve assembly efficiency and lower the overhead for each product. The effectiveness of AR-assisted assembly operations was proven [33], where the researchers performed a comparative study on object assembly using traditional paper media, monitor-based media and HMD-based AR media. For the purpose of providing timely assembly guidance information, its rendering has to follow the assembly procedures, meaning that the system would need to know "when" and "where" to render "what" information so that the guidance can be correct and as intuitive as possible. Hence, there are two research issues to be addressed, namely, the recognition and tracking of assembly components, and the interaction among the operator, the components, and the system.

In assembly data management, an assembly tree is usually applied to determine the hierarchical assembly sequences. Yuan et al. [34] developed a Visual Assembly Tree Structure (VATS) for their assembly guidance system. Information such as the component name, description, and images can be interactively acquired and rendered to assist the assembly operations. An information authoring interface was also presented.

Regarding the assembly component recognition and tracking approaches, most reported AR-assisted assembly guidance systems rely on the ARToolKit markers, which can be attached on the assembly components or the component containers [35, 36]. Research shows that the tracking and rendering performance provided by ARToolKit can meet the application requirement quite well. A Binary Assembly Tree (BAT) structure was applied to facilitate information rendering. ARTag markers have been employed [35, 36] to achieve an assembly platform. Researchers have investigated other approaches to identify assembly components. In the system developed by Yuan et al. [34], the operator needs to identify the components according to a set of images of the components, and actively enquire the information related to the components.

Furthermore, research has been conducted on the interaction between the operator and the system. In the system reported by Yuan et al. [34], an information panel is rendered on the screen or on an ARToolKit marker, and the operator would need to use a stylus with a color feature as a pointer to activate the virtual buttons on the panel to request for the relevant assembly data. Valentini [37] focused on the interaction mechanism using a 5DT dataglove during virtual assembly in an AR environment. The research focused on the grasping and manipulation of virtual assembly components based on the identification of three typical manipulation gestures normally encountered during assembly operations, namely, grasping a

Fig. 30.6 An assembly guidance implementing near field RFID technology [40]

cylinder, grasping a sphere, and pinching. Upon a successful grasping operation during virtual assembly, two circumstances are considered, namely, to move an assembly component freely in the workspace or an assembly constraint.

Chimienti et al. [38] described a standard development procedure for AR assembly training systems, including the steps such as the analysis and subdivision on assembly jobs, assembly instruction generation, etc. Andersen et al. [39] presented an edge-based pose estimation method for the correct rendering of the assembly operations on sub-assemblies that have been accomplished. Pruned model based on the given CAD models were generated off-line, and Chamfer matching method was applied to estimate the pose of the assembly parts. Near-field RFID technology was implemented in the application of assembly guidance in an augmented reality environment [40]. Aiming at providing just-in-time information rendering and intuitive information navigation, methodologies of applying RFID, infrared-enhanced computer vision, and inertial sensor have been discussed in this research (Fig. 30.6).

2.3.4 Robot Control and Programming for Industrial Applications

Industrial robots have been used for tasks that are beyond human operators due to safety, accuracy requirements, etc. In many robot applications, such as welding, optimal paths for the end effectors (EEs) are needed to minimize the task completion time and/or energy consumptions. CAD and VR environments have been investigated for robot control, path planning, programming and simulation [41,42]. Online programming of the paths is achieved by guiding the EE of a robot manually through a preliminary path via several key points. Optimization of the path can be achieved off-line later. VR-based robot control and programming systems have a few limitations. Firstly, depending on the modeling of the environment, certain factors may be neglected by the operator when guiding the EE in the virtual environment, and they cause problems that can only be identified after the offline optimization process. Secondly, VR-based path programming systems have lower tolerance to environment changes due to the fact that modeling of the environment is needed.

AR has been applied in robot programming in industries due to its ability to provide real-time feedback to the operator's actions according to the real

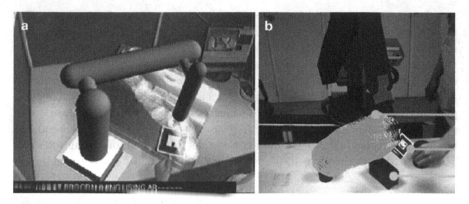

Fig. 30.7 AR robot programming and path planning system [46]

environment. Chintamani et al. [43] used AR technology to help the operator identify the misalignment between the axes of the hand controller (HC) and that of the EE of a remote robot. Reinhart et al. [44] implemented an AR-assisted task-level programming approach, which has shortened the cycle time greatly. Ong et al. [45] applied a collision-free volume (CFV) which are specified during the online guiding of the operator, and an optimized EE path can be generated according to the CFV (Fig. 30.7a). Fang et al. [46] used a marker cube during the manual guiding to facilitate 3D key point insertion and editing actions (Fig. 30.7b).

3 AR Approaches for Rapid and Flexible Manufacturing

3.1 Factory Facility Layout Planning

Research on facility layout planning (FLP) focused on improving the manufacturing efficiency and flexibility by optimizing the layout of facilities, such as machines, material storages, etc., according to certain constraints. FLP is usually achieved based on 2D blueprints 3D computer graphics-based software and VR-based systems. Facility layout is still an open research issue, and a number of research studies focus on the formulation of the problem and the development of approaches to solve the problem [47]. However, conventional FLP software and VR-based systems have a few limitations. Parallel processing of the layout planning process and the layout plan evaluation cannot be carried out due to the lack of realism using computer-based and VR-based systems. Secondly, user interactions provided by these software remains weak [48].

AR can be applied to achieve online FLP with real-time rendering and review of the newly proposed facility arrangement. However, till now little research has been conducted in applying AR to solve the FLP problems. A mobile platform was designed and developed for space planning using the MR technology [49]. The mobile platform incorporates a computer with a touch monitor, a video camera and an inertial sensor to facilitate the planning tasks. Poh et al. [50] applied marker-based interaction methods to allocate physical constraints between mechanical components. Pentenrieder et al. [51] considered the planning of workshops using markers with detailed discussions on the accuracy, functionalities, etc., for the planning application. A pilot study conducted in an automobile industry was presented in this research. Lee et al. [52] developed a FLP system using mixed reality (MR) technologies based on a commercial digital manufacturing software. They focused on the handling of the simulation data in the MR environment.

3.2 Maintenance

Maintenance activities, e.g., preventive and corrective maintenance, are performed according to pre-defined procedures according to the maintenance tasks. The maintenance workers need to be trained in the respective procedures, and they sometimes need to seek help from supporting systems and experts when they are on site. The training of maintenance tasks can be achieved using traditional 2D printed materials and VR-based simulation systems [53]. However, VR technologies cannot be applied for maintenance guidance where interactions with real machines are required. AR technology shows merit in the maintenance applications in two aspects. Firstly, user interfaces can be rendered in a ubiquitous manner so that the worker perceives the instructions with less effort. Secondly, user interactions in the AR environment can facilitate maintenance data logging and management and allow remote collaboration to be achieved intuitively.

Henderson and Feiner [54] developed an opportunistic control (OC) model and applied this model in the development of a TUI for maintenance applications. According to the user study, the OC-based user interface improves the performance with shortened task completion time. Lee and Rhee developed a ubiquitous car service system framework using AR technology with three layers for the manipulation of interaction, context, and service, respectively [55]. User context, such as the preference profile of the user, was considered in this research. Marker-based tracking and information retrieval from product technical information system was applied in the system. The system was implemented for the scenario of a user who needs to repair his mal-functioning car on the road.

Authoring is an important step in remote collaboration applications as experts need to provide instructions to the maintenance worker. Zhu et al. [56] developed an online authoring tool where online authoring is performed by the experts on still keyframes. Using parallel tracking and mapping (PTAM) as the tracking and registration framework, the highlighted objects in the environment can be tracked so that the authored information can be displayed in consistency with the objects (Fig. 30.8).

Fig 30.8 An AR-assisted remote maintenance system [56]

4   AR Approaches in Manufacturing Applications

4.1   Hardware Configurations

Azuma presented the hardware configuration of using the well recognized HMD device in AR applications [57]. Other hardware configurations have emerged, including the monitor-based configuration, the projection-based configuration (e.g., SAR), and the mobile device-based configuration. Researchers select the configuration that suits their applications best. The SAR and the mobile device-based configurations have become more popular recently, mainly because they allow the users to move freely in the physical space without the necessity of wearing hardware or staring at any screens.

4.2   User Interactions

TUI methods using physical artifacts, such as markers, marker cubes, etc., have been developed to facilitate natural interactions in AR applications. TUI methods are applied more commonly in applications where interactions with physical components are needed, such as the physical mock-ups used in the application of design review [13, 14]. More functions have been incorporated in tangible devices to enhance realism, such as physical mock-ups [13, 14] developed with buttons, tactile feedback actuators, etc. Lee et al. [58] used two marker cubes as tangible interfaces for the user's hands. The movement of the two hands can be recognized using the ARToolKit tracking method. Buttons are added in the cubes for function triggering. Two common assembly operations during the assembly of a toy, namely, screw driving assembly and block adding assembly, has been achieved as a pilot study in this research.

In another approach, fingertip detection and gesture detection have been applied in AR applications in order to realize intuitive manipulation and interaction between the user and the augmented virtual artifacts. Fingertip detection was applied by Park [13] to determine the triggering of button functions. Gestures derived from two fingers were applied to manipulate virtual assembly parts by Wang et al. [31]. A pinch glove attached with markers, conductive materials and vibration motors was developed for hand gesture detection and tactile feedback rendering [59]. The glove can provide natural manipulation of virtual objects for applications such as assembly. Dual-hand AR or MR-based assembly tasks may not outperform the cases when only one hand is used in terms of task completion time and operation accuracy [60]. However, using two hands in AR assembly training and guidance systems provides a higher level of realism to the practical assembly tasks, and thus it shortens the time needed for the operator to switch the context from the AR-based system to the real assembly stations.

4.3 Occlusion Handling

Occlusion between 3D objects is normally solved using depth comparison methods. Xu et al. [61] discussed the handling of occlusion between physical and/or virtual elements in an AR-based assembly environment. Depth images of both virtual and physical elements are calculated and compared pixel by pixel to obtain correct rendering on the premise that CAD models of all the assembly parts are available. A model-based depth comparison method was applied [27] on the premise that the cutter will not be occluded by the workpiece during machining processes. Based on the registered cutter position in the image plane, a bounding box is defined and the pixels inside this bounding box are examined one by one to determine the rendering to be the real scene from the camera captured image or the virtual scene from the OpenGL rendering buffer.

The occlusion of the hand by virtually rendered objects was solved by rendering the skin color region on top of other virtual objects, such as in the application of the design review by Park [13].

4.4 Tracking and Registration Methods

According to the applications, different tracking and registration methods have been applied. Fudicials, such as the ARToolKit markers are applied widely in the industrial applications. For single marker-based applications, tracking will fail easily if the marker is occluded in the image plane. Thus, multiple markers, such as the ARTag markers, have been applied to ensure consistent rendering of virtual objects in the scene. Lee et al. [52] used circular shaped safety signs to estimate the camera pose for image registration in a factory layout planning application using circular contour extraction and inverse projection methods.

To overcome the problems mentioned above, natural feature-based tracking methods have been applied in some applications. A hybrid tracking method using template matching and KLT tracker was applied by Zhang et al. [27] to track the moving worktable in CNC machining processes. The PTAM tracking method was applied in the maintenance application [56]. A contour-based markerless tracking method was applied [62] for car engine maintenance where contours are extracted from CAD models under different camera viewpoints and varied illuminations.

5 Future Trends

Based on the literature review, several future trends in the research of AR-based industrial applications are identified.

Researchers have been putting effort to achieve AR applications using specific interaction methods and interfaces that are identical or similar to the traditional methods applied in the industries. The purpose is to facilitate smooth context switch between the AR environment and the real environment. Applications with intensive user interactions can benefit from this research trend, such as in the area of design, assembly training, maintenance, etc. A physical-virtual tool was developed to facilitate the air brushing actions carried out by a designer [63]. Specifically, the designer holds a pistol-like device in his dominant hand to air brush a physical model using the design pattern he selects from a stencil. This system was developed under the SAR configuration, where design patterns are projected onto the hand-held stencil. A foam sculpting system was developed [64] focusing on capturing the sculpting actions of the designer to generate digital models of the workpiece in real time. The system allows the designer to use tools and materials that are traditionally used, namely, a hot wire cutter and a block of foam.

Research on AR industrial applications is towards mobility using handheld devices that are either commercially available products or specially designed for the applications. Hakkarainen et al. [35] reported a study on the possibility of using mobile phones for an AR-assisted assembly guidance system. A client/server architecture was set up using a Nokia mobile phone and a PC. Considering the limited processing capability of the mobile phone, the PC handles the rendering of complex CAD models, and static rendered images are sent to the mobile phone for fast rendering. A mobile device, namely MARTI, was developed incorporating a UMPC and a camera [65]. The MARTI device provides a two-handed gripping structure to ensure comfortable handling of the device.

Some researchers focused on improving the development efficacy of AR-based systems. Engelke et al. [66] discussed several aspects during the development of AR-based training systems.

References

1. S. K. Ong, M. L. Yuan, and A. Y. C. Nee, "Augmented Reality Applications in Manufacturing: a Survey," International Journal of Production Research, Vo. 46, No. 10, 2008, pp. 2707–2742.
2. H. Salzmann, and B. Froehlich, "The Two-User Seating Buck: Enabling Face-to-Face Discussions of Novel Car Interface Concepts," Proceedings of the IEEE Virtual Reality 2008 (VR'08), 2008, pp. 75–82.
3. Y. Chen, J. Liu, and X. Tang, "Sketching in the Air: A Vision-Based System for 3D Object Design," 26th IEEE Conference on Computer Vision and Pattern Recognition (CVPR2008), 2008, pp. 1–6.
4. M. Xin, E. Sharlin, M. C. Sousa, "Napkin Sketch – Handheld Mixed Reality 3D Sketching," Proceedings of the 15th ACM Symposium on Virtual Reality Software and Technology (VRST2008), 2008, pp. 223–226.
5. D. Saakes, and P. J. Stappers, "A Tangible Design Tool for Sketching Materials in Products," Artificial Intelligence for Engineering Design, Analysis and Manufacturing, Vol. 23, Special Issue 3, 2009, pp. 275–287.
6. M. Anabuki, and H. Ishii, "AR-Jig: A Handheld Tangible User Interface for Modification of 3D Digital Form via 2D Physical Curve," Proceedings of the 6th IEEE and ACM International Symposium on Mixed and Augmented Reality (ISMAR2007), 2007, pp. 97–106.
7. M. Haller, P. Brandl, D. Leithinger, J. Leitner, T. Seifried, and M. Billinghurst, "Shared Design Space: Sketching Ideas using Digital Pens and a Large Augmented Tabletop Setup," Proceedings of the 16th International Conference of Advances in Artificial Reality and Tele-Existence (ICAT2006), 2006, pp.185–196.
8. Anoto Digital Pen, http://www.anoto.com/(accessed on 11 January 2011).
9. S. K. Ong, and Y. Shen, "A Mixed Reality Environment for Collaborative Product Design and Development," CIRP Annals, Vol. 58, No. 1, 2009, pp. 139–142.
10. L. X. Ng, S. K. Ong, and A. Y. C. Nee, "ARCADE: A Simple and Fast Augmented Reality Computer-Aided Design Environment Using Everyday Objects," Proceedings of IADIS Interfaces and Human Computer Interaction 2010 Conference (IHCI2010), 2010, pp. 227–234.
11. J. Chastine, K. Nagel, Y. Zhu, and M. Hudachek-Buswell, "Studies on the Effectiveness of Virtual Pointers in Collaborative Augmented Reality," Proceedings of the IEEE Symposium on 3D User Interfaces 2008 (3DUI2008), 2008, pp. 117–124.
12. S. Lee, and H. Hua, "Effects of Viewing Conditions and Rotation Methods in a Collaborative Tabletop AR Environment," Proceedings of the IEEE Virtual Reality 2010 (VR2010), 2010, pp. 163–170.
13. J. Park. "Augmented Reality based Re-formable Mock-up for Design Evaluation," Proceedings of the International Symposium on Ubiquitous Virtual Reality (ISUVR2008), 2008, pp. 17–20.
14. H. Takahashi and T. Kawashima, "Touch-sensitive Augmented Reality System for Development of Handheld Information Appliances," International Journal of Interactive Design and Manufacturing, Vol. 4, No. 1, 2010, pp. 25–33.
15. G. Caruso and G. M. Re, "Interactive Augmented Reality System for Product Design Review," Proceedings of the SPIE - The International Society for Optical Engineering, Vol. 7525, 2010, pp. 75250 H-1–12.
16. H. Aoyama and Y. Kimishima, "Mixed Reality System for Evaluating Designability and Operability of Information Appliances," International Journal of Interactive Design and Manufacturing, Vol. 3, No. 3, pp. 157–164.
17. Y.-G. Lee, H. Park, W. Woo, J. Ryu, H. K. Kim, S. W. Baik, K. H. Ko, H. K. Choi, S.-U. Hwang, D. B. Kim, H. Kim, and K. H. Lee, "Immersive Modeling System (IMMS) for Personal Electronic Products using a Multi-modal Interface," Computer Aided Design, Vol. 42, No. 5, 2010, pp. 387–401.
18. A. E. Uva, S. Cristiano, M. Fiorentino, G. Monno, "Distributed Design Review using Tangible Augmented Technical Drawings," Computer Aided Design, Vol. 42, No. 5, 2010, pp. 364–372.

19. M. Fiorentino, G. Monno, A. E. Uva, "Tangible Digital Master for Product Lifecycle Management in Augmented Reality," International Journal of Interactive Design and Manufacturing, Vol. 3, No. 2, pp. 121–129.

20. M. Bordegoni, F. Ferrise, and M. Ambrogio, "Haptic Interaction and Interactive Simulation in an AR Environment for Aesthetic Product Design," Proceedings of the 3rd International Conference on Virtual and Mixed Reality (Held as Part of HCI International (HCII2009), 2009, pp. 293–302.

21. N. Li, S.-H. Kim, J.-H. Suh, S.-H. Cho, J.-G. Choi, and M.-H. Kim, "Virtual X-Ray Imaging Techniques in an Immersive Casting Simulation Environment," Nuclear Instruments and Methods in Physics Research Section B: Beam Interactions with Materials and Atoms, Vol. 262, No. 1, 2007, pp. 143–152.

22. J. Cheng, Y. Gong, and J. Yang, "Research of Simulation for Tunnel Boring Machine Based on Virtual Reality," Proceedings of 2009 International Conference on New Trends in Information and Service Science (NISS2009), 2009, pp. 1038–1041.

23. K. Watanuki, and L. Hou, "Augmented Reality based Training System for Metal Casting," Journal of Mechanical Science and Technology, Vol. 24, No. 1, 2010, pp. 237–240.

24. A. Olwal, J. Gustafsson, and C. Lindfors. "Spatial Augmented Reality on Industrial CNC-Machines," Proceedings of the Engineering Reality of Virtual Reality 2008, 2008, pp. 680409-1–9.

25. A. Olwal, C. Lindfors, J. Gustafsson, T. Kjellberg, and L. Mattson. "ASTOR: An Autostereoscopic Optical See-Through Augmented Reality System," Proceedings of 4th IEEE and ACM International Symposium on Mixed and Augmented Reality (ISMAR 2005), 2005, pp. 24–27.

26. K. Weinert, A. Zabel, E. Ungemach, and S. Odendahl, "Improved NC Path Validation and Manipulation with Augmented Reality Methods," Production Engineering, Vol. 2, No. 4, 2008, pp. 371–376.

27. J. Zhang, S. K. Ong, and A. Y. C. Nee, "Development of an AR system Achieving in situ machining simulation on a 3-axis CNC machine," Computer Animation and Virtual Worlds, Vol. 21, Issue 2, March/April 2010, pp. 103–115.

28. A. Seth, J. M. Vance, J. H. Oliver, "Virtual Reality for Assembly Methods Prototyping: A Review," Virtual Reality, Vol. 15, No. 1, 2011, pp. 5–20.

29. H.-S. Park, H.-W. Choi, and J.-W. Park, "Augmented Reality based Cockpit Module Assembly System," Proceedings of the 2008 International Conference on Smart Manufacturing Application (ICSMA2008), 2008, pp.130–135.

30. S. Li, T. Peng, C. Xu, Y. Fu, and Y. Liu, "A Mixed Reality-Based Assembly Verification and Training Platform," Proceedings of 3rd International Conference on Virtual and Mixed Reality (VMR 2009, held as part of HCI International 2009), 2009, pp. 576–585.

31. Z. B. Wang, Y. Shen, S. K. Ong, and A. Y. C. Nee, "Assembly Design and Evaluation based on Bare-Hand Interaction in an Augmented Reality Environment," Proceedings of the 2009 International Conference on Cyberworlds (CW09), 2009, pp. 21–28.

32. A. C. Bound, D. J. Haniff, C. Baber, and S. J. Steiner, "Virtual Reality and Augmented Reality as a Training Tool for Assembly Tasks," Proceedings of 1999 IEEE International Conference on Information Visualization, 1999, pp. 32–36.

33. A. Tang, C. Owen, F. Biocca, and W. Mou, "Comparative Effectiveness of Augmented Reality in Object Assembly," Proceedings of the ACM CHI 2003 Human Factors in Computing Systems (CHI2003), 2003, pp. 73–80.

34. M. L. Yuan, S. K. Ong, and A. Y. C. Nee, "Augmented Reality for Assembly Guidance using a Virtual Interactive Tool," International Journal of Production Research, Vol. 46, No. 7, pp. 1745–1767.

35. M. Hakkarainen, C. Woodward, and M. Billinghurst, "Augmented Assembly using a Mobile Phone," Proceedings of the 7th IEEE International Symposium on Mixed and Augmented Reality (ISMAR2008), 2008, pp. 167–168.

36. T. Salonen, J. Sääski, M. Hakkarainen, T. Kannetis, M. Perakakis, S. Siltanen, A. Potamianos, O. Korkalo, and C. Woodward, "Demonstration of Assembly Work using Augmented Reality," Proceedings of the 6th ACM International Conference on Image and Video Retrieval (CIVR 2007), 2007, pp. 120–123.

37. P. P. Valentini, "Interactive Virtual Assembling in Augmented Reality," International Journal of Interactive Design and Manufacturing, Vol. 3, No. 2, 2009, pp. 109–119.

38. V. Chimienti, S. Iliano, M. Dassisti, G. Dini, and F. Failli, "Guidelines for Implementating Augmented Reality Procedures in Assisting Assembly Operations," Proceedings of the 5th IFIP WG 5.5 International Precision Assembly Seminar (IPAS2010), 2010, pp. 174–179.

39. M. Andersen, R. Andersen, C. Larsen, T. B. Moeslund, and O. Madsen, "Interactive Assembly Guide Using Augmented Reality," Proceedings of the 5th International Symposium on Advances in Visual Computing (ISVC2009), 2009, pp. 999–1008.

40. J. Zhang, S. K. Ong, and A. Y. C. Nee, "RFID-Assisted Assembly Guidance System in an Augmented Reality Environment," International Journal of Production Research, Vol. 49, No. 13, 2011, pp. 3919–3938.

41. J. N. Pires, T. Godinho, and P. Ferreira, "CAD Interface for Automatic Robot Welding Programming," Industrial Robot: An International Journal, Vol. 31, No. 1, 2004, pp. 71–76.

42. Y. Wang, Y. Chen, Z. Nan, and Y. Hu, "Study on Welder Training by Means of Haptic Guidance and Virtual Reality for Arc Welding," Proceedings of the 2006 IEEE International Conference on Robotics and Biomimetics (ROBIO2006), 2006, pp. 954–958.

43. K. Chintamani, A. Cao, R. D. Ellis, and A. K. Pandya, "Improved Telemanipulator Navigation During Display-Control Misalignments using Augmented Reality Cues," IEEE Transactions on System, Man, and Cybernetics, Vol.40, No. 1, 2010, pp. 29–39.

44. G. Reinhart, U. Munzert, and w. Vogl, "A Programming System for Robot-based Remote-Laser-Welding with Conventional Optics," Annals of CIRP, Vol. 57, No. 1, pp. 37–40.

45. S. K. Ong, J. W. S. Chong, and A. Y. C. Nee, "A Novel AR-based Robot Programming and Path Planning Methodology," Robotics and Computer-Integrated Manufacturing, Vol. 26, No. 3, 2010, pp. 240–249.

46. H. C. Fang, S. K. Ong, and A. Y. C. Nee, "Robot Programming using Augmented Reality," Proceedings of the 2009 International Conference on CyberWorlds (CW09), 2009, pp. 13–20.

47. A. Drira, H. Pierreval, and S. Hajri-Gabouj, "Facility Layout Problems: A Survey," Annual Reviews in Control, Vol. 31, Issue 2, 2007, pp. 255–267.

48. J. Bénabès, F. Bennis, E. Poirson, and Y. Ravaut, "An Interactive-Based Approach to the Layout Design Optimization," Proceedings of the 20th CIRP Design Conference 2010, 2010, pp. 511–520.

49. G. A. Lee, H. Kang, and W. Son, "MIRAGE: A Touch Screen Based Mixed Reality Interface for Space Planning Applications," Proceedings of IEEE Virtual Reality 2008 (VR2008), 2008, pp. 273–274.

50. Y. L. Poh, A. Y. C. Nee, K. Youcef-Toumi, and S. K. Ong, "Facilitating Mechanical Design with Augmented Reality," 2005 Singapore MIT Alliance Symposium, 2005, pp. 17–18.

51. K. Pentenrieder, C. Bade, F. Doil, and P. Meier, "Augmented Reality-based Factory Planning – an Application Tailored to Industrial Needs," Proceedings of the 6th IEEE and ACM International Symposium on Mixed and Augmented Reality (ISMAR2007), 2007, pp. 31–42.

52. J. Lee, S. Han, and J. Yang, "Construction of a Computer-Simulated Mixed Reality Environment for Virtual Factory Layout Planning," Computers in Industry, Vol. 62, No. 1, 2011, pp. 86–98.

53. B. Arendarski, W. Termath, and P. Mecking, "Maintenance of Complex Machines in Electric Power Systems Using Virtual Reality Techniques," Proceedings of 2008 IEEE International Symposium on Electrical Insulation (ISEI 2008), 2008, pp. 483–487.

54. S. Henderson, and S. Feiner, "Opportunistic Tangible User Interfaces for Augmented Reality," IEEE Transactions on Visualization and Computer Graphics, Vol. 16, No. 1, 2010, pp. 4–16.

55. J. Y. Lee, and G. Rhee, "Context-Aware 3D Visualization and Collaboration Services for Ubiquitous Cars using Augmented Reality," International Journal of Advanced Manufacturing and Technology, Vol. 37, No. 5–6, 2008, pp. 431–442.

56. J. Zhu, S. K. Ong and A.Y.C. Nee, "Online Authoring for Augmented Reality Remote Maintenance," Proceedings of the 12th IASTED International Conference on Computer Graphics and Imaging (CGIM2011), 2011, pp. 87–94.

57. R. Azuma, "A Survey of Augmented Reality," Presence: Teleoperators and Virtual Environments, Vol. 6, No. 4, 1997, pp. 355–385.

58. H. Lee, M. Billinghurst, and W. Woo, "Two-handed Tangible Interaction Techniques for Composing Augmented Blocks," Virtual Reality, 2010. (Available online first at http://www.springerlink.com/content/33gpv053w763n77q/; accessed on 11 January 2011).

59. J. Y. Lee, G. W. Rhee, and D. W. Seo, "Hand Gesture-Based Tangible Interactions for Manipulating Virtual Objects in a Mixed Reality Environment," International Journal of Advanced Manufacturing Technology, Vol. 51, No. 9/12, 2010, pp. 1069–1082.

60. A. Kotranza, J. Quarles, and B. Lok, "Mixed Reality: Are Two Hands Better Than One?" Proceedings of the ACM Symposium on Virtual Reality Software and Technology (VRST2006), 2006, pp. 31–34.

61. C. Xu, S. Li, J. Wang, T. Peng, and M. Xie, "Occlusion Handling in Augmented Reality System for Human-Aided Assembly Task," Proceedings of the 1st International Conference on Intelligent Robotics and Applications (ICIRA2008), 2008, pp. 121–130.

62. J. Platonov, and M. Langer, "Automatic Contour Model Creation out of Polygonal CAD Models for Markerless Augmented Reality," Proceedings of the 6th IEEE and ACM International Symposium on Mixed and Augmented Reality (ISMAR2007), 2007, pp. 75–78.

63. M. R. Marner, B. H. Thomas, and C. Sandor, "Physical-Virtual Tools for Spatial Augmented Reality User Interfaces," Proceedings of the IEEE International Symposium on Mixed and Augmented Reality 2009 (ISMAR2009), 2009, pp. 205–206.

64. M. R. Marner, and B. H. Thomas, "Augmented Foam Sculpting for Capturing 3D Models," Proceedings of IEEE Symposium on 3D User Interfaces 2010 (3DUI2010), 2010, pp. 63–70.

65. B. Stutzman, D. Nilsen, T. Broderick, and J. Neubert, "MARTI: Mobile Augmented Reality Tool for Industry," Proceedings of the 2009 World Congress on Computer Science and Information Engineering (CSIE2009), 2009, pp. 425–429.

66. T. Engelke, S. Webel, U. Bockholt, H. Wuest, N. Gavish, F. Tecchia, and C. Preusche, "Towards Automatic Generation of Multimodal AR-Training applications and Workflow Descriptions," Proceedings of the 19th IEEE International Symposium on Robot and Human Interactive Communication (RO-MAN2010), 2010, pp. 434–439.

Chapter 31
Military Applications of Augmented Reality

Mark A. Livingston, Lawrence J. Rosenblum, Dennis G. Brown,
Gregory S. Schmidt, Simon J. Julier, Yohan Baillot, J. Edward Swan II,
Zhuming Ai, and Paul Maassel

Abstract This chapter reviews military benefits and requirements that have led to a series of research efforts in augmented reality (AR) and related systems for the military over the past few decades, beginning with the earliest specific application of AR. While by no means a complete list, we note some themes from the various projects and discuss ongoing research at the Naval Research Laboratory. Two of the most important thrusts within these applications are the user interface and human factors. We summarize our research and place it in the context of the field.

1 Introduction

This chapter reviews military benefits and requirements that have led to a series of research efforts in augmented reality (AR) and related systems over the past few decades, beginning with the DARPA-funded research of Ivan Sutherland that initiated the field of interactive computer graphics. We will briefly highlight a few of the research projects that have advanced the field over the past five decades. We will then examine in detail the Battlefield Augmented Reality System at the Naval Research Laboratory, which was the first system developed to meet the needs of the dismounted warfighter. Developing this system has required advances, in particular in the user interface (UI) and human factors. We summarize our research and place it in the context of the field.

Military operations are becoming increasingly diverse in their nature. To cope with new and more demanding tasks, the military has researched new tools for use during operations and during training for these operations. There have been numerous goals driving this research over the past several decades. Many of the military requirements and capabilities have specifically driven development of

M.A. Livingston (✉)
Naval Research Laboratory, Washington, DC, USA
e-mail: mark.livingston@nrl.navy.mil

B. Furht (ed.), *Handbook of Augmented Reality*, DOI 10.1007/978-1-4614-0064-6_31,   671
© Springer Science+Business Media, LLC 2011

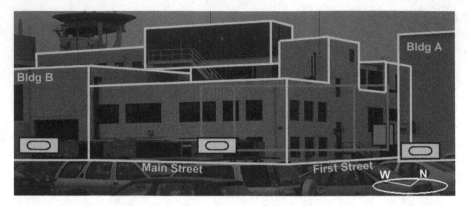

Fig. 31.1 This concept sketch shows information important for military personnel to establish and maintain SA: building and street labels, friendly (*light rectangles*) and enemy (*dark square*) icons, and a compass

AR systems. Thus we begin this chapter by discussing some military needs and challenges for which AR has been proposed to help. The following sections review some specific military applications of AR and examine some of the critical issues limiting the incorporation of AR in military applications. We conclude with a discussion of implications for the field of AR.

1.1 Situation Awareness

The environments in which military operations occur have always been complex, and modern operations have only served to increase this complexity. Dynamic scenarios help create the "fog of war," according to the oft-quoted phrase. It is difficult to keep track of the many friendly and opposing forces operating in an environment. Keeping track of the past, present, and future during such a military operation has been termed *situation awareness* (SA) [7]. The time scale considered to be part of SA varies, but the three categorical times remain. Even keeping track of basic information such as the locations of friendly forces, building and street names or identifiers, and orientation with respect to a global coordinate system become challenging, but critical, tasks. Early designs in our human-centered research process attempted to show multiple layers of geometric and human terrain that might be of interest to dismounted personnel (Fig. 31.1).

The Marine Corps Combat Development Command Concepts Division once described the issue as follows

> Units moving in or between zones must be able to navigate effectively, and to coordinate their activities with units in other zones, as well as with units moving outside the city. This navigation and coordination capability must be resident at the very-small-unit level, perhaps even with the individual Marine [60].

On top of this, recent trends towards asymmetric conflicts have witnessed civilians getting caught in the midst of battles – or worse, purposefully used as human shields by terrorists who do not operate under conventional rules of engagement. These asymmetric battles have become much more common in recent conflicts, and this trend is expected to continue. Increasingly, such battles are fought in dense urban environments, which are inherently more challenging to understand. The nature of battles in 3D urban structures and involving combined air-ground forces further stresses the cognitive load of the individual infantryman, pilot, or sailor, whether in command of some portion of the forces or reporting up the chain of command. With the ability of AR to augment one's view without obscuring that environment, AR became a natural paradigm in which to present military information. Head-up 3D visualization within urban structures was considered a key benefit over 2D map visualizations. This is similar in spirit to the insertion of the first-down line in broadcasts of (American) football; seeing the line as play unfolds gives viewers much greater awareness of the meaning of the play.

1.2 Information Overload

The counter-point to having myriad bits of information that give one a complete picture of the past history, current status, and potential consequences of actions in the environment is having too much information to process. Military commanders often compare information processing in the battlespace to attempting to sip water from a fire hose. The condition of *information overload* occurs when one is unable to process the information presented into coherent SA. With the rapidly expanding ability to collect data in (near) real-time about many locations and provide data abstractions to the warfighter at levels from the command center to individual field personnel, the danger of information overload has grown significantly.

The nature of AR is (generally) to add information to the user's view of an environment; clearly, the issue of information overload requires that this be done in a careful manner so as not to impede the user's ability to achieve or maintain SA. One corollary to this requirement is that the information presented to each user must be appropriate for that user's role in the team's mission. A commander may need to understand the global situation and how the various teams are expected to move through an environment, whereas a private on patrol may only be concerned with a very limited area of the environment. Similarly, a medic may need health records and a route to an injured soldier, whereas a forward observer may need a few days' worth of reconnaissance information in order to detect unusual or unexpected enemy actions. Ideally, an AR system (or any information delivery system) would be aware of these various tasks, the mission plans (including any contingencies), and the current roles any particular user may be fulfilling at a given time.

It should also be evident at this point that an AR system for military applications bridges two somewhat disparate fields. SA implies the introduction of visual representations of data. This type of data abstraction is in itself a major sub-field within the field of computer graphics. Overlaying information is a fundamental characteristic of AR, and this sensory integration can both limit the types of abstractions that make sense for a given application and push the application designer to create new methods of understanding perceptual or cognitive cues that go beyond typical human sensory experiences.

1.3 Training

When conceiving of virtual training, most people immediately think of immersive virtual environment systems, rather than AR and its overlaying of information on the real world. One research thrust that is gaining interest is the use of wearable virtual reality systems for embedded training. For example, a warfighter en route to a deployment may wear a system like the Land Warrior system [17] containing a wearable computer and head-mounted display designed for the display of SA information. But the system could load a virtual training application to better use this travel time. Systems of this type include VICTER [5], DAGGERS and ExpeditionDI® [52], Virtual Warrior [25], Nett Warrior [26], and COMBATREDI® [14].

AR offers some practical advantages over virtual environments. Embedding virtual training applications in existing live-action training facilities can reduce modeling (and rendering) requirements and other infrastructure costs. Modeling an accurate virtual environment and the unknown fidelity requirements of such a model make this an expensive need for immersive virtual environments. Furthermore, this AR facility would maintain the natural haptic cues one gets from walls and other real objects. Virtual environments often require unnatural (e.g. joystick-based) navigation methods; AR eliminates this and allows the user to walk normally, albeit by requiring a large tracking range. Given that AR may one day be an operational tool, using it for training follows the goal for the military to "train as you fight." AR allows for more realistic interaction among multiple trainees, since they see each other through their natural vision (as opposed to an avatar representing a particular person). Finally, instead of using personnel resources to take the roles of potential adversaries or having trainees learn against empty space, a warfighter could train against avatars.

A projection-display based version of mixed reality (MR) training was implemented in the Future Immersive Training Environment Joint Capability Technology Demonstration [48]. In the first implementation, avatars appear on projection screens within a real training environment, technology that is often known as spatial AR. This limits flexibility in the location of avatars, but still supports effective training. The ability to reduce the number of personnel required for effective training (by substituting avatars for real actors to play opposing forces) translates into cost savings. One advantage of the use of AR for this training is that the amount of infrastructure that must be changed from a live-action training facility is small compared to that required by an immersive virtual environment training facility. An improved version of the system used video-based, head-worn AR displays that incorporated a computer vision-based tracking system to reduce the errors in registration of the avatars to the real environment. Registration error could cause avatars to be improperly occluded by the real environment or appear to float above the ground. One limitation of this system is that it currently allows only small units to train together, either a fire team (four people) or squad (thirteen). Another limitation is the size, weight, and power requirements of the head-worn apparatus.

In general, the disadvantages of AR for training are that, like virtual environments, AR systems are not easy to implement, and the technology has struggled to meet some of the minimal requirements in order to be a useful system. Several ongoing research projects are aimed at improving the displays and tracking systems that are critical components for an AR system. Some aspects of AR technology, such as the display, have more stringent requirements than immersive training simulations. So while AR clearly has powerful potential as a training tool, whether it is best for a particular application is not so clear.

A related concept to the planning or rehearsal of a mission is the analysis of a completed mission for future training. In the military, such an analysis is known as *after-action review* (AAR). Both virtual environments and AR generate data that may be used for this type of training. In the same way that AR could reduce the modeling costs associated with virtual training, AR might help reduce the expense of setting up a formal AAR.

Another possible use in training is for specific skills that are basic to numerous military roles. Patrols use particular search patterns to maintain awareness of potential threats. While actors could be trained to approach from specific directions, it can be a more repeatable and cost-effective system to implement virtual avatars for training such a fundamental skill. In this way, basic requirements in military training can be met in an individual instructional phase, allowing each trainee to progress at his or her own pace. It also affords the instructor the ability to test specific difficulties a trainee has had in the past in a repeatable fashion.

1.4   Quick-Reaction Forces

Another increasing emphasis for military operations is the faster pace at which decisions must be made, while the cost of poor decisions can be catastrophically high. If an AR system can present exactly the right pieces of information, better and faster decisions can be made and turned into correct actions. This operates at multiple levels: an individual on an operation might make a better decision about whether an approaching vehicle is a threat, a squad might be able to come to the aid of another unit that is under fire, or a battalion can take advantage of a quickly-configurable AR training facility and be ready to respond to an opportunity that is available for only a brief time. Without such information, perhaps the advantage of pro-active maneuvers will be lost, an operation would be too high a risk to undertake, or decisions have a lower probability of positive outcomes (e.g. a higher rate of losses). Because AR can theoretically present training scenarios with low configuration cost in terms of the scenario (if not the AR infrastructure with current technology), it offers hope for the future of quick-reaction forces.

2   AR Projects for the Military

The concept of a display system indistinguishable from reality was introduced by Ivan Sutherland [57]; a preliminary realization of this "Ultimate Display" for the visual sense was described subsequently [58]. The system included not only the head-worn display (HWD), but also an image generation subsystem and a tracking subsystem for the user's head and one of the user's hands. Thus it marked the starting point for both virtual environments and AR research. It is interesting to note that this first HWD was an AR display, not a completely immersive display suitable for immersive virtual environments.

The system required other novel hardware, notably a "clipping divider" that could properly render perspective views (well before commodity graphics cards became standard) and two position tracking systems (mechanical arm and ultrasonic). One important difficulty noted in early tests of the system was the ambiguous nature of the 3D images. Users visualized a cyclo-hexane molecule; those familiar with the shape had no trouble recognizing it, but other users misinterpreted the shape. This foundational work foreshadowed the difficulties faced by later systems being applied to military applications.

2.1   The "Super Cockpit"

The first specific application of AR technology was for fighter pilots. The Super Cockpit was the forerunner of the modern head-up display still used now by fighter pilots and available in some passenger cars. The original implementations used both virtual environment and see-through display metaphors, to enable the pilot to use the system at night. The system was developed at Wright-Patterson Air Force Base beginning in the late 1960s [21].

Visibility out of a cockpit is limited, and airborne tasks such as low-altitude navigation, target acquisition, and weapons delivery require pilots to reference landmarks on the terrain. However, sensors mounted on the aircraft can create visibility in areas that are occluded by the aircraft structure, or in conditions such as low light that prevent the pilot from seeing the real world. The system superimposed flight and target data into the pilot's visual field and provided sound cues to assist localization.

The key feature of this system was providing spatial awareness for the pilot to understand and incorporate into his course of action a variety of incoming data streams. The horizon became visible through the cockpit window, rather than being conveyed on an indicator on the instrument panel. Targets, navigation waypoints, and threats could similarly be registered to their 3D locations. The concept was that such a view would improve upon using a dashboard display, leaving the pilot to mentally merge the virtual map with his visual field. This is not an easy task and would have required the pilot to take his eyes off the real environment many times in order to align the virtual information. Another feature provided a rear-view mirror, similar to the standard mechanism in a car.

Early versions of the system pointed out the need for study of the human factors of such systems. Spatial reasoning is a complex task, even more so under the physical duress of flight and the emotional intensity of combat. An intuitive interface could take advantage of the natural abilities of many people to reason in three dimensions, rather than have them reason in two dimensions and try to apply that to the real environment. This 3D spatial reasoning is also not a trivial task, but pilots are screened for high spatial reasoning ability, so it seems natural to supply them with an inherently 3D view.

2.2   Aspen Movie Map

One long-standing goal of military training is for forces to know the environment in which an operation will take place, enabling them to navigate and make decisions much faster than if they had to focus on a possibly inaccurate mental map and consider the choices available to them. The interactive movie map was an early attempt to provide this "mechanism for pre-experiencing an unfamiliar locale that allows the acquisition of spatial knowledge to take place in a meaningful, natural, and accurate way" [47]. The Aspen Movie Map [49] was the first of these systems, building on the newly-available optical video disc technology of the 1970s to enable interactive computer control of the display of video frames. In this regard, the movie map shares many characteristics with video-based AR systems; the major difference being the spatial and temporal separation of the user from the displayed environment. However, as this was intended to investigate training applications for the military, it sparked much research in virtual environments and AR, including some of the systems discussed below.

The goal of this system was to convey a sense of being in Aspen, CO to the user, such that the user would know how to navigate in the town without ever having been there. Thus the UI and the controls offered were important components of the system. Most relevant to our discussion of AR and MR was the overview map mode, in which the user could trace the route taken or specify a route for the system to follow; these graphics were merged with aerial overviews. Speed and direction were controlled through a scrollbar-like widget on the touch-screen display. The user could zoom in on the map view, change the season through a toggle switch, or engage a slide show about a specific building from the map.

In an informal user evaluation, subjects who experienced Aspen through the interactive movie map were found to sketch similar maps of Aspen as residents made. Similarity was judged in terms of the number of errors, degree of uncertainty, and level of detail (especially along the main street). It appeared that the movie map users composed their maps based more on linear paths than on areas. This was perhaps a consequence of the linear, grid-like street system of the town, which gave the only available travel routes in the movie map. These users were more likely to be unsure about distances from the movie map, and even when using the system, noted uncertainty about distance traveled along the real terrain and the number of degrees turned, even to the point of some being unsure whether they had turned 90° or 180°. One user sketched an extremely accurate map from the movie map, so at least the potential for learning the space seemed to be a feature.

2.3 Battlefield Augmented Reality System

The overall goal of the Battlefield Augmented Reality System™(BARS) was to do for the dismounted warfighter what the Super Cockpit and its successors had done for the pilot. Initial funding came from the Office of Naval Research. The challenges associated with urban environments were a particular concern: complex 3D environment, dynamic situation, and loss of line-of-sight contact of team members [35]. Unambiguously referencing landmarks in the terrain and integrating unmanned systems into an operation can also be difficult for distributed users [39, 40]. All of these examples show the impairment of SA in urban operations [60]. The belief was that the equivalent of a head-up display (such as in the Super Cockpit) would help solve these. By networking the mobile users together and with a command center, BARS could assist in establishing collaborative SA by a dispersed team.

This raises numerous issues in system configuration. BARS includes an information database, which can be updated by any user. Sharing information across the area of operation is a critical component of team SA. We designed an information distribution system [10] so that updates would be sent across the network. We enabled BARS to communicate with semi-automated forces (SAF) software [9] to address the training issues discussed above. We chose to use commercially-available hardware components so that we could easily upgrade BARS as improved hardware became available. We built UI components so that routes could be drawn on the terrain in the command center application and assigned to mobile users, or drawn by mobile users and suggested to the commander or directly to other mobile users. Typical AR system issues like calibration [3] were investigated.

The BARS research program helped spawn ongoing efforts in both operations [16] and training [50]. Land Warrior [13] shares some capabilities of team SA and has been praised for eliminating confusion in time-sensitive target missions and stopping fratricides in terrain that prevents squad elements from seeing each other. Specific research efforts within BARS for the UI and human factors aspects are the focus of the next section.

2.4 C-130 Loadmaster Training

Flight simulators have become standard tools for training pilots, but other aspects of military flights were also considered to have the potential to benefit from virtual training systems. The USAF Air Education and Training Command conducted a project to determine if AR was an effective tool for training C-130 loadmaster normal and emergency procedures. A C-130 is a military transport aircraft typically used in cargo and resupply operations by numerous countries. The loadmaster is a cargo handler and rigging expert that delivers cargo by airdropping equipment and personnel out of the back of the C-130 [24]. Current training for this job uses ground-based fuselages mounted in a hangar, without wings or tail but with the appropriate working interior. However, the number of training devices and the fidelity of existing devices was judged insufficient to meet the training objectives.

A system was built from commercially-available hardware components and custom software. Head-worn AR displays were mounted to standard-issue flight helmets for students of the training. After a calibration phase, 15 students were trained in procedures for engine start-up and another 15 students in procedures for cargo airdrop. After this training, the students were asked to evaluate the effectiveness of the AR system as a training tool. Six instructors were also asked to evaluate the AR system. A third scenario, simulation of smoke and fumes in the cargo compartment, was shown to students but not included in the evaluation. Questionnaires were used to gather evaluation data.

The overall reaction to the AR system was positive [24]; 63% of the students said that AR was an improvement over the current instructional training. The visualization capability in the AR system was judged to be "far superior" to "checklists and class discussions." However, only 68% thought the AR display was comfortable to wear. Although only six students had used AR prior to this study, 21 recommended it for future use in the training. Among the six instructors surveyed, there was unanimous agreement that the AR system enhanced student training and gave a realistic portrayal of events in the aircraft. Three instructors felt that the training they received on the use of the AR device was less than adequate. Only two of the instructors had never used AR before. Students criticized the AR display as hampering their vision and being too dim. The helmet and display assembly were also judged to be uncomfortable. Finally, students commented that the reaction time of the software was too slow. One missing piece of data that the evaluators were not able to collect were the grades received in the training course to determine whether the AR training had helped students achieve better grades. Lessons learned from these surveys were used to upgrade the AR system. New software and hardware (including display goggles) will be tested in 2011 on a larger group of students. Future evaluations will use surveys, interviews, and reviews of student training records to judge the efficiency and effectiveness of the AR training for loadmaster procedures.

2.5 Summary

In addition to the applications described here, military tasks encompass a wide range of roles that are filled in other professions as well. Industrial and manufacturing applications are discussed elsewhere in this volume. Maintenance and repair of military vehicles is a critical element of mission requirements. Many military vehicles feature a complex, special-purpose set of equipment that makes repairs especially challenging. One particular difficulty can be the densely-packed interior of the vehicles. An evaluation of a prototype AR system for repair of an armored personnel carrier turret [29] found that six recent graduates of a US Marine Corps mechanic's course exhibited faster task location times with AR guidance versus an electronic manual running on a notebook computer and versus the use of a head-worn display with head-fixed (i.e. non-registered) graphics. The study also found that head motion (translation and rotation) was lowered with the AR system versus the electronic manual. The head-worn display may have induced the users to move less than they would have otherwise, so the cause-and-effect relationship must be investigated further. Medical applications are another field in which military interest in AR technology has a long history. The Ultrasound Augmented Reality project [55] is one noteworthy example of a project supported by military research funding.

The remainder of this chapter will describe the multi-faceted BARS program's points of emphasis. The next section discusses case studies of how BARS has been or could be instantiated. The following section describes a number of research efforts in the UI and human factors aspects of the BARS system instantiations. These were motivated by difficulties encountered in implementing the prototype applications and were viewed as critical problems to solve in order to transition these applications out of the lab and into the hands of real users.

3 BARS Case Studies

BARS was originally envisioned as a system for operations, but it became clear that there was great benefit in taking some of the concepts into the training domain as well. These are two vast areas of military applications. As noted above, the military has long supported AR efforts in medicine, maintenance and repair, and other areas that are of interest but not exclusive to the military. In this section, we present four examples of applications built from the BARS software and infrastructure.

These discussions will discuss hardware as appropriate, mostly from the point of view of the requirements or benefits of certain technologies. Since some of these applications were pursued for a finite period of time which has long since passed, some specific hardware would now seem to be an anachronism and will thus be omitted from the discussion.

3.1 Dismounted Warfighter Operations

Military operations in urban terrain (MOUT) present many unique and challenging conditions for the warfighter. The environment is extremely complex and inherently 3D. Above street level, buildings serve varying purposes (such as hospitals or communication stations). They can harbor many risks, such as snipers or explosives, which can be located on different floors. Below street level, there can be an elaborate network of sewers and tunnels. The environment can be cluttered and dynamic. Narrow streets restrict line of sight and make it difficult to plan and coordinate group activities. Threats, such as snipers, can continuously move and the structure of the environment itself can change. For example, a damaged building can fill a street with rubble, making a once-safe route impassable. Such difficulties are compounded by the need to minimize civilian casualties and damage to civilian targets.

A number of research programs have explored the means by which navigation and coordinated information can be delivered to dismounted warfighters. Many of these approaches are based on handheld maps or opaque head-mounted displays (HMDs). For example, Land Warrior introduced a head-worn display that combined a map and a "rolling compass" [27]. Unfortunately, these methods have a number of limitations. They obscure the user's field of view and do not truly represent the 3D nature of the environment. Moreover they require the user to integrate the graphical display within the environment to make sense of it. This work is sometimes difficult and distracting from the current task. We believe a mobile AR system best meets the needs of the dismounted warfighter [35]; we began assembling hardware and writing software to build prototype wearable systems (Fig. 31.2).

Through the ability to present direct information overlays, integrated into the user's environment, AR has the potential to provide significant benefits in many application areas. Many of these benefits arise from the fact that the virtual cues presented by an AR system can go beyond what is physically visible. Visuals include textual annotations, directions, instructions, or "X-ray vision," which shows objects that are physically present, but occluded from view. One important design consideration was not to limit the perceptual capabilities of the warfighter, so we chose optical see-through displays and worked with display manufacturers to reduce the loss of peripheral vision around the display. However, optical systems require significant range of brightness in order to be effective in the wide range of outdoor lighting conditions (day or night).

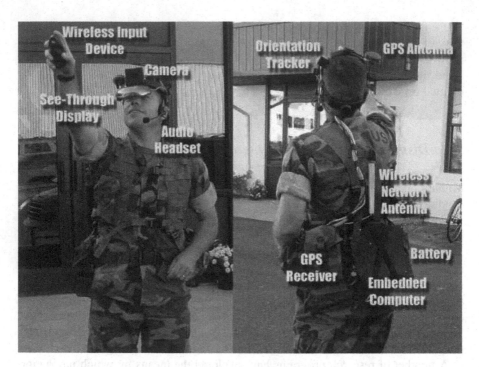

Fig. 31.2 We built this early prototype of our wearable AR system from commercial components. This and similar realizations were used in the research described later in this chapter

3.2 Mounted Warfighter Operations

Military vehicles are also increasingly operated in complex urban environments, forcing vehicle operators to face many of the same SA challenges as dismounted troops. Vehicle commanders are trained to maintain SA by cross-referencing two-dimensional map products, both digital and paper, to the live tactical environment outside the vehicle. Even for experienced operators, this process can be time-consuming and error-prone in the urban environment. AR systems are designed to merge the relevant aspects of the spatial data in the digital map environment into a view of the live tactical environment. A well-designed AR system will display spatial data intuitively with the real world. In a military vehicle, AR systems can enhance the SA of commander, driver, or gunners.

Vehicles are particularly well-suited for AR systems. Typically, the limitations of power, size, and weight that constrain wearable systems are less critical in the vehicle-mounted AR system. In addition, advanced military vehicles may already provide key components such as high-performance GPS and inertial navigation systems, external imaging sensors, digital computers, and video display screens. An early prototype of our vehicle-borne AR implementation is shown in Fig. 31.3.

Fig. 31.3 An early prototype for a vehicle-mounted system included a four-antenna GPS unit on the roof for position and orientation and mobile computers inside for computation and display

Optical see-through AR systems must overcome some unique challenges to be effective in vehicle-mounted systems. The most obvious solution is a "head-up display" as previously discussed in reference to military aircraft. The display device could be mounted in the windshield in front of a vehicle commander. The primary issue with this approach is maintaining alignment of the symbols with the real world, since motion of the operator's head will create significant errors in registration caused by parallax. Fighter aircraft overcome this issue by constraining the pilot's position using an adjustable seat and a harness or placing the display in the fighter's helmet, which is in turn tightly worn on the head. Registration can be accomplished dynamically by tracking the operator's head with a tracking system and combining that information with the vehicle position and attitude to create the visual overlay. This approach adds complexity to the overall system and limits the operator view to a narrow window. Another solution involves having the user wear optical see-through displays inside the vehicle and then tracking the operator's head movements. This approach is currently being utilized by several military aircraft platforms, including the USMC AH-1Z and the Joint Strike Fighter. The approach is highly effective for providing real-time SA but the high costs to develop, purchase, and maintain such systems prevent it from being used in most land vehicles.

Fig. 31.4 The Meissa software displays cues for SA and threat potential

Video AR applications can provide similar functionality with less cost and complexity. The Meissa project at the Naval Research Laboratory looked to develop a simple AR system that could be installed in USMC and US Army HMMWV vehicles to enhance the vehicle commander's SA. The system comprises a wide field-of-view camera installed behind the windshield, a commercially-available attitude GPS system, a rugged vehicle PC, and an LCD touch screen display. Custom-developed software merges symbols representing static and dynamic geo-spatial data onto the live video feed from the camera (Fig. 31.4). The end result is effectively a Head-Down-Display for the commander, which provides a SA alternative between two-dimensional map products and optical see-through options.

3.3 Embedded Training

MOUT training requires that trainees operate in urban structures with or against other live trainees. Often the training uses simulated small-arms munitions and pits instructors against students in several scenarios. Many military bases have "towns" for training that consist of concrete block buildings with multiple levels and architectural configurations. AR and MR can enhance this training by providing

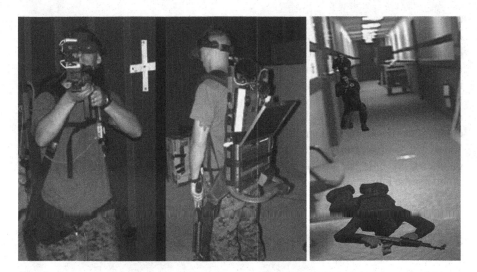

Fig. 31.5 (*Left*) The wearable prototype for our embedded training uses a similar set of equipment as our earlier backpacks. (*Right*) Virtual forces in the embedded training system must appear to exist in the real world and be subject to gravity and other laws of nature

synthetic opposing forces and non-combatants. MR MOUT [30] provided virtual targets on a realistic set using MR (similar to the FITE project, described above). This does not require the trainee to wear an AR display but nearly eliminates portability. Training transfer work [54] found that a "sensory-multiplexing" approach, in which the system takes advantage of the user's ability to gather information from multiple senses simultaneously – assuming the sensory input makes sense – increased the effectiveness of the training in the environment. We theorized that an AR trainer, getting many of these sensory inputs for "free," could be especially effective.

Using AR for MOUT training is a difficult undertaking. Once one has cleared acceptance and logistics issues, there are many technical challenges to face. Many of these challenges are the same as those as described earlier when AR is used for operations – wearable form factor, accurate tracking indoors and outdoors, and so on. One unique challenge to using AR for training operations is that the simulated forces need to give the illusion that they exist in the real world (Fig. 31.5).

Model fidelity is limited by the modeler's time and the rendering capability of the training computer. For mobile devices, it is only recently that sufficient capabilities have existed to display more than a few models with geometric and textural details. However, since only the virtual forces need to be drawn in an AR training application, rather than the entire environment, these resources can be focused on virtual forces. Lighting of the forces should match the environment, which requires measurement of the natural light, rendering capability to reproduce it, and a display algorithm that can make the rendered image appear as desired on the display. This last issue is problematic for optical see-through displays. Finally, the virtual objects must properly occlude and be occluded by real objects. Optical see-through displays again present difficulties here. Whereas in operational contexts, seeing objects through walls might be an advantage, in training, this would break the illusion. Modeling the environment can provide the ability to occlude graphics with real objects by simply not rendering graphics where they are computed to be hidden from view; this is a standard property of the depth buffer in graphics hardware. Only a few research prototype optical see-through displays can fully occlude the real environment, by using a second display surface to become occlusive where desired. Video AR systems can provide this capability, at a cost of limiting the user to the geometric and color resolution of the camera that captures the real environment. We opted for the latter choice in our embedded training prototypes.

3.4 Forward Observer Training

The USMC's Fire Support Team training begins with small-scale (1:40) pneumatic mortars on a field. The purpose of this training is to hone the communication skills between the forward observer and the Fire Direction Center (FDC). In the current training plan, a forward observer visually locates targets, identifies and determines grid coordinates using binoculars and a map, and recommends a call for fire to the FDC. Once the shots are fired, the training instructor (not a part of the operational fire support team) determines the accuracy of the shots and the effect on the target: catastrophic hit, mobility hit, or no effect. The calls for fire are adjusted until the team has the desired effect on the target. Before the introduction of the AR system, the team fired upon static and unrealistic proxy targets.

One system [11] was demonstrated at Quantico Marine Corps Base in October 2004. It provided a head-mounted display for the forward observer and a touch screen for the instructor, each showing virtual targets on the real range. Figure 31.6 shows the observer's view of virtual targets and buildings on the range. The observer can have the computer simulate a magnified view (including a reticle) that binoculars provide, to determine target identity and grid coordinates. The targets move along preset routes and are started and stopped by the instructor through a simple interface. As before, the forward observer calls for fire on the targets and a round is fired. The instructor sees where the round lands in the augmented touch screen view and designates the effect on the target. Through the dynamic shared database the forward observer sees that effect and revises the call for fire. Inserting AR into the training plan resulted in no significant changes to the duties and actions of the participants, but it enabled them to fire on moving targets.

The virtual targets for training were received well by trainees and instructors at Quantico; however, rigorous studies and measurements of effectiveness are yet to be done. The system can also insert virtual terrain and control measures into the display, and both capabilities were preliminarily tested at Quantico.

Fig. 31.6 The forward observer training application shows virtual targets and buildings

4 Human-Centered Research

As with the Super Cockpit [22] and Aspen Movie Map [47], we found that BARS could not succeed in the applications described above without innovation in the UI and human factors of the hardware and software. For BARS research, we followed a user-centered approach [37]; thus, we conducted a domain analysis [40]. In this section, we summarize a number of research thrusts in these arenas, with references to papers for readers interested in further details. These efforts were motivated by difficulties faced in the applications, as noted in the discussions below.

4.1 Depth Perception and Occlusion Representation

Among the things our initial domain analysis [23] indicated as a potential advantage for AR for dismounted troops was the ability to show where distributed troops were in an urban area of operations. Later, client interest included the ability to communicate points of interest in the environment to distributed team members (without the benefit of line-of-sight contact between team members). Both of these goals require the AR system to identify objects that are occluded from the user. This became a central focus of the BARS research program.

The metaphor of "Superman's X-ray vision" has long been applied to the capability of AR to depict a graphical object that is occluded by real objects [56]. There are three aspects to the problem of displaying cues that correspond to occluded virtual objects. First, the alignment or *registration* of the graphics on the display must be accurate. This is a defining aspect of AR [2]. Second, the ordinal depth between the real and virtual objects must be conveyed correctly to the user. Because we selected optical see-through HWD for operational reasons, we needed to replace the natural occlusion cue for depth ordering. Third, the metric distance of the virtual object must be understood to within a sufficient accuracy that the user can accomplish the task. This requires the cues that are provided to be sufficiently accurate to estimate distance. Further, each successive aspect depends on the previous ones.

We began our investigation with a study that identified graphical cues that helped convey the ordinal depth of graphical objects [36]. We found that changing the drawing style, decreasing the opacity with increasing distance, and decreasing intensity with increasing distance helped users properly order graphical depictions of buildings that corresponded to occluded buildings on our campus. This task was detached from the real world, however, so our next experiment used a depth-matching task with the same graphical cues. This enabled us to measure metric distance judgments and forced our users to compare the depth of graphical objects to the real environment. We verified that users were behaving similarly with virtual objects as with real objects [38], and then studied distance estimation [59]. We found an underestimation of distance at medium-field distances of 5–23 m (similar to results for virtual environments), but overestimation beyond these distances. We found that the presence of an occluder increased the absolute distance error about 8 cm for every meter of distance from the user versus when no object occluded the region surrounding the virtual object's location relative to the real environment.

We next moved our experiment to the outdoor scenario for which BARS was intended and that this series of experiments was designed to solve. Because we were seeing such strong linear perspective cues in our indoor (hallway) environment, we decided to test whether replicating this cue would assist users in estimating the distance (Fig. 31.7). Our results [43] showed that users underestimated distance indoors, but overestimated distance outdoors. This differed from our previous indoor data, which showed a switch from underestimation in the medium-field but overestimation at far-field distances.

An analysis showed that the difference between the two data sets overall was significant. A closer analysis comparing the distances revealed that only for a reference object at approximately 33 m was the difference for a particular distance significant. Thus we considered experimental conditions that were changed to suggest reasons for this difference in user behavior with respect to under-or over-estimation. The most obvious difference was the orientation of the reference

Fig. 31.7 (*Left*) The indoor portion of our most recent AR depth perception featured strong (real and virtual) linear perspective cues. (*Right*) The outdoor portion of the experiment tested the utility of only the virtual perspective cues, with limited success for distant targets.

objects. For the earlier experiment, we oriented the reference objects vertically, and the near edge of the virtual object (also oriented vertically) was a few inches away from the real reference objects. When the experiment was replicated for an outdoor environment, it became difficult to keep the reference objects upright, so we oriented both the real reference objects and the virtual targets horizontally in both indoor and outdoor environments. This separated the real and virtual objects by a couple of feet (as seen in Fig. 31.7). It is also true that for the second experiment, we compressed the distances slightly to fit into a smaller experimental space. One of these changes appeared to cause the difference in the indoor data.

The more important result from this experiment, however, was that the linear perspective cues caused users to reduce their estimation of the distance of the virtual object for only the most distant reference objects. In the outdoor environment, this improved the performance, since users were overestimating the distance. However, for the indoor environment, this increased the error, since users were consistently under-estimating the distance already. At distances of under 25 m, the linear perspective cues seemed to make no significant difference in the users' performance.

To bring this series of experiments full circle, we needed to return to the ecologically valid task of the MOUT scenario. In our most recent experiment, we made one more important change in the experimental design [45]. We used military standard map icons [18], and applied the drawing styles discovered early in our sequence of experiments to these icons. We compared this to several other techniques for displaying occluded information that had appeared in the AR literature. The opacity and drawing style techniques were not as effective as newer techniques (Fig. 31.8). A *virtual tunnel* [4] built by drawing virtual holes in known occluding infrastructure led to the lowest error in interpreting the ordinal depth of a virtual squad icon amongst real buildings. The next best technique was one we devised for this study, a *virtual wall* metaphor with the number of edges increasing with ordinal depth. However, both of these techniques led users to perceive the icons as closer than they were intended to be. A *ground grid* technique which drew

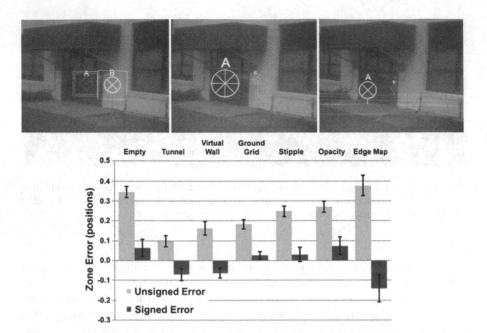

Fig. 31.8 The new techniques for displaying personnel locations occluded from line-of-sight contact performed well. The top row shows the virtual tunnel (*left*), virtual wall (*center*), and ground grid (*right*) techniques. The graph shows the performance by users in our study. Negative signed error indicates users thought the objects were closer than they were

concentric circles on the ground plane (of the nearly flat experimental environment with the 18 cm deviation) resulted in the signed error that was closest to zero, even though users made more errors in this condition.

We observed other significant effects (not published elsewhere). The type of icon (friendly or enemy) had a significant effect on signed error – $F(1, 13) = 43.935$, $p = 0.000$ – but no significant effect on unsigned error – $F(1, 13) = 0.584$, $p = 0.458$. These results were echoed in our finding of a significant interaction between icon type and occlusion metaphor for signed error – $F(6, 78) = 7.651$, $p = 0.000$ – but not for unsigned error – $F(6, 78) = 1.536$, $p = 0.178$. The cyan friendly icon was interpreted to be closer than it really was, whereas the red enemy icon was interpreted to be slightly farther than it really was. The colors were matched to the MilStd2525c document, but not corrected for the AR display, which pushes the cyan (used for friendly icons) toward the purple while pushing the red (used for enemy) slightly more toward the orange [44]. This may have caused some change of apparent brightness, which in turn affected the perceived distance from the user.

We asked further for users to estimate (in meters, feet, or yards) the difference in depth between the two icons. A significant main effect of occlusion metaphor on unsigned distance error – $F(6, 78) = 13.426$, $p = 0.000$ – was found, but not for signed error – $F(6, 78) = 0.555$, $p = 0.765$, which raises concern that users got confused about which order implied a negative number should be entered. Users were most accurate with the ground grid, which explicitly shows the absolute egocentric distances. We also saw a main effect of occlusion metaphor on response time – $F(6, 78) = 2.660, p = 0.021$. Users were fastest with the empty design (mean response of 2.70 s), closely followed by the virtual tunnel (2.78 s). The ground grid (3.71 s) and virtual wall (3.73 s) were slower than all methods except an overlaid edge map (which inspired the virtual wall). We did not sub-divide response time into the sub-tasks of depth for each icon and the distance estimation task, and it is possible that users conceived all three answers before entering any responses for a trial. Finally, we noted a standard practice effect: users were faster with successive blocks of trials (where blocks had a constant occlusion metaphor). We recorded subjective workload responses, but did not find a significant main effect. We did see some slight evidence – $F(6, 78) = 1.832, p = 0.104$ – for users to feel that (in this order) the virtual tunnel, virtual wall, and ground plane had the lowest workload (measured by NASA TLX [28]).

To summarize this discussion, we found good designs for display the information that can help dismounted personnel meet some of their SA needs. This line of research represents how an interesting ecological problem suggested by subject matter experts can spark an interesting scientific question, which can be pursued independently or in the context of that specific application. While even the most recent test did not provide a final answer, it gave us great insight into directions for how the scientific and ecological questions inform the design of military AR applications.

4.2 Information Filtering

The issue of information overload, as noted above, can become a primary difficulty in MOUT. The physical environment is complex, 3D, and dynamic, with people and vehicles moving throughout. In addition, these entities may be hostile, neutral, or friendly to troops – and even these relationships may change depending on the recent course of events. Thus one may think that more information would be of obvious assistance to the military personnel engaged in such operations. But the amount of information can become too much to process in the dynamic pace of military operations, to the point where it inhibits the ability of personnel to complete their assigned tasks. We have thus developed algorithms for restricting information that is displayed to users.

Based on interviews with subject matter experts over the extended course of the project, our filtering algorithm evolved from a region-based filter [31] to a hybrid of the spatial model of interaction [6], rule-based filtering, and the military concept of an area of operations. The resulting algorithm [45] enables sufficient flexibility to update the area of operations, the user's area of interest, the area in which a threat has potential impact, and of course the user's position and orientation in

Fig. 31.9 (*Left*) Showing all information and labels in the database can overwhelm the user and prevent a Marine from achieving SA. (*Right*) Our information filter uses semantic keys and the concept of area of operations to limit the information shown, which enables the user in this case to discern the location of enemy tanks – spotted by another user – much more easily

the environment. Objects are displayed when their impact can be felt within the user's area of interest (a spatial calculation) or the rule-based filter determines that the information is vital (Fig. 31.9).

Compounding the difficulty of having too much information is the issue of how well registered the annotating graphics are to their proper location. As noted above, this underlies the presentation of depth, but it also supports the filtering operation. If graphics can be properly aligned, then the cognitive load to understand the graphics' meaning or information content is reduced, enabling the user to understand and integrate the merged real and virtual image. Thus more information can be shown (assuming a consistent level of registration). We studied techniques to compensate for improper registration [46] and how much mis-registration might be acceptable in certain military tasks [34].

In the UI architecture, we had to determine how to merge the sometimes competing directives from the components. We began with a simple architecture, proposed a complicated mediation architecture [32], but then settled back to a simple pipeline architecture, assisted by incorporating the occlusion representation into the information filter [45].

4.3   Object Selection

In order to query, manipulate, or act upon objects, the user must first select these objects. BARS allows a user to select objects by combining gaze direction (using tracking of the head) with relative pointing within the field of view using a 2D or 3D mouse or eye tracker. The complex nature of the selection operation makes it susceptible to equipment error, scene ambiguities, and user error. Equipment error includes tracking noise, drift, latency, and insufficient resolution for the desired precision. Scene ambiguities arise from the geometric environment, such as when objects overlap in their projections to the current viewpoint. In BARS, with the "X-ray vision" paradigm, these occlusion relationships complicate matters more than many applications. Human error includes imprecision due to lack of experience, poor motor control skills needed for fine-grain selections, and fatigue developed during a session. All these errors lead to selections that were not intended.

To mitigate these errors, we designed a multimodal (speech and gesture) prob-abilistic selection algorithm [53]. This algorithm incorporates an object hierarchy (e.g., in the BARS object database, a door is a child of a wall, which is a child of a building, and so on), several gaze and pointing algorithms, and speech recognition. The pointing algorithms rank the objects by distance to the pointing vector, a weighting scheme combining size and distance to the pointing vector, and a weighting scheme combining distance to the view plane and pointing vector. For each pointing selection, the user issues a voice command including the type of object to be selected. The speech recognizer returns a ranked list of candidate objects that it interpreted as what the user intends to select. The object hierarchy, in conjunction with the voice commands, reduces the search space for which object is being selected. The algorithms are combined using a weighted voting scheme to disambiguate any remaining selection discrepancies. We estimated best weighting assignments by evaluating the algorithms through a series of user experiments.

4.4   Collaboration Techniques

From its inception, BARS was envisioned to include a command-and-control (C2) application that would enable a commander to maintain SA of the mobile users in the field; this is also a critical aspect of a military scenario. Commanders naturally have more information about the entire area of operations and situation that subordinates in the field do not have. A C2 application can enable them to get a bird's-eye view, which can be useful for understanding positioning or routes on the ground plane, or they may see the environment from a particular mobile user's vantage. They can direct personnel out of harm's way or to come to the assistance of personnel who encounter a crisis. They can see conflicts between units and perhaps through this capability, reduce friendly fire incidents. We implemented a route-drawing feature in the C2 application, enabling the commander to place waypoints on the ground plane simply by clicking the mouse.

Virtual globe applications can provide an excellent platform for this type of C2 application; we found Google Earth to be suitable due to the 3D building layer and the API that enabled rapid prototyping of environments and an application [1]. We simulated having sensors in the environment by merging in live camera views onto this simple 3D terrain. We computed the projection of the camera's image onto known geometry to approximate a live view of the environment (Fig. 31.10).

Mobile users also need to collaborate directly with each other. From our interviews with domain experts, we learned how military personnel often draw maps

Fig. 31.10 A command-and-control (C2) application might show icons for forces and live sensor (including camera) data over a mixture of satellite imagery and virtual terrain

in the dirt in order to coordinate a new plan of action. We decided to extend the map view mode of our mobile AR system to incorporate this paradigm. The map view has always been a popular feature of our and others' AR software [20]. Technically, this breaks the first-person paradigm that is often considered a fundamental aspect of AR; we give an essentially 2D view of the world by raising the virtual viewpoint high, directly over the user's position. We then extended the route-drawing feature of the C2 application into the mobile application's map mode, and gave users the ability to communicate these objects through the data distribution system. As with all objects, routes are subject to the filter parameters and rules. We then found that our domain experts reacted more positively to viewing the filter results in map mode than in the head-up AR view. This became a good way to preview the filter results.

4.5 Evaluation of Vehicle AR for IED Awareness

Several important results were identified during the development, testing, and demonstration of the Meissa system. Testing showed that in a moving vehicle environment, the AR display should be considered an enhancement, not a replacement, for the map display. The two-dimensional map provided excellent SA at greater distances. The AR display was most effective at closer distances where the camera could see clearly. Meissa was designed to allow the user to toggle between using the map or AR display as a primary display with a smaller window visible for the alternate view. Also, a significant effort was made to ensure that symbols were consistent between the two views, to allow the operator to switch quickly between views without losing SA.

A somewhat surprising result identified during the operational demonstrations was the enthusiasm the operators had for the Meissa mission recording capability. Operators appreciated the real-time SA, but they were often more interested in the Meissa system's ability to record video, geospatial data, events, and audio annotations. These features allowed for much more effective AAR using the AR technology to overlay aspects of the recorded mission. The geo-registered video also enabled much more accurate extraction of valuable intelligence from missions than the hand-written notes and human recollection used in most military patrols. The mission recording capability of Meissa was not an initial focus of the research and development effort, but based on user feedback this technology became a focus of subsequent development efforts.

4.6   Urban Skills Evaluations

To determine the suitability for mobile AR for urban skills training, we conducted two evaluations. The first evaluation considered the training transfer to teams of novices for the task of clearing multiple rooms [12]. The second, expert evaluation, designed using lessons learned from the first, looked at skills improvement of experienced warfighters, Corporals and Lance Corporals with combat experience. Room clearing [19] is a task in which a four-person fire team methodically enters a room and engages any threats in that room. Each member of the team enters the room a certain way (cross, hook, etc) and has a particular area of responsibility within the room.

The novice evaluation used two-person teams; scenarios were designed such that the missing team members would have had no responsibilities in the small rooms in the experiment. The primary independent variable was the training mode: with AR or without AR. Eight teams participated, receiving their training through a video, demonstration of techniques by a subject matter expert, and then practice in their assigned training mode. All participants wore the AR backpack, but only teams assigned to AR training practiced against virtual forces (Fig. 31.11); the other teams practiced against empty rooms. Teams were encouraged to perform several repetitions of the task in the 15 min allocated to practice. After the instructional period ended, the subjects moved to another part of the test site to be evaluated. Here, participants performed six room-clearing scenarios against real people. Each scenario had enemy and neutral forces in different positions. The subjects and the people playing the enemy and neutral forces traded fire using "laser-tag-style"

Fig. 31.11 Virtual enemy forces populated the training rooms for the urban skills evaluation teams randomly selected to train in the AR condition

weapons. This weapon system counts the number of hits on the subjects and on the enemy and neutral forces. The participants wore the AR backpacks solely for tracking and logging the users' actions.

While there were no main effects on objective or subjective performance measures designed by our subject matter expert, we did find an interesting interaction between training method and the number of trials performed. The dependent measure that showed this interaction was visual sweep. Visual sweep is a composite of both speed and effectiveness in the participant's initial entry into the room, and was created based upon recommendations from our SME. It is the angular rotation (based upon the head tracking data) of the participants during their initial 3.5 s in each room. The brevity of this time period was enough to capture the subjects' first sweep of the room, but eliminated all motions that they made after finishing their initial sweep, when the subjects would turn and discuss the situation, or turn completely around and leave the room. A test of simple main effects revealed that on trial 1, the AR group had a significantly smaller room sweep compared to the non-AR group. However, on the last trial, the AR group's room sweep was significantly larger than that of the non-AR group. In essence, novice subjects who trained against AR-generated forces were learning to look at more of the room to be cleared than novice subjects who trained against empty rooms.

We simplified the expert evaluation to allow us to collect more detailed data and to make practical the task of performing the evaluation off-site. Subjects were evaluated individually, and the scenarios were set up such that the threat was always in the subject's area of responsibility. This evaluation had three training conditions: with AR, without AR using a live enemy, and without AR using static targets.

The purpose of these studies was to measure the usefulness of AR at the application level and to set the stage for future work. This evaluation used a pre-test, a training period, and a post-test for each subject. The test periods ran the subject through six scenarios each. The training period contained 24 scenarios to be completed regardless of time needed rather than a fixed time period as in the first evaluation. In this evaluation, the subjects were experienced warfighters, mainly Corporals and Lance Corporals. This subject pool was more homogeneous than that of the novice evaluation, and due to their experience and expert knowledge in room clearing, we could focus on skills improvement rather than training transfer. The pre- and post-tests were always against live threats regardless of the training condition. As before, the scenarios were designed such that the single user would only face threats in that user's area of responsibility, retaining the spirit of the room clearing doctrine.

We ran 24 subjects through our three training conditions: AR (seven subjects), live (eight), and static targets (nine). We did not see any significant results, and the trends noted in the data seemed to indicate the difficulties our Marine subjects had with the AR system rather than measurements of the effectiveness of the application as a concept. One benefit of testing on enlisted Marines was getting feedback from people who would use a system like this if it were fielded. The most frequent comment was that subjects had difficulty sighting with the AR-based weapon. This feedback reflected the difficulty of achieving precise registration. Other comments focused on the poor visibility through the video-based AR display (which prompted the basic perception experiments described in Sect. 4.7) and on ergonomic issues. But subjects liked the concept, and the manpower savings that could be realized by replacing human actors with virtual enemy forces in training could be significant. As noted above, this aspect of the BARS project has been carried forward into other programs, currently sponsored by the Office of Naval Research.

4.7 Basic Perception

One of the problems encountered by users in our urban skills evaluation was an extreme difficulty in seeing clearly through the video AR display we selected in order to overcome the occlusion issue noted in Sect. 3.3. This prompted an investigation into exactly how well users could see through the AR displays. We began to consider several aspects of basic perception in AR displays: contrast sensitivity, color perception, and stereo perception. (Users also noted problems with depth perception, an issue addressed in Sect. 4.1.) It should be noted that these issues occurred in a controlled laboratory setting, whereas military operations may occur at any time of day or night and will likely involve both indoor and outdoor settings. This increases the range of background lighting conditions under which good visibility of both the real and virtual portions of the AR scene must be maintained.

Visual acuity is perhaps the most basic visual capability that can be measured. An optometrist determines this through a series of recognizable targets (often letters or simple shapes) at a standard contrast value. Contrast sensitivity accounts for

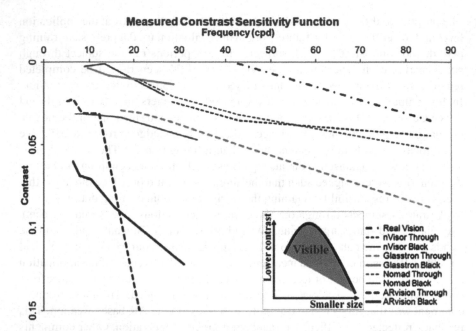

Fig. 31.12 The measured contrast sensitivity function (CSF) shows that AR displays severely reduce users' visual capabilities relative to their natural vision. The inset next to the legend shows the canonical form of the CSF we have sampled

the varying size requirements for different levels of contrast. But such a *contrast sensitivity function* for AR has two forms: one can measure the ability of the user to see the graphics presented on the AR display or measure the ability to see the real environment through the AR display. Full details of our analysis to date [33,44] may summarized as follows (Fig. 31.12). Some optical see-through displays inhibited the user's ability to see the real world. Some graphical presentations were interpreted at the visual acuity one would expect from the geometric resolution of the display device. The video AR display (which was used in the urban skills evaluation) did not fare well in either measure, owing to the camera resolution and display quality in commercial products of the time. However, even with moderate contrast levels, users were not able to achieve performance that would have corresponded to the maximum visual acuity score for which the stimuli could test; this acuity was in turn below that implied by the pixel resolution of the displays. Thus it is fair to speculate whether poor visual quality of the display devices could be blamed for difficulties in any of the applications or evaluations we conducted.

Color perception can also be a key display property for military applications and a particularly novel hazard for optical see-through displays. Black in a rendering buffer becomes transparent on an optical see-through display, allowing the real world to be seen. So one can easily imagine that dark colors will be perceived improperly. But even bright colors do not fully occlude the real-world background, and thus they too are subject to incorrect perception depending on the color (or mix

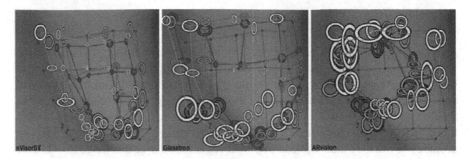

Fig. 31.13 The perceived color gamut for three AR displays shows the distortion that optical see-through displays nVisorST (*left*) and Glasstron (*center*) as well as video-overlay display ARvision (*right*) cause in the perception of colors, both of the graphical overlays and of real-world objects

of colors) that appears behind them in the real environment. We measured the color distortion seen in AR displays, two optical see-through and one video. We found that all three displays distorted colors that were seen on white or black backgrounds, and that this occurred with both graphics presented on the displays and real-world targets seen through the displays. With our particular devices, the video AR display and one of the optical see-through displays were particularly limiting of the color brightness, making all colors appear closer to gray than they were intended to be. Additionally, the video AR display caused high variance in user responses to our color matching task (Fig. 31.13).

Stereo presentation of graphical images has often been considered a requirement for AR displays. The belief is that in order for the user to perceive graphics as representing 3D objects existing in the surrounding 3D environment, the graphics must be in stereo. One limiting factor in whether a user is able to fuse two images for the left and right eye is vertical alignment. Using nonius lines, we detected errors in alignment ranging from a few hundredths of a degree (well within the tolerance of the human visual system) to four tenths of a degree (an amount that would likely cause eye fatigue or headaches if the user were to force the images to fuse). Simple geometric corrections applied to one eye were sufficient to alleviate these errors [41]. We then were able to measure the stereo acuity that users experience with AR displays, again finding that the differences in depth that a user could detect between real and graphical imagery were well above thresholds in normal human vision of real objects [42]. This gave us further evidence of the limitations relative to normal human vision caused by a commercial AR display.

5 Challenges of Designing Military AR Applications

We begin our summary of applications of AR to the military with a discussion of the aspects of military operations and personnel that make designing AR applications a challenging problem.

5.1 Mobility

Among the greatest technical challenges for BARS was mobility; this also makes
BARS somewhat unique from several other military applications of AR. A pilot or
boat captain moves or turns his or her head in a constrained domain. Dismounted
and vehicle-mounted personnel have a much freer range of movement relative to
fixed infrastructure that is central to their tasks. This requires the tracking system
to be usable nearly anywhere on the globe, in theory. To achieve the kind of
accuracy in tracking that will lead to proper registration over this range is of course
a heavy requirement. In the BARS program, we tested technologies including GPS,
magnetic systems, inertial systems, video-metric systems, and hybrids of these
without finding a solution that we felt was robust and accurate enough to achieve
the kind of results we could get in a laboratory setting; these in turn were barely
sufficient to perform controlled versions of the tasks we envisioned as being of
potential value to military users of AR. Note that pilots are in particular known
for having a high dynamic range in their head orientation; we expect dismounted
personnel on a patrol could exhibit similarly sudden movements, further stressing
the tracking system.

Another crucial difficulty created by the need for mobility was finding a suitable
display device. We tested numerous head-worn displays. As noted above, optical
see-through devices have the obvious advantage of permitting the user to take
advantage of peripheral vision around the display and natural vision where the
graphics are not present. Video overlay displays were judged to be advantageous for
training systems because we could completely control the occlusion relationships
between real and virtual entities. But to use either type of display outdoors requires
that the brightness of the display be sufficiently high to be visible in bright sunlight.
At the same time, a display must be usable at night without being visible to a third-
party observer who may be hostile to the user; any light emitted by the display
becomes a danger to the user. And, as we found, these displays reduce human visual
capabilities in several ways.

Another consideration of the mobility requirement is the size, weight, and power
requirements of the AR system components. While these metrics have been rapidly
improving thanks to the efforts of hardware designers and manufacturers, reducing
the amounts of each of these required to drive the AR system will always be a
worthy goal for mobile AR. Within the BARS research program, we focused our
efforts on other aspects than the hardware requirements, preferring to communicate
our requirements to hardware vendors who were interested.

5.2 User Profiles

One challenge that heavily affected our research – especially on the UI for BARS –
was the array of tasks and experience that BARS users were expected to have.

Even when focusing on a dismounted task of maintaining SA, the type of role the user plays in the organization may differ significantly enough to warrant very different information being presented. A fire team leader (with three subordinates) may need different information about neighboring units than a company commander (typically responsible for approximately 125 subordinates). A medic, supply specialist, forward observer, or interpreter might need a very different set of information about the surrounding environment, people encountered, or the plans for the immediate future (the third aspect of SA).

Another consideration is the background or previous experience with computer graphics that the user is likely to have. There is a significant difference between designing for a dismounted Marine private (typically a male of age 18–20 years) and a field commander with 15 or more years of experience in the military. The private is likely to have grown up with computers and be a frequent player of video games, especially the first-person shooter games that are often similar to training tools for basic strategy and techniques. He is more likely to be comfortable with novel computer interfaces and will be familiar with the standard voice and gesture commands that are used to communicate with friendly forces in the battlefield. Field commanders are more likely to be an experienced leaders and military strategists. Most served as field officers but (for the time being) are less likely to have grown up using computers and mobile electronic devices on a regular basis. They integrate reports from forces in the field, and they resolve conflicts between pieces of information (which can be reasonably easy) and between evaluations of the situation (which were shown to be harder to resolve for pilots and air traffic controllers [51]). They may be less comfortable using even traditional computer interfaces but will have familiarity with standard protocols for voice communication with field officers and with superior officers in the C2 center.

5.3 Task Context

One overriding concern for operational applications for military AR systems is that the users will be working in a high-stress environment. This argues for having a simple UI that does not distract the user's attention from the task at hand. By this, we mean that the physical actions required to perform functions in the UI and the ease of understanding the presentation of information must be as simple and intuitive as possible. For the functions, we focused on using the metaphors and commands (voice and gesture) that military personnel currently use to build the UI for BARS. For the understanding, we eventually settled on building on the standard military icons in our most recent implementations, and conducting human factors evaluations as an integral part of the research and development process.

One issue in the UI was that dismounted military personnel generally need their hands free to perform existing military tasks or protocols. While gestural commands may be incorporated as commands to the AR system, interacting with the AR system should intrude on military protocols as little as possible. However, the higher the level of a commander, the less likely that his hands will be occupied with such tasks. Thus, it becomes reasonable that the UI could include more commands that require hands-on operation of the AR system for such personnel.

5.4 Collaboration Between Distributed Users

As noted above, one of the most important tasks that was identified as a potential area for BARS to improve the team's SA was to highlight the locations of users who were not within line-of-sight contact. This is a frequently-occuring challenge for MOUT, which are themselves a more frequently-occurring aspect of military operations. Thus we constructed an information database and distribution system and focused the UI visualizations on troop locations and routes. We also built a UI for reporting new or changing information, such as the sighting of an enemy or conflicts between the urban terrain database and the real environment. While this action required a more complicated UI than would be advisable for certain tasks, it is appropriate for forward observers and other personnel.

This dynamic aspect leads to another type of collaboration, that of synchronizing movements and routes. This is also an important aspect of MOUT. Routes and lines of fire for one unit should not intersect those for friendly units without careful consideration of the timing and danger that this implies for both units. During MOUT, available routes can change dramatically and quickly, increasing the difficulty of keeping movements synchronized. Since the dynamic nature of military operations means that it is nearly inevitable that the initial plan will need to be adapted to the situation on the ground, keeping SA of troop locations and movements is a challenging task. AR has the potential to assist dismounted or mounted personnel with this aspect of SA. An important, connected issue to this is length of routes. In one study [8], routes and directions communicated during an operation were generally short, with close contact between units encouraged. When teams must refrain from communications, the duration and distance potentially grow, complicating the task of avoiding conflicts between movements. Control measures such as phase lines, and the progress of other units towards these points of synchronization along respective routes, are another potentially useful visualization that adds to the collaboration between distributed users.

6 Summary

The field of AR has a long and rich history of applications specific to military tasks, dating back to the beginning of the field. In addition, the military has helped to push the technology forward in numerous application areas from medicine to maintenance and repair. AR technology has been demonstrated to have the potential to benefit military applications. However, the military problems are difficult and, for mobile AR systems, more complex than civilian applications. Hard AR research and systems research challenges remain to produce useful prototypes.

It is true that – as with many other applications of AR – military applications have often been limited by the hardware available to system designers and builders. But just as critical to the success of these applications has been the user interface and human subject evaluations (which often reveal limitations of the hardware). BARS focused much effort on these two aspects of AR design and implementation, while trying to shape the interests of hardware vendors to coincide with the demands of the envisioned military applications. One can see similar threads in the other military-specific AR applications discussed here. Indeed, one of the most famous AR applications (at least within the research community) failed not for primarily technical reasons, but for lack of user acceptance [15]. The physical and psychological stress inherent to military tasks increases the importance of these aspects of the AR system.

With all the efforts underway, there is reason to believe that AR will one day find a place in the standard gear of military personnel. It remains to be seen whether AR equipment can make itself critical enough to the individual soldier or Marine to be issued to all personnel, or whether only a unit leader (fire team, squad, company, or battalion) needs to see the augmented common operating picture through the lens of augmented reality.

Acknowledgements A complex system such as BARS cannot be constructed by even a modest-sized team such as the author list of this text. Numerous employees, interns, and university collaborators have been an integral part of the research over the past decade: Marco Lanzagorta, Doug Maxwell, Steven Feiner, Blaine Bell, Deborah Hix, Joseph L. Gabbard, Tobias Höllerer, Blair MacIntyre, Enylton Coelho, Ulrich Neumann, Suya You, Reinhold Behringer, Catherine Zanbaka, Aaron Kotranza, Robert Dickerson, Jane Barrow, Evan Suma, Brent Daugherty, Dennis Lin, Bryan Hurley, Elliot Cooper-Balis, Adam Lederer, Jason Jerald, Erik Tomlin, Eric Burns, Donald Charity, Joshua Eliason, Jesus Arango, and Scott Frees. In addition, the authors would like to thank Henry Fuchs, Pete Muller, Steven Feiner, and Randy Mayberry for assistance in the preparation of this manuscript.

Current affiliations for the authors no longer affiliated with the Naval Research Laboratory are: Lawrence J. Rosenblum, National Science Foundation; Simon J. Julier, University College London; Dennis G. Brown, USAF Materiel Command, Warner Robins Air Logistics Center; Gregory S. Schmidt, SPADAC, Inc.; Yohan Baillot, Simulation3D, LLC; J. Edward Swan II, Mississippi State University; Paul Maassel, Reallaer, LLC. Interested readers may contact Mark A. Livingston for further information.

References

1. Ai Z, Livingston MA (2009) Integration of georegistered information on a virtual globe. In: IEEE International Symposium on Mixed and Augmented Reality 2009 (Poster Session)
2. Azuma RT (1997) A survey of augmented reality. Presence: Teleoperators and Virtual Environments 6(4):355–385

3. Baillot Y, Julier SJ, Brown D, Livingston MA (2003) A tracker alignment framework for augmented reality. In: IEEE International Symposium on Mixed and Augmented Reality, pp 142–150
4. Bane R, Höllerer T (2004) Interactive tools for virtual x-ray vision in mobile augmented reality. In: International Symposium on Mixed and Augmented Reality, pp 231–239
5. Barham P, Plamondon B, Dumanoir P, Garrity P (2002) VICTER: An embedded virtual simulation system for land warrior. In: 23rd Army Science Conference
6. Benford S, Fahlén L (1993) A spatial model of interaction in large virtual environments. In: Third European Conference on Computer-Supported Cooperative Work, pp 109–124
7. Bolstad CA, Endsley MR (2002) Tools for supporting team sa and collaboration in army operations. Tech. rep., SA Technologies
8. Bowman E, Cosenzo K, Hill SG, Grynovicki J, Branscome TA, Brelsford M, Savage-Knepshield P (2006) C4ISR on-the-move testbed 2005 experiment: Human factors analysis. Tech. rep., Army Research Laboratory, Human Research and Engineering Directorate
9. Brown DG, Baillot Y, Julier SJ, Maassel P, Armoza D, Livingston MA, Rosenblum LJ (2004a) Building a mobile augmented reality system for embedded training: Lessons learned. In: Interservice/Industry Training, Simulation, and Education Conference
10. Brown DG, Julier SJ, Baillot Y, Livingston MA, Rosenblum LJ (2004b) Event-based data distribution for mobile augmented reality and virtual environments. Presence: Teleoperators and Virtual Environments 13(2):211–221
11. Brown DG, Baillot Y, Bailey MP, Pfluger KC, Maassel P, Thomas J, Julier SJ (2005) Using augmented reality to enhance fire support team training. In: Interservice/Industry Training, Simulation, and Education Conference
12. Brown DG, Stripling R, Coyne JT (2006) Augmented reality for urban skills training. In: IEEE Virtual Reality Conference
13. Cox M (2008) Land warrior: Now or later? Army Times Retrieved from http://www.armytimes.com/news/2008/10/army_landwarrior_101308w/, 22 December 2010
14. Cubic Corp (2011) Combatredi®. Retrieved 12 January 2011 from http://www.cubic.com/cda1/prod_&_serv/defense/training_products/virtual_training/combatredi.html
15. Curtis D, Mizell D, Gruenbaum P, Janin A (1998) Several devils in the details: Making and AR application work in the airplane factory. In: Augmented Reality: Placing Artificial Objects in Real Scenes (Proceedings of the First International Workshop on Augmented Reality
16. Defense Advanced Research Projects Agency (2010) Urban leader tactical response, awareness and visualization. http://www.darpa.mil/i2o/programs/uvis/uvis.asp, retrieved 22 December 2010
17. Department of the Army (2001) Operational requirements document (revised) for land warrior
18. DISA Standards Management Branch (2008) Department of Defense interface standard: Common warfighting symbology. http://assist.daps.dla.mil/quicksearch/basic_profile.cfm?ident_number=114934
19. Division UMCD (1998) Military operations on urbanized terrain (MOUT). Marine Corps Warfighting Publication No. MCWP 3-35.3
20. Feiner S, MacIntyre B, Höllerer T, Webster A (1997) A touring machine: Prototyping 3D mobile augmented reality systems for exploring the urban environment. In: First International Symposium on Wearable Computing (ISWC), pp 74–81
21. Furness LTA (1969) The application of head-mounted displays to airborne reconnaissance and weapon delivery. Tech. Rep. TR-69-241, U.S. Air Force Avionics Laboratory, Wright-Patterson AFB
22. Furness TA (1986) The super cockpit and its human factors challenges. In: Proceedings of the Human Factors Society 30th Annual Meeting, Human Factors and Ergonomics Society, pp 48–52
23. Gabbard JL, Swan II JE, Hix D, Lanzagorta M, Livingston MA, Brown D, Julier S (2002) Usability engineering: Domain analysis activities for augmented reality systems. In: Woods AJ, Bolas MT, Merritt JO, Benton SA (eds) Proceedings of SPIE: Stereoscopic Displays and Virtual Reality Systems IX, Vol. 4660, pp 445–457

24. Gardley M, Bishop L, McCollon B, Clemons L, Mayberry R, Kohler T (2008) Loadmaster training utilizing augmented reality. Tech. rep., Air Education and Training Command, Randolph AFB

25. General Dynamics Corp (2010) Virtual warrior. Retrieved 02 December 2010 from http://www.gdc4s.com/content/detail.cfm?item=d3ae855e-74ab-4af0-8c56-abad8be8ea0 f&page=1&ParentPageID=177d49b8-73c6-479f-94e8-f79826e1d422

26. Gould J (2010) Infantry battalion tests nett warrior. Army Times Retrieved from http://www.armytimes.com/news/2010/10/infantry-battalion-tests-nett-warrior-103010w/, 22 December 2010

27. Gumm M, Marshakm W, Branscome T, McWesler M, Patton D, Mullins L (1998) A comparison of solider performance using current land navigation equipment with information integrated on a helmet-mounted display. Tech. Rep. ARL-TR-1604, Army Research Laboratory, Aberdeen Proving Ground

28. Hart SG, Staveland LE (1988) Development of NASA-TLX (Task Load Index): Results of Empirical and Theoretical Research, North Holland Press, pp 239–250

29. Henderson SJ, Feiner S (2011) Exploring the benefits of augmented reality documentation for maintenance and repair. *To appear in* IEEE Transactions on Visualization and Computer Graphics http://doi.ieeecomputersociety.org/10.1109/TVCG.2010.245

30. Hughes CE, Stapleton CB, Moshell JM, Micikevicius P (2002) Challenges and opportunities simulating future combat systems via mixed reality. In: 23rd Army Science Conference

31. Julier S, Lanzagorta M, Baillot Y, Brown D (2002) Projects in VR: Information filtering for mobile augmented reality. IEEE Computer Graphics & Applications 22(5):12–15

32. Julier S, Livingston MA, Swan II JE, Baillot Y, Brown D (2003) Adaptive user interfaces in augmented reality. In: Proceedings of Workshop on Software Technology for Augmented Reality Systems

33. Livingston MA (2006) Quantification of visual capabilities using augmented reality displays. In: IEEE International Symposium on Mixed and Augmented Reality, pp 3–12

34. Livingston MA, Ai Z (2008) The effect of registration error on tracking distant augmented objects. In: International Symposium on Mixed and Augmented Reality

35. Livingston MA, Rosenblum LJ, Julier SJ, Brown D, Baillot Y, Swan II JE, Gabbard JL, Hix D (2002) An augmented reality system for military operations in urban terrain. In: Interservice/Industry Training, Simulation, and Education Conference

36. Livingston MA, Swan II JE, Gabbard JL, Höllerer TH, Hix D, Julier SJ, Baillot Y, Brown D (2003) Resolving multiple occluded layers in augmented reality. In: IEEE International Symposium on Mixed and Augmented Reality, pp 56–65

37. Livingston MA, Swan II JE, Julier SJ, Baillot Y, Brown D, Rosenblum LJ, Gabbard JL, Höllerer TH, Hix D (2004) Evaluating system capabilities and user performance in the battlefield augmented reality system. In: Performance Metrics for Intelligent Systems Workshop (PerMIS), National Institute of Standards and Technology

38. Livingston MA, Zanbaka C, Swan II JE, Smallman HS (2005) Objective measures for the effectiveness of augmented reality. In: IEEE Virtual Reality, pp 287–288

39. Livingston MA, Brown D, Julier SJ, Schmidt GS (2006a) Mobile augmented reality: Applications and human factors evaluations. In: Virtual Media for Military Applications (RTO Meeting Proceedings No. RTO-MP-HFM-136), Research and Technology Organisation, Neuilly-sur-Seine, France, pp 25-1—25-16

40. Livingston MA, Julier SJ, Brown D (2006b) Situation awareness for teams of dismounted warfighters and unmanned vehicles. In: Proceedings of SPIE: Enhanced and Synthetic Vision, Vol. 6266

41. Livingston MA, Lederer A, Ellis SR, White SM, Feiner SK (2006c) Vertical vergence calibration for augmented reality displays. In: IEEE Virtual Reality (Poster Session)

42. Livingston MA, Ai Z, Decker J (2009a) A user study towards understanding stereo perception in head-worn augmented reality displays. In: IEEE International Symposium on Mixed and Augmented Reality, pp 53–56

43. Livingston MA, Ai Z, Swan II JE, Smallman HS (2009b) Indoor vs. outdoor depth perception for mobile augmented reality. In: IEEE Virtual Reality
44. Livingston MA, Barrow JH, Sibley CM (2009c) Quantification of contrast sensitivity and color perception using head-worn augmented reality displays. In: IEEE Virtual Reality
45. Livingston MA, Ai Z, Karsch K, Gibson, MSC, USN LO (2011) User interface design for military ar applications. Virtual Reality (UK)
46. MacIntyre B, Coelho EM, Julier S (2002) Estimating and adapting to registration errors in augmented reality systems. In: IEEE Virtual Reality, pp 73–80
47. Mohl R (1981) Cognitive space in the interactive movie map: An investigation of spatial learning in virtual environments. PhD thesis, Massachusetts Institute of Technology
48. Muller P (2010) The future immersive training environment (FITE) JCTD: Improving readiness through innovation. In: Interservice/Industry Training, Simulation, and Education Conference
49. Naimark M (1979) Spatial correspondence – a study in environmental media. Master's thesis, Massachusetts Institute of Technology
50. Office of Naval Research (2010) Human performance training and education thrust. http://www.onr.navy.mil/Science-Technology/Departments/Code-30/All-Programs/Human-Performance-Training.aspx, retrieved 22 December 2010
51. Orasanu J (2005) What neeeds to be shared in shared situation models? In: DoD Human Factors Engineering Technical Advisory Group Meeting 54
52. Quantum3D, Inc (2010) Expeditiondi®. Retrieved 02 December 2010 from http://www.quantum3d.com/solutions/immersive/expedition_di.html
53. Schmidt GS, Brown DG, Tomlin EB, Swan II JE, Baillot Y (2006) Probabilistic algorithms, integration, and empirical evaluation for disambiguating multiple selections in frustum-based pointing. Journal of Multimedia 1(3):1–12
54. Schmorrow C, Cohn L, Stripling R, Kruse A (2004) Enhancing virtual environments using sensory-multiplexing. In: Interservice/Industry Training, Simulation, and Education Conference
55. State A, Livingston MA, Hirota G, Garrett WF, Whitton MC, Pisano ED, Fuchs H (1996) Technologies for augmented reality systems: Realizing ultrasound-guided needle biopsies. In: SIGGRAPH '96: Proceedings of the 23rd Annual Conference on Computer Graphics and Interactive Techniques, pp 439–446
56. Stix G (1992) See-through view: Virtual reality may guide physician's hands. Scientific American 267(3):166
57. Sutherland IE (1965) The ultimate display. In: Proceedings of the IFIP Conference, pp 506–508
58. Sutherland IE (1968) A head-mounted three-dimensional display. In: AFIPS'68: Fall Joint Computer Conference, pp 757–764
59. Swan II JE, Livingston MA, Smallman HS, Brown D, Baillot Y, Gabbard JL, Hix D (2006) A perceptual matching technique for depth judgments in optical, see-through augmented reality. In: IEEE Virtual Reality, pp 19–26
60. Van Riper PK (1997) A concept for future military operations on urbanized terrain. Available from http://www.globalsecurity.org/military/library/policy/usmc/mout.pdf

Chapter 32
Augmented Reality in Exhibition and Entertainment for the Public

Yetao Huang, Zhiguo Jiang, Yue Liu, and Yongtian Wang

1 Introduction

Augmented Reality (AR) is a branch of virtual reality, which has received great attention since early 1990s. A virtual reality system tries to immerse its user inside a computer-generated environment, whereas an AR system integrates virtual objects into the real world in real time and tries to let its user believe that the virtual and real objects coexist in the same space [1]. Augmented reality technologies have great potentials in many fields of application [2, 3]. Here we focus on its applications in exhibition and entertainment.

With the development of global information infrastructure and living standard of people worldwide, cultural and entertainment needs of people are growing all the time. From the late twentieth century, we can see the transition of many countries and regions from production-led to consumption and entertainment-led development. Cultural creative industry which contains digital entertainment and cultural exhibition is regarded as a new trend of technology revolution after communication and internet technology. Entertainment and exhibition industry provide not only methods of relaxation for the public, but also a mass of job opportunities. At the same time, they can create hundreds of millions of economic value, and growth of many technologies in research and development of related industries. In recent years, the development of exhibition and entertainment industry has great a potential to become a sunrise industry. They have many features as huge market demand, high costs, high investment, high added value, and high degree of internationalization.

Augmented Reality also has its own characteristics, and many of those characteristics just meet the needs of exhibition and entertainment industry. Among the characteristics, these points below are believed as important advantages:

Y. Huang (✉)
Beihang University, Beijing, China
e-mail: 6666@bit.edu.cn

B. Furht (ed.), *Handbook of Augmented Reality*, DOI 10.1007/978-1-4614-0064-6_32,   707
© Springer Science+Business Media, LLC 2011

- Better feel of immersion
  Virtual reality tries to build a virtual world, including the virtual view, virtual sound and so on to simulate the senses of human in the real world. However, real world is already in augmented reality. Augmented reality should only try to make the virtual objects seem like real ones in real surroundings. That will provide a better feel of immersion of modified world for users.
- Maintenance of real world
  In many applications, real world can be changed, for example, in video game. However, in some special fields, real world cannot be changed freely, even slight alteration, for example, in exhibitions of culture heritage. Augmented reality keeps the real world without any change as a background, so it maintains the real scene to the utmost.
- Appealing and particular experience for users
  Mixed view of both real and virtual world provides a new experience which enhances one's current perception of reality.
- No need to build the complicated virtual surroundings
  In augmented reality system, only some artificial information about the environment and the objects are put onto top layer of the real world view. Thus, much work to build complicated scene of surroundings is needless.

On the other side, the purpose of exhibition is to show the information of objects as much as possible. The purpose of entertainment is to make users feel interesting, relax, and pleasantly surprised. Thus, we can easily find that augmented reality is suitable for exhibition by combining real scene and virtual information in an appealing way, and also for entertainment with an interesting and particular mean of immersion. Meanwhile, applications and needs in exhibition and entertainment, especially for the public, also encourage a great improvement of AR technology.

This chapter presents applications of augmented reality in both exhibition and entertainment fields. In doing this, we describe their classifications and representative cases in the two separated fields. Some key technologies associated with these systems are also briefly described.

2 Augmented Reality in Exhibition

In the field of exhibition, we are always confronting with the challenge to present objects in an appealing and understandable way. Classical presentations like signboards and graphics as passive elements become arid and cannot satisfy the demands of visitors during the last years. Therefore, new technologies are increasingly used, like for example virtual reality and other means of human-computer interaction. Visitors highly appreciate these new technologies, and augmented reality is one of the most important and novel technologies. Typical applications of augmented reality in exhibition include museum guidance, cultural heritage reconstruction, digital art, and commercial exhibition showcase.

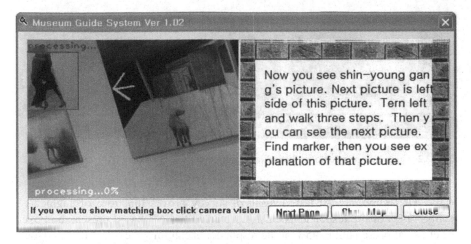

Fig. 32.1 Dong-Hyun Lee's system

2.1   Museum Guidance

Museum guidance is to lead visitors through the exhibition space in a sensible order. AR guidance system function seeks to find a new way besides 2D map or pure audio description for visitors to guide them to their points of interest in a museum.

In [4], T. Miyashita presents a very exciting project of the Louvre – DNP Museum Lab (LDML). The AR-guide can be used by any museum visitor during a 6-month exhibition on Islamic art. In this paper, T. Miyashita concluded related works in advance, and introduced tracking technologies [5] and mobile devices [6] used by other researchers. Then, hardware and software are presented in detail. Some technologies like markerless tracking, hybrid tracking, and an ultra-mobile-PC were used. Presentation room and route guidance are two basic functions involved in the system for the public in museums. LDML is an integrated project of augmented reality museum guide. It shows the possibility of AR-guide in such a traditional museum for the public.

Dong-Hyun Lee has also done an augmented reality system on portable PC. The purpose is to guide the users to exhibits of their interest for selective viewings [7]. In his system, an inertia tracker and a camera are used for tracking. Users could input their interests, and then location of the next exhibit of interest may be informed to the users as well as additional multimedia information about the interest exhibits. The information and direction to the next interest exhibit is shown in Fig. 32.1.

Another AR-based system in museum is done by Michael Grafe for interactive exploration. He described the view system, tracking system and user interface in detail [8]. At the Heinz Nixdorf Museums forum in Germany, augmented reality system is developed to show the underlying information of the exhibit, for example, the hidden part of a PC, or introduction text of a graphic board. Besides introducing the whole system, in [8], a user survey was done to figure out user acceptance

Fig. 32.2 Complementary color game in French museum

of the AR technology. At last, a result of survey proves functions of augmented reality. "74% of the respondents clearly preferred the AR-based presentation over the classical presentation. 95% of the respondents can imagine that AR technology can also be used with other exhibits."

After Michael Grafe, in [9], a specific examination has been done to find if an augmented reality guide can enrich museum visits. This work has been done in the French funded ANR GAMME project. An ergonomic experimentation has been conducted where real visitors use their augmented reality prototype. The complementary colors game is shown in Fig. 32.2, to help the visitor have a better understanding of complementary color. Because of its precise design of experiments, their result has power of persuasion. At last, this paper proposes some implications about the future usage of augmented reality in a museum context. For example, three recommendations as follows, comparing the distinguishing aspects of an artwork with other works, exploring the creation process of a work by indicating the relevant and sometimes hidden details, supplying visitors with some professional information. These suggestions which are on basis of user survey are very useful to the latter development of applications for the public.

In fact, museum guidance is not only useful for visitors, but also meaningful for users as presented in [10]. AR system can be a tool for behavioral analysis, for instance, stay time and activities on a spot to form long-term activity logs.

2.2 Cultural Heritage Reconstruction

An ideal AR system for digital reconstruction should allow users to walk around the cultural relics and see some relevant and hidden information with a vivid AR view freely. Allowing users to do such activities is remarkably meaningful for both public tourism and study. Funded by the European Union, the AR navigation systems used at the ancient Greek Parthenon [11, 12] and the Pompeii exemplify the usefulness of AR. In Pakistan, digital reconstruction has also been made for Buddhist historical sites [13]. There are also many other researches on cultural heritages by AR technology [14–16]. No matter which kind of devices they used as a

Fig. 32.3 Cultural heritage layers

terminal, portable and wearable computer [17], or mobile phone and PDA (Personal Digital Assistant) [18–20], they open a huge potential use in cultural heritage by AR for public.

Michael Zoellner has done an integrated work named as "Cultural Heritage Layers" [21]. The main idea is to use existing historic content from archives and superimpose them seamlessly on reality at the right spot. These locative layers are context sensitively telling the location's history and create the impression of a time journey. He used the vision-based tracking technology for registration. And all computations and display are on an ultra mobile PC. The augmented reality view is illustrated on Fig. 32.3. In the same way, "Re-Living Las Vegas" [22] is a project focused on the underrated, and often untold, history of Las Vegas and the so-called golden music age of the city. Moreover, their experience can be reused and adapted to different contents.

Furthermore, [23] has discussed how an augmented reality can be designed to match the requirements of users. After showing mobile AR guide in cultural heritage, they discussed an approach of user research process by documenting field notes in a 5W1H and organized findings in POEMS (People (P), Object (O), Environment (E), Messages/Media (M), and Services (S)). And some conclusions of an augmented reality system should be are drawn as: "it can enhance the actual world without over-dominating it; address the actual tourist's problem in the context of use, and create new social environment for the tourists."

A fixed-position viewing system called AR-View is developed for certain outdoor applications of augmented reality [24]. AR-View which is developed at Beijing Institute of Technology, is already used for the public in China. Some details are in introduced as follows. Display system of AR-View is operated in the same way as a scenery-viewing telescope often seen on the commanding point of a park or on the visitor's platform of a television tower, but its main function is augmenting the real scene with virtual objects rather than magnifying it. With its position fixed, the viewing system has two degrees of freedom for angular movement, namely azimuth and pitch, which can be detected by two rotary encoders. As illustrated in Fig. 32.4a,

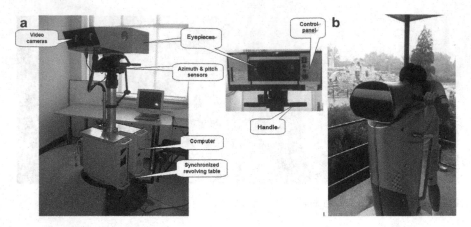

Fig. 32.4 AR-View for cultural heritage

the viewing system is equipped with two video cameras to capture the video streams of the real world for left and right eyes respectively. The video signals are sent to the computer, which renders the virtual objects at the right positions in each frame of the real scene images in real time according to the output of the azimuth and pitch sensors. The composite video streams are then displayed on two LCDs and imaged by the eyepieces to the corresponding position of the real world for the user to observe. On the control panel of the viewing system, there are buttons for the user to switch among the real scene, the augmented scene and a totally virtual scene, and to zoom in or zoom out.

Figure 32.4b is a picture of the second generation of the fixed-position viewing system which is lighter and more compact. Before this generation, user survey was carefully designed and conducted in Yuanmingyuan Relics Park of China, to find what should be improved for public use. Considering results of user survey as a feedback, the new design was much more convenient and comfortable to use and prepared for commercial public use in the field of cultural heritage.

2.3 Digital Art and Commercial Exhibition

The collision of art and technology can often inspire new ideas and creativity. Human-computer interaction, multimedia rendering technology has formed a growing new media art. Helen has shown his augmented reality installations, "Wonder Turner" and "The Amazing Cinemagician," in Ontario Science Centre Idea Gallery, Toronto, from May to September, 2010. Evolutions of the two installations are introduced in [25]. To encourage the digital art with augmented reality, ISMAR conference started a new session of art and media for this new trend of applications.

Fig. 32.5 Augmented reality for commercial exhibition showcase

"Augmented Shadow" by Joon Moon, "Flick Flock" by Wendy Ann Mansilla, "Sound Walk" by Julio Lucio Martin and some other digital art installation are shown in ISMAR 2010 art gallery.

In recent years, this new trend certainly affects the commercial exhibitions. We can classify this kind of application as commercial exhibition showcase and new product release conference. In this field, some companies with AR technology have done a lot of remarkable applications.

For commercial exhibition showcase, new vehicle is the most used with AR technology. Renault flagship store on the Champs Élysées uses AR technology to shows its new products, which attracts many customers. As shown on Fig. 32.5a, a little girl could freely rotate a card to look around a new Renault sports car, and others could crowded round to get a better view. Metaio, a Germany company, has also done similar showcases for Toyota. Furthermore, if that is icing on the cake, LEGO Showcase named as digital box which they designed can be regarded as a real boon in Fig. 32.5b. When we buy a LEGO toy, we can only find its look by 2D cover image. However, digital box can show a virtually built-up and fully animated for customers before they buy and build it. Not only in real stores, but also on web stores, augmented reality can show products better in a proper and vivid way. Moët&Chandon is a famous French winery. Now, through its corporate website, we can use a champagne bottle to discover the heritage and world of Moët&Chandon as shown on Fig. 32.5c. Even the world leading sports brand, Adidas tries "The Adidas Originals Augmented Reality Game Pack" online to broadcast its idea.

Realtime operation is a key feature of augmented reality system. Thus, on the stage for a new product release conference, augmented reality show its attraction on this side. Total Immersion, a famous augmented reality company, helped Alstom which is a world leader in transport infrastructure and power generation to show a live presentation with 3D special live effects. When emcees gave presentations on an empty stage, virtual objects, what they talked about, are magically appear around they, of cause on a big screen as shown in Fig. 32.6. In 2010, Mazda China also used augmented reality on its new product release to introduce Mazda 6.

Fig. 32.6 Augmented reality in live show

3 Augmented Reality in Entertainment

Nowadays, digital entertainment plays a more and more important part in our daily life, and becomes a new growing point to support economic development. Meanwhile, new technologies and creative ideas are more and more used to give a special experience in digital entertainment to win the support of the public and the market. Among them, augmented reality, which has a new interactive mean and vivid view, achieve a rapid development in entertainment in both personal entertainment device and multi-user theme park attraction.

3.1 Personal Entertainment Device

Personal entertainment devices can be classified as arcade, video game player, handheld game console, mobile phone. Augmented reality is already applied in those fields, and details will be introduced as follows.

In the field of video game player, PlayStation of Sony, Xbox360 of Microsoft, and Wii of Nitendo are called top three together. When Wii come out, it becomes a bestseller soon because of its new interactive way, even though its computing ability is not as good as the other two. Then, represented by PlayStation, augmented reality game began to operate on video game players. "The Eye of Judgment," the first augmented reality game as we know, is published on PlayStation3 in 2007 with multiuser supported. Vision-based tracking with markers by camera is used in this game. In 2009, another augmented reality game on PlayStation3, "Eyepet"

Fig. 32.7 Augmented reality games on video game player

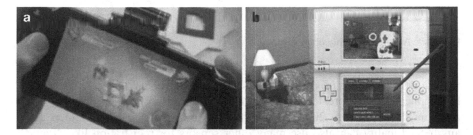

Fig. 32.8 Augmented reality games on handheld game console

is developed for kids as shown in Fig. 32.7a. Virtual pets are superimposed in real rooms, and can be interacted with users like touching and feeding. "PS Move" also integrated many other somatosensory games by using AR technology. Developed by Microsoft Xbox, "Kinect" is officially published in 2010 as shown in Fig. 32.7b. With a depth camera, it could do a lot of work and inspire many new ideas of augmented reality game.

In the field of handheld game console, PlayStation Portable (PSP) is a product of Sony, which could add an extensional camera for capturing real scene. "Invizimals" is a hunting game on PSP by using augmented reality in 2009 as shown in Fig. 32.8a. It uses a marker-based tracking method with the camera. Meanwhile, Nitendo also announced a new augmented reality game "Ghostwire" on its DSi handheld game console. This game makes good use of the characteristic of augmented reality. Superimposing ghosts into real rooms of users, players should try to catch ghosts by its own camera in their own rooms as shown in Fig. 32.8b.

In the field of mobile phone, smart phone emerged gradually as its computing and display abilities evolved. Early, many researchers developed augmented reality game on Nokia's Symbian system, for example augmented reality system for cultural heritage on Nokia N95 smart phone [26]. Designed by Apple, iphone contains many sensors and touch screen. Its function and open platform also inspires developers plenty of interactive ideas. Thus, iphone becomes a new hot spot, after it is released. From online store, we can download many augmented reality games, for example, "firefighter 360" which could make you a firefighter fight in your

Fig. 32.9 Augmented reality on mobile phone

real garden as shown in Fig. 32.9a. "Layar," as shown in Fig. 32.9b, is another hot application on store to provide location-based information nearby by using augmented reality from 2009. Although vision-based tracking is common used, augmented reality can also use many other sensors for registration like "Layar," for example, GPS, compass, and accelerometer.

3.2 Multi-user Theme Park Attraction

Multiuser theme park attraction is large-scale entertainment equipment in particular parks. In twenty-first century, with continuous progress of science and technology, large-scale entertainment equipment began to change gradually from simplex mechanical motion to mechanical motion coordinate with multimedia. Therefore, new interactive technologies are largely used in theme parks.

"Dark Ride" is the term used within the industry to describe theme park rides in the dark. However, a dark ride describes an indoor amusement ride where riders in guided vehicles travel through specially lit scenes that contain animation, sound, music, and special effects, so that it needs not to be dark. As shooting is integrated in dark ride, for example, "Buzz Lightyear's Space Ranger Spin" and "Toy Story Midway Mania" in Disney, augmented reality technology tries to be used in this type of attractions. In 2005 Aichi Expo in Japan, the first multiuser dark ride attraction by augmented reality as we know was shown in Hitachi exhibition hall. Several players can play together without disturbing each other. Each of them wears a head mounted display and a handheld device in which six freedom of degree tracking devices are contained. They designed three theme scenes and virtual objects to interact with for players. Similarly, "Animaux" in the theme park "FuturoScope" in the southern France is the first attraction of augmented reality dark ride which is long-term open

Fig. 32.10 Augmented reality in theme park

to the public from 2007. Virtual animals are superimposed in real scenes, so that players can hold a telescope to see the mixed view as shown in Fig. 32.10a.

In 2008, an augmented reality dark ride system in Guangdong Science and Technology Center, China, is open for the public named as augmented reality adventure in Guangzhou City. The AR adventure game is the first multi-user novel AR game for public use in China. Its wide-area vision-based tracking technology is discussed in details in [27]. Walls and ceiling are equipped with the coded infrared markers. A tracking camera and scene cameras are fixed in the HMD. With the help of novel inside-looking-out tracking system, each user could use its own individual system without being disturbed by others. It was initially designed to allow the visitors to move around freely, but later changed to sit the visitors on a trailer for safety reasons. In [28], see-through HMD system for display is discussed in details. The virtual world and interactions are managed by Virtools. Registration between real and virtual world is also realized in Virtools with tracking data as represented in [27]. Four users in a mini-train travel around the three scenes, i.e. Pearl River boat tour, underwater world adventure and flying over Guangzhou, and enjoy the combined real and virtual views in HMD. As illustrated in Fig. 32.10b, four users were seated in the train. They could see the interactive virtual fish superimposed in the real artificial seabed scene.

Interactive live show is another kind of augmented reality application in theme park for the public. AR-immersive cinema at the Aula Natura Visitors Center is designed to merge past and present and immerse users into history [29]. On the other side, a 3D interactive live show is designed by Total Immersion to allow one performer interact with virtual objects and change the physical world around them in real time. The interactive 3D live show is come out in 2009, which is the highlight of Tomorrow City Theme Park in South Korea. With a camera trained on the audience, the performer can pull video of audience members directly into the show. This type of augmented reality for pubic entertainment seems to be stable and have a good potential use in theme parks, even in new product release conferences and theatrical evenings.

4 Conclusions and Future Directions

This chapter describes augmented reality applications in the field of exhibition and entertainment. Augmented reality is an applied technology of many cross-cutting areas. Meanwhile, it can be certainly used in many fields. Here, we focus on entertainment and exhibition, because needs of them are partly close. For exhibition, we discuss augmented reality applications in museums, cultural heritage relics and commercial showcases. It could provide extra and extensive information by a friendly and intuitive way. Some typical instances are introduced in details. For entertainment, we firstly classify this area into two fields of personal device and multiuser installation. Then, augmented reality applications in video game player, handheld game console, and mobile phone are carefully discussed. At last, multiuser theme park attractions with augmented reality are introduced, like dark ride and interactive 3D live show.

From discussions above, we can easily find that augmented reality is suitable for entertainment and exhibition. It gives a better immersion feel and appealing form by combining real and virtual world together. Those are meeting the needs of both fields. For example, commercial showcase and video game console want to beat all other ordinary ones and attract audients. And augmented reality in new product release and live show in theme park are all trying to show audience an interesting and unforgettable information or experience. Nevertheless, augmented reality in the two fields has different requirements. Augmented reality in entertainment should be more playable, while it in exhibition should focus on its functions and convenient use for users.

Therefore, when we develop an augmented reality entertainment system, we should pay more attention to its design and plan on playability, then the vivid mixed reality view rendering. On the other side, actual and useful function should be considered firstly for its applications in exhibition. Lastly, user survey is needed for its massive use for the public. Nowadays, many applications are emerging on the online store of iphone. As a personal device, its computing ability and display indeed inspires lots of imaginations, and bring a bright future of augmented reality applications in entertainment and exhibition for the public.

References

1. Azuma R. T., "A Survey of Augmented Reality," In Presence: Teleoperators and Virtual Environments, Vol.6, No.4, 1999, pp.355–385.
2. Julier S., et al., "The Software Architecture of a Real-Time Battlefield Visualization Virtual Environment," IEEE Virtual Reality 99, 1999, pp.29–36.
3. Lintu A., Magnor M., "An Augmented Reality System for Astrnomical Observations," IEEE Virtual Reality 06, 2006, pp.119–126.
4. Miyashita T., et al., "An augmented reality museum guide," 7th IEEE International Symposium on Mixed and Augmented Reality 2008, 2008, pp.103–106.

5. V. Lepetit, and P. Fua. "Monocular Model-Based 3D Tracking of Rigid Objects: A Survey," Foundations and Trends in Computer Graphics and Vision, Vol. 1, No.1, 2005, pp 1–89.
6. E. Bruns, B. Brombach, T. Zeidler, O. Bimber, "Enabling Mobile Phones to Support Large-Scale Museum Guidance," IEEE Multimedia 2007, 2007, pp 16–25.
7. Lee DongHyun, and Park Jun, "Augmented reality based museum guidance system for selective viewings," Proceedings - 2nd Workshop on Digital Media and its Application in Museum and Heritage(DMAMH 2007), 2007, pp 379–382.
8. Grafe M., Wortmann R., Westphal H., "AR-based interactive exploration of a museum exhibit," First IEEE International Augmented Reality Toolkit Workshop. Proceedings (Cat. No.02EX632), 2002.
9. Tillon A.B., Marchand E., et al., "A day at the museum: An augmented fine-art exhibit," Proceedings of the 2010 IEEE International Symposium on Mixed and Augmented Reality-Arts, Media, and Humanities (ISMAR2010-AMH), 2010, pp 69–70.
10. Okuma T., Kourogi M., Sakata N., Kurata T., "Reliving museum visiting experiences on-and-off the spot," Proceedings of the Sixth IEEE and ACM International Symposium on Mixed and Augmented Reality, 2008, pp302-303.
11. Vlahakis V., Ioannidis M., et al., "Archeoguide: An Augmented Reality Guide for Archaeological Sites," IEEE Computer Graphics and Applications, 2002, Vol.22, No.5, pp52-60.
12. Dahne P, Karigiannis J.N., "Archeoguide: system architecture of a mobile outdoor augmented reality system," Proceedings of the IEEE and ACM International Symposium on Mixed and Augmented Reality, 2002, pp263-264.
13. Mehmood A., Shahid A.M., "Digital reconstruction of Buddhist historical sites (6th B.C-2nd A.D) at Taxila, Pakistan (UNESCO, world heritage site)," Proceedings Seventh International Conference on Virtual Systems and Multimedia, 2001, pp 177–182.
14. Pace P., Aloi G., Palmacci A., "GITA: new architectures for interactive fruition of historical and artistic contents on wireless multi-technology platform," 2008 International Symposium on Ubiquitous Multimedia Computing, 2008, pp 45–50.
15. Nakasugi H., Yamauchi Y., "Past viewer: Development of wearable learning system for history education," Proceedings International Conference on Computersin Education, 2002, pp1311–12.
16. Allen P., Feiner S., Meskell L. et al., "Digitally modeling, visualizing and preserving archaeological sites," Proceedings of the Fourth ACM/IEEE Joint Conference on Digital Libraries (IEEE Cat. No.04TH8766), 2004.
17. Reitinger B., Zach C., Schmalstieg D. "Augmented reality scouting for interactive 3D reconstruction," 2007 IEEE Virtual Reality Conference, 2007.
18. Schall Gerhard et al., "Handheld Augmented Reality for underground infrastructure visualization," Personal and Ubiquitous Computing, Vol.13, No. 4, 2009, pp281-291.
19. Güven Sinem, Feiner Steven, "Interaction techniques for exploring historic sites through situated media," Proceedings of IEEE Symposium on 3D User Interfaces 2006, 2006, pp111-118.
20. Pace Pasquale, Aloi Gianluca, Palmacci Antonio, "A multi-technology location-aware wireless system for interactive fruition of multimedia contents," IEEE Transactions on Consumer Electronics, Vol.55, No.2, 2009, pp342-350.
21. Zoellner M., Keil J., Drevensek T., Wuest H., "Cultural heritage layers: integrating historic media in augmented reality," Proceedings of the 2009 15th International Conference on Virtual Systems and Multimedia (VSMM2009),2009, pp193-196.
22. Antognozzi M., Bottino A., De Santi A., Lera V., Locatelli M., Cook D., "Re-Living Las Vegas: a multi-user, mixed-reality edutainment environment based on the enhancement of original archival materials," 2009 IEEE International Conference on Virtual Environments, Human-Computer Interfaces and Measurements Systems (VECIMS 2009), 2009, pp 292–297.
23. Ying-Wei Toh, Ji-Hong Jeung; Young-Hwan Pan, "A combined user research process for designing mobile AR guide in cultural heritage," Proceedings of the 2010 IEEE International Symposium on Mixed and Augmented Reality - Arts, Media, and Humanities (ISMAR2010-AMH). 2010, pp 71–72.

24. Wang, Y., Liu, Y., et al., "Fixed-Position Augmented Reality Viewing System for On-Site 3D Digital Reconstruction," Chinese Patent ZL 2005 1 0105577.X., 2005.
25. Papagiannis H., ""Wonder Turner" and "The Amazing Cinemagician" Augmented Reality and Mixed Reality Art Installations," Proceedings of the 2010 IEEE International Symposium on Mixed and Augmented Reality - Arts, Media, and Humanities (ISMAR2010-AMH). Science and Technology, 2010, pp27-32.
26. Omar Choudary, et al., "MARCH: mobile augmented reality for cultural heritage," Proceedings of the seventeen ACM international conference on Multimedia (MM09), 2009.
27. Huang Yetao, Weng Dongdong, Liu Yue, Wang Yongtian, "Key issues of wide-area tracking system for multi-user augmented reality adventure game," Proceedings of the 5th International Conference on Image and Graphics(ICIG 2009), 2010, pp646-651.
28. Dongdong Weng, Yongtian Wang, Yue Liu, Jing Chen, Dewen Cheng, "Display systems and registration methods for mixed reality applications," Proceedings of the SPIE - The International Society for Optical Engineering, Vol.7428, 2009, pp742805-742809.
29. Portalés Cristina, Viñals María J., Alonso-Monasterio Pau, Morant Maryland, "AR-immersive cinema at the aula natura visitors center," IEEE Multimedia, Vol. 17, No.4, 2010, pp 8–14.

Chapter 33
GIS and Augmented Reality: State of the Art and Issues

Olivier Hugues, Jean-Marc Cieutat, and Pascal Guitton

Abstract In this chapter we propose a joint exploration of Geographic Information System (GIS) and Augmented Reality (AR). Thanks to some factors, we will detail hereafter, these two domains have greatly converged in recent years further to certain factors which we shall detail hereafter. We then outline applications combining GIS and a display technique using AR in order to identify the scientific issues, as well as the functional and technical issues. Starting from this extensive state of the art of existing work, we propose a new functional classification, before concluding with different perspectives.

1 Introduction

Until recently Augmented Reality (AR) was still seen as a technology used only by researchers in laboratories, but it is now becoming increasingly accessible to a public at large. This technology can be observed according to two different axes: a technological axis and a functional axis. On the one hand, the technological perspective leads us to observe that AR is based on three main pillars. The first pillar corresponds to hardware technologies. Miniaturisation, the multiplication of various different sensors and the increased performance of equipment have enabled this technology to be implemented using many different devices. The second pillar corresponds to software technologies. Progress in image analysis [1,2], new ever higher performance algorithms [3–7] and new multi-sensor data merging methods [8–11] enable this technology to better satisfy expectations. Finally, the third pillar, corresponds to data and access to these data. Data relocation, supported by cloud computing and ubiquitous computing [12], provides easier access to information from anywhere and at any time. On the other hand, by observing

O. Hugues (✉)
ESTIA Recherche, MaxSea, LaBRI, France
e-mail: o.hugues@net.estia.fr

B. Furht (ed.), *Handbook of Augmented Reality*, DOI 10.1007/978-1-4614-0064-6_33,   721
© Springer Science+Business Media, LLC 2011

AR according to the functional axis, it is possible to consider it as an interface between the user and the machine [13, 14]. In this respect, as is commonly the case with user-machine interfaces, such a process cannot exclude seriously taking into account user-based parameters and those linked to the environment. According to [15], "using a new technical device modifies our sensory-motor coupling with the environment; and at the same time it modifies our perception". However, we cannot "only" apply ourselves to better perceiving since perception is not an aim in itself, but a way to achieve an action objective [16]. Indeed, the issues (which we shall examine later on) which a GIS is able to satisfy aim to be pragmatic. It is in this context that Information Systems (IS) and more particularly Geographic Information System (GIS) are used in this context. The architectures of these systems therefore now need to be reorganized based on these three elements: the user, the environment and the data. On the one hand, technological developments have enabled a new functionality in addition to those already present in IS: locating data in time and space. On the other hand, mobile computing has added an extra essential component: locating the user in time and space. This technological revolution requires the implementation of methods and architectures which are coherent with the entities at stake. We shall begin by showing how AR suffers from a major lack which GIS can fill. We then propose to define GIS and to show what they can contribute to AR. Finally, after a state of the art of different applications combining GIS and AR for which we propose a new classification, we shall present an analysis of the stakes of this type of applications.

2 Augmented Reality: A Still Emerging Technology

We shall not discuss in this chapter the different definitions proposed for AR and we invite readers to refer to the Chap. 1 of this manual on the Basis of Augmented Reality. We can however note a certain distinction between communities which deal with this technology. On the one hand, AR is seen as a non-immersive approach (in opposition to Virtual Reality). Instead of proposing a fully digital environment, AR modifies the world perceived by the individual by add some digital informations [17, 18]. On the other hand, AR is not seen as being opposed to Virtual Reality (VR), but rather as an extension which involves mixing real and virtual information in the same scene [19,20]. By considering this second point, the authors of [21] have identified five barriers which must be overcome by those involved:

Techniques   Need to improve technical developments. This corresponds for example to the reliability and interoperability of different technologies used in order to be able to easily integrate them in demonstrators and test new applications.

Methodology Lack of methods in order to analyse and to evaluate needs in terms of AR systems and available solutions.

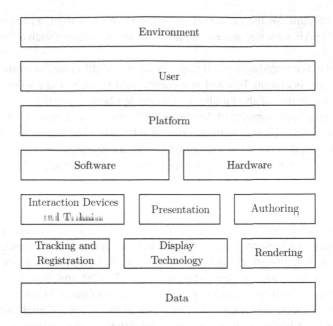

Fig. 33.1 Blocks of an Augmented Reality system. Based on the [24] diagram

Evaluation	Poor quality of clearly functional applications and limited proof of their added value. Answering a question by an industrialist – "What are the advantages of a stereoscopic system?" – is not easy.
Safety	Applications often call into play the safety and health of users.
Usability	Potential difficulties due to the non-intuitive nature of certain interfaces.

Although these difficulties are encountered in Virtual Reality too, [22] considers *"that these limitations are also characteristic of AR technologies"*. In this context, [15,23] have identified the three main elements which occur when using a technical device. The first element, hierarchically the most important, is the *user*. Then, the *device* or platform, which is described in terms of resources and finally the *environment* which is defined by a series of objects, people, events and phenomena peripheral to the user's activity, but which have an impact on the system or user's behaviour. Considering all these elements, we can complete the diagram proposed by [24] which initially represents the building blocks of an AR system, by adding some functional building blocks (Fig. 33.1). We add a "Data" block at the bottom of the diagram, a "Hardware" block as well as a "Software" block to clearly identify the importance of developing both hardware and software for this type of application. We thus add the "Platform" block, directly made up of two previously mentioned blocks, to clearly identify one of the three pillars described in Sect. 1. Less technical, but just as important are the user and the user's environment, which are to be taken into account for the design of an AR system. Although certain blocks are not specific to AR systems, associating all these blocks enables such a functionality to be created.

As stated in the introduction, AR requires the use of different hardware technologies[1] which are becoming less and less cumbersome, costly and energy-consumer. Indeed, the explosion of the number of various applications using AR is linked to the technological development of devices (mobile phones, webcams, OLED screens, CCD sensors, etc). Morover, certain forms of AR[2] also need access to data sources (digital 3D or 2D models, video, images, sounds, symbols or event text). The applications also need to access space and time location metadata, both local and online. AR, as a man-machine interaction paradigm [13, 14], enables information to be offered to users with associations of different types[3] between digital entities (generated by computers) and physical entities (our natural environment). The rate of evolution of technological devices was therefore necessary, but insufficient. Apart from hardware, AR requires sources of information content to be relevant. Although the evolution of hardware has already begun, the explosion of localised information platforms accessible to the public at large [25–28] and even [29][4] enables the necessary lacks in the development of AR technologies to be compensated. Although from a technological point of view AR aims to "link" digital entities to the physical world, it is obviously necessary to have these digital entities. And despite the fact that generating digital models is quite long, costly and tedious, GIS offer an abundant source of digital information which AR can use. Obviously, the processing of different sources of information affects the evolution of AR. Issues arising from information sources can create difficulties on these systems like data updating times for example [31].[5]

3 "IS" is Included in "GIS"

A lot of different definitions have been proposed during technological evolutions to define IS and this multitude of definitions stems from the difficulty in defining objects and subjects involved in this type of application [32]. Due to the diversity of layers (hardware, software, dataware and humanware), we can for example find in the literature both functional [33] and technological [34] approaches. Generally, we consider Information Systems (IS) from a functional point of view as an organised series of elements which provide information [35] to be grouped,

---

[1] We invite readers to refer to this manual's "Technological" chapters.

[2] We invite readers to refer to the Chaps. 1 and 2 of this manual to find out about all forms of AR.

[3] These associations can be in space, in time, semantic or a combination of these types of associations.

[4] Company which in 2010 opened an Android based AR application development platform [30].

[5] This application is based on website date. Data may sometimes only be updated every 2 h.

classified, processed and disseminated. These systems have been developped until they achieve a level of complexity as it requires many adaptations with regard to interfaces (abstraction, symbolisation, etc).

4   From IS To GIS

GIS arc information systems (IS) which can organise and present spatially referenced alphanumerical data. GIS encompass four components named *"Personal"*, *"Software"*, *"Data"* and *"Hardware"* in [36]. Based on different databases, these systems provide digital geographical information to be *acquired* digitally. They enable the *analysis* of geographical data by handling and interrogation. They *display* this information using visualisation techniques which make it easily understandable. Finally, they sometimes enable future phenomena to be anticipated. GIS face to several technical issues:

Acquisition Import of digital data captured on site.

Archiving   Management of the database (integrity, coherence...).

Analysis   Handling and interrogation of data. Data may target objects of all types, phenomena, events, etc. GIS globally enable five questions to be answered.

        Where: The geographical location of a set of elements or a specific element.

        What: The type of set of elements or element in the region of interest.

        How: A set of elements or an element concerning the distribution of entities and their links in the region of interest to be spatially analyzed.

        When: Enables a temporal analysis to be carried out on a series of elements or a specific element.

        And if: Enables a uchronic analysis to be carried out.

Display   Visualization of information contained in the database in order to make it understandable by the user. Different abstractions are created to make the system lighter (vector, raster, resolutions multi-scale, symbolization, etc). This component can thus be considered as a virtual environment, close to a form of Virtual Reality since it is a digitally created environment.

Quality   Whether internal (adequation between a card/BDD and what it should have been) or external (adequation between the card/BDD and the needs of its user). Quality has been subject to many discussions for almost 30 years [37].

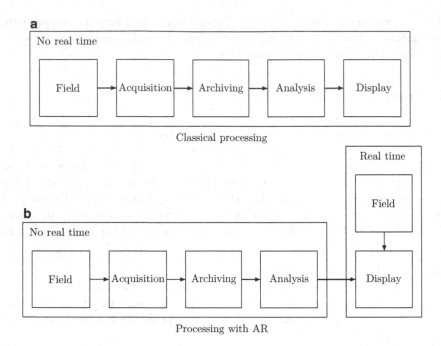

Fig. 33.2 GIS data processing chain

It is possible to consider the "Field" (the environment which is concerned) as being the natural environment or a sub-element of this, and the display of data by the GIS as a virtual environment made up of digital entities semantically linked with the real environment. The symbolisation of data leads to a difference of representation between the natural environment and the artificial environment which does not facilitate the matching of information for users. It should however be noted that, as defined by [19], technologies are available to limit this gap between reality and a digital world. It is partially, for this reason that AR takes on its full meaning as a technology which reduces the gap between the physical world and the digital world since, by definition, AR brings together digital entities and physical entities in both time and space [20,38]. The final aim of using this technology combined with a GIS is therefore to act on the "Display" phase of GIS. With the combined use of AR and GIS, we try to reduce the semantic gap between real data and digital data (Fig. 33.2).

More than a link between GIS data and the environment, adding an AR display system completely modifies the way GIS are used. In classical cases, the display system requires two input vectors:

1. User request
2. Display parameters (factors of scale, abstractions, symbolisations, etc.)

For the display system using AR, adding a new component must be taken into account:

1. User's position and orientation

To obtain information from GIS, the user should not only launch the right request, but also choose the right position and orientation. Geographic Information System therefore offer a vast field of action for AR. We can now find a wide range of applications combining AR and GIS. In the next section we take a look at the different applications combining GIS and AR according to a taxonomy directly taken from the literature.

5 Joint Use of GIS and AR

Developing a GIS using AR for its display induce some technological, methodological, industrial and commercial challenges. Indeed, associating these two types of technologies requires both the common and specific stakes of these applications to be taken into account. From a technological point of view, it is necessary to perfect new adapted hardware and software architectures. It is also necessary to develop new interactions and visualizations of geographical digital data. It is also useful to study the implications of the use of AR techniques on a GIS (and vice versa). Exploring the synergy between digital geographical data and AR becomes inevitable and the development of new GIS methods specific to this type of application should be created. Many different fields such as tourism, environment, civil engineering, road and sea navigation are interested by this type of application.

5.1 Towards a Functional Classification

If we consider AR, seen as a set of technologies enabling different associations of digital entities and physical entities to be implemented, we can consider AR using two approaches. Furthermore, we know that developing an AR functionality indoor or outdoor do not involve the same stakes [39]. In our application context, combining GIS and AR, we can initially extract two categories from the literature.

1. Indoor exploration of geographical data.
2. Outdoor exploration of geographical data.

However, we propose a different classification, which is much more specific to the joint use of GIS and a display system using AR. We hope that this classification, whose initial aim is to describe and compare, will be considered to be generative [40]. In this context of geographical information, we need to distinguish between the source of this information and its representation. Indeed, the map is not the territory. We therefore propose separating applications into two major groups. The first includes applications which aim at handling geographical

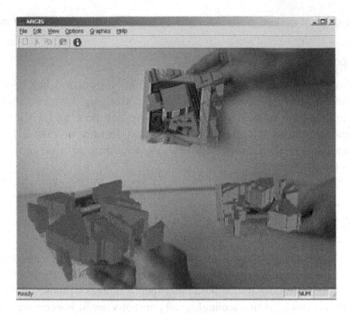

Fig. 33.3 Exploring geographical data by modifying the point of view [41]

data. Digital augmentations target GIS data. In this case we are referring to an *Augmented Map* (AM) functionality. These applications translate the modification of the display system's sub-component intended to take into account user requests to then update the display of data. The second characterizes applications which aim at enabling users to work more efficiently in their environment. The target of digital augmentations is not representing the environment as in the first case, but the environment itself. We therefore refer to an *Augmented Territory* (AT) functionality. These applications translate the modification of the sub-component of the display system enabling the application's data with location in time and space to be updated.

5.2 Augmented Map

We called the first functionality of our classification *Augmented Map*. The aim of an application of this type is to enable one or several people to explore geographical data coming indifferently from the physical world or the digital world. For example, the prototype proposed by [41] is a system for presenting geographical information. Data are described by 3D digital models. Presented as a specific GIS framework for presenting geographical data inside or outside, the experiments proposed only show the indoor application by proposing handling data via markers (Fig. 33.3). This approach enables these data to be explored according to different points of view by handling markers.

Visualisation of data   Interaction ("Paddle Interaction")

Fig. 33.4 Visualisation and interaction with geographical data [42]

In [42], the authors propose two possibilities to collaboratively explore geographical data. The first one is an interface which combines AR and the user's hand
tracking through image analysis. Users can thus look at a real geographical map
(paper) and see a 3D model adjusted on this map (Fig. 33.4a). The second one offers
different interaction techniques (zoom, move, notes, etc.) by using for example the
zoom tool metaphor so users can explore data (Fig. 33.4b).

In [43], the authors use the vision-based AR technique[6] popularized by [44].
They also propose several techniques to explore the geographical data of a NASA
mission to the moon using "telescopic" (baguette) interactors. Markers are used as
metaphors (Fig. 33.5) from real life (zoom tool) or from computing interfaces like
sliders to vary the linear value of certain parameters.

Another example (based on detecting points of interest [45, 46]) proposes using
AR combined with a PDA to facilitate the use of a paper map. Video content or
images are thus offered to users in context with the paper map. In addition to these
augmentations, they offer interactions like exploring images according to a selected
point on the map (Fig. 33.6).

In [48], the authors propose comparing paper maps and electronic maps. They
propose to compare these two means of consulting geographical information by
distinguishing four main categories: *functionalities* and *content* as well as *use* and
interaction. This analysis enables the authors to conclude that both approaches
(paper and digital) are complementary in many cases. This conclusion leads the
authors to develop a prototype using a PDA and marker-based positioning to consult
the geographical data on a mobile's electronic map.

---

[6]Single camera position/orientation tracking with tracking code that uses simple black squares.

Fig. 33.5 Interaction metaphors (slider example) [43]

Fig. 33.6 Exploring an image from the map [47]

5.3 Augmented Territory

We call the second functionality of our classification Augmented Territory. The aim of an application of this type is to provide one or several people additional information to explore our natural environment. For example, in [49], the authors propose two indoor AR applications. The first helps explore a building (Fig. 33.7a)

Help finding your way inside a building

Help finding a book in a library

Fig. 33.7 Two marker-based AR applications

and the second is an application to help browse through a library (Fig. 33.7b). These applications are based on a marker system.

In [50], we can see an AR system whose camera is fitted on a helicopter. The helicopter flies over buildings and sends the video back to the ground as well as its position and orientation wirelessly. Once the data (video, position, orientation) have been collected, they are added to a database enabling, for example, the names of buildings to be displayed on the video. The demonstrator suffers from a huge lack of precision when adding the virtual information in the video. The authors of [51] propose an AR demonstrator with indirect vision enabling this geographical information to be incrusted (street names and numbers, names of monuments, etc.) as illustrated in Fig. 33.8 in a video flow available to the user through a screen (indirect vision AR). Geographical data is extracted from the English database maintained by [52]. Retiming is carried out by combining a GPS for the position and an internal navigator for orientation. Access to data is by Wifi. Work has been done on placing the labels and synchronising the orientation.

[53] describes an application where users are informed about their position, the name and altitude of surrounding summits. Users look at the summits of mountains through the screen of their mobile phone and the Peak.AR application provides useful information by incrusting text labels (Fig. 33.9).

ARVino is a demonstrator resulting from the Tinmith project [54] for the augmented visualisation of geolocated wine-growing data. Presented at ISMAR05, [55] propose solutions to avoid colour overloads in virtual information as well as managing the transparency of these objects with the aim of not concealing data from the physical world (Fig. 33.10).

In [8], a Real-Time Kinematic GPS, more precise than a classic GPS, enables the team to propose a demonstrator christened "Geo-Media", allowing the physical world to be mixed with artistic virtual objects. Augurscope is an interface also using a GPS and inertial sensors so as to propose a virtual environment whose point

Fig. 33.8 View of monuments from Westminster Bridge (London) [51]

Fig. 33.9 Peak.AR: an application combining AR and GIS on mobiles

Fig. 33.10 Example of ARVino demonstrator augmentation [55]

of view (in the virtual environment) depends on the point of view in the physical environment (Fig. 33.11). It is used in [56] for an application enabling the public to explore a medieval castle.

ARGIS is a project for visualising information during a project for building an aerodrome [57]. Besides the classic retiming mechanism for virtual geographic information on the video flow by detecting points of interest, they propose an "X-ray" augmented visualisation enabling users to see what the naked eye is unable to see (Fig. 33.12).

With regard to visualising buried geographical data, [58] proposed in 2008 an indirect vision Augmented reality application resulting from the Vidente project and enabling underground pipes to be visualised (Fig. 33.13a) via an UMPC (Fig. 33.13b).

It is partly to satisfy the stakes previously described in Sect. 5 that [59] propose a flexible client-server solution where geographical data and 3D models are located on the server and the data display and presentation components are located with the client. We also find in [60] a geographical information management strategy whose three tier architecture enable these data to be used for a collaborative Augmented Reality application (two users) and reusing data for other applications. The demonstrator is an application to assist in exploring a town or city (Fig. 33.14).

An environmental change visualisation application using AR and geographical data is proposed by [61]. They propose augmenting geographical data via an erosion

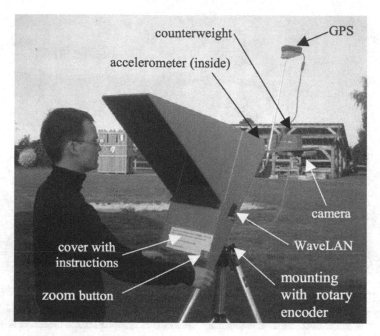

Fig. 33.11 Augurscope details [56]

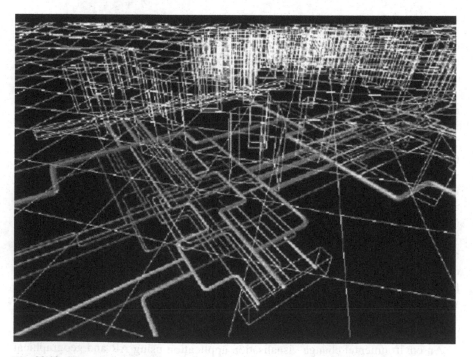

Fig. 33.12 "X-ray" visualisation mode for information on a building site [57]

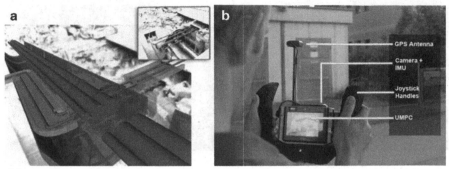

View of a model georeferenced on site

UMPC (Ultra Mobile Personal Computer) enabling underground information to be visualised

Fig. 33.13 Visualisation of underground infrastructures

Fig. 33.14 Example of augmentation during whilst following a route in a town or city [60]

model enabling users to understand damage on the environment over time. In [61], the authors propose a method allowing a physically realistic yield of GIS data using AR. Sea navigation is one of the most attractive fields concerning the use of GIS. Although still subject to debate with regard to traditional paper maps, the adoption in 2009 by the IMO maritime safety committee [62] of amendments introducing a rule forcing all vessels making international voyages to carry on board an electronic mapping system confirms this interest. However, few applications in the field of shipping use AR in their information display components. The "Ship

Scene augmented with AIS information   A vessel augmented with AIS information

Fig. 33.15 Example of AIS augmentation [31]

Augmented maritime scene [63]   Augmented maritime scene [64]

Fig. 33.16 AR in assisting sailing

Ahoy!" application by [31] is a mobile application which recovers AIS[7] targets from a specialised website and displays these data by basing retiming on the GPS position and the terminal's magnetometer. Since data is only updated approximately every hour, the application is difficult to use and is only available with an internet connection.

We can mention work by "Technologie Systems Inc." which proposes an application using AR to help plan missions [63] of which an example of augmentation can be seen in Fig. 33.16. Another approach, which we have developed in [64, 65], enables visual data using the same definition set to be merged in certain conditions. We use mapping and a georeferenced video flow to merge these two sources so that users can simultaneously have whichever of the two sources of information they need (real or digital).

In the field of cars, we can mention Wikitude Drive [27] which is an application which uses the Android operating system [30] and which must be installed on a mobile platform mobile with a video sensor and GPS. Blaupunkt [66] has been selling an assisted driving device whose display uses an embedded video sensor since 2009 (Fig. 33.17).

---

[7]Automated message exchange system between vessels.

Wikitude Drive   Blaupunkt assisted driving

Fig. 33.17 Assisted car driving application combining GIS and AR [27, 66]

5.3.1 Building One's Own Augmented Territory

All the applications presented above are determinist. Augmentations are planned by the designer. Users are only able to carry out very limited modifications on the symbolism or types of augmentations. However, there are also applications enabling users to define their own *Augmented Territory*. Through web interfaces or creation modules directly integrated in applications, certain solutions enable users to build their own augmentations, eg. Layar [25], Wikitude [27], Tonchidot [26], Qualcomm [29] and Junaio [28] are applications sold as AR "search engines". These applications offer users the ability to define layers of information or points of interest (POI) defined by users themselves. When these layers are activated in the interface of different respective applications, the latter use hardware resources for the platform on which they are installed (GPS, gyroscope, accelerometer, video sensor, etc.) to position POI on the mobile's video flow. Using the latest surrounding tweets for the position of restaurants, hairdressers or cultural venues, these platforms provide a framework for development allowing each individual user to create his or her own *Augmented Territory*.

6 Conclusion

In this chapter we have proposed to explore two domains which have converged due to certain factors which we have detailed. We have proposed a functional classification of these new applications enabling them to be described and compared. Combining GIS and display techniques using AR presents many challenges both with regard to technologies (hardware, software), methods (visualising geographical data, interaction with major data sources, etc.) and industry. There are still a number of issues remaining to be solved in order for both of these technologies to be able to take full advantage of their respective progress.

References

1. J.-C. Gonzato, T. Arcila, and B. Crespin, "Virtual objects on real oceans," *GRAPHICON'2008*, vol. Russie, Moscou, December 2008.
2. J. Platonov, H. Heibel, P. Meier, and B. Grollmann, "A mobile markerless ar system for maintenance and repair," in *ISMAR '06: Proceedings of the 5th IEEE and ACM International Symposium on Mixed and Augmented Reality*, (Washington, DC, USA), pp. 105–108, IEEE Computer Society, 2006.
3. C. Tomasi and T. Kanade, "Detection and tracking of point features," Tech. Rep. CMU-CS-91-132, Carnegie Mellon University, April 1991.
4. S. Smith and J. Brady, "Susan - a new approach to low level image processing," *International Journal of Computer Vision*, vol. 23, pp. 45–78, 1995.
5. D. Lowe, "Object recognition from local scale-invariant features," in *Computer Vision, 1999. The Proceedings of the Seventh IEEE International Conference on*, vol. 2, pp. 1150 –1157 vol.2, 1999.
6. H. Bay, T. Tuytelaars, and L. V. Gool, "SURF: Speeded Up Robust Features," *in ECCV (1)*, pp. 404–417, 2006.
7. J.-M. Morel and G. Yu, "A new framework for fully affine invariant image comparison," *SIAM. Journal on Imaging Sciences*, vol. 2, no. 2, pp. 438–469, 2009.
8. Y. Takaya, H. Mugibayashi, M. Satomi, T. Kobayashi, and A. Sekiguchi, "Geo-Media: The interactive augmented-reality system for outdoor use with VRS-RTK-GPS," in *Proceedings of the Tenth International Conference on Virtual Systems and Multimedia*, pp. 1262–1271, 2004.
9. S. You and U. Neumann, "Fusion of vision and gyro tracking for robust augmented reality registration," *IEEE Virtual Reality Conference*, pp. 71–78, 2001.
10. T. Auer and A. Pinz, "The integration of optical and magnetic tracking for multi-user augmented reality," *Computers and Graphics*, vol. 23, no. 6, pp. 805–808, 1999.
11. W. Piekarski, B. Avery, B. H. Thomas, and P. Malbezin, "Hybrid indoor and outdoor tracking for mobile 3d mixed reality," in *ISMAR '03: Proceedings of the 2nd IEEE/ACM International Symposium on Mixed and Augmented Reality*, (Washington, DC, USA), p. 266, IEEE Computer Society, 2003.
12. D. Schmalstieg and G. Reitmayr, "The world as a user interface: Augmented reality for ubiquitous computing," *Central European Multimedia and Virtual Reality Conference*, 2005.
13. W. E. Mackay, "Augmenting reality: A new paradigm for interacting with computers," *World Proceedings of ECSCW'93, the European Conference on Computer Supported Cooperative Work*, vol. 7, 1996.
14. W. E. Mackay, "Augmented reality: Linking real and virtual worlds a new paradigm for interacting with computers," *In proceedings of AVI'98. ACM Conference on Advanced Visual Interfaces, New York: ACM Press*, 1998.
15. M. Auvray and P. Fuchs, "Perception, immersion et interaction sensorimotrices en environnement virtuel," *In A. Grumbach & E. Klinger (Eds.), Réalité Virtuelle et Cognition. Numéro spécial de Intellectica*, vol. 45, no. 1, pp. 23–35, 2007.
16. H. Bergson, *Matière et mémoire. Essai sur la relation du corps à l'esprit*. Première édition : 1939. Paris : Les Presses universitaires de France, 1965, 72e édition. Collection : Bibliothèque de philosophie contemporaine, 1939.
17. P. Wellner, "The digitaldesk calculator: Tactile manipulation on a desk top display," *In proceedings of ACM Symposium on User Interface Software and Technology (UIST'91)*, pp. 27–33, November 11-13 1991.
18. E. Dubois, *Chirurgie Augmentée, un Cas de Réalité Augmentée; Conception et Réalisation Centrées sur l'Utilisateur*. PhD thesis, Université Joseph Fourier, Grenoble, juillet 2001.
19. P. Milgram, H. Takemura, A. Utsumi, and F. Kishino, "Augmented reality: A class of displays on the reality-virtuality continuum," *Telemanipulator and Telepresence Technologie*, vol. 2351, pp. 282–292, 1994.

20. R. Azuma, "A Survey of Augmented Reality," *Presence: Teleoperators and Virtual Environments*, pp. 355–385, August 1997.
21. J. R. Wilson and M. D'Cruz, "Virtual and interactive environments for work of the future," *International Journal of Human-Computer Studies*, vol. 64, no. 3, pp. 158–169, 2006. Interaction with virtual environments.
22. M. Anastassova, *L'analyse ergonomique des besoins en amont de la conception de technologies émergentes*. PhD thesis, Ecole doctorale "Cognition, comportement, conduites humaines" (ED261), Université René Descartes - Paris 5, Décembre 2006.
23. G. Calvary, J. Coutaz, D. Thevenin, Q. Limbourg, L. Bouillon, and J. V, "A unifying reference framework for multi-target user interfaces," *Interacting with Computers*, vol. 15, pp. 289–308, 2003.
24. O. Bimber and R. Raskar, *Spatial Augmented Reality: Merging Real and Virtual Worlds*. A K Peters, Ltd., July 2005.
25. Layar, "http://www.layar.com/," 2010.
26. Tonchidot, "http://www.tonchidot.com/en/," 2010.
27. Wikitude, "http://www.wikitude.org/team," 2010.
28. Junaio, "http://www.junaio.com/," 2010.
29. Qualcom, "http://www.qualcomm.fr/," 2010.
30. Google Android, "http://www.android.com/," 2010.
31. PinkFroot, "Ship ahoy! : http://my.pinkfroot.com/," September 2010.
32. D. Maguire, "An overview and definition of GIS," *Geographical Information Systems: principles and applications*, vol. 1, pp. 9–20, 1991.
33. D. Maguire and J. Raper, "An overview of GIS functionality," *Proceedings of GIS Design Models and Functionality Conference*, p. 10, 1990.
34. S. Zlatanova, A. A. Rahman, and M. Pilouk, "3D GIS: current status and perspectives," *Symposium on Geospatial Theory, Processing and Applications*, 2002.
35. R. De Courcy, "Les systèmes d'information en réadaptation," *Québec, Réseau International CIDIH et facteurs environnementaux*, vol. 1-2, no. 5, pp. 7–10, 1992.
36. P.-A. Ayral and S. Sauvagnargues-Lesage, "Système d'information géographique : outil d'aide à la gestion territoriale," *Techniques de l'Ingénieur. Référence H7415*, 2009.
37. R. Devilliers, A. Stein, Y. Bédart, N. Chrisman, P. Fisher, and W. Shi, "30 years of research on spatial data quality - achievements, failures and opportunities," *Transaction in GIS*, no. 557, 2010.
38. R. Azuma, "Overview of augmented reality," *International Conference on Computer Graphics and Interactive Techniques*, 2004.
39. I. Zendjebil, F. Ababsa, J.-Y. Didier, J. Vairion, L. Frauciel, M. Hachet, P. Guitton, and R. Delmont, "Outdoor Augmented Reality: State of the Art and Issues," *10th ACM/IEEE Virtual Reality International Conference (VRIC2008), Laval: France*, pp. 177–187, 2008.
40. M. Beaudouin-Lafon, "Instrumental interaction: an interaction model for designing post-wimp user interfaces," in *CHI '00: Proceedings of the SIGCHI conference on Human factors in computing systems*, (New York, NY, USA), pp. 446–453, ACM, 2000.
41. F. Liarokapis, I. Greatbatch, D. Mountain, A. Gunesh, V. Brujic-okretic, and J. Raper, "Mobile augmented reality techniques for geovisualisation," in *Proc. of the 9th International Conference on Information Visualisation, IEEE Computer Society*, pp. 745–751, IEEE Computer Society, 6-8 July 2005.
42. R. Hedley, Nicholas, M. Billinghurst, L. Postner, R. May, and H. Kato, "Explorations in the use of augmented reality for geographic visualization," *Presence: Teleoper. Virtual Environ.*, vol. 11, no. 2, pp. 119–133, 2002.
43. K. Asai, T. Kondo, H. Kobayashi, and A. Mizuki, "A geographic surface browsing tool using map-based augmented reality," in *VIS'08: Proceedings of the 2008 International Conference Visualisation*, (Washington, DC, USA), pp. 93–98, IEEE Computer Society, 2008.
44. ARToolKit, "HITLAB, http://www.hitl.washington.edu/artoolkit," 2010.
45. J. Shi and C. Tomasi, "Good features to track," *IEEE Vision and Pattern Recognition*, June 1994.

46. J. P. Rolland, Y. Baillot, and A. A. Goon, "A survey of tracking technology for virtual environments," *Fundamentals of Wearable Computers and Augmented Reality*, pp. 67–112, 2001.
47. G. Reitmayr, E. Eade, and T. Drummond, "Localisation and Interaction for Augmented Maps," *Symposium on Mixed and Augmented Reality*, 2005.
48. V. Paelke and M. Sester, "Augmented paper maps: Exploring the design space of a mixed reality system," *ISPRS Journal of Photogrammetry and Remote Sensing*, vol. In Press, Corrected Proof, pp. –, 2009.
49. G. Reitmayr and D. Schmalstieg, "Location based applications for mobile augmented reality," *ACM International Conference Proceeding Series; Vol. 36*, 2003.
50. H. Kim, B. Jang, J. Kim, J. Kim, and D. Kim, "An outdoor augmented reality system for understanding remote geographical information," *International Conference on Artificial Reality Telexistence*, vol. 7th, pp. 154–158, 1997.
51. A. Radburn, "A mobile augmented reality demonstrator," *Ordonance Survey*, 2006.
52. Ordnance Survey, "OS MasterMap," 2010.
53. S. Research, "Peak.ar : http://peakar.salzburgresearch.at/."
54. W. Piekarski, "Tinmith Project," 2010.
55. R. King, Gary, W. Piekarski, and H. Thomas, Bruce, "Arvino — outdoor augmented reality visualisation of viticulture gis data," in *ISMAR '05: Proceedings of the 4th IEEE/ACM International Symposium on Mixed and Augmented Reality*, (Washington, DC, USA), pp. 52–55, IEEE Computer Society, 2005.
56. H. Schnädelbach, B. Koleva, M. Flintham, M. Fraser, S. Izadi, P. Chandler, M. Foster, S. Benford, C. Greenhalgh, and T. Rodden, "The augurscope: A mixed reality interface for outdoors," *CHI Minneapolis, Minnesota, USA*, April 20-25 2002.
57. Y. Guo, Qingyun, Y. Luo, W. Zhang, and L. Xu, "Application of augmented reality GIS in architecture," *The International Archives of Photogrammetry, Remote Sensing and Spatial Information Sciences*, vol. XXXVII, no. Part B5, pp. 331–336, 2008.
58. G. Schall, E. Mendez, E. Kruijff, E. Veas, S. Junghanns, B. Reitinger, and D. Schmalstieg, "Handheld augmented reality for underground infrastructure visualization," *Personal and Ubiquitous Computing, Special Issue on Mobile Spatial Interaction*, vol. 13, pp. 281–291, Mai 2008.
59. T. Romao, N. Correia, E. Dias, A. Trabuco, C. Santos, R. Santos, E. Nobre, A. Câmara, J. Danado, and L. Romero, "Augmenting reality with geo-referencend information for environmental management," *In Proc GIS'02, Virginia, USA*, pp. 175–180, 2002.
60. G. Reitmayr and D. Schmalstieg, "Data management strategies for mobile augmented reality," in *Proceedings of International Workshop on Software Technology for Augmented Reality Systems*, pp. 47–52, IEEE Computer Society, 2003.
61. P. Ghadirian and I. D. Bishop, "Integration of augmented reality and gis: A new approach to realistic landscape visualisation," *Landscape and Urban Planning*, vol. 86, pp. 226 – 232, March 2008.
62. "International Maritime Organization (IMO) http://www.imo.org/."
63. C. Benton, R. Nitzel, and T. Zysk, "Merging ocean/maritime models and arctic operations using mission planning toolkits and augmented reality," pp. 1–6, sept. 2008.
64. O. Hugues, J.-M. Cieutat, and P. Guitton, "An experimental augmented reality platform for assisted maritime navigation," in *AH '10: Proceedings of the 1st Augmented Human International Conference*, (New York, NY, USA), pp. 1–6, ACM, 2010.
65. O. Hugues, J.-M. Cieutat, V. Pilnière, and P. Guitton, "SIG maritime augmenté (SIGMA) un système enactif de réalité augmentée," *12e Conférence Internationale Ergonomie et Informatique Avancée (Ergo'IA 2010)*, Octobre 2010.
66. Blaupunkt, "http://www.blaupunkt.de/," 2010.

Index

B. Furht (ed.), *Handbook of Augmented Reality*, DOI 10.1007/978-1-4614-0064-6,
© Springer Science+Business Media, LLC 2011